A *Backwoods Home* Anthology:

The Seventh Year

Published by
Backwoods Home Magazine
P. O. Box 712
Gold Beach, OR 97444

Copyright 1996, 1999, 2006, 2008 by Backwoods Home Magazine

Editor: *Dave Duffy*

Senior Editor: *John Silveira*

Art Director: *Don Childers*

Contributors:

Tom Kovach, Martha Belding, Margaret Wright, Martin Waterman, Alice Yeager, James O. Yeager, Massad Ayoob, Harry Styron, Annie Duffy, Anita Evangelista, John Silveira, Lee Harbert, Thomas C. Tabor, Harry G. Nemec, Marjorie Burris, Terrie Clark, Richard Blunt, Ruth Adler, Albert H. Carlson, Matt McEachran, Jan Palmer, Connie Glasheen, Paul Jeffrey Fowler, Bill Palmroth, Tanya Kelley, Maurcia DeLean Houck, Barbara Fallick, Edna C. Norrell, Dynah Geissal, Anne Westbrook Dominick, Sally Denney, Jacqueline Binford-Bell, Jim Hildreth, Inez Castor, L.A. Wallin, L. Gordon Stetser Jr., Ben Sizemore, Michael Clayton, Rev. J.D. Hooker, Michael J. Tougias, Craig Russell, Jacqueline Tresl, Mark Tresl, R.E. Bumpus, Skip Thomsen, Joy Lamb, Sharon Griggs, Robert L. Williams III, Sylvia Gist, Lance Bisaccia, Marna Meagaen, Jennifer Stein Barker, Christopher Nyerges, Dave Duffy, Angela Jenkins, Jayn Steidl Thibodeau, Mary Kenyon, Raul Castellano, Rodney L. Merrill, Branley Allan Branson, Steve Anderson, Lydia Mayfield, James Robertson, Marcia Brown, Linda Gabris, Janell Henschel, Sandy Lindsey, Don Fallick, Allyn Uptain, Robert L. Williams, John Fuchs, Mary Jo Bratton, Micki Warner, Olivia Miller, Lance Barker, Mark Klammer, Lynn Klammer, Robert K. Henderson, Edith Helmich, Jan Cook, Judith W. Monroe, Charles A. Sanders, Darlene Campbell, Dana Martin Batory, Carole Perlick, Darlene Polachic, Reuben O. Doyle, Robert E. Kramer, Marjorie (Sultzbaugh) Harrison, Olive L. Sullivan, Wilma Hinman, Diane M. Calabrese

Introduction

As I write this introduction to the Seventh Year Anthology, we are completing our tenth year as *Backwoods Home Magazine*. In these ten years we've watched the hysteria come and go about the ways the world as we know it will end. There's been global warming, the New World Order, and a collision with an asteroid, among other things. Most recently, there was Y2K. But we're all still here, the world is still intact, and our lives go on.

In all this time *BHM* has refused to ride any of the bandwagons of doom and gloom. We have instead stayed with our basic philosophy of independence and self-reliance, knowing full well that this is not just the proper way to prepare for bad times, it is the recipe for everyday living.

Quality how-to articles involving building, growing and storing food, alternative energy, homeschooling, guns, etc., with a sprinkling of the self-reliant philosophy of Libertarians like ourselves, have been our mainstay since issue Number 1 and will remain so in the foreseeable future.

So we are hoping that within these pages you will find articles that will enrich your life, make you more self-sufficient, and, if the world does end, ensure you are the first on your block to be the last on your block.

John Silveira
Senior Editor

This anthology is dedicated to

*Ruth Bosco of North Hutchinson Island, Florida,
who kept her son, John Silveira, on the straight and
narrow despite his friend, Dave Duffy.*

Profiles

Contents —

Issue Number 39

Issue Number 40

JAN/FEB 1996
No. 37

Backwoods
Home magazine

practical ideas for self-reliant living

Earn a college degree at home

$-Saving home food storage

Successful homeschooling

Quilt making is fine art

Plants to purify your home

Protect yourself from lightning

Rid your pond of annoying weeds

Grow mouth watering persimmons

DON CHILDERS

$3.95 US•$5.50 CANADA

My view

The new frontier

A week before putting this issue to bed, John Silveira, Lance Bisaccia, Don Childers, Richard Blunt, Martin Waterman, and I engaged in a furious exchange of ideas, stories, and art that affected a half dozen key articles in the issue. Not surprisingly, we made decisions quickly and effectively, much like any capable group of managers would make decisions about the business of any successful company.

Surprisingly, to many people, we made them while participating in what futurists like to call "the virtual office," an office created purely by electronics. We communicated by computer, FAX, and phone. Rarely were any of us in the same building; in fact, Bisaccia was 40 miles away in Ashland, Childers was 700 miles away in southern California, Blunt 3,000 miles away in Connecticut, and Waterman 3,300 miles away in New Brunswick, Canada. Unfortunately, every time I turned around, Silveira was right there behind me.

This wasn't some kind of experiment we were engaged in. It has just evolved as a convenient and quick way to put together the magazine, without any of us having to leave home. What is most remarkable about it is the fact that only six years ago, when this magazine was founded, almost no one was conducting business this way, let alone a small business like us with only four full-time employees.

This virtual office is part of the new technological frontier that is currently being settled, not just by businesses like this magazine, but by entire families engaged in the most ordinary pursuits. My daughter, Annie, regularly communicates via computer and modem with her friends across the country, and my wife, Lenie, keeps the family checkbook on the computer. *BHM's* column about the electronic frontier, which started last issue, will show you many other ordinary things done with the new technology.

A lot of people who live in the country, however, seem to shy away from this new frontier, in part because it appears threatening and complicated, terribly unlike that simpler, less complicated way of life the country often promises.

The fact is that this new technology is not only pretty simple to use, once you take that initial step to try it out, but it is also fairly inescapable. It is changing the entire landscape of our future every bit as much as previous frontiers we encountered changed things. You can no more escape it than you can escape the fact the world is round, rather than flat.

Luckily, it's not something you want to escape anyway. Computers, modems, FAXs, and the rest of the new technology are the new improved tools of the future. If we think

Dave Duffy

we're too old to use them, our children certainly aren't. And just as, 150 years ago, we wouldn't have sent someone from Massachusetts out to the frontier without the proper tools—a plow, a woodstove, and a rifle—because you'd be ensuring the likelihood they'd fail, nowadays you'd be irresponsible to send your children out into the world without ensuring they were armed with the ability to use a computer.

Remember that old saying: "God created man, but Colt made them equal." That's how I feel about computers, especially when it comes to making a living. Today, entire businesses are being run by ordinary people out of their living rooms with nothing more than a computer and perhaps a connection to the Internet. Thanks to the computer this magazine is able to compete successfully with much bigger ones. Only 10 years ago it took a small fortune to start a magazine; today it takes a $1500 computer.

Just as the early days of the western frontier were a place where an individual could cut out a fortune for himself, in these early days of the electronic frontier, there are thousands of places where enterprising men and women can make a living—or fortune—for themselves.

But, for everyone who went west in the early days of our country, hundreds—even thousands—of others played it safe and stayed behind in Boston, New York, Baltimore, and other safe cities. And, just as the western frontier was finally pronounced closed, someday the electronic frontier will lose its vastness and promise, and all the opportunities for the little guy will be gone.

I suppose this is especially good advice for anyone contemplating a move to the country but having trouble figuring out a way to make a living. Take a hard look at creating a job with a computer. We'll try to help with our new column.

NASA says these plants will help clean the air in your home

By Tommy Kovach

In researching ways to clean the air in space stations, NASA (the National Aeronautics and Space Administration) discovered that many common houseplants and blooming potted plants eliminate significant amounts of harmful airborne gases.

In addition to absorbing carbon dioxide and releasing oxygen into the air as part of the photosynthesis process, plants also absorb benzene, formaldehyde, and trichloroethylene. These are three of the worst offenders polluting the air of new homes and offices, or those with new furnishings.

Synthetic building materials and furnishings such as carpet, fabrics, laminated counters, plastic-coated wallpaper, and other materials can "off-gas" pollutants into the interior environment. When buildings are well insulated and sealed tightly to conserve heat or air-conditioning, the pollutants are trapped indoors.

If you live in a newer, energy-efficient, tightly sealed home, or if you work in a building with new furnishings or where the air feels stale and circulation seems poor, the liberal use of houseplants can help.

Most of the plants on the NASA list evolved in tropical or subtropical forests, where they received light filtered through branches of taller trees. Because of this, their leaf composition allows them to photosynthesize efficiently under relatively low-light conditions, which in turn allows them to process gases efficiently.

Soil and roots also play an important role in removing airborne pollutants. Microorganisms in the soil become more adept at using trace amounts of these materials as a food source when exposed to them for longer periods of time. Effectiveness can be increased if lower leaves covering the soil are removed so as much soil as possible is in contact with the air.

The best results in air purification were obtained when small fans pulled air through a charcoal filter in the soil. This cleaned better than foliage alone or in combination with a passive pot of soil. However, even without the fan and filter, houseplants did remove trace pollutants from the air.

The recommendation generated by the NASA studies is to use 15 to 18 good-sized houseplants in six- to eight-inch diameter containers to improve the air quality in an average 1,800-square-foot house. The more vigorously they grow, the better job they'll do.

Although all houseplants probably are beneficial, not all are equally efficient cleaners, and one cannot assume they will remove all harmful pollutants. For example, no plant is of much help in removing tobacco smoke.

But plants do a good enough job of removing air pollutants to cause us to view houseplants as more than just an attractive feature in decorating the interior environment of homes and offices.

Here is the list of indoor air-cleaning plants compiled by NASA:

- **English ivy** (*Hedera helix*)
- **Spider plant** (*Chlorophytum comosum*)
- **Golden pothos** (*Epipiremnum aureum*)
- **Peace lily** (*Spathiphyllum "Mauna Loa"*)
- **Chinese evergreen** (*Aglaonema modestum*)
- **Bamboo or reed plant** (*Chamaedorea sefritzii*)
- **Snake plant** (*Sansevieria trifasciata*)
- **Heartleaf philodendron** (*Philodendron scandens "oxycardium"*)
- **Selloum philodendron** (*Philodendron selloum*)
- **Elephant ear philodendron** (*Philodendron domesticum*)
- **Red-edged dracaena** (*Dracaena marginata*)
- **Cornstalk dracaena** (*Dracaena fragrans Massangeana*)
- **Janet Craig dracaena** (*Dracaena deremensis "Janet Craig"*)
- **Warneck dracaena** (*Dracaena deremensis Warneckii*)
- **Weeping fig** (*Ficus benjamina*) Δ

It took a lot of weed-eating fish & work to make our lake usable

By Martha Belding

Do you have a pond or lake so choked with weeds you can't put a hook in it? We've been there. We live on Silver Lake, a four-mile long lake with an average depth of 10 feet, in southwest Washington. Three years ago it had aquatic weed to the surface on most of it. It was lost to weeds.

The local teacher of marine biology identified 97 varieties of aquatic weed in Silver Lake over the summer months. Not all species of weed grow at the same season. Aquatic weed in the lake grow like vegetables in a garden; each has a predominate season. But by July Silver Lake was unusable with aquatic weed to the surface on most of the lake.

A study by Washington State University (WSU) in 1989 said Silver

Lake would be a meadow in 10 years. We who live on the shore figured its demise would come much sooner, for weed had covered the lake bottom and grew to the surface on most of it. Weed growth had stopped fishing and restricted boating. The WSU study said Silver Lake was in a state of eutrophication, a word none of us ever heard of but we learned that eutrophication means dying from lack of oxygen, caused by excessive weed growth. We learned eutrophication can be a natural event usually taking many years to accomplish, but often hastened by actions of man, such as fertilizing tree farms, gardens, and lawns around the lake.

We tried everything to get rid of the weeds. We had weeds cut with a weed cutter, which the salesman was more than happy to demonstrate. The cutter

and barge, which we would need in order to haul weed to shore, cost $75,000. But the weeds grew back more dense the next year after our demonstration of weed cutting, for each piece of weed left in the lake grew.

Some tried chemicals. One man living on the east shore put a commercial herbicide in the lake in front of his house and his neighbors almost had apoplexy. We are a diversified group of retired people, mill workers, and loggers. The chemical drifted. It was expensive, costing several thousand dollars, so he told us, for he had a large frontage. The weed grew back in a year and the applicator came back to add more. He needed a state permit for this and several neighbors were up in arms when a sign was posted, "Don't eat the fish for four days."

We looked into dredging. Our state says water from dredge spoils must not drain back into the lake. We pointed out that the water in the spoils came from the lake, but our Department of Ecology said spoils

Dumping amur in Silver Lake to rid the lake of weeds

must be deposited outside the watershed. This would take a lot of hauling of mud. Dredging itself was estimated to cost five-million dollars.

Mowing weeds with fish

Then we investigated the white amur. The amur is a fish labeled exotic, non native to the United States, so requires a permit from your State Fisheries to use. The amur (Ctenopharyngodon Idellus) "grass carp" originally comes from the Amur River between Russia and China and were written about in Marco Polo time as a vegetarian fish. They are said to be a tasty fish of white meat with not as many bones as a common carp, and amur have been used in Europe for

*Author scooping weeds
from Silver Lake*

centuries as a food fish. Amur have scales like the European carp, but are silver with the face of a Bass. They mow weed rather than pull it by the root.

They are strong and can break a five-pound test line at the sight of a net. They are curious and will strike at lures and jump when cornered. We have seen them jump three feet over a net when we tried to remove some to weigh them. They jumped over the net, around it, and under it. We sent the video of the operation to the T.V. show, America's Funniest Video, but nothing came of it. Otto Cunningham, a commercial fisherman in Melba,

Idaho says he has seen amur jump six feet when cornered.

We obtained from the Washington Department of Wildlife a permit to put 8" amur in a pen in the lake to see if they would eat the weed. After all the weed in a pen was gone, none jumped the fence to a place where the weed was abundant. They apparently only jump to escape.

They have predators. When 8 to 10-inch amur were first introduced at Silver Lake we lost many to the Eagles and Osprey which live on the south shore. We also lost some to otter in the creeks which feed the lake, but as the amur grew larger, and they grew 18 inches in 2 years, the Eagles could not lift them and amur became too quick for them.

They are sterile

Triploids, an amur with three chromosomes, thus sterile, are now required by most states. The Diploid, or original two-chromosome amur, was used in Florida in experimental areas and in other southern states in the Sixties and Seventies, but because one amur can produce a million eggs, the threat of over-production has been held over the head of the amur since its introduction into the United States.

However, we can find no proof of reproduction in the United States except in strict laboratory settings. Here the eggs are stripped from the hen and fertilized with sperm from the male, and the chromosomes of the eggs are altered by pressure.

When seeking approval for the amur, we had to run down many "It's rumored that" theories about reproduction to get the amur into Washington. But the specter of over production raised its head until a fellow named Steve Malone in Lonoke, Arkansas, incorporated a method of altering the chromosomes in the egg of the amur which made the egg produce a Triploid. Now, only the Triploid is permitted in most states.

The powers that be—Fisheries Departments, both state and national— are taking no chances with over production and each amur which leaves Arkansas to be shipped to a state permitting Triploids must be certified by the U. S. Department of Fisheries as disease free and sterile.

But, you may ask, how do I get amur for my lake or pond? Getting them may depend upon where you live. Check with your own Fisheries Department and your local fish biologist.

California requires approval by the Legislature, and only three southern California counties use them under the term research. That system, we are told by those working with amur in California, will change as soon as the California Fisheries Department sets a policy regarding the amur permitting process. Resistance to using the amur is strong in some areas. We are told that in northern California it is the commercial salmon fishermen most concerned about the impact of the amur on the salmon industry. Those working with the amur in California feel this will change in a few years as more is made known of the effects of amur on all types of fisheries.

Stocking your pond

For you who live in a permitted state or one of the three counties in California where amur are permitted, here's how you rid your pond or lake of weed using the amur.

1. Contact your local District of State Fisheries and Game and apply for a permit to use amur. In Washington this costs $22. You will have papers to fill out listing location and size of pond, etc.

2. You must prove the amur cannot escape into another body of water. You may need to build a fence or retaining structure if your body of water drains into another.

3. Decide how many fish you need. It's better to under stock than over

stock. Our Fish and Wildlife says it is very happy with the results here.

Some of us feel we may be over-stocked and have contacted a commercial fisherman to advise us on removal of surplus fish, if necessary. He tells us he wouldn't try to remove amur in summer or spring, when they are lively and very difficult to catch but rather work in winter when amur are lethargic and he would try to net them.

You stock per vegitated acre. If you have a two-acre pond with one acre of it in weed, you consider only the one acre when discussing stocking. Ten fish per vegetated acre seems to be pretty standard, but all ponds and all weeds are different. If you start with five per vegetated acre, you can always add more. You will want cover for other fish.

Eight to ten inches is a good size for amur. Early spring is the best time to stock. It has been our experience that the amur will hibernate when weeds die down or water temperature drops below 55 degrees.

4. Order amur from a supplier. We got ours from Bob Hooper, at Hooper-Stepthens, Route 2 Highway 31 So, Lonoke, Arkansas, 72086, phone: 501-676-2435. Our cost was $3.37 each, delivered, and we got a lot of them. If you have only a few, yours will cost more per fish. A short order may cost as much as $8 a fish. Amur can be air-freighted or delivered by truck supplied by the seller. In southern California call Mike Mesometo at the Imperial Valley Water Resource Lab in Brawley, California, 619-339-9565. His supply is limited, and as I write, he has only 1,000 amur in the 8" to 10" size for sale. Paul Beatty, PO Box 13212, Palm Desert, CA, 92261, Phone 619-568-5499, supplies for small ponds in that area. In Idaho contact Otto or Richard Cunningham, Cunningham Fish Farms, H.C. 79 Box 100, Melba, Idaho 83641. Phone: 208-495-2654. The Cunninghams have many kinds of fish for sale, but spring is the best time to place an order. In other states ask your Fisheries Department for addresses of suppliers. Many states have wholesalers.

Soft weeds only

If your stocking rate is right, your pond should be free of weed in two years. We're talking soft weed here, Milfoil, Elodea, etc. The amur's' teeth are in their throat and they don't eat lily pads or hard stems. We've watched them suck in the weed and spit out the stem. If the lake is over-stocked and they have absolutely nothing else to eat they will uproot a Lily Pad bulb for the new shoots, but its not a preferred food. Preferred foods vary with the water content. What is preferred in Silver Lake may not be the preferred aquatic weed in yours, but we didn't find any "soft" weed they would not eat. We were told by Brad Caldwell, who did the Colorado study, that the same species of weed in two ponds side by side supplied by two different water sources resulted in different plant species preferred. He wonders if it was the chemicals in the weed which caused this.

Life expectancy of the amur seems to be about 10 years, although some have lived 15, but we've been told they eat their weight each day and can eat themselves into a short life span. You will eventually need to restock. Most users we've talked with who have used the amur for several years recommend one or two per vegetated acre for maintenance restocking.

All of this is well and good for those in states which permit the amur.

For you who are not fortunate enough to live in a state where the amur are permitted, take heart. Until four years ago, Washington, where we live, was such a state, and we worked to get the amur approved for the state and thus Silver Lake by educating agencies. This is how we did it.

We told them all, by letter and phone, that Silver Lake, with 3200 surface acres of water, is well known as primarily a bass lake which also has abundant pan fish such as perch, trout, blue gill, and crappie. But no one could fish it, for the aquatic weed grew to the surface on 90 percent of the lake and we couldn't travel 1,000 feet in a boat without cleaning the motor of weed. We couldn't fish, even with a "weed" hook we used a year earlier. Sailing was out, and we wanted the amur in Silver Lake.

Some time ago, I read an article in a magazine about Bill Whiting in Arkansas raising an aquatic weed eating fish, the white amur.

I wrote to Bill Whiting and asked. "How can we get amur in Silver Lake?" Bill answered, "In

The amur are 8" to 10" when released into the lake

Washington, you won't. It's illegal." He added, "from your letter it sounds like you have milfoil." (He was right.) He wrote, "Milfoil will spread like cancer..." (It did). "...and there is no way to stop it without the fish." This was a blow. He added, "Amur do not eat anything other than vegetable matter, and they will not reproduce. The real reason the fish are not being used is that vast amounts of federal and state monies are available to do and re-do the same research over and over. As long as the money is there they will keep funding their own research."

Boy, was he right on that one.

Form a citizens group

It was soon obvious that we would need clout to deal with bureaucrats and agencies who either never heard of the amur or who wanted status quo, so we formed a citizens group with one goal, to put the amur in Silver Lake. We named our group COWSLIP, an acronym for Clean Out Weeds Silver Lake IS Possible. A Cowslip is a plant which grows in a swamp and we were rapidly getting a four-mile swamp in our front yard. Our slogan was "Save Silver Lake for the Generations Which Will Follow." And we used it.

We soon had 90 families as members. We sent letters to our state senator, Department of Fisheries, Wildlife Department, Department of Ecology, and the county commissioners, saying we want the amur.

Fighting the "studies"

Then we ran smack dab into the world of studies that Bill Whiting told us about. We learned that companies are built on money from studies and universities thrive on them. Studies are big bucks. Results of studies make books, which we doubt many people read. We were stymied while Washington College of Fisheries studied the amur, with hefty million dollar grants from the Washington Department of Ecology (DOE). California people who worked with the amur told us Washington was reinventing the wheel. We moaned and we waited.

DOE had $45 million a year for clean water grants, much of it going to studies and a small part earmarked for rivers and lakes. We found the track record for implementing studies and actually cleaning up lakes was dismal to say the least.

DOE said we must update the last study of Silver Lake if we wanted to apply for a grant to buy amur. An earlier study said the lake was dying from too many weeds. The new study by

WSU said, sure enough, the lake was dying from too many weeds. But this study gave us a chance to educate the WSU team about the advantages of using the amur. WSU agreed the amur was the way to clean up Silver Lake and said so in the conclusion of their study, though they still could not be used legally in Washington. About this time the people at Devils Lake in Lincoln City, Oregon, wanted to use the amur and we went to their meeting. They paid for the air flight of Scot Henderson, Director of Arkansas Fisheries, to Oregon to explain the use of the amur in Arkansas. We heard him tell them he felt, 10 or 12 amur per vegetated acre would clean up Devils Lake in two years. The citizens formed a group, named it PAL, and arranged to pay the group doing the Washington study, Washington College of Fisheries, a sum, we heard, of $200,000 to become a study lake so they could stock Devils Lake with the amur. They were told to by the College of Fisheries study team to use 40 amur per acre.

Our own study

While waiting for studies to be finished so we could proceed, we got a permit from the Washington Department of Wildlife to build a pen, in the name of research, in Silver Lake and stock it with amur to learn if amur would eat the weed which covered all of that area. COWSLIP stood the cost of $600 for fencing in two pens 100 feet by 40 feet in two different areas of the lake, using chicken wire, iron posts, rock and a lot of labor. Bob Hooper sent us seven amur by air freight. The board of COWSLIP celebrated with champagne as the first amur were put in Silver Lake.

In two years the area inside our pen where we had six amur was completely free of weed and was home to large schools of fry, bass, crappie, perch, and blue gill. In our pens they were safe from predators. And the hungry

amur, with all grass gone, did not touch them.

"But the amur will eat other fish," some doubters told us. We answered, "They're vegetarians; if you put a cow and a horse in a pasture, when the grass runs out the cow won't eat the horse." We proved the hungry amur would not eat fry. We also proved we overstocked the area, for **all** the grass was gone, and we wanted some for habitat. Finally, the five-year study of the amur by the College of Fisheries was finished. The conclusion? They need to study a larger lake and DOE obliged with another half-million dollars to study a lake near the DOE office, for five more years they said.

This was a low point of our project, and we called all those people we had been writing to and said "NO WAY" would we wait another five years. We started a campaign for pledges for $70,000 to buy 17,000 amur, which we decided would be a good starting number. Some of our more imaginative neighbors said we would use the local Volunteer Fire Departments' water wagon and go to Arkansas and get the amur and volunteered to do so. The Lake was unusable and what did we have to lose other than our freedom? Our 92-year-old neighbor volunteered to be the patsy and go to jail. We wrote to all those we had asked for help in the past. Our state senator, Linda Smith, called a meeting of all the agencies to meet at Silver Lake. Members of those agencies, including the state Director of Wildlife came to Silver Lake and it was decided we would not need to wait another five years but could get the amur the next spring. Our stocking rate must be set by the College of Fisheries who did the five-year study. After studying the amur five years they should be the experts. Right? Those doing the study said we should use 50 amur per vegetated acre and every acre in the lake was vegetated by this time. Fifty fish per acre was a long way from the 10 we expected to use. They decided Silver Lake had 1,610 acres of surface water. We knew we had 3,200 acres which meant we would get 26.6 amur per acre not 50.

Financing

Now we needed money to buy the fish. Our donations and pledges would not stretch to cover 50 or even 26 per amur acre, plus a retaining structure. So, we went after the state grant money in the Clean Water Fund, much of which had been going for studies. We made an application which gave points for approval of a grant and we scored very high on public participation. We scored very high on need. We scored low on public access, an absolute necessity, said DOE, for a grant, for the only public access was the Washington Fish and Wildlife boat launch. The grant money was to be distributed and granted through the Washington Department of Ecology, (DOE) which held the purse strings, and DOE said our county must participate by furnishing 25% of the funding, one half of which could be in in-kind services, such as use of an office, etc.

Our county commissioner said no. The county would not provide public access to Silver Lake or pay 25% of the cost of providing fish. We pointed out to him that the WSU study said the project should cost $675,000 including the cost of a new study of $198,000, and the county would be reimbursed for administering the grant. The county said okay and hired a project manager at $50 an hour. DOE was willing to loan $1.2 million for the project. So the cost of the project was budgeted—not the $675,000 proposed by WSU but $1,701,500, with the county to pay $425,375, one half of which was to be cash or $212,688.

Studies which were estimated by WSU to be $198,000 went to $555,000. When we asked why, we were told because the money was there. We were told by the county administrator of the grant that we were "going for the whole thing."

But unless you get involved with studies you won't need money in that large amount to put amur in your pond or lake. The people at Ilwaco, Washington, determined they needed amur for their county lake, Black Lake. They figured they could clean it of weed with amur for $4,500, and were going to do it with community fund raisers. We had no problem getting pledges (which we released when DOE came in with a grant.) The determination to save our waterways and lakes is strong with the general public, and once the word is out that someone is doing something about it, you have no problem getting support; we didn't.

Success

May 16, 1992, 83,000 amur 8 to 10-inches long were put in Silver Lake with much fan fare. A parade proceeded the delivery truck, which came from Lonoke, Arkansas, and arrived five minutes before the start of the parade. COWSLIP outfitted it with a sign, "Silver Lake or Bust." The local volunteer firemen led the parade with the fire truck covered with kids and balloons. Honking vintage cars followed, and on a barge in the lake local Old Time Fiddlers played 'Turkey in the Straw.' COWSLIP fed the crowd 400 hamburgers, 400 hot dogs, and 400 sodas, all of which were paid for with money COWSLIP members earned working at the Freeway Rest Stop giving out cookies and coffee for donations from travelers. The introduction of amur in Silver Lake and the celebration accompanying it made the headlines of the local weekly paper.

Two years after introduction of the amur, all the weed was gone. The WDFW fish biologist in charge of Silver Lake says that there has been no impact on other fish. In fact more and larger fry abound for they have more oxygen and more chance at getting to "critters" they eat. Bass fishing has never been so good as the first year of weed removal. A recent count shocked the WDFW, as they found

more bass and pan fish and larger bass then they expected. The eight to ten-inch amur which we put in the lake grew to 24 inches in two years and weighed an average of six pounds. They ate a lot of weed.

Pitfalls

Don't overstock or you'll have a mud hole. Amur are mowing machines. Start small and add amur as needed. The fish are sterile and you will eventually need to restock.

The amurs' natural habitat is a river and its natural instinct is to go up river to spawn. Though the Triploids' chromosomes have been altered to make it sterile, the urge to spawn is apparently still there. Be certain your retaining structure is especially secure in the spring. In May we saw thousands of amur (it seemed like every amur in the lake) at our retaining structure nudging the iron posts. Some escaped. We had a diver replace moved rock.

Unless the structure is firmly planted in the hard pan, amur can dig under it. They dig under Lily Pads for roots, so it stands to reason they can dig in soft mud under your retaining structure. In the pen COWSLIP constructed, we used chicken wire fencing bent outward one foot at the lake bottom so rock of at least 10 inches in diameter could be placed on it. This confined amur in a pen even when grass was gone and they could see weed on the other side. They can dig and will, so secure the bottom of your retaining structure with rock.

As I write, I'm looking at water skiers, fishermen, and kids swimming and laughing. Was it worth it? You bet. We got our lake back. You can too. Δ

> *The power to tax involves the power to destroy.*
> —John Marshall
> 1755-1835
> Chief Justice, U.S. Supreme Court

Commonsense precautions help keep kids safe

By Margaret Wright

Children in nature are like little peas in a pod, safe as long as they are secure in their little shells . . . but they can get in serious trouble when the shell is open. Having raised children in backwoods and suburban settings, I can attest to the fact that there is no better place to raise a bunch of happy, healthy offspring than a country home. Usually the only time problems come up is when complacency sneaks in and we become too comfortable with our surroundings. Even though we live far off the "beaten path," away from the busy streets and all the terrible possibilities that lurk there, we still have to be careful. Children, in their innocence, need special care and training to enjoy the freedom associated with the backwoods lifestyle.

Toddlers are always at risk of wandering away. They can disappear in seconds and can travel great distances. Our neighbor's two-year-old daughter was lost between the place her dad was cutting wood and the family home, a distance of about 300 feet. In just a matter of minutes, her parents knew she was missing. After a massive search, she was located about three miles away in the opposite direction from the house. Those little legs can go a long way in a big hurry.

Bells on the shoes and bright clothes are two ways to see and hear the child easily. Fences, of course, are a good barrier to keep them from following the family dog or the pretty butterfly off into the trees, but a fence will only contain the child who consents to be contained. For us, it seems that a redheaded youngster cannot be confined no matter what we do, so we just watch him closely.

If for any reason you think your toddler is out of his safe area and you cannot find him, call for help right away. Emergency personnel would

much rather help locate an "easy find" than one who is seriously lost.

Are they safe to eat?

Keeping the children's play area free of not-so-healthy plants can be an ongoing problem. I am especially wary of the mushrooms that flourish after the rains of spring. Some of them really do look quite appetizing, but would be pretty hard on the tummy. Rake in hand, I go on mushroom patrol regularly. I mash them up and spread the mess around for compost.

My grandson picked all the beautiful red peony flowers this year. Of course they were in full bloom and he said "Yummy." I tried to convey to him all the reasons why we do not pick Mamaw's flowers, and I asked him if he was going to do it again. He promptly said "*Yes!*" They did look good enough to eat, but I never dreamed someone would try it.

Children learn quickly that sweet peas and raspberries right off the vine

taste real good, but they can't tell the difference between the good and the bad plants. We teach them they are not to pick anything to eat unless they ask first. Of course, Papaw's strawberries are taboo under any circumstances. He is the only person allowed to pick them. (Wonder why he is not the only person allowed to *weed* them.)

I always planted a bed of Little Marvel peas for my children, and they loved to stand in the garden eating them. Now they are teaching *their* children to eat Mamaw's peas. We have to watch closely that they don't pick them too soon, but it's fun. The little fellows can pick any raspberries they can reach. The older kids have to help me pick, and then they can glean the leftovers for the day.

Every year we have an ongoing lesson on edible plants. Children like to go hiking, looking and comparing all the plants they find with the pictures in the book. I use the books, A Golden Guide to Weeds from Golden Press and A Field Guide To Rocky Mountain Wildflowers, published by Houghton Mifflin. They have color pictures, and the descriptions give a lot of useful information. You can find both books in used book stores for a couple of dollars each. Making a notebook with pressed plants, each labeled with its name and use, has been a school assignment for each of my children. They really enjoyed doing the project, and they learned a lot.

It is necessary to adjust perimeters as the children get older. Our four-year-old is allowed to ride his bike on the paths and in the lane that goes from his house to Great-Grandma's. We spray-painted a big red line across the driveway about 30 feet from the main road, and this keeps the kids away from the traffic. Bright clothes are a good idea at this age, too. The four- to six-year-olds are probably more apt to wander out of curiosity.

Lost? Wear a whistle, hug a tree, sing a song

We taught our son to "hug a tree": if he is lost, the child is to find a big, friendly tree, then sit and hug it till someone finds him. We also taught Benjamin to sing "Row, Row, Row Your Boat" if he was scared or lost. Most children know this song, and a singing child is easier to find than a quiet one. (It works, even though I never expected the proving ground to be K-Mart.) Also, a child tired from screaming for help is more apt to go to sleep and will be harder to find.

Woods have animals. When we move into the wildlife's territory, we need to be very careful not to intrude too much. Never are children to interfere with the wildlife in any way. If they think something is sick or hurt, they come tell an adult, and we investigate and decide what needs to be done. We took care of an orphaned "Bambi" one year, and that was a neat experience. Only under extreme circumstances should we have to intervene where nature is concerned.

My children always wore a whistle when going out to help dad cut firewood. We knew they would be in alien territory, and a whistle would come in handy if they became separated. We still use whistles a lot if we are going out of our safe zone. Adults can become lost, too.

We have all heard the stories of survival when the victim said, "I remembered my mom said...." So I never hesitated to remind the budding woodsmen of some little safety tip as they went off to be Daniel Boones. The reply was always, *"Aw Mom,"* but several times they used some tid-bit I had reminded them of, to keep themselves safe and healthy.

A big cow bell hangs by the front door. I use it for calling in the troops. When I haven't seen or heard from someone in a while, I just step out and shake that old bell. Voices respond from all over. It has saved me a lot of steps, not to mention wear and tear on the throat. The bell also works great in an emergency. After cutting my hand cleaning veggies one morning, I was a little woozy. I rang that old bell and had plenty of help in a flash. In the reverse case, if the child is in the house and I am outside, they can ring the bell for attention. I do get a little upset if they ring the bell because they want a treat, but I can live with a few false alarms.

Tree houses are fine but make them safe

Tree houses are an absolute requirement for a backwoods home with children. Make sure they are a reasonable height. (The house, not the kids.) I didn't think we needed one like Swiss Family Robinson, so we had a building inspector (me) keep a watch on the progress of the construction. Walls are important. The height of the walls should be such that the kids cannot easily fall over them. Clearing out from under the structure is critical. A stack of firewood or building lumber can increase the injuries if a construc-

tion worker should tumble. It helps to fill in under the tree with sand or other materials that can soften the fall if it happens. When Benjamin fell out of his tree house, the doctor told us he sees several kids a year that have toppled out of tree houses. I personally think safety harnesses and hard hats should be required, but that probably would be hard to enforce. We do have two absolute rules: No throwing things off the tree house, and you have to come in the house to go potty (or at least down on the ground).

You shoot it, you eat it

The tree house age also seems to be the BB gun stage. Gun safety should be in effect no matter what the type of gun or its potential for causing injury. Our hard and fast rule is: If you shoot something, you *will* be prepared to clean it and eat it. I know for a fact that rule has saved many a little bird's feathers (though it did not help big sister's car window).

Older (elementary school age) kids need wider spaces, and we taught them to stay where they could see the house. It depended on the direction they took, but usually they could wander off a safe distance and still feel independent. Remember that the look of the terrain changes with the seasons, and the children need to be reminded of that. Several winters ago, Benjamin became lost in a snow storm because the neighbor's fence, ten acres away, was buried in the snow.

We are very careful to respect the neighbors. The young explorers are repeatedly warned about going on private property, and we never go over, under, or around a fence. We always try to be good neighbors, and teaching the children "neighbor etiquette" can prevent problems.

Teenagers, those invincible people who cannot get hurt (yeah right) are a special concern. Teaching them woods safety should be initiated from the time they are little, but if they're new to the woods, you have to play catch-up.

Since firewood is our source of heat, we have to maintain chain-saw and ax safety procedures. To maintain chain-saw safety, there is one law in effect: they are not allowed to touch it. Just a simple *No!* The ax is OK after they are taught how to use it. We make sure they never chop wood with other kids around.

Keeping the tools picked up is an ongoing problem, but we try real hard. I made a fence out of wood pallets around the wood pile area, and that makes a great place to store the tools. I put the handles down through the top of the pallets so they are out of the way and I can find them. This also protects my garden tools from the little ones dragging them off.

Wood piles are dangerous

A wood pile is an accident waiting to happen. Never let any child climb on a wood pile. We try real hard to keep them away from the stacked wood altogether. Woodpiles, no matter how well stacked, can shift and fall. A little body cannot withstand the crush of the wood. (Every parent and older child should learn CPR. First

Aid is a nifty mini-class for a home-school support group.)

With the tree house injury, I learned that emergency personnel are not equipped with radar to find me way back in the boonies. We measured with the car, from the main highway to the county road and then from the county road to our drive, so we could tell them exactly how to find us. We also put red plastic streamers on the newspaper boxes out by the county road, so there is no room for misunderstanding where we are located. (This also helps if you are selling eggs, etc.)

The perimeter for the older kids was expanded as they grew. Starting out with the fenced yard, it grew to be the area around the house. Then their area was the confines of our property. Being bordered by National Forest can present a problem, so be sure the landmarks are visible year-round. A season-by-season hike will help kids become acclimated to the new appearance of things.

Now that Benjamin is a teenager, he is woods smart, but we are still careful. Rules are in place not only for his safety, but for other people also. He always rides his motorcycle with a

buddy. They are only allowed to have two people on a cycle in an emergency. (Yes, running out of gas is acceptable.) Even if it's Dad, they always have to tell someone where they are going and an approximate return time.

Whether he's hiking, hunting, or riding his motorcycle, we make sure Benjamin has all the proper gear. I also include a small fanny pack with identification, a first aid kit, and a personal alarm. He can turn on the alarm if he crashes and needs help or if he is lost. I think it might also deter a bear or other beast if necessary. Even if it serves no purpose, it makes me feel better.

No matter how well prepared we are, something will always come along to remind us how vulnerable we are. Each new experience teaches something useful, and we just regroup and add the new information to the old.

While not taking away the freedom and innocence of childhood, we need to teach our kids as much as we can to take care of themselves. Caution, not paranoia, should be the guide. Give 'em a big hug and turn them loose to learn and enjoy their environment. Δ

Feeling nostalgic? Now you'll rave! Here's the story of Burma Shave.

By Martin Waterman

I can remember taking a trip as a child and seeing my first Burma Shave signs. Technically speaking, after 1963 all the 7,000 or so sets of signs were supposed to have been taken down. Still, my discovery may not have been unusual, since even today sightings abound (though they're not as frequent as Elvis sightings). It could be possible that some of the thousands of signs that dotted the countryside were never taken down, or perhaps (and more likely) they are the work of some nostalgic farmers who recreated them.

Like many great success stories, Burma Shave started by happenstance. Burma Shave, a brushless shaving cream, was concocted by the Odell family. Its predecessor product, a liniment called Burma Vita, was not doing very well in sales, due to competition and to the fact that it could only be sold to people who were ill. It was suggested that it would be more profitable to market a product that could be used every day, such as Lloyd's Euxesis from England. This was the original brushless shaving cream that was available world-wide. A chemist was hired (Burma-Vita was one of grandfather Odell's homemade concoctions) and after about 300 mixtures were tried, Burma Shave was born.

However, inventing the product was not the key to success, and the product almost died several times because of poor marketing. One of the marketing schemes was called "Jars on Approval," in which the Odell boys would enter a man's office and give him a jar of Burma Shave on this basis: if he liked the product he would pay them 50¢ the next time they saw

him. If he didn't like Burma Shave they would take back the unused portion and "remain friends."

Then one day, Alan Odell came up with a suggestion. He suggested roadside signs like the ones he had seen on road trips when he was out trying to sell Burma-Shave. However, his father would not hear of such an idea, and was sure that the boy was just homesick because of all the travelling he was doing. Alan continued to lobby for his idea and finally his father gave in and gave him $200 to try out his idea.

The year was 1925, and the automobile had people beginning to take to the roads of America. Second-hand boards were purchased, cut into 36-inch lengths, and painted. The original signs did not have a rhyme. Typically, four consecutive signs would read,

SHAVE THE MODERN WAY
FINE FOR THE SKIN
DRUGGISTS HAVE IT
BURMA SHAVE

The signs were put up in a hurry before the ground froze solid on the two roads leading out of Minneapolis. There were about a dozen sets of signs put up on the two roads.

Not too long after that, the first repeat orders for Burma Shave were received from drugstores because the people who travelled the two roads

where the signs had been installed were purchasing Burma Shave from area drugstores. At this time, the business was broke, so the company was incorporated and 49% of the stock was sold to raise capital. Within three weeks, the shares had been sold, and in early 1926 the first sign shop was set up.

The signs continued to bring success and became more and more humorous. The six consecutive signs, when placed 100 paces apart, created something unique in advertising. Of course, in later years as the roads got better and cars got faster, the size of the signs and the distance between them had to be increased.

The consecutive signs commanded the attention of those reading them longer than any single sign could ever hope to do. The entertaining signs helped make long journeys more entertaining, and people became addicted to reading them.

By having the rhymes build suspense until the fifth sign, Burma Shave forced those reading the signs to focus their attention on reading the full series of signs so that the message could be understood and savored like a good joke. For instance:

THE BEARDED LADY / TRIED A JAR
SHE'S NOW / A FAMOUS
MOVIE STAR
BURMA SHAVE

or

IF YOU THINK / SHE LIKES
YOUR BRISTLES
WALK BARE-FOOTED
THROUGH SOME THISTLES
BURMA SHAVE

Eventually, the signs spread to every state, with a few exceptions. No "official" signs appeared in Arizona, New Mexico, or Nevada because of low traffic density. Massachusetts received no signs because winding roads and excessive foliage made it hard to find enough locations to justify placing them there.

The slogans were very powerful, so much so that the Burma Shave Company did not even feel the effects of the Depression. The rhymes aimed at motivating potential purchasers of Burma Shave were not just cute, but were probably some of the best advertising slogans ever written. Some of them suggested to men that they would do better with the women if they used Burma Shave:

SHE EYED / HIS BEARD
AND SAID NO DICE
THE WEDDING'S OFF
I'LL COOK THE RICE
BURMA SHAVE

or

A CHIN / WHERE BARBED WIRE
BRISTLES STAND
IS BOUND TO BE
A NO MA'AMS LAND
BURMA SHAVE

Another good example is

USE THIS CREAM / A DAY / OR TWO
THEN DON'T CALL HER —
SHE'LL CALL YOU
BURMA SHAVE

Not overlooking the spending power of women, the company put up rhymes to lure them to purchase Burma Shave for the men in their lives:

A CHRISTMAS HUG
A BIRTHDAY KISS
AWAITS / THE WOMAN
WHO GIVES THIS
BURMA SHAVE

Others slogans suggested that there was no better product or substitute for Burma-Shave:

SUBSTITUTES / ARE LIKE A GIRDLE
THEY FIND SOME JOBS
THEY JUST / CAN'T HURDLE
BURMA SHAVE

Though the Burma Shave Company prospered, there were many challenges, too. Not only was there fierce competition, there was also the need to come up with a continuous supply of superior verses. This was solved with an annual contest that paid $100 for each verse used. There were thousands of entries sent in, resulting in many rhymes of high quality. Judging the entries eventually became difficult because in some years there would be more than 50,000 entries. This forced Burma Shave to hire some advertising copywriters to help in the selection process.

With the trend toward better automobiles and roads, the traffic accident rate began to climb. In response, the company created some slogans stressing traffic safety. In fact, some of the best Burma Shave rhymes were written with public service in mind:

PAST / SCHOOLHOUSES
TAKE IT SLOW
LET THE LITTLE / SHAVERS GROW
BURMA-SHAVE

or

IS HE LONESOME / OR JUST BLIND
THIS GUY WHO / DRIVES
SO CLOSE BEHIND?
BURMA-SHAVE.

Still other good examples include

MANY A FOREST / USED TO STAND
WHERE A / LIGHTED MATCH
GOT OUT OF HAND
BURMA SHAVE

and

THE ONE WHO / DRIVES WHEN
HE'S BEEN DRINKING
DEPENDS ON YOU
TO DO HIS THINKING
BURMA SHAVE

There are some funny stories in the history of the Burma Shave Company.

In Los Angeles, free sample jars were handed out to men as they entered a wrestling match. However, when one of the wrestlers angered the crowd, some of them started to throw their jars into the ring. Fortunately (and probably miraculously) no one was hurt . . . a close shave for the company, so to speak.

A similar occurrence happened at Ebbets Field in New York. Tubes of Burma Shave were handed out to fans entering the game, but when the umpire made a call unfavorable to the Dodgers, he was pelted with the tubes. The game had to be interrupted until the groundskeepers could remove the tubes.

Another problem that arose was that the Burma Shave signs had a tendency to disappear near college towns. To remedy this, special bolts were used, so that a special tool was necessary to unbolt the signs, and the posts had crosspieces attached to the bottoms to act as anchors.

Another problem in rural areas was the tendency for hunters to use the signs for target practice. Some destruction was also caused by small animals that took to chewing on the signs. However, much more damage was attributed to horses that found them to be an ideal height for back scratching. A horse would maneuver itself beneath the bottom edge of a sign and then begin to scratch the itch. This would often result in a broken sign. This problem was solved when many of the signs were raised from nine feet to ten.

Still another problem occurred when the Burma Shave Company tried to mock the rising trend of coupon advertising with the following rhyme:

FREE OFFER! FREE OFFER!
RIP A FENDER / OFF YOUR CAR
MAIL IT IN FOR
A HALF-POUND JAR
BURMA-SHAVE

Fenders began to arrive in the mail and by express, and local people scavenged the Minnesota junkyards and brought in fenders. Some fenders from toy cars also came in, and without exception, everyone who brought or sent in a fender received a free half-pound jar of Burma Shave. Of course, the publicity from the bumper offer was priceless and further helped to establish the company as part of America's roadside culture.

Perhaps the company went too far with the following rhyme spoofing science fiction and curiosity about outer space:

FREE - FREE / A TRIP / TO MARS
FOR 900 / EMPTY JARS
BURMA-SHAVE

The manager of a supermarket in Appleton, Wisconsin, took up the challenge and wrote to the company asking where he should send the 900 jars for his free trip. The company sent back the following reply: "If a trip to Mars you'd earn, remember, friend, there's no return."

In reply, the enterprising supermarket manager accepted. He turned the project into a fantastic promotion for Burma Shave that had children and adults swarming the supermarket. The promotion included no less than a rocket plane on display and little green men on the roof firing toy rocket gliders into the parking lot.

It was decided by the Burma Shave company to send the manager and his family to Mars. The real destination was to be Mars, Germany. (Even though it is spelled *Moers*, it is pronounced *Mars*.) Again, the publicity was enormous, especially when the manager showed up wearing a silvery space suit and a bubble on his head. The company, of course, provided him with extra jars of Burma Shave so that he could barter with the Martians.

Another reason the ad campaign was so successful is that the company would not put up any signs that offended anyone. Some of the signs showed a measure of humility:

ALTHO / WE'VE SOLD
SIX MILLION OTHERS
WE STILL CAN'T SELL
THOSE COUGH DROP BROTHERS
BURMA SHAVE

It is said that all good things must come to an end, and this was the case with Burma Shave. There were a number of factors that led to the decline of the product. After World War II, increasing costs and decreasing sales began to be felt by the company. People were travelling faster on the highways and times were changing. The signs just weren't working anymore, and the company started to advertise with other media.

The real end to the roadside rhymes came in 1963, when the company was sold to Phillip Morris to become an operating division of American Safety Razor Products. The decision was made to remove all the signs as soon as possible, especially since any remaining signs would mean that rent money would still be owed to farmers. The end of the signs was popular fodder for the news media, and many stories were written about the demise of this American institution. A set of signs was donated to the Smithsonian Institution to preserve this part of Americana. Below are a few more of the 600 rhymes that were used on roadways throughout the country.

WE'VE MADE / GRANDPA
LOOK SO TRIM / THE LOCAL
DRAFT BOARD'S AFTER HIM
BURMA SHAVE

OUR FORTUNE / IS YOUR
SHAVEN FACE / IT'S OUR BEST
ADVERTISING SPACE
BURMA SHAVE

PEDRO / WALKED
BACK HOME, BY GOLLY
HIS BRISTLY CHIN
WAS HOT-TO-MOLLY
BURMA SHAVE

WHEN THE STORK
DELIVERS A BOY
OUR WHOLE / DARN FACTORY
JUMPS FOR JOY
BURMA SHAVE

THE POOREST GUY
IN THE HUMAN RACE
CAN HAVE A
MILLION DOLLAR FACE
BURMA SHAVE

THIRTY DAYS / HATH SEPTEMBER
APRIL / JUNE AND THE
SPEED OFFENDER
BURMA SHAVE

IF DAISIES / ARE YOUR
FAVORITE FLOWER
KEEP PUSHIN' UP THOSE
MILES-PER-HOUR
BURMA SHAVE

SUBSTITUTES
CAN LET YOU DOWN
QUICKER / THAN A
STRAPLESS GOWN
BURMA SHAVE

THE BIG BLUE TUBE'S
JUST LIKE LOUISE
YOU GET / A THRILL
FROM EVERY SQUEEZE
BURMA SHAVE

"NO, NO," / SHE SAID
TO HER BRISTLY BEAU
"I'D RATHER / EAT THE MISTLETOE"
BURMA SHAVE

TRAIN APPROACHING
WHISTLE SQUEALING
PAUSE!
AVOID THAT / RUNDOWN FEELING!
BURMA SHAVE

UNLESS / YOUR FACE
IS STINGER FREE
YOU'D BETTER LET
YOUR HONEY BE
BURMA SHAVE

THIS CREAM / MAKES THE
GARDENER'S DAUGHTER
PLANT HER TU-LIPS
WHERE SHE OUGHTER
BURMA SHAVE

IF YOUR PEACH
KEEPS OUT / OF REACH
BETTER PRACTICE
WHAT WE PREACH
BURMA SHAVE

TO KISS / A MUG
THAT'S LIKE A CACTUS
TAKES MORE NERVE
THAN IT DOES PRACTICE
BURMA SHAVE △

The Fuyugaki persimmon — it really is "food for the gods"

By Alice B. Yeager
Photos by James O. Yeager

In our small orchard there is one tree bearing fruit that can only be described as *luscious*. This is the Fuyugaki variety of Japanese persimmons. The taste of a ripe Fuyugaki persimmon bears a faint resemblance to that of an American wild persimmon. Fuyugaki fruit has a flavor all its own—sweet and wonderful—something to be anticipated and enjoyed. The scientific name for the genus of these trees is *Diospyros*, meaning "food for the gods"—a very appropriate description.

Fuyugaki flesh has a good texture, and the fruit may be eaten before it's fully ripe without any puckering effect, as it is non-astringent. When ready for harvesting, the fruit will turn a dark red with a blue blush and be slightly soft to the touch. The interior is reddish-orange and holds its color well when cooked or frozen. Keep a napkin handy when eating a Fuyugaki persimmon, as the fruit is juicy—kind of like a ripe Elberta peach or a mango. The persimmons are large, often weighing a pound or more apiece.

The Fuyugaki tree is a medium height tree maturing to about 25 to 30 feet high. It is an excellent summer shade tree, as well as a fruit tree, and it is not necessary to plant more than one tree for pollination. Fuyugaki is self-pollinating, as are most Japanese persimmon trees.

The leaves are a little larger than those of the American native persimmons, but they have the same oblong shape, sharp-pointed with smooth margins. This is a deciduous tree, and with the coming of cold weather, the leaves turn a vibrant orange-bronze color.

Trees bloom in mid-spring after leaves have appeared. The flowers are somewhat inconspicuous, being small, cream colored, four-lobed, and semi-bell-shaped. However, bees are drawn to them, making persimmon trees—both wild and tame—a boon to bee-keepers.

Japanese varieties of persimmons do not have the wide climatic range of the common American persimmons, which cover a large range of territory from Connecticut to the Gulf states and as far west as Southeast Iowa and West Texas. The Japanese cultivars are mainly recommended for Zones 7 to 10.

In our part of Zone 8 (southwest Arkansas), we have had only one fruitless season. In 1987, due to a freak late-April freeze, fruit of all kinds was wiped out in a large portion of the South and Southwest. That freeze killed all of the tender foliage on our Fuyugaki tree, and although the tree did renew its leaves a month later, it produced no flowers.

Soil requirements for Japanese persimmon trees are about the same as for peach trees, and persimmon trees will thrive in ordinary soil. Rich soil or soil high in nitrogen causes these trees to produce more foliage than fruit. A well-drained sandy loam is ideal. The pH preference is 6.0 to 8.0. Trees should be planted about 20 feet apart, making them suitable for most home orchards. First fruits should be harvested in three to four years, depending on growing conditions.

Once established, Japanese persimmons don't seem to require a great deal of care, as they are relatively disease- and insect-free. As with all trees, there will be an occasional dead limb or one that is weak and sagging toward the ground. These should be removed to promote good health and appearance.

The only pest problem we have had with the Fuyugaki tree has come in the form of fall webworms. These one-inch-long caterpillars form weblike nests (similar to those of the Eastern tent caterpillar) on the ends of branches. If not brought quickly under control, these culprits will proceed to defoliate a goodly portion of the branches. We break their webs with a stick, puff some Sevin dust at them and that's usually the end of the caterpillars.

For some reason, we seldom see a bird-pecked fruit. Maybe the native birds haven't developed a taste for this foreign import.

Unless cross pollination occurs because of wild trees in the area, fruits will be almost seedless. Usually seeds are very small and useless as far as propagation is concerned. To secure a worthwhile tree, a gardener should purchase a grafted variety from a reputable nursery.

When ordering trees by mail, I always request that roots *not* be severely pruned. Some nurseries insist on following a practice of close root-cropping, but I have found from experience that trees with only a stub of a root are very slow to take hold and grow when planted and may even die. That's money down the drain, to say nothing of the time and effort involved. However, most reputable nurseries will replace plants if the gardener reports the problem within a reasonable length of time.

A good example of the negative side of severe root-pruning occurred when I ordered our Fuyugaki tree. The tree arrived with only a stub of a tap root and did not put out a leaf for an entire year. During the summer, I kept the soil moist and mulched. To be sure the tree was still alive, I checked from time to time, gently rubbing the trunk in a small area until I could see the

The hand in this picture gives the scale: this fruit is big.

green life color just beneath the surface of the young skin-like bark. I was encouraged by the fact that the trunk felt cool to my hand—not dry and lifeless. The next year, leaves appeared and the tree slowly began to recover and grow. (In gardening circles this type of human behavior is known as *keeping the faith.*)

When planting a Japanese persimmon tree, remember to give it plenty of root space—*i.e.,* dig the hole somewhat larger than actually needed. Notice the soil line at the base of the trunk and plant accordingly. When placing the soil around the tree, fill the hole about halfway and then water generously. Put in the remainder of the soil and water again. This will remove any air pockets, and soil will settle in around the roots.

A young tree needs plenty of moisture to carry it through prolonged dry spells. Until it can develop a good root system, a small dam about 18 inches in diameter should be made around the tree so that water may be directed to developing roots. A thick mulch of organic matter—straw, grass clippings, etc.—is very beneficial during the summer. Not only does mulch shade the soil, but it keeps grass and

weeds from infringing on the tree's moisture supply.

Fuyugaki fruit is versatile. Besides being eaten fresh, it may also be used in other delectable ways, such as pies (see recipe), puddings, fruit salads, and so on. The persimmons may also be pureed and frozen for later use. (Discard skins before processing.) Japanese persimmons rank high in

Two ripe Fuyugaki persimmons weigh in at a little over a pound apiece.

Vitamin A and potassium, making them a very healthful fruit to eat fresh.

Food for the gods! What more can I say?

This nursery carries at least 17 varieties of Japanese persimmons, among them the Fuyugaki:

Chestnut Hill Nursery
Route 1, Box 341
Alachua, FL 32615

And here's the recipe I promised you:

Fuyugaki persimmon pie

1 unbaked 9-inch pie shell
1/2 cup sugar
2 tablespoons flour
1/2 teaspoon ginger
1/2 teaspoon nutmeg
1 1/2 cups pureed Fuyugaki pulp
  (Do not puree skins.)
1/4 cup evaporated milk
1 egg, slightly beaten
1/3 cup chopped pecans (optional)

Sift dry ingredients together and combine with persimmon pulp. Add milk and egg. Stir until smooth and pour into unbaked pie shell. Bake at 375° F for 45 to 50 minutes, or until knife inserted in center comes out clean. Optional: Pie may be taken from oven just before completely done, sprinkled with chopped pecans (or other nuts) and returned to oven to finish baking. Δ

If all mankind minus one were of one opinion, and only one person were of the contrary opinion, mankind would be no more justified in silencing that one person than he, if he had the power, would be justified in silencing mankind
—John Stuart Mill
1806-1873

Ayoob on firearms

By Massad Ayoob

My choice for the ideal backwoods gun is the four-inch .44 Magnum handgun

I've packed many a handgun from the backwoods to the plains to the desert and the bushveld, but as middle age and experience (the collected aggregate of our mistakes) come together for me, I'm down to one primary backwoods handgun. It's the Smith & Wesson .44 Magnum with four-inch barrel.

Yes, this handgun can kick—but hear me out. First, in the same sense that you can load a .357 Magnum revolver with light .38 Special ammo, you can load the .44 Magnum with mild .44 Special. The latter cartridges give you about the power of an old Army .45 automatic, and very mild recoil in the big Smith & Wesson revolver. It feels like you're shooting .38s.

You can load the gun with .44 Special Winchester Silvertip hollowpoints and have an excellent home defense handgun. I've seen 10-year-old girls and arthritic older women fire this round from .44 Magnum S&Ws with no discomfort or fear. Will it be powerful enough? Col. Jeff Cooper, the master gunfighting instructor, has publicly recommended the .44 Special revolver as the ideal police service handgun. One of Cooper's contemporaries was Elden Carl, the famous combat master. Carl shot his way to fame with the Colt .45 automatic, but the revolver he actually carried on patrol as a deputy sheriff was a Smith & Wesson .44 Special with four-inch barrel.

When you've paid your shooting dues and have learned to tolerate more recoil, you can move up to the Magnum loads for hunting, long range

shooting, and protection from large animals. Ross Seyfried, former world champion combat shooter and professional big game hunter, carried a four-inch Model 29 .44 Magnum behind his right hip every day when he made his living as a cattleman. His big concern wasn't shooting a deer while out in the pasture; it was having to shoot a big steer if one went berserk.

A similar job description was in the mind of Seyfried's mentor Elmer Keith, the legendary gun expert who was almost single-handedly responsible for the development of the .44 Magnum by Smith & Wesson. As both a cowboy and a professional hunter, Keith had multiple occasions to shoot maddened horses, livestock, and in at least one case a game animal, off his body. A rifle was too long or too far from reach to bring to bear in these situations. Each time, the gun that saved Keith's life was a heavy caliber sixgun.

When the .44 Magnum came along, the Smith & Wesson factory presented Keith, the developer, with the very first one, a blue steel specimen with four-inch barrel. This or one identical was his carry gun virtually daily for the rest of his long, rich life.

Why the .44? First, it is very accurate at long range and retains its power there. In 1987 in the Eastern Transvaal in South Africa, I shot an impala with my 4" 629. The 320-grain SSK hunting bullet drilled completely through him and knocked him flat, at a range of 117 yards. Keith reported much bigger animals shot through and through at much greater ranges with his own .44 Magnum handloads.

Massad Ayoob

Handgun hunting experts feel that within a hundred yards, a .44 Magnum revolver puts about the killing power of a .30/30 rifle on your hip. The better ones will shoot four- to six-inch groups or tighter at that distance, which is better than most experienced hunters can do with an open-sighted .30/30 rifle at the same distance.

Second, if you run a risk of being threatened by large, dangerous animals—the livestock-turned-bad that Keith and Seyfried had to deal with, or bears, or big feral dogs—the .44 Magnum gives you the punch you'll need to stop a sudden, close threat before you or yours get mangled.

The four-inch barrel gives daily portability when holstered on a sturdy belt, and the holstered revolver is short enough that it doesn't get in the way on horseback or when sitting in a vehicle. The shorter barrel also allows for a quicker draw in an emergency.

Numerous single action revolvers are made in this caliber, but they're slow to load or reload in an emergency (punch out the empties one at a time, reload the fresh cartridges one at a time), and the hammer has to be thumb-cocked before each shot. The swing-out cylinder of the Smith & Wesson lets you load two rounds at a time—or all six with a speedloader—and you punch all the empties out at once with a single stroke of the ejector rod. The double action design lets you rip off six shots as fast as you can pull the trigger in a short-range emergency, without having to cock your Smith & Wesson.

There are other emergencies the gun can handle. A friend who's a farmer had a hand badly mangled in a machine accident. To this day he's convinced that if he had been carrying one of his .41 or .44 Magnums, he could have hammered six shots into the motor of the device and "killed the machine" before it maimed him for life. Unfortunately, he didn't have it on. Today, one of the big S&W Magnums is constantly on his hip as he goes about his farm duties.

There are other double action revolvers that take the big Magnum cartridge, the Ruger and the recently discontinued Dan Wesson, but they're both larger, bulkier guns than the S&W. I've found the Model 29 (blue or nickel finish) and Model 629 (stainless) to be the lightest and most compact when fitted with four-inch barrel.

I now switch off between two S&W .44s for backwoods use. Both are the stainless 629 format. One is standard out of the box, and particularly accurate; it delivered that 117 yard shot for me in

Africa and is my preference during hunting season.

The rest of the time, the version I use is S&W's Mountain Gun, now back in production. It's the lightest of the big Magnum revolvers, with its four-inch barrel gracefully tapered, the edges of its cylinder radiused, and the grip frame rounded off to a .38-size round butt configuration. Recoil isn't that bad once you're used to it, and it's very comfortable to carry. I normally wear it discreetly concealed in an ARG (Ayoob Rear Guard) inside-the-waistband holster from Mitchell Rosen. The reasons for this, and the "etiquette" of carrying handguns in backwoods environments, are things we'll discuss in more depth in this space before too long.

For me, I can't think of a better back-trail companion. The versatile ammunition options in the full range of .44 Special through the most potent .44 Magnum rounds give you a single gun that can cover any emergency, from a rampaging grizzly bear to trespassers who think *Deliverance* was a training film and have their eye on the lady of the house. Δ

A BHM Writer's Profile: Annie Duffy

Annie Duffy, age 17, grew up with *Backwoods Home Magazine*. As publisher Dave Duffy's daughter, she began working with the magazine at age 6 by helping to stuff envelopes for mailings to potential subscribers.

At age 7 she wrote her first small article for the magazine, and at age 13 originated the magazine's *"Where I live"* column for teenage readers.

Since then she has worked in every aspect of the magazine, including writing and editing articles, working in the mailroom, tending the magazine's booth at the many trade shows we do around the country, and setting articles in the desktop publishing program used for final copy.

Now 17 and a high school senior, her main interests are singing (she takes voice lessons and is a member of her high school choir), dancing (she takes an after school swing dance class), writing, and computers.

A BHM Writer's Profile: Dave Duffy

Dave Duffy is the founder, publisher, and editor of *Backwoods Home Magazine*. He built his own home in a remote area of the Siskiyou Mountains of southern Oregon while launching the magazine, and that served as BHM's first office. Since the home was 10 miles from the nearest electric utility pole, Duffy installed a photovoltaic system to produce sun-generated electricity to run the computers and printers to publish the magazine.

Born in Boston, Duffy spent his first 29 years there, where he worked as a journalist for several daily newspapers. He then moved to Nevada and California, working as a journalist for newspapers and later as a writer and editor for the Department of Defense.

Unhappy with working for others and living near cities, he spent several years of vacations and long weekends building his hideaway in southern Oregon. He eventually fled the rat race for the woods. In 1989, he started *Backwoods Home Magazine* to help others do the same.

Homesteading on the electronic frontier

By Martin Waterman

Find information fast on the Internet

This is just a personal observation, but I've noticed that many of my rural-based friends tend to favor using the Internet *news groups* while friends from the city favor the *World Wide Web*. Perhaps this gives credence to the idea that country folk are more friendly than city folk, since participating in a news group is more like going over to your neighbor's and chatting over coffee,

while the Web tends to be more commercial and impersonal...more like getting coffee at the drive-thru at a fast food restaurant.

Using the Internet

On the other hand, perhaps this country preference for news groups comes about because of the new learning challenges making the change to backwoods living presents. Many people who make the change have to start from scratch as they learn about producing their own food, power, buildings, and the other things they need. This requires a lot of information, much of which is not readily available. Even those who have been living the rural lifestyle are continually seeking information, as they consider new technology (as well as valuable older technology) for various projects.

Fortunately, the Information Highway can provide ample amounts of information in a short amount of time. In the majority of instances, this is a cost-effective and efficient way to receive information, since it only takes a few moments to post your questions on the appropriate news group, and then you can get on with your affairs. When you check your e-mail or news group postings later, you will probably be surprised at the wide range of responses, as well as the areas from which they came.

Independent energy

Like most people, when I need answers to my questions, I don't want to have to wait weeks for a catalog, or run up my long distance phone bill, or spend time hunting at the library. I want the answer *now*. Recently, I've been assembling information on independent energy and have found the Internet to be most obliging.

One news group which I find particularly useful is **alt.energy.renewable**. Topics usually include the latest technology and uses of wind- and solar-generated power. There is always information on other aspects of producing your own energy as well, and recently there was a fascinating discussion on how to build a wind generator from oil drums for either pumping water or charging batteries. Another very important topic that is discussed in this news group is where to go on the Internet for related information or to find suppliers. That

makes it a good starting point to find information about renewable energy resources or to supplement your knowledge.

The best thing about the site is that people post messages to give reports or to ask questions about their alternative energy experiences, installations, and plans. You can often learn more from reading about other people's personal experiences than you can from studying other types of technical media.

Using the Web

You can also find a great deal of useful information on the World Wide Web. Using *Webcrawler,* a popular and easy-to-use Internet *search engine* on the Web, I entered the words "alternative energy" and clicked on the Search button. It instantly returned a list of 662 Internet sites.

The first one I visited was the Alternative Energy Equipment Exchange, a very useful site located at **http://www.wetlabs.com/aeex/sintro.html.** AEEX has a free service in the form of *alternative energy classifieds.* You can post equipment you have for sale or look for equipment that you may require. AEEX provides classifications for solar energy (photovoltaics, solar hot water, solar cooking, solar heating, etc.), wind power (wind generators), storage batteries (lead-acid, nickel-iron, nickel cadmium, alkaline, fuel cells, etc.), hydro-electric power (water power), and other independent energy resources. All ads remain on the system for one month, and you can repost as often as you like.

I found another interesting independent-energy-related Web site at Solstice: Sustainable Energy and Development Online. It's located at **http://solstice.crest.org/index.html**.

Solstice bills itself as "the site for energy efficiency, renewable energy, and sustainable technology information and connections." Solstice is sponsored by the Center for Renewable Energy and Sustainable Technology in Washington, DC, and in addition to being a site with lots of information, there are also links to other related sites on the Web.

(Editor's note: the Net Links page of our *BHM* Web site will take you to the energy-related Internet addresses mentioned here, among others. Our Web address appears at the end of this article.)

Your own news group

You can't please everyone, so inevitably there will be those who have a need for a news group that is not already available. In some cases, there may be a demand for just the type of news group you're looking for. Let's say you want to start a news group called **rec.icefishing**. The first thing to find out is if the group already exists in one form or another, or if a similar group such as a fishing news group has a constituency of frost-loving fisherfolk. If the proposed group is of local interest, without wide appeal, your next line of action is to see if your local provider wants to set up a local group for you and your ice-fishing friends.

If you want your news group to be distributed on a world-wide basis, things get a little more complex. There is a formal procedure which usually includes voting by a panel. If you want information about how to start your own news group, you can get it by going to the news group called **news.announce.newusers**. You will find an article posted there called "How to create a new USENET news group." This is a very good news group to visit, because it has many documents for beginners that tell about the "netiquette" of posting messages and replying to postings, as well as general information about USENET News.

Web weather

Everyone seems to be spending more and more time on the World Wide Web. My *Web browser*, *Netscape* (the program that allows me to see the Web), also allows me to *Bookmark* my favorite sites. This is important, since many Web sites have inconveniently long addresses, and often, if you find a site you like, you may not be able to find it again. I have about 50 sites Bookmarked. I just click on "Bookmark" on the Menu Bar, and the Bookmark Menu opens, displaying the list of sites I've marked. Then I click on the Web site I want to go to on the list. This also saves online charges, and you don't have to remember layers of linked sites or how you cyber-surfed to the site the last time.

The Web site that I frequent the most is the weather site for my area. I find that it is very accurate, since it is updated three times a day. It is the same information that our goofy weatherman receives, and I like the idea that I don't have to synchronize my day so that I can turn on the idiot box to catch his routine, just to find out if we will have frost or rain. In addition, I only need the particulars for my area, and most weathermen focus on city weather, where most of the population resides; they don't pay much attention to the rural areas. At one time, one of the most popular sites on the Internet was the satellite weather maps, because they look so cool. However, they are really not much use to the average person.

You can easily find a weather site for your area by doing a search using the *keyword* "weather." I like the convenience of being able to get the weather when I need it. For the last few years, I've planted my crops using the rain and frost forecasts given on the Internet. I have found that they are very accurate. We have a short growing season here, so being able to get my crops planted as early as possible without risk makes a big difference in

how much I will harvest throughout the season.

E-mail from hell

I am often asked about the Internet, and people say to me things like, "You must love computers." If fact, I hate the bloody things. I would rather be outside on a sunny day tearing up the field with a plow, planting, or being with friends and family. I look at computers and the Internet as tools that enhance my rural existence and allow me to make a living, just like a tractor does. But no one comes up to me and says, "You sure must love your tractor."

What does this have to do with e-mail? I'll tell you. Electronic mail has saved me a bundle on postage, and it's faster than the conventional "snail mail." However, I recently had an experience which reminded me how frustrating computers and the new information technology can be.

I had always thought of e-mail as an uneventful way to send and receive messages, until I experienced what can best be described as The E-Mail from hell. It all started innocently enough. An editor wanted to borrow a piece of software so that he could take some screen shots of it for a review I had done. I had done a lot of customizing on this software, including many add-on components. I used Norton Desktop to compress the file, but it was still over five megabytes in size. I sent the file as an *attachment* to an e-mail message. As sometimes happens, I got knocked off the Internet. I have never tracked down the reason for this, but it seems to occur most often during high-traffic times. This was Sunday evening, and it took me three tries to send my e-mail.

A few hours later, I logged on to check my e-mail and found that the address I sent it to was incorrect, so the *Mailer Daemon* wanted to send the file back to me. (That's its real name; it's a program that bounces back messages that have technical problems.) There was nothing I could do. I kept trying to receive the file, but I kept getting knocked off the Internet before the half hour needed for transferring the file was up. I knew that if I did not accept this e-mail, I would not get any of my other e-mail that was backing up behind it.

Finally, I called my provider and he hunted down that e-mail message in the bowels of their computer server and unceremoniously killed it on my behalf. I would have loved to see it die. This simple exercise had ended up costing me several hours, with about three hours of wasted on-line charges. This story has two morals: (1) electronic communication is not a perfect science, and (2) if you are e-mailing

large files, make sure you have the right address.

The Internet is really changing social structures, and many people are meeting who normally would never come in contact with each other. Recently I visited a friend who'd met her current boyfriend on the Internet. I asked her if it was serious, and she nodded and said, "I'll say, we're even sharing a hard drive."

(Questions, comments, and information of interest to *Backwoods Home* readers can be sent via the Internet to Martin Waterman at waterman@nbnet.nb.ca, or to other editors of *Backwoods Home Magazine* at backwood@snowcrest. net. *BHM*'s Internet address on the World Wide Web is http://www.snowcrest.net/backwood/index.html.) Δ

A BHM Writer's Profile: Maurcia DeLean Houck

Maurcia DeLean Houck is a nationally known author with more than 1,500 credits in a variety of national magazines and newspapers. She is a 1999 inductee in the Marquis Who's Who in the East and is an active member of the National Writer's Association. Maurcia is a contributor to two books, Family Travel Guides (Carousel Press, 1995) and The Grandparent's Answer Book (Chariot-Victor, 1999). Her first solo book project, If These Walls Could Talk, is scheduled for release later this year by Picton Press.

E-mail from readers

It caught us a bit off guard: we never anticipated that our Electronic Frontier column would draw so many responses so fast. So far, most of the responses are concerned with getting connected with the Internet and finding information on it. Here are a few examples.

Andrew G., from New Brunswick, Canada, wanted to know what resources were available to those who were interested in a "backwoods home" type of lifestyle. I told him that the *Backwoods Home* Web Page (http://www.snowcrest.net/backwood/index.html) would be continually adding links to sites that would be useful to those contemplating the move, or those already enjoying the lifestyle. This column will also offer useful sites. Upcoming topics include homeschooling and doing business on the Web.

Heidi M. wrote, "A little over a year ago, my husband, our dog and I moved from Los Angeles to the Rocky Mountains. Our goal is a ranch, upon which we can be self sufficient." Heidi works from home for a California-based computer training and consulting company, but like many people, she has found being online intimidating. One of her questions was how to get on the Internet.

The first—and one of the best—sources of information is the nearest computer store. Someone there will know who the Internet providers are for your area. However, some computer shops become agents for some of the providers, so shop around and make sure you're getting the best possible prices and services.

One of the hottest e-mail topics was finding connectivity at a reasonable price in rural areas. Many of the messages came from people who already had access to the Internet via America Online and Compuserve but found the access to be expensive and complicated. John D., from Arizona, was frustrated because he uses Compuserve, and although he uses an 800 number, it is not toll free.

If you are already on the Internet, check out the Web site **http://www.tagsys.com:80/Providers/**. You can also ask people and businesses in your town that have Web sites, since they probably have arrangements with providers that are close at hand.

The business of being an Internet provider is growing by leaps and bounds, and although most of the growth has taken place in the cities, it is spreading fast to rural areas. Only recently did *Backwoods Home Magazine* find an Internet provider with a toll free dial-up near them, but you probably don't live as remote as they do.

Around the corner is wireless and cable technology, which I will write about in future columns. Δ

When it comes to land contracts — be careful! Here are some critical points to consider.

By Harry Styron

You've finally found your country dream place. The seller has treated you with great courtesy. What's more, he'll finance your purchase with a land contract.

No need to deal with the endless fees, requirements, and delays of lenders. Even if you qualify for a loan, the broken-down farmhouse won't meet most lenders' guidelines. And the bank or mortgage company has absolutely no interest in financing the unconventional house you're dying to build.

The land contract, or *contract for deed*, seems to be just what you need. The real estate broker tells you that it is the customary device in the area for owner-financing. Just put 15% down, move in and start making payments.

But did you ask these questions?

1. What happens if the seller gets Alzheimer's disease or a divorce or dies or goes bankrupt?

2. What happens if you pay on the property for nine years on a ten-year contract, then are disabled and cannot continue? Do you have any equity? If so, do you have to file a lawsuit to get it?

3. If a highway comes through and takes part of the property, who gets the condemnation money? If a neighbor files a re-zoning application, who gets notified? Do you have any right to protest?

4. Is there another way to do the deal with owner-financing?

If you asked these questions and obtained clear answers, you may be having serious doubts as to whether you want to buy land on contract. The truth is that courts look on such contracts with disfavor because of all the grief they cause for sellers and buyers. The statutes and case law regarding such contracts vary from state to state. Even within a state, it may be impossible for a lawyer to give a clear answer to one or more of these questions, because the law on that point is unsettled.

What happens when the seller's capacity changes?

A land contract looks much like a contract to purchase real estate with a long-delayed closing. So you sign it, make a down payment, and begin making payments. Now who owns the property?

Ownership has suddenly become complicated. In the best possible arrangement for a land contract, the seller signs a deed to the property in your favor when you make the down payment and sign the contract. The deed is held by a reputable escrow company whose job is to collect your payments and to record the deed when you have made all the required payments. At this point, the seller has legal title to the property and *record title* (your name doesn't show up in the county land records), and you possibly have equitable title, or a right of unknown extent that it would be unfair to deprive you of.

Suppose the seller, two years later, becomes mentally incapacitated due to disease, injury, or age, and suppose he has never signed the deed and placed it in escrow. He is put in a nursing home, and Medicaid picks up part of the tab for his care, thereby obtaining the right to reimbursement from his assets. He dies. Medicaid searches the land records and finds that he owns the property where you live. Medicaid wants to sell the property at auction. You find that your payments have been cashed by the seller's son. Maybe you can get it all straightened out, but it costs you $15,000 in legal fees and months or years of anxiety.

Maybe you make ten years' worth of payments on the ten-year contract, then find out the seller doesn't remember who you are. His son (or somebody) was cashing your checks. You want your deed, but the record owner of the land can no longer write or tell anyone what your deal was. The son wants the land for himself.

Suppose the seller's son or spouse claims that the seller was not legally competent at the time you signed the contract. Though it was not apparent to you at the time, because you didn't know the seller personally or the true value of property in the area, he truly had been slipping and sold the property to you well below market value. The real estate broker collected a commission out of the down payment and is now difficult to locate. The court agrees with the seller's family and orders them to return your money and a little more and rescinds the purchase. You have no title insurance, so you get a nice bill from a nice lawyer.

Maybe the seller has all his marbles, but gets into financial trouble elsewhere. He is forced to file for liquidation in bankruptcy court. The bankruptcy trustee doesn't like your land contract and begins legal wrangling to get you out so he can liquidate the seller's interest in the property to get money to pay the seller's creditors. Maybe you "win" in court, after a drawn-out, expensive battle.

The seller gets a divorce. The divorce decree fails to mention the property. You need the ex-wife's signature on the deed to get good title, if only so you can sell the property. You can't find her. Or you find her and she wants to know what's in it for her. Or you learn that she's disabled or dead.

I once encountered a situation in which both selling spouses had signed the deed, but there was a mistake in it. Meanwhile the wife had died, so obtaining a corrected deed was impossible without opening a probate court case and having a personal representative appointed for the sole purpose of signing the corrected deed.

Where's the equity?

You've paid 173 of the 180 payments, but you can't continue. Using an ordinary amortization schedule, you would have paid off 95% of the principal. You miss a couple of payments and get an eviction notice. Where's your equity?

The answer is very much dependent on the state the land is in. For example, land contracts caused so much trouble in Oklahoma that the legislature determined that they were the equivalent of a deed, note, and mortgage, giving the buyer-borrower the same right to his equity as though he had financed the property with a note and mortgage. The buyer-borrower would get to prove his equity in court.

In Missouri, however, some judges say that the buyer-borrower forfeits all equity if he misses even the last payment, if that's what the contract says, and it usually does.

This is one of the reasons sellers who provide financing do so with land contracts. They can get a higher than market price and interest, and if the buyer cannot keep it up, the seller gets to keep the down payment and equity. Often this type of seller will never sign a deed, much less put one in escrow; the defaulting buyer finds out that he has no easily-realized rights and simply disappears. The seller can then do the same transaction again.

The seller may have another motive. He may not have clear title to the land, and he knows that on a land contract the eager buyer is less likely to obtain

a title search. He may be attempting to evade the effect of a "due-on-sale" clause in an existing mortgage on the property, which would require him to pay off the existing mortgage when he sells the property. If you buy the property and the seller defaults on his first mortgage, you must immediately pay off the seller's mortgage to avoid losing the property.

Who gets the condemnation money?

What does the contract say? If it says anything, it will say that the seller gets it. That's because people with both money and brains don't buy property under such contracts. It may say nothing about condemnation or fire insurance proceeds or such matters: the seller feels secure because the property remains in his name at the courthouse and the poor schmoe who bought it won't have the money to assert his rights.

Unless the land contract is recorded in the land records at the courthouse, or a memorandum of the land contract is recorded, the highway department won't have any reason to notify the buyer of the condemnation. The seller may sell some of the buyer's land to the state without the buyer knowing about it. If the buyer finds out, he is faced with suing both the seller and the state.

If the buyer's name doesn't show up in the county land records, the buyer won't receive notice of nearby re-zoning applications. If the buyer tries to protest, he may have to overcome the hurdle of proving his interest before his protest will be heard.

Another problem is property taxes. The contract probably obligates the buyer to pay them, but the owner receives the tax bill (as well as reassessment notices). The buyer forgets about the obligation. The owner doesn't pay the taxes. The property is sold at tax sale without the buyer being aware. The buyer finds out, but has an uphill battle to prove his redemption rights.

Is there another way to do owner-financing?

Of course. Many owner-financings are accomplished in the conventional manner. The owner-seller conveys the property to the buyer-borrower by *warranty deed*. The buyer obtains an *owner's policy of title insurance*. The buyer signs a *note* and *mortgage* (called a *deed of trust* in some states) in favor of the owner-seller. Some sellers don't want to do it this way because they never have; the way they've done it has worked real well for them each time they sold the property and then took it back and sold it again.

Installment sale agreements and *leases with options to purchase* are common ways to document transactions in which title stays with the seller and the agreements clearly specify the requirements for conveying the property to the buyer. These agreements should also clearly establish the buyer's equity in the property as payments are made, as well as specify who is obligated to pay taxes and insurance and who is entitled to insurance and condemnation proceeds. From the buyer's point of view, it's advisable for the buyer and seller to sign a *memorandum of the contract*, if the contract is not to be recorded, which states that the buyer has an interest in the land and is entitled to notice of legal proceedings affecting the land. This memorandum should contain a *legal description* of the real estate and the buyer's mailing address,

and it should be recorded in the county land records.

If a land contract or contract for deed is the only and last resort, make sure that the seller places a deed to the property in escrow, with all necessary signatures and notary acknowledgments, along with instructions for the escrow agent to record the deed upon your satisfying the terms of the contract.

Be sure to get competent legal advice before signing checks or contracts. Office supply forms are usually biased heavily in favor of the seller and are often very difficult to interpret. Real estate brokers are generally fountains of legal misinformation. If you don't get informed answers to the questions posed in this article, ask someone else. Law and custom vary so much from place to place that the experience and knowledge you gained in one place may only mislead you in another place. Δ

A BHM Writer's Profile: Don Fallick

Don Fallick has been writing for *Backwoods Home Magazine* since issue number eight, but he's been reading *BHM* since the first year. He built his own home on his first homestead in western Colorado in 1976. Since then, Fallick has lived in Wisconsin, Washington State, and Utah. His homesteading activities have included owner-built construction, homeschooling, independent energy, horse-power, harvesting wild foods and game, homebased business, cooking, and "raising everything but his standard of living."

Fallick and his bride Barbara have 10 children betwen them. All have been home-schooled. When he is not writing for *BHM*, Don works as a surveyor and substitute school teacher. At one time or another, he has also been a carpenter, nurse aide, factory worker, locksmith, editor, and commercial pilot. He has a wide range of interests, and says that he tries to do "everything that interests him." Current projects include a lengthy "how to" book, three books of guitar music, and two children's stories.

A BHM Writer's Profile: Anita Evangelista

In 1985, Anita Evangelista moved to a farm in the Missouri Ozark Mountains from a house not far from downtown Los Angeles, and has been there ever since. Over the years she, her husband Nick, and their two children, Jamie and Justin, have raised everything from sheep to rabbits. Anita has written for a variety of magazines, everything from *The Twilight Zone* to *The Los Angeles Times* to *Fate* to (of course) *Backwoods Home*. She has also written six books, including the best-selling How to Develop a Low-Cost Family Food System, How to Live Without Electricity—And Like It, and Backyard Meat Production. Much of her writing is based on personal experience. She is also a registered nurse and a licensed EMT. Anita is listed in Who's Who in the Mid-West, Who's Who Among American Women, and Who's Who in America.

A BHM Writer's Profile: Rev. J.D. Hooker

Rev. J.D. Hooker is a longtime contributor to BHM and one of our most prolific writers. He draws on his backwoods experiences of gardening, building, fishing, hunting, and making an independent living. Home for him is back off a gravel road in rural Dekalb County, Indiana, along with his wife of 26 years. They have four daughters, one granddaughter, and two grandsons. On their small acreage they raise burros, and wolf/German shepherd hybrids—a unique and highly competent type of working dog. Rev. Hooker also serves as the voluntary head of a Baptist Youth Ministry in the area.

"I see so awfully many kids living in towns" Hooker says, "who've never had any concept of life away from the sidewalks and the crowds, that every day I'm even more convinced that living an enjoyable backwoods lifestyle really is the best possible way to raise a family. Fortunately for me, my wife has always agreed with that philosophy as well; which is why we now have decades of experience in independent living."

Where I live
By Annie Duffy

Salvaged wood makes a good goat shed

Last September I acquired three Nubian goats, a doe named Missy, and two kids named Tara and Peter, from my neighbor, Sue Tickle. I was planning to keep them with my horse, Buddy, and my donkey, Donna Quixote, but as hardy as the horse and donkey were, the goats needed shelter from the cold weather, wind, and the threat of cougar. So I decided to build them a goat shed.

For several evenings in a row I planned, after dinner, the specific characteristics that I wanted to build into the shed.

- It had to be big enough to house six goats (I have three more in Utah that will be coming here soon.).
- It needed a sturdy feeder since goats often like to jump right inside the feeder when they eat.
- A shelf inside would be nice, because goats like to sleep above the ground.
- It would need a tall fence of its own, inside the corral, because the goats are such good jumpers they would jump over the corral fence.
- It also needed ventilation, but not so much that it created a draft.

I finally came up with a 6 by 16 1/2-foot building design with a shed roof and windows on two sides.

Since I didn't have much money, I salvaged some long, wide boards my dad had laying around from previous building projects. Most of them were loaded with bent nails. While I pulled nails out, Dad ripped the wood down to size with his table saw. I only had enough scrap wood for a foundation, so when two by fours went on sale at a lumber store in town, we stocked up.

Although I helped my dad build our Oregon office, I still needed help in building the shed, so I volunteered my dad for the job. We finally built the shed inside our horse corral nearest to my bedroom window. We built the foundation on top of cinder blocks and homemade concrete piers. When Dad and I finished the foundation, my friend Rich Perrigo took over while my dad went off to install a septic tank for the house.

I built the shed out of two by fours and some old plywood siding my dad had laying around. The wall studs and roof joists were built two feet apart. I even used the siding for the floor, because my dad didn't have any regular flooring. Dad found some 1/2-inch plywood for the roof, and we bought some asphalt shingles to cover it.

I made several mistakes that I learned from:

- The shed size (6x16 1/2) is not sized correctly to nail on the standard 4-foot wide sheets of plywood easily, so Rich and I had to cut a lot of small pieces of plywood. I should have made the shed 8x16.
- The shed is only 6 feet deep, which made it difficult to build an 8-foot wall while it lay on its side on top of the foundation.
- I also nailed the siding of one of the walls on before it had been raised, which was a mistake

Annie pulls nails out of salvaged lumber.

because the wall became so heavy it was difficult for Rich and me to raise it. After that we waited until the wall was up to nail on the siding.

But the shed came out great anyway. While Rich and I were nailing shingles onto the roof, I kept my longeing whip with me, since my horse had already decided that the shed was for him.

When we finished the shingles, Rich cut pieces of 1x1 pine to trim the windows and door. On the inside of the windows, we stapled chicken wire to keep the goats in at night and to discourage predators from entering. On real cold nights we will nail plastic over the opening, and cut sheets of plywood to fit.

Right now, a few old lawn chairs are serving as shelves for the goats, and a couple of buckets serve as feeders, but in the spring we'll build some permanent furniture. The shed looks great, and the goats love it. Δ

These are Jacob's sheep

By Anita Evangelista

A city-dwelling visitor to an Ozark "hobby" farm looks over the green, rolling hillside at the grazing flock of white commercial sheep.

"How pastoral," he says with a touch of wistfulness. (He has no idea of the labor that has gone into making that pretty picture a reality—the seeding of the field, the hay mowing, the sheep worming, the shearing and hoof trimming, the nights spent shivering in the cold, waiting for lambs to be born.)

"I wish I could be...." He stops and stares at the flock. "Is that a goat? Or what?"

"Or What" raises his black-and-white spotted head again, and the spectacular set of horns becomes visible, even at this distance.

"Wow!" the visitor says. "It's an antelope or something!"

"It's a Jacob sheep," the farmer says, trying to keep his voice level. "Jacob sheep."

The visitor looks hard at the four-horned spotted animal.

"Jacob who?"

Jakes have been known, at least as a unique color variation, since Biblical times. The story in Genesis tells how Jacob worked for his father-in-law and was allowed to take all the spotted animals from the solid-colored herd for his own use. In a dream, God told Jacob that the use of spotted rams on those solid-colored ewes would produce spotted offspring and increase his flock—and the first recorded instance of genetic selection occurred.

While no one knows if today's Jacobs are descendants of this original line (there are spotted sheep with drooping ears and "fat tails" still living in the Middle East), the name of the first purposeful breeder of spotted sheep lives on in these animals.

Jacobs have been raised as estate sheep and "lawn mowers" in England for centuries. These sheep may be the result of cross-breeding British breeds with a spotted African sheep, or they may be a Spanish breed washed ashore during the wreck of the Spanish Armada. In 1970, there were so few Jakes remaining in England that a breed-preservation registry was formed. Recently, British breeders introduced Dorset sheep blood into a

number of their lines, resulting in a much larger, meatier animal than the original sheep.

North American Jakes

In North America, Jakes vary significantly from their European cousins, probably from the introduction of domestic lines such as the Navaho-Churro. They've been known in this country at least since the turn of the century, with several importations from England and Scotland taking place in the interval.

As a four-horned (*multi-cerate*) sheep, Jacobs are dramatic examples of diversity among breeds and a living testimony to the vast genetic stores available to commercial breeders. The breed is unusual in that two-horned, no-horned (naturally polled), and even individuals with up to five or six horns may appear within bloodlines. Females (ewes) also are horned, though theirs are significantly smaller than ram's horns and are easier to break off during head butting contests.

Because the American breed has only in the past several years acquired a "breed standard" or "typical look," many lines of Jakes show considerable variation in spotting, head shape, body conformation, and even in ear size. (There are lines with ears so tiny that they appear to have no ears.) Some lines are tall and angular, some are short and tubby. It is not unusual for Jacobs to have crystal-blue eyes as well, although brown shades are more common.

The six-pound fleece of a typical Jacob ram is open and can be parted to reveal a medium-fine, lustrous, soft wool three to seven inches long. Unlike many other breeds of British origin, there is no heavy undercoat.

The spots are what set Jacobs apart in any flock. Basically a white-colored sheep with black (often surface-faded to brown) spots, the color of the fleece is a reflection of the animal's underlying skin color: pink under white wool, grey or black under dark wool. Pure

Jacobs also carry black eye or cheek patches, a dark nose or muzzle, and black knee spots, although there is considerable variation within lines on this, too. There is no wool on the animal's face or forehead, just hair; animals with wool before the horns probably are the product of a recent outcrossing to some commercial breed.

Just because a sheep carries four horns and has spots doesn't make it a Jacob. A number of other minor breeds have four horns, including the Navaho-Churro, and spots occur with a certain regularity in offspring of Dorset and Merino origins. Both sellers and buyers have traded all sorts of odd lots, including Barbados hair sheep crosses, as Jacobs.

The American Livestock Breeds Conservancy was instrumental in initial preservation efforts for this breed. As early as 1985, when a nationwide survey found that fewer than 5,000 Jacobs were born annually, Jakes were put on the ALBC's "Watch List." In 1988, a separate Jacob Sheep Breeder's Association grew out of the ALBC's efforts, and a specific breed description was established to help standardize the breed, and to provide guidelines for breeders and buyers.

Jacobs are a small to medium sheep, with rams weighing between 120 and 180 pounds, ewes slightly smaller at 80 to 120 pounds. Animals are fine-boned, long-framed, and smoothly muscled, with straight backs. Legs must be free of wool below the hocks and white in color, with or without black patches. Ears are small and erect.

On adult sheep, the white patches should be white—that is, without significant "freckling," and the black patches as dark and sun-resistant as possible. The wool shouldn't have "quilting," a difference in length between white and black fibers. The wool should be about 60% white and 40% black, with a fleece weight of around three to six pounds. The fleece is low in natural oils, lustrous, and has little or no hair and no *kemp* (thin,

wiry hairs). Occasionally, pure Jake lambs are completely white, including their horns (but this is not desirable).

Rams should carry two or four black or black/white horns growing clear of the face in a wide, sweeping curl, with flesh between the upper and lower set of horns. Although some lines produce offspring with "fused" horns, where two horns are growing together on one or both sides, this is not desirable. The ram's scrotal sack is short, with testicles held closer to the body than in modern breeds. Some rams have the large "Roman" or bulging nose typical of improved modern breeds, and are acceptable as such—but they are considered "less primitive" than rams with the more slender, triangular head of the earlier breed.

What you don't see

What you don't see in Jacobs is their internal or innate qualities: the breed is hardy, thrifty, and produces a very lean meat. A typical lamb carcass, processed when the animal weighs between 60 and 80 pounds, can readily produce between 30 and 40 pounds of nearly fat-free meat, especially if the lamb was raised without grain supplements. The meat is generally a darker red, almost baby-beef-like, in comparison with paler commercial meats. In spite of its natural leanness, the meat is quite tender and delicious. It should be cooked at 325°F with moisture for best results.

Most Jacob ewes lamb successfully without much intervention, the result of the breed having remained fairly primitive through the years. (Commercial sheep producers may have to "pull" a third of their lambs.) Ewes produce sufficient milk for their single or twin lambs, but not so much milk that udder problems develop. Triplets are not common, with twins more usual with this breed. Lambs are often born with a hairy-looking coat to start with (depending on lines), or even a combination hairy-wooly coat. This grows out into ordinary wool before long. Hairy lambs, in my flock at least, seem to take the early spring cold a little better than wooly ones—but all the Jake lambs are significantly hardier, quicker to get to their feet, faster to nurse, and more lively than lambs of commercial breeds.

An interesting thing about crossing spotted Jacobs with white commercial sheep is that the offspring will often be mostly-black wooled. A white "cap," white heel patches, and white tail are often the only pale areas on the resulting animals—and that particular coloration is a sure indicator of a first-generation Jacob cross. If these crosses are then bred back to a spotted Jacob, a high percentage of these second-generation offspring will be spotted, too.

One animal geneticist has suggested that Jacobs are not actually a "white sheep with black spots," but are a "black sheep with white marks." Even though this seems to deny the evidence of our eyes, it appears to be a genetic truth. It's perfectly apparent every time one of those mostly-black crosses arrives in the world. The same geneticist has opined that, since all-white Jacobs are fairly rare in a genetically black-wooled breed, folks should hang on to any all-white Jake lambs and try to produce all-white lines.

In terms of general health, the breed as a whole is remarkably vigorous and long-lived. It's not uncommon to find productive Jacob ewes well into their teens, while most commercial sheep are washed up at eight years of age, and some more modern breeds are pooped out by the time they're six. We recently suffered the loss of one of our oldest ewes, who was by all accounts over eighteen—and she'd produced a lamb last year!

There are, however, inheritable problems in these sheep, as there are in all breeds. Probably the most significant of these is "split eyelid deformity." While there are variations of how extreme this condition becomes, it is

simply a division in the sheep's upper eyelid. It may occur in one or both eyes. It appears to be the result of a stage in fetal development during which the lamb's horns and skull are forming. Skulls of animals with the deformity show a division line running from the eyeball socket to the base of the horn. It's seen more often in four-horned animals.

In the mildest cases, there is only a slight "bump" or "dip" in the edge of the lid. In the worst cases, the eyelid is divided clear to the animal's "eyebrow" area. The sheep can experience irritation to its cornea or eyeball if the deformity causes eyelashes to rub on the eye—and with a severe split, the eyeball is exposed to dust, weed seeds, and other damaging irritants. The worst possible effect from split eyelid is blindness, which may take years to become evident.

It's not quite known how this condition is passed on, since from year to year its incidence in lambs may vary. Some years, all the lambs in the flock will be free of the condition; other years half or more lambs may be varyingly affected. In extremely severe split eyelids, veterinarians can suture the division together—there's no long-term damage to the lambs. It is probably wisest to not use animals for breeding that continuously or frequently produce lambs with split eyelids.

On the plus side, Jacobs appear to be fairly resistant to parasitic intestinal worms—they often require less de-worming than commercial sheep in the same flocks. They also have particularly sturdy hooves, so there is less susceptibility to "foot rot" and other hoof problems; very little hoof trimming needs to be done.

Most commercial sheep producers vaccinate their stock for numerous contagious sheep diseases, including vibriosis, clostridia, black leg, red water, tetanus, rabies, and so forth. Organic sheep raisers may or may not vaccinate as consistently. If a particular sheep disease is endemic in your

area (ask vets and local University Extension officers), I'd suggest vaccinating against it. As mostly-organic sheep raisers, in the past we've only vaccinated against overeating disease and tetanus (CD/T)—and infrequently at that. However, with the rise of antibiotic-resistance in many livestock and human diseases, we may make greater use of the preventive value of vaccinations in the future. Vaccinations can be mail ordered from vet suppliers, if you don't mind giving shots yourself.

The fleece is unique

That fancy Jacob fleece is, perhaps, what makes the breed most desirable for the small backyard flock—not only is the wool unique, it is also particularly easy to hand spin into yarn or felt into thick pads. Because it's low in natural grease, the wool can be spun directly "off the sheep," without initial washing, carding, or special handling. I've spun Jacob wool using a simple drop spindle and a regular spinning wheel, and it is a delight because of its natural lightness, springy body, and just enough oil to make it flexible.

While wool prices vary from year to year, Jacob fleeces are not that common and tend to command higher prices. I've seen clean "raw" or freshly-shorn Jacob wool sell for $3 to $8 per pound to handspinners—but that's at private "niche-market" sales. Commercial wool co-ops, where most of the nation's shepherds sell their white fleeces, discount colored wools and may only offer 10 to 15 cents per pound for your fancy Jacob fleece—so most Jake owners either use their wool at home or sell it to handspinners.

As a minor (or heirloom) breed, Jacobs also represent a genetic base which is significantly different from the majority of commercial breeds. Where commercial sheep must grow quickly to a marketable size—and consequently require grain and quality hay inputs—the Jacob is slower-growing and can do quite well on pasture and occasional supplementation when fields are sparse. This thriftiness is one of the features of Jakes which endeared them to the hill shepherds of Scotland. It may also become an important trait for crossbreeding into commercial lines of sheep, if costs of grain and hay should increase in the future. Furthermore, the characteristic Jacob leanness could become very desirable if consumers demand lean lamb that is both juicy and tender. With agriculture changing constantly, the hardy Jake may hold an unsuspected answer in crossbreeding programs.

Heterosis is the term used to describe the result of crossbreeding two dissimilar lines or breeds, which produces offspring which are superior in specific traits to either parent. In heterosis, we often find such offspring to be both hardier and quicker to mature than either parent. This hybridization effect can produce the maximum heterosis when a two-breed crossbred animal is bred to a pure animal of another breed—and, to my knowledge, there are virtually no Jacob breeders engaged in this kind of experimentation. Would it be possible to produce a black fine-wooled sheep the size and meat quality of a 300-pound Suffolk, by crossing Jacobs to Suffolk-crosses? With time and careful selection, the resultant prolific, fancy-wooled animal could revitalize the small flocks on many "hobby" farms — but no one has yet undertaken this particular venture. There's room for an incredible amount of crossbreeding experimentation with

Jacobs; it will probably fall to backwoods producers to do this work.

At a typical $100 to $350 for purebred Jakes, the cost of these animals is comparable with purebreds of other breeds. As a sheep with an unusual look, special fleece, and innate traits of remarkable hardiness and productivity, they are *not* comparable...they excel!

For more information

American Livestock Breeds
  Conservancy
PO Box 477
Pittsboro, NC 27312
(919) 542-5704

Jacob Sheep Breeders Association
Janine Fenton, Secretary
6350 ECR 56
Fort Collins, CO 80524
(303) 484-3344

Jeffers Veterinary Supply
PO Box 948
West Plains, MO 65775
1-800-JEFFERS (533-3377)
24-hour Fax: (417) 256-1550
Ask for a catalog. Δ

A BHM Writer's Profile: Dynah Geissal

Dynah Geissal is 48-years old, is married, has three grown children, a son-in-law, and one grandchild. She and husband Bob have been subsistence farmers for 21 years and figure they are 90% food self-sufficient.

On August 1, 1994, they bought 40 acres of bare land in the mountains of western Montana. Since then they have lived in a tipi at 4600 feet while building shelters and pens for the livestick and beginning work on their home. They carry water from their hand-dug well and their only electricity is from a single solar panel, providing two lights and a radio.

A BHM Writer's Profile: Connie Glasheen

Connie Glasheen is a wife, mother, and grandmother who loves to garden. A large orchard, vegetable and flower gardens keep her busy, along with tending to her sheep and cats. One of her goals is to become as self-sufficient as possible.

A BHM Writer's Profile: Harry Nemec

Harry is the father of Chester and husband to Elizabeth Nemec. He is a self-reliant reconstruction engineer, farmer, fabrication & welder, volunteer firefighter, instructor, and poet. Nemec prides himself as an author who paints pictures with words and enjoys writing from actual experience.

How I've started my child in a program of homeschooling

By John Silveira

(This is the first of many articles on homeschooling that will be written by the staff at *BHM*. In future articles we will discuss hands-on approaches to teaching reading, writing, and arithmetic along with science, history, geography, and everything else your child is expecting you to provide in the way of an education before you send them off into the world. — Editor.)

Homeschooling? I'd considered it for my daughter for years but I worked full time in an office for a defense contractor. With all the hours I spent either there or on travel, I didn't have the opportunity. So her birthdays passed like a progression of lemmings marching off a cliff, each one irrevocably lost, and the chance to ever homeschool her was slipping away.

Then, one day I was out of that job and I was working full time for *Backwoods Home Magazine*. This new job took me 700 miles away from home for several weeks each month. But the working conditions were different and after about a year I realized I could make time for homeschooling.

The decision to do so came at the end of the last school year. But with it came the realization that I didn't know quite how to start. I spoke with a lot of people. I listened to what was said, and the advice boiled down to a practical approach:

> Assess your child
> Assess yourself
> Have a plan

Assess your child

In assessing my daughter, I first wanted to find where her weaknesses lay. I met with her eighth grade teacher. She told me Mary's math skills were poor. This surprised me because, when she was very young, it was her math skills that made me realize she wasn't retarded.

Nine years earlier, when she was entering kindergarten, Mary was diagnosed as having childhood schizophrenia with symptoms of autism and

several learning disorders. But over the years many people had been impressed with her math skills and her ability to calculate numbers in her head. Now I was being told she's not good with numbers. How could that be?

I discovered that every time she wanted to multiply numbers, she did the calculations from scratch. No one had ever bothered to have her memorize a multiplication table. I asked how she could reach the age of 15 and not know a standard multiplication table. I also asked where I had been while she wasn't learning it. This is a skill that should be committed to memory in childhood. Even as a mathematician, I never recalculated something so fundamental. I had all the basic stuff memorized.

This became the initial focus of my attack. I started out teaching her the multiplication table from 1 to 12. I wrote all the permutations of multiplication of two integers, from 1 to 12, on index cards. There are 144 of them. And she's being tested on them. It's one of the things we go over on our long drive to Oregon and our return to Ojai. She has other weaknesses, from her penmanship to her reading comprehension. I've made it my business to know these things so we can work on them.

Next, I wanted to find what she's good at. I want to focus on her skills so I can encourage her. I also want to make use of them.

For example, I was surprised to find out she can write stories. She had been writing them one after another for several years—then she'd throw them away.

"I didn't know you wrote stories."

"Well, I like to write, Dad."

"Why do you throw them away?"

"You'd get bored with them after you'd read them 20 times, too, you know."

Her logic was at once both compelling and annoying. But I wanted to see her stories and gauge her progress.

"From now on," I announced. "Everything you write goes into your binder."

She still throws some away, but channeling this skill of hers makes it easier for me to help develop her language skills. It also makes an unusual way for me to test her. For one thing, though most students hate essay questions, for Mary it's a natural way for me to quiz her.

So, for her first history quiz, she had to write me a story about a typical day of an indentured servant girl in Colonial America—and include all the detail from the readings I had given her.

Assess yourself

I found that I had a mixed bag of skills and drawbacks—as any parent is going to have—when I started home-schooling. On the plus side, I used to be a math teacher. When I got my college education, I thought I was going to become a physicist, so I have a background in the hard sciences. This part of her education will be easy. How I teach her math and science will become part of future columns.

On the minus side, though I now write for a living, I'm a self-taught writer. Worse yet, I know little if anything about grammar and punctuation. And I'm a lousy speller. (Dave, the publisher, thinks it's funny that to teach my daughter punctuation I'm finally going to have to learn how to do it myself.)

I was also a terrible student and, though I write a great deal about history, there are incredible holes in my education. So, along with punctuation, I'm going to have to teach my daughter things I don't know.

In future columns, we will deal with strategies of how to teach subjects you don't know.

Have a plan

I decided there are six areas of concentration this year:

1. I want Mary to develop her math skills. I want her to learn algebra.

2. I want her to read with comprehension.

I once read that literacy among white Americans 150 years ago was 98%—though most Americans didn't go beyond the sixth grade. (Blacks are excluded from this figure because they usually weren't even allowed to read in those days.) We think of time bringing progress and it would seem that in a century and a half the gap between 98% and 100% would have narrowed. Instead, it's widened. Literacy among high school graduates today is dismally low. Even a large percentage of college graduates have poor reading skills.

This is despite the fact that the way people get most of the information in their lives—even if they're sitting in front of a computer screen—is by reading.

So, if you can't think of a lesson today, make 'em read.

3. I want to expand her practical vocabulary skills. Not simply to add to her mental baggage a plethora of hyperpedalian polysylabics, but to learn the precise use of words including the proper use of everyday words, such as when to use *well* instead of *good*, *may* instead of *can*, *ensure* instead of *insure*. When I was a boy, my mother hounded me with the differences between commonly used words. If your parents did this also, then it's time you started too.

I also want her to expand her everyday vocabulary. I give her two words a day. I don't pull them out of thin air. Any time she asks what a word means, it automatically becomes a word on her list. The first two words were *escalate* and *vocabulary*. Last

night's words were *interior* and *exterior*.

4. I want her to develop her writing skills. After 15 years working for Department of Defense contractors, I've discovered that most people cannot convey their thoughts clearly and concisely in writing. How are you, as a homeschooling parent, going to instill this in your child? You'll find that just as you don't have to be able to cook to know when something doesn't taste right, you don't have to be able to write to know when something doesn't read right. We are going to cover the *who*, *what*, *when*, *where*, *why* and *how* of writing.

5. I want her to have a feel for history and understand the significance of the impact of that history on our culture.

6. I want her to understand the concept that has done more to make the modern world "modern" than any other concept—the "scientific method." I want her to understand what science is, and what it is not.

Among the things that rankle me more than anything are statements people make about science that betray their ignorance. Among them is: "Science and religion are just alike; they are no more than sets of beliefs we choose to take on faith." Another is: "Science is just a bunch of statistics."

But the worst are the "alternative sciences" of various political and social movements that serve only to blind your child to an understanding of the real world. It's long been my plan to write a piece for *BHM* titled, *How we know what we know*. It's about what science is and what it is

---

Use No. 3 for index cards

My daughter knew the capitals of about five states when I started homeschooling. We are now making 50 index cards with the name of each state on one side and its capital on the other. Later, the cards will be useful for adding more information about the individual states when we study them in detail.

---

not, the problems it can solve and the problems it can't. Mary will help me write it.

There's one more thing I plan to do. I plan to get Mary involved in my job. In the past we've had articles about how to involve your child in your job to further his or her homeschooling. Recently, we even had an article about using apprenticeships (Issue 31).

For my part, since I do research for my feature pieces, Mary's become part of the researching. She has to help look things up and tell me why they're relevant to my article. The little girl who had no idea how to use an encyclopedia was suddenly looking up the information on the Prohibition era.

The daughter of the *BHM* publisher, Annie Duffy, is being homeschooled and part of her homeschooling is to write a teen column for the magazine.

Cultural literacy

Not included above, and one of the hardest things I'm going to face is making my daughter familiar with her culture—what's recently become known as cultural literacy. It used to go by the name of general knowledge, except it's not so general anymore.

I found this out while working for one defense contractor in the '80s. I had brought in a quiz from a magazine. The headline asked, "What do you know that your high school-aged children don't." It was simple questions from geography and world history and included such questions as: To the nearest half-century, when did the Civil War take place? Who was

Calvin Coolidge? On what continent is Kenya located?

"According to this article," I said to my fellow employees, "less that half of all high schoolers can answer more than half of these questions." I read the 20-odd questions.

One fellow, who had just received his degree in math, laughed and said, "I hate to say it, but I don't know the answers to most of those questions."

In turn, several others made the same admission. Many of them also had degrees. But what they all had in common was that they were young.

It was the older people in the group who could answer almost everything. Many of them weren't degreed, and one was a high school dropout. Yet, they generally knew the answers. How could this be?

The answer came quickly. The older people remembered learning these things in school. The younger people had never heard of them.

Resources and tools

Your local school system. When I started this, the good news for me was that California has made provisions for homeschooling. The bad news is that the school district where we live gives no support to homeschoolers after the 8th grade. My daughter is entering the 9th.

Still, I've found ways to take advantage of the school system. They've told me what books they're using and two teachers even gave me copies of their syllabuses for the school year.

Homeschooling or not, I want to at least come close to tracking what they're doing in the public school I took her from. Something unforeseen may mean I have to put her back into the school system and I'd like her to at least be familiar with the material her fellow students are studying.

Also, even though I'm a mathematician, I'm not going to try to set up her entire math curriculum. Others have already put a great deal of time and effort into composing problems and

---

If your child learns nothing else, she should learn:
(1) to read with comprehension
(2) to write clearly and concisely
(3) to be able to solve problems algebraically
(4) what science is and is not
(5) enough to be culturally literate
(6) how to use a computer

---

the sequence of lessons, and some of them have done very well. I'm not going to try to reinvent those. Geometry, if we get to it, is such a subject.

Computers. Those awful machines we're so afraid of are here to stay. Maybe we, as adults, can ignore them. But our children can't. They're going to be part of the world they're growing into. Ignoring computers would be seriously shortchanging them because computers are going to be the tools of survival in the future.

There's another aspect of computers that make them useful. There's a tremendous amount of educational software out there and more and better software is being developed—typing programs, programs that test spelling and math skills, even games that require a certain knowledge of history to play.

The online services have educational interest groups where you can meet parents like yourself, and your children can meet other students.

Nowadays, you can even find the *Encyclopedia Brittanica* on the Internet.

If you can afford a computer, buy one. If you can't, see if you can get your kid access to one at the local library, at a friendly local school, or even through a friend.

In another week Mary and I will drive south for home. Maybe you'll see us go by. I'll be stearing. She'll be going through her index cards.

Next issue, I'll show you how to teach your child a fundamental concept in algebra— what an equation really is, and how to use equations to solve problems. Δ

Think of it this way...

By John Silveira

Just how good of a bet are those lotto tickets?

I looked at the newspaper and tried to match up the lotto results printed there with my picks. I sighed. "Boy, I sure would've liked to have won that one."

O.E. MacDougal, the poker player, was on the other side of the office disassembling his shotgun to put a plug in. We were going duck hunting in the morning. "Ever buy any of these lottery tickets?" I asked him. "The pot last night was worth about $20 million."

He looked across the office and I held up my ticket so he could see it.

"Is that one of those California Lotto tickets?" he asked.

"Yeah. Ever buy them?"

He smiled. "Every once in a great while." He went back to disassembling his shotgun.

"Do you think they're a good bet?"

He looked up again. "No."

"Then why do you buy them?"

"I don't buy them often, but when the jackpot's way up there, even I get suckered in."

"Suckered in? Why, aren't they such a good deal?"

"Well, in the first place, half the money in the pool goes right to the state. So your return is already cut in half."

"Well, at least they give you the other half. And you've got to admit that the other half goes to a worthy cause—education."

He paused for just a moment. "Well..." I thought he was going to say something but he just said, "Okay," and went back to putting the plug in his shotgun.

"What were you going to say?"

"Well..." I could see he was still reluctant to say it. "In the first place, they actually keep all the money."

"No they don't. They pay out prizes. On this jackpot—$20 million—they'll pay it out at $1 million a year for 20 years." I could tell by the way he was looking at me there was something I wasn't getting.

"Okay," he said, "but look at it this way. What if you had $20 million and you felt inclined to loan it to me at 5% interest and all I had to do was make interest payments for 20 years?"

"That would be a pretty low interest rate."

"That's right."

"Let me see..." I did the calculation in my head. "That would mean you'd give me $1 million a year."

"Correct. And with the final payment I'd give you $1 million and what else?"

"The principal. The original $20 million."

"Now, consider the lottery. The state holds the $20 million prize money and gets to use it at 5% a year. In the 20th year they give you the last 5% payment and..."

I thought a few seconds. "And nothing."

He just looked at me.

"They get to use your money at 5% a year and, after 20 years they keep the principal," I said.

"You could look at it that way."

I looked at my ticket again. "I never thought of it like that before."

The plug was in the shotgun and he was reassembling it.

"You know, you have a way of throwing cold water on a lot of things. I'll bet now you're going to say that there's something fishy about the money they give to the schools."

He worked the slide a few times. "Well, actually, the money doesn't go to education—though I know they say it does."

"What do you mean?"

"The way the lottery was presented to the voters was that the proceeds were going to be added to the school budgets, over and above the taxes that were collected for the schools. But what happened was that they saw how much lottery money was going to the schools, then they cut the existing state contributions to the schools by roughly the same amount. The schools don't actually get any more money."

"How do you get away with that?"

"It's the way government works. The same thing happened with the funds raised by the civil forfeiture laws. Supposedly, the funds raised by civil forfeiture—that is, the money and property raised from suspected criminals—was going to be added on top of police budgets. But what happened was that the police budgets were cut by the exact same amount as the money the police raised by confiscations.

"It created a situation where the police in some police departments now have to make civil forfeiture quotas. Otherwise, their budgets will come up short and jobs will be lost."

I threw the losing lotto ticket into the trash. "So you're saying that the state runs a lottery to raise money for education, but they don't actually give any extra money to education, and they only pay interest on the prize money—for 20 years—before they confiscate the principal?"

"You could think of it that way." Δ

Shiitake mushrooms for food and for cash — you "plant" them by inoculating logs

By Lee Harbert

The Japanese have been growing mushrooms for their nutritional and medicinal value for over 2000 years. They eliminated the work and worry of growing them on compost by cultivating Shiitake mushrooms on the logs of deciduous trees. Today, Shiitake mushrooms (*Lentinus edodes*), are exported from Southeast Asia and grown all over the world. They are used in Chinese and Japanese cuisine (in both fresh and dried form), sold by health food stores, and used for a variety of medicinal purposes. The ancient process of cultivating Shiitake mushrooms has not changed; only a few of the techniques have been updated and modified to accommodate different growing conditions.

You begin by *inoculating* a log with the Shiitake *spawn*. The log should be a hardwood: white oak, red oak, chestnut oak, sugar maple, sassafras, sweet or black gum, and other members of the oak family work well. Shiitake *does not* grow well on soft hardwoods like aspen and willow, or on conifers. The log should come from a healthy tree, and be three to eight inches in diameter, and three to five feet long. You cannot use old or diseased wood, and it should be a log that has been cut recently. The best time to cut the tree is between early fall and early spring, just before the buds begin to open.

Inoculation of the log should be done in early spring. Outside daytime temperatures should be above 40° F, but temperatures falling below freezing at night are fine. Drill 20 to 40 holes in the log, one inch deep. Holes should be drilled at six- to eight-inch intervals within the row, along the length of the log. The rows need to be spaced one to two inches apart, and offset to form a diamond pattern (see illustration). If you are using *dowel spawn*, drill a 5/16 inch hole, and lightly tap the spawn into the hole with a hammer. If you are using *sawdust spawn*, drill your hole 7/16 inch and insert the spawn with your fingers. Using an inoculation tool works best when inserting sawdust spawn. The

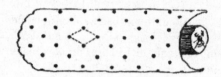

"Diamond" drilling pattern used to make holes for inoculation. (Surface of log is shown in "exploded" view only for purposes of illustration.)

spawn should be packed into the hole until it is level with the bark surface.

Now you must immediately seal the holes, using cheese wax melted at about 300° F. Do not overheat the wax. The flashpoint of wax is 450° F, and overheating can occur easily. If the wax starts to smoke, turn down the heat. Use a wax dauber, or wax baster, to apply a thin layer of hot cheese wax over the spawn, making sure the surface is sealed. A tag may be attached to the log showing the month, year, and variety of spawn used. You will find it handy to identify the log with a lot number or serial number, if you are cultivating for commercial sale.

Once the log is inoculated with the spawn, place it outdoors in a shaded area, where it will remain for about a year. The area should be close to where you live, with cold running water available. The logs may be covered lightly with burlap or pine boughs to retain moisture. They should be stood on end, crowded together against a sawhorse or other support, on a wettable surface of sod, bare earth, or leaf duff. This allows them to soak up ground moisture from rain and snow. The upper ends of the logs will be moistened by dew, snow, frost, and rain. During this period (known as the *spawn run*), provide extra moisture as needed. If the tops of the logs develop cracks from drying, provide moisture to them. Restand or reposition any logs that fall.

It takes about a year for the Shiitake fungus to *colonize* the log. When the fungus is ready to produce mushrooms, white patches will appear on the ends and around the inoculation holes. A temperature change, like that produced by a thunderstorm or rainfall, will induce fruiting (appearance of mushrooms) naturally. You can force the fruiting by submerging a warm log (about 85° F) in cold water (about 65° F) for 12 to 36 hours.

Restack the logs in a way that will allow for ease in picking the mushrooms. Your mushrooms should be ready to pick within one to two weeks. It is possible to induce fruiting two or three times a year, in six- to twelve-week intervals. A log should produce two to three pounds of Shiitake mushrooms over a period of three to six years. Once the log is decayed, it will not produce mushrooms, and it should be left to decompose on the forest floor or in your compost pile.

If you are interested in growing Shiitake mushrooms for your own use or for profit, here are some helpful books:

Shiitake: The Healing Mushroom, by Kenneth Jones, published by Healing Arts Press.

Medicinal Mushrooms, by Christopher Hobbs, published by Botanica Press.

Growing Shiitake Mushrooms in a Continental Climate, by Joe Krawczyk and Mary Ellen Kozak.

And here are four sources for Shiitake mushroom spawn, cultivation tools, reference books, processed Shiitake mushroom products, and just plain good advice:

Paul Goland
Hardscrabble Enterprises
HC 71, Box 42
Circleville, West Virginia 26804
304-358-2921

Joe Krawczyk & Mary Ellen Kozak
Field & Forest Products, Inc.
N3296 Kozuzek Road
Peshtigo, WI 54157
715-582-4997 (M-F 8-5 Central)
Fax 715-582-0101

Persimmon Hill Farm
HCR 1, Box 220 SFT
Lampe, MO 65681

Greenwood Nursery
Box 686-A
McMinnville, TN 37110.

Successfully cultivating a Shiitake mushroom crop takes time, patience, and persistence. Paul at Hardscrabble Enterprises and Joe and Mary Ellen at Field & Forest Products have started thousands of interested growers and would be happy to talk with you. Δ

A BHM Writer's Profile: Martin Waterman

Martin P. Waterman, a frequent contributor to *Backwoods Home Magazine*, writes on the science of gardening and horticulture. He also writes on technology such as computers, communications, and genetics, and how these sciences influence our lives.

Waterman is a rural based writer living in British Columbia, Canada. He spends much of his time writing, gardening, breeding hardy fruit for the north, or on the Internet where he can be reached at:

martin_waterman@bc.sympatico.ca.

A BHM Writer's Profile: Jan Cook

Jan Cook has been with *BHM* since the beginning, as a writer, an editor, and was the principal typist for entire issues. She is still the crafts editor for the magazine.

A technical writer for the Department of Defense for 17 years she is also completely addicted to machine embroidery and will write about it for future issues.

Jan says she's a cut-to-the-chase kind of person with little tolerance for things that are supposed to work but don't. She believes in life's simpler things, like poems should rhyme and people should be as good as their word.

A BHM Artist's Profile: Don Childers

Don Childers, who retired from the magazine in 1999, is the artist who painted most of *BHMs* scenic covers. He had spent many years working for the Defense Industry, painting mock-ups of military equipment still in the planning stage. The stealth bomber and fighter, the HARPOON and TOMAHAWK cruise missiles, and a variety of other once secret weapons are among the many mock-ups he painted at various stages of their development.

He is also an amateur astronomer who has built many of his own telescopes, an amateur inventor of a graphic arts tool to sharpen exacto knives, and has illustrated various historical books. Many of his paintings have been sold to private collectors, and many more hang on the walls of admirals and generals around the country. The Dijon Museum in France exhibits one of his paintings, and several hang in English pubs. Don is moving to Colorado to retire.

Try these bread recipes that are part of our heritage — and still delicious today

By Thomas C. Tabor

Of all the pleasing culinary odors emanating from a homemaker's kitchen, possibly the most enticing of all is the aroma of fresh-baked bread. What could be better than trying to get a bite before the melting butter has a chance to slip off the edge and onto the plate? I know from my own experience that loaves of homemade bread seldom have a chance to cool before someone is tempted into taking the first slice.

Somehow the pleasures and rewards of home bread baking go beyond the smells and flavors of the product itself. Most of us relate bread baking to early times when life was less complicated and an individual's worth was assessed in terms of the truth and of the basics. For good reason, a lot of us cling to those times, even though they were not really as easy and carefree as we choose to remember them.

Historically, bread baking was not just confined to the home and did not always take the shape of today's loaves. Unleavened breads were often prepared for soldiers and sailors, as well as for cowhands and explorers. In the mid-1800s, army forts sometimes employed full-time bakers who supplied the men and their families with daily rations of bread. Possibly the most common product they produced was called the *sea biscuit*, or *hardtack*. Outside of a firearm, this was one of most important survival items anyone could have in those days. It could be kept for months or even years without preservatives or refrigeration. As long as these hard biscuits were kept free from moisture and bugs, they would last almost indefinitely. In some cases, sea biscuits have been uncovered in archaeological digs, biscuits that were baked over 100 years before. Many times these were perfectly preserved and probably could still have been eaten. If moisture got in, however, it would encourage the growth of bacteria and result in quick spoilage. For that reason, proper packaging was imperative for survival.

Some leavened varieties of loaf breads were produced as well, but these were sometimes considered more of a delicacy, particularly in the case of sailors, scouts, cowboys, trappers, and soldiers. Homesteaders probably used more leavened loaf breads than anyone else during these early years. Due to the yeast and the moisture within this type of bread, it could not be kept more than a few days after baking, making it impractical for those on the high seas or on the trail.

By today's standards, a few of these early forms of bread aren't all that tasty. For example, hardtack is something that you might want to try, but to prepare it for the family on a

Like most kids, Laura Borgman of Ridgefield, WA, enjoys a piece of fresh homemade bread with jelly.

steady basis . . . I think not. On the contrary, however, breads like bannock, soda biscuits, gritted and sourdough breads are still considered quite good. In most cases, these aren't really all that difficult to make. The following are a few time-proven recipes that you might like to try for yourself.

Hardtack or sea biscuits

2 cups of whole wheat flour
1 cup of water
1/2 tablespoon of salt
1 tablespoon of butter

Mrs. Edna Grover of Vancouver, WA, still bakes bread the old fashioned way in her wood cook stove.

Note: If you want to extend the life almost indefinitely, leave out the salt and butter.

Gradually add the water to the flour and other ingredients and mix or knead the dough only until clear of lumps, no longer. Continued kneading beyond this point will cause the bread to be not as light, flaky, and brittle.

Roll the dough out to a thickness of around 3/8 inch, then stamp or cut into whatever shapes you prefer. Traditionally, the most popular shape seems to be squares, but sometimes they were made in round shapes as well. These should be three or four inches in diameter. After cutting, make perforations by sticking a fork or other sharp object in the surface repeatedly. This helps to prevent puffing. Puffing causes air voids to form, and in early times these areas were inviting places for insects to set up housekeeping. Place on a greased cookie sheet and bake at 450° F for 25 to 30 minutes. The finished product should be light yellow or tan in color.

When struck on a hard surface it will actually "ring," and it will float in water, a sign of a "good" product.

A word of warning: If you decide to give hardtack a try, you should understand that these are extremely hard little biscuits. Many a broken tooth has resulted from trying to bite one. The proper way to eat hardtack is first to soak or dip it in some form of drink. For example, give it a dunk or two in your coffee, tea, or water first. You don't want this visit to the past to be followed by a visit to the modern-day dentist.

Bannock

Another form of frontier bread is *bannock*. It originated in the north country and is still commonly used by many people today. I have prepared this type of bread many times while camping and on hunting trips. Unlike hardtack, which requires some form of oven for baking, bannock is cooked over the fire in a frying pan, and if properly prepared can be quite tasty. In many cases, the mix was made up beforehand and carried on the trail either in saddlebags or inside the bedroll. When it was time to eat, the mix could be added to a little water and cooked in a skillet over the campfire. While not necessarily a requirement for good bannock, a cast iron skillet seems to produce the best product. Bannock is easy to make and requires very little expertise to turn out a great product.

1 1/2 cups of flour
1/2 tablespoon baking soda
1/2 tablespoon salt
3/4 cup of water

Simply mix the dry ingredients thoroughly, then add the water. Knead until all lumps and dry spots have disappeared. Form into a patty and place in a hot, greased frying pan. Fry until it is cooked through. Bannock tastes best right out of the pan, while still warm, but it's also good cold.

Parker House Rolls

The American tradition of Parker House Rolls dates back to 1855, when Boston's famous Parker House Restaurant was opened. Here's one version of this roll:

6 to 6 1/2 cups of flour
1/2 cup of sugar
2 teaspoons of salt
2 packages of active dry yeast
1/2 cup butter
1 egg

Combine in a large bowl 2 1/4 cups of flour, sugar, salt, and yeast. In another bowl combine 2 cups of hot water (130° to 150° F), 1/2 cup butter and 1 egg. When the butter is softened, pour the wet ingredients over the dry ingredients and beat two minutes, occasionally scraping the bowl. Fold in one cup of flour, or enough to make a thick batter. With a spoon, stir in the additional two cups of flour to make a soft dough. Turn the dough onto a lightly floured surface and knead for approximately 15 minutes. Place the dough in a greased bowl and let rise for 1 1/2 hours. Then punch the dough down and shape it into rolls. Let it rise until rolls have doubled in size. Bake in 375° F oven for 18 to 20 minutes. This recipe makes about 3 1/2 dozen.

Sourdough bread

An old favorite, sourdough bread has been with us for many years and is many peoples' idea of the perfect accompaniment to a meal. In Alaska during the gold rush it became the preferred bread of the miners. Soon the label "sourdough" was attached to the miners themselves.

Step one

> 1/2 cup of sugar
> 1 cup of water
> 1 1/2 cup of flour

Mix above ingredients into your starter. (See below for starter.) Cover and let stand at room temperature for 10 to 12 hours. Remove 1 1/2 cups and place in a covered jar in the refrigerator to replenish your stored starter.

Step two

> 1/3 cup of sugar
> 1/2 cup of vegetable oil
> 2 teaspoons of salt
> 1 1/2 cups of water
> 4 cups of flour

Mix sugar, vegetable oil, salt, and water gradually with approximately four cups of flour or until a hearty dough is made. Knead thoroughly until no lumps remain. There is no such thing as "too much kneading" — the more the better. Place dough in an oversized, greased bowl and cover with a towel. The dough should be allowed to rise at room temperature. This is best accomplished overnight. The next morning, punch your dough down and divide into loaves. This recipe will make about three normal sized loaves. Place in greased baking pans and allow to rise again until size has doubled. Bake at 350° F for 45 minutes. A little butter allowed to melt over the top of the loaves is the final stage and will add flavor.

Corn bread

Corn breads have been around as long as our country, particularly in the southern states. Try this recipe for a tasty addition to your country meal.

> 2 1/2 cups corn meal or stone ground meal
> 1/2 cup flour
> 1 teaspoon of salt
> 2 teaspoons of baking powder
> 1/2 teaspoon of soda
> 2 tablespoons of melted margarine or shortening
> 1 cup of buttermilk (approximately)

Mix ingredients, adding enough buttermilk to make a thick batter. Pour into greased baking pan. Bake in a 425° to

450° F oven for approximately 30 minutes or until brown. An iron skillet will help ensure excellent results.

Soda biscuits

Biscuits similar to these can be found on many a country table throughout rural America and are great for sopping up gravy. Soda biscuits seem to have their roots in the southern states, where the delicacy of biscuits and gravy are a top seller on most restaurants' breakfast menus.

> 2 cups of flour
> 1 teaspoon of salt
> 3 teaspoons of baking powder
> 1/4 teaspoon soda
> 1/3 cup shortening
> 1/2 to 3/4 cup of buttermilk

Mix flour, salt, baking powder, and soda. Cut in shortening until thoroughly mixed. Add just enough buttermilk to make a soft dough. On a floured board, knead six to seven times. Roll out and cut into biscuits. Melt about two tablespoons of shortening in a baking pan. Put in biscuits and turn immediately to grease the tops. Bake for 10 minutes or until brown.

Gritted bread

Corn has been added to breads for many years, either as a substitute for flour or as a supplement. Here is an example of a distinctively different product as a result.

> 2 cups gritted corn (see below*)
> 1/2 cup sweet milk
> 1 teaspoon of sugar
> 1 teaspoon salt
> 2 tablespoons of soft butter
> 1/2 teaspoon baking soda
> 1/4 cup flour

Mix ingredients together, adding flour as needed. Bake in greased iron pan at 400° F for approximately 25 minutes.

*Gritted corn is made by scraping ear corn with a grater. The corn must be past roasting ear maturity, but not too hard. If a grater was not available, homesteaders sometimes made one by puncturing a piece of tin with a nail. This porous scraper was then used to grate the corn while still on the cob.

Sourdough starter

Maintaining a starter was an important responsibility for the early American homemakers. The recipes—and starters—were generally passed from mother to daughter. In the event a homesteader's starter turned bad or was lost for any one of many reasons, it was sometimes necessary to travel great distances in order to get one from a neighboring family.

Here is a more modern starter that uses a small amount of yeast to get started. While the yeast gives you a jump ahead, the end product is much the same as any other, more traditionally begun starter.

> 1 tablespoon of active dry yeast
> 2 1/2 cups of warm water
> 2 1/2 cups of unbleached white flour

Dissolve the yeast in a glass bowl containing one cup of lukewarm water. Stir in the flour and remaining warm water and mix well. Cover and let stand four to five days in a warm place. Temperature should be between 75 to 90° F. A windowsill is a great place, as long as it doesn't get too warm. If it gets too hot, the yeast will be killed. Until it's needed, the starter can be stabilized in the refrigerator.

Sourdough potato starter

After boiling several potatoes for your evening meal, pour off the still-warm water. Allow to cool until lukewarm and add flour to produce a thick batter. Let stand for at least 24 hours or until it smells yeasty. The starter can be stabilized in the refrigerator. This method was commonly used historically when potatoes were available. Δ

A BHM Writer's Profile: Alice Brantley Yeager

Alice Brantley Yeager was born near Akron, Ohio, to parents who were "plant people" and she was introduced to plants at an early age. Her family moved to Texarkana, Arkansas, when the Great Depression came along, money was still in short supply, and gardening was almost a necessity for most folks if they had space for a garden and Alice displayed her natural gifts with plants including wild food plants.

After two years of college, Alice worked for the Navy Department in Washington, DC, before World War II, and the Southwestern Proving Ground in Hope, Arkansas during the war.

After the war, she worked as a freight agent for some commercial trucking companies and as an Arkansas real estate agent. She is now concentrating on being an artist and a garden writer as these are the things that give her the most personal satisfaction. "When you think about it, there are few occupations wherein one is allowed to eat one's subjects and what is better than a juicy tomato or cool cuke?"

Alice married her photographer husband, James Yeager in 1955 and they have one daughter, Leah Y. Gray, living near Houston, TX. Leah and her husband, John, have two daughters Sarah Kathleen and Alexandra Hope, ages 8 and 11.

A BHM Writer's Profile: James O. Yeager

James O. Yeager is retired from 35 years of government employment with the Department of the Army as an engineer. He has fallen on hard times and is now employed by his wife, Alice, as a not-too-well paid photographer. He was born in Morgan City, LA, but shortly after his birth the family moved to Texarkana, Arkansas, to settle on a portion of the original Yeager estate homesteaded by his grandfather. James and Alice live on an inherited 20 acres of the same property.

An interest in photography was kindled in childhood when box and bellows cameras and black and white photos were the norm. After he and Alice married, she began writing for a small gardening magazine and used him as her photographer. He bought more and more expensive equipment: lenses, flashes, reflectors, tripod, monopod and other accessories. "Full gear with accessory vest is comparable to someone going on safari." His present career proves there's life after retirement. "Photography teaches both patience and to quickly take advantage of the moment. Butterflies flutter. Shadows move. Breezes won't let plants stand still. Harvested greens and flowers wilt. Bugs never cooperate. People get disgruntled when asked to stand too long in the sun." James has seen it all.

Here's a cold storage house as good as our ancestors built

By Harry G. Nemec

Back in the early seventies, my wife and I decided to invest in our own ideas to "get ahead." I was not earning enough money. We had tried second jobs, but that wasn't cutting it either. We could exist and plod along, I could see that. It took every cent I was earning to pay our living expenses. That meant we would not have any savings. We needed a way to use our talents as an investment.

We decided to venture out into the woods of central Pennsylvania. We purchased a five-acre parcel of mountain land and a cabin, since we could afford it. The reason we could afford it was because there was no electricity, no running water, and no plumbing. An old cookstove was the source of heat and cooking. Water was available from a spring a short walk from the house.

The property was far enough away from the mainstream of life to be a cheap place to live. It was a desolate hunting area, and as such, a luxury for some people, an extra place to get away to at times. For us, it was an

opportunity to have a place to get out of the rain until we could afford to fix it up for year-round living. We discussed the best way to capitalize on our investment. We could clear some land, grow our own food and sell the excess, raise chickens and sell eggs. We would make it into a five-acre farm.

During the first year, we obtained electricity, and with that, power to run the pump (which meant running water and inside plumbing) and automatic heat. We were becoming civilized. We had an acre of level woods cleared, and we planted a general crop. We were becoming a farm, and no farm is complete without a place to store potatoes and root vegetables.

I was determined to make the hunting cabin and mountain ground into a five-acre farm. All I needed was a barn, a storage house, a tractor, and a patch.

With the completion of the inside plumbing and automatic heat, we could move on to the next projects. The second was the patch, which involved clearing land and planting crops. With our crops planted, we

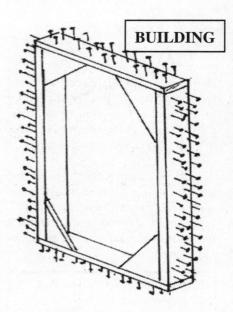

"Porcupine" door frame

needed a storage facility so they would feed us all year and until the next crop came in.

After considerable study on the subject of food storage, moisture, ventilation, and rodents, I went on to look at the many types of construction. I chose to use what I had at hand—natural mountain field stone.

I was told that the stone found on the ground wasn't good enough for the project because it had been weathered and wouldn't hold the concrete. Since I had all that stone just lying around, it didn't matter to me if they were right or wrong; I was going to do it my way. The way I figured it, since our ancestors built barns, houses, fence rows, and everything else using the stones that were lying around, I could too. Their buildings and fence rows are still around. Maybe the roofs have caved in and wood rotted away, leaving the shells of what were buildings years ago. I could use the same material they used and have a storage house for the cost of concrete and some sweat.

My mind was made up. I was going to use the stones that were all over the place. Next I had to figure how many stones I needed, but that meant I had to know how big this thing was going to be. How much of what was to be stored? Now the real thinking began. I reverted back to the basics: What do we buy that we can grow? I studied

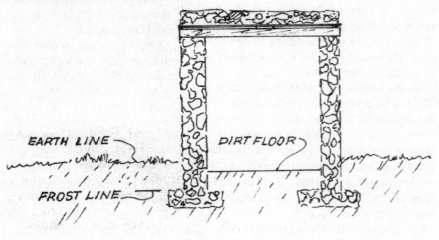

Cross section of cold storage house, seen from the end

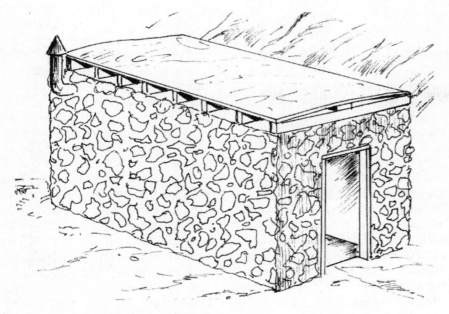

This view of the cold storage house shows the 2x4s on top of the walls, supporting the plywood roof. The concrete roof was poured on top of this plywood.

our shopping habits: potatoes, carrots, beets, apples, yams, cabbage, onions, and the like. I could grow them and store them. I computed the mainstays and came up with 400 pounds of potatoes. (We usually used five pounds per week, and I added some to plant, and surplus). I then went to the store and looked at the pile of 20-pound bags, and measured the volume that made up 400 pounds. I figured that I could put 400 pounds of potatoes into a bin measuring two feet wide and five feet tall by three feet deep, or thirty cubic feet.

I measured in the same fashion for everything I was planning to store in the building. I then converted the total cubic feet into dimensions that would comprise the inside of the building. The result of my calculations showed that the cold storage house would have to be six feet by eight feet, with a six-foot ceiling, or 288 cubic feet. This measurement included walk-in space.

The next part of the project involved building materials. To determine how much stone I would need for this project, I used the same measuring technique as I had used to measure the space requirements for the contents of the cold storage house. I had to determine the thickness of the walls and

make an allowance for the depth of the wall into the ground to the footer (or foundation), minus the space for the door. I had enough stone to start, and I would find more while digging.

I chose a portion of the land that had been used previously as a place to push unused ground while leveling for the house, since it faced the patch. I staked off the area, allowing for the thickness of the walls. Then I grabbed the pick, shovel, friendly digging iron, and gloves.

The initial day's digging went fast, as I was digging from the side of a small depression into a steep rise. I did not need shoring, since the rise was only six feet or so. I was able to throw the dirt right into the patch.

Because of the purpose of the building and the design of the walls (more than a foot thick), the footer had to be 24 inches wide and 6 inches thick, and it had to be down below the frost line (in our area, 34 inches).

The dirt floor acts like a chimney, permitting earth-temperature, moisture-laden air to flow into the cold storage building. It is this moisture-laden air that prevents the stored food from drying out or freezing.

The design calls for a ventilation pipe to provide an air passage for the ventilation of the moisture coming out

of the ground through the dirt floor. If the footer isn't deep enough, frost will use the passage through the vent pipe, freezing everything in its path.

In a couple of weeks I had the footer dug, and a sizable pile of rocks that I'd found in the digging.

I mixed the concrete for the footer, using the same formula I had used for an earlier septic tank project (one part concrete, two parts sand, three parts stone), and reinforced it with scraps of re-bar, stones, and fence wire.

The stones were protruding out of the footer, ready to accept more stones that would make up the wall.

Since I was using concrete rather than mortar, I had to let each day's mixing set before I could continue. I was thankful for that.

I placed the stones vertically, in such a fashion that there was a space between them. I was building two walls with a small space between them. When that concrete hardened, I filled that space and put up more vertical stones, creating another space. Before I set each stone in place, I tried it several ways to get the most vertical coverage out of each stone. Then I wet the stone and set it into a "cushion" of concrete and propped it into place so the concrete could set.

Every day I would come home from work and mix up a batch of concrete and set some stones. Eventually, the ugly hole began to take the shape of a crude building sticking out of the side of the rise in the ground.

I began in the corners, setting stone that would comprise the walls against the dirt sides of the hole first, since all I had to do was climb over the footer rather than go around the wall to work on the other wall. (I had figured that the raw stone would hold the concrete just as well a few months later as it would right that instant, just as long as I had used a wet concrete mixture and a dampened stone.) It got to the point that I was sorting rocks to find the perfect rock for the next placement. I then began to try breaking off some of the rock imperfections, rather than spending so much time finding the best fit.

Sorting a pile of football-sized rocks every time I needed another rock seemed like a waste of time, so I drafted my wife to assist. She sorted while I set the rocks. That lasted for a couple of hours; then I was sorting and setting the rocks by myself again. (I may have insulted her by discarding a rock that didn't fit where I had wanted it. She was better at sorting the laundry and stuff like that, anyway. I remember some words about where I could find more rocks that she didn't need to hand me.)

By that time, the structure was taking shape, and the walls were high enough that I could begin planning for the roof and ventilation pipe. The pipe hole had to be planned so that varmints couldn't gain access to the food that was going to be stored inside. I used a three-inch pipe and put a quarter-inch wire mesh screen inside the pipe to keep varmints out. The ground floor of the structure would provide a "warming" effect in the cold winter weather and circulate the natural moisture around the food that was stored. The vent pipe permitted this air flow. Failure to have air circulation permits fungus to grow and ruin the stored food.

Getting back to the roof construction: Once the vent pipe was positioned, I straddled the six-feet-apart upright walls with 2x4s on edge about a foot apart and put a furring strip lengthwise in the middle (to pre-stress the poured roof). I covered that with half-inch plywood, tacking it on the edges to form a slight bow.

Since the 2x4s were on top of the walls, there were open gaps between them at the ends, between the top of the wall and the plywood roof. I filled in these gaps with concrete and small stones. I was now ready to work on the front wall, which would contain the door.

I measured the door frame using an old door I found out back. I made a 2x8 frame around the door and tacked it together so that it would remain square (or as square as the door, anyway) by nailing triangle pieces on all four corners.

I had left a roughed-out opening in the front wall, and I placed the 2x8 frame in the opening to be sure of the fit. Then I removed it and carefully drove 20-penny nails halfway into it from the outside, all the way around it, so that the heads would hold onto the concrete. The frame resembled a porcupine until it was set into place. This frame was first held in place by bracing, and then by filling in the voids in the stone wall with a concrete mixture between the stone wall and the nails. I then installed the doorstop trim on the inside of the frame, using a common furring strip.

The door I used was now going to fit into the 2x8 frame. Next, I had to frame it out to make it into a thick insulated door. I made a 2x4 frame on it, filled the openings in the frame with insulation, then put a piece of half-inch plywood on the open side of the frame. Before I fastened it all together, I put the door in place and tried to open it. I discovered the side that opened out needed a bevel to ensure a snug fit. I removed the screws holding the panel to the frame, made the bevel adjustment (hitting the opening-side 2x4 a couple of times with my hammer) and trimmed the plywood after it was fastened. I put on strap hinges and rope for a handle.

With the door on and the plywood roof not yet completed, I had an opportunity to remeasure and determine if I needed more head room. I was pleased to find that my measurements had worked out perfectly.

The final stage in the completion of the cold storage building was to pour concrete onto the roof. I nailed some scrap lumber around the edges of the form to prevent the concrete mixture from running off. I gathered all the scrap metal I could find, including an old bed spring. I cut everything into appropriate sizes and laid it all in a checkerboard weave pattern in the roof form. I mixed a batch of concrete and poured it into the form over the metal pieces, which I had wet down pretty well. I then put a layer of wet rocks into the still-wet cement, pushing them as far down into the concrete as I could.

At the end of the week, I removed the form edges and examined the seal. I even hit it a couple of times with a hammer to check it out. It was "rock solid." Time to build the bins and shelves.

That year we filled the cold storage house and had pears until after Christmas, tomatoes until February, potatoes until March, and some to plant. We also had beets, carrots, turnips, and apples. We ate healthier from then until we left our farm. Δ

"Exploded" view of the insulated door, showing
the old door, the framing, the insulation, and the plywood panel

Our homestead motto: Make-do

By Marjorie Burris

During the Depression years of the late 1920s and the early 1930s, there was a common saying in our part of the country: "Use it up, make-do, or do without." "Use it up" meant don't waste anything. "Do without"—well, we all know what that means. But *make-do*—ah, *that* was the challenge.

Make-do in 1995 lingo is almost explained by "recycle"—but not quite. "Recycle," to most minds, means "Turn it back to the manufacturers so they can melt it down and use it again." *Make-do* has a broader meaning: it requires a bit of imagination, a bit of ingenuity, and sometimes a bit of humor. It can even have a spirit of adventure about it.

When I was a girl, if we needed anything, we didn't just go down to the store and buy it . . . Oh, no! We were very careful how we spent the few dollars we managed to earn, so we looked around to see if we had anything on hand we could utilize to do the job. This make-do spirit has lived with me all these years, and we find it is still a very good motto on our old homestead today. In fact, we enjoy seeing how creative we can be to use whatever we happen to have on hand. Here are five examples of our make-do philosophy.

Bed springs fence

After we bought our land, we found 50 metal army cots of World War II vintage crammed into the barn loft, all with springs too saggy to use as beds. When we needed angle iron, we would cut a bed apart and hang the springs on a nail on the side of the barn. We had quite a collection of springs.

Early one April morning, as we were making garden, the rancher who ran cattle on the Forest Service land around us stopped by and said he was turning his herd into our range the next day. We had no fence around our garden, and since this is open range country, it was up to us to either make a fence or give up on gardening. Having neither the time, the money, nor the inclination to rush to town for barbed wire, we decided to use the bed springs to make a "temporary" fence. That was 20 years ago. Our bed-springs fence still stands, and since it is the only section of the garden fence which has never been breached by range cattle or jumped by the local deer, we have no immediate plans for replacing it. What is "temporary," anyway? A month? Twenty years? A lifetime? I suppose it depends on where you stand to view the universe.

And we've not had a remark about our fence for at least ten years now. It used to be the unimaginative visitor would say, "What's that?" The imaginative visitor would say, "What a good idea!" And the smart-aleck visitor would say, "I know some people like to sleep on their side, but isn't this a bit much?" Yep, make-do sometimes requires a sense of humor.

Bathtub raised garden

We found ourselves short of time early one spring when an unexpected break in the weather made an early planting possible. A heavy blanket of unmelted snow prevented us from tilling the garden, and since we had always wanted to try a raised garden bed, we thought this would be a good time to make one. But what to use?

We didn't have the time to stop and cut boards on the sawmill for a frame, and go to the store and buy concrete blocks? Heavens, no! Then we spied the bathtub our son Duane had hauled up to the homestead when he remodeled his bathroom. Why not?

We leveled a place on the sunny south side of my little wash house, set the tub close to the house and hid the ugly ends with a false rock wall. I covered the bottom of the tub with fist-size rocks, then we filled the tub with topsoil. Since the tub held only a small amount of dirt, I could easily amend our very acid soil with a sack of limestone, and for the first time I could raise lettuce. We quickly found out that the birds and ground squirrels like lettuce, too, so Husband made a tall wire frame to cover the top of the tub and attached the frame to the side of the building,

Our funny raised garden is only a few steps from our kitchen door, so it is easy to plant and tend even when we can't get to the big garden. Fresh lettuce early in the spring is such a treat. (But yes, I still do have to wash the lettuce before eating it, even if it is raised in a bathtub.)

Big tank wood bins

With the purchase of our land, we also inherited two big metal tanks that had once been used for water storage. Time and neglect had turned the bottoms of the tanks into lace, making them unusable when they stood upright. But tipped over . . . well, we needed a woodshed, anyway. The problem was, how to get the big tanks off their six-foot-high platforms and down the hill, then down the road to a place near the buzz saw where we cut wood.

Husband and I were finally able to hook chains and cables around a tank and pull it off the platform with the tractor, but the big, awkward thing refused to be pulled meekly along behind the tractor. Every rock or root it hit rolled it sideways or endways until finally it got away from us completely and rolled downhill and got wedged between a rock and a tree, which squashed it out-of-round.

We were not happy. We shoved, pushed and tugged, dripped sweat, and almost cried until we got tank number one into place. Took half a day.

Then we sat down with a glass of iced tea and were pondering how to move the second tank when two of our sons, their wives, and two good friends drove in and wanted to know what was going on. We explained. They laughed, "Pull it off the platform and we will move it." We pulled the tank down, they swept all the debris out of it, and then all six adventurous young adults lined up in the tank and began walking, making the tank roll. When they came to a steep downhill slope, part of the team turned around and walked uphill, making an effec-

tive brake. In no time at all they jockeyed that big tank into place exactly where we wanted it. I could tell from the squeals and laughter coming from inside the tank that our "Big Tank Walk" was every bit as much fun as any carnival ride.

We positioned the tanks facing south, so not much rain and snow blow onto the wood. The tanks' lacy bottoms allow the wind to circulate through the wood and dry our fuel. And when we have both tanks full we know we have enough wood cut for the winter. We like our big tank wood bins.

Barrel & rock fence posts

We needed to put up a pig fence, but *fence* meant *posts*, and *posts* meant *digging*, and *digging* meant *hitting rock* and *rock . . . Rock?!* We've got *lots* of *rock!*

But rock has to be contained someway. We used all the wire mesh concrete reinforcing we had to make cylinders for rock posts, but we still needed more posts. What about all those barrels stashed away in a far corner of the pasture? Yes, the ones that some thoughtless hunter had used for target practice some time or another. Not much good for holding liquids, but perfect for holding rocks.

We put the more attractive wire cylinder fence posts on the front side of the pig pen and used the barrels on the back side where they don't show much. The pigs did not knock down any of the posts, so we considered our make-do fence posts well done. They certainly saved us a lot of time and energy.

Wheels for hose hangers

We are blessed with a good spring with gravity flow pressure, but we have to use lots of hoses and sprinklers to spread the water around. That means we have hoses distributed all over the place, and when cold weather sets in we have to drain all those hoses

and hang them up. That takes *many* hose hangers.

Also on our property we found about 20 old wheels (yes, this was a *junky* place) that had lain so long the tires were almost fused onto them. We couldn't get the tires off, so we took the wheels to the service station and the attendant removed the tires on his machine for two dollars a wheel. We thought this was a good price considering the work involved, and the station disposed of our old tires as well.

The wheels make perfect hose hangers and it makes us proud that we are able to use the antiques instead of letting them lie around.

This is just a sample of our make-do. Perhaps you have an interesting make-do project you'd like to share with *Backwoods Home*. Why don't you write Dave a letter and tell him about it? Maybe you can give the rest of us some ideas, too. Δ

A BHM Writer's Profile: Charles Sanders

Charles A. Sanders, 44, his wife Patti, and three children live in southern Indiana on 39 acres of pasture and timberland. They raise beef, poultry, an orchard, and a large garden. The surrounding countryside and woodlands provide the addition of deer, squirrel, rabbit, and wild turkey for the family. He has been an Indiana Conservation Officer for over 23 years.

In addition to having articles in BHM, he has been published in *Back Home, Fur-Fish-Game, Good Old Days, Outdoor Indiana Magazine,* and several local newspapers and publications. Other writing projects are underway.

In addition to writing, his other interests include fur-trapping, American history, radio, winemaking, and devising handy projects in the workshop.

The saga of Benjamin, the backwoods, homeschooled boy who wanted to get a job

By Margaret Wright

Raised in the woods of Northern Idaho, home schooled by loving, protective parents, he was a happy, carefree child for the first sixteen years of life. The sixteenth summer, reality hit, and he discovered his "toys" were costing more, and Mom and Dad were expecting contributions of a higher percentage than in the past. Hence, the idea to get a real job came into Benjamin's mind.

Odd jobs for people in the area around our home no longer brought in the amount of money needed to support his hobbies. After searching the newspapers for several weeks, he found an ad for a job that sounded suitable for his training, with a schedule that would fit his lifestyle. The local theme park (15 miles away) was hiring teens to fill in for the regular summer workers who were leaving for school and college.

We stopped one day on the way home from town to pick up an application. I was always on the lookout for learning experiences, so I figured it would be good practice filling out the forms. After all, we always knew the day would come when our offspring would be ready to fly from the nest. I helped him fill in all the little lines with the details of his existence. Pretty basic stuff.

However, I cringed when we came to the "education" part. I have an unshakable belief in keeping the children at home under the care of their parents. Benjamin's older sister was home schooled and has done very well, but this was the first test of how the outside world would react to *this* child—and I was a wee bit nervous. Our son was going to be judged on a decision that we, his parents, had made when he was a little bitty thing

so many years ago. We just wrote in the two words "home schooled" across the "education" blanks.

The paper sat around for a few days. He reminded me for the umpteenth time, "Did you mail it yet?" Oh well, it would be a disappointment for him, but that's learning, too, so I sent it in.

I had actually forgotten it when the phone rang a few days later and a gentleman asked for Benjamin. I took the message that Benjamin was to meet him at his office the next day at eight a.m. for an interview. I could have swooned at that point. I wanted to yell at him, "No, no, you cannot take my child from me," but I controlled myself and got the information.

We were up earlier than usual. Benjamin was in a high state of anticipation. I was suffering from an extreme condition called anxiety. OK, I told myself, there is a slim possibility of his being hired. What do we need

as far as paper work? I had no idea, so I called the park's personnel office. We were told to bring his birth certificate, social security card, and a picture ID.

Picture ID? Why would he need that? The office lady says, "The federal government says everyone has to have one before they can be employed."

"No, we don't have a school picture ID." (I always knew the same kid would come down the stairs every day to do his school work.)

"Well, what about a year book?" Yeah, right, for one kid. (We did draw his picture a long time ago and write a story about him.)

"OK," she says, "He can work one day without the ID," while Mom figures something out.

Off to the theme park we went. After a 15-minute interview, Benjamin came back to the truck with his work schedule and announced he was going to be rich. One of the managers told me he'd had several home schoolers work for him over the years and they work out just fine and are very self-motivated. I was relieved to hear that. At least now I know it's not a permanent scar on my child's unblemished record.

Actually, most people do give good recommendations for home schoolers. I don't know why I was anticipating problems.

We were sent over to Personnel to fill out the mountain of paper work and produce our documentation that this child exists. I produced his birth certificate, social security card, immunization records, and a picture ID with fingerprints. It had been made by the Sheriff's Department and was to be used in the event he was ever stolen and we decided we wanted him back.

Well, everything was in order, but the ID would not work. *Fingerprints,* no less, and the government says No. It might not be him. Well then, why did the Sheriff's Department put their seal on it?

Plan B: Into town to the driver's license bureau. Yes, we could get a picture ID, but we needed three proofs of who he is, along with a certified, homogenized, and pasteurized birth certificate from Boise. I had one, but it wasn't the right kind of copy. They want the kind that costs $10 and takes 30 days to get here. OK, I've got "my copy" of the birth certificate, birth announcement that was in the paper, church blessing certificate, immunization record, and a Medic Alert Card I carry in my wallet that matches the number on the bracelet he wears. Nope, not enough proof he's who I said he was. (Look, do you want to see the Caesarean scar; it's a beaut.)

Plan C: Go get a passport! Now that's simple compared to Plan B. We can get the pictures made, only $30. Yes, I can get them that day. Then to the courthouse with my folder of info and the clerk there says, "No problem." Pay them $40 and he will have a

passport in two weeks. Let me get this straight: I can't get this kid a personal ID card from Kootenai County to work in a local theme park, but I can get him a passport that will let him travel all over the world? The answer to that was, "Go figure!"

If not for the time frame involved, I would have done the passport thing. After all, isn't a mother supposed to pull out all the stops for her child?

Benjamin is showing signs of wilting by now, but that's OK. "Don't worry son, I'll get you that job if I have to call the Governor."

We stopped by the Sheriff's Department on the way out of town, and the sweet, portly gentleman safely hidden behind six inches of bullet-proof glass just smiled and said, "Sorry, we don't do personal ID's any more. We have 15 or 20 parents a month needing help with the same problem." (At this point, I can see why he's behind that glass.)

Back to the theme park (on the second tank of gas for the pickup that morning). I tell the Personnel Manager my tale of woe, and she is as distressed as I am at this injustice. She digs out the Federal Regulations Book that has all these rules, and as we are reading down the list of items that so far have given me nothing but a headache, we find that a person under the age of 17 can use a statement of identity from their personal physician as to who they are and the date of their birth. This will circumvent the requirement for a Personal Picture ID!

OK...Plan D: Back to town, (22 miles) to storm the doctor's office. (Hang in son, we're on a mission!)

The receptionist could probably tell by my demeanor that I was getting close to murder or suicide (depending on the outcome of our visit), and she proceeded to offer all kinds of help. She made several copies of Benjamin's records and stamped them with the doctor's "stamp of approval." She even signed with her own name, saying that might help.

By now Benjamin was tired and hungry and even said maybe he didn't want a job.

"Are you kidding? This is a matter of pride and principle, and I will get you hired and working if it kills both of us!" This from a devoted mother who just a few hours earlier was close to tears because her little fledgling was going out into the big bad world.

Back to the theme park, and through the gate for the thousandth time. Except this time they just waved us through without any questions. (By the way, this time the parking attendant had me park in the handicapped space. Go figure.)

Down to personnel. . . . Well praise be to the gods that watch out over fools and children with kamikaze mothers, all the paperwork passed inspection and he got his coveralls with a T-shirt and a little badge that had his name on it.

Back home after nine hours of our (my) non-stop mission, I settled down with two aspirins and a coke, when reality hit. "Oh, no! What have I done?" My sweet, innocent child whom I have protected with my life has been thrust out into society to fight the tigers, and I'm the one that made sure it happened.

Just then the phone rings and that sweet little voice says, "Hi Mom, it's Benjamin." (Like I didn't know who he was . . . after all, now I have proof!) "I'm having a blast. They let me use the big weed eater!"

It's official, my fledgling has flown the nest and I am so glad we kept him at home as long as we could. Δ

For this resourceful couple, primitive survival skills are a path to self sufficiency

By Terrie Clark

"Just do it!" says John McPherson, echoing the ad for athletic gear. He's not referring to aerobics, though: he's talking about deciding to live a more self-reliant lifestyle. He speaks from experience, and he knows that some of the biggest obstacles are the fears that can come when you temporarily lose sight of your goal.

John says making that decision, that initial break, is the hardest part of making such a lifestyle change. He concedes that making that decision for himself may have been easier than for most. John made his choice shortly after being discharged from the Army in 1972. He was 28 years old and single. He'd been around the world a couple of times and, like an 18-year-old just out of school, he was without responsibilities or obligations to anyone except himself.

Today John and his wife Geri are living the lifestyle of their choice in a log cabin they built on 40 acres of native prairie in northeast Kansas.

Some of the first visible indications of the McPhersons' lifestyle as you approach their home are the rail and pole fences, the windmill and water tank, and the solar panels on the roof. A further look around reveals the semi-permanent grass shelter (9x9x17) they built three summers ago, and right in front of the house you see John's flint-knapping area. Inside the house, you find the primitive stone tools they used to hollow out a 20-foot log canoe, the earthenware pots and the baskets Geri has made from materials she gathers within 200 yards of their house, and the wood stoves and kerosene lamps.

John and Geri strive for the ultimate in self-sufficiency, reaching back to primitive skills. In earlier times, people lived by making whatever they needed from materials the natural

*John and Geri McPherson
(Photo by Ann Turbin)*

world provided. They made traps, cordage, cookware, and tools. This level of self-sufficiency has always been John and Geri's goal. It has led them to acquire the necessary knowledge and mastery of the day-to-day skills required to provide for themselves should they unexpectedly find themselves "naked in the wilderness." Although they don't live at this level continuously, they consistently use the primitive skills they've mastered, keeping them as natural as flipping a light switch or starting a car.

As a boy growing up in New York state in the Appalachian mountain area, John spent his free time camping, hunting, fishing, and daydreaming of living a wilderness life in a self-built log cabin. In 1964, he joined the Army Paratroopers, and those boyhood dreams seemed forgotten.

While in the Army, John was injured during maneuvers and suffered a ruptured disc in his back. He underwent surgery to correct this condition. Fourteen months later, he was serving a tour in Viet Nam. The injury, the subsequent surgery, and the tour in Viet Nam combined to limit his activities. Unable to continue jumping, he was transferred out of his airborne unit and re-assigned as a platoon sergeant of a headquarters company.

Geri in the kitchen

After his discharge from the Army, John again had serious trouble with his back and was assessed as partially disabled. Two years later he underwent a second surgery, and three years after that was assessed 100% disabled retroactive to his last hospitalization. His back is a condition he's learned to live with. In almost constant pain, he wears a back brace and has learned his limitations — what he cannot do at all and what he can do within limits. The disability check he receives from the Veterans Administration pays for the physical work he can't do himself and has to hire out.

After eight years of military life, John found himself out of the Army and alone. In only a few months he went from being a gainfully employed family man with a wife and son to being unemployed and single.

The next several months were a time of transition. John went back to college for a semester before getting a job as a newspaper photographer. During that time he contemplated what he wanted to do for a living, and his thoughts kept returning to the wilderness. He realized a rare opportunity lay before him: responsible only to and for himself he could freely ask,

A selection of earthenware containers used for cooking and storing water

"What do I want to do for the rest of my life? What am I looking for?" He had seen different jobs, lifestyles, and cultures. He had some knowledge and talent. His answers kept taking him back to the wilderness, and to a free, independent, self-sufficient lifestyle. He knew he wanted that log cabin from his boyhood dreams, but the next question was more specific: "What exactly do I need to know?"

Although John had grown up appreciating the wilderness, he realized he had no knowledge of living self-sufficiently. He didn't know how to cut logs, build a cabin, produce or gather his own food, or live without electricity. His plan was to support himself as a newspaper photographer while he learned what he needed.

He hit the library and the newsstands, looking for information on living self-sufficiently. *Mother Earth News* became a primary source of information. Living in a small, rural Kansas town provided an opportunity to learn from older people. He started gathering old tools and working for local farmers, helping them with crops, fences, tending livestock. He spent a summer helping a friend build a house, and he learned about pouring concrete. He installed a wood stove in his house, both as supplemental heat and to begin the transition away from gas. He bought a chain saw and started learning which trees made good

firewood and how to cut them. He planted a garden and started learning to preserve his own food.

An early milestone came for John in 1975 when he got rid of his television. He found he had been spending more time watching what he wanted to do than he spent doing it. That same year he made his first bow, tanned a calf skin, and made his first friction fire.

A lump sum payment from the Veterans Administration in 1977 provided the small down payment John

A 20-foot dugout canoe nearing completion. It started as a 30" diameter cottonwood, chopped down, squared into a beam, and hollowed out— all with stone tools.

A stairway made from logs, using a chain saw, hammer, and chisel. The steps are set into the split log.

*Geri de-hairs a skin
while John splits wood*

needed to buy the land where he now lives. He had become self-sufficient and knowledgeable enough to start building his own house and to raise his own food.

One of John's goals was to build the house without using electricity, to use

*A collection of tools used in
various projects. Nearly all of
them were made using primitive
methods (such as burning holes
with fire made with a hand drill).*

only chain saws and hand tools. In 1978, John's back was still strong enough to cut the trees he needed for the first course of logs. He cut the trees, squared them off, and laid the logs on the concrete walls. He made the roof flat, planning to build up from it sometime in the future.

The initial house was a 736 square-foot walk-out basement. Planning to build in stages, John moved in the next year (1978), as soon as he had a floor and roof. It was another milestone. He and his (former) wife were living without electricity. They had a large garden (40' x 100') and canned all their food, and they raised and butchered their own hogs and steers. They used a propane refrigerator, wood heating and cooking stoves, and kerosene lamps.

They hauled water in gallon milk containers from the town of Randolph, two miles away, until the water system was completed three years later. Planning a simple gravity-flow system, John had a well drilled and purchased a windmill for $300 from a friend. The base of the windmill is 10 feet above the floor level of the house. The hardest part of installing the system was jackhammering the 142-foot water line trench from the tank to the house. Three feet of limestone and flint had to be cut through to lay the line. Unable to do that work himself, John recalls, "I rented the jackhammer and bought a lot of beer for my friends."

In 1985, John and his second wife parted ways. She began moving more into the modern world and John, moving more toward the primitive, began making the Mountain Man Rendezvous circuit. For the next couple of years, John attended the Rendezvous and taught brain tanning, bow-making, and friction fire techniques. It was following one of these rendezvous that John wrote and published his first book, Brain Tan Buckskin. In 1987, he wrote and published his second book, Primitive Fire and Cordage. It was also at one of these Rendezvous

*When gathering, you need a way to
carry things. Here are some of the
couple's baskets, most of which can
be made in a short time. The large
one on the left took about three hours,
including the carrying strap.*

that he and Geri met. Traveling the same road, they were married in December 1987.

Construction on the upper level of the house was begun in 1990. Unable to cut and haul the logs, John purchased milled logs. John and one of his older friends, 70-year-old Argel Pultz, were the only full-time workers. The work took its toll on John's back,

*Sharp, useful tools can be made using
the ancient art of flint knapping. Here
are some examples of John's work.*

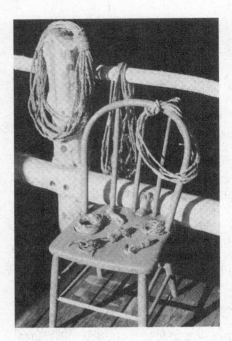

Making cordage is an essential primitive skill. Here are examples ranging from a short fishing line to a 60-foot ³/8-inch rope—all made by hand from locally-gathered natural fibers.

and he almost had to hire the work done. He learned his limits: as long as he didn't do too much at one time and quit whenever his back told him to, John found he could do the work. The addition, including a loft, added another 976 square feet of living space to the house. Later, John and Geri added another bedroom and library (448 square feet) making the complete house 2,160 square feet.

Although John would still like to retreat to the mountains and live a truly primitive life in the wilderness, his back condition doesn't permit further withdrawal from modern society and medicine. The success of his first two books convinced him, instead, to write a series of how-to books on primitive skills. Because there was such a lack of information available when John began his quest for self-sufficiency, sharing what he and Geri have learned is very important to them.

John chose to publish his books under the name Prairie Wolf, the Indian name for the coyote, because the coyote hasn't just adapted to the modern world, it has thrived.

The original series contains ten how-to books covering the subjects of tanning, fire and cordage, bows and arrows, obtaining sustenance, cooking methods, containers, tools, and semi-permanent shelters, all done primitively, directly from nature. John wrote the first two books himself, and he and Geri together wrote the others. The series was consolidated in 1994 into one large volume: Primitive Wilderness Living & Survival Skills.

As a complement to the book, John and Geri have also produced six videos showing the skills of brain tanning, primitive fire and cordage, the primitive bow and arrow, dressing a deer, primitive shelters, and the Asiatic composite bow.

Writing and publishing challenged the McPhersons' electricity-free lifestyle. At first John wrote the books using a typewriter and took the manuscript to a typesetter. That proved to inefficient, but running a computer without reliable energy was worse. After their third book, the McPhersons purchased a home computer system. The computer reduced production costs and gave them more control of their final product, but getting power to it was a problem.

They began by using a generator, but soon tired of the noise. Someone offered to set them up with a solar system at cost, in trade for a week of Primitive training, and they jumped at the opportunity. Their system consists of two 4-foot-square sections of panels and six, 6-volt golf cart batteries. This provides ample power for the two computers and for the VCR system they added for their video production.

Along with writing the books come the tasks of publishing and marketing. Unable to find a publisher willing to buy and produce the books the way John wanted it done—with all the photographs included—John began marketing the books himself. He has

Naturally made buckskin

built mailing lists, identified retail outlets, and learned to utilize direct mail advertising. (More self sufficiency.)

Teaching primitive skills and tending to the details of marketing their books and videos consumes much of John and Geri's time . . . more than they would like. They prefer to spend their time perfecting and enhancing their primitive skills or researching, through doing, material for their next book.

This fall John will gather cedar logs to start a new project, a 10x12 log cabin. A nearby landowner wants to take down some trees, so John will take advantage of the harvest. He and Geri will also spend some time perfecting the log canoe that they and local youngsters have spent the last two summers making, using only stone tools.

With the onset of cold weather, indoor activities will resume: making pottery, bows, and arrows, tanning hides, reading and writing. Geri is currently writing a novel that is set during the Stone Age. The work calls upon her knowledge of primitive skills, lending a unique perspective to her descriptions of the daily activities of aboriginal people. John and Geri are also researching Volume II of their how-to book, the next phase of their journey to self-sufficiency.

The McPhersons' book, Primitive Wilderness Living & Survival Skills, and their videos are available by writing to Prairie Wolf, PO Box 96C, Randolph, KS 66554. You can also order their book through *Backwoods Home*. Δ

Beans — they may be a poor man's meat, but they are also the gourmet's delight

By Richard Blunt

During the last half of the 20th century people have become as concerned with nutritional value as they are with the quality of taste and pleasure in the food they buy. Before the last World War most of us didn't know the difference between a vitamin and calorie. Today it is a familiar sight to see folks waltzing through the supermarket and spending more time comparing the nutritional information of various foods than actually shopping. My 10-year-old daughter can recite the names of the eight essential amino acids in one breath, without mispronouncing one of them. I don't even know who taught her.

With all of the nutritional awareness in this country, it baffles me that beans don't seem to be fully recognized as an inexpensive, very available food source that is low in fat and calories, and high in complex carbohydrates and fiber. It also has enough essential amino acids to qualify as a fair source of usable protein. Beans can easily be prepared using simple basic recipes that will produce some wonderful tasting hors d'oeuvres, soups, salads, casseroles, stews, and desserts. There are few other foods that are so versatile.

For those model gourmands striving to etch their name in the great book of gastronomical mythology, you can enter the holy war of the French cassoulet and create your own version of this classic meat and bean casserole, baked in an earthenware pot. The French will spend whole evenings discussing the virtues of a true cassoulet, with the same dedication that football fans exhibit when defending their favorite team in the Super Bowl. Not only that, but they do it in French.

In the recipe section I have included a version of the Castelnaudry cassoulet. It doesn't fall into the "easy to prepare" category of bean recipes, but I assure you that every minute spent in preparation of this classic dish will be returned twice-fold in taste, aroma, and absolute eating pleasure.

Poor man's meat?

At one time beans were called "poor man's meat," but the sweeping interest in Mexican and Mediterranean food in this country has taught us that beans are everybody's food. At one time if asked how we ate beans, many of us would answer, "baked," instantly calling to mind the old franks and beans tradition. Without a doubt Boston Baked Beans has been a signature of American cuisine as few other dishes have been. But I find many folks can't deal with the

syrupy sweetness of this dish and will avoid beans in general because of this association. My daughter Sarah was one of these people until I started experimenting with different bean recipe concepts while working on this column.

Baked beans are a favorite item around our house, and poor Sarah was often forced to eat a second choice on the nights when baked beans were on the menu. When she found out that I was writing this month's column on beans, she was not happy. It finally dawned on me to ask her what it was that turned her off to beans. She answered, "They're too sweet and a little bitter."

I reminded her that one of her favorite snack foods was the spicy bean dip, hummus. She looked surprised and said, "That's not beans."

After realizing that beans were not the culprit, Sarah and I went to work and created a recipe called, Beans for Sarah. If baked beans offend your palate, and you would like to create a simple dish that accents the natural sweetness and hardy flavor of the common bean, you will love this recipe.

Flatulence

At the risk of sounding inappropriate, I would like to say a few words about an often embarrassing consequence of consuming any variety of dried bean. Flatulence is not life threatening, although I was once in a crowded elevator in Boston's Harbor Towers when the area suddenly filled with that mixture of hydrogen, methane, and hydrogen sulfide gases, carrying those offensive skatole and indole odors. After only one minute of exposure in such a confined space, I confess that I was a little concerned for personal safety.

Intestinal gas is the result of sugars, starches, and fiber reaching the large intestine without being digested. Once there, the harmless bacteria residing in the bowel eat them and give off those bothersome gases as a byproduct of this process. One of the most prolific sources of intestinal gas are what scientists call raffinose sugars. Unfortunately they are found in large amounts in dried beans. These sugars require a specialized enzyme (alpha-galactosidase) to break them down. However, our bodies don't produce this enzyme, so our intestinal bacteria are left to the task and produce the gases as a byproduct.

There are a number of "gas preventer" products on the market that may help if you are troubled by flatulence. Being one who is troubled with gas, I decided to try one. One company makes little bean-shaped pills that, much to my surprise, cut down on the volume of gas and eliminated that uncomfortable bloated feeling. Unfortunately, odor was still a problem. Over the last few months I have learned a few tips that also help to reduce gas generated by bean consumption.

1. Cook your beans completely. By completely I mean soft without being mushy.

2. Discard the water that you soak the beans in. This water is loaded with raffinose sugars.

3. Many bean recipes call for the addition of onions, cabbage, and other potential gas producing vegetables like broccoli. Try reducing some of these ingredients.

4. Always carry a book of matches (no joke). A lit match produces ozone which oxidizes those mortifying odors.

5. Learn to point to someone smaller than yourself when you're the culprit.

6. If all else fails, make friends with other bean lovers, and hang with them as much as possible.

Cooking tips

As I stated above, beans benefit most from simple, basic cooking techniques. With this in mind you will find my list of cooking tips short and uncomplicated. To develop the best flavor and consistency in all of your bean recipes:

1. Spend a few minutes to plan your bean usage for any period of time. Cook a large enough quantity of beans to cover your needs. Drain, cool, cover, and refrigerate or freeze them until you are ready to use them. This is called the "bean pot method." When the pot is empty repeat the process. Keep in mind that most beans always taste better and have a better texture a couple of days after being cooked.

2. Do not soak beans overnight. There is no advantage to soaking beans for more than four hours. I have discovered that black beans require as much cooking when soaked as they do without soaking.

3. Invest in a couple of earthenware bean pots and casserole dishes. Beans cooked in this type of pot have a flavor that cannot be achieved using a metal pot. As a matter of fact, the great authority of Mexican cuisine, Diana Kennedy, suggests that beans should never be stirred with a metal spoon. When the great ones speak, I listen.

4. Do not add salt or any acid sauce to beans until they are thoroughly cooked. Accomplished chili and Boston Baked Bean makers have discovered that adding partially cooked beans to the acid environments of tomatoes or molasses will prevent the beans from getting any softer no matter how long they are cooked.

5. Cook beans very slowly in a covered pot. Most beans require 1 1/2 to 2 1/2 hours of slow cooking time. Faba, garbanzo, and soy beans will need about 3 hours.

The recipes that I have selected to share with you all call for a type bean, and these recipes are selected and developed to suit my personal taste preferences. If you do not have the type of bean that is called for, replace it with the bean of your choice.

Not all beans are created equal; each type has a special flavor and texture. I am sure that if you have not already developed a preference for any particular type of bean, it will not be long before you do. I prefer the taste of any variety of common bean (navy bean, pea bean. pinto bean, mung bean, kidney bean to name just a few) over the taste of the broad bean (lima bean or faba bean). I avoid faba beans because my father's side of our family has had problems with Favism, which is a type of anemia caused by the consumption of faba beans. In severe cases, simply inhaling the pollen of this bean's flowers is enough to cause problems.

Because of my own preferences and concern for my health, the cassoulet recipe I am going to present is far from being classic. The classic version calls for faba beans as a first choice, with lima beans as a distant second. Having said that let's begin the recipes with this French classic.

Cassoulet

Despite the fact that this dish can cost big bucks at any French restaurant, it is in reality a basic country food that calls for ingredients that are common in many French kitchens. Even if you decide to pass on preparing this for your next family get-together, I think that you will enjoy reading about how complex simple food can be.

This recipe calls for a goose confit (pronounced con-fi) which is another name for preserved goose. When prepared properly, this stuff holds in the refrigerator for months.

Most recipes suggest that it be held in the refrigerator for 3 or 4 months before using it. Even though the meat is cooked in, and preserved in, a large volume of fat, the finished product is fairly low in fat and has a wonderful flavor. I included this in the recipe because it is one of the few luxury foods that I enjoy. But I don't feel that a cassoulet will fail without the inclusion of the goose confit so you will see that I have listed it as optional in the list of ingredients for the cassoulet.

Ingredients for Goose Confit

1 goose (about 10 pounds)
2 Tbsp Kosher salt
6 whole black peppercorns
1 bay leaf

Method

1. Cut the goose into quarters and remove as much fat as possible. Place the fat in a heavy-bottom pot and melt it slowly. Add the goose quarters, salt, peppercorns, and bay leaf. Cover the pot and cook over low heat for two hours. Remove from the heat and allow to cool without stirring.

2. When the goose has cooled and the fat settled but is not yet stiff, spoon some of the fat into a large preserve jar or stone crock. Lay one of the goose quarters in the jar and cover it with more fat. Continue this sequence until all of the goose quarters are in the jar and covered with about a half inch of fat. Use only the fat, do not disturb the meat juices. Cover the jar tightly and age in the refrigerator for at least 4 months. I recommend 5 months.

3. Now, pretend it is five months later, and you are ready at last to create your classic Castelnaudry cassoulet. If you really want your cassoulet to be a winner, I suggest that you carefully consider the sausages you select. The character, taste and texture of the sausage selection, is in my opinion, the signature of the individual cook. The taste and texture of sausage mixtures vary according to continent, country, region, town, hamlet, neighborhood, street, as well as religious, ethnic background, and taste preferences. So please feel free to use the type of sausages that represents your region and personal tastes. Keep in mind one type of sausage should be a type that will hold its character when cooked in liquid for a long period of time. The other should be somewhat spicy and roast well.

Ingredients for cassoulet

1 pound of dried white kidney beans (or other white beans)
water to soak the beans
2 Tbsp salt free butter
4 Tbsp extra virgin olive oil
2 medium white onions diced fine
4 cloves of minced garlic
1 Tbsp flour
4 raw ham hocks
1 pound kielbasa (boiling sausage)
4 oz lean salt pork
8 oz piece of fresh pork shoulder or butt
1 1/2 cup fresh diced plum tomatoes (peeled and seeded)
1 large bouquet garni (fresh basil, thyme, flat leaf parsley tied together in a piece of cheesecloth)
2 whole cloves
4 whole black peppercorns
3 cups fresh beef stock
3 4 oz center cut pork chops
3 4 oz loin lamb chops
1 pound venison sausage or other course textured spiced sausage
4 pieces preserved goose (this is the optional confit)
2 medium white onions sliced

2 medium carrots chopped
1 cup bread crumbs
3 Tbsp soft unsalted butter

Method

1. Pick over the beans and discard any that don't look right, then soak the beans in cold water for at least 4 hours.

2. Heat the butter and olive oil in a heavy-bottom pan, add the diced onion and garlic and cook over a medium heat until the onions are translucent. Stir in the flour with a wooden spoon and cook the mixture for five more minutes.

3. In a large earthenware casserole (at least 4 quarts or larger) combine the onion mixture, ham hocks, kielbasa sausage, salt pork, pork shoulder, fresh tomatoes, drained beans, bouquet garni, whole cloves, peppercorns, and enough beef stock to just cover the mixture. Cover tightly and bake in a preheated 325 degree oven for 2 to 2 1/2 hours or until the beans are completely cooked.

4. Remove the beans from the oven and reset the oven to 375 degrees. Combine the pork chops, lamb chops, venison sausage, preserved goose, sliced onions and carrots, and 4 oz of beef stock in a large roasting pan.

5. Roast them all together removing each meat as it becomes cooked, and setting it aside in a covered container. Discard the onion and carrot. Since the goose is already cooked, it can be removed as soon as it becomes hot.

6. Remove the kielbasa sausage, ham hocks, and pork shoulder from the beans. Cut the fat from the ham hocks and discard it. Scrape off any meat from the hocks and return it to the beans.

7. Add any pan juices from the roasted meats, along with the venison sausage, pork chops, and lamb chops. Cover the casserole and return it to a 325 degree oven for one hour.

Final Preparation

8. Remove the casserole from the oven and separate all the meats. Spread the beans in a large shallow casserole; slice the sausages, and pork butt to desired thickness. Arrange the meats on top of beans in a desired order. Make it cute.

9. Mix the bread crumbs with soft butter and spread evenly on top of the cassoulet. Bake in a 375 degree oven until brown. Serve immediately. It will serve 5 to 6 adults

One final word: Try not to cut any corners when you make this for the first time. If you do, you will never experience the real delight of this wonderful dish. Good luck.

Beans for Sarah

This is one of those bench-job recipes that gives me a tremendous sense accomplishment and satisfaction when they turn out right. The recipe also marks a milestone in my life. My daughter offered to help me research and assemble a recipe for the first time ever. The delicate balance between the strong taste of cabbage and the light sweetness of Granny Smith apples is a result of her natural ability to taste a food and suggest accurately what is missing.

Ingredients

1 1/4 cups dried pinto beans
Water to soak beans
3 Tbsp extra virgin olive oil
12 oz green cabbage (diced small)
2 cloves minced garlic
1 1/2 cups low salt chicken stock (fresh or canned)
1 cup apple cider
1 large onion (diced medium)
1 large carrot (peeled and diced medium)
1 stalk of celery (diced medium)
1 bay leaf
3 whole cloves
4 oz piece of lean salt pork (optional, for additional flavor)
1 cup peeled, seeded, and diced fresh plum tomatoes
1 cinnamon stick (broken in half)
1/4 cup apple brandy (optional)
3 Granny Smith apples (peeled, cored, and diced medium)

Method

1. Soak the beans for 4 hours in water. Drain and discard water.

2. In a heavy-bottom pan heat the olive oil and saute the cabbage and garlic until the cabbage is tender.

3. In a large heavy-bottom pot, combine beans, chicken stock, apple cider, onion, carrot, celery, bay leaf, and cloves. Bring to a boil over high heat and remove from the heat immediately.

4. Transfer the bean mixture to a bean pot or earthenware casserole, add the salt pork, cabbage mixture, tomato, cinnamon stick, and apple brandy.

5. Cover the casserole, place it in a 325 degree oven for one hour, then add the apples and bake until the beans are tender, about 1 1/2 hours. Total cooking time 2 to 2 1/2 hours.

Poor man's pierogi with red beans

Here is what seems to be an unlikely combination. I first tasted this hearty meal in October of '65 while fishing for striped bass on Race Point Beach on Cape Cod with four market fisherman during a midnight high tide. The bass hung in, chasing bait fish for about two hours, and I nearly worked myself into a coma trying to match these pros cast for cast. At about 2:30 A.M. things started to quiet down and I walked out of the surf and collapsed from exhaustion on the sand. After my unknown fishing companions stopped laughing, one of them came over and asked me if I would

like to share some "poor man's food" with them. I was cold, wet, and very hungry; plus they had a warm fire and I didn't. A giant man with a ragged graying beard, and a soft friendly voice, reached out to shake my hand, "How ya doin' big guy, my name is Howard. Hope you like Pierogi and red beans, cause that's all we got." The five of us sat for the next half hour and feasted on this wonderful and simple dish, spooning cold noodles onto our plates from a large casserole and topping them with hot kidney beans seasoned with smoked chourico sausage.

This brief interlude was suddenly interrupted when a bunch of hovering sea gulls signaled the return of a school of bait fish. This meant that the stripers were not far behind. So I was left sitting next to a waning fire and an empty pot of beans, while these supermen returned to the surf. I laid down and went to sleep.

I fished with Howard every fall for about ten years, and badgered him until he taught me to make his "poor man's food." Both of these recipes are best when prepared and allowed to mellow in the refrigerator for a couple of days.

Ingredients for the noodles

12 oz (dry) medium egg noodles
4 oz unsalted butter
1 1/2 lb green cabbage (diced medium)
1 large white onion (diced medium)
4 cloves of minced garlic
1 Tbsp fresh ground black pepper (no kidding)
1/4 tsp ground nutmeg
6 dried juniper berries (crushed)
1 oz warm gin
1/2 cup fresh beef stock

Method

1. Cook the noodles in lightly salted boiling water until just tender, drain and cool under running water. Set aside.

2. Melt the butter in a large fry pan over medium heat and add the cabbage, onion, garlic, black pepper, and nutmeg. Saute until the cabbage is tender and translucent.

3. Combine the juniper berries with the warm gin in a flame proof bowl. Ignite the gin with a match and allow the flame to burn out. Combine this with the beef stock and add to the cabbage mixture.

4. Reduce the heat and cook the cabbage mixture for about 30 minutes, or until the cabbage is very tender. Stir every few minutes to prevent burning.

5. Combine cabbage with noodles in a large casserole, cover and refrigerate until the beans and sausage are ready.

Ingredients for the red beans and sausage

1/2 lb dry red kidney beans
water to soak the beans
3 large ham hocks
2 cups water

1 cup light fresh beef stock
1 cup of your favorite beer or ale
1 cup celery (diced medium)
1 1/2 cup onion (diced medium)
1 cup red bell pepper (diced medium)
2 bay leaves
8 oz smoked chourico sausage (cut into 1/2 inch pieces)
2 tsp dried cilantro
2 cloves minced fresh garlic
1 tsp chopped fresh mint
1 tsp dried oregano leaves
1 tsp ground coriander
1/2 tsp cumin powder
1/2 tsp cayenne pepper
1/2 tsp black pepper
2 fresh tomatoes (peeled, seeded, and chopped)

Method

1. Soak the beans for at least 4 hours in cold water 2 inches above the beans. Drain and discard soak water.

2. Place the ham hocks, water, beef stock, ale, celery, onion, red pepper, and bay leaves, in a large heavy-bottom pot, cover, bring to a boil, reduce the heat and simmer until the meat is fork tender.

3. Remove the ham hocks and set them aside. Add the beans to the stock, bring to a boil, cover, reduce the heat and cook the beans over a low heat until just tender.

4. Remove the meat from the ham hocks and combine with the sausage. Stir these meats into the beans along with the remaining ingredients. Transfer this mixture to a large earthenware casserole, cover and place into a preheated 300 degree oven. Bake until the beans are very tender and the sauce has thickened. This should take from 1 1/2 to 2 hours. Check the casserole occasionally and, if the beans become dry, add more beef stock as needed.

5. During the last half hour that the beans are cooking, place the noodle mixture in the oven to heat.

6. Serve the red beans and sausage over the noodles.

Before closing, let me add that you shouldn't be alarmed by the heavy seasoning in these dishes. Beans are a heavy carbohydrate food. Strong flavors like the soy based sauces of China, the curries of India, and the chillies of Peru and Mexico are designed to flavor beans and other starches. These starchy foods both absorb and dilute the strong flavor of the seasonings in the sauces. On the other hand, these same sauces, when served with meats, are really potent. So don't be bashful with the flavor enhancers when cooking with beans.

Good luck until next issue. Δ

A BHM Writer's Profile

Richard Blunt

Richard Blunt is the *BHM* Food Editor. His articles in *Backwoods Home Magazine* are more than just collections of recipes, they are instructions for how to create a dish then how to vary it to suit your tastes with explanations of how each step and ingredient affects the final product. His column is written to appeal to all readers, from beginners who want to learn how to cook well to experienced chefs who want to experiment and broaden their horizons.

Blunt is well qualified for the task. His career in the food industry spans more than three decades. What began as a desperation job as a teenage pot washer in Cambridge, Massachusetts, developed into a thirty-year learning experience that has found him presiding over the kitchens of exclusive restaurants in the Greater Boston area. Since then, he has worked as senior manager for three large food management companies, and he is currently Assistant Director of food service at a large hospital in Massachusetts. He lives in Connecticut with his wife and three children.

A BHM Writer's Profile: Marjorie Burris

Since 1970, when Marjorie Burris and her husband bought their 40-acre homestead in the central Arizona mountains, necessity has forced them to learn self-sufficiency. They use native plants for medicine, cure their own meat, and maintain and repair all their equipment.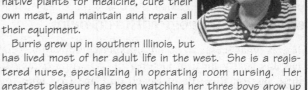

Burris grew up in southern Illinois, but has lived most of her adult life in the west. She is a registered nurse, specializing in operating room nursing. Her greatest pleasure has been watching her three boys grow up in the backwoods. Now they bring their own children to the homestead to pass along backwoods values and skills.

Burris began writing after she retired from nursing. Her articles and stories have appeared in *Backwoods Home Magazine* and other publications.

The amazing aloe

By Ruth Adler

"Ouch," shouted Mary, as she inadvertently spilled hot coffee on her hand. Instead of running to the medicine chest for a commercial ointment, she snipped off a large leaf from the aloe vera plant on her kitchen windowsill ledge and squeezed the gel-like liquid on the burn on her hand.

Silly? An old wives tale? Perhaps, but aloe has proven effective for Mary and many others to soothe minor burns or even sunburn. Prompt application of the clear gelatinous interior of a split stalk of aloe to burns and cuts almost guarantees a fast, painless, no-scar recovery.

The versatile aloe plant is native to South Africa, where it grows in tall, grass-like stalks. The plant belongs to the lily family and varies from species a few inches high to giant forms growing 30 feet tall. The thick, fleshy leaves are armed with spines along the edges and are sharply pointed at the tip. In mild climates, they are used in landscape planting, and they are familiar greenhouse perennials in cooler sections of the country.

In herbal medicine, the raw pulp of the aloe is used as a balm for burns, scrapes, sunburn, and insect bites, as well as to promote healing of these injuries. A university research team even found the aloe to be the most efficacious treatment for minor radiation burns.

The aloe today is renowned for its use in skin care products, burn salves, and suntan lotions. Some cosmetic companies recommend their products for smoothing wrinkles on the face and neck.

Test the legendary power of the aloe yourself by growing this Biblical plant in your own home. It is easy to grow, readily available at any nursery, and simply thrives under all conditions, even the warm atmosphere of dry air and central heating in our homes. Give it lots of sun, and water it moderately during summer and winter. There is no need to keep the plant almost dry during the cold months, as there is with other succulents.

When watering, avoid dropping moisture into its rosette of leaves. Feed it with a 20-20-20 fertilizer mixture once every few months.

If you would like to retain some of the gel in the refrigerator for your convenience, here is how to go about it: Remove a large leaf, cutting it off close to the base, and wrap it in plastic, but leave the cut end open. Use a rolling pin to press the gel out of the plant onto a piece of foil. Then, using a spoon, carefully scrape the gel into a clean, covered container and put it in the refrigerator until it's needed. When you use it, spoon a small amount out of the jar and then put it back in the refrigerator.

The aloe plant is capable of sending out large clusters of bell-shaped blossoms from early March until July, but it is rare to have this occur in your home.

You can easily propagate new plants, too. The aloes send up suckers from their base. These small plants can be dug up with some roots attached and then placed into their own pots filled with a light well-drained soil.

Enjoy the versatile aloe plant in your own home and judge for yourself its healing attributes, its easy care, and its beauty. Δ

A BHM Writer's Profile: Ilene Duffy

Ilene Duffy is the Business Manager for *Backwoods Home Magazine*, and she also has written articles and book and video reviews. As the main proofreader for each issue, she is responsible for the remarkably low number of typographical errors that appear in *BHM*.

Ilene formerly worked as a bilingual kindergarten and first grade teacher for nine years in California. She gave up teaching to become *BHM's* business manager shortly after she married the magazine's publisher, Dave Duffy. She says the biggest benefit of working with the magazine is the freedom it offers her to work at home so she can be with her three young sons, and to raise her family in a quiet, country setting.

Since the magazine has moved to Gold Beach in Oregon she has become a fresh and salt water fishing enthusiast, catching and cooking king salmon from the Rogue River and catching and cooking the many bottom fish from near the Gold Beach Reef, located a few miles offshore. She buries the fish carcasses in her big garden to help her vegetables grow.

Everybody *talks* about lightning — and yes, there *are* things you can *do* about it

By Albert H. Carlson

What was a beautiful sunny day with large white billowing clouds low on the horizon has turned progressively darker. The clouds are now almost black, and the temperature has dropped. You are now sure that you are in for a real storm . . . but not just any storm: a *thunderstorm.* One with a spectacular light show and driving rain. In fact you are about to come face to face with nature's largest and most regular display of electricity, *lightning.*

Static electricity builds up on the clouds as they move through the sky. Charges of *several million volts* are not uncommon. Whenever a charge builds up, it will seek to neutralize itself. This is because all systems attempt to come to rest in the state that requires the lowest energy. In the case of the earth and the surrounding environment—of which the sky is a part—the lowest state for electricity is usually found in the earth itself. This is normally called *earth ground.*

Because the air itself is an *insulator* —meaning that current does not readily flow through open air—the charge in the clouds must reach large values before it will *arc* across the air. Another example of this type of phenomenon is the spark jumping the gap of a spark plug in your car. When electricity arcs, it is visible to the naked eye and can be heard. When it happens in the sky, it's called lightning and thunder.

Lightning contains *a lot* of power. Lightning typically delivers 100,000,000 volts and can create heat along its path of up to 60,000 degrees F. Bolts of lightning most often branch out many times like a large Christmas tree. They usually occur singly, but occurrences of two and three simultaneous bolts have been captured on film.

Lightning usually takes one of two forms: *cloud-to-cloud* and *ground strikes.* Most lightning is from one cloud to another. This is to be expected, because there is a smaller distance from cloud to cloud than there is from a typical cloud to the ground. The resulting lightning can come in sheets and light the sky. Ground strikes are less common, but much more frightening. They frighten us because cloud-to-cloud strikes don't hit us (or things near us), whereas ground strikes may.

Air as insulator

Air belongs to a class of materials called *insulators.* All materials fall under one or the other of the following classes: *conductor, semiconductor,* and *insulator. Conductors* allow electrical current to flow easily. *Semiconductors* resist electrical current flow unless a foreign substance, called a *dopant,* is added. Dopants are usually phosphorus or boron. *Insulators* resist electrical current flow vigorously.

Current *will* flow through an insulator *if* there is a sufficient voltage difference at either end of the insulator. We can measure how well an insulator resists the flow of current; the resistance is measured in *ohms* per unit area. If an insulator has a rating of 10 ohms per unit area and is 15 units long, the total resistance is 150 ohms. It's easy to see that if the distance between two clouds is 1000 meters, while the distance between a cloud and the ground is 3000 meters, then the resistance between the clouds is smaller than the resistance between the cloud and the ground.

Because air is an insulator, in order for lightning to arc to the ground, there has to be a *whole lot* of power behind it to break down the insulator and create an intermediate state of air called *plasma*. Lightning follows a path that it continuously creates in front of itself made out of plasma. A small bolt reaches the ground, and then a *much larger return bolt* flows from the ground (or the object struck), back along the exact same path. Therefore, anything that gets hit by lightning gets hit *twice* . . . double the fun and double the damage.

Light, heat, ionization, explosion

In a lightning strike, electrical power can manifest in one of four ways: *light, heat, ionization*, and *explosion*. Lightning is very bright, of course. Some of the power in the lightning bolt is *dissipated*, or used up, in the characteristic light associated with it. A similar phenomenon is used to make light in light bulbs. As current flow through the bulb's filament, light is produced, along with heat. Remember that when a tree is struck by lightning it usually catches fire. That's the *heat* in the lightning bolt. Think of the lightning bolt as the filament. Heat isn't as big an effect as it might be (given all that power), because lightning is a *transient*, or temporary, occurrence.

Sometimes a smell of *ozone* is in the air after a lightning strike. Ozone is a form of oxygen in a different configuration than the one we're used to. It has the chemical formula O_3 (that is, the ozone molecule is made up of three oxygen atoms), while normal air is O_2. So much power is dumped into the air that it actually rips air molecules apart (an example of *ionization*) and rearranges them.

The last sign is *explosion*. When lightning strikes something, so much power enters the thing that is struck that the power can't all be absorbed. The object of the strike tries to convert the power into heat and can't handle all the heat. The result is an explosion.

When lightning strikes an object, a great deal of current suddenly flows through the object being hit. Current has several by-products, including heat, fire, explosion, vaporization, and electrocution. Heat results because everything has electrical resistance. Even metal (a conductor) has a minute amount of resistance, although it is much smaller than in non-conductors. Power is dissipated across a resistor, and the power that is used up changes form and becomes heat.

Since all materials have some kind of resistance, when lightning strikes an object, an enormous amount of heat can be created. Whenever the heat exceeds the *flash point* of a flammable material, it will catch fire and burn. Paper, for example, burns at 451 degrees F, hence the name of the classic novel Fahrenheit 451. This explains why trees and wooden buildings catch fire when hit by lightning. If sufficient energy is transferred (as heat) from the lightning bolt to the object that is struck, the moisture in the object becomes gas. That gas expands so rapidly that pressure builds up, and the object explodes. A tree that gets hit and explodes suddenly becomes a wooden grenade, complete with shrapnel, and may drop large limbs on someone standing beneath it.

With sufficient current, the muscles in the body contract. When the muscles contract, the body can involuntarily strike things. This can result in secondary injuries if something hard or sharp is hit, and you could conceivably hit yourself. Muscle contraction begins at about 0.02 amps, less than the current required to light up one light-emitting diode. As long as the current is applied, the muscles remain contracted. The same mechanism is used by the brain to make the body move. Only 0.07 amps are required to stop the heart, a condition known as *electrocution*. As little as 175 volts can stop the heart if the victim is wet with sweat or other ionized moisture. Electrocution can happen quickly and be complicated by burning and destruction of tissue along the path of the current.

If you feel it coming, *dive!*

Can you tell when you are about to be struck by lightning? There is often a warning: a feeling similar to what happens when you touch a static electricity generator, or when you take the clothes out of the dryer and separate a staticky sock from a towel. This is to be expected, since lightning starts as static electricity that breaks down the air to neutralize the charge. The result is that people about to be hit can feel the hair on their bodies stand on end and sometimes report a tingling sensation.

If you are in a storm and feel this, *act immediately*. This is all the warning you are going to get. Get as low as you can to the ground. If you are not the highest point around, you are less likely to be hit. If you can find a nearby ditch or draw, get into it. *Rolling* to the ditch is much smarter than *running* there. Rolling in something wet will also help to get rid of the charge accumulation on your body. Avoid holding on to anything metal. If you have a tool in your hand, drop it. If you are touching a metal object, get away from it. If you are on a roof, get off. Don't do anything that will make you a more attractive target for the lightning.

It's easy to detect an oncoming storm with your TV. Turn on your set to Channel 2 and turn the sound all the way down. Next, adjust the set so that the contrast turns the screen just barely black. Lightning will cause the screen to flash white. This works because lightning emits energy on a lot of frequencies at the same time (*broad band emissions*). Since even the small portion of the lightning energy emitted as radio frequencies is huge, your TV antenna picks this up and tries to interpret it as a picture. The worse the lightning, the more frequent and brighter the screen flashes will be. This will give you some idea when a bad storm is heading your way without having to expose yourself to the weather.

Lightning rods

Some damage to buildings and land can be averted by employing *lightning rods*. The role of lightning rods is to *attract* lightning and direct its energy to a safe target: the ground. The idea is that you can control where the lightning hits and steer it away from people, property, trees, and livestock. The key to using the lightning rod effectively is to put it up high and *ground* it well. Plan on using three or four on a building to make it really safe.

Lightning rods are lengths of heavy metal, sometimes with radiating metal fingers, that are mounted at the highest point of a building or other structure. They are connected to ground with a heavy wire cable through a stake or ground rod. There is a range of commercially available rods with mounting brackets that work well. See your local hardware or building supply dealer.

After mounting your rod on the highest point of the structure, you must connect it to the ground. Actual earth is the ground that you need. Remember that there will be a *whole lot* of power running through the cable. If you use a small wire, *it will melt,* and then the only path to ground from the lightning rod will be the structure you are trying to protect—so don't skimp. You need to use a large cable to connect the lightning rod to the ground. Cable is used, instead of wire, because of the large current that will have to pass to ground if the lightning rod is struck. Since the resistance of wire or cable is directly related to its diameter (higher resistance

for lower diameter), and since the purpose of the unit is to attract lightning by making the path to ground as easy as possible, it stands to reason that the larger the cable, the better. Large lightning rods have cables as large as 3/4" to 1" in diameter. Smaller rods typically use 1/8" to 1/4" diameter cables. Rods that pound right into the roof of a house can usually get away with 1/8" diameter cable. Rods that mount to the roof with a bracket should have 1/4" diameter cable, minimum.

Almost all cable used for lightning rods is stranded cable made of steel. Copper cable is sometimes used when and where available. Although copper tends to have less resistance than steel, it also tends to be more expensive. The difference in resistance is minimal in practice, so use whatever is cheaper. Smaller-diameter wire may be insulated, but don't count on larger cable having any insulation. When mounting the rods, connect the cable and loop it around the base of the rod and then through the mount, if there is one.

Usually the cable is terminated to either a stake in the ground or a buried ground rod. The best metal to use for this purpose is copper. Stakes should be at least four feet long and 1/2 inch in diameter. Rods should be at least six feet long and 1/2 inch in diameter. Count on changing these every four to eight years, depending on the amount of moisture in the ground.

Do lightning rods work? You bet! They are in use from Chicago to Florida. Wherever you have frequent lightning you will find—and should be using—lightning rods.

Power surges

Lightning can hit a power grid or generator. This happens all the time throughout the world. Lightning is attracted by the alternating voltage when it drops to its negative value. Typical power grids are 110/120 volt three-wire systems (although there are

also 220 and 440 volt systems). Part of the regular variation in voltage in the system is one of the wires going to the negative peak. In a 110 volt system, voltages will vary between 110 and minus 110 volts. Normally the earth is at *ground* (0 volts), so called because that is the normal voltage of a plot of dirt. As the power lines go below 0 volts, lightning will be more strongly attracted to them. When lightning hits the grid or generator, the energy has to go somewhere, and that somewhere is right into your house! If you haven't protected your home and electronics, there is a good chance that components in one or more of your electrical devices will be destroyed. The more common lightning strikes are in your area, the greater the chance that this will happen to you.

These *power surges*, or *transients* (so called because they are short and powerful), can be handled by using a couple of strategies. The first is to use a *surge protector* on all of the electrical appliances in the house. Many commercial models are available at Radio Shack, building supply stores, and other electrical or computer supply houses. These detect surges and react in a very short time, usually from *micro-* (1/1,000,000) to *nano-* (1/1,000,000,000) *seconds*. You must manually reset the protector each time it is tripped. Costs range from $10 to $100 for five outlets on the strip.

More electrically handy people put *dual transorbs* and *metal oxide varistors (MOVs)* between the power lines and the point of entry to the house. *Note:* Don't attempt this yourself, unless you really know what you're doing; otherwise, call in a professional.

Transorbs are components that carry current after a certain voltage is exceeded. This is called the *trip voltage*. The transorb keeps the voltage between the two lines at a set voltage and won't allow it to go any higher. This prevents your appliances from being damaged by the application of too great a voltage at their inputs.

Transorbs can absorb a lot of current but turn on more slowly than MOVs. They are rated in the number of kilovolts that they can handle. Never use a smaller-rated unit than 1.5 kV. The 5kV units are good all around choices to maximize protection and minimize cost. Most power grids, or power distribution systems, have voltage variations of 10% - 20%. This means that a 110V grid can vary between 88V and 132V, so rate the trip voltage for the transorbs at least 30% above the *nominal*, or rated normal voltage, for your grid. Make sure that you use the type of transorbs for AC (alternating current) lines.

MOVs react very quickly to surges but have the tendency to allow the voltage between power lines to get further apart. In other words, they don't clamp well if the inputs vary slowly. Their operational characteristics specify the normal voltage applied to them. As with transorbs, specify the operational voltage at least 30% over the nominal grid voltage.

MOVs and transorbs are placed between individual power lines. And it's worth saying again: Don't attempt this if you are unsure or unfamiliar with electricity. Remember always put **SAFETY FIRST**.

Counting the distance

There's an old saying that you can tell how far away lightning is by counting the time between seeing the flash of lightning and hearing the thunder. This is absolutely true. The propagation of sound through the air is about 300 meters/second (about 1000 feet/second). Light travels much faster, about 30,000,000,000 meters/second (just over 186,000 miles/second) and is in effect instantaneous. Counting each second ("one one thousand one, one one thousand two") will give you a rough idea of the time elapsed. Dividing the number of seconds by five will give the distance to the lightning in miles.

Protect yourself

Protecting yourself during a lightning storm is easy. All you need to do is remember a few simple rules:

1. If possible, don't go out in a thunderstorm. This means that you need to be aware enough of the weather to know when one is coming.

2. If you *are* out in a storm, make sure that you are not the highest point. Stay off the top of hills. Don't make yourself look taller to the lightning by holding things up or holding on to trees or structures. Stay off roofs.

3. In a thunderstorm, don't take refuge under a tree. The tree may be hit and explode and turn into shrapnel, or fall on you.

4. Stay away from metal. Metal generally attracts lightning. This also means that you should not shower or bathe during storms. Your pipes are made of metal, and current flows through wet things, including people.

5. Don't sit on the toilet if you can help it. You're sitting right in the way of a direct ground.

6. Pay attention to your body. It will tell you if you are about to be hit. When you feel the warning signs (a feeling of static electricity, hair standing on end, a tingling sensation), take action *immediately*: get low (roll into a ditch if possible).

7. Don't talk on the telephone. The phone lines are not immune to lightning strikes.

8. If you are in a high-lightning area, such as Florida, use lightning rods on your buildings and install surge protection for your house and electronics.

You might survive a lightning strike (many people have), but it's a heck of a lot nicer if you don't have to try.

(Albert Carlson is an electrical and computer engineer. He is currently designing control systems with embedded computers and finishing work on an advanced degree in artificial intelligence.) Δ

A BHM Writer's Profile: Jennifer Stein Barker

Jennifer Stein Barker has been cooking since she was a youngster in Vermont. She has always loved the backwoods, and moved to a rural site six weeks after arriving in the Pacific Northwest in 1973. Since settling down in remote eastern Oregon with her husband, Lance, she has spent her time working as a part-time botanist, cook, and writer. In 1994, she wrote and published The Morning Hill Cookbook.

Jennifer and Lance have a large garden in an area where summer frosts are common. Meeting this challenge has been a learning experience. With row cover, early and late-season techniques, and selection of frost-tolerant types, they are able to grow a large selection of berry crops, leafy greens, cabbage-family vegetables, alliums (onions and garlic), and root vegetables. Growing the food with which she cooks has shaped Jennifer's whole foods recipes. You won't usually find recipes for corn, beans, and squash in her articles because she doesn't very often have them. What you will find is recipes for foods often ignored by cookbook writers: carbohydrate-based recipes with greens and roots, and whole grain baked goods. They are often cooked in the ethnic styles of the areas where they grow the best. In the last few years, Jennifer has become very interested in solar cookery. She has an array of solar cookers at her home in the Blue Mountains. She has been working on a second cookbook, The Morning Hill Solar Cookery Book, which is now being home published.

Propane is a multi-purpose fuel, and it has many key advantages

By Matt McEachran

Propane—or L.P.G. (Liquefied Petroleum Gas)—can be a wise fuel choice for you and your backwoods home, barn, or garage for a variety of reasons. It's fairly cheap, environmentally friendly, and best of all, you don't have to live near town, as with natural gas, because there are no pipes to run.

Propane is a by-product of oil. When you burn it, you are mainly releasing water, carbon dioxide, and hydrogen back into the air instead pollutants. It burns much cleaner in your car than gasoline, and a lot cleaner than your oil furnace.

It is also much cheaper to use in your home than electricity. Propane itself is not cheaper than natural gas, but to install natural gas pipelines in a backwoods home can cost thousands of dollars, compared to the couple hundred that propane will cost to install.

Where I live in Ontario, the price of propane varies from around 28 cents a liter to 40 cents a liter, depending on your usage and the local economy. It varies widely in the United States as well, from 80 cents per gallon to $1.20 per gallon. Depending on your particular region, you may save a lot compared to oil.

Another factor to consider with propane is that most companies will give you a greater discount, the more propane you use in your home and vehicles. So buying more appliances that use L.P.G. will actively save you money.

Propane appliances today are much more efficient than they were even 10 years ago. You can buy propane-powered furnaces, water heaters, stoves, refrigerators, fireplaces, room heaters, clothes dryers, barn/garage heaters, lights, and even air conditioners.

Another plus is that these appliances can be converted to natural gas very easily. If natural gas *does* come by your house in a few years, it's a lot easier and cheaper to convert your propane appliances than to sell your oil appliances and buy new ones.

Most propane appliances today offer high efficiency (80 to 85% efficiency). Also, direct vent appliances can be installed without the use of your chimney. Instead, they can be vented with B-vent directly through an outside wall. This is great if you are heating your house with a woodstove and can't share the chimney.

Another great thing about propane is this: if you heat your house with a woodstove but that one room in the basement is always cold, it is easy to install a room heater.

Whenever possible, buy as many appliances as possible at once, or let the salesmen know that you plan to buy more in the near future. Most places give good discounts when you buy several appliances at once.

Power failure no problem

Another great advantage of propane is if there is a power failure, you still have heat and a refrigerator and a cookstove that work. A couple of years ago, a winter storm knocked out the power in our neighborhood. We suffered no hardships, as our appliances burned propane, but our friends weren't so lucky. They called us around 8:30 AM to tell us that they were all in winter jackets and blankets. They had no heat and they could see their breath in their house. They came over and ended up staying with us until late that night, when the power was restored.

Propane fuel is great—but how much does it cost to get it? That too

will vary, depending on where you live. In Ontario, the average price to set in a tank and put 10 feet of copper underground to your house is around $100. Then to be safe, add $2 a foot to run copper from your furnace, stove, etc. to your outside wall. Depending on the number of appliances being installed, your hours of labor will vary, at an average of $30 to $45 an hour.

It's good to have a salesman give you an estimate. He should be able to come to your house and give an accurate estimate as to how long it will take to install and how much it will cost. He can also tell you the best locations for your appliances, according to safety regulations and cost.

When planning your system, be sure to allow for add-ons to your system. The salesman or installer should already have this planned, but be sure and ask. All this usually means is installing a larger size of copper pipe than currently required and adding a tee or two in the copper line near possible expansion sites.

For your vehicles, too

Not only is propane an inexpensive and clean way to fuel your *home*, but it is also an alternative fuel for your *vehicles*. In Ontario, propane is almost half the price of gas, but in some states it is more expensive than gas. However, as with your home, a larger volume used will give greater savings. If you buy propane for your car from a gas station that sells propane on the side, they likely won't give you a discount at all. If you use 75 to 100 liters and up, go to a store that mainly sells propane. A discount of a few cents a liter can save a lot of money at the end of the month.

You may decide that your car does not use enough gas to bother to switch over to propane, and if it's anything like mine (which barely holds 30 liters), you'd probably be right. But that old pickup truck that gets 15 miles per gallon is a great candidate to save some major cash.

Propane is especially good for homesteaders because the tanks are usually much larger than a regular gas tank. My little car holds 30 liters, but it's not uncommon for me to pump 250 liters into a truck. Obviously, this can save on the trips to town. Also, because propane burns cleaner, you can save on oil changes, spark plugs, and engine tune-ups, and even have fewer muffler replacements.

Pay attention to safety

While propane is perfectly safe to use in your home and vehicles, it can be dangerous if used improperly, just like any other fuel.

It's highly flammable but has an odor added to it so that you can tell if it is leaking. If you do smell propane in your house, turn off the tank and then call the company from your neighbor's house. Even the spark that sometimes happens when you turn off a light switch is enough to ignite propane.

When doing construction on or around your house, be sure you know where the propane lines are. You don't want to hammer a nail through a copper line as you hang a picture or put down a floor in your kitchen.

All lines in the house should be labeled as propane, and the copper from the tank to your house should be at least 15 inches deep, and you should keep this line in mind when digging or doing construction.

In a town not far from where I live, a man unknowingly drove a stake into his propane line, cutting it in half, while adding a porch to his house. The vapor eased its way through the ground and through a crack in the wall and filled his basement with vapor. When he went downstairs half an hour later to stoke the woodstove, a spark ignited the vapor, and both the man and his wife were killed. Windows exploded to 30 meters away, and the first story floor was blown up to the ceiling.

Things you can do yourself

There are some repairs that you can do yourself, and at $40 per hour you can save a lot of money.

One easy way to save is to have the installer show you how to light the pilot light on your appliances. Pilot lights shouldn't go out unless you turn them off, but occasionally they do, and it always seems to happen after 5 pm on a cold winter night. It'll take you about a minute to light it yourself, which is a lot easier and cheaper than paying the after-hours call-out fee.

Another simple thing is to check the level of propane in your tank. Many propane companies have automatic delivery, but if your company doesn't, or if you live too far away, calling in a few days early, when your tank is around 25 to 30% full, can save you from running out on a weekend or at night.

By now you know that calling a repair man after 5 pm or on a weekend costs you extra. If your furnace or stove gives you trouble at one of these times, try to wait until the next business day before calling the repairman. It's amazing how many people call in on weekends for minor problems that could have waited until Monday, and therefore have to pay the extra call-out fee.

Paying bills on time is a good way to get breaks when you need them and even some discounts. Good customers get good deals on repairs and extra time when something comes up and they need to pay their bill a little late.

For the most economical, environmentally friendly, and convenient way to heat your backwoods home, cook your food, and even light up your porch, be sure and check out the advantages propane can give you. Δ

Try these smaller breeds of multi-purpose cattle

By Jan Palmer

In 1902, Rand, McNally & Co. published a book entitled <u>Practical Farming and Gardening</u>. Although many things have changed over the past 93 years, many things have remained the same.

Some of the changes? In the book, one of the top beef breeds listed is the Polled Durham. Among the top dairy breeds was the Dutch Belted. Today those breeds are revered by only a handful of "rare breed" enthusiasts. Also in the cattle section was a section for "dual purpose cattle," which might be better described as "multi-purpose," in that they do more than two things. These breeds are the Brown Swiss, Red Polled, and Devon. All three breeds excel at producing meat and milk, as well as draft oxen. Ninety-three years later, these three breeds can still earn their keep on a small farm.

Brown Swiss cattle

The Brown Swiss was described then as "gray or brown with dark extremities except muzzle which is 'mealy.' Bulls are usually darker colored than cows." Cows weighed from 1,200 to 1,400 pounds, with bulls from 1,600 to 2,100 pounds. That isn't much different from the description of today's Brown Swiss. The book describes their disposition as "dull," but "docile" might be a better word today.

Brown Swiss cows are money-makers in the milk race. Their disposition makes them good family cows, and they're known for their longevity. It's not unusual to see mother, daughter, and granddaughter in the same herd. One of the breed's production leaders is "High Spruce Stretchy Eve," an "elite" cow with an average production per day of 59.4 pounds of milk since two years of age. She tested in one lactation at 1,668 pounds of butterfat and 1,037 pounds of protein.

According to the Brown Swiss Breeders Association, consumers today are looking for low-fat milk without compromising taste and nutrition. A look at the grocery store dairy case confirms this. Within the span of ten years, they predict that demand for skim milk will increase nearly 60%, while low-fat milk will claim an additional 27% of the market. Demand for cheese is also expected to increase.

A brochure from the Association contains a quote that many farmers will applaud: "Type conformation today means more than just a pretty cow. It means she is functional and she is sound. It means she will be in the herd for more than just a few years." Many Swiss breeders in the breed directory have under 30 cow dairies.

If you're interested in finding out more about the Brown Swiss breed, write to the Brown Swiss Cattle Breeders' Association, P.O. Box 1038, Beloit, WI 53512-1038. They can give you more in-depth information and a list of breeders.

Devon cattle

The Brown Swiss has plenty of beef, but that often gets overlooked because of the emphasis on that breed for dairy production. The opposite is true of another of the breeds, which has been developed for beef instead of dairy. The Devon has a long history of multi-purpose talents. According to the Devon Association, records of the red cattle in the Devon section of England (their homeland) date from as early as 23 B.C. In 1850, Colonel John T. Davy of "Rose Ash" in north Devon published the first herd book. His people had been involved in the breeding of purebred Devons for at least 150 years prior to that.

The British favored the Devon for its adaptability, foraging ability, and high quality, tender meat. In 1623, the Pilgrims brought the Devon to America. Their hardy foraging ability fit the questionable grass conditions that the settlers were unsure of. Their moderate but rich milk production

Brown Swiss milking cow. Photo courtesy of the Brown Swiss Cattle Breeder's Association

gave them the ability to feed a calf and a family, and their docility and strength made them useful oxen. The Devon made the westward push, and in 1884 the American Devon Cattle Club was established.

The ability to use forage instead of grain, ease of calving, good conformation, and good beef are important characteristics the Devon still possesses today. A good yearling bull was advertised at 50 inches at the shoulder, 58 inches from the point of the shoulder to the pins, and 1,020 pounds. Thus, like the Swiss, the Devon is a larger breed suitable for use as a draft animal, as well as for milk and meat.

Added to the above characteristics are the points of fertility, early maturity, disease resistance, and hardiness, as well as climate tolerance, and the Devon shows qualities that are still fashionable today, despite being in the "rare breed" status. For more information on these useful cattle, write to the American Minor Breed Conservatory, P.O. Box 477, Pittsboro, NC, 27312.

Red poll cattle

A slogan adopted by the Red Poll cattle producers perhaps best testifies to the breed's multi-purpose billing: "More red meat—The milk to make it pay." In the final quarter of the 18th

Red poll bull. Photo coutesy of the American Red Poll Association.

century, English farmers of Norfolk and Suffolk counties had selectively bred two strains or stocks of cattle for their area. The Norfolk cattle were excellent beef cattle, while the Suffolks were known for milk production. About 1880, a tenant farmer, John Reeve, wanted to upgrade his cattle and mated a Suffolk bull to his polled red cow of Norfolk blood. This started a trend.

Polled red cattle were recorded as far back as Biblical times. F.G. Taber of New York imported four foundation cattle in 1873. Before 1900, about

300 Red Polls were imported, and the breed's popularity soared. Numbers diminished with the onset of the world wars, and by the 1960s breeders had adapted to breeding for meat to keep up with demand. In 1972, Red Polls were moved to a beef-emphasis breed.

They are all red, of any shade except with a yellow hue. White is acceptable in but not above the switch of the tail. They are relatively short-haired and polled. In breeding condition, bulls are 1,800 to 2,000 pounds, with cows being 1,200 to 1,500 pounds. Red Polls are well muscled and alert, vigorous and hardy with good temperaments. A century or more of selection for manners has culled out mean, nervous, or flighty animals, making them safe for personal care in a small, family owned situation. The milk is small curd, fine fat white milk said to be nearly "naturally homogenized." The American Red Poll Association can be reached at P.O. Box 3519, Louisville, KY 40232.

The size of these three breeds, combined with their other abilities, make all three breeds excellent candidates for the homestead. The qualities described here can help the small farmer today gain a productive lifestyle, just as they did for farmers nearly a century ago. Δ

Devon cow. Photo courtesy of The Reverend Bruce Alexander

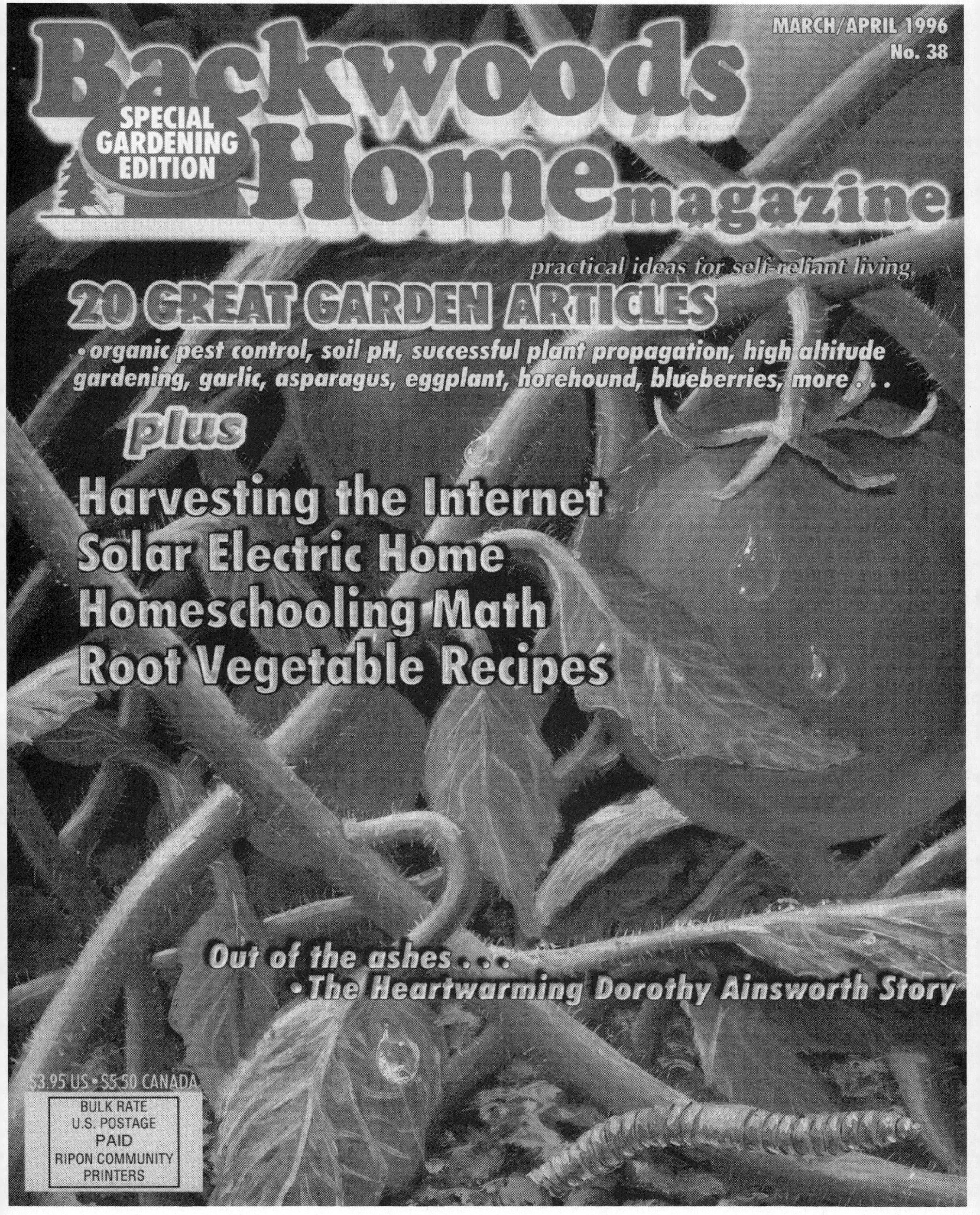

MARCH/APRIL 1996
No. 38
Backwoods Home magazine
SPECIAL GARDENING EDITION
practical ideas for self-reliant living
20 GREAT GARDEN ARTICLES
• organic pest control, soil pH, successful plant propagation, high altitude gardening, garlic, asparagus, eggplant, horehound, blueberries, more . . .
plus
Harvesting the Internet
Solar Electric Home
Homeschooling Math
Root Vegetable Recipes
Out of the ashes . . .
• The Heartwarming Dorothy Ainsworth Story
$3.95 US • $5.50 CANADA
BULK RATE
U.S. POSTAGE
PAID
RIPON COMMUNITY
PRINTERS

My view

The tax problem

From my viewpoint, taxes are the major problem in this country, from how high they are, to how they are collected, to how they are spent. If we could solve America's tax problem I think most of our other troubles would fade away.

Cut taxes by cutting waste

We obviously need to cut waste. No sense collecting taxes we don't need. Our most recent federal government shutdown revealed that at least 260,000 furloughed federal workers are nonessential. Not only was I not inconvenienced by the government shutdown, but I actually felt a sense of relief that many of the bureaucrats were safely locked out of their offices. I even took a survey of people I know, and I could find no one who was inconvenienced by the shutdown. In fact, I did not find one person who thought it important to reopen the government.

It seems clear then that most of those federal employees should be permanently furloughed so they can go out and get productive jobs. That would certainly save a lot of tax money.

Don't conceal taxes

The new year just happened to begin during the government shutdown, and we woke New Year's Day to read in our newspapers that the 10% tax the federal government puts on airline tickets bad expired and could not be renewed until the budget impasse was solved. That reminded everyone of the hundreds of other hidden taxes the government collects from us--on everything from gasoline and auto tire taxes to cosmetic and alcohol taxes.

A major portion of government taxes arc hidden. Virtually every product you buy has a hidden tax on it because corporations, acting as unwilling government tax collectors, pass on their high taxes to us in the form of higher prices.

Personally dole out taxes to recipients

But the most significant way to solve the tax problem lies in the way taxes are doled out to the recipients. Rather than continuing to use the impersonal approach of having government act as the intermediary between the taxed and those who get to spend the tax, we need to substitute a personal approach. Starting with our paychecks, tax payers should personally hand over their taxes to the beneficiaries so we get a firsthand understanding of what is really going on.

Picture this scenario: You get your full paycheck from your employer in cash take some of the money and put it in your pocket so you can buy things for your family, then take the remaining--those federal and state taxes that used to go the government--and personally hand it out to tax recipients. Maybe there'd be a line of people with their hand out going by you.

First would be a thin welfare mother carrying her baby with two more young children in tow. "Here you are," you'd say to her as you handed over a wad of bills. "Go have another kid; there's plenty more where this came from."

Next would come along a well-fed corporate farmer in his $800 suit and 10-gallon hat. You'd hand him an even bigger wad of bills, thanking him profusely for taking part in America's agricultural subsidy program in which big farmers are paid not to grow too much of one crop.

Then maybe a tall and erect member of the National Education Association (NEA) would come by and you'd hand her some money so she could use it to lobby Congress to stop the home school movement in America, or use it to buy television time to stop a school voucher initiative in some state.

And don't forget the distinguished member of the American Association of Retired Persons (AARP). He needs his tax dollars so he too can lobby Congress--to make sure Congress doesn't cut Medicare or social security payments to AARP members.

And what about those social security taxes? You'll want to put some of your money into that social security trust fund that's supposed to be there for your own retirement. But that's when you'll find out the trust fund doesn't even exist. It's all just a big flim flam game, a con that every senator and congressman-Republican or Democrat-knows about. In fact, congressmen don't even participate in it; they have a real retirement plan.

Then you'll go through the rest of the line, handing out a few bucks here, a few there to all the rest of the drug addicts, the political action committees, and other worthy people getting slopped at the tax trough.

Once we went through this personal process of doling out our money in the form of taxes to the various people government has deemed worthy to get them, some of us might decide we didn't want to pay some of our taxes. That's when we'd get reminded of another cruel aspect of the tax problem: taxes are not voluntary.

In fact, should we protest paying some of these taxes and decide to fight then we'd find ourselves not in a court of law but in a tax court run by the Internal Revenue Service. Virtually no one wins in the IRS court. Because you see, in the end the government holds a gun to our head when it comes to paying taxes. We really have no choice.

Does all this make you mad? Good!

It's cheap and easy to multiply plants by using these propagation techniques

By Connie Glasheen

Are you looking for cheap, easy ways to increase the number of plants in your garden? I am, and I've found some plant propagation techniques that really work: *cuttings*, *layering*, and *division*. What's really nice about these three methods is that the baby plants will be identical to the parent plant. I only need to get one plant, and then I can produce enough starter plants for my gardens, plus have leftovers to sell or give away.

Cuttings

Let's start out with cuttings, the method I like to use the most. Usually *stem cuttings* are the way to go, but you can also try *root cuttings* (very easy with fleshy-rooted perennials like day lilies). There are three types of stem cuttings:

- Softwood (I use this most often)
- Semi-ripe
- Hardwood

Softwood cuttings are usually done in spring and early summer, before the plant gets too woody and hard. You're looking for soft, succulent new growth, not a plant that is droopy and limp from lack of water.

Choose a stem or branch that is about two to three inches long, and use a knife or razor blade to sever it from the parent plant. Cut below a leaf node. Don't use scissors, as the inside tissue will get bruised and probably rot.

Most cuttings need to be planted right away so they don't lose much moisture. (There are always exceptions to every rule. In this case, geraniums and cacti and succulents *like* to

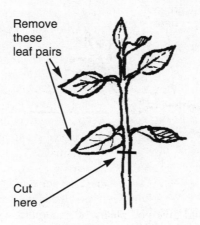

Remove these leaf pairs

Cut here

Making a softwood cutting

dry a little and scab over before planting.) If you aren't able to plant immediately, just put the cutting in a plastic bag and leave in a cool, shady spot up to a couple of days.

When potting up the cuttings, strip off any leaves that would be below the soil when planted. That way they won't rot and cause problems. Leave the tip intact.

Some people swear by using *rooting hormone* powder and others don't. This powder contains synthetic versions of natural plant hormones called *auxins* which stimulate root formation. One envelope costs about a dollar and will last for years. Just dip the cut end into the powder, shake off the excess, and pot up the cutting.

Another way to encourage root formation is to water with *willow water*. Just soak willow branches in water for a couple of days, and the water will contain the auxins also. I've used pussywillow and weeping willow, so this method doesn't seem to need a particular variety.

The soil you use for potting up your cuttings can be well-rotted compost,

sand potting soil (dries out quickly), or plain garden soil. I use a mixture of compost and garden soil. No matter what you use, one thing must be constant: it needs to remain moist.

I usually pot up my cuttings in four-inch plastic pots, one cutting per pot. When I use seed-starting flats, I can fit about 30 cuttings in a flat. I make a hole in the soil with a pencil, stick the cutting in, then firm the soil around the cutting and water it. Keeping the cutting in a warm place will hasten the rooting process. When I see new leaves forming and rapid growth, I know it has worked.

Semi-ripe cuttings are usually taken in mid-summer to mid-fall. The stem tops are soft and succulent, and the bottoms are starting to become woody. Pinch out any flower buds, because you want the plant to concentrate on making roots, not flowers.

Sand is usually the best type of medium to root semi-ripe cuttings. On average, these cuttings take from 5 to 25 weeks to root, so keep checking to make sure they are moist (but not wet). This works for conifers, heaths, heathers, laurels, and roses. Often these are rooted in cold frames, and you will see lots of new growth in spring, when you can move them to their permanent spot.

Hardwood cuttings are cuttings from fully ripened wood. Look for a healthy, ripe one-year-old stem (a stem that grew that current year) with bark that doesn't give when you pinch it. It should be about eight to ten inches long. (This is only a guide; it works with shorter or longer pieces.)

Make a straight cut below a leaf node or bud. Now on the top make a slanted cut. This way you know which

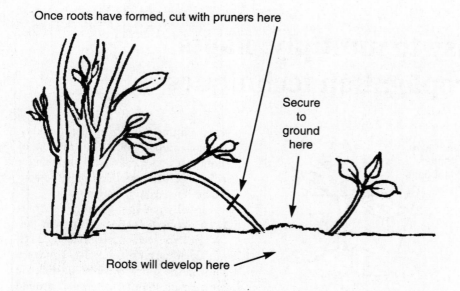

Once roots have formed, cut with pruners here

Secure to ground here

Roots will develop here →

Layering

is the top and bottom. Dip in rooting hormone and plant in a well-drained site, preferably facing south so it will warm up quickly. Plant and firm in the soil. Since these cuttings take months to root, we're lucky that they don't need any winter protection. Stem cuttings can be taken from thick-stemmed plants (usually houseplants). When you cut the stem, make sure you have a couple of nodes. You can plant it vertically (making sure it's right-side-up) or horizontally (half-buried).

When these cuttings root, you'll see new leaves emerging. Allow time for the new plant to establish healthy roots, then re-pot.

Root cuttings are used with fleshy-rooted plants like day lilies, iris, and dahlias. Avoid grafted or budded trees or shrubs, as you'll get rootstock, not the plant you see on top. To do this, pick a time when the plant is dormant, so it won't suffer from the disturbance. Lift small plants from the soil and brush off enough of the soil so you can see what you're doing. On larger trees and shrubs, just scrape away enough of the soil to expose a couple of roots you can use. Choose pencil-thick roots. Two or three roots

should give you plenty of material to work with and will not cause too much distress to the plant. Make clean cuts and don't let these dry out. Bag the cuttings if necessary and replant the parent plant as soon as possible.

Back to the cuttings: Trim off thin side roots and cut into sections two to three inches long, with the bottom straight and the top slanted so you know which end goes up and which goes down. Pot into planting medium, firm soil, then water. There's no need for rooting hormone, and if you're not sure which is the top, then plant horizontally. Cover with a thin layer of

soil. You'll soon see buds forming on the surface, but be patient and let them grow a little bit before transplanting.

Division

Some plants can be divided into several pieces, each growing into an entirely new plant. This process is easy, and one plant can yield six or more plants. Dividing is best done in early spring when the plants are growing rapidly. They re-establish themselves quickly. Carefully dig up the plant with a garden fork or shovel. Remove some of the soil with your fingers, trying not to damage small, sensitive roots. Some plants can be separated with your fingers, while others will need to be cut apart with a knife. Using two garden forks back to back, try prying the clump apart. Divide again if needed. Day lilies can usually be divided with the garden forks, but some of the ornamental grasses will need to be cut. Make sure each section has several strong shoots and plenty of roots.

The centers of clumps sometimes become very woody (bearded iris comes to mind). Just discard any woody centers and replant the vigorous outside sections.

Layering

Simple layering is taking a stem still attached to the parent plant, weighing

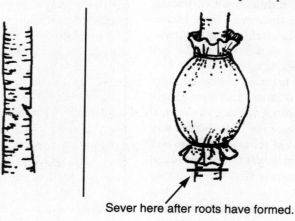

Sever here after roots have formed.

Air layering

or pinning it down to the ground, and covering it with soil so that new roots form. Then, once roots have formed, you sever the stem from the parent plant.

Raspberries, currants, and blackberries do this easily, and it's most successful during the active growing period.

Cultivate the soil around the mother plant so it's nice and crumbly. Choose the stem to be layered and remove any leaves that would be underground. It should be a young, supple stem that won't snap when bent over. To encourage rooting, wound the stem slightly by scratching off a little of the bark. Use a coat hanger wire bent into a U or a large stone to peg the stem into place, then cover it with soil. Roots will form during the following season, and then you can separate it from the parent.

Tip layering mimics what blackberries do in the wild. Take a supple shoot with a healthy, strong growing point, bend it to the ground, and peg it down or dig it into the soil. A new tip will quickly form. Allow good root formation to occur before severing.

Air layering

Air layering is used on plants that don't have supple stems. Rigid stems would snap if the other methods were used, but air layering will work and provide you with new plants. Usually you see this done with large houseplants that have outgrown the space they're in.

Choose the place on the stem where you intend to produce new roots to create a new plant. The stem should be sturdy but young. Make a diagonal cut, taking care not to go all the way through. Insert rooting hormone into the cut, then insert a small piece of wood (a toothpick works well) to keep it open a bit.

Wrap damp sphagnum moss around the cut, then put plastic wrap around it. This will keep it nice and moist, and will create a greenhouse effect for

warmth. After roots have formed, sever beneath the cluster of roots and pot up your new plant.

These are some of the ways you can easily propagate plants and increase your plantings, both indoors and out. Don't give up if one way doesn't work. Keep experimenting until you find the ways that work best for you and your plants. Δ

Yard Work

I planted
Two common purple lilacs
And two rosebushes,
A Mr. Lincoln and a Peace.
I planted
Catnip for Christopher Marlowe.
I planted larkspur
For Pat and
Spring Beauty for me and
Some old stalks of
Chrysanthemum that may
Or may not survive.
I put in some Shasta daisies.
None of them look well.

I want to plant
Old-fashioned roses—
I want a thicket
By my front door, a hundred
Feet tall and full of blackberries.

I want blue spruce and
Daffodils and
Barking dogs and roots
That go down so deep—

I want my hands in warm soft loam,
My back to the sun, and mostly
To be left alone.

**Olive L. Sullivan
Pittsburg, KS**

A BHM Writer's Profile: M. C. Wright

Born and educated in a small town in southern Mississippi, Margaret Clark (M.C.) Wright still has the accent to prove it. She was raised by her grandmother and a loving nanny while her mom worked outside the home. Wright married her high school sweetheart; they have been together 32 years. She is mother to four children and "Mamaw" to seven grandchildren. Her youngest child, Benjamin, is still at home.

Wright and her family have travelled extensively, following the electrical construction trade. They landed in Idaho 20 years ago and are still there. Wright has worked with several rural ambulance services as an emergency medical technician.

Basically a mother earth type, Wright homeschools her children, cooks from scratch, sews, quilts, gardens, and takes care of the animals. Her favorite attire is a denim skirt, sweatshirt, and Birkenstocks with socks, which she describes as a real fashion statement. She began writing after taking some journalism classes—a hobby turned serious. She says, "I love the idea of other people being interested in my lifestyle, and hope I can inspire them to follow their dreams."

Soil pH is the secret of a good garden

By Marjorie Burris

A garden with the correct soil pH can produce a beautiful, bountiful harvest, but a garden with the wrong soil pH barely produces stunted, runty plants that scarcely keep alive, let alone bear fruit. It's easy to determine your soil's pH, and the more you find out about your garden, the better you will be able to garden. Playing by ear may be great for musicians, but when it comes to gardening, guesswork doesn't pay.

What is pH?

Literally, pH is shorthand for the French words *pouvoir hydrogène,* which mean the "power of hydrogen." The pH value tells you the concentration of hydrogen ions in a substance. The more free hydrogen ions there are in a substance, the more *acid* it is.

Hydrogen ions are counteracted by hydroxide ions which are symbolized by the chemical shorthand "OH." The more free hydroxide ions there are in a substance, the more *alkaline* it is.

In pure water, there are enough hydrogen ions and hydroxide ions to almost neutralize one another. The measurement of hydrogen ions in a liter of pure water is 1×10^{-7}. Written out, that is 0.0000001. This means that each liter of pure water has one ten millionth of a gram of H^+ and the equivalent amount of OH ions in it. This is just too awkward to write out all the time, and since the logarithm of ten millionth is 7, we say the pH of water is 7. Thus chemists have developed a scale of 0 to 14, with 7 being *neutral.* Values from 0 to 7 indicate acidity and values from 7 to 14 indicate alkalinity. Most common vegeta-

bles grow best on a soil that has a pH of 6.5 to 7, which is only slightly acid to neutral.

How to test for pH

Hydrogen ions make things taste *sour*; vinegar is a good example. In the old days, a farmer might taste his soil, and if it tasted sour, he knew it was acid. In contrast, hydroxide ions make things taste *brackish* or *bitter*. Baking soda is a good example, and if the soil tasted bitter, the farmer knew his soil was alkaline. This is a rough test, and although it is not too reliable, it is better than no test.

A slightly better test for pH is the *litmus paper* test. Litmus paper is paper which has been impregnated by a solution made from ground-up lichens. It is purplish in color and is neutral in itself. A few drops of acid solution on the paper will make it turn red. An alkaline solution will make it turn blue. (There is also red and blue litmus paper, but this is simply the neutral purple paper which has been treated by a few drops of acid to make it red or a few drops of alkali to make it blue.)

To use litmus paper in soil, simply press the paper against the damp soil and watch for the color change. This test indicates whether soil is acid or alkaline, but not *how* acid or alkaline. Still, it is more accurate than the subjective taste test. Litmus paper can be purchased at most good drug stores and is not expensive.

Most good full-line nurseries and seed companies sell *pH meters* and *soil test kits* at reasonable prices. Considering the value of knowing how to amend your garden soil correctly, they are well worth the cost. I've seen two or three different makes of meters, but they all work on the same principle. Each uses a probe which, when inserted into the soil, triggers a needle to record the pH. They do not use batteries.

The soil test kits come with test tubes and tablets and work very much like swimming pool test kits. They give an indication of the level of *usable* nitrogen, phosphorus, and potassium in the soil, as well as the pH. Most kits contain enough tablets for several tests, some of them up to 40 tests.

My 1995 seed catalogs from Burpee's and Gurney's both list pH meters and soil test kits. If you want more information, here's how to contact them:

Burpee Seed Company
300 Park Ave.
Warminster, PA 18991-0001
Phone: 1-800-888-1447
Fax: 1-800-487-5530

Gurney's Seed Co.
110 Capitol St.
Yankton, SD 57079
Phone: 1-605-665-1930
Fax: 1-605-665-9718.

As I write this I don't have my latest Vesey's seed catalog (it's a company specializing in short season seeds), but their 1994 catalog lists a pH meter. Their address and phone:

Vesey's Seeds, Ltd.
P.O. Box 9000,
Calais, ME, 04619-6102
Phone: 1-800-363-7333
Fax: 1-900-566-1620

Many private laboratories and state agricultural extension services of state universities do soil analyses, but I have found them to be expensive and slow in returning their results, so I prefer my own little soil testing kit.

How to amend acid soil

People who live in cool, moist climates where the trees are conifers will probably find their soil to be acid. Moisture leaches the alkaline calcium salts away from the soil, and coniferous trees do not use much alkaline material, so they can't *return* alkaline material when the leaves and wood decay. Also, the soil will be poor in nitrogen, because the long winters hamper the growth of nitrogen-fixing bacteria. Of course, other soils can be acid, too, so a test is the only accurate way, not only to find out if the soil is acid or alkaline, but to what *degree* it is acid or alkaline.

Acid soil first of all needs a replacement of calcium salts, and probably the best and easiest-to-get source of calcium is limestone. Limestone is better than slaked lime or quicklime, because limestone breaks down more slowly. Slaked lime and quicklime are so alkaline they give the soil too much calcium too quickly and can injure the soil. Wood ashes, bone meal, dolomite, crushed marble, and oyster shells are also good sources of lime.

Often, just correcting the pH will release enough nitrogen, phosphorus, and potassium to raise a good garden, but if testing after using a lime source shows a lack of these nutrients, there are certain materials that are better for acid soils than others. Organic matter is a good way to start replenishing the

soil, but pine needles, sawdust, wood chips, and most deciduous leaves (especially oak) are very acid and should be composted with limestone or wood ashes before using.

Good sources of nitrogen for acid soil are steamed bone meal, blood meal, animal manures, and green manures. Buckwheat is tops for building poor, acid soils. Lespedeza and sour clover are also useful. Phosphorus sources include bone meal, ground rock phosphate, raw sugar wastes, and dried blood, as well as green manures.

Potassium (also called potash) sources include green sand, sea weed, potash rock, buckwheat and millet straw, wool wastes, and wood ashes as well as the green manures.

How to amend alkaline soils

Alkaline soils, often found in desert and semi-arid regions, have an accumulation of soluble salts, usually chlorides and sulfates of sodium and calcium and magnesium and sometimes potassium, all of which are toxic to plants. Also, alkaline soils will usually have a hard-pan under the surface, which "adds insult to injury," as the old saying goes.

The first step in reclaiming alkaline soil is to work humus into it. Here, the acid leaves, pine needles, wood chips and sawdust (but not wood ashes) used raw are of great value. Peat moss is another great source of acid humus. Gypsum is useful for breaking up many kinds of hard-pan and is very acid.

Most alkaline soils are lacking in nitrogen, and since sawdust and wood chips take a lot of nitrogen to decompose, additional nitrogen is needed when these are used. An excellent source of acid nitrogen is cottonseed meal. Animal manures, especially poultry manures, are very helpful. Horse manure makes humus, but doesn't supply much nitrogen.

Blood meal and bone meal supply both nitrogen and phosphorus. Sea weed, potash rock, and green manures add phosphorus and potassium. Green manures that are especially good for alkaline soils include most of the grain crops. Alfalfa is probably the best, because it likes a flooding type of irrigation that washes away the harmful salts, and its long roots reach down and break up hard-pan. Bermuda grass, sweet clover, maize, barley, sugar beets, cotton, rye, and sorghum are all helpful in amending alkaline soils.

Grow plants that like your soil's pH

Although most common garden plants like a pH between 6.5 and 7, there are some that will thrive best in either a moderately acid soil or a moderately alkaline soil. When you know the pH of your soil, you can concentrate on those plants that will grow best in your soil.

Common acid-soil plants that do best between pH 4 and 6 are radish, sweet potato, watermelon, and berries such as blackberry, blueberry, cranberry, huckleberry, and raspberry. Peanuts and pecans also like an acid soil. Plants that like a somewhat acid soil, but can tolerate a neutral soil are pumpkin, rice, turnip, and apple.

Moderate alkaline-soil plants are peas, beans, beets, cabbage, cantaloupe, cauliflower, celery, cucumber, lettuce, onion, parsnip, rhubarb, salsify, and squash.

Because soil is continually changing, you will want to test your garden periodically to see how your treatment regimen is working. Some plants use more of one nutrient than another, and you may need to replenish more of that element. Even just standing idle can alter a soil's make-up from year to year. Get to know your soil, and you will enjoy gardening all the more. Δ

Here are some thoughts on finding your dream place — garden and all

By Alice B. Yeager
Photos by James O. Yeager

Every gardener (and would-be gardener) has a dream, and it usually centers around a neat cottage with flower beds, a manicured lawn, a small orchard, and a weedless garden spot. From the latter two come all sorts of picture-perfect fruits and vegetables, aromatic herbs, berries—you name it. Maybe there's a small grape arbor, too, always abundantly hung with fat, fragrant clusters of grapes just waiting to be harvested. Sometimes a small flock of well-behaved chickens rounds out the dream.

Many people are looking forward to just such a place when they retire. Others are wanting to move out of neighborhoods that are changing for the worse. Same may be looking for that first real home—you know, the place where one puts down roots and raises almost all of one's food—a "Green Acres" type of place.

There are pitfalls to selecting the right spot, especially when it comes to choosing Home Sweet Home with an eye to gardening. The most important garden requirements center around *soil*, *water*, and *location*.

Soil

If one wants that garden of perfection, good soil is a *must*. When viewing property, it is well to be armed with some facts about soil. If nothing else, at least know the difference between clay, loam, and sand. Otherwise, you may end up with something you didn't count on.

Take a close look at the garden spot to determine if it has recently been under cultivation. If the owner is still on the premises, he/she can be of

Home-grown tomatoes—everyone's favorite. Celebrity is a good variety.

tremendous help as a source of gardening advice. If the place has been abandoned for some time, take a close look at the weeds and grass, as there will undoubtedly be plenty of those. If they're healthy and shoulder-high, chances are the soil is fertile. Your job will be to conquer all the seedlings that will came up. (Lotsa luck!) If there is a great supply of nut grass, look out. That may be the reason the garden spot was abandoned. When nut grass invades, some gardeners finally just throw up their hands and quit. It is a devilish opponent.

A sandy loam soil that is rich in humus is usually regarded as the best soil for general gardening. If an organic gardener has spent years working with the soil, you can bet it will raise almost anything.

Of course, sometimes that neat little place you have your heart set on may have *hidden* problems as far as the garden is concerned. Unless you can actually see the place during the peak of the gardening season, you will have to take the word of the seller or the real estate agent as to the soil's fertility. Experienced old-timers can reach down, take a handful of dirt, smell it, run it through their fingers, and tell a lot about the possibilities. To the novice, this doesn't mean much, and

Gardeners love to bring in a variety of fresh vegetables for culinary use. This basket contains squash (2 varieties), cucumbers, tomatoes, beans, and sweet peppers.

that's how some places are unloaded on unsuspecting buyers.

If you aren't sure about the soil and have questions, it would be a good idea to ask the County Extension Agent to run some soil tests for you. He can give you some practical advice as to what (if anything) is needed to make it produce those savory squash, plump tomatoes, and pounds of potatoes.

If the real estate salesman hints at other buyers waiting in the wings, don't panic. Any salesman anxious for a commission will occasionally employ this tactic, particularly if the payment is due on his Cadillac.

Water

There is hardly a garden anywhere that doesn't require watering now and then, and some more than others. Take into consideration the source of water for the garden. If it is city water, be prepared to deal with high water bills in the summer if you want your garden to keep producing during dry periods. If there is a well with a pressurized water system, so much the better.

It is surprising how many people never consider the subject of water when being shown property. They assume that if water faucets are in sight, everything must be all right.

Water is a very important item, especially when considering property

Fruit tree blossoms in springtime are beautiful, and they herald a harvest that can result in canned fruit and honey on the shelf to enjoy until next harvest.

in a rural setting. How long has the well been in use? Does the water get low during long dry spells? Is the water hard or soft? How new is the pump? Has the water been tested for bacteria lately? Where is the septic tank located? (You'd be surprised at what goes on underground.) These are only a few general questions about water, and quality varies from area to area and from hill country to the lowlands.

Above all, ask if you may taste the water. That should give you a good idea as to its value for kitchen use. A seller with a good water supply is never hesitant about giving information regarding water. If you have reason to be suspicious of the water, ask the County Agent about having it tested. It's better to be safe than sorry.

Location

A desirable garden area should be open to the sun and slightly sloped for good drainage. It should not be closely surrounded by tall trees that cast shade a good part of the day. *Some* shade is helpful, particularly during hot afternoons, but most vegetable plants require at least a bare minimum of six hours of sunshine per day. Nearby large trees will also sap moisture and nutrients from the soil.

Gardens clinging to the sides of hills are risky sites and an awful lot of work. Some of them may be interesting, but those are for folks who enjoy challenges, like to haul topsoil, and have no other place to garden. Hard rains can play havoc with hillside gardens. And hillsides dry out fast.

An ideal location for a garden is near the house for convenience. A

Here's a neat Ozark homeplace. The shade trees are well away from garden, leaving it open to the sun.

cross-country runner might not mind a garden located 200 feet away from the kitchen, but most of us don't feel that way. And remember, those pounds of splendid vegetables are going to get heavier the farther you carry them. If you live where there is competition from animals for food, a garden handy to the house is easier to patrol.

Naturally, most real estate salesmen like to show property at its best—nice day, preferably in spring when orchard trees are blooming, gardens are being started and there's plenty of upbeat activity going on. (If house and outbuildings have had a fresh coat of paint, fine and dandy.) This is all very well, but if possible, view the place of your dreams during bad weather, especially during a time of heavy rain. That will bring to light any hidden horrors regarding the garden spot. If it's under a foot of water and fast becoming a lake, beware. Sometimes the situation can be corrected by trenching to give water an outlet. It depends on the lay of the land.

If you can't visit the place during wet weather, try the hottest day of the year during a drought. If plants are dehydrated and the ground dulls a pick-axe, you're going to have to do a lot of building-up to get that wonderful loose soil for which we all strive. Over a period of time, mulching with organic material will help, as it will assist in retaining moisture and will return nutrients to the soil as the mulch breaks down. Also, earthworms will be attracted, enhancing the soil's aeration and fertility.

Earthworms are another indication of just how rich the soil is. Assuming that the soil is in pliable condition on the day you inspect the garden area, dig around a bit and take a look at the earthworms. Are they vigorous, plump and plentiful? Good sign. Are they few, skinny, pale, and barely able to move? Very poor soil. If you find no earthworms at all, it could mean they have been wiped out by chemicals.

But take heart, drawbacks are not permanent except in extreme cases, as almost any soil can be made productive if a gardener will make an effort to improve it. There is plenty of advice obtainable on every side: bookstores, magazine racks, experienced gardeners, County Extension Offices, libraries, and so on.

Pollution

In addition to soil, water, and location, there is another gardening factor that is increasingly of concern—one that wasn't even discussed years ago. *Pollution*. Rare is the real estate salesman who will point out the possibility of contaminated soil or water. Prospective buyers should be wary of neighborhoods that have "For Sale" signs everywhere and no apparent reason for them.

One should make it a point to find out which industries are located in the area. Are there paper mills, steel mills, toxic dumps and such in the vicinity? Don't be fooled by nice names like "Resource Recovery" (municipal incinerator), "Sanitary Landfill" (dump), and so on.

Once soil and water are contaminated, it takes a long span of time to clean them up—much longer than a gardener wants to wait. If you find a homey little place that suits you to a "T" but has the likelihood of pollution attached to it, flee without hesitation. Who wants the pleasure of gardening overshadowed by the Grim Reaper.

The foregoing is but a sampling of things to consider when one is intent on pursuing one's dream. Above all, don't try to cultivate more space than you can manage. Nothing is more frustrating than trying to keep things under control in one end of a garden while in the other end, weeds and grass are having a heyday producing next year's crop of gremlins.

Remember, under the right conditions, gardening is fun and rewarding, both mentally and physically. So, if you're serious about having that dream place, go for it. Δ

A BHM Writer's Profile: Skip Thomsen

Skip's been writing homesteading books and articles since 1980, starting out with some stories in the original *Mother Earth News*. His first real book was <u>More Power to You</u>!, self-published about 10 years ago. There were others in the meanwhile and another since, but <u>The Modern Homestead Manual</u> was published in '93. His first homesteading experiences were in Oregon, and the one that inspired the <u>Homestead Manual</u> was his 108-acre scratch-built homestead in North Central Oregon. 1993 was also the year the Thomsens had had enough snow, ice and cold for their lifetimes and they finally decided that they were never again going to burn anything to stay warm, and they moved to rural Hawaii.

Skip is newly remarried (for the last time!) and the happy couple just bought a little home near the ocean in a tiny community where papayas, oranges, mangoes, and avocados are everywhere, and tomatoes grow all year 'round. The Big Island is a golden opportunity for those considering a comfortable, affordable, self-sufficient lifestyle, and that's going to be the topic of an upcoming article. Meanwhile, the Thomsens spend as much time as possible playing in the crystal clear, warm ocean and enjoying the tropical sun.

PV pioneer describes his successful solar home

By Paul Jeffrey Fowler

My wife Lea, my three-year-old son Terry, and I live in a passive solar home nestled in a remote corner of a small town in the Berkshire Hills of western Massachusetts. Our house is located 1.3 miles and $20,000 away from the nearest power line. To get to our land, we drive up and over the highest hill in Worthington on a one-lane gravel road. Bob and Karin Cook, our only year-round neighbors in the 2,500 acres of land that surround us, live a third of a mile up the road.

I was born and raised on a pretty little 120-acre farm in Worthington. Unfortunately, my parents had to sell the farm I was to have inherited, just before I graduated from college. Several years after college, I returned to Worthington when my parents left me their mobile home on the lower corner of the old farm.

The trailer was of poor quality construction. I have always been someone who thought I could make something out of nothing, but I could not find anything worth saving in that trailer. I soon bought the small house just up the road which a friend and I had built several years before for my sister and her family. It was a better structure, but like the trailer, it was located at the bottom of a narrow valley.

A perfect solar site

At the time, I avidly read all the material I could find on solar energy. I could never successfully redesign the small house into a passive solar home, because there was too little sun in that valley. In 1981, I found a nine-acre piece of land for sale with perfect south-sloping solar exposure. The only drawback was that the nearest power line was 1.3 miles away at the main road.

For years I had also been reading about wind machines and alternative energy systems. I looked at this land, so far from the power line, as a chance to do it all: build a passive solar home and power it with alternative energy. In a few months I had sold my two properties, moved to a tent on my new land, and begun to build my new energy-efficient home.

When I bought the land, I expected to install a wind machine to produce electricity. I had determined that it was a good wind site. I purchased a large generator for the building project and planned to replace it with an alter-

The author with his wife Lea and son Terry in front of the heat-storing stone wall in the sunspace

native energy system when I had time to design and install one. I never really expected a power line to come down the road to my house. Therefore, the whole house was designed from the beginning to be an alternative energy home, in addition to being energy-efficient. In 1982, I discovered solar electric modules and abandoned the inherent problems of a wind machine on top of a 90-foot tower. Besides, the sun shines more often than the wind blows.

Today, our house is powered by a large solar electric system. We have been more fortunate than most people who own solar electric systems. For one thing, our first systems were purchased back in the days of state and federal tax credits. Furthermore, my early research into solar electric systems evolved naturally into a successful business which sold solar electric systems throughout the Northeast.

Solar electric modules on the house and garage

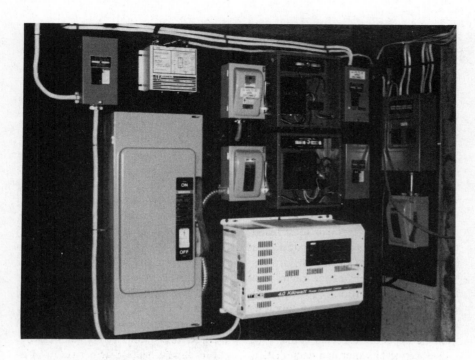

System controls and 4000-watt sinewave inverter

Therefore, later expansions of our system were purchased at wholesale prices from our business. On the other hand, we were the pioneers who suffered the trials and errors of an emerging technology.

The system

On the south side of our house above the first floor windows are mounted 24 33-watt, nine-year-old Mobil Solar modules. For years, these were the sole power source for our solar electric system. Four years ago we added eight 48-watt Hoxan modules on the south side of the garage. At the time, our business offices were upstairs in the large building, and two of the three garage bays warehoused our inventory. The growing business required a lot of power to run computers and office equipment. Three years ago, we sold the remaining shares of the business, and it moved across town, leaving us with the additional electricity from the eight Hoxan modules for our home loads.

Our combined solar arrays are rated at 1,200 peak watts. This rating means little to anyone but a solar electric engineer with a program to size systems. In practical terms, after we derate the modules for actual operating temperatures, and account for losses associated with charging lead-acid batteries, we have a daily summer average of 4,800 watt-hours to power loads in our home. In the winter, when the average insolation is low, we have a daily average of 2,400 watt-hours. Quite logically, we have approximately 3,600 watt-hours in the spring and the fall.

Figuring the angles

Our site is at 42° latitude. The standard angle to mount the modules on an adjustable mounting structure is latitude minus 15° in the summer (27° above the horizon), latitude in the spring or fall (42°), and latitude plus 15 degrees in the winter (57°). For a non-adjustable mounting structure, the array is typically installed at 42°, to obtain the greatest amount of power over the whole year. We have chosen to mount our modules on non-adjustable structures at the winter adjustment of 57°.

Winter is the hardest time for our solar electric system. The insolation is low in the Northeast, and the short days require longer lighting loads. We are purists and do not depend on a generator to charge our battery bank in the winter. Instead, we have sized our system to meet our conservative winter loads and know we will have extra electricity in the other three seasons. Therefore, it is not necessary to adjust our arrays for the other three seasons to get additional power. The steep 57° angle of our arrays produces 20% extra power in the winter, because the modules can also pick up reflected sunlight from the snow on the ground.

Both the garage and house arrays have their own charge controllers and the associated fuses and disconnects to satisfy the requirements of the National Electrical Code (R). They both charge the same large battery bank in the basement of our house. The controller for the smaller garage array turns off before the controller for the house, so that the charging is somewhat "tapered" as the batteries approach full charge.

Our battery bank is composed of 32 6V (6-volt) 200-amp-hour golf-cart batteries wired in a 24V configuration. Many people in the industry recommend larger batteries. We sold the best quality Trojan golf-cart batteries in our business for years. We had fewer failures with them than with the larger Trojan L-16 batteries. The golf-cart batteries have the same plate composition as the larger L-16 batteries, but they are mass produced, so they cost 30% less per amp-hour. Our batteries are now 6½ years old. We expect them to last over eight years, while L-16 batteries are expected to last ten years.

Our solar electric system and home are wired to code and inspected. Our house wiring has about one circuit per room to power a selected 24V efficient lamp or lighting fixture. This wiring system and DC (Direct Current)-rated circuit breaker box are left over from our earliest solar electric system. Some of these lights are used every day, while others now serve only as backups. The house is also fully wired for 120VAC (Alternating Current). This electricity is supplied by a 4000-watt, sine-wave, Trace 4024 inverter powered by the large 24V battery bank.

Conservation is the key

Our solar electric home uses about one-third as many watt-hours per month as my last grid-connected home. We live at a similar level of comfort in our present home, because our electrical usage has been decreased by the design of our home and the choices we have made for efficient appliances. Well-planned conservation is the real key to a successful independent home. The electricity we produce costs about 30¢ per kilowatt-hour after we factor in the costs of all the components and their maintenance and life expectancy. Solar electricity becomes a money-saver for us only after we consider our conservation and the $20,000 we would have to pay the utility company up-front to extend the power line to our home.

We pride ourselves on having an alternative energy home that does not appear to be different to someone who visits for a weekend. We have no complicated systems of switches and *do's* and *don'ts* to follow. Conservation is designed into the system.

Solar heating

Our well-insulated, passive solar home is heated by the solar gain of our south-facing windows. The solar energy heats the house to 75° even on sunny days of subzero weather, which are quite common in our cold New England winters at 1700 ft. above sea level. Solar heat is stored in interior stone walls and in a concrete slab that is covered with Vermont slate. The

balance of our heat is provided by two cords of wood burned in our basement wood stove. We have none of the standard electrical loads of running a furnace and its circulating fans or pumps.

We have eliminated other common large electrical loads. We use a propane refrigerator, stove, and tankless hot-water heater. Our home was designed to utilize daylight. Most walls and ceilings are white, so no additional electric lighting is needed until sunset. Our electric lighting is carefully placed in all the rooms. We have chosen fixtures and lamp shades that efficiently transfer the light from the bulbs to the room, reducing the need for large bulbs or many lights in a given area. Wherever possible, we utilize compact fluorescent bulbs.

Our source of water is a deep drilled well 200 feet from our house. Because the static water level is 30 feet below grade, our best choice for pumping water was a standard 120VAC submersible pump. Our electrical loads would be less if we had a shallow well that could be pumped by an efficient low-voltage pump, or if we had a gravity-fed water supply, as our neighbors do. But we are fortunate to have crystal-clear pure water from a high-yielding well. We recently reduced our water budget and its associated electrical loads by installing a new washer that uses less water and by designing an efficient underground watering system in our raised-bed garden.

Normal appliances, plus a bit of planning

We have the common 120VAC appliances found in most American homes, such as a clothes washer, color TV, VCR, vacuum cleaner, computer, and stereo. We chose them carefully for efficiency. In addition, we think about each appliance's use, to keep in balance with our seasonal production of electricity. When possible, we have given extra consideration to certain

appliances. I now mostly use my notebook computer, which uses 15 watts, while my desktop computer uses 100 watts. Our 25-year-old Electrolux vacuum cleaner sent our ten-year-old Electrolux into retirement when I found it used 400 watts compared to 900 watts. A few months ago we purchased a Staber clothes washer because it uses 250 watt-hours per load instead of the 450 watt-hours per load needed by our standard model.

When the house was two-thirds built, I bought my first inverter and immediately sold the generator. The rest of the house, buildings, and additions were built with power tools powered by solar electricity. We own all the usual carpentry tools from drills and a circular saw to a screw gun and a router, plus some larger ones like a table saw, a radial-arm saw, and a planer. In the past, we carefully selected these tools to not exceed the surge capability of our inverter. Our new 4,000 watt inverter will start any of their large motors easily. The electrical energy used by these large wattage tools is not terribly significant, because they are running a very small amount of time during any given work day. However, we do plan our projects for the right time of year. When a project requires shiplapping the siding for a garage, or planing boards for a floor, we do the job during a sunny spell, or during a season of abundant sunshine.

We have no freezer. A standard freezer is too inefficient, and we feel the efficient low-voltage models on the market would still put a large strain on our system in the depth of winter, since we choose not to use a generator. We do have a one-cubic-foot deep-freezer in our gas refrigerator. For six months of the year, we eat fresh vegetables from our garden, utilizing cloches to extend our growing season. For seven months of the year, we can use our large walk-in cold-storage room as a giant refrigerator and almost root cellar. This area is cooled by passive air circulation whenever the outside temperature is

Propane refrigerator and freezer

lower than the temperature in the cold storage room.

Living in an independent home with solar electricity is incredibly different from living in a grid home. A family in a grid home can use as much electricity as they want. If Grandma comes in January, a grid home can crank up the electric heat in the extra room. An alternative energy system requires an investment in a system that can produce a certain amount of electrical energy. After that, living is a matter of balancing the loads to the system's production and seasonal variances.

Over the years, I have watched some people live naturally in alternative homes and other people move or pay to bring in the power line. Sometimes one member of a couple loved the alternative-energy life while the spouse could not adapt. Lea, Terry, and I are successful in our independent home because our home and our solar electric system are well-designed, and because we work together naturally keeping our homestead in balance. The efficient raised-bed garden, the chickens, the passive solar house, the solar garage, the solar electric system, and our philosophy of life function interdependently.

(Paul Jeffrey Fowler is the author of <u>The Evolution of an Independent Home: The Story of a Solar Electric Pioneer</u> and <u>The Solar Electric Independent Home Book</u>, both available from Backwoods Home Magazine [order form on page 96]. He is also the founder of Fowler Solar Electric, Inc.) Δ

A BHM Writer's Profile: Robert L. Williams

Robert L. Williams has been a freelance writer/photographer for more than 30 years. A former professional baseball player and a teacher for three decades on the high school, college, and university campus, he has sold several thousands of articles and photographs to leading national and international magazines. Among the publications that have purchased his writing and/or photos are Money Magazine, House Beautiful, Southern Living, Our State, Sandlapper, Modern Maturity, American Legion, Rotarian, Our Navy, Elks Magazine, the Compass, Hughes' Rigway, Grit, Capper's Weekly, Baseball Digest, and others.

The author of 36 books, either published or under contract, Williams has written books published by G. P. Putnam, W. W. Norton, TAB. McGraw-Hill, Allyn and Bacon, Donning Publishers, Berkley Publications, Herald Books, Hastings House (subsidiary of United Publishers Group), Loompanics, and Southeastern Publishing, Inc. His books include how-to, self-help, autobiography, history, labor history, a college English textbook, pictorial histories, mystery and suspense novels, baseball nonfiction, and general interest novels.

Some of Williams, titles include <u>Starting Over</u>, <u>The Thirteenth Juror</u>, <u>Daytrips in the Carolinas and Georgia</u>, and, most recently, <u>100 Practically Perfect Places in the North Carolina Mountains</u>. He is also author of a book on how to build log houses.

At present, Williams is editor and author for Southeastern Publishing Corporation. He continues to write for *Backwoods Home Magazine* and for a series of travel and general-interest magazines.

A BHM Writer's Profile: Robert L. Williams III

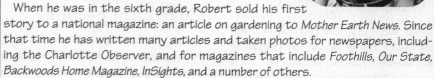

Born in 1976, Robert L. Williams III was among the youngest writers/photographers ever to be published. At age 3 he had first appeared on NBC's Today Show where Tom Brokaw and Jane Pauley introduced him to the American public as the youngest photographer in history to be published. At age 4 he was selling photos to many magazines, book companies, and newspapers. At age 5 he was under contract with the Vivitar Corporation as a photographer, and that same year he had a one-man show at the Las Vegas Convention Center at the World Photo Marketing Trade Fair.

When he was in the sixth grade, Robert sold his first story to a national magazine: an article on gardening to *Mother Earth News*. Since that time he has written many articles and taken photos for newspapers, including the *Charlotte Observer*, and for magazines that include *Foothills*, *Our State*, *Backwoods Home Magazine*, *InSights*, and a number of others.

He had co-authored a hiking book (along with his parents) that is now in its sixth printing. He has also written a mystery/suspense novel based on events related to the tornado that destroyed the family home. Now in college, Robert was among 20 Honors Students selected at Cleveland Community College. He is now a junior at Gardner-Webb University. Robert makes his home with his parents in Belwood, North Carolina.

Homesteading on the electronic frontier

By Martin Waterman

Harvesting the Internet for gardening information

Cicero, the much noted Roman statesman and orator (106-43 B.C.), said, "If you have a garden and a library, you have everything you need."

I wonder what he would say if he were alive today to see and use the Internet. He would have almost instantaneous access to thousands of libraries, universities, government agencies, web sites, and news groups around the world. Of particular interest to him might be the many Internet sites that have information on gardening, farming, and other aspects of horticulture.

So I'm going to take you on a tour of a few dozen of those horticultural related Web Sites and news groups to show you what they are like. I have chosen most of them based on the fact that I have used them and found useful information and, of course, some new friends. For veteran users this will provide some new places to surf and check out. For those who have not yet made the jump into cyberspace, I hope this will give an indication of the type of resources that are available.

There has been much press about the dark side of the net and many fluff pieces in the media about the "gee whiz" or "what a wonderful novelty" aspects of the Internet. The fact of the matter is that those who know how to use the Internet use it to save money, make money, and enhance their lives. In many instances, my own circumstances for example, it is one of the key factors that permits me to enjoy a rural lifestyle.

News groups

The benefits of the news groups is that since they are interactive, you can get answers to your questions in a very short amount of time from the people who use the groups. If it is an active news group, one with many users, you will also be blessed with numerous answers reflecting diverse opinions from people around the globe. This will usually give you a number of alternatives to explore. Usually when I post a garden question, which is something I often do as a garden writer and avid gardener, I usually get more answers than I need within a very short amount of time, usually under a few hours.

News group members not only exchange ideas, they often exchange seeds, cuttings, and plants making the news groups a terrific resource for those seeking hard-to-find or specialty plants. There are many news groups that deal with gardening and related issues. Press the "Usenet" button (or use a news reading program), then type in any of the names of the news groups described below.

alt.agriculture.fruit is a good resource for those who grow tree fruit, berries, and grapes. One of the most common questions I receive is how a grower should go about marketing their fruit, and this is a topic often discussed. Of course, any cultural or pest problem can also be discussed, and I have found people who use this group to be very knowledgable and helpful.

alt.agriculture.misc usually discusses farm issues. If you are a serious grower or farmer, you will find a supportive community of like-minded individuals.

alt.bonsai is strictly for the bonsai enthusiast, a discipline which many gardeners like to try now and then. Some of the rural people in my area are doing well starting bonsai plants and selling them to nurseries and garden centers.

alt.landscape.architecture discusses landscaping issues from plant selection to heavy duty landscape construction projects. It's also an active place at times for those who are seeking landscape work.

rec.food.preserving is one of my all-time favorite news groups. When I have an abundance of apples, beans, grapes or any other type of produce, I check into this group which discusses preserving foods. It is great fun to swap recipes, and I have received some real good ones. Many of the people who post are masters at preserving food, and I highly recommend this group.

rec.food.veg.cooking is another excellent resource for those who are blessed with bountiful harvests and are looking for new ways to serve up those legendary country meals.

rec.gardens is the mother of all gardening groups. There is constant debate on splitting off subgroups such as for house plants, but for the most part this group covers a broad range of topics. During gardening season I have seen it with as many as 1000 postings.

rec.gardens.orchids is for orchid enthusiasts. I never knew there were so many orchid fans until I checked out this group. If you like orchids, this is the place. Members will steer you to orchid WWW pages with spectacular photographs.

rec.gardens.roses is for the rose connoisseur. This is another one of my favorite groups, and I lurk to see what new and historic varieties I might consider trying.

rec.ponds is about ponds. Many will argue that no country place is complete without a pond. This group is dominated by gardeners in search of the perfect backyard pond. Discussions include fish, water lilies, aeration, waterfalls, plants, algae, and other issues.

sci.agriculture discusses the science of farming but is also a useful resource for serious gardeners.

sci.bio.botany is the place I go if I have a gardening question that is quite scientific or complex in nature or just to learn tons of interesting things about the plant world. This is an excellent place for those who love botany or are interested in the scientific aspects of plants. Recent discussions have included the study of botany in terms of geometric forms, restoring and creating ecosystems, and misting propagation.

Software problems

Obviously, if you are finding gardening information online, you are using a computer and software. There are news groups for all the major software packages. These are excellent places to visit, especially if you are having software problems.

One day I had a problem with WordPerfect, and even though I still had free technical support, it was late and I would have had to pay for a long distance phone call. I remembered seeing a WordPerfect user group, so I went onto the Net and quickly found it. I was surprised that numerous other people were having the same problem and the solution was posted. I had my answer in less than a minute. When there is no information posted on my problem, I post a question and then go about my business. The traffic is heavy on some of the news groups and often I have my answer in less than an hour.

Even if you are not having problems, the software news groups are a wise place to check from time to time. Discussions cover new releases, add on products, tricks to make programs more efficient, and often commentary and dialogue from the developers themselves. Information is also available on where to download drivers or other products or information that can make the program perform better.

WWW garden pages

Using my web browser, Netscape, I hit the "search button" and chose Web Crawler as my search engine. I typed in the word "gardening" and was presented with over 800 links to pages that were either on gardening or had a mention of gardening. Obviously, I could have done a more specific search such as for the word "peppers," "composting," "tomatoes," or any other better defined gardening topic. I once made the mistake of doing a search for "apple" forgetting it was a major computer make so I have learned to define my searches better. When I find a site I like, I "Bookmark" it. This way I need only look at my bookmark menu and point and click on the site to find it. This means I don't have to redo a search for a particular or favorite site.

When I want to look for new gardening web sites, I usually will start with a search using one of the many search engines. Many of the sites that are found usually contain links to other sites. Some of the sites can be quite extensive, especially if it belongs to a university or large organization such as the Brooklyn Botanical Gardens.

With so many sites it is hard to choose a favorite so I will give an example of a few I just used and have used before.

Books that Work makes gardening software (3D Landscape) and has a Gardening Web Directory Page **http://gardening.com/urls/toc.html**

It has links to many of the most popular gardening sites, such as Botanical Gardens, where you can take a visual tour and view plant material and general gardening sites. It also has links to insect and entomology sites to help you identify insect pests, as well as links to botany, landscape, environment, and gardening catalogs and supply pages.

The Internet Gardening site **http://learning.lib.vt.edu/garden.html** also contains a number of links, including the Royal Botanical Gardens at Kew in Australia and the University of Delaware Botanical Gardens. In the colder winter months, I really do like taking the tour of botanical gardens from the warm comfort of my computer.

http://garden.burpee.com/ is the address of Burpee Seeds. More and more seed companies are putting their wares on the net. Burpee's site features their new blue rose, blue corn, and blue poppy. It sure beats filling out a card and mailing it by snail mail and having to wait several weeks for your seed catalogs. In addition to the seed catalogs, other garden related companies such as Troybuilt, which sells tiller, are also going online.

Another good place to start is the Yahoo index of gardening sites **http://www.yahoo.com/Recreation/ Home_and_Garden/Gardening/** It is probably the most thorough gardening directory on the World Wide Web.

This last week, I used several WWW sites. This included The USDA-ARS Pesticide Database **http://www.arsusda.gov/SRLHome.**

html since I had some questions about how fast certain pesticides break down. This site serves pesticide companies, farmers, environmentalists, gardeners, and other interested parties. The database covers hundreds of pesticides including more than 95% of the most popular ones. For each pesticide, the database describes up to 16 chemical, physical, and biological features that influence its breakdown rate and likelihood of entering surface or groundwater. The data is designed to be utilized for use in crop and soil computer models, which account for soil, temperature, and other local factors that affect pesticides.

Another interesting site for starting out is the GrowRoom **http://a1.com/growroom/**. The factors that make the GrowRoom such a good starting point is that it has some very useful links. A new addition to the GrowRoom is a list of hydroponic suppliers worldwide, currently about 200. There are also links to others, and a place where frequently asked questions are answered. GrowRoom's website continues to grow and will soon contain book reviews and product critiques of the commonly available hobby hydroponic units as well as indoor lighting, light moving devices, and hydroponic plant nutrients.

Gardening magazines

Many gardening magazines are going on the net, offering samples of their articles as well as links to other sites. The Growing Edge Magazine deals with hydroponics and issues for advanced gardeners **http://www.teleport.com/~tomalex/** Don't forget that you can also visit *Backwoods Home Magazine* **http://www.snowcrest.net /backwood/** and don't forget to bookmark it as it grows to include more links, articles, and features.

The University of Southern California has a site that heralds the type of sites we may see in the future. It is called CyberEden and allows any-

one, (providing they register) to operate a computerized robot arm from their home computer in order to care for a small garden.

The project is co-directed by the USC school of engineering, and the project has already won a prize for excellence at a recent computer exhibition. The address to the site is **http://www.usc.edu/dept/garden/**

Before I visited the site I had wrongly anticipated a scene out of the Jetson's. When I arrived I found myself at the controls of a robot arm that is anchored in the middle of a large circular planting box.

The procedure to participate in the TeleGarden is to first fill out an e-mail application so that you can be a member of the TeleGarden cooperative. After joining, you can plant seeds and then water them regularly. One of the interesting things about this technology and social experiment is that nothing stops one member from planting in the same space as another, or even crushing a plant they don't like. One of the objectives of this site is to slow down Internet surfers with short attention spans and provide a place where they can become more involved.

Asking which garden sites to go to is sort of like asking for a good place to go camping in North America. The answers are vast, and they vary depending on preferences. You can also use Archie and other software (included in most Internet Suite software packages or available as freeware or shareware over the Net) to access almost 10,000 universities. Many of them have extensive horticultural information including the latest research and information on how to grow commercial crops. Cornell University is a favorite of mine, especially for fruit growing information.

The more you can focus on a particular piece of information, the more effective your searches will be. When you find information that you like, you can save it to a file and then read it offline to help keep your connect charges down.

Eventually, you can build your own Bookmarks directory of sites that support the type of gardening you do. The Internet has had a great influence on the types of crops I grow and how I grow them. It has become a quick reference encyclopedia, a learning tool, entertainment, and, of course, a place to visit with like-minded individuals.

(Questions, comments, and information of interest to *Backwoods Home* readers can be sent via the Internet to Martin Waterman at waterman@nbnet.nb.ca, or to other editors of *Backwoods Home Magazine* at backwood@snowcrest. net. *BHM*'s Internet address on the World Wide Web is http://www.snowcrest.net/ backwood/index.html.) Δ

A BHM Writer's Profile: John Silveira

No one at BHM knows what Silveira does but he may be responsible for the Y2K crisis. In his younger days, he served as the village idiot in a number of New England towns until, by law, those positions were made elected offices. He lists his accomplishments as almost graduating from high school, his extensive collection of autographed pictures from Elvis Presley impersonators, and his fourth-place finish in a Gary Coleman look-alike contest. John would like to hear from desperate women with low self-esteem who would think he was a good catch.

When John grows up he wants to be a superhero.

Eating crow isn't that bad

By Bill Palmroth

To most of us, the term "eating crow" has to do with someone being forced to retract an emphatic statement or admit that he or she is wrong. Yet crows have been eaten, literally, by a surprising number of people around the world.

In England, young crows are considered a great delicacy. In France and Germany, crows are shot at any age, young or old, and used to put in vegetable stew. They are also used in bouillon soup.

In North America, however, most of us think of the crow as a pest, and it is rarely eaten. That's unfortunate because, when properly prepared, crows are very good to eat. Young crows have a very tender and mild meat much like squab, young pigeon, or woodcock, and it is every bit as good.

Check your state's game laws before hunting crows because in some sections of the country these birds are protected by law.

Here are a few suggestions on the proper preparation of crows for the table:

The older birds should always be skinned instead of plucked. This is much easier if the feathers are not taken off. Only the meat of the breast and legs should be used. Young birds may be roasted like squab but the use of butter or slabs of bacon is absolutely necessary as crow is inclined to be quite dry.

Crow broth

The breast and legs should be browned a little in butter and then boiled with small quantities of celery until tender. Use water in normal proportions according to the quantity of broth desired and the available amount of meat.

Sandwich spread

This mixture is worth trying. The boiled meat should be carefully inspected and all bones removed. It should then be run through a meat chopper. To the well-minced meat add small quantities of mustard, finely chopped onion, salt, pepper, and a bit of mayonnaise. A dash or two of paprika will add to the mixture, and it may be kept for a reasonable length of time in the refrigerator.

Crow stew

Brown some large onions in bacon fat at the rate of one large onion to the average bird and add the meat, salt, and pepper to taste. Smother for a few moments in the onions and add enough water to cover the meat. Let it simmer over low beat until tender and stir in some sour cream mixed with a teaspoonful of flour. Your other favorite ingredients for stew can then be added.

To prepare crows similar to squab, clean them thoroughly, rub with salt and pepper, and add a bit of lemon juice. Some cooks have been known to add some finely-crushed juniper berries in place of the lemon juice. You may also want to stuff the young birds with whole mushrooms.

Wrap the bird completely in strips of bacon, tie together, and boil or roast like squab. The breast of crow squab may also be dipped in egg and bread crumbs and fried like cutlets.

If you try these recipes and don't agree that the birds are really quite delicious, I'll be the one eating crow.

Protect those young trees from frost and vermin

By Tom R. Kovach

Young trees that are only several years old have thin bark and are easily damaged. They need protection, especially in the winter months.

One of the problems is sunscald, which occurs when temperatures are above freezing in the daylight hours, but drop to freezing temperatures at night. This sudden change in temperature kills cells in the bark, causing afflicted areas to die and peel off during the next growing season. To prevent this from happening the trunks should be wrapped with material which either shades the trunk or reflects the sun to prevent excessive warming. You can use aluminum foil, waterproof tree wrap, or burlap.

Another problem for young trees are nibbling animals such as rabbits and mice. Dave DeCock, a County horticulturist in Fargo, North Dakota, says that fruit trees are usually the first trees attacked by rabbits. And if a tree gets eaten off below the graft, it will usually die.

Rabbit and field mice damage can be avoided or at least reduced by wrapping the tree trunks same as you would for sunscald. Or you can spray or paint on common repellents. These are available at garden stores.

You can make your own repellent by mixing 85 percent raw linseed oil, 5 percent household detergent, and 10 percent water. Apply with a small sprayer or with a paint brush. You should reapply after heavy snow melts but that should not be a problem during the winter.

You can also fence each tree by using a cylinder of 1/2-inch mesh fencing. This will deter rabbits, says DeCock, but a finer mesh fencing or a solid retainer is needed to repel the field mice. Δ

Don't have a cow! (Get a steer instead.)

By Tanya Kelley

Shortly after we moved to our farm and began our struggle for self sufficiency, we had made considerable progress. The chickens were laying plenty of eggs, our first pig was back from the butcher, and the garden had provided us with more than enough produce. The eating was definitely good, but we still had strong hankerings for beef. Unfortunately, the price of beef feeder calves was well out of reach of our limited finances.

When a friend mentioned that Jersey calves were selling for veal at the auction for around $20, the wheels started turning. Why couldn't we raise a Jersey for beef? A little research was in order. I soon discovered that Jerseys were not considered practical to raise for beef because they did not get as big as the beef breeds. That seemed to be the only complaint. So, despite the snickers, long looks, and

flat-out "It'll taste terrible" comments of some "experts," we decided to take the plunge.

The results were well worth the effort for anyone. If you are considering raising your own dairy beef, here are a few of the lessons I learned. I think you'll be pleased with the results.

Buying a calf

Buying a healthy bull calf can be tricky. Fortunately, we had a friend who went and purchased our first one for us. When she presented me with an emaciated-looking (to my eye), wobbly calf, I thought she was crazy. Our vet reassured me that calves just come that way. In fact, day-old calves that look well-fed have often been *over*fed. Overfeeding can cause *scours*, which is often fatal.

There are several things to look for. Check for scours (diarrhea). Manure should be ploppy, runny, and brown.

If it is a yucky yellow and watery, steer clear of that calf. If the calf has scours, his legs and tail will probably be a mess.

The umbilical cord should not be swollen, infected, or hard, and there should be no ruptures. The calf should breathe clearly, with no rattles, and there should be no green or white discharge. A clear, slimy coating of the nose is typical. Shriveled-looking ears and tail indicate the calf is suffering from a vitamin deficiency. The feet should seem sturdy. The calf should have bright eyes and seem perky. And don't let the wobbly walk fool you—if he gets loose, he can run faster than you or me. Trust me.

It's a good idea to check with the locals about the reputation of nearby auctions and breeders. Occasionally you can get source recommendations from your vet, extension agent, or feed dealer. Your vet will also be able to advise you of any problems common to your region, such as selenium deficiencies.

Bringing baby home

When you get your calf home, it is a good idea to give a shot of penicillin and vitamins if the calf has had no colostrum. Dip both the navel and hooves in a 7% iodine solution to toughen them and prevent infection. Your vet can recommend any other precautions you might need to take.

We buy calves in the spring, only because it is more pleasant weather for bottle feeding. We stack bales of hay in a corner of the barn to make a cozy temporary stall. It cuts down the drafts and lets us keep a closer eye on them for the first week or so. Calves can take cold, but they must be kept dry and out of drafts. We bed them in deep straw. You can also use sawdust, but make sure it's not dusty. We don't

This steer has the smooth hips and filled-out brisket (chest) that show he's gotten his growth.

*This day-old calf looks pretty skinny, but that's normal in
a healthy calf. With proper care, he'll gain weight quickly.*

put calves together if they're more than six weeks apart in age.

Feed a good quality calf milk replacer with a 40 to 60% fat content. Get a bottle and some calf nipples, available at your feed store. We usually start our calves out with three pints of warm water or electrolytes for the first 12 hours and give half-strength milk replacer for the next two feedings. We feed three times a day for four days and then twice a day, three pints, morning and night. Calves usually know how to eat, and can drain a bottle in nothing flat. The sucking reflex is strong, and so is the urge to butt the bottle. When they are nursing on a cow, that butting stimulates the milk to let down. When they butt on the bottle, it can stimulate you to drop the bottle, or even get whacked with it.

When the bottle is empty, they still want some more. No matter how pathetic they seem, don't feed them more or let them suck on an empty bottle. Let them suck on your fingers if it will relieve any guilt, and remember that overfeeding can cause scours. You can gradually increase the milk to four to six pints, starting on the eleventh day.

Clean the bottles and nipples with hot, soapy water. Rinse well and turn upside down to dry. As an extra precaution, I rinse the bottles with bleach and water every few days. Again, rinse well.

At four days, introduce grain. It may take several tries, but they do catch on. From that point on, the calf should have free access to a calf starter or grain mixture with a supplement. Check with local feed manufacturers to find the best quality and value. We have had considerable success with Moorman's feed supplements mixed with grain we buy from a local farmer. We begin with one part corn, one part oats, and one part Moorman's Mintrate for Cattle.

Leading and "steering"

Train the calf to a lead . . . while he still weighs less than you. Start with a calf halter and two people to help (one to pull and one to push). Keep a steady tension on the line until the calf steps (or is gently pushed) forward.

Let the relief from the tension be the "reward." Keep repeating until the calf steps forward willingly.

Continue leading on a regular basis. Don't wait until the day you have to take your steer to the vet unexpectedly, or he gets loose and you have to take him home. An ill-mannered, gallumphing, 800-pound steer will go pretty much where he pleases. With or without you.

Peppermint candies given as treats occasionally can be helpful. The first time, you may have to put it in the steer's mouth. After that, you can just crackle the plastic wrapper and he will follow you anywhere. That crackling noise can be the deciding factor when you are 10 feet away from a loose steer that is contemplating a gallop through your neighbor's flower garden.

Dehorning and castration

You might decide to forgo the dehorning, but one whack with a grown steer's head will probably cause some serious regrets. Steers play rough, and they have no idea how fragile people can be.

Castration is a must. If the steer is not castrated, the hormones will taint the meat. There are banding kits, or you can have the vet band or cut them. We have used both methods and definitely prefer banding. While slower, it seems to be relatively pain-free, and it doesn't attract flies. You can have the vet come out, or save the cost of a farm call by packing your 70-pound calf into a small pickup or even into some cars. (Put down plastic!)

At four weeks (depending on the weather), we usually move our calves to an outside pen with a three-sided 12- by 12-foot run-in—plenty of room for two calves. The pen itself is 25 by 50 feet, made of four-foot woven wire. Unfortunately, we learned early on that steers can do a lot of damage to our neighbor's yard. Sturdy fence and gates are definitely in order. Good neighbors are also a plus.

You can keep your calf in open pasture, but the quality of the meat will be lower, and so will the weight gain. The more grass the calf eats, the less corn he will eat, and that results in a lower weight gain.

You can wean the calf off the bottle and get him drinking from a bucket. To do this, dip your fingers in the milk and hold them just above the milk. When the calf starts sucking, gradually lower your hand down below the surface of the milk. After considerable snorting and choking, most calves will allow you to remove your fingers. I usually have to repeat finger feeding several times. I have come to the conclusion that, while bottle feeding may be messy, bucket feeding is more time consuming and results in calves that never really seem to lose the desire to suck on everything.

Depending on how well the calf is doing and how much grain he is consuming, you can wean at about six weeks. Usually at this time, the calf will be eating 1½ pounds of grain a day. Take him off the milk gradually by diluting it and offering him plenty of water with a little milk replacer mixed in. As the calf starts drinking the water and eating more grain, cut back on bottle feedings. It takes a week, but most calves make the transition quite smoothly. However, we did have one calf that refused to eat grain and glutted himself on the milk water. It was difficult, but at eight weeks old, we finally eliminated all milk replacer and made him go cold turkey. Within 24 hours, he got the picture.

Generally, we don't feed our calves a feed supplement with antibiotics. According to most manufacturers, feeds with antibiotics will result in a faster weight gain, but we decided we didn't want to unnecessarily bombard our animals or our food with antibiotics. The only other medication we use is a wormer at four months. Again, consult your vet for recommendations.

At two months, gradually change feed proportions to one pound mintrate per calf, no oats, and all the corn they can eat. They get one flake of hay a day. The roughage helps them digest better, resulting in faster weight gain.

We have a large wooden feed bin that allows us to dump up to 150 pounds of corn in at a time. We top dress the corn each day with mintrate. In addition to unlimited grain, keep plenty of water and a large mineral salt block available at all times.

Any changes in feeding must be gradual. Sudden changes to grass, different brands or amounts of feed, or large amounts of garden waste or table scraps can cause illness or diarrhea.

Do not feed yard clippings. Innocent-looking plants can be deadly. My friend's Jersey nibbled on some yew and was dead within the hour. Apparently yews contain arsenic.

Cleanup

Our calves are usually in an outside pen which requires only a rare cleaning. When winter really hits, we move the steers into the barn. On good weather days, they go in the pen for the day and into the barn for the night. The worst stall cleaning I have had to do takes me about 15 minutes a day and results in one wheelbarrow load of garden fertilizer. I pick out the wet and dirty spots and add two or three flakes of straw. We use a bale or a bale and a half of straw a week for two calves for about 16 weeks of winter.

Keeping records

It's a good idea to keep a record book of your feed purchases, vet expenses, animal costs, weight gains, and other data. Tracking spending can show you where there is room for improvement, and best of all, you can feed your friends the best steak they ever ate, and then gloat about the ridiculously low cost.

Weigh the calf by picking him up and standing on bathroom scales. Then subtract your weight to get the calf's weight. Obviously, you won't be able to weigh the calf by this method for long. You can take your steer to a local scale to track weight

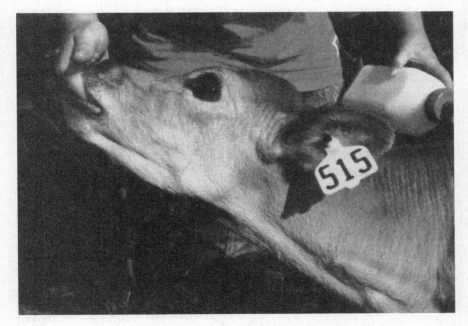

He's finished his meal of milk, but he still wants to do some sucking, so he's making do with fingers for a while.

gain, but there is a simpler (though less accurate) way to track progress.

Many feed stores and vets will give measuring tapes that measure weight by measuring "heart girth" (around the steer, just behind the front legs). You can track progress with these, but the weight may not be accurate. Our first steer weighed 70 pounds less at the butcher's than the tape indicated.

Tracking our first calf showed us that we finished him off with an average weight gain of 1.8 pounds per day, at a total cost of less than 85¢ a pound. He weighed 879 pounds at butchering. Our take-home beef was 468 pounds. Our techniques have improved, and our current steer appears to be gaining 2.1 pounds a day. Our cost will probably finish out at about 90¢ a pound, due to increased grain prices. The cost includes the purchase of the calf, feed, vet expenses, straw, and butchering. Try to find hamburger at 90¢ a pound . . . let alone steak.

Finishing and butchering

Improvements in our procedures have enabled us to bring our current steer to be finished in about 13 months. Our first steer took 16 months.

Knowing when your steer is finished can require some educated guessing. When your tape is registering a weight between 900 and 1000 pounds, you're probably right there.

Check that the brisket (the chest) is no longer just loose folds of skin, but is filled out. Ribs should be well covered and the hip points should be smooth and not protruding. At that point, you *can* continue feeding him to a higher weight gain, but the gain will be of a higher ratio of fat to meat, so it's not cost-effective.

Not all butchers are the same, so it's a good idea to get references. Find out costs, custom butchering procedures, options for packaging, smoking, deboning, and labeling procedures—both for customer identification of

meat and for the different cuts. Find out how far in advance you must arrange the butchering date. Some butchers offer pickup or can refer you to someone to pick up your steer.

Custom butchering can make the biggest difference between your beef and commercial beef. Commercial beef is often butchered and then placed in heat-shrink plastic bags where it can be held up to 30 days before being sold. You can have your beef hung for one to two weeks to allow the fiber of the meat to break down, resulting in a very tender meat. You can also choose the fat content of your hamburger.

Most butchers are happy to explain the different cuts and other options. We usually take all the meat, even cuts we don't use, such as the brain. We give our neighbor any cuts we don't use, as well as several prime cuts. It helps make up for some of the bald spots in her yard. We have the bone scraps cut for the dog, and we bring the beef fat home for making soap. The one thing most butchers don't give back is the hide. That is included as part of the cost of butchering.

A home freezer may be large enough to store your meat, but renting a local locker may be a better choice. There are no worries about freezer failure, and you still have room for your frozen vegetables. We rent a locker for $5 a month at a local grocery store. Once a month, I pick up a few weeks' worth of meat and store that in the freezer at home. That has eliminated the temptation to eat all the steaks first and the liver last. We pick up a balanced order and we don't go back until we're out.

The guilt trip

"Look at those sad eyes. How can you stand to eat him?" "Don't your kids cry?" These are things we hear from people. At first, we did feel a twinge of guilt. Then I realized that if we hadn't bought the calves, they

would have been used as veal. We name them, we take good care of them, and then they fulfill their purpose in life. It may seem harsh, but if people weren't eating beef, there wouldn't be many cattle around. They don't make great house pets.

Just in case I feel the empty-stall syndrome, I buy my new baby calf a few days before the older one leaves. By the time he goes, he is big, smelly, and rough, and I'm ready for him to leave.

Food for thought

Self sufficiency aside, there are other advantages to raising our own beef. We found that beef is beef, no matter what the size or breed. In fact, the smaller size is an advantage—one steer provides enough beef for our family for one year. We don't have an extra side of beef that we must sell.

More benefits: Our beef was fed with no drugs or steroids. He was not pasture fed, then finished with corn, as is commercial beef. From the beginning, he was only free-fed corn, which resulted in a faster growth rate. That in turn allowed us to butcher at an earlier age, resulting in the most tender beef we have ever tasted.

One word of warning: You might be tempted to invite friends to dinner to show off your delicious bounty. If you do, be prepared for a lot of unexpected dinner guests. Home-grown beef is just too tempting to resist. Δ

Try these organic controls for garden pests

By Tom R. Kovach

More and more gardeners are using organic methods to control garden pests. This is because insecticides, fungicides, and herbicides can do more harm than good.

For controlling **spider mites, strong water sprays** from the garden hose will do the trick. Put a nozzle on the hose and spray every few days. This will work on your evergreens, which are often beset by mites in hot, dry weather. It will also work for roses and a number of other shrubs and plants.

There are a number of ways to control **slugs**. You can just **pick them and drop them into a can of soapy water**. A good time to accomplish this is **after dark** with a flashlight. That's when they're out. **Beer** also works. Just sink some saucers of beer into the earth. When they fill up with drowned slugs, renew the beer. Also, you can scatter **ashes** around plants, a few inches from the stems. This works well for tomato plants. Do it early in the season, and when the band of ashes gets too smooth, scatter more ashes. This also discourages **root maggots**.

Here is an old U.S. government list with some homemade concoctions for controlling garden pests organically:

For **aphids and mites**, use a **spray made of soap and water**.

Use **garlic oil spray** to fight **onion flies, aphids and thrips**. Onion and chive solutions can also be used.

Mineral oil applied to corn silk with an eye dropper eliminates **corn earworms**. Wait until silks have turned brown before applying.

You can kill **slugs and snails** by sprinkling them with **table salt**.

For **cabbage maggots**, use **hot pepper, salt, and sour milk sprays**.

Coriander and anise oil emulsifiers help control **mites and aphids**.

Sticky bands around tree trunks will trap **tent caterpillars** and keep **cankerworms** from crawling onto the leaves of the plant.

To keep **leafhoppers** away, encase your plants in **cheese cloth or muslin** frames.

Cut short **cutworms** by placing **paper or tin can collars** around plant stems and forcing them firmly into the soil.

Aluminum foil strips placed between rows will keep **insects** out of your vegetable gardens.

Remove and burn affected plant parts to keep an insect infestation from spreading.

If a lily plant suddenly turns brown, you should **immediately remove it** from your flower bed. The browning is a sign of root rot or other diseases that can easily spread to your other lilies.

To keep **aphids** away from your roses, place a **garlic** clove on the ground next to the rose.

Some of these methods work better than others. It just takes a little experimentation. But it beats having to use chemical means of control. Δ

A BHM Writer's Profile: Olivia Miller

Olivia Miller is proud to be from rural Alabama and, as a freelance writer, enjoys writing for agricultural publications. She's published in <u>Horse Women</u>, <u>Progressive Farmer</u>, <u>Successful Farming</u>, <u>Turkey Call</u>, <u>Forest Farmer</u>, and <u>Catfish Pond Harvest</u> to name a few. Olivia is an adjunct professor at the University of Memphis, and is married with three children.

A BHM Writer's Profile: Darlene Polachic

Darlene Polachic is a freelance writer from Saskatoon, Saskatchewan. Besides writing, she enjoys gardening and needlework.

Stop bugs Nature's way

By Maurcia DeLean

First it hit the green beans. Next the carrots, and before long even the lettuce and beets showed signs of an insect invasion. On quiet evenings I was sure I could hear the munching sounds of bugs feasting on my garden.

That's what *almost* sent me scurrying to the local garden supply shop for a load of insecticide. But I didn't. And you don't have to either—if you opt to follow the advice of old-time bug-proofers.

Yesterday's farmers didn't use poison to stop bugs. They didn't have any. Instead, they saved their crops from becoming the "salad de jour" to the local insect population by giving Nature a helping hand at building its own resistance.

Before beginning any type of pest control, it's a good idea to check to see if the insects eating your plantings are still around. Most are hit and run eaters, doing most of their damage before pupating. To check for lingering pests, look at the leaves on your plants. Are the new leaves undamaged? Or are the chewed edges brown and dry? Chances are the insects you most have to worry about are gone. If, however, the leaves have fresh cuts, excreting sap, your garden is still at risk.

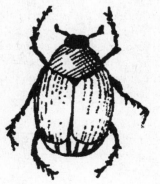

Japanese beetle

There are several safe, practical, and inexpensive ways to stop bugs from ruining your garden splendor.

Prevention

The first, of course, is prevention. Something as easy as **cultivating the soil prior to planting** in early spring exposes burrowed eggs and larvae to the local birds, cutting down on the season's insects. **Scraping trees of**

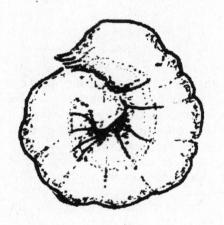

Cutworm

egg masses, too, can help leave your garden insect-free.

Beneficial insects

If, however, you need help curbing a current problem, you may need to encourage natural resistance by attracting beneficial insects to your garden. **Predators and parasites** are

Predatory wasp

good for controlling the insect population in gardens, because they feast on other insects, not your plants.

For example, to control **aphids, gypsy moths, mealybugs**, and **Mexican bean beetles**, introduce a **parasitic wasp** to your garden.

Spined soldier bugs get rid of **Colorado potato beetles**, while **mites** handle **fungus gnats** quite well.

Beneficial bugs can be purchased at garden stores or through a number of catalogs.

Companion planting

Companion planting, too, can help to stave off an insect invasion. For a list of companion plants, see the box in this article.

Barriers

Using barriers to protect your plants is simple and effective. **Floating covers** are lengths of synthetic fabric draped over the top of your plants. They offer excellent protection for young seedlings.

Top five garden pests

Pest	Host
Aphids	Fruits, vegetables, flowers
Caterpillars	Fruits, vegetables, shade trees
Colorado potato beetle	Potatoes, tomatoes, eggplant
Cutworms	Early seedlings
Japanese beetle	Small fruit, vegetables

Companion planting

helps control the insect population by attracting predators

Companion plant	Where to grow	Controls
Dandelion	Border	Potato beetles
Catnip	Border	Aphids, fleas, beetles
Marigolds	Interplant	Root nematodes, aphids, beetles
Southernwood	Border	Moths, beetles
White clover	Interplant	Cabbage root flies

Collars protect against most species of **cutworm,** but not climbing ones. Cutworm collars are stiff cardboard or plastic cylinders that encircle the plant stems at ground level.

To get rid of **gypsy moths** and non-flying bugs, try **tree bands.** These barriers are placed around the trunks of trees to prevent bugs from climbing and attaching their larvae to the trunk.

As you can see, there are a number of barriers and traps available to keep insects at bay. Check your local gardening supplier to find the method best for you.

Organic sprays

If it's a fast and effective cure you seek to thwart bugs, try one or more of the following homemade organic recipes to chase away even the hungriest chewers:

• **Hot pepper spray:** Mix ¹/₂ cup ground hot pepper with 2 cups water. Strain and spray on plants.
• **Garlic oil:** Finely chop 15 cloves of garlic. Soak in one pint of mineral oil for 24 hours. Use as a spray.
• **Buttermilk/wheat flour mix:** Mix one pound of wheat flour and ¹/₂ pt. of buttermilk, add six gallons of water. Spray.
• **Molasses mixture:** To kill just about anything, spray molasses, diluted in 50 parts water, on your plants.

Since more than four out of every five species in the animal kingdom are insects, it's no wonder we gardeners feel outnumbered at times . . . we are! But that doesn't mean we have to resort to using insecticides that poison our plants along with the bugs. Try out some of these old fashioned remedies instead. And enjoy a bug-free season. Δ

Combat aphids by *planting* garlic

By Barbara Fallick

Garlic is extolled for many virtues, but many people find the odor repulsive. Aphids also find garlic repulsive— and that's good.

Every spring, my cherry trees become infested with aphids. Leaves curl up and are dotted with the black aphid bodies. The leaves are sticky to the touch. Garlic is a simple and thorough remedy to this problem.

Purchase ordinary garlic bulbs from the grocery store. I plant mine in the fall with my other bulbs. *Organic Plant Protection* by Rodale Press says to plant them early in the spring. Evidently, either time will work. Split the garlic bulb into cloves and plant each clove individually around the base of the tree about five inches from the base and five inches from each other. Plant them approximately two inches deep.

The garlic plant itself does not give off an odor, nor does it affect the flavor of the fruit. In my climate of hard winters, my garlic plants do not reproduce themselves the following year, so I have to replant every year. In some climates, they will reproduce every year. Home-grown garlic has a better-mannered taste than the store variety, and is therefore a boon to medicinal and culinary uses.

Though garlic is the most potent, other plants which also work as aphid repellents are chives and other alliums, pennyroyal, spearmint, southernwood, tansy, coriander, anise, nasturtium, and petunia.

Now, can anyone tell me what to do about the white worms that get into the cherries? My trees are very tall, and even organic spraying is not a viable option. Δ

From humble stew to curried root soup, root vegetables are an overlooked delight

By Richard Blunt

A few days before Christmas my mother called wanting to know what time I planned to pick her up Christmas day. I reminded her that I planned to pick her up Christmas eve. Then she asked me what we were having for Christmas dinner and I recited the menu. She said, "That sounds delicious, but aren't you forgetting something?"

Up to this point I'd been happy with the menu, but her question made me hesitate. I read the list again. "I don't think so."

"You forgot the root vegetables," she said. "Richard, Christmas dinner is a special meal. Even though you and I were not rich, we always ate well during the holidays because of the wonderful fresh turnips, parsnips, rutabagas, Jerusalem artichokes, and other root vegetables the neighbors shared with us from their gardens every winter. When you got married I gave you copies of your favorite winter vegetable recipes. Why don't you pick one of those. It doesn't matter which one. They're all good."

I told her that it sounded great to me, and after we hung up I started digging through my files for the recipes. After an hour, I found an old dusty manila envelope with the following note hand written on the front. "These recipes were given to me by your grandmother when I got married. You and I have enjoyed the magic of these recipes for many years. I hope that you will share with your new wife the tradition of simple but elegant foods that have been so much a part of our family tradition. Love, Mom."

I opened the envelope and found recipes with names that I had completely forgotten about: Yankee pork and roots, maple baked rutabaga, southern yam pie, curried root soup, Jerusalem artichoke bisque, and humble stew. It rekindled memories of tastes and textures almost forgotten. All of these recipes called for a variety of vegetables that thrive in cool moist climates of the Northeast where I grew up.

After reading a few, I got excited. I sat at my kitchen table and felt a funny kind of enthusiasm as I drew up a shopping list. My daughter, Sarah, was also getting excited as she watched me, even though she didn't know what was going on.

"Come on," I said when I'd finished my list. She followed me out to the car and we headed for the best local farm stand in the Farmington Valley, "Pickin' Patch," where I assumed everything I needed would be on the shelf. In the back of my mind, however, I was a little worried that the holiday shopping rush would have depleted the supplies

before I got there, so on our way I stopped off at a couple of supermarkets just to see what they had.

It was to my surprise and disappointment that all I found in these stores were some waxed rutabagas, a few withered bunches of red beets, and some parsnips that had not been cold-stored properly so they had a flat, starchy taste.

I guess this shouldn't have been a surprise because most would-be fresh vegetables available in the northeastern markets during the winter months are the globe-trotting, ethylene-stimulated varieties that are the product of someone else's summer. We eat tomatoes from Mexico that are picked green and never really ripen, storage grapes from South America that fall off the stem when you pick them up, and deep red strawberries from New Zealand that have more color than taste but are a temptation to any shopper. And I will admit that I, like most other people, am not willing to go without lemons, oranges, melons, and bananas at any time of year, so I purchase this ersatz-ripened fruit myself.

Still, in spite of all these techno-ripened fruits and vegetables, there are some vegetables, grown right here in the Northeast, that we ignore. They are vegetables that ripen in summer but improve in flavor and texture with proper storage, making them worth serving in winter. Irish potatoes, sweet potatoes, onions, and winter squash are good examples.

I had high hopes that I would find some of these at the Pickin' Patch. But, when I finally arrived there, my disappointment deepened. I found no root vegetables at all. Sarah sensed my mood and the excitement faded from her face. I asked the owners if and when they would be restocking. They told me most root vegetables don't sell, so they stopped planting them several years ago.

Then I went to see Randy Morse, a respected farmer who operates a popular farm stand in Southbridge, Massachusetts. I asked him why many root vegetables were so hard to find. What Randy said went something like this:

Many folks think of root vegetables such as salsify, Jerusalem artichokes, celeriac (or celery root), and parsnips as cheap produce. Growing vegetables for cold weather harvest takes skill, patience, and a lot more land than the finished crop can support with sales. Plus, cold weather harvesting is hard, dirty work.

Don't get me wrong, buying vegetables that are grown and harvested locally is the most economical and nutritionally sound way to go. But that kind of quality will never be available at bargain basement prices. Popular, high yield vegetables like sweet corn, squash, and pumpkins offer the local consumer reduced prices because local farmers sell a lot of these crops.

Most of my customers are only familiar with the well known root vegetables like carrots, potatoes, and onions. So that's what we stock. It's a shame, but I would have a hard time convincing many of my customers that a parsnip exposed to a moderate frost is as sweet and tasty as a young early summer carrot, and it's a more versatile vegetable in the kitchen.

Good words, Randy. I agree.

I had to travel all the way up to the wholesale market in Haymarket Square, outside historic Faniel Hall in Boston, to find what I wanted. So given all the trouble I went to, let's put them to use and try a few root vegetable recipes.

The first recipe produces one of my favorite flavor and texture combinations. It combines a broad spectrum of balanced vegetable flavors in a mixture that requires very little herb or spice enhancement. To enhance this mixture too much would mask the delicate flavor balance of the vegetables. This version does not contain any meat, but I have used this vegetable mix as a base and added lamb, pork, or beef and a little more stock to make a real appetite pleasing

winter stew. Serve any version of this stew with fresh corn bread or hot biscuits.

Humble stew

Ingredients

1 cup dried red beans
6 cups plus 8 cups of cold water
3 cups fresh beef, chicken, or vegetable stock
1/2 cup dry red wine
8 Tbsp margarine or butter (I prefer butter in this recipe)
8 oz onion, peeled and diced medium
4 oz celeriac, coarsely grated
4 cloves fresh garlic, peeled and minced
4 Tbsp flour
4 medium carrots, peeled and cut into 1/2 inch pieces
4 small to medium fresh beets (without greens), peeled and cut into 1/2 inch chunks
1/2 lb peeled rutabaga cut into 1/2 inch pieces
4 medium parsnips, peeled and cut into 1/2 inch pieces
1 tsp dried basil leaf
1/2 tsp dried oregano leaf
kosher salt to taste
freshly ground black pepper to taste
1/4 tsp cayenne pepper (more or less according to taste)
2 cups canned whole plum tomatoes (with the juice), diced medium

Method

1. Soak the beans in the six cups of cold water for at least four hours. Drain and rinse beans, discarding the soaking water. In a large sauce pot combine the beans with eight cups of fresh water and bring to a boil. Reduce the heat and allow the beans to cook slowly for about 45 minutes. Rinse the partially cooked beans in cold water to cool, drain and set aside.

2. Combine the stock with the wine and heat almost to the boiling point over a medium heat.

3. Melt the butter in a large sauce pot, and add the onion, celeriac, and garlic and saute them for about two minutes or until the onion becomes translucent. Stir in the flour and continue cooking the mixture over a low heat for another two minutes. Add the hot stock to this roux while stirring with a wire whisk. Cook over a medium heat until the sauce thickens.

4. Add the remaining vegetables, beans, basil, oregano, salt, black pepper, cayenne pepper, and plum tomatoes. If you have a large earthenware casserole, transfer the vegetables into the casserole, cover and place in a 350 degree oven for 45 minutes to an hour. Or simply cover the sauce pot, reduce the heat to low, and cook the vegetables on top of the stove about 45 minutes, or until everything is tender.

If you want to experience a great one dish meal, cook some of your favorite rice or noodles and serve these vegetables on top with some grated cheese.

Curried root soup

This is a real departure from the delicate pureed soups that are usually made with root vegetable combinations. It has a full taste, rounded off with a slight tingling nip from the addition of several spices that make up a mild but noticeable curry mixture. This is also a soup that improves in flavor when allowed to rest in the refrigerator overnight.

Ingredients

3 medium beets (separate the greens and save), peeled and diced medium
1 lb carrots, peeled and diced medium
8 oz parsnip, peeled and diced medium
1 lb rutabaga, peeled and diced medium
8 oz russet boiling potatoes, peeled and diced medium
4 medium leeks (white part only)
2 qts fresh vegetable, chicken, or beef stock (if you don't have fresh stock, low salt canned stock can be substituted)
5 Tbsp unsalted butter
2 cloves fresh garlic, minced
1/4 tsp ground cumin
1/4 tsp cayenne pepper
1/8 tsp ground ginger
1/8 tsp mustard powder
1 pinch turmeric
1/4 tsp powdered coriander
2 Tbsp flour
2 Tbsp fresh lemon juice
reserved beet greens, chopped
Add kosher salt and fresh ground black pepper to adjust seasoning.

Topping ingredients

1 medium onion, peeled and chopped fine
1/4 cup flat leaf parsley, chopped fine
2 cups plain yogurt

Method

1. Separate the greens from the beets, wash, drain, and chop the greens and set them aside
2. Slice leeks in half lengthwise and dice into 1/2 inch pieces.
3. Combine the vegetables with the stock in a large pot and bring to a boil. Reduce the heat and cook until all the vegetables are just tender. Remove them from the heat and strain the stock into another container. Set the stock and half of the cooked vegetables aside.

4. Puree the other half of the vegetables in a blender or food processor and set these aside.
5. Melt the butter in a large heavy bottom pot, add the garlic and saute over a medium heat for about one minute. Now, add the spices and flour while stirring with a wire whisk. Cook this seasoned roux over low heat, to prevent browning, for about two minutes.
6. Slowly add the stock to the roux while stirring with a wire whisk to prevent lumps from forming. Heat this mixture to a slow boil while stirring constantly. Cook over a low heat until the stock shows signs of thickening, then add the chopped beet greens, lemon juice, and diced vegetables. Continue to cook for about 10 minutes or until the greens become tender.
7. Remove the soup from the heat and add the pureed vegetables, stirring gently with a wooden spoon to mix.
8. Adjust the seasoning with kosher salt and fresh ground black pepper to suit your taste.

To serve, combine the chopped onion and parsley in a serving bowl and the yogurt in another bowl and bring them to the table as condiments. Heat the soup to a serving temperature 165-175 degrees. *Do not boil again.* Sprinkle a little parsley and onion on each serving along with a dollop of yogurt.

Cajun baked turnip

My mother was a master at creating recipes for turnip and rutabaga. Of all the root vegetables in the world these are the two that give me taste fatigue the quickest. So my mom would do her best to keep me from groaning every time I saw these two vegetables come to the table. Not all of her creations did the job, but I will share with you one of those monotony breakers that is still one of my favorites.

Ingredients

2 lbs white turnip, peeled and diced
6 Tbsp unsalted butter
1/4 cup red bell pepper, diced medium
1 tsp whole grain mustard
2 Tbsp brown sugar
1/2 tsp kosher salt
1/4 tsp garlic powder
1/8 tsp ground nutmeg
1/8 tsp cayenne pepper
1/4 tsp dried thyme leaf
1/4 tsp dried basil leaf
1/4 cup distilled apple cider
1/4 cup whole wheat bread crumbs

Method

1. Wash and peel the turnips and dice them into 1/3 inch pieces.

2. Cook the turnip pieces in lightly salted water until just tender. Drain and set aside.

3. Melt the butter in a heavy bottom skillet, add the diced bell pepper, and saute until the pepper is tender.

4. Combine the mustard, brown sugar, salt, garlic powder, nutmeg, cayenne pepper, thyme and basil with the apple cider and blend with a fork. Add this mixture to the sautéed bell pepper.

5. Toss this mixture with the blanched turnip in a suitable oven casserole. Sprinkle the whole wheat bread crumbs on top and bake in a 375 degree oven for about 20 minutes, or until the top is lightly browned and the turnip is to a desired tenderness.

Jerusalem artichokes with brown rice

The Jerusalem artichoke is not the most eye appealing vegetable, which is probably why most retail markets don't carry it. It also requirse special handling once it is removed from the ground. It has a very short shelf life.

In spite of its short comings, this vegetable is an absolute delight to eat in many ways. If you decide to grow some, you will experience a culinary delight similar to picking a fresh ripe tomato or ear of corn from your garden and eating it on the spot. Taste doesn't get any better.

If you can find some Jerusalem artichokes that are fresh, don't bother peeling them. Just wash them with a stiff brush and work them into this recipe.

Ingredients

```
4 Tbsp extra virgin olive oil
1 medium carrot, peeled and diced small
1 small red onion, peeled and diced small
1/4 cup fresh mushrooms, diced
2 cloves garlic, minced fine
3 cups Jerusalem artichokes, scrubbed and diced medi-
   um
1/4 cup long grain brown rice
1/2 cup fresh chicken stock
1 Tbsp lemon juice
1 Tbsp fresh mint, diced fine
kosher salt and fresh ground black pepper to taste
```

Method

1. Heat the oil in a large skillet. Add the carrots, onion, mushrooms, and garlic and saute for about 5 minutes. Add the Jerusalem artichokes and continue to saute until the artichokes are just tender.

2. In a suitable oven casserole combine the vegetable mixture with the rice, chicken stock, lemon juice, and mint. Add kosher salt and fresh ground pepper to taste. Cover the casserole and bake in a preheated 350 degree oven for about 20 minutes, or until the rice is tender

Sweet potato salad

Here is another taste lifter that helps to give new life to a vegetable that can get boring when just served cooked. Raw sweet potatoes and yams are great mediums for strong and flavorful sauces. I like a variety of spicy vingairette dressings.

Ingredients

```
1 cup grated raw sweet potato or yam
2 cups diced apple
1/4 cup celeriac (diced)
1/2 cup broken walnuts
1/4 cup seedless raisins
1/4 cup dried apricot diced
your favorite lettuce
```

1. Combine the grated sweet potato, apple and celeriac. Add the walnuts, raisins, and the diced apricots and toss gently to mix.

2. Chop the lettuce and arrange it on a platter with the sweet potato salad on top of the lettuce.

Here is one of my favorite dressings for this salad.

Walnut vinaigrette

Ingredients

```
1/4 cup extra virgin olive oil
1/2 cup walnut oil
1/4 cup of your favorite herbed vinegar
1 Tbsp apple brandy
kosher salt and fresh ground black pepper to taste
```

Method

1. Whisk the oils, vinegar, and brandy together and season to taste with salt and pepper. Refrigerate for 1 hour before using.

I hope you readers will try some of these neglected root vegetables and maybe even make room for some of them in your garden this spring. See you next time. Δ

Shadows

Tending my garden in the last hour of evening
I stop to rest
and see against the rays of setting sun
shadow figures from the past.
Indians who once tilled this soil work beside me;
hoeing only the corn, the squash and beans
they leave the rest to me.

**Wilma Hinman
McCune, Kansas**

Be a purple martin landlord — and find lots of uses for gourds

By Edna C. Norrell

The purple martin is one of nature's marvels, one of the most amazingly acrobatic birds on wings. Late afternoon, just about sunset, they put on a show that will leave you wishing you had wings. They drift, seemingly effortlessly, glide on a breeze, rise till they are no more than specks against the sky, fold their wings and zoom unerringly to their gourd home. I have yet to see a squabble due to mistaken entry.

Besides being fantastic entertainers, martins have a practical use: they eat nothing but flying insects, their favorite being mosquitoes. Since they can be found in all the lower 48 states and Canada, you can have purple martins as tenants no matter where you live.

We have offered them all kinds of dwellings, from single bird houses to high-rises, and we find they prefer earthy bottle gourds to the more expensive homes. Gourds are low cost and can be found easily at flea markets, yard sales, and farm stands. Or if you have a plot of dirt, grow your own. The gourds need at least 150 growing days; the longer the gourd stays on the vine, the thicker the shell will be. For your martin colony, choose gourds whose shells are at least ¼" inch thick and 8" to 12" in diameter.

When the gourds are dry enough that the seeds rattle, cut a two-inch doorway about halfway up the side of the gourd. Scrape out the seeds and membrane. Long tongs are handy for this. Drill three holes in the bottom for drainage. Drill two holes in the neck, 2" down from top, and thread through a piece of clothes hanger or baling wire to hang the gourd by. Paint the gourds white; this makes them more attractive to the renters and keeps the inside cool on sweltering days.

For one colony you will need

- 24 prepared gourds
- a 4" cedar or pressure treated pole 15 ft. long
- 8 runners (1x1 cross pieces, 4 of them 3 ft. long and 4 of them 4 ft. long)

For the tilting design, add

- two pressure-treated 2x4s
- 2 machine bolts ½" in diameter and 8" long with
- 6 washers and
- two nuts

Sink the cedar pole upright at least three feet deep. If you wish, you can anchor it in cement. At the top of the pole, nail two of the shorter crosspieces at right angles to each other, using two nails per crosspiece to prevent tipping. Hang a gourd on each end of each runner. To keep the gourds from sliding off, hammer in a nail 3" from the end of each runner.

Nail the second pair of crosspieces directly under the first, hanging the gourds as above. In similar fashion, use the longer crosspieces to make the third and fourth tiers. Hang two gourds from each side of the longer runners. This results is an attractive pyramid-shaped gourd structure.

Some landlords feel the need to lower the pole periodically to check the nests and to clean them out when the birds have flown. If this is your desire, build a base for the pole that allows you to tilt it down. Sink two 6 ft. lengths of pressure treated 2x4 lumber on end 2½ ft. into the ground, preferably in concrete. The 2x4s should be parallel, the space between them ¼" greater than the pole diameter. To hold the pole in place with

The author's 300-unit purple martin apartment complex

machine bolts, drill a set of ½" holes 6" from the top of the 2x4s, and drill a second set one foot from the soil level. Drill corresponding holes through the pole. Mount the pole with two machine bolts, placing washers on each side of the pole and at the end of each bolt before threading on nuts. The top bolt will serve as a hinge when you remove the bottom bolt to tilt the pole down to clean out the gourds or replace broken ones.

We have never used the base described above; it comes from an expert in the field of purple martins. We leave the gourds as the martins leave them when they leave for their migration to South America in the fall. We never clean them out, either: we think the birds like to find their homes just as they left them, straw and all. When the homes need a new coat of paint, we use ladders to climb the poles for the job. Should one become too old to be sturdy in a wind storm, we replace it. Otherwise, we leave them alone.

The martins start gathering in late July or the middle of August, and take off on the first leg of their long journey. They make stopovers in Florida and south Alabama for a few weeks' rest and food stock-up, then they're off across the long stretch of water to their winter quarters. In February and March, the first scouts come back. On their heels is the flock, chattering as they come back to the same gourds they left last summer. How they do this is beyond understanding.

Useful gourds

Gourds are useful for many things besides purple martin homes. They are great for crafts that are fun for everybody from the wee ones to Great Grandma. They can be found in all sizes from the huge bushel basket to the tiny nest egg, with all lengths and shapes of necks. No matter what you have in mind to make, you are sure to find a gourd just right for your project.

They are easy to find too, at flea markets, fairs, yard sales, and on the farm where they are grown. Should you want to grow your own, plant them in mounds some ten feet apart each way, as the vines are great runners and make half a dozen to twenty gourds to a vine. Allow them to stay on the vine until the vine is dead and the gourds are dry. If you pull them when they are green, they are certain to rot.

When dry, the gourds can be cut and sawed easily. If you are buying your gourds, look for ones with thick shells and ones that don't mash in when pressed on the sides. In making objects like vases and holders for tooth brushes, crayons, pencils, and pens, cut off the tops or handles about halfway down. With long tongs, pull out the dry membrane and seeds, then wash the gourd and allow it to dry thoroughly before sanding and painting or shellacking. To make faces, do not cut the gourd, just sand it and it's ready for decorating.

Native American vases and bowls are popular and easy to make. For a vase, cut the neck off down to the body of the gourd or about halfway down. Paint earth colors, deep brick red, tans, or browns. You can make designs by cutting paper in shapes like rectangles, squares, or circles. Trace these on the gourd, outline in black and shellac all over. Beautiful! Vines, flowers, and mountain streams cut from magazines make wonderful decorations. Glue them right on the gourd and shellac all over. Just use your imagination in this, and you will have a masterpiece in no time!

Faces are the most fun to do. I have seen some gourd faces that actually resembled people I knew! Grandpa and Grandma, the old fashioned kind, are great to make. Grandpa needs a small or short nose, a gray yarn mustache, and a fringe of gray hair topped by a straw hat. Bore a hole beneath the mustache and poke in the stem of a corncob pipe.

Grandma has gray hair, spectacles, and a sunbonnet. Glue on eyes made of black buttons or felt.

Santa Claus has a long white beard of yarn or long fiber cotton for his beard and hair, glued on beneath his red cap. Mrs. Claus wears her spectacles and her hair in a bun atop her head.

Choose a gourd with a long slender handle for Ichabod Crane or Pinocchio. Ichabod sports a black hat and Pinocchio a white one with a black band, both glued to the head side of the gourd.

Remember all these characters are using the handles of the gourds for their noses, so hats, hair, etc. are glued to the side of the gourd.

Look for a penguin-shaped gourd, paint on a black tuxedo, white shirt, and black bow tie. An artificial carrot end will make a great beak, or you might want to paint on a mouth with a small hole drilled for his pipe or plastic cigarette. A black top hat completes his costume.

Back on the farm, few farmers were without a long handled dipper gourd. Nowadays these make wonderful conversation pieces when entwined with vines, flowers, and a tiny bird perched in the doorway and hung on the wall of your kitchen or dining room.

All these crafts, from the decorated waste basket to the penguin, make great gifts or yard sale items. They will win prizes at fairs, or it's fun just to keep them. Just go out and get the gourds and let your imagination go. You will have fun and keepsakes too! This activity will keep kids busy for hours, using water colors and Elmer's glue. Grandma can present Grandpa with a good likeness of himself. Altogether, it is a great project and so much fun to do. Δ

It's springtime in Montana

By Dynah Geissal

The dawn comes gray and foggy, with a breeze . . . warm for March, but chilly still. The eastern sky is bright where the sun will top Mount Sentinel in another half hour. Only a few patches of snow remain, although the nearby mountains are bare for only the lower hundred feet.

The redwing blackbirds came back during a warm spell in January, but disappeared when a blizzard and 30-below temperatures followed right on their heels. Now, in the first week of spring, they're back in full force. There is a pair above the bedroom window. They seem to be competing with the red rooster who is displaying his prowess to the adolescent chickens in the brooder pen by the house.

Sleep tugs at me but no, it's time to start the day. I heard the first curlew last night. The pintail with the broken wing is back. She stayed all through the fall until the creek froze. I thought she had died, but now with the water moving again, she's back. She walks in the solemn line of domestic ducks, even though she can fly now. She's only a quarter their size.

The meadowlarks are mating, and their songs brighten the morning. The whole elm tree is alive with redwings. They like the cattails, but there won't be any for a couple of months yet. The great horned owl that lived in the barn all winter has moved to her nesting tree by the river. It's a huge old ponderosa, and the nest is way up in a hollow with a convenient dead branch for a perch. I like to examine the pellets underneath to see what she's been eating. Mostly it's mice but sometimes birds, and I've found many snail shells in the pellets. I think they must have been eaten by something that was then eaten by the owl. I saw her

mate in the hills above my house several times this winter, but I never could find where he lived. He hunted rabbits in a copse of trees up there and seemed unafraid when I approached.

I've noticed before that animals react differently to a person on snowshoes. There's a herd of deer that regularly graze with the cattle, and even though they come quite close to the house, they will never tolerate my approach. One day, though, I passed them when I was snowshoeing. They showed curiosity but not fear and they went on grazing as I moved away.

There's a female coyote that comes every year in late winter to catch voles. For a couple of months she will come every day. I think she must be feeding a litter to be so brazen. She moves among the cattle with their newborn calves but never threatens them, and they seem unconcerned— except once when the calves gathered around the coyote in curiosity. The mothers moved in on a run and the coyote moved off a ways.

One time I was snowshoeing and I saw the coyote. She was upwind of me and moving toward me. She had to have seen me, but she kept coming without any hesitation until we were only about a hundred feet apart. She suddenly leaped into the air in surprise and trotted off; I guess she had finally caught my scent.

I heard the swans flying over. When I was doing the milking, I heard a group that was so high that I couldn't

see them, but there's no mistaking that sound. Later, when I was feeding the horses, I heard the sound again, and this time I could see them as little more than pinpoints against the clouds. There used to be a hundred or more that stopped on the creek for a month or so before going on to the Arctic. A gas spill in '82 put an end to that. The oil company assured me that the creek had returned to normal a year later, but the fish are only starting to come back, and I don't think the swans ever will.

Spring in Montana—not much snow in the valley, not much green for a couple more months, but the sap's running, the rough-legged hawks are soaring and whistling in pairs, along with the redtails and the marsh hawks. To some people it may look bleak, but if they looked closely, they'd be amazed at all the stirrings of life.

I raked off the flower beds, but they were still embedded in ice under the mulch. I dug up the coldframe, but four inches down, the earth was solidly frozen. The carrots are still crisp and sweet in the garden under their bags of leaves. The dirt I brought in to start plants sprouted hundreds of hollyhocks as soon as the soil warmed. Everything is on the verge. Just a little longer. I tell myself to be patient and to enjoy this period of anticipation. Soon it will be warm and we will be trying to cram everything we can into our short summer. Δ

You definitely want to grow your own asparagus

By Anne Westbrook Dominick

Just like the sugars in corn and peas, the sugars in asparagus start the starch conversion as soon as it's harvested. The bottom line: you can't buy asparagus that tastes as good as what you raise and harvest yourself. A perennial of long duration (we're talking decades here, even centuries), a good growing asparagus bed requires a busy start-up to get it well established. But if you like store-bought spears even a bit, a dish of fresh cut ones will make a dedicated "bedder" out of you.

That's what asparagus needs, a bed in full sun out of roto-tilling areas. Some people, like my father, establish it as an adjunct to the north end of their vegetable garden; others, like me, give it its own spot in the landscape. When figuring where to put it, know that asparagus reaches five to eight feet in height, topped with dense feathery plumage that can screen out unsightlies. Song birds also enjoy it as a safe place during August and September.

Choices

Starting an asparagus patch forces even more decision making: Should I start with seeds or crowns? A *crown*, a one-year-old established root system with visible spears ready to grow, will give a few eatings the second year; seeds take till the third year. Crowns cost more and demand immediate bed preparation; seeds offer more for the dollar and can wait another year for their permanent piece of the property. I've done it both ways. Crowns offer quick gratification; seeds offer a more relaxed project with a bit of prolonged adventure.

A second decision: what variety? The stand-by line is Washington—Mary and Martha are the best

known—and for good reason. Asparagus' arch enemy, a fungus called *rust*, will always win if it can get a spore in the stalk. Evidenced by dusty orange blisters on the spears and foliage, it exists throughout the United States . . . but Washingtons are immune. Hybrids touting more, longer, and better yields now flood the market and confuse everybody. Many carry the Washington genes, but the catalogues selling them don't tell us which ones.

Now we can even choose all-male selections (seed or crown format) that will give us more, bigger, and better spears, since they won't be "thinking reproduction." However, some evidence indicates all-male hybrids are over-sensitive—too much cold or heat does 'em in.

I started my last patch with Martha Washington crowns nine years ago in northern New England. This year I've started another bed of Martha Washington in southern Arizona, and they're already showing their strength. I'm feeling the urge for a bit of variety, so next year I'm going to start some hybrid seeds in my perennial-seed-starting patch, enlarge Martha's

bed, and move those new companions in with her the following year.

Planting

To prepare a bed for crowns, dig a ditch eight to ten inches deep. A traditional two- to three-foot deep trench is no longer "in," so forget it (thank goodness). To figure the ditch's length, allow a foot and a half between plants. Rows should be three feet apart. Chop some compost or cured manure into the ditch's bottom and cover with a bit of soil, forming a mound for each root. To plant a crown, place the top at the peak of the mound, drape its roots uniformly into the lower areas, and cover with about two inches of dirt tucked in snugly around the roots. As spears appear, which should happen in one to two weeks, keep covering them until the trench is full.

To start asparagus by seed, plant them an inch deep at the beginning of the growing season in a place where you can keep tabs on them. For me, that was the first week in May in the northeast and the start of the rainy season (the beginning of July) in the southwestern desert. Germination can be speeded up by soaking the seeds for a day or so before sowing. When they're up, thin to about three inches apart, keep weeds from competing, and let them grow the year away. A year later, move them to their prepared permanent bed.

The harvest

Unfortunately, asparagus can't be harvested the year its crowns are set. The second year, they can be picked for a couple weeks—enough for a couple good meals. By the third year, they should be strong enough for a full harvest lasting two to two and a half months. Should the spears become spindly (pencil thickness) before then, stop harvesting, and let them gain for next year's crop.

Asparagus is most succulent and delicious when six to eight inches tall. To harvest: right before cooking, cut the stalk at—or just below—ground level, being careful not to injure future spears. After harvesting, I get rid of the spear's tough, stringy end by tapping lightly, starting at the root end with a paring knife in half inch increments until the knife slips through. Throw away that bottom end and what's left will melt in your mouth.

Preparing for winter

To prepare for winter, mow the entire patch to the ground anytime after the first frost. Because asparagus is a heavy eater, spread a generous covering of compost or manure over them at this time. That gives the nutrients an early start leaching down to the roots for next season's robust start. Chicken manure, which is too strong for many plants, is ideal for asparagus. In areas where the soil is acidic, an annual liming is beneficial. Wood ashes are even better since they not only sweeten the soil (keep it around neutral—pH 6.5 is ideal), they also contain potassium and other important minerals. Where the soil is alkaline,

an annual dose of sulphur will keep the level where asparagus likes it best.

Asparagus can co-exist quite happily with most weeds and, being the long-term perennial it is, that's a good thing. Weeds in general and witch grass in particular are more of a problem to the gardener than to the asparagus, but these can be controlled somewhat by early shallow cultivation followed by mulching.

Salting asparagus is now unacceptable. You might say, "Well, of course," but more than a few people still do it. Recently, when I was moaning about the accursed grass takeover in my asparagus patch, a gardening friend whose advice I had always taken as gospel rather smugly told me how he controlled his: 400 pounds of salt. His patch is 20 by 40 feet. Sure, the salt will kill a lot of weeds and even give asparagus a one or two year boost. After that, not only will the asparagus go into decline, the soil will have been ruined for years to come, and some salt will have leached into surrounding areas—a very large area if it gets into the ground water. Smart people still advocate stupid things, and lesser ones, like me, do consider following their advice. This is one we shouldn't follow.

Actually, asparagus, once established, will maintain itself for years. As long as we get the plants well placed and growing strongly, we don't have to do much more than what we feel comfortable doing. Few weeds bother it. Poor soil really doesn't faze it. The best I ever ate was from a mighty poor hay field near the Canadian border in northern Maine. That bed had been abandoned when its people had moved up the hill to build a proper house over 75 years ago. Δ

The Ichiban Hybrid eggplant is a real producer

By Alice B. Yeager
Photos by James O. Yeager

Have you ever tried year after year to grow a particular type of vegetable, but it always seemed to turn out wrong? Finally you throw up your hands in disgust and question your sanity for even thinking about trying again. This used to be my track record with eggplants.

My young eggplants always looked good in their neat peat pots, giving me enough encouragement to believe that plants of such fine caliber would surely perform well in the garden. After transplanting to a well-composted spot, the plants continued to show great promise. With the help of a pest deterrent, they would survive the onslaught of flea beetles, blister beetles, and others of ill intent. What couldn't be controlled was the Arkansas summer weather with its periods of high humidity, drought, and miserable heat. However, I would manage, with the aid of mulch, water, and perseverance to actually harvest a couple of purple fruits literally worth their weight in gold, considering all the effort it took to raise them. It's times like those that can make you wonder if your mama raised a fool.

The eggplant variety Ichiban Hybrid first came to my attention some years ago while I was afflicted with the annual Hope-Springs-Eternal disease. This malady is common in winter among avid gardeners, causing them to rivet their attention on seed catalogs for days at a time. Ichiban was advertised as an oriental variety bearing huge crops of long, cylindrical fruits—unlike the plump types I had been attempting to grow. Skeptically, I thought I'd give eggplants another try, and, if Ichiban failed, that was it!

Ichiban Hybrid eggplant is prolific.

No more time-wasting attempts at growing eggplants.

Fortunately, Ichiban Hybrid measured up to its description and is now a welcome part of our garden selection each year. It has far out-produced others such as Black Beauty and Dusky (which, in my case, hasn't been too hard to do). Ichiban is very prolific, beginning its production by early summer and continuing until frost. I have yet to find an Ichiban fruit with the slightest bitter taste, regardless of its stage of maturity.

Getting started

I prefer to start eggplants indoors several weeks ahead of the last anticipated frost date in our area (Zone 8), thus giving them a head start so that they are about four to six inches tall when transplanted to the garden.

Young Ichiban plants are handsome with their velvety, grey-green leaves, and they grow off with a flourish when they are out on their own. Being tender plants, they are not transplanted until the weather has warmed and the soil has lost its chill.

Eggplants like a sunny spot, but will tolerate some partial shade. They seem to appreciate some relief from hot summer sun and will thrive alongside taller plants such as trellised cucumbers or pole beans. Six or eight plants will produce enough fruit for the average size family.

Ichiban needs a sandy loam soil with plenty of humus and good moisture retaining qualities (but not boggy). Well-rotted barnyard manure or rich compost dug into the ground a few weeks in advance of planting will boost production. Eggplants require soil with a pH factor of 6.0 to 7.0, so they fit in very easily with the soil needs of many other home garden vegetables.

Young plants should be spaced about two feet apart. I like to apply a mulch of organic material—pine needles, leaves, etc.—to cut down on grass and weed growth. Also, the mulch will attract earthworms to do the chore of cultivation. (Why do all that work when there are eager and meticulous tillers willing to work for nothing but good living conditions.) Adding to the mulch from time to time helps in other ways, too, as it keeps plants and fruit from getting dirt-splashed during heavy rains and prevents soil from being washed away from the roots.

They grow tall

Ichiban plants grow tall in our garden and require staking. Usually, a four-foot stake driven solidly into the ground at the time of planting is sufficient, and it is needed if plants are to remain upright while laden with fruit. Strips of old nylon pantyhose come in handy for use as ties, as they do not restrict the circulatory system of the plants. Tomato cages work well, too. Place them over the young transplants and they will grow up through the cages, supporting themselves as they grow.

During prolonged periods of drought, even mulch won't take the place of needed water. Eggplants must have a moderate amount of moisture to produce their fruit properly. When leaves continue to droop after sunset, it's time to give the ground a good soaking. During extended hot, dry periods I sometimes water every two to three days to ensure survival of the plants. Given adequate attention, Ichiban will do you proud all summer long.

In southwestern Arkansas, our worst eggplant enemy is the flea beetle—that small black pest that eats tiny holes in the leaves of many plants, causing them to look like they've been punched with a myriad of pins. Flea beetles are very hard to find, as they have a protective habit of jumping as soon as a leaf is disturbed. At the first sign of leaf damage, it is imperative to use a good garden dust or spray, as the cagey beetles can play havoc with eggplants. I lightly dust with 5% Sevin dust, and usually one or two applications are enough to discourage the beetles. I try to garden as organically as possible, so I don't like to resort to a great deal of spraying and dusting. I prefer instead to leave pest control to the birds, chameleons, and toads that patrol the garden.

Ichiban fruits are dark purple and elongated with a slight curve. They may reach a length of 10 to 12 inches and about 2 to 2½ inches in diameter and still be of good texture and taste, although the recommended harvesting size is six to eight inches. I use a sharp pair of clippers to remove the fruit from the plant, as the stem is woody and not easily broken by hand. Plants will continue bearing until fall, although the last fruits will not be of prime quality.

Eggplant is high in potassium and low in calories. Thanks to publicity created by the great number of chefs appearing on TV and writing books, eggplant is at last receiving the recognition it deserves. It is very versatile and may be used in many ways—battered and sautéed, stuffed, marinated, stir-fried, and so on. It is excellent to dice and use in vegetable soup. However, don't fool yourself into thinking that because eggplant is low in calories, it can be combined with cheese, sausage, and other tasty ingredients and still result in a low-calorie dish. If you gain a pound or two from such a delicious combination, don't blame the eggplant!

Seed Sources:

Park Seed Co.
Cokesbury Road
Greenwood, SC 29647-0001

Vermont Bean Seed Co.
Garden Lane
Fair Haven, VT 05743

J. W. Jung Seed Co.
Randolph, WI 53956

Eggplant supreme

This is a special mixture to enjoy during fresh vegetable season.

2 Tablespoons olive oil
2 medium Ichiban fruits, peeled and sliced crosswise in ¼" slices
2 large ripe tomatoes, cut in small chunks
1 medium onion, chopped
8 okra pods cut crosswise in ½" slices (optional)
2 medium bell peppers, coarsely chopped
1 small hot pepper, minced
6-8 fresh basil leaves, chopped (or 1 teaspoon dried sweet basil)
1 small bay leaf
½ teaspoon salt (optional)
1 cup grated cheese (use a favorite that melts well)
Optional: 2 cups coarsely chopped, leftover cooked chicken, lamb or other meat

In a medium size cast iron skillet, heat the oil until the bottom of the skillet can easily be coated by turning from side to side. With the exception of the cheese, put all ingredients in the skillet and simmer covered until vegetables have reached a semi-firm but not mushy stage. (Lift the lid occasionally and stir the mixture to be sure it isn't sticking and to bring all the vegetables to the same stage of doneness.)

Distribute the grated cheese over the hot mixture and stir just enough to melt the cheese. Serve hot over cooked noodles, brown rice, spaghetti, or whatever suits your fancy. Δ

For something different in your garden, try ground cherries

By Sally Denney

Looking for an interesting annual fruit to grow in your family garden? *Physalis peruviana*, also known as ground cherries, may be just what you are looking for. Physalis plants are as easily grown as tomatoes. From transplanting, the hardy plants take only 70 days to harvest the first fruits. Six plants furnished my family with enough fruit for pies, jam, and plenty to freeze for winter use.

While similar to tomatoes in their growing habits (they are a close relative in the nightshade family), ground cherries are not a true tomato. Their seeds resemble cherry tomatoes. The one- to two-inch fruits are enclosed in a papery husk that turns golden yellow when the cherry-sized fruit inside is ripe. When picking the fruit, you will soon discover why the Amish call them "ground cherries." Jostling the plant causes the ripe fruit to fall to the ground. On the ground is where the gardener will find the sweetest fruits. Once picked, the husks slip easily from the cherries and expose plump, golden-yellow fruit.

The flavor is delicately exotic. Some seed catalogs say the taste is strawberry-like when eaten fresh. I conducted an at-home taste test, and every answer was different when I had my taste testers (my family) describe the taste. Their answers ranged from "a faint pineapple taste" to "a hint of kiwi." No matter what each discriminating taster found in the fruit, a pint of husked cherries quickly disappeared from my kitchen counter as the family grabbed handfuls on their way in or out.

For first-time growers, I recommend starting the seeds indoors six to eight weeks before your last frost. Doing

this helps distinguish the seedlings from weeds and keeps the gardener from pulling them out by mistake.

My transplanted plants grew to around 24 inches tall with heavy foliage and flowers. For a while I wondered if they were called ground cherries because the plant hugged the ground before shooting upwards. The plants are very productive and gave my family of seven plenty of fruit.

We mulched our plants with grass clippings. Insects did not bother the plants, but ants loved the sweet fruits. When the pods were left too long on the ground, I would find that ants had beaten me to the harvest.

This year I plan to do one thing differently: I will place an old sheet under the plants during the peak harvest, so I can pick up the fruit with less effort.

The Amish are fond of ground cherries. Nearly all their cookbooks have at least one recipe for ground cherry pie. While living in Hawaii, my daughter discovered that the Hawaiians call ground cherries "poha" and make jam from them.

Seed catalogs list them under a variety of names, such as "Strawberry Husk" and "Winter Cherry." Gurney's Seed and Nursery Co. lists it as "Yellow Husk Tomato" in their "Fun to Grow Novelties" section.

Since discovering the fruit, I've acquired a few favorite recipes for ground cherries.

Hawaiian poha jam

3 lb. poha (ground cherries)
1/4 cup water
1 cup sugar per cup cooked poha
1 Tablespoon lemon juice

Husk and wash fruit. Combine with water and cook slowly for 30 minutes, stirring frequently. Remove from heat and let stand overnight. Measure pulp and juice and combine with an equal quantity of sugar. Return to heat and cook slowly, stirring occasionally for one hour. Add lemon juice and continue slow cooking until product reaches jelly stage. Immediately pour into hot sterilized glasses and seal. (I froze my jam.)

Ground cherry pie

4 cups ground cherries
1/4 cup lemon juice
    (or depending on taste preference, 2 drops almond extract)
1 cup water
3/4 cups sugar
3 Tablespoons cornstarch

Put cherries, flavoring, sugar, and 1/2 cup water into a saucepan; heat to boiling. Mix 1/2 cup water with cornstarch and add to hot cherry mixture. Cook until thick. If too thick, add a little more water. Pour into an unbaked pie crust. Adjust top crust. Bake at 375° until crust is baked. Δ

What you do to one side of an equation, you do to the other to keep it balanced

By John Silveira

Years ago I taught high school algebra. I was young then and even before the first day of school I was sure I had the secret to what it would take to get a classroom full of students to understand algebraic concepts. I expected that every one of them would understand what I was teaching. And there would be no lost souls in my classroom.

Then reality raised its ugly head. From the first day, the concept the students had the most trouble with was one of the core concepts in algebra: how to work with an equation. About half my students did manage to grasp the concept well. But the rest, to varying degrees, found it confusing, including several for whom it seemed a complete and eternal mystery.

Not understanding what an equation is is a major shortcoming for math students. Day in and day out, they have to solve equations, even while they're learning other algebraic concepts. And the ability to deal with equations carries over later into classes like trigonometry, calculus, statistics, physics, and chemistry. Many students take no more math than they absolutely have to because they never feel at ease when working with equations.

It was discouraging. I wanted to be a good teacher. But I have to admit I never came up with a satisfactory solution that made the concept easy back then.

It's been years since I taught a high school class. But I am now a homeschooling parent with a high-school-aged daughter. So it was with great trepidation that I decided to teach her algebra. Because of her learning problems (that resulted in years of special education classes where algebraic concepts aren't even considered), I realized I may once again be butting my head up against a wall.

So I decided that before I introduced her to an algebra text, I would fix in her mind the concept of an equation.

Adding and subtracting

That first day, I sat down beside her and drew a picture on a piece of paper. It was a balance scale.

"Do you know what this is?" I asked.

She looked at it.

"It's a balance scale" I said.

She nodded and said, "It's for weighing things."

"That's right. This balances if there's an equal amount of weight on both sides. If I add more weight to one side, that side goes down and the other side goes up." I tipped the picture as if throwing the scale out of kilter. "If, instead, I take weight away from that side, it goes up and the other side goes down." I tipped the picture the other way.

"So, if I add one pound to this first side," and I tipped the picture so that side was down, "how much do I have to add to the other side to make it balance—or be equal?"

"One pound," she answered, and I made the picture even.

"And if, instead, I subtract two pounds from the other side," and I tipped the picture the other way, "how much would I have to subtract from this side to make it balance—or be equal?"

"Two pounds," she replied, and I tipped it back.

"That's how equations work. You have to keep both sides equal to keep them even. The word *equation* comes from the word *equal*. That's why the equal sign appears in every equation."

I wrote

$$=$$

on the paper.

"Just think of everything we do for the next few weeks as trying to make a scale balance."

She nodded.

"Now, here's a problem: Say you were walking down the street with a bag of apples and you met your sister, Meaghan. She hands you three more apples and asks you to put them in your bag and take them home with you. When you get home, you suddenly wonder how many apples you started out with.

"How many apples did you start with?"

She looked at me like I was crazy. "I don't know. You didn't tell me."

"Then let's call the number you started with, 'x'," I said and I wrote

$$x$$

on the paper.

"And Meaghan gave you three more…"

I wrote:

$$x + 3$$

"Then you count the apples in the bag and there are 13. So you know the number of apples you started with is 'x' and Meaghan gave you three more and now you have 13."

I wrote "= 13" after the "x + 3" and we now had:

$$x + 3 = 13$$

"That's an equation."

She leaned closer. "That's an equation?"

The first addition and subtraction test

$x + 6 = 11$

answer (x = 5)

$x + .51 = .98$

answer (x = .47)

$x + .18 = .48$

(This was the first "trick question" because I expected her to write the answer as .30—which she did—and, without lingering, I pointed out that when it's money, it's .30 but that we can really write decimals like this as just .3)

answer (x = .3)

$x + \$23 = \$100$

answer (x = \$77)

$6 + x = 11$

(This was another trick question because for the first time the number was first and the unknown second. She rolled right through it.)

answer (x = 5)

$x + 3 = 6$

answer (x = 3)

$x - .14 = .26$

(Once again, I have a chance to show her that .40 can be written .4)

answer (x = .4)

$x - 123 = 123$

answer (x = 246)

$x - \$19 = \$ 38$

answer (x = \$57))

$x - 1000 = 1$

answer (x = 1001)

I nodded. It was like showing a primitive native in New Guinea a cigarette lighter.

"If I write this…"

$$x + 3 = 13$$
$$\underline{ -3 \quad -3}$$

"then I'm taking 3 from both sides of our equation—like taking 3 pounds away from both sides of a scale to keep it balanced—and we get x+0 on one side—and anything plus zero is whatever you started with…" so I wrote an "x" down, "and 13-3 is 10…" So now we had:

$$x + 3 = 13$$
$$\underline{ -3 \quad -3}$$
$$x = 10$$

"So, I started with 10 apples," she said.

I nodded.

Then I said, "Suppose I asked you to hold 47¢ for me, and you put it in your purse with your change. Suddenly, you're wondering how much of that money is yours. You count all the money and find there's $1.37. What are we going to call the money you had?"

I didn't wait for an answer. I told her. "We'll call your money x," and I wrote on the paper.

x

"So, your x plus my 47¢ equals $1.37." I wrote:

$$x + .47 = 1.37$$

"So, if we take the 47¢ from both sides of the equation—just to keep it balanced, mind you—we have:

$$x + .47 = 1.37$$
$$\underline{ -.47 \quad -.47}$$
$$x = .90$$

"What you're trying to do is find out what x, 'the unknown,' is," I emphasized. "You're trying to get it by itself. We call that 'isolating' it. But anything you do to one side of the equation you have to do to the other to keep it balanced."

I was sure she wouldn't remember this the first time we did it. Or even the second or third time. But she made progress as I repeated similar exercises all week and it inexorably sunk in. The emphasis was always that

to solve the equation we are trying to isolate the unknown *and* if we have to add or subtract on one side of the equation to get the unknown alone, we have to do the same to the other side of the equation.

Most of algebra is just mechanical. I hoped that once she realized this she would be less intimidated, so that solving equations would become automatic for her, just as it is for me.

Multiplying and dividing

One of the truly amazing things I discovered when I taught high school was that students sometimes got the solution to a problem but didn't know how they got it—until I told them how.

Situations similar to the following happened many times:

I'd query a student, "You have a bag with marbles in it. You haven't counted them to see how many. Someone says, 'I'll triple the number of marbles in the bag,' and he does. Then he hands the bag back and you count the marbles in it and there are 117. How many were in there when you started?"

The student would think, then reply, "Thirty-nine."

"How did you get that answer?"

He would look at me for a few moments, then say, "I don't know."

And believe me, he didn't. This happened again and again with many students. I couldn't accept 'I don't know' as an answer. Sometimes I even imagined that every third student in my class was the Rain Man.

But I finally realized that the problem was that they just didn't have the tools to figure out how to explain it. And that was my job, to show them algebraically how they did it and demonstrate that the method worked all the time.

So it happened with Mary. I asked her that very same question, and, when she couldn't explain to me how she got the answer, I showed her how she did it:

x

I wrote, is the number of apples originally in the bag.

3x

is the number of apples in the bag after the number has been tripled. And after she counts the apples, she discovers

$$3x = 117$$

is the equation.

She watched me do this, then I divided both sides by 3 to get the x alone.

$$\frac{3x}{3} = \frac{117}{3}$$

When the 3x is divided by 3, the 3s cancel out leaving just the x. But you have to divide the 117 by 3 also, which results in 39. So,

$$x = 39$$

It made sense to her.

With this fresh in her mind, I asked, "If you had another bag with apples and you gave it to me, and I said, 'I'm going to increase the number of apples 5 times,' let's see how you'd write it. Since you don't know how many apples were in the bag, how do you write it?"

She wrote

$$x$$

"And I multiplied it 5 times. How do you show that?"

She wrote a 5 before the x.

$$5x$$

"And let's say you now count the number of apples and there are 15. How would you show what that 5x is equal to 15?"

She added an = and the 15.

$$5x = 15$$

"That's it," I said. Now, to get the 5 off the x you have to do the opposite of multiplication to get rid of it."

"So I divide by 5?" she asked tentatively.

"That's right."

"So, x = 15," she said.

"But you only divided the 5x by 5. To keep it an equation, you have to do the same to both sides to keep it balanced. So, if you divide the other side, where the 15 is, you get…?"

"Three?" she asked.

We worked several examples like this and I constantly pointed out that when her unknown was multiplied by a number, she had to divide *both* sides of the equation to get rid of it.

These problems were beginning to come easy to her.

"Now, let's say we have a box of cookies," I said, "and you have 5 friends come over. I decide to divide the cookies evenly among the 6 of you and you discover you each have 7 cookies. How many cookies were there originally in the box?"

"42," she replied.

"How did you get that?"

She thought a minute. "I don't know."

"Well, let's say you didn't know there were 42, then the number of cookies is our unknown. How are we going to represent our unknown?"

"With x?"

I wrote

$$x$$

on the paper.

"And there were 6 of you I divided them among, so

$$x/6$$

is how many you each got. And when you counted what you each got it was equal to…?"

"7 each."

"So this…" and I wrote

$$x/6 = 7$$

"…is the equation. And since we're dividing by 6, we have to do the opposite of division to get rid of the 6. And the opposite of division is…?"

"Multiplication," she said.

"So we multiply both sides by 6

$$6 * x/6 = 6 * 7$$

"What's 6 * x/6?"

"I don't know," she said.

"What's 6 times 1 over 6?"

"One."

"What's 6 times 2 over 6?"

"Two."

"What's 6 times 5 over 6?"

"Five."

"So, how about 6 times x over 6?"

"X?"

"That's right."

"It's like what we learned when we learned to multiply fractions," she said. "The numbers cancel out."

"That's right. In this case the 6s cancel out.

"And what is 6 times 7?" I continued.

"42."

I wrote

$$x = 42$$

The delight she was beginning to find in these exercises was twofold. First, we get along well, so she likes working on these things with me. But second, and of greater importance to me, is that she sees everything I'm teaching her so far still consists of mechanical rules she can memorize. Because of this second point, she is not intimidated like many of my high school students were.

The first multiplication and division test

6x = 24	*answer* (x = 4)
5x = 125	*answer* (x = 25)
x/2 = .48	*answer* (x = .96)
x/11 = 10	*answer* (x = 110)
4x = 1	*answer* (x = .25 or 1/4)
4.5x = 10.8	*answer* (x = 2.4)
x/2 = 6.5	*answer* (x = 13)
2x/3 = 6	*answer* (x = 9)
x/2.5 = 7.5	*answer* (x = 18.75)
x/2.5 = 1	*answer* (x = 2.5)

But I'm going to have to stay with this everyday. Only repetition will reinforce the principles until they become second nature to the student.

Combining operations

It was a small step to combining operations, i.e., combining addition or subtraction with multiplication or division.

However, there is a difference between the equations

$$2x + 6 = 30$$

and

$$2(x+6) = 30$$

In the first, x = 12, and in the second x = 9. I thought about how to approach this for a day then I decided to leave out problems that required parenthesis until later. I was still concentrating on how to get her to understand the concept of balancing equations. I would deal with more complicated equations later.

I sat down with Mary and wrote:

$$2x + 6 = 30$$

The first thing I did was explain that these are the easiest of the equations that involve either addition and subtraction along with multiplication and division. Then I showed her how to solve it. First eliminate anything that's added or subtracted; then it's just like the other problems she did. So I wrote

$$2x + 6 = 30$$
$$\underline{-6 \quad -6}$$
$$2x + 0 = 24$$

which resulted in

$$2x = 24$$

which is a type of problem she's already familiar with.

We worked many of these problems. Then I quizzed her.

In fewer than three weeks she had as good an understanding of what an equation was as the best of my high school students and, looking back, I realize that if I could step back in time and sit down with each of those confused ones individually, they all would have understood the concept.

Later on I'll teach her things such as: if she has to take the square root of one side to get an answer, then she has to take the square root of the other side. But that's later.

Now, Mary, for all the problems she has had in school before I started homeschooling her, might have been one of those students who would have caught on to what equations are all about, anyway. But the fact is, as we go off into factoring, exponents, and solutions to special equations like quadratics, I'm assured she won't be hampered by a lack of understanding of what equations are.

Summary

If you can get the following in your child's head, you'll have gone a long way toward taking the mystery out of algebra.

1. An equation is nothing more than a balance scale for numbers.
2. Whatever she does to one side of an equation to get the unknown by itself, she has to do to the other side; otherwise, it doesn't balance.

For now, all she has to know is that, if she has mixed operations, i.e., when addition or subtraction are mixed with multiplication or division, she subtracts or adds numbers to each side of the equation before she divides or multiplies. I will teach her how to deal with terms that are in parenthesis, next.

If you don't know algebra

It is an unfortunate truth that to teach algebra, you have to know a lot about it yourself. The solution to teaching it if you never learned it, or you did learn it but you can't remember it anymore, is beyond the scope of this article. But please don't expect to just send your kid off in a corner with a book and expect her to learn it without guidance.

It is possible to learn it along with your child. I and about 20 other students once survived a semester of probability and statistics taught by a man who had never had either course in college. He managed to teach us, though he was always just a few weeks ahead of the class. But he was a man who already had a great deal of experience with mathematics.

The astute reader will realize I haven't dealt with problems that involve negative numbers, like

$$x + 6 = 3$$

The first test combining the operations

$3x + 6 = 60$	
	answer $(x = 18)$
$2x - 7 = 13$	
	answer $(x = 10)$
$5 + x/4 = 6$	
	answer $(x = 4)$
$x/10 - 10 = 10$	
	answer $(x = 200)$
$11x + 5 = 5$	
	answer $(x = 0)$
$5 + x/11 = 5$	
	answer $(x = 0)$
$x/3 + 6 = 19/3$	
	answer $(x = 1)$
$x/3 - 5 = 10$	
	answer $(x = 45)$
$x/2.5 + 6 = 13.5$	
	answer $(x = 18.75)$
$x/2.5 - 6 = 1.5$	
	answer $(x = 18.75)$

Interesting math terms

There are two words I'm sneaking into Mary's vocabulary. One is *inverse*. The inverse of a number in addition and subtraction is the number you must subtract or add to get zero. So, the inverse of 3 is -3 because 3-3=0. The inverse of -7 is 7 because -7+7=0.

When it's only addition and subtraction that are involved, zero is called the *identity* because when a number has zero added to or subtracted from it, the number is unchanged. 3 + 0 = 3 and 7 - 0 = 7. Zero is called the identity.

The inverse when you're multiplying and dividing is the number you must divide or multiply by to get 1. So, under multiplication and division, the inverse of 3 is 1/3 because 3*1/3=1 and the inverse of 1/7 is 7 because 1/7 * 7 = 1.

When we are talking about multiplication and division, there is a different kind of identity. Here, 1 is the identity because when you multiply or divide a number by 1, you get the number back. So, 3 * 1 = 3 and 7/1 = 7.

I'm not asking her to memorize these terms yet. But I use them as I explain these things to her. And, like a visitor to a new land who is learning to pick up the language, she is gradually using them too.

which results in a negative number for an answer, nor problems like

$$-3x = -6$$

which involves division or multiplication with negative numbers.

Negative numbers are not something my daughter is yet familiar with. On my list of priorities was to first teach her how to work with equations.

In future issues I will deal with other concepts my students had difficulty with, including "the order of operations" which are the rules for knowing which operations to perform first: addition, subtraction, multiplication, division, exponents, numbers in parenthesis, etc. And we'll learn to deal with those infamous and nefarious negative numbers. Δ

High altitude gardening — it's a challenge but these helpful tips can get you started

By Dynah Geissal

High altitude gardening is definitely a challenge, but it can also be very rewarding. For those of us who live in the mountains and are striving for self sufficiency, it is a necessity. Attitude is important for success: Trying to "conquer the elements" is possible to a certain extent, but it's self-defeating, prone to failure, and extremely frustrating. On the other hand, working *with* Nature is rewarding and leads to a feeling of harmony with the earth and the seasons.

With this in mind, forget about tropical and sub-tropical crops until you are proficient at growing the cold season ones. Experimenting can be fun, but first learn to provide basic food in these somewhat adverse conditions.

Choose your site

Give a lot of attention to your choice of site. Ideally, it should be south-facing with water nearby. It should be part-way up a slope so that it is not in a frost pocket, but not up so high that the winds can scour it. The slightest slope has an effect on the sun's ability to heat the garden. In addition, the garden should be fairly close to the house. Not only will it receive more attention that way, but also there is less chance of destruction by deer or bears.

Be sure your chosen site gets plenty of sun. You may have to clear away some trees. If your topsoil is as shallow as mine is, you will want to begin building it up from the very beginning. Someone gave me a load of topsoil. In addition, I worked in rabbit manure and bedding from the chicken house. Fresh chicken manure can burn

plants, but mine was mixed with large amounts of straw and I had no problem. Keep in mind that if you import topsoil, you may also import weed seeds.

Unless you have running water, you'll have to carefully evaluate water availability for your garden. We positioned ours as near to our springs as we could without having it waterlogged after a rain.

Choose your seeds

It is very important to purchase seeds from a company that specializes in high altitude or cold season gardening. I always use seeds from Garden City Seeds in Victor, Montana, and I've had great success with these. Not only are they bred in and for a cold climate, but the company also provides lots of helpful information.

Consider also that a plant variety that matures in 60 days in a mild climate may take 75 days in a place where the ground stays cool and the nights are always cold. When the air is thin, temperature variations are extreme, and the seeds you plant need to be suitable. For example, it's August as I write this. Yesterday, the

high was 87° and the low 27°, and that is very common. Clear, sunny days bring the extremes, while cloudy days are much more moderate. Most varieties that do quite well in other parts of the country are not going to prosper under these conditions.

Your high altitude garden will basically consist of greens, roots, pea crops, cabbage family crops, and some herbs.

Starting your garden in the fall will give you a head start. Prepare the soil as you would for a spring garden. If your soil is acid, work in plenty of ashes, as well as bedding and compost. When the weather is cold, but the ground has not yet frozen, plant spinach, lettuce, peas, and snow peas. In your herb garden, try parsley, chives, chervil, coriander (cilantro), chamomile, mint, and dill. All of these herbs are self-seeders, so after the first year you may not have to replant.

If your area has snow all winter, you will not need to mulch. If it doesn't, pile on the compost and bedding, so that the seeds don't germinate during an early thaw. Not all these crops will do well every time, but you should have enough success to make it worthwhile.

When to plant what

Garlic should always be planted in the fall where growing seasons are short. It's OK if your garlic starts to grow before the ground freezes. Cover the garlic with about six inches of mulch.

When the ground begins to thaw and the first wild plants are peeping through the top layer of the warming soil, you can plant peas and snow peas and sugar snaps. When they start to sprout, add mulch for protection. If you add mulch too early, the seeds will stay too cold to germinate. On the other hand, nights in the 20's will damage or kill your plants, so pile the mulch lightly around your plants with just the growing tops above. It will take experience to get this right, and even with experience, there will sometimes be failures. We're really pushing the season here.

In late April, plant root crops such as carrots, parsnips, and onions. This is also the time to plant parsley. These crops are planted late enough that by the time their long roots are growing well, the ground should be thawed (say early May).

In May or early June, plant lettuce, spinach, radishes, and turnips. The ground will be warm enough now so that these seeds will benefit from a layer of mulch. Not only will mulch keep the seed beds moist, but it will keep them protected from the cold night air, thus hastening germination and growth. As they push up through the mulch, you will not have to pile more on, as they will be able to withstand frost.

In mid-May, plant potatoes, using extra large chunks of seed potatoes. These should be planted five inches deep and covered with a six-inch layer of mulch. As the plants grow, continue to add mulch, so that only the tops of the plants are exposed. In that way

only the tops will be lost to frost, and the rest of the plant will live.

In early June, plant beets and set out cabbage, broccoli, Brussels sprouts, kale, and collards.

In mid-July, plant second crops of lettuce, spinach, and radishes. If lettuce freezes, let it warm up naturally before picking it.

If you have snow cover, you can dig out Brussels sprouts, kale, and collards as you need them. Otherwise, cover with mulch to prevent freezing and thawing.

Carrots can be left in the ground all winter if they are covered with bags of leaves. Just lift a bag and pull up as many as you need.

To store cabbage, dig a pit, line it with straw, and place your cabbages inside. Cover with straw and then bags of leaves.

Leave parsnips in the ground and use them as soon as the snow melts.

If strawberries and raspberries grow wild where you live, you can probably grow domestic varieties. Choose varieties carefully and mulch in the winter unless you have continuous snow pack.

Try growing rhubarb and Jerusalem artichokes, too. Rhubarb is a hardy perennial, and Jerusalem artichokes will usually come back year after year, since it is unlikely you can dig up the tuber from every plant.

Cold frames and greenhouses will extend your growing season for lettuce, greens, chives, and parsley, but unless you want to use supplemental heat, it's probably not worth the effort to try other vegetables. Even if the plants stay alive, the growth will be so slow that it won't really be worthwhile.

Some people get great enjoyment from seeing what they can coax into growing under adverse conditions. If you're one of those people, go for it. First, though, concentrate on the easier plants that are more likely to provide sustenance for you and your family. Δ

Goats don't eat zucchini

By *Jacqueline Binford-Bell*

I was raised by an earth mother who always seemed most at home when she had her hands in dirt. By contrast, *my* feet seldom touched the ground, and my head was always in the clouds, filled with some grand dream or make-believe world. The only time I came in touch with the earth was to trip over it.

Adulthood did not seem to change that much. I merely wrote down my daydreams and called myself a writer. The spring and summer of 1972, I was writing my first novel, and despite my weaving and angora goat raising, I was less connected to the world than most. I would turn 27 that June, but I was more a child of fantasy than at seven. Paul Simon sang of "slip-sliding away," and I knew what he meant. To ground myself quite literally, I decided to emulate Mother and plant a garden.

What I knew about gardening came from the back of the Burpee seed packages I purchased at the local feed store. A growing season was that period when the ski area six miles up the road was not open. Dirt was dirt, even if it did come in a variety of colors from yellow ocher to Indian red to burnt umber. That at least I had noticed during my watercolor painting period. And I was never the one to read directions until all else had failed.

I had not even taken notice of my mother's gardens since second grade. That was her last garden before we left the lush Missouri River basin of my childhood. That half-acre garden in my memories was weed- and bug-free and magically produced crisp, cool sweet peas which I plucked and ate on early morning strolls down the

rows, as I went off to climb my favorite oak tree and dream away the day with a favorite book and Boy, my beloved English setter.

That I no longer lived on a grassy plain of peat with scattered hillocks of oaks and black walnut, but on a steep mountainside of rocks covered with Ponderosa pine should have given me my first clue that the reality of a garden would be quite different from my fantasy. That first garden, like those of Robert Frost, grew rocks best.

Cucumbers, I found, did not like the chilly mountain nights, and the corn was not knee-high by the Fourth of July and never reached *Oklahoma*'s mythical elephant's eye. Beans and peas sprouted well but quickly fell prey to my small flock of Angora goats. Solomon, Sheba, and Babylon would have gotten the lettuce, too, but the wild rabbits beat them to it. (The rabbits went *under* the chicken-wire fence and the goats went *over* it.)

Cabbage mites got the cabbage, cauliflower, and broccoli. Frost claimed the pumpkins, and the melons seemed

to have just given up soon after sprouting. The only plant that seemed to thrive was zucchini. The dark green plant with its curious long fruit survived the arid soil, low humidity, chilly nights, and rarified air as if it were a weed.

When it first began to thrive, in fact, I thought it must *be* a weed. I had forgotten I had planted the zucchini, since the goats also had eaten my row markers. I would have pulled it up, but by then *anything* green was welcome. If nothing else, it would please the goats, who took great delight in stealing forbidden fruit while I daydreamed during their daily outings from the pen. But the goats studiously ignored it, preferring even the Russian thistle that grew wild at the garden's perimeter.

And so, undaunted by even my novice gardening efforts, the zucchini plants flourished. In the middle of summer it began to produce a seemingly endless harvest of squash, a vegetable I had at that time seldom eaten by choice and never cooked.

My neighbor, a retired widower from Georgia who seemed to be quietly and endlessly amused by my garden, had given me the package of zucchini seeds and came regularly to check on their progress and chuckle at mine. When I professed not to know what to do with the long green vegetable, he gave me a recipe for zucchini bread. It was delicious, but it only used two cups of the abundant vegetable for two loaves. Zucchini soup, a recipe found in my collection of cookbooks, used more. Zucchini sauteed with onion used it most easily but proved the least palatable. Zucchini breaded and fried like at the neighborhood Italian restaurant was my favorite, but it soon grew tiresome.

Finding new ways to use it became a challenge, and I was soon substituting it for almost anything in my favorite recipes: zucchini pickles and zucchini pie and zucchini salsa (and a natural dye for handspun Angora goat hair that unfortunately was a failure.)

Friends who had previously enjoyed coming to dinner began turning down invitations and sent me recipes and cookbooks instead. Soon I had so many ways to cook zucchini that I considered writing my own cookbook on the subject. The same friends smiled indulgently at that and encouraged me just to keep thinking and call them later. The zucchini plants ultimately succumbed to the mountain winter, and so my friendships were saved.

After my horticultural failure that summer, I am not sure why I planted a garden the next year, unless (as Mother maintained) it is that I am just plain stubborn and unwilling to let anything defeat me. Or perhaps I was so detached from reality that I was unaware I had failed. I had, after all, produced a bounty of zucchini. In part, I think, it was the memory of watching the zucchini grow the year before that re-ignited the desire to plant the next spring. Like Thoreau at Walden Pond, a tiny part of me at least "...wished to live deliberately, to front only the essential facts of life." For Thoreau it was in watching beans grow that life and the seasons became real, and for me it was zucchini that brought me (even fleetingly) from my imaginary worlds to the earth on which I was forced to live. It is gardening that keeps me from just flying away.

I have planted numerous gardens since then. I have learned about growing seasons and climatic ranges and acidity of soil. I have gardened on the rich soil of the Piedmont Plateau of North Carolina and in the dark peaty soil of the Missouri River Basin and have learned to adapt my seed choices to the peculiarities of the area . . . but I have always planted zucchini, and I have never seen it fail to produce.

I now live at 8000 feet above sea level in the heart of the Sangre de Cristo Mountains of Northern New Mexico, where my garden must be a 90 day wonder. I have mastered the techniques of forcing plants that like longer seasons and wetter and warmer summers. I have gone from the basic vegetables to gourmet varieties I cannot get in the local store. Every January, when winter is raging outside my window, I compile my seed orders, and as spring begins to claim temporary victories in March, my first seedlings are sprouting in plastic trays lined up along every window.

A BHM Writer's Profile: Linda Gabris

Linda Gabris is a full time freelance writer and creative writing instructor. Her articles, fiction, and poetry have appeared in publications across North America. She has hosted an outdoor column for a number of years and especially enjoys writing features about nature and outdoor recreation.

Despite all that, it is the lowly zucchini, hastily cast into the ground and given no special consideration, that never lets me down and oddly provides me the greatest pleasure. If the goats would eat what I do not want and cannot use, it would be a perfect plant. Δ

A BHM Writer's Profile: Ruth Adler

Alder has been a free lance writer for the past 30 years. She is also a former secretary and newspaper reporter. She has had 150 articles, features, and stories published over the years. Some magazines that published her manuscripts are Country, Country Folk Art, Almanac for Farmers and City Folk, Fashion Accessories, Grit, Capper's, and Mature Living.

Grow horehound for the health of it

By Jim Hildreth

Growing food is a large step along the road of self-reliance, and growing medicine comforts each step along the way. Horehound, *Marrubium vulgare,* should be made to feel at home in all gardens. It's an attractive perennial herb with time tested medicinal benefits and other desirable traits. It's easily grown, and being a perennial, it grows bigger and better every year.

The ancient Egyptians first recorded growing horehound and using it to relieve cough symptoms. They derived its name from Horus, their god of sky and light. The Greeks credited the herb with curing bites of mad dogs, calling it "hoarhound." The Anglo-Saxons referred to the herb as "hare hune," meaning "a downy plant," undoubtedly due to the plant's wooly appearance, and they used it to combat the effects of rabies. Horehound's latinized generic name, *Marrubium,* actually derives from the Hebrew word "marrob," meaning "bitter juice." The herb is one of the five ritual bitter herbs of Passover.

Time-tested cough remedy

Horehound has been used to treat everything from snake bites to jaundice, but it's the herb's use as a cough remedy that's withstood the test of time. Our grandparents attest to taking horehound cough drops and cough medicine years ago, and it remains an effective remedy to this day.

It's not fussy

That's the good news. The great news is that horehound flourishes on its own with little help from the gardener. Ideally, horehound grows best in organically rich soil and a location that receives full sun. That doesn't mean, however, that the herb fails in anything less than the perfect growing environment. In fact, my 10-year old horehound planting grows beautifully in partial shade. It thrives in my organically rich garden soil, but I wouldn't hesitate to plant it in poor, sandy soil either, because it adapts quickly to harsh conditions.

Horehound grows up to two feet tall with fuzzy, light green, heavily wrinkled, inch-long leaves. It serves as an accent in the herb garden when planted behind lower growing, darker colored oregano and thyme and in front of taller, darker beebalm, feverfew, or aconite. It produces tiny white flowers that grow in whorls on the stems the second year after planting. The flowers attract pollinating bees to the garden, and their small size proves extremely inviting to beneficial predatory and parasitic wasps.

Divide and multiply

Plant divisions establish horehound quickly and easily in the home garden. Ask a fellow gardener's permission to divide one or more of his or her healthy, mature plants. The technique is simple. Drive a spade through the center of a mature horehound plant. Then push the spade into the soil around the plant division and lift it and its root ball carefully from the ground, taking care to minimize root damage. Take the division home and plant it in full sun or partial shade. Firm it into the soil to elimi-nate air pockets and water thoroughly with a dilute solution of liquid seaweed to reduce transplant shock and further reduce air pockets between the soil and roots.

Horehound may also be started from seeds planted indoors during early spring for transplanting in mid-to-late-spring or direct-seeded outdoors during late spring. Moisten the soil, then plant the seeds 1/8" deep. Cover them with fine soil, water again, and maintain even soil moisture until the seeds sprout and grow several inches tall. Thin seedlings to stand a foot apart or spread them throughout the herb and vegetable gardens to attract beneficial insects.

Horehound doesn't require much attention once it's established. It tolerates drought extremely well and doesn't

require heavy feeding, which helps explain why it grows readily along roadsides, on dry grasslands, and in the "difficult" areas of the garden. Nevertheless, I give horehound the royal treatment: organically rich soil, monthly dousing with liquid seaweed and fish emulsion, and compost side dressings in spring and fall. It receives 1/2" of water per week during this area's dry summer season. This drought-tolerant herb could survive on a lot less water, but I find that it grows faster and stronger when given an even weekly supply.

Harvest and storage methods are fairly standard. A light harvest may be taken the first year from seed. After that, heavy-handed harvests two or three times a season do no harm to the plants. For the best medicinal properties, cut stems just as the first flowers open. To maximize horehound's potential to attract beneficial insects, allow the plants to flower for a few weeks before harvesting. Either way, cut the stems to within three inches of the ground. Hang dry in a cool, shaded place, shuck the leaves and flowers from the stems, and store in a cool, dark place in airtight containers.

Making medicine

I find making horehound cough medicine very gratifying. It increases self-reliance by eliminating the need for over-the-counter commercial cough medicines and saves money in the process. It provides an effective cough remedy without the usual drowsiness or other side-effects found in commercial preparations.

Make horehound cough medicine by steeping a couple ounces of fresh horehound or an ounce of dried material in a pint of hot water for 10 minutes, stirring occasionally. Strain the liquid into a bottle and add honey to taste. I usually add as much honey as there is liquid, but keep in mind that horehound tastes very bitter. Adding twice as much honey as there is liquid

A BHM Writer's Profile: Angela Jenkins

Angela Jenkins lives in Glendale, Kentucky, and works at the Elizabethtown Community College, in the college library, as a technician. Angela writes on a free-lance basis and has previously published short stories and poetry as well as magazine articles. She is a member of two writers groups and is on the board for ECCO, the college literary magazine.

A BHM Writer's Profile: Craig Russell

Russell's formal training is in history and biology and those interests come together in old breeds of livestock, old garden and agricultural plants, gathering wild foods, and doing things the old way that have become his avocation.

Given the time he's a rambler and a roamer with an interest in old trails and far places. Sometimes he is a caver and a climber as well.

Currently he's president of the Society for the Preservation of Poultry Antiquities (SPPA).

makes a better-tasting concoction. Shake the solution while it's hot to thoroughly mix it. Store it in the refrigerator. Hot horehound tea with honey and lemon feels great on a sore throat, too.

Horehound certainly earns its keep in the garden. Planted once, it increases in size every year thereafter, providing the planting scheme with attractive wooly foliage. Its ability to attract beneficial insects helps gardeners maintain a chemical-free garden, and its medicinal properties give welcome relief from coughs and sore throats—all that from a low-maintenance, perennial herb.

Seed sources

The following companies sell horehound seeds and will send a catalog free for the asking:

Abundant Life Seed Foundation
P.O. Box 772
1029 Lawrence St.
Port Townsend, WA 98368

Nichols Garden Nursery
1190 North Pacific Highway
Albany, OR 97321-4580

Mellinger's, Inc.
2310 W. South Range Road
North Lima, OH 44452-9731

Park Seed® Company
Cokesbury Road
Greenwood, SC 29647-0001 Δ

Visit our popular website at:
http://www.backwoodshome.com

Blueberries are an affordable luxury

By Alice B. Yeager
Photos by James O. Yeager

Blueberries are an affordable luxury that almost anyone can grow—that is, anyone with a little extra yard space. They are a functional as well as an attractive addition to the home landscape, and if one has an unused lot or more in land, blueberry bushes can be downright lucrative.

When we began to grow blueberries for our own use a number of years ago, the only blueberries in our Southwestern Arkansas area were wild, hard to find, and referred to as "summer huckleberries." They were found in hilly, wooded places in the company of chiggers, ticks, and snakes.

Having been treated to delicious blueberry pie up north, I often wondered why I seldom saw anything made from fresh blueberries in my part of the country. After some research, I found out that our part of Arkansas is somewhat south of the best blueberry growing areas. However, I also learned that some varieties had been developed that were especially suited for the South (Zones 8 and 9). As a group, these varieties are known as "Rabbiteyes."

I ordered early, midseason, and late varieties of blueberries in the hope of having some of them perform well here. As it has turned out, I wasted neither time, effort, nor money, as our blueberry bushes have consistently given us plenty of fruit for our own use as well as to share with friends. By having different varieties, the harvest season is stretched, so that fresh blueberries are available over a longer period of time.

In our piney woods area, we are ideally situated for growing blueberries. All blueberries must have well-drained, acid soil, as their pH requirement is not over 6.0. They don't do their best in ordinary garden soil, as the pH is a little too high—fine for cucumbers and okra, but wrong for blueberries.

Blueberry bushes will grow in full sun or semi-shade. Our blueberry patch is in an area that receives light shade part of the day, which makes picking a pleasant chore on warm days. Shaded areas are impractical for large pick-your-own operations, where blueberries are grown by the acre.

The fact that these plants will tolerate some shade makes them very desirable for the homeowner who would like to use a few bushes in his landscape plans. Being acid-loving, they can be worked in very nicely near azaleas, camellias, cape jasmines, etc. As a fringe benefit, blueberry bushes close out their annual performance with a bright display of red color in late fall.

A few simple rules for planting blueberries

A few simple rules need to be followed when planting blueberry bushes: Never crowd the roots, but dig holes large enough to extend a few inches beyond the actual rootspread. Plant bushes at the same depth as they were grown in the nursery. This is easily seen by the soil line at the base of the plant. Assuming the soil is the proper pH and no additives are needed, fill in the hole halfway with dirt, water thoroughly, then complete filling with dirt. Water again to get rid of any air pockets around the roots.

If you live where summers are drought-prone, make some small dams about 15 inches in diameter around the plants so as to direct water to the roots. Young plants should not be allowed to suffer for lack of water, as they may die or be stunted.

Blueberry bushes appreciate heavy mulches of a mixture of leaves and pine needles. A steady diet of this organic material is all that is needed as far as feeding is concerned. It is also a good way to use yard rakings to advantage. The plants are shallow-rooted and do not need cultivation, although they should always be kept free of invasive vines or weeds.

These plants do not require large spaces, and they may be planted five to six feet apart. Depending on the variety, they will grow from four to eight feet tall. Blueberry plants are very simple to maintain, as they do not require a great deal of pruning. Some nurseries recommend cutting off the low, bushy side growth at the end of the first year. Others say to keep the shorter branches pruned off mature plants in order to encourage the young side-shoots. In our case, being non-commercial and averse to a lot of work, we have found that keeping bushes clean of dead branches and lightly pruning when necessary is sufficient.

Our blueberries are among the most trouble-free plants we have. It has never been necessary to use any sprays. If your area is subject to problems of some sort—rust, fruit fly maggots, etc.—it would be wise to consult a county extension agent and seek out a *non-toxic* control.

Plants will begin bearing in earnest in about three years from planting. They need cross-pollination, so more than one variety should be planted. Most nurseries have special offers combining three or more varieties. By having early, mid-summer, and late varieties, the harvest season can be stretched over a goodly portion of the summer. Surplus berries can be turned

A plump bunch of Woodard blueberries just right for picking

into jam or syrup, or frozen for later use in muffins or other recipes.

Rabbiteye varieties

Our Rabbiteye varieties include Woodard, Tifblue, Delite, and Homebell. Woodard is a choice variety that reaches a height of about five feet. It is a heavy bearer and heralds the beginning of the blueberry season—early June in our Zone 8A. Berries are large, medium-blue, and slightly tart.

Tifblue is a taller plant than Woodard and begins ripening its berries while Woodard is still producing. Tifblue is prolific and has round, sweet, powder-blue berries. I love to sample these blueberries while "working" in the blueberry patch.

Another of our very good blueberries is the Delite variety. It begins to ripen about the first of July and gives a good harvest. Berries are round, medium blue, and a tiny bit tart. Plants tend to be more upright in growth than the others.

Homebell is a unique blueberry and one that I no longer see listed by nurseries. The berries are round and black and have a huckleberry flavor. It ripens about the same time as Delite. It is not a heavy yielder, but its flavor is superb.

Besides those of us who tend the bushes, there are other competitors for blueberries. Birds are fond of the ripe berries, but they redeem themselves by policing the bushes for insects. Frankly, I don't mind the birds and leave the remainder of the crop for them when it thins down. (Small pay for such diligent workers!)

If birds become too much of a nuisance at the peak of the season, they are easily discouraged by loosely tying pieces of *dark* sewing thread at random between the branches. This creates the effect of a strong spider web and frightens them away without harming them. One should be careful not to tie thread (particularly nylon thread) around the branches too tightly, as it can restrict the circulatory system of the branches, resulting in dead limbs.

Blueberry patches are a boon to beekeepers, as the first hint of the opening of the small, bell-shaped flowers brings scout bees to the plants. Until blossoms drop, our blueberry bushes are abuzz with bees.

They're not huckleberries

Blueberries are often erroneously referred to as "huckleberries," but the two are different. Blueberries ripen in summer and huckleberries ripen in late fall. Blueberries have hardly-noticeable seeds and huckleberries have fairly large seeds. Pies made from huckleberries have great flavor but are like trying to eat buckshot. Hence the name "crackerberry." Huckleberries are seldom found in cultivation, but tend to be regarded as wild food.

I have noticed that some restaurants in mountain resort areas like to list huckleberry pie on their dessert menus. This gives a down-home, living-off-the-land touch to the menu. Believe me, if they really served *huckleberry* pie, patrons would never order a second piece!

Due to the Rabbiteye introductions, a number of blueberry farms are now flourishing in the South, indicating that blueberry production may soon be numbered among our major farm industries. Before the new varieties were created, blueberry-growing was mainly confined to Zones 4 to 7. Unlike most orchard production, it does not take many years before blueberry acreage can begin to show a profit. Bushes are easy to maintain and "pick-your-own" is the order of the day, thus relieving owners from having to hire extra labor to harvest the crop.

Whether one is the owner of several acres of blueberry bushes or a small patch, there's nothing better than hot blueberry muffins on a cold, miserable day. (See recipe below.) Forget the weather—it's blueberry time. Enjoy!

Some sources for Rabbiteye varieties

Stark Bro's Nurseries
P.O. Box 10
Louisiana, MO 63353-0010

J. W. Jung Seed & Nursery Co.
235 S. High Street
Randolph, WI 53957-0001

Henry Fields Seed & Nursery Co.
415 N. Burnett
Shenandoah, IA 51602

Gurney's Seed & Nursery Co.
110 Capital Street
Yankton, SD 57079

Blueberry muffins

Step 1

1 cup whole wheat flour
1 cup unbleached flour
4 teaspoons baking powder
1/2 teaspoon nutmeg
1/2 teaspoon cinnamon

Mix together and set aside.

Step 2

1 cup milk
1 beaten egg

Mix and set aside.

Step 3

1 cup sugar
1/4 cup melted butter or oleo
1 teaspoon grated lemon rind
1/2 cup chopped pecans

Mix and then combine all ingredients.

Step 4

1 cup fresh or frozen blueberries
(If frozen, thaw before using.)

Gently stir blueberries into combined mixture. Too much stirring will crush blueberries, so mix only until berries are distributed throughout the mixture.

Fill greased muffin tins 2/3 full and bake at 375° F for 20-25 minutes. Makes 18 muffins. Δ

A BHM Writer's Profile:
Mary Kenyon

Mary Kenyon, her husband David, and their children live and learn in the country near Petersburg, Iowa. Mary is the homeschooling mother of six children as well as a freelance writer and author of Homeschooling From Scratch (Gazelle, 1995). The Kenyon family owns a home-based business selling quality used books through the mail. For a list of books the Kenyon 's sell, send $2. OO to; Once Upon a Time Family Books, P. O. Box 296, Manchester, Iowa 52097.

A BHM Writer's Profile:
Robert Bumpus

Nebraskan by birth, Bumpus has lived most of his 70 years in California, but since 1990 he has lived in Oregon. He and his wife bought 3.5 acres just off Highway 101 near a game park. Heavily timbered and overgrown with brush, they have been clearing it ever since.

They raise most of their own meat plus garden and orchard stuff. Drilled their own well, built outbuildings, etc. His wife says they are too old to pioneer but he says he's having a ball.

Married since 1948, they have nine children and a host of grandchildren and great-grandchildren.

Bumpus has been a fruit worker, a cowboy, a gold miner and gold dredger, he has worked in security for an aerospace corporation, worked for the Yuba City, California, police department, been an auto and truck mechanic, and has spent time working in the big California timber. He presently does odd jobs for widow ladies and is co-pastor of a small nondenominational church. He says he is anti-abortion, anti-tree hugger, and a Republican with strong Libertarian leanings, and he hates the way Oregon is being liberalized by former Californians.

Bumpus also belongs to a writers group in Coos Bay, Oregon, and writes short stories and poetry.

The duck dilemma: they're a lot of fun, and they *do* eat those slugs — *but . . .*

By Inez Castor

It all started innocently enough. All we wanted to do was keep the slugs from eating everything we planted. Here in the Pacific northwest, slugs can destroy an entire planting of seedlings in a single night. Since my husband and I are organic market gardeners, our options are limited; most of the things that kill slugs are on the "prohibited" list.

For a while, we hand-picked the slimy creatures at dawn and dropped them into a bucket of water and yeast, but it became apparent that I could spend every morning of my life at this Sisyphean task and still not harvest produce fit to sell. Crushed oyster shells helped a little, and so did agricultural lime. Strips of plastic permeated with salt worked well, but they were much too expensive for people trying to earn a living on one acre of land.

It was at this point, early in March and well into the slug season, that our friend Donna offered us what appeared to be a perfect (and inexpensive) solution. All we needed was a few ducks, and she had eggs due to hatch in a few days. Of course, they wouldn't be much help in the first few months, but by the time the rainy season started again, they would virtually eliminate our slug problem.

At first we were hesitant, knowing nothing about ducks except that they flew over us twice a year. Donna voiced the prevailing attitude, one that we were to encounter time and again: "Ducks take care of themselves; you don't have to do anything but throw them a little feed now and again." Right.

Finally, convinced that we were being unduly pessimistic and suspicious, I brought the first four ducklings home the day after they were hatched. At the last minute, Donna told me that they'd need to stay in the house until they exchanged their soft baby down for real feathers, but I didn't pay much attention.

Busy falling in love

I was busy falling in love with a tiny being whose bill was the size of my pinky fingernail, and whose webbed feet were so delicate that every blood vessel showed. It all seemed quite simple; they could live in a box in my office. So I carefully packed them home in a bucket to show David, already feeling protective and maternal. David, ever the practical soul, wanted to know what I intended to do with them now.

"Why, they're going to solve our slug problem," I stated confidently.

"Sure they are, but I meant what are you going to do with them *right* now. We have *slugs* bigger than they are."

"Don't worry about a thing. Just bring in that old box the chipper came in, and put it in my office. I bought starter mash for them at the feed store. It's kind of expensive, but they'll grow into the regular food soon."

Did I mention that I tend to get rabidly enthusiastic about everything I start?

We lined the chipper box with an old plastic tablecloth and put thick pads of newspaper in the bottom. Since baby ducks love water but tend to drown if it's more than two inches deep, we gave them a cake pan full of water. We put food in a cereal bowl and rigged a trouble light for warmth.

We released our fluffy yellow babies into their palatial new home and stood back to watch. They fluttered frantically the length of the pool, through the food dish, and back through the water, peeping and pooping all the

way. Within minutes it was apparent that we'd have to change their food, water and papers several times a day. At the end of the first week we were out of newspapers, we'd gone through five dollars worth of food, and the entire house reeked of duck.

But they were delightful; there was none of the mindless pecking at each other that chickens are known for. They simply made more mess than anything that size should be capable of.

At the end of two weeks, we began putting them outside for most of the day. We bought a hundred-foot roll of two-foot poultry wire to make them a playpen, justifying the expense by telling each other that the rest of the roll was bound to come in handy for something. Now we only had to change their box once a day, and preparations began for their move to the great outdoors. We began hand-feeding them small slugs, which they seemed to consider a rare delicacy.

We dismantled the old pumphouse that wouldn't fit the new pump, and turned it into an A-frame. The idea was to tuck them in at night and cover the front with poultry wire.

At two months, the ducks moved into the garden on a permanent basis, free to forage during the day, bedded down in their A-frame at night. What a relief! No more catching them and schlepping them into the house every evening. No more need to leave the doors and windows open day and night in order to breathe. We had nearly $100 invested in food, wire, and incidentals, and the only slugs they'd eaten had been served to them on a cabbage leaf, but things were looking up.

We slid almost imperceptibly from spring into a peaceful summer, and it looked as if everything was working out just fine. The ducks followed us around the garden waiting for us to turn up goodies, and they actually ate slugs—lots of slugs. It's amazing how far a slug can stretch with a duck on either end.

We began giving them cracked corn at half the price of starter mash. Of course, they seemed to waste a lot of it, and we were feeding every sparrow and squirrel in northern California, but that was all right. They were definitely going to take care of the slug problem.

The pleasure of watching them work

All the initial expense was worth the pleasure of watching them work a carrot bed, bills buried in the soil, tails up and twitching, chuckling self-importantly deep in their throats. It was a sight guaranteed to bring a gardener's blood pressure down.

As the ducks gained confidence, strength, and weight, a new problem surfaced. Ducks have large, flat feet, suitable for trampling seedlings. It didn't help that our ducks were Pekins, the largest and heaviest type. What's more, wherever we'd been disturbing the soil (as we tend to do when planting seedlings) was where the ducks wanted to be. Have you ever tried shooing ducks out of a raised bed that's thirty feet long and four feet wide? They panic, flap, squawk, then run the length of the bed—several times. I began to detect a malicious gleam in their eyes as they danced among the seedlings.

They also wanted to come in the back door. They hung around the porch like teenagers on a street corner. I have an aversion to wasting all that fine fertilizer by tracking it into the kitchen, so we ran a strip of wire the width of the property between the garden and the house.

We bought four more rolls of wire to surround various areas of the garden that we wanted free of ducks. Wide beds, indeed, entire sections of the garden were fenced off with lopsided lengths of poultry wire supported by bamboo stakes. Now we were gardening in a maze, having to step over at least two fences in order to get anywhere. There were occasional accidents, but the system worked quite

well as long as we paid close attention to where we were walking. It was the work of only a few minutes to move a length of wire from one spot in the garden to another.

One day I watched David, a heavily laden bucket in either hand, march down the path, suddenly step high and swing the buckets over a bit of empty air, then continue on his way. He hadn't noticed that I'd moved the wire.

In mid-summer, the job of putting the ducks to bed became an exercise in frustration. There's a limit to how long I'm willing to chase ducks, and I reached that limit in early August. They simply didn't want to go to bed on warm summer nights, and I really couldn't blame them a bit. They were now too large to tempt hawks and owls, and I figured that if we couldn't catch them, neither could anything else.

An intruder strikes

This pleasant interlude came to an abrupt end one morning when our two females were found dead. We suspected weasel, because the villain had simply opened the throats and sucked them dry.

We buried the girls and began construction on a pest-proof pen up near the house for the drakes, who were suddenly willing, even eager, to be put to bed in the evening. The new pen required a roll of six-foot wire and ten posts at $3 each.

Our drakes were lonely, and Donna happened to have more ducks than she needed, so she gave us a gray pair of uncertain lineage and Stella, a mallard with the raucous voice of a middle-aged barfly.

A week later, the gray female was dead, the pitiful little corpse left beside the "pest-proof" pen. It was at about this time that I began losing all sense of perspective.

I dug a trench and buried the bottom six inches of the fence. I used a complex series of bungee cords and wires to secure the gate. I left the bedroom window open at night so I could hear the ducks should they be disturbed. And I began jumping up to run out naked at every night sound. (You can get away with that sort of thing in the country.)

The dog was as crazy as I was, and together we ran howling into the night several times a week. It didn't save James, who never made a sound while becoming dead.

It did, however, save Fella, the remaining Pekin. One night dog and I ran shrieking from the house, only to see a raccoon struggling to drag Fella through a hole he'd excavated near the gate. I snatched Fella by one leg, and the raccoon was gone. There I stood with a horribly injured duck and an inability to "finish the job."

Though the feathers never grew back on his head and neck, and he held his head cocked strangely, Fella survived. We put the food dish on an old wheel to get it up where he could reach it without straining his damaged neck muscles.

Donna came through for us again, donating Lady, a Pekin female, to keep Fella and the rowdy Stella company. By this time the pen was more impregnable than the local maximum security prison, but that's another story. We began to relax, and I slept through the night again.

Then we came home from town one day to find that a pair of stray dogs had killed all three ducks. David began digging the inevitable hole while I, blubbering, gathered up our little friends.

I moped for a week. The garden was too still, too predictable. Besides, it would soon be slug season again, and we had several hundred dollars invested in this "final solution" to the slug problem.

The simple truth is, I enjoy ducks. It's not possible to watch them waddle down a path without smiling. A freshly filled wading pool will bring on a veritable circus of diving, flapping, darting, and preening; it's a show I'd pay to see. There is no meanness in

A BHM Writer's Profile: Terrie Clark

Terrie Clark is an account executive at commercial printing firm in Manhattan, Kansas. It was through her work there that she became acquainted with and wrote about John and Geri McPherson and their primitive life-skills lifestyle.

A graduate of the University of Kansas with a degree in Environmental Studies, Clark has appreciated calling Kansas home. After residing several years in rural Doniphan County, she and her two daughters currently live on the outskirts of Manhattan, which lies in the heart of the Flint Hills and Tall Grass Prairie region of central Kansas.

Before moving to Manhattan in 1992, Ms. Clark worked in livestock publications both as an advertising executive and as a writer. Her special interests include environmental issues, individual's rights, equality, and self-sufficiency. She especially enjoys meeting and writing about people who live their passion, like the McPhersons.

them. When Fella was injured and couldn't keep up, they stayed near him as if in moral support.

I'm hooked on ducks!

So we looked at our dwindling bank account and began discussing the idea of fencing the entire place. While we stood in the front yard arguing passionately, me for a fence and David for a woodshed, a strange mongrel ran around the corner of the house with the cat food dish in his mouth.

We invested over seven hundred dollars and a month's labor in fencing.

We bought three grown mallards, and they've brought the garden back to life. We watch them patrol their territory during the day, tuck them in at night, and harvest slime-free produce. In a pen in the greenhouse, safe and warm under lights, are four Swedish Blue ducklings, warming up in the bullpen, so to speak. We sure do enjoy our ducks.

But don't let anyone tell you that ducks are a cheap solution to the slug problem. Δ

A BHM Writer's Profile: Carolyn Beck

Carolyn A. Beck has written since high school and is a graduate of the Institute of Children's Literature. She has been married 36 years and has three sons plus one grandson.

She has become a Certified Oregon State University Master Gardener where she has had the opportunity to write several publications for the Extension Service which were produced for public use.

She has also researched people who had lived in Oregon after surviving the civil war to assist a professor at the University of Maine with a college level Civil War, The Blue and The Gray.

The article she wrote for BHM, "Orphaned Kittens Need Special Care," was inspired after finding a dead mother cat on the road. Later, she heard the kittens crying, and took them home. Not knowing the first thing about how to care for motherless kittens, she started researching. Since then has helped several other batches of motherless kittens to survive.

Scrap poly pipe can be transformed into "training wheels for trees"

By L.A. Wallin

Along about the time of year that northern gardens and fields are covered with deep snow, orchard and seed catalogs begin clogging mailboxes. It seems like everybody and their cousin is offering special offers on new varieties . . . a sure sign that spring is not too many months away.

In our area, the giant chain stores have a contest with each other to be the first to set up nursery departments in early April. Truckloads of young fruit and shade trees arrive each week, both bareroot and container-grown.

During the past 15 years, we've purchased and planted about 100 fruit trees. We bought some at full price, early in the planting season. The rest we bought at a discount, just before greenhouses were stored for the summer. Like lost kittens and puppies, they just seemed to find their way to our homestead. With extra care, most of these trees have survived, and we are well on our way to food self-sufficiency.

Some of the trees had been trimmed and properly shaped by the growers who raised them, but the limbs on a few of them looked as if they had been enclosed in small-diameter tubes. They were growing almost straight up, not spreading a bit. Left alone, they would have been certain to produce hard-to-pick crops. They needed helping hands.

We tried various methods of holding the supple limbs for a few months, while they acquired a new direction in life. We notched short lengths of wood lath, and tried to keep the sticks braced between the boughs. That's a difficult task in our windy area.

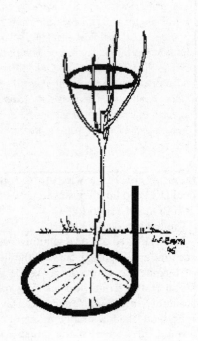

The newly-planted tree in this diagram is benefitting from both the limb rack and the irrigation ring.

Then a new wrinkle on the ancient Hula Hoop theme flashed through our minds. We had a pile of scrap pieces of black poly water pipe, in various diameters and lengths. They were left over from building our own home, and from scavenger tours . . . orphans just looking for something to do.

Limb racks

For our "limb racks," we carefully curled 54" long sections of 3/4" diameter poly pipe into circles. We joined the ends of each loop by pushing them onto a round, 4" long hardwood stick. Then we slowly heated the pipe with a small propane torch to heat-shrink it onto the connector.

Next, we placed the units in the center of the limbs which needed to be spread, one to each tree, carefully pulling and pushing them into position. With one of us holding limbs and pipe, the other tied branches to the poly with used baler twine. Care was taken not to girdle the thin bark of the boughs.

We left the new hoops in place for a few months. In late autumn, they were removed. The limbs remained where we wanted them, for better open space in the center of the new fruit trees. The poly pipe rings, little affected by ultraviolet sun rays, were stored for use in future years.

And that's not the only use we found for that scrap pipe.

Underground irrigation rings

For several years, we have made circular irrigation rings of poly pipe, which are buried about a foot deep in the soil around new trees. Surrounding the newly planted trees, they allow water to seep down to the root zone, without encouraging unwanted, nutrient-robbing weed and grass growth near the surface of our orchard. This brings on better root growth, as they spread in a wider range than with simply irrigating near the main stems. With the loops, we can slowly inject diluted liquid organic fertilizers and reduce concern about burning tender subsurface growth.

Our irrigation loops are about 6 1/2 feet in diameter. We usually use the larger sizes of poly pipe for these. The ends of each loop are pushed onto opposing male ends of poly pipe tees. The loop is laid on a flat, horizontal surface. The third male end of the tee is aligned so that it rises vertically. A separate piece of poly pipe, about three feet long, is slid over this end. Then, as with the limb racks, we slowly heat the pipe with a small propane torch to bond it onto the connector. Next we turn the circle over and use a 1/4 inch drill bit to bore a string of holes into what will become the lower edge of the loop. We make the holes about an inch apart.

When planting a new tree, we dig a seven-foot-diameter hole in the ground, about three feet deep. The tree is placed in the hole, and the cavity is backfilled around the roots with a mixture of soil, a small amount of fine gravel, and well-composted manure.

One of the poly loops is installed around each tree on a gravel bed, much like a sewer drain field. We place each wheel about a foot below the orchard surface, using a bubble level to get it as flat as possible. The vertical standpipe rises about two feet above ground, and serves as an inlet for a nozzle made of a piece of copper tubing attached to a garden hose.

The rest of the new tree hole is filled with the soil mixture, tamped lightly to remove air pockets, and topped with moisture-conserving mulch of old sawdust and shavings. When we irrigate our trees, we adjust the faucet so that only a medium stream of water enters the standpipe. Since the buried loop has many perforations to spread the water, there is little risk of eroding the soil which surrounds each tree. Buried that far from the surface, the loop allows us to safely rototill the ground around the trees. It has worked well for us.

Both above and below ground, we're proud of our "training wheels for trees."

L.A. Wallin and her husband live in an earth-bermed, rock-and-turf-roofed, solar-electric-powered house. They lived in a tent for three years while building their house. Country hard-scrabble raised, during the past 15 years they have developed many alternative methods of surviving tough times. Δ

Lilacs can provide a reliable "thermometer" for planting

By L. Gordon Stetser Jr.

Because the dates of killing frosts can vary by as much as two weeks within a mile, you're taking a chance if you depend on gardening books, seed packets, or weather forecasters when you schedule your planting.

According to Dr. L. P. Perry of the University of Vermont, "It's safer to use your own garden to determine your planting schedule." The Persian lilac is a most reliable thermometer: when the leaves unfurl, it's time to plant root crops and lettuce; when the flowers bloom, put in tender plants like melon, corn and tomatoes.

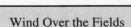

If you don't have a lilac bush, take a look around your yard this spring. Are the daffodils blossoming when you put in lettuce, for example? Then if all goes well with the harvest, use your daffodils as a when-to-plant indicator next year. Δ

Wind Over the Fields

Even here in the city, when everything quiets enough in three a.m., there is a moment of hesitation, a stuttering of sorts, and the wind comes.

Gentle at first, like someone giving gas to a new car and then with force

"Let's see what she can do."

It runs through streets and loiters dangerously on front porches, opening and slamming screen doors, moving quickly over rooftop shingles and concrete telephone lines, whispering

"There were fields here once."

Ben Sizemore
Hamilton, OH

When you're laying out your farm, careful planning pays big dividends

By Jan Palmer

Planning the layout of your farm can make the difference between an enjoyable enterprise and an unsuccessful financial drain.

Hopefully, you'll have time to become totally familiar with your land in all kinds of weather and seasons. Only time will tell what your land is capable of handling. Here in northeast Oklahoma, the challenges are different from those faced by someone in western Washington or northern New York. Yet there are many similar problems, and homesteaders can learn from each other, no matter where they live.

Before buying materials, we sat down with pen and paper and listed enterprises we wanted to get into or try. Some of them can share a space (such as a couple of jenny donkeys and sheep), while others should be kept separate (such as pigs and horses—rooting by pigs could cause injuries to horses if they stepped in a hole). We found that many enterprises we would undertake would involve small numbers of the particular animal. For example, we plan to raise a few pigs for our own use, but our needs will be much different from those of a commercial hog ranch.

In arranging your homestead, if you're lucky enough to be able to start from scratch and put buildings, fields, etc., where you want them, you have more options than the person who gets an existing spread.

How close to the house?

The more time you spend with a particular enterprise, the closer you'll want it to be to the house. For example, for milking goats, you'll either want to run water and power to the milking area *or* set up an area near the house with just light and basic power, allowing you to carry the milk in and wash pails and such in the house. The pig enterprise, on the other hand, should be some distance *away* from the house, and keeping the pigs in a sanitary manner will help reduce many of the problems associated with keeping hogs.

We set our chicken house and yard about 25 feet from the house for ease of caring for the birds, ease of carrying water (no water run to the yard yet), and as extra security against predators.

Shelter for the animals

Some enterprises can be done without a barn, but shelter should be provided for all types of stock. Outdoor rabbit hutches are popular on homesteads, and offer housing that can be moved from time to time if need be. Pigs can get along fine with a three-sided shelter, as can sheep, although if you have babies on the way in colder climates, be sure it is warm enough in the shelter to keep them from freezing.

What's normal?

Find out what is normal for your area. For example, most planning books we've ever seen suggest three-sided sheds to be facing south for maximum sun. In our area, however, some of the coldest winds come from the south, and seldom from the east, so our sheds will be facing east instead of south. We aren't alone in that decision: a red angus ranch near here also has all their shelters open on the east side. We put up temporary structures facing south, and they were whipped to shreds by the south winds, so take heed. Your area might have stronger east winds or west winds, but no book or article can take the place of the advice of the local farmers and/or extension office. Planning ahead now can save you dollars later—as well as the frustration of doing all the work over again.

If you have an area that is naturally low-lying, you might consider putting in a pond. This could serve as livestock water and almost always increases the value and looks of your property. Be advised, though that if you hire it done it will be expensive ($3,000-4,000 in our area). If you haven't bought acreage yet and want a pond, you might want to consider buying land with a pond already on it.

Planning the garden

If you plan on putting in a garden, as many homesteaders do, you will probably want to locate it within a reasonable distance from the kitchen, to help make harvesting easier. An alternative, which will cost more money, is to have a small "second kitchen" out by the garden with running water and basic harvesting supplies (canning or freezing). With that setup, you can take the waste (corn shucks, leaves, etc.) straight out to the stock and the produce into the house to the pantry or freezer.

One of the best investments you can make in starting your operation is getting a soil test, usually available from the county extension service. In some areas, they're free; in our area it costs $8. It can tell you the true condition of your soil and what you need to add, if anything.

Make note of soil conditions: the spot where you want to put the garden might not be ideally suited for growing. Our planned garden area was *wet,* and when it did dry it was like concrete. What little did grow didn't develop as it should have. (We *didn't* start by getting a soil test.) We solved part of the problem by raising the growing area up, using raised beds in tires, which we got free for the hauling from a local tire dealer. The disadvantage to this is that it means hand tilling, because it's not possible to get a tiller down inside the tires. An alternative might be to ring the garden area with old tires, then raise the entire area if you have the fill to do it.

Make use of fertilizer from your livestock and put it on the garden to help enrich the soil. Many people suggest using geese for weeders and chickens to go after the bugs. It's been our experience that geese would rather eat the lettuce than the weeds growing next to them, but the chickens do a good job at keeping the bug population down. They do scratch, however, and might redistribute newly planted seeds, so you'd best keep them out of the garden area until plants are well established. This also keeps them from eating your corn seeds and other treats.

Be sure to check restrictions on your property. For example, you may not be permitted to locate any buildings within so many feet of a property line. Plan the layout with consideration for the neighbors, to help keep peace in the neighborhood. Of course, some neighbors are easier to get along with than others. Some don't mind the "country air" as much as the noise, which can be pretty loud at feeding time. Install fences that keep your stock where they should be. The first time your goat gets into the neighbor's flower bed could cause the last peaceful communication with the neighbor.

Consider a compact setup to allow as much room as possible for grazing. It might not be a bad thing to carry water 150 feet to the goats in the summer, but when it's below freezing and you're already cold, you might be tempted to give them less than they need.

Old homesteads in the Northeast had connected buildings, so that in severe weather there was no need to go outside at all. This offers some unusual solutions, but also creates some problems. The biggest is the risk of fire, particularly if hay is stored in the barn. A fire in the barn could quickly spread to the house, or vice versa. Another issue is the increased chance of pests (such as flies or mice) coming into the house. Planning ahead and talking to people who have had such structures is the best way to find out the disadvantages so you can work on eliminating the problems if you like this type of structure. Another possibility is to have an attached area for small stock, with the larger stock in another barn away from the house.

Idea books

There are many books available to give you different ideas and perspectives for planning your homestead. Here are some of them:

Big House, Little House, Back House, Barn, by Thomas C. Hubka, $21.45. The history and cultural significance of the connected farm building tradition of New England. Small Farmer's Book Service, P.O. Box 2805, Eugene, OR 97402

Horse Barns Big and Small, by Nancy W. Abrosiano and Mary F. Harcourt. Horse barn designs and considerations; could be adapted to other barns or combination barns. Breakthrough Publications, 310 North Highland Ave., Ossining, NY 10562

The "Have More" Plan, by Ed and Carolyn Robinson, $7. Enterprise and planning for the homestead for self sufficiency. Good ideas for sun porches for turkeys, small hog setup, and more. Lots of good information. Prices are different now from when it was written, but the information is just as good. Storey's Books for Country

Living, Dept 60, P.O. Box 38, Pownal, VT 05261-9989

Building Small Barns, Sheds & Shelters, by Monte Burch, $11.65. Planning barns, shelters, sheds. Storey's Books, address above.

Fences for Pature & Garden, by Gail Damerow, $14.95. Choosing, planning, and building fences. Storey's Books, address above.

Buildings for Small Acreages, by James S. Boyd, $22.60. This is 289 pages of plans with materials lists for farm, ranch, and recreation structures. Storey Books, address above.

These books are just a start, and some might be at your local library or book store.

May your homestead be productive and a joy to your family. Plan now for lasting success. Δ

A BHM Writer's Profile: Steve Anderson

Steve Anderson is 46-years-old and has been married 27 years (to the same person the whole time). For the last 21 years he has lived, gardened, worked, and raised four kids in the small central Maine town of Charleston. For 10 years he and his wife owned their own business, a retail food/restaurant, but for the last four years he has spent most of his time as a freelance writer and outdoor photographer.

Follow these eight easy steps to a successful eggplant harvest

By Michael Clayton

The following methods can be used with a variety of crops. The information is very detailed for the first time gardener, but it contains a specific method which may be of interest to the seasoned gardener.

Step one. Selecting the variety is fairly simple with eggplants. You choose either purple or yellow (the yellow eggplant's fruit is green when harvested), long and thin or egg shaped, depending on personal choice, and a long or short season variety depending upon the length of the growing season in your area. If you are going to save the seed, do not choose a hybrid variety.

Step two. To prepare the soil for indoor planting, mix four parts topsoil with one part cow manure and add some peat moss. Make sure that the cow manure is well decomposed. Mix the soil and other ingredients well and put into containers.

Step three. To plant the seed, about six weeks before time to transplant (you transplant when the weather is warm and all danger of frost has passed), take the seeds out of their container and get the containers with the prepared soil. Take a pencil or your finger and make a hole 2½ times deeper than the seed's length. Put three or four holes per container. Place a seed or two in each hole. Cover and pat down gently, then water. To speed germination time, place in a sealed plastic bag. Check every few days for germination.

Step four. When the seeds come up, remove them from the plastic bag and place them in a warm, sunny location. Water as needed. Warning: Do not over-water or the plant stems may rot. In about four weeks, thin to the strongest plant in each container.

Step five. When the weather outside is warm and all chance of frost has passed, pick a sunny location, clear it of trash and cut the weeds, then dig up the area, removing the remaining weed parts. The digging can be accomplished either by tilling or by digging with a shovel. Make sure that all large clods are broken up. Take a garden rake and rake the area level, removing any remaining trash.

Step six. To transplant the eggplants, dig a hole two feet by two feet and about two feet deep, or you can dig a trench if you want. Place in the hole two shovels of cow manure, two shovels of compost, one shovel of wood ashes, and a handful of lime. Place the soil back into the hole and dig in the ingredients until you can no longer see the added components in the soil, then rake it level. If planting directly outdoors, see step three.

With a trowel, dig a small hole slightly larger than the soil ball (the soil in the planting container). Fill the hole with water and let it soak in. Water the eggplant in the container and then remove it. Place it in the hole and cover slightly above the soil ball.

If you goof and a cold snap is coming, take a clear two- or three-liter plastic cola bottle and wash it out. Cut it so it will fit over the eggplant and remove its cap. Place the bottle over the eggplant with the edge of the bottle cutting slightly into the ground.

Step seven. Harvest the eggplant fruit when they are the size that you desire but have not yet changed color. If purple ones have brown stripes, or if yellow ones are turning yellow, they are no good.

Step eight. To gather seed, wait until the eggplant fruit have changed color. If you are not sure, just let them fall off the vine: then they are ready. Cut the eggplant fruit lengthwise into four equal parts and remove the seed. Place the seed on a pan or paper. (The seeds will probably stick to whatever you dry them on, so keep that in mind when choosing the surface.) Do not dry the seed in the oven, because the heat will kill it. After about a month of drying, place the seed in a sealed container, such as an envelope. Note: When you let the fruit mature, the productive energy of the plant will go down, so you need to use only one or two plants for seed production. Do not save the seed of a hybrid. Δ

Tobacco has some uses that might surprise you

By Rev. J.D. Hooker

Before I actually get started here, I'd like to say something: I really hope that no one takes this article as my encouraging anyone to take up tobacco use. If you don't already use it, you'd be so much better off never even to try it that you'd be absolutely stupid to start.

However, I'm sure that many readers of this magazine are already regular tobacco users, and tobacco has some other, very good uses. So I'd like to pass along some of what I've learned about growing it and using it on the homestead.

While anyone who tried telling you that homegrown tobacco was *good* for you would be a liar, I honestly think that it might be less unhealthy than the commercial product. If you watched any of the televised documentaries about the tobacco industry, or read any of the stuff all over last year's newspapers, I'm sure you're well aware of the tremendous number of additives put into cigarette tobacco. Some of them are sufficiently poisonous to be illegal as food additives. I'd say we can safely assume that cigars, pipe tobacco, snuff, etc., are just as "chemically enhanced."

I can definitely tell you that homegrown tobacco is much healthier for your wallet than any similar commercial product. For less than the cost of a single pack of cigarettes or pipe tobacco, you can purchase a packet of seeds and grow a whole year's worth of tobacco.

Even folks who'll never consume any form of tobacco might want to consider putting in a row or two of this versatile plant. It has some pretty valuable uses, aside from human consumption, and it's even an attractive ornamental.

It's a wormer...

Long before I'd considered trying to grow my own, I'd heard many older farmers recommending tobacco as being highly superior to any commercial wormer for every sort of livestock. In fact, the US Army Special Forces Medical Handbook recommends tobacco for human use as an antithelmetic (worm expeller) if standard medicines aren't available.

For myself and other folks I've talked to who've tried this, feeding a couple of large leaves (or an equivalent amount of shredded stems) each month to each hog, goat, cow, pony, or whatever really does seem to eliminate any problem with internal parasites.

With severe infestations, this sometimes needs to be repeated every few days for a while. Still, this treatment seems much less severe, with fewer debilitating effects, than commercial wormers. As a preventive medicine, a couple of large leaves every month or so not only works great, but the animals act like it's a terrific treat. Goats, cows, and such seem to have a strong liking for tobacco. (Cats and dogs and other carnivores don't seem to agree.)

Serious overdosing seems close to impossible using tobacco as a wormer. About the worst I've ever seen happen has been an occasional bout of temporary diarrhea.

...it's a pesticide...

Brewed into a strong tea-like solution and poured or sprayed on and around garden crops, fruit trees, rose and berry bushes, etc, tobacco is also about the best herbal pesticide there is. If you have any sort of insect problem, your own homegrown tobacco can offer as good a solution as any expensive commercial product. (If you consume your tobacco leaves, I've found the woody stems and stalks just as effective for this.)

Recipe: Add two ounces of dry (or three ounces of fresh) tobacco to a gallon of boiling water. Remove from heat and allow to steep several hours, or overnight. Strain, pour into containers, and cover. Spray or mist plants lightly as needed.

...and it's a bug bomb

Here's another thought to consider when deliberating whether to put in your own tobacco crop. Many years ago, lots of Native Americans would toss a handful of tobacco atop a pile of glowing coals. Burning like incense, the tobacco smoke would permeate their dwelling. In their belief, this helped drive out any "evil spirits" that might be present. Given the insecticidal, germicidal, and other properties modern science has shown to be present in tobacco smoke, they were absolutly right (if you consider germs, bacteria, and insect "vectors" as "evil spirits"). You might want to try this should the need arise; it's cheaper than disinfectant or bug bombs and just about as effective.

Grow your own

If any of this has given you an interest in growing your own crop of tobacco, there are a few preliminary steps you'll need to go through to get started.

First you need to find a source for tobacco seeds. I haven't run across very many garden catalogs that even offer tobacco seeds, while the few that do normally carry only a single variety. But here's a source where they carry quite a few tobacco varieties, as well as an array of other Native American type seeds:

Native Seeds/SEARCH
2509 N. Campbell Ave. #325
Tucson, AZ 85719

Write and ask for a copy of their seed listing. We plant some of each tobacco variety they carry every year. You'll most likely find some corn, vegetable, or grain varieties you'd be interested in trying in their listing while you're at it. (Their Santa Domingo Blue flour corn is something else I highly recommend.) NSS is an organization that I heartily endorse. They've preserved a considerable number of useful and valuable seed varieties that would probably have been lost to us without their efforts. (If you are of Native American descent, you'll want to check out their discounts.)

Preparing beds

Anyway, once you've obtained your seed supply, you'll need to prepare some planting beds. All tobacco varieties will cross very readily, so unless you won't mind buying more seed every year, you'll want to keep the types as widely separated as possible.

I like to get my tobacco beds ready the preceding fall. I work large quantities of manure, leaves, grass clippings or spoilt hay, compost, and wood ash thoroughly into the soil. You don't ever want to plant tobacco in the same place two years in a row, nor should you follow tomatoes, peppers, or potatoes with it, since the few diseases and organisms that attack tobacco plants can winter over from any of these. Because of their nitrogen-fixing abilities, any type of bean or pea makes a good crop to precede tobacco.

Start your tobacco seeds indoors, in pretty much the same manner and at the same time as you would tomatoes. The seeds are almost as fine as dust, so I use a pair of tweezers to pick up just a very few at a time for planting. Once the final frost date for your area has passed and the soil is well warmed up (about a week after you'd put out tomato plants), your tobacco seedlings are ready to be planted. Space them about three feet apart in rows four or five feet apart. Mulch very heavily, both between plants and between rows, as the young plants can't compete well with weeds.

"2nd batch" manure tea

Once a week, through the entire growing season, I feed the tobacco crop with a "second batch" of manure tea. Here's what I mean: Fill a feed sack about 1/2 full of manure and tie it shut. Place this in a 55-gallon drum, fill it with water, and allow it to steep overnight. In the morning, use this first batch to feed some other garden crop. Then, using the same manure and fresh water, steep overnight once again. This milder "second batch" seems to work wonders for tobacco. The somewhat depleted manure then gets added to the compost pile.

You'll find that flower buds start to form at the tops of the plants. The first time this occurs, select a few of your best looking plants to let flower and go to seed. Keep the buds trimmed off of all the rest, as this forces more of the plant's energies into producing more and larger leaves.

Harvest and cure

After a while, you'll notice a few leaves at a time yellowing and starting to die off. As each leaf yellows, trim it off. Tie these leaves in bundles and hang the bundles in a dark, moist place (a root cellar works well enough) to "cure."

Wait at least a couple of months if you intend the tobacco for smoking, then shred up one of the leaves and try it out. If the flavor seems pretty good to you, your tobacco's ready to use. If it doesn't seem very good, let it mellow by curing longer. Keep sampling it occasionally until you decide it's just right for your own taste.

As the leaves cure to my liking, I shred them up and pack them into half-gallon canning jars. Adding a thick slice of apple or pear to each jar helps the tobacco stay moister and fresher. These fruit slices need to be replaced every couple of weeks. Since not all of your tobacco will finish curing at once and you'll be keeping the jar lids screwed on, you should find your homegrown supply keeping in pretty good shape for a year or more.

Stalks, stems, and whatever leaves that aren't just perfect go through our chipper/shredder for use as livestock wormer, pesticide, etc. If you're only interested in growing tobacco for these purposes, you can just put the entire plant through the shredder.

I'm not sure of all the laws regulating tobacco, but I wouldn't recommend trying to sell any of your homegrown smoking or chewing tobacco. For your own private use, though, whether you're stuffing a pipe or worming a herd of goats, I don't believe you should run into any problems, as long as you're over 18. Selling or giving away tobacco seeds to other adults is OK so far, as well.

If the present governmental assault on the tobacco industry, along with all of the deadly-sounding adulterants, the skyrocketing prices, and the Surgeon General's warnings, haven't been enough to convince you to give up tobacco altogether, why not try growing your own? If nothing else, you'll know that it's additive free and you'll save yourself quite a bit of money. Δ

Whose garden is this anyway?

By Michael J. Tougias

The sugar peas had recently flowered, and now the pods were approaching the two-inch mark. Fledgling cabbage, kale and lettuce plants were green with promise; spinach and beets were on their way. But when I rushed to my garden after a day in the city, I found only stems sticking out of the ground like so many dragons's teeth.

It had to be a woodchuck. No rabbit systematically works his way down row after row, leaving only the nub of a stem in his wake.

My first defense was to erect a fence. It cost about $50 and took a few hours to build, but it was a small price to pay to protect my crops. And it worked, for all of two days. Then the woodchuck, also known by the fitting name of groundhog, tunneled under the chicken wire and sheared off the cabbage and kale. From there he moved on to the spinach, beets, eggplant and parsnip greens. I asked a local fanner for advice. He chuckled and said a groundhog could go over a fence as well as under one. He suggested I buy a humane, "live" trap, saying, "I guess woodchucks need to eat like the rest of us; after all, they're as much God's creatures as we are." Then he added, "If you do catch 'im, make sure you kill him; I don't want him coming over here.

I bought the trap, an expensive investment at $60, but it worked-on a skunk. I never used it again.

My garden still held peppers, beans, squash, tomatoes and strawberries. It was a far cry from my original bounty, but worth protecting, so I escalated from defense to offense. Groundhogs make their burrows with two entrances so they have a handy escape route should a fox enter their home. It didn't take long to find an entrance.

While I examined it, the hog himself came barreling down the hill and disappeared into the second hole no more than 5 ft. away from me. I hadn't expected my adversary to act this way or to be so large. He was much bigger than my neighbor's cat, grown fat, no doubt, on lettuce, cabbage, beans and my beloved sugar peas.

Now that I'd found his base, I began my attack. I put mothballs and rags soaked in ammonia down the hole to drive him out. They didn't work. I tried sealing the hole with boulders. He pushed the small ones aside like petty worries; the big ones he dug around. And always he was eating. My well-nourished enemy grew not only larger, but bolder, too. One day I sat under our maple and looked out at the pitiful remains of my vegetable garden-decimated tomatoes, trampled strawberries and a few lonely squash. The hog emerged from the woods, sniffed the air and bounded toward the garden, stopping only when I threw a rock at him. I chased him into his hole, grabbed the biggest boulder I could find, and pushed it into the entrance. And stepped on a hornet nest.

It was psychological warfare, and the short, furry guy was winning. My mental outlook was as desolate as my garden. I thought about the chuck constantly; even at work. I envisioned him back in my garden and wondered which plant of mine he was devouring. Friends asked for a daily "groundhog report," and when I got home in the evening, I greeted my wife with the same terse question: "Did you see him?" By now my garden looked like the Sahara, and I'd been pushed to my limit. I didn't care anymore about a kinder, gentler garden with a picturesque fence separating his territory from mine in a microcosm of peaceful coexistence. I didn't care anymore about humane trapping. I didn't even care to drive him out of his happy home with ammonia and mothballs. This was war, and I was taking no prisoners. I wanted him, and I wanted him dead.

Shooting the critter was out of the question since I lived in a suburban setting, but I had another weapon in my arsenal-bombs. Yes, bombs. My local farm and garden store carried rodent smoke bombs complete with fuses and detailed instructions. The trick was to drop the bomb into the hole and then cover the opening with dirt so the noxious fumes would asphyxiate the groundhog. But I forgot to seal the exit hole, and the fumes escaped. On my second try, I sealed the hole but extinguished the bomb with the dirt. But the third time ... ah, sweet success. Days went by, and not a woodchuck in sight.

A week later, as I sat under my maple tree, lord of my acre once more, a movement caught my eye. And there he was, my nemesis, perched like a squirrel with lunch in his paws. He had the last laugh; right beneath the tomato plants was the entrance to yet another burrow.

Well, at least I'm in good company. Thoreau had problems with groundhogs at Walden Pond. Commenting on his bean patch, he lamented, "My enemies are worms, cool days, and most of all woodchucks. I plant in faith and they reap." Walter Harding, in his excellent biography, "The Days of Henry Thoreau," tells us that Thoreau became so exasperated with the woodchuck that, "Abandoning his not-too-strongly-held vegetarian principles, he trapped, killed and ate it as a culinary experiment."

Don't tempt me. ∆

For some surprises in your garden, grow potatoes from seed

By Craig Russell

The underground tuber of the potato plant is the modern world's most important vegetable. In the garden, potatoes are normally grown by planting small potatoes or cutting larger "seed" potatoes into sections, making sure that each section contains an "eye" or sprout, and planting these.

Despite the fact that everyone is familiar with potatoes, and many people have seen their white-, pink-, or purple-petaled flowers with yellow centers, many gardeners seem to be unaware of the small, green, tomato-like fruits these flowers can produce.

As a result, every few years another article shows up about someone's potatoes and tomatoes "crossing." While the two vegetables are related, and both are members of the nightshade family, they do not cross, or hybridize. However, the seeds from potatoes can be grown like tomatoes, often with surprising results.

Wild potatoes are found in South, Central, and North America. The majority come from the cool regions of the Andes and the west coast of South America. The domestic potatoes are certainly hybrids, and botanists have traced their closest relatives and what they believe to be the bulk of their ancestors to central and southern Chile. Wild potatoes and even domestic varieties from the Andean area are much more variable in shape and color than the typical round or oval white-fleshed domestic types common in the rest of the world.

However, these variable types have contributed to the genetic makeup of our modern potatoes, which are seldom genetically pure. Modern potatoes maintain their characteristic type only because they are reproduced vegetatively (as described above), not from seed. Seeds which result from pollination reshuffle the genes, and when planted can result in tubers quite different from the parent types. Other characteristics such as flower color may also vary.

If you try the methods described in this article, and one or more of the resulting plants produces potatoes you like, save some of the tubers and plant them like other "seed potatoes." In this way, you can actually start your own varieties. Besides the typical potatoes, you may get flat and wavy or even odd and grotesque tubers. Even those that aren't very practical can be fun.

Seeds from a patch of a single variety may produce considerable variation, although most will show at least some similarity to the parent type. Still, I've had several shapes and skin colors and yellow- as well as white-fleshed tubers from seed collected from a patch of typical roundish, brown-skinned, white-fleshed potatoes. The greater the diversity of the possible pollinators, the greater the possible variation of the offspring. With seeds collected from a patch containing brown-, red-, whitish-, and blue-skinned potatoes of several shapes, and with blue- and yellow-fleshed as well as white-fleshed tubers, the variation has been astonishing. Not only were the original characteristics reshuffled, purple skins and white-fleshed potatoes with red or blue tints were added, and unusual shapes were rather common. I can't make any promises on what you will get, but waiting to find out is part of the fun.

While some gardening books suggest pinching of the flowers or fruits of a potato plant to prevent their drawing energy away from the tubers, I've never found this to be a problem. As far as the fruits go, looking around the potato patch late in the season will probably reveal some, but many of our modern potatoes seem to have been selected for not being very prolific in terms of fruit production. Some of the plants I've grown from seed are much better in that respect, with almost every flower producing a fruit. In any case, you may be able to improve production by giving the pollinating insects a hand. Use a brush or some soft feathers to transfer pollen from one flower to another when the potatoes first bloom.

When the fruits are ripe (they stay green but become lighter colored), open them and squeeze the seeds onto a paper towel. When dry, this may be marked, wrapped, and stored until spring, or the seeds may be removed and stored in an envelope or a small plastic bottle.

Note: Do not eat the fruit. They look like tomatoes, but *like all above-surface parts of a potato plant, they are potentially toxic*.

In the spring, start the seeds in flats or peat pots like tomatoes or peppers and when well started transfer to the garden. You too can have some real "seed potatoes." Δ

MAY/JUNE 1996
No. 39

Backwoods Home magazine

SPECIAL
BUILDING
EDITION

practical ideas for self-reliant living

11 GREAT BUILDING ARTICLES

Lessons of a Log Home
Your Own $78 Garage
Concrete Dome Home
Chainsaw Lumber Mill
Cheap Brick Walkway

Chutney, Jam & Pickles
Classic Backwoods Rifle
How Smart are Computers

$3.95 US · $5.50 CANADA

DON CHILDERS

My view

The age of misinformation

Recently I exhibited this magazine at a three-day Natural Health Show in Pasadena, California. The show, according to its sponsors, was meant to educate people about natural alternative approaches to health and healing, which is not a bad goal. The show, however, was anything but educational. It was largely an exercise in disinformation, with many vendors handing out phony documentation backing up exaggerated health claims for their products. The products ran the gamut from cures for cancer to water that would help the drinker live for 100 years.

In many respects the show was no different than the environmental and New Age shows I've gone to in the past. These shows too are largely platforms for charlatans to expound theories based on nonsense and to sell solutions based on pseudoscience. The most bizarre of the shows are the New Age affairs, where serene-looking people parade around with metal triangles over their heads, claiming to be communing with the cosmos. People at these shows are into exploring their inner and outer selves, their consciousness and unconsciousness. They like to talk in generalizations about how modern man must get beyond modern science and achieve harmony with the energy of the universe. Psychics and modern day holymen abound at these shows.

If you'd like to see a first hand example of what I am talking about, go into almost any bookstore and examine the plethora of books dealing with miracle cures, spirituality, and cosmic consciousness. They are not sold as science fiction, but as factual how-to descriptions of how the world really works. For those of you who understand the value of real science, that is, the science that has given us modern medicine and things like automobiles, airplanes, and computers, a close examination of this fantasy science may make you laugh. There must be a lot of stupid people out there, you might say.

It may be stupid science that these shows and books are full of, but I am meeting an alarming number of not-so-stupid people who seem to believe in some of this stupid science. Just the other day a friend of mine, who dreams of one day travelling to other star systems much like the actors on Star Trek do, started telling me that mankind must rethink science so it can get beyond the limitations of present day science.

I asked him what he thought science was, but he beat around the bush with generalized explanations until I realized he couldn't tell me. When I tried to explain to him that science isn't some theory you reinvent, that it is a method that allows you to discover the way the real world around us works, he protested that I was thinking about science in an old fashioned way, that the only way mankind was going to advance, both physically and spiritually, was by reorienting our thoughts towards a new reality.

This type of mumbo jumbo made no sense to me, and I realized it was the same type of mumbo jumbo spouted at the shows and in the New Age books. The only thing that was different was that it was being uttered by someone who I thought had both feet on the ground.

The popularity of these charlatan shows, the New Age books, and the mumbo jumbo explanations they put forth to explain their version of reality are, I think, part of a sad epidemic that is gripping much of modern society—a reliance on information that has nothing to do with reality. It is as if the clock is turning backwards to more ignorant times when superstition ruled the world. The shows and the books, in a very real sense, are a rehash of the ancient religions and cults that once drained off much of mankind's mental resources while doing nothing to improve the lot of people.

I think it is important for all of us to keep in mind that science is not some religion that has become popular during the last 300 or so years, ever since Englishman Robert Boyle and others began using the scientific method to discover how the physical world works. Science is not something you reinvent to suit your view of the world; it is simply a method of discovering how the physical world works.

Science is based on the scientific method, which demands that theories be subjected to verifiable experiments. The scientific method can be practiced by Christians, Buddhists, Hindus, Muslims, Jews, atheists, and agnostics. A Buddhist in New Delhi performing the same experiment in organic chemistry as a Christian in New York will get the same result. It's not a matter of opinion; it's a matter of verifiable fact.

It is this scientific method that has made possible all the modern technological inventions and discoveries of mankind, from vaccines for disease to increased ways to pull food from the soil to virtually every convenience in your house that turns on with the flick of a switch. The discoverers and inventors of these wonderful things run from Louis Pasteur to Jonas Salk, and they all used the scientific method. Name me one new age mystic who has done anything other than line his own pockets with other people's money?

This modern day reliance by so many people on this new conglomeration of fantasy sciences is disturbing because it represents a giant leap backward for society. The scientific method is the greatest invention since fire, and we can't turn our back on it now. There are more problems to be solved and they are not going to be solved by some New Age prophet pretending to commune with the cosmos.

This issue of *BHM*, which contains many how-to articles about building your own home, contains more real science than all the New Age books put together. Δ

Make your own lumber with a chainsaw mill

By Jacqueline Tresl
Diagrams by Mark & Jacqueline Tresl

These are trying times for those of us who need to buy lumber. The prices of good boards are at an all-time high. The E.P.A. is shutting down the mills that make plywood. The timber companies have less old growth forest to choose from. Most of the affordable timber is being cut from new-growth pine. In the Midwest, the standard 2x4 is made primarily from spruce. Boards made from cherry, oak, or poplar are expensive. The easy solution to this lumber crisis is for the woodworker to make his own boards from the trees of his choosing.

There are many methods for making boards from trees. Most of them require costly equipment or contracting out the work. The portable sawmills that will make boards in the back yard cost several thousand dollars. If the back-yard woodsman chooses to cut down his own trees and send them off to the mill, transporting the trees to the mill and bringing the finished boards back home is expensive.

The affordable and practical solution for the carpenter who needs lumber is to make his own boards at home with

Milling a board with a chainsaw lumber-maker

his chainsaw. With a large saw and a special device fitted onto the chainsaw bar, any kind of board can be made for just pennies. This device, known as a chainsaw lumber-maker, will mill through any tree, no matter how large or tough, making boards of any length or thickness.

The construction of a chainsaw lumber-maker requires a bit of steel and pipe and a few bolts (Figure 1). To make the mill, a rectangular frame, slightly shorter than the length of the

chainsaw bar, is welded together from square and channel steel stock.

Once the frame is welded, two recesses need to be ground into the centers of the channel stock pieces which make up the two short sides of the rectangle (Figure 2). In these recesses, two pieces of half-round pipe are welded into the channel stock. These half-round pieces will act as sleeves to accept the two pieces of whole round pipe. The round pipe will be adjusted up and down according to how thick the miller wants his board.

Next, two short pieces of square tubular stock are welded onto the ends of the whole round pipes. These short pieces should be four inches longer than the width of the chainsaw bar. To make the square stock stronger, reinforce it by welding a 3/8" steel plate onto the center of the underside of the short square tubular stock. Then, from the center line, measure an equal distance out from both sides and drill holes using a 5/16" drill bit to provide for a 3/8" tap and bolt size. Drill through the plates and the one side of

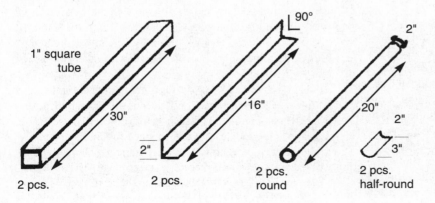

1" square tube

30"

2 pcs.

90°

16"

2"

2 pcs.

2"

20"

2 pcs.
round

2"

2"

3"

2 pcs.
half-round

Figure 1: The pieces

the square stock as shown in Figure 3. These pretapped steel plates will act as the bolting surface for the chainsaw's bar.

In order to bolt the welded frame onto the bar, remove the chainsaw's body from the bar. Drill four holes, two on each end of the bar, centered to match the pretapped holes on the reinforced square tubular stock. Bolt the mill onto the chainsaw bar through these reinforced holes by using four $^3/_8$" machine bolts. Then lower the rectangular frame onto the round pipe which is welded onto the short square tubular stock which is now bolted onto the bar. With the mill bolted onto the bar (Figure 4), the bar is put back onto the chainsaw body.

The rectangular frame can now be adjusted up and down to set the thickness of the milled board. To make these adjustments, two muffler clamps, one above the other, are placed around the half round and the whole round pipe (Figure 5). To set the correct measurement for the sleeves, measure from the chainsaw bar to the part of the rectangular frame that rides against the log (Figure 4). By loosening the clamps, the round pipe can be moved up or down to adjust the board thickness. Once tightened, the clamps will keep the pipe from moving up and down while milling. This enables the miller to make boards of uniform thickness.

Note: Not all chainsaws are suitable for a mill attachment. The chainsaw engine must be at least five cubic inches. The style of the saw must be such that it can be refueled in the milling position, with the bar parallel to the ground. The saw must have a 30" bar or longer. The longer the bar, the wider the boards that can be milled. A 36" bar will mill boards 24" wide. The chain must be chisel style and be ground square with a hook angle of 40 to 50 degrees.

Before lumber-making can begin, one side of the tree to be milled will need to be made flat. This initial cut is different from all subsequent cuts,

because the mill must first have a flat surface to rest on. This beginning cut is made with a *starter board*.

A starter board is a board at least ten feet long with steel sides running the length of both sides of the board (Figure 6). The length of the starter board determines the length of the boards that can be milled. A ten-foot starter board is the best length for most situations. The board is two inches thick, and the channel iron running the length of it will act as a guide for the mill to be pushed along. Once the initial cut is made, the top surface of the log will be flat, and the starter

board won't be needed again until a new log is started.

A starter board will last for years. If three or four ten-foot starter boards are made, they can be set end to end and a 30- or 40-foot tree can be milled, providing lumber long enough to make beams. With the chainsaw lumber-maker, any length board is possible, as long as that same length of starter board (or boards) is available.

To mill lumber, the chainsaw is started and then laid horizontally either against the starter board or the flat surface of the log. The bar is guided carefully into the log's end as the

Beams, joists and walls were made with a chainsaw mill.

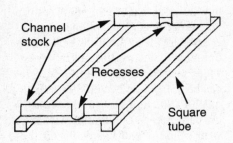

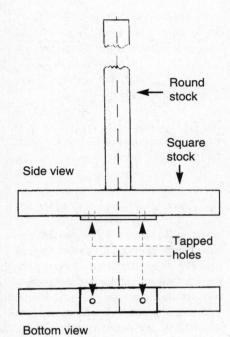

Channel stock

Recesses

Square tube

Figure 2: The frame

Round stock

Square stock

Side view

Tapped holes

Bottom view

Fig. 3: The surface to which the chainsaw bar is bolted

cut begins. The saw will be easier to guide through the log if the tree slopes slightly downhill away from the miller. The mill only needs to be steadied and pushed gently until it reaches the end of the cut. At the log's end, the throttle is released and the chain eased out.

When milling softwoods, board production is fast. Twenty pine or poplar boards can be milled before lunchtime. With dense trees like locust or elm, milling goes a bit slower, and the chain will need to be resharpened more often. Yellow

poplar is a great choice for backyard lumber-making, as it is a soft hardwood, and its variegated colors make it a superior choice for woodworking projects. Since poplar grows quick, tall, and straight, it has enough strength to carry stress loads, yet mills easily.

Boards milled with a chainsaw lumber-maker are smooth and do not need to be planed. Freshly-milled boards are stacked 20 tall with a one-inch air gap between boards. For the highest quality lumber, the boards should be kept under cover and away from excessive moisture. Lumber made from dead trees can be used in two weeks. Green wood needs to cure at least three months. If the boards are intended for flooring, they can easily be tongue-and-grooved by using a dado cutting blade on the table saw.

The lumber-maker frame itself requires no maintenance. The saw chain needs to be kept sharp, and it will be over seven feet long, so chain sharpening is the most tedious part of

lumber-making. The chain will need to be sharpened after every eight hours of milling, and a new chain bought after every 5,000 board feet milled. If the trees to be milled are dragged home in the dirt, the chain will get dull much faster.

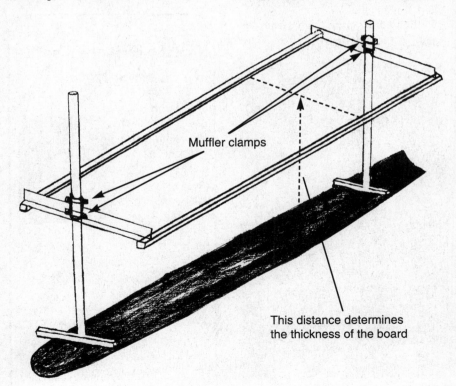

Muffler clamps

This distance determines the thickness of the board

Figure 4: The assembled mill frame is bolted to the chainsaw bar.

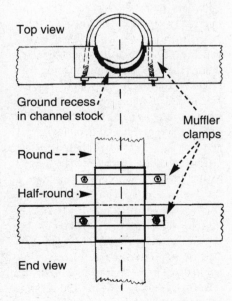

Top view

Ground recess in channel stock

Round

Half-round

Muffler clamps

End view

Fig. 5: Muffler clamps hold settings to determine thickness of boards.

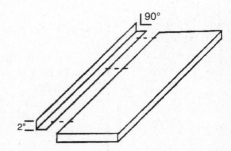

Figure 6:
The metal-edged starter board
makes the first cut flat and straight.

The mill is potentially quite dangerous. Good safety measures during its operation are important. Besides the need for safety glasses and ear protection, the miller must never become distracted or take his attention from the mill. Seven feet of rapidly moving saw chain can be lethal.

Once the woodworker owns a chainsaw lumber-maker, he will never need to buy lumber again. Houses can be built from the substructure to the roof just from the trees in the back woodlot. If 12-inch-wide roof beams or 4x4 posts for footings are needed, the lumber-maker can mill two or four sides off of a tree by moving the starter

Starterboard, chain, and mill

board. Logs can be milled flat on two sides to make tight-fitting walls for a log house, leaving less space to be filled in with chinking.

Milling boards from the back yard is great for the environment: it recycles

unwanted or dead trees, and trees can be cut out selectively, allowing smaller trees to fill in the open areas without clear-cutting an entire forest. Trees that might have been left to rot can be milled into beautiful lumber.

With the chainsaw lumber-maker, the carpenter has unlimited choices of species and size of boards for his projects. The days of picking through crooked, inferior boards at the lumberyard will be over. And no more sticker shock at the cash register over a pile of 2x4s. Backyard lumber-making will save the woodworker hundreds of dollars and allow his creativity to soar. Δ

I've often wished that I had clear,
For life, six hundred pounds a
* year;*
A handsome house to lodge a
* friend,*
A river at my garden's end,
A terrace walk, and half a rood
Of land set out to plant a wood.

—Alexander Pope
1688-1744

A BHM Writer's Profile:
Carole Perlick

Carole Perlick has had a varied work career. She worked as a nurse for 20 years as well as running a grocery-liquor store for her husband. Carole also managed a 72-unit apartment building in southern California. Since retiring with her husband of 40 years, Carole has enjoyed a new hobby of writing for *BHM* and currently has a weekly column with a local newspaper. She and her husband live on Copco Lake in California.

Guiding the lumber-maker through a cut

Here's a "helping hand" for your chainsaw lumber mill

By R.E. Bumpus

Anyone who has ever operated a chainsaw lumber mill will agree that, while they *do* produce lumber, the amount of physical exertion required can give you second thoughts about the high price of "store bought" boards. This simple, inexpensive, and mobile accessory can make the difference between actually using your mill and leaving it on a hook in the tool room.

All that's required is two lightweight pulleys, one long post and one short post, a five-gallon plastic bucket, and a length of ¼" rope. The rope is strung through the pulleys and the handle of a weighted bucket and attached to the mill frame. The weight of the sand-filled bucket exerts pull on the mill and allows you to operate as if you had a helper on the stinger end of the chainsaw (see diagram).

The weight of the sand in the bucket is adjusted to accommodate the variables you'll find in sawing lumber. The type of wood, the diameter of the log, the capabilities of your chainsaw, and the type of cutting chain on the saw all affect speed and ease of producing lumber. Generally speaking, the larger the saw, the more lumber you can produce.

The long post is planted 10 or 12 feet from the end of your saw log. The short post is planted against the end of the log to stabilize the operation. The pulleys are attached to the top and near the bottom of the long post. The rope is first tied to the bottom frame of the top pulley, then run down through the plastic handle of the bucket (which turns easily and therefore acts as an intermediate pulley), back up through the top pulley, down through the bottom pulley, and then to the mill frame, where it is attached by means of a hook. (You can make a suitable hook from a doubled wire coat hanger.)

When you're running a chainsaw mill, a bucket of sand can "lend a hand."

If you find your post is not tall enough to allow sufficient fall for the bucket weight to pull the mill all the way through the cut, just attach another hook at the appropriate place on the rope. Δ

You have to look beyond the building code to create really pleasing stairs

By Skip Thomsen

This article isn't about how to build stairs, or even about the technicalities of designing stairs. There are lots of books available that already do an admirable job in these areas. (See end of this article.)

What we are going to discuss is the *aesthetics* of stairs, and the value of stairs that goes way beyond their function of providing a means to get from one floor to another. This is the information that's left out of all the technical books, and it is exactly this information that makes the difference between a technically-correct, code-legal staircase and one that is a work of art and a pleasure to use.

An interior staircase can be the focal point of a room. An exterior stair can light up the face of a whole building.

Photo 1

More often than not, stairs appear to have been designed merely to take up the least amount of space possible or to get them out of sight or out of the way. Many times they appear to have been designed as an afterthought: "Now that we've got a second floor, where are we going to put the stairs?"

A staircase can be so visually inviting that it beckons one to try it out, to see where it leads. Stairs can be interesting and comfortable to walk. A staircase can even be designed to have a landing that affords a unique view of a room or out of a special window. But too often, staircases are basically boring, many are uncomfortable and/or tiring to walk, and some are downright dangerous. Many staircases are even intimidating, by being too steep or dark or narrow.

So what are the ingredients of the perfect staircase? The basic ingredients are safety, comfort, eye-appeal, and visual and functional integration into the design of the room or building. All of these elements are amazingly simple to put into practice.

There are just a few fundamental rules that, when adhered to, will produce a safe, easy-to-walk, comfortable staircase. The visual aspect is admittedly a little more subjective, but there are some basic guidelines that apply here, as well.

Getting started

In new construction, it's fairly easy to design a staircase that meets all these requirements. The real challenge is coming up with a good design when a second floor is added to an existing building, or an additional staircase is planned for an existing upper floor.

Although I promised that this would be a non-technical article, I'm afraid that we have to start with one technical rule as the basis on which to build all staircases. The most fundamental rule of designing any staircase is the "Rule of 25." It goes like this: any staircase will be safe and easily walkable if the height of two risers plus the width of one tread equals 25 inches. Sounds too easy, doesn't it? But it really works.

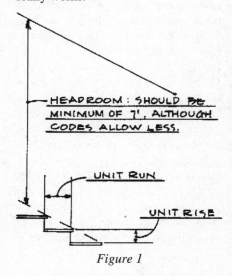

Figure 1

First, let's make sure we are all talking the same language here. *Rise* and *run* are stair-speak terms. *Unit rise* is the height from the floor to the top of the first tread, and/or the height from the top of any one tread to the top of the next one. *Unit run* is the width of each tread, or the distance from the face of one riser to the face of the next one. *Total rise* is the height from the floor-surface to the next floor-surface serviced by the staircase. *Total run* is the length of the staircase, or the combined lengths of all the treads. (See Figure 1.)

The minimum unit rise for a normal staircase is usually 4", and the maximum, except for service stairs (that aren't used often) is 7". Service stairs can go as high as 8", but that is considered a steep staircase. The most comfortable range for the average

Photo 2

staircase and the average person is between 6 and 7 inches.

Techno-stuff

For a staircase to be comfortable to walk at a natural pace, the wider the tread gets, the lower the riser must be. Conversely, the higher the riser, the narrower the tread. For example, to determine the best width for the treads of a staircase that will have a 7" unit rise, use the Rule of 25: 7+7=14, then 25-14=11. A staircase with a 7" unit rise will need an 11" unit run (or 11" wide treads) to be comfortable and safe to walk by the average person.

Another example: Let's say you would like to maintain 12" treads (unit run) on your entry stairs. Let's do the math: 25-12=13, and 13 divided by 2 equals 6½. The unit rise, or the height of each step, will then be 6½".

This amazing rule is not just somebody's opinion or an "old wive's tale," either. Try walking various staircases and taking note of ones that are comfortable and just seem to naturally fit your feet and gait. Then measure the rise and run. Now try measuring some that seem awkward. You will find that the Rule of 25 applies every time.

Another detail, and this is one that's covered in every building code (for good reason), is that *each unit rise must be the same.* Different building departments will specify different limits here, but they usually specify ¼" or ⅜" maximum variation. Personally, I keep mine within ⅛". It's surprising that such a little variation in step-height can make such a difference in walkability, but it really does. When you go up or down stairs, you automatically adjust your gait for the height of the steps. If you get to one that isn't the same as the rest, you will almost surely trip. Going up, you'll catch a toe on a high step or lose your rhythm on a low one. Going down uneven staircases has caused many people serious falls.

OK, that takes care of the technical stuff. From here we go beyond the technical and venture into the aesthetic and psychological aspects of stair design.

The planning stage

In the design phase of a new building, consider the staircase as an archi-

Photo 3

tectural feature of the building. Properly done, an attractive staircase can transform an otherwise ordinary-looking building into a showplace. Exterior, or entry stairs should be inviting. From the first moment they come into view to one who is approaching the building, the stairs should welcome the visitor. From a design point of view, this means that the stairs should not only be gradual and easy to climb, but they must present a gracious invitation.

The easiest way to offer graciousness in most areas of construction design is to make the particular element a little more generous than is absolutely necessary. Sounds simple, but it works. If an entry stair needs to be four feet wide to satisfy code requirements, make it six feet wide. Or wider. Another little detail that almost always enhances any staircase is to make the bottom step or two a little wider than the following ones.

Photo 2 illustrates both these points. First, this staircase, which could have been three or four feet wide and still satisfy legal and safety requirements,

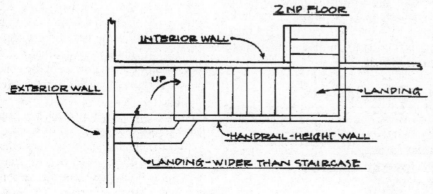

Figure 2

is in fact a little over six feet wide. Look at the picture and imagine it being only three or four feet wide. See the difference? It would have presented an even more inviting face at eight feet wide. Notice that the bottom wooden step wraps around the posts, and the concrete step is a bit wider than the wooden one. The staircase seems to "flow" out onto the ground like the open arms of a waiting and welcome embrace. Adding a feeling of graciousness to a staircase by making the first few steps wider than the following ones works well in most cases, but care must be taken here to avoid making a staircase appear to be "narrowing," which is distinctly intimidating. The object is to open up the first few steps of an already inviting staircase.

Interior stairs

The same principles of widening the base of a staircase apply to interior stairs. There are several ways this can be accomplished. One of the most effective, especially if the staircase runs down alongside a wall, is to have it turn ninety degrees into the room by way of a landing that is a foot or two wider than the staircase itself. Then the first one or two steps up to that landing are the full width of (or wider than) the landing. (See Figure 2 .)

The ninety-degree turn at the bottom of a staircase that runs parallel to a wall has another benefit, too. A staircase is always more inviting if it opens into the space from which its traffic arrives. In other words, the bot-

Photo 4

tom stairs should face into the room serviced by the staircase.

Go that extra mile

Often, designers and builders will keep everything in a building to code minimums to cut down costs. (Guess why tract houses all look the same.) The small extra cost of making a staircase a little wider than required by the building code is soon forgotten, but the convenience, feel, and ambiance it provides is permanent. It's best to avoid narrow stairs in any place where they will be used often. Consider the probable uses of a staircase. Will furniture have to be carried up and down? Appliances? Will there be a likelihood of opposing traffic?

The same thing applies to steep staircases. Most staircases are steeper

than they need to be, and most are that way just because the designer either didn't want to put in the extra effort required to make a more comfortable staircase fit in the same space, or the builder wanted to "keep things simple and cheap." Often, it does take some extra time and effort to plan the perfect staircase. And it almost always involves a little extra labor and cost to build it. But in my experience of designing and building (and selling) custom homes, it has always been worthwhile. I believe that my staircases have been instrumental in selling my homes. It's not that a buyer exclaims, "Wow! That staircase! I've got to have this place!" What happens is that people are drawn to the overall feel of the place, and even though they don't realize it, the stairs have a lot to do with it.

The width-to-length ratio is one of the most important details to take into consideration when designing any stairs. A long, narrow staircase looks intimidating in most circumstances. If a lot of stairs are needed because of a big elevation change, break up the staircase with landings. Keep each run of stairs fairly short, with about eight steps being a maximum if at all possible.

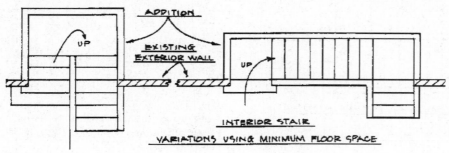

Figure 3

Different styles

Stairs can be open, enclosed, all-wood, carpeted, or combinations of these. An example of a combination approach is pictured in Photo 3. The bottom of this staircase is a three-step-up landing (not shown). From there, the open, wooden run goes to a second landing, from where the remainder of the steps are enclosed and carpeted to match the second floor. The staircase affords several interesting views of the room below (Photo 4).

A lot of the visual interest in this particular staircase comes from the materials and assembly techniques used in the open stairs (Photo 1). The wood is nearly knot-free fir with the exception of the end-caps on the treads, which are dark cedar. The staircase was finished with several coats of high-quality spar varnish. A staircase like this is admittedly very labor-intensive, and a much simpler way would have been to enclose and carpet it all the way. But this staircase was designed not only to be a focal point of the room, but its openness visually subtracted less space from the room.

An example of a fully-enclosed, carpeted stairway, and the visual interest it supplies to a small building, is shown in Photo 5. This relatively small (1400 sq. ft.) home has expansive views like this throughout, giving the feeling of a much larger, more open space. Stairways are the perfect medium to make these views possible.

There are three landings in this staircase, so the whole unit takes up very little floor space, yet the riser heights are a comfortable 6½". Every cubic foot of space under the staircase has been utilized, too.

Notice the stair lights in some of these staircases. They are inexpensive, and make it possible to illuminate the stairs with very low-wattage lamps. A light is placed near the edge of each landing and in the middle of each run longer than three or four steps.

In some cases, an interior staircase can be constructed outside of the actual building. This technique works in new construction, but is especially well-suited to an upstairs add-on, as no existing floor space is taken up by the staircase. (See Figure 3.) The supporting structure for the staircase can be cantilevered from beneath the building, or it can be hung from the existing wall structure.

An interesting point to keep in mind for second-floor spaces like apart-

Photo 5

ments or offices is that an exterior access to these spaces is not only a convenience, but it gives whoever lives in or uses that space a feeling of autonomy and independence. Having to go through someone else's space to get to your own is often uncomfortable. It's much more pleasant to have your own entry.

Handrails

Another essential ingredient of any staircase is the handrail. The dimensional limits of handrails are spelled out in the technical stair-design books, and are also strictly enforced by the building codes . . . but again, there are other considerations that go beyond

the code requirements. These include not only aesthetics, but thoughtful little details that can make the handrail more than just something to hold onto.

Handrails should be designed to complement the staircase itself and any adjacent trim. When designing a handrail, picture yourself holding onto it and sliding your hand along its entire length. The no-splinters part is obvious, but not so obvious is the ability to run your hand along the railing without hitting the mounting hardware or brackets, encountering tight spots not quite big enough to pass a large hand comfortably and safely, and having the railings start and end so that they fall to hand naturally.

Another very important and often overlooked aspect of designing and building handrails is that they need to be rigid and well braced. A handrail, especially one that is more than a few feet from the ground, can feel very scary if it moves even slightly when leaned upon. Properly done, a railing or handrail shouldn't yield at all under anything that could be considered normal pressure. And for sure it better not fail if someone falls against it (like they always do in the movies).

A very short bibliography

Rob Thallon's Graphic Guide to Frame Construction has a terrific section on the technical-design aspects of every kind of stairs imaginable. (The Taunton Press, ISBN: 1-56158-040-6) I've been building houses for more years than I can remember, and this book is still my most valuable reference. You can build a frame house from the ground up with just this book as your guide. The text is clear, it is supported by excellent illustrations throughout, and the index is super.

(Skip Thomsen describes himself as a "sort-of-retired designer and builder of one-of-a-kind homes that are individually crafted to be at ease with their immediate environment." All photos, drawings and stairs are by the author.) Δ

Here's a mighty creative way to protect your plants from animals

By Joy Lamb

A huge brown beast stared at me as I drove through our apple orchard toward the house. I parked, walked quickly into the house, and said to my husband, "Tom's bull is munching on our apple trees."

He shot past me out the door, yelling, "Call Tom and tell him to get over here now!"

The next half hour was spent running this way and that. We chased south and withdrew to the north. We herded south and blocked on the east and west. Finally the bull, several cows, and one fat sheep were escorted out of our orchard and into their own pasture. During this process, the bull nonchalantly stepped over a three-foot fence and trampled my garden. Later, while discussing the event with Tom, we decided that we were glad that most of our vegetables, flowers, and shrubbery had been spared. The apple trees were left standing with only minor damage to the foliage and fruit.

This incident was only one of many animal-related problems we had faced since we had become backwoods homeowners. Deer stripped new growth off young fruit trees, cats used vegetable plots for litter boxes, and visiting dogs dashed through flower and vegetable gardens, trampling as they went. Even our own dog loved to dig in planted areas rather than the natural wooded areas. We were frustrated. My husband built fences higher and higher around the orchards. This was useless, as deer can jump amazingly high. I planted shrubs, flowers, and vegetables, only to have them torn up by dogs. The cats loved the freshly worked soil, and rabbits nibbled at what was left. And this was not the

Fencing is laid in two sections around a fruit tree. The tree can be watered, fertilized, sprayed, and harvested with the wire in place.

first time we had been invaded by bovine beasts. What were we to do?

At first we tried fences. We fenced groups of trees, we fenced islands of flower gardens around the house, and we fenced vegetable plots. We created a botanical zoo with plant cages all over our property. The fences kept the dogs out but did not faze the cats, cows, and rabbits that wandered through. The deer were not even slowed down by the fences, no matter how high we made them. The fences were unsightly and very inconvenient when we were caring for the plants and trees. We became vigilant plant guards, but decided we did not want to dedicate our lives to this pursuit, espe-

cially our lives between 10 p.m. and 6 a.m.

We thought through the problem and came up with a solution. We immediately put into action our "Protect Trees and Plants from Four-Legs Plan," and very soon we knew we had a plan that worked.

We had used livestock fencing attached to wood and metal stakes for fences. We removed the stakes, cut the wire fencing into workable sizes, and just *laid it on the ground* in the areas we wanted to protect. Once an animal puts a foot on the wire, it backs up. We were and still are amazed at how well this works.

Our dog will not enter the areas covered with wire, so no more uprooted

Sections of fencing can be laid right over small plants.

and trampled plants. No more holes dug under trees. The cats find better areas to scratch, and best of all, the deer keep away from our trees. It is so nice not to have all the new growth eaten off the trees. We have not had a visit from a bull, cow, or sheep since we laid the wire, but we think it will work for them, too. We have found bear spoor in the areas furthest from the house, but our trees and their fruit have remained undamaged. I still see rabbits in the clover surrounding the apple trees and in the native undergrowth, but there have been no holes dug around the wire-protected trees. We have not detected any damage to the fruit trees or the gardens caused by rabbits.

Since we heartily recommend our method to anyone wanting to protect their plant life from four-legged animals without using harsh methods, the rest of this article will provide specific information about it.

Use livestock fencing

A 12- or 14-gauge field fencing works well. It is sturdy and holds up well. It can be cut readily with a wire cutter and is rigid but bendable. There are many kinds, heights, lengths, and hole sizes available. The twisted wire is cheaper and easier to work with than welded wire. My personal favorite is a three-foot-high, 12½ gauge, non-climb fencing that has 2" x 4" holes.

Wire fencing can be purchased at feed stores, hardware stores, and garden shops. The price depends upon the gauge, whether it is twisted or welded wire, the size, and the amount. A 330' roll of twisted wire field fencing with 2" x 6" holes at the bottom and 6" x 6" holes at the top sells, in my area, for $104. A 100' x 3' non-climb 12½ gauge fencing that has 2" x 4" holes sells for $85. I saw 50' x 3' of 14-gauge welded wire fencing for $23.

Save and reuse previously used wire fencing. There are no definite size requirements for the fencing. We often use whatever is on the scrap pile.

Cut into workable sizes

Get out the wire cutters, pliers, tape measure, and work gloves. Besides the fencing itself, that is all you will need to implement the method. "Workable size" means something that you can handle. This obviously varies from person to person and depends on the size of the area and the plant that is to be protected. You need to remember that you will have to be able to remove the fencing to work the soil. Don't worry about the size of the pieces if you are using scrap fencing. Just do the best you can with what you have. The wire can be overlapped lying on the ground or joined with a twist of the pliers if need be.

For garden areas:

Roughly measure the area. If the fencing can be cut in one piece, great. If not, cut the fencing into the largest sections possible that will cover the area. However, the pieces should not be so large that you cannot handle them comfortably. Arranging the fencing is discussed below.

For trees and shrubs:

Cut two pieces of fencing, each about 6' x 3'. It is better to use two pieces rather than one, because it is easier to remove. However, we have sometimes placed one smaller piece of fencing over a newly-planted bare root tree. The wire can always be cut later.

Placing fencing over bare or just-seeded soil is easy. Just lay it down and bend over the ends, poking them into the soil

Care needs to be taken so as not to damage plants when placing the fencing over trees, shrubs, or growing vegetables and flowers. Some cutting will be required to make the fencing fit over or around them. At any cut, poke the wire ends into the ground to secure it and to make it safer for you. Overlap fencing as needed for coverage.

Most watering, fertilizing, spraying, and weed control can be done with the wire in place. After all, people wearing shoes can walk on the wire.

When major work needs to be done, such as harvesting, tilling, or planting, simply lift the wire fencing from the ground and replace it when you are finished working. If you originally cut the wire into sizes that you can handle, removing and then replacing it is very easy to do.

We have been pleased with the results of this method at our house. We hope you will be, too. Δ

Your family can afford a computer: buy it used

By Sharon Griggs

You don't have a new car, you shop at rummage sales, and you gladly accept hand-me-down clothes for your kids. So why are you considering buying a brand new $2000 computer system? Don't let some salesman who has charged his credit cards up to the limit and needs the sales commission tell you that you need the newest, most impressive machine with all the bells and whistles.

There are people out there who are upgrading their systems and who will sell their old computers cheap. Often they are sold with software and accessories such as printers that don't come with a new computer. These are things that you would end up having to go out and buy extra and install, if you bought a new computer.

You say you are home-schooling your youngsters and you want them to be computer literate. Or you are running your own home-based business, and you want a computer for that. Or you want to get on the "information superhighway."

Well, believe it or not, you can probably do all these things for under $500, and maybe less if you are willing to shop around. In fact, I bought an old Texas Instruments

computer at a garage sale for $10 that is perfect for learning basic programming on. Sure, I had to hook it up to an old TV (it didn't have a monitor), but it came with all kinds of illustrated books about basic programming. I even learned how to program graphics as well as words. You won't get that kind of information with your new gee-whiz right-out-of-the-box computer. And you won't be afraid to try things on a cheap old machine, daring things that you would be afraid to risk on an expensive new computer.

But you say you want a little newer technology. You want to be able to hook up a modem and explore the on-line world about your areas of interest. Here's where you really get lucky. Newer, faster modems are being put on the market all the time and people just gotta have 'em. Slower modems are getting cheaper, and faster ones are quickly being discarded and replaced with even faster ones. And there are "trial-run" offers all the time from on-line services that let you get on-line for 10 hours free. Why not try them all? A used 386 IBM-compatible computer or a used Mac should be plenty good enough to get you there. Like driving a good used car, you go a little slower, but you get there just the same.

Heard about Windows 95? Well, there are older versions of Windows out there, and lots of older computers have the older versions of Windows on them. When you buy one of them, you can upgrade, or you can use the old version while they work the "bugs" out of the new version.

There is also a world of free and cheap software available (such as *shareware*). Just be sure the software is "registered," or legal. In fact, some of the folks who started computing by using some of the older, cheaper programs are so attached to them that they wouldn't give up their old favorites for all the new ones in the world. You may find that you feel the same way about some of these "oldies but goodies."

Really broke? Believe it or not, you don't even have to buy a computer to compute. You can try one out at some public libraries or community colleges for free. One library near us has a computer that is hooked up to the Internet, and anyone can use it. There are also computers there that can be used for word processing (typing) or for bookkeeping for your business. Just buy a floppy disk and bring it with you. Usually someone will be glad to help you get started and get into the tutorial programs on the computer that teach you how to compute step by step, with demonstrations. There are also free classes at the library on how to get on and use the Internet. They attract a lot of "non-techies." In fact, my youngest son (who likes to work on the innards of computers and such but who normally hates to sit down at a keyboard) really likes exchanging points of view on-line with people in other countries.

Don't let a lack of funds slow you down. You too can start computing "on the cheap" and enjoying it as much as we do. Δ

Would you believe . . . a canvas roof?
It's simple, quick, durable, and cheap

By Rev. J.D. Hooker

Have you ever wondered what-ever happened to all of those big canvas covers from all the Conestoga wagons that crossed the Plains? Well, sure, most were temporarily utilized as tents, until some more permanent dwelling was erected. But eventually, the vast majority of those wagon covers ended up being used as the roofing material on some permanent structure. Often they were used on the central portion of the house (they weren't really big enough for an entire house roof), or atop a stable or other outbuilding

Actually, when properly installed, this sort of roofing is just as watertight, good looking, and long lasting as most of the more expensive roofing materials available at the lumber yard, but it's much quicker and simpler to install.

I think that probably this type of roofing was simply forgotten (like many other good ideas) as newer materials hit the market. As late as the 1950s, some of the "do it yourself" encyclopedias gave instructions for installing canvas roofing. And in many areas where building codes have been around long enough, you'll find canvas roofing covered by the codes. If your area has a long history of building codes, you could just skip reading the rest of this article, and take a look in your county's code book. The information is likely to be practically identical.

Installing a canvas roof

To install a long-lasting canvas roof doesn't require much in the way of equipment. Here's what you'll need:

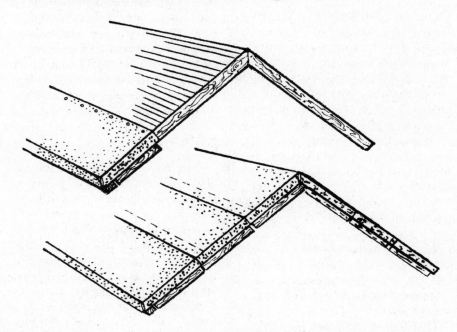

Stretch and paint one course at a time. Tack only the top edge of each course to the surface of the roof—let the other edges lap over the edges of the roof and nail up with furring strips. Allow subsequent courses to overlap eight inches. When all the courses are in place, apply the second and third coats of paint.

- Enough canvas or other cloth to cover the required area
- Some tacks or staples
- Maybe some furring strips and nails
- Enough exterior-grade paint to apply two or thee coats over the entire roof
- Probably a ladder or two
- A roller or paint brush

Now, before you start shaking your head in disbelief, thinking that this sort of roofing can't hold up very long, you should consider a few points. First, the coverings for the old-style wood-and-canvas canoes were simply cloth and paint, and some of the better maintained ones are still serviceable. And as late as World War II, many countries were putting fighter planes into the skies with exterior skins made only from painted canvas. Some of these planes are still flying.

You wouldn't hesitate to consider fiberglass, a sort of glass cloth held together by hardened resins, as a durable material. While painted canvas hasn't nearly the strength of fiberglass, it is basically the same principle, and capable of standing up to the weather at least as well.

Installing a canvas roof really does not take a lot of labor or figuring, either. To illustrate how to put on one of these roofs easily and properly, I'm going to detail how we installed a canvas roof on one of our hog farrowing huts.

This is a pretty small building, roughly ten by twelve feet, so for the cloth covering we just used old cotton bed sheets, purchased for next to nothing from a Salvation Army store.

Actually, for any smallish roof, up to about 400 square feet (20 x 20 or so), lightweight cloth of this sort is ideal. For larger projects, you'll need to use heavier-weight material, like regular canvas or duck cloth.

On our farrowing hut, the first course was installed the same way you'd put on regular roll roofing, except that it lapped over the sides and the bottom edge, being held in place by thin wooden furring strips. Only the top edge was tacked in place. A heavy coat of paint was then applied to that course. (Make sure you really saturate the cloth when applying the first coat of paint, to bond it to the roof sheathing.)

The second course overlapped the ends of the roof, and was secured in place with furring strips, in the same manner. It also lapped down for eight inches over the first course, and again only the upper edge was tacked down. This course was also given a heavy coat of paint.

That took care of one half of the roof, and the whole procedure was repeated on the other side. A narrower piece of cloth was cut to cover the roof's peak, where the cloth from the two sides didn't quite overlap. This was again fastened in place with furring strips where it lapped over the sides, but wasn't tacked down at all to the roof's surface. A heavy coat of paint was applied to this also.

For the next few hours we tended to other things that needed to be done. Then, once the first coat of paint was dry to the touch, we applied a second coat of the same paint. Then we did a third coat, after the second had dried. We were now finished.

About a week later, we got hit by a terrific thunderstorm, one of those real bucket-and-firehose downpours. I checked the canvas roof carefully, and couldn't find any sign of a leak, not even a damp spot underneath. But I hadn't expected to, because this was not my first experience with canvas roofing.

Maintenance doesn't amount to much, either. You just look at your roof from time to time. After several years, you'll notice that it will start looking sort of tired and faded. As soon as you think the roof looks like it could use it, just add another coat of paint. How long before you'll need to repaint will depend on the quality of the paint you used to start with. So the length of time between re-paintings can be anywhere from a year or so to a decade or more.

Milk paint

When the Conestogas were arriving in the western states and giving up their canvas tops for roofing material, probably the most commonly used paint for this purpose was home-produced milk paint. It wasn't anything like in the movies anyway—very few wagons were ever hauled by horses. Most were pulled along by oxen, or by three- or four-year-old cows. So most settlers could readily come by enough milk to produce their own paint in quantity.

Milk paint is just as simple to make today, and though it's not as long-lasting as the *best* commercial paints, it will outlast by far any of the *cheaper* commercial grades of paint. The best recipe I've found for mixing up this sort of paint is as follows:

- Thoroughly stir two quarts of builder's lime, *or* three quarts of sifted white hardwood ashes, into four gallons of skim milk.

- Next, stir in one gallon of linseed oil.

- You can also add any sort of water-soluble powdered dye, to make just about any color you want.

- Strain this paint through a piece of cheesecloth (or something similar), to remove any lumps or undissolved powder.

- *Use within two days.*

You might think this doesn't sound like much of a paint, but this mixture

bonds to wood, cloth, crockery, and such with unbelievable tenacity, and it dries to a hard, tough, plastic-like finish. In fact, many original pieces of colonial furniture, painted with this same finish, have survived 200-plus years of daily use with absolutely no signs of finish wear or fading. (Of course, they weren't exposed to the elements outdoors.) So it's well worth trying, if you have enough surplus milk to give it a shot.

Exterior grade varnishes, or polyurethane finishes, are also excellent choices for use on canvas roofing.

Gutters and windows

If this has stirred up your interest in this type of roofing, you might want to consider a couple of other uses for painted canvas as well. First, there will probably be a goodly amount of water running off your roof during rainy spells. Without proper gutters, this can lead to some real erosion problems, leaky foundations, etc. So just add some wooden gutters while you're at it, and simply extend your canvas roofing as a lining for the gutters, making them nice and watertight.

And here's another use, for anything like a chicken coop, where letting in light is important, but you don't really have to have windows you can see through clearly. You can make durable, translucent windows by tightly stretching lightweight cloth (like those Salvation Army bed sheets) on a wooden frame and then coating it with clear varnish or polyurethane. These windows will let in plenty of light; they're just not very good for seeing through. You can even make "multi-pane" or "double-glazed" windows if you want.

That's about all there is to it. Just about anyone can put a long-lasting, watertight canvas roof on just about any building, without investing a whole lot of time, money, labor, or materials. Δ

There are *lots* of tomato varieties — choose the ones that suit your garden and your taste

By Alice B. Yeager
Photos by James O. Yeager

When the ground warms up and frost is a thing of the past (at least for a few months), gardeners' thoughts turn to tomatoes. Actually, there seems to be great haste from coast to coast to see who can harvest that first plump ripe tomato. This pits neighbor against neighbor and friend against friend. Some folks grow an early-ripening variety for the pure pleasure of gloating when they are the first in their neighborhood to pick a ripe tomato.

The first fruits of the season aren't always the tastiest, however. Wait until those mid- and late-summer tomatoes ripen. There's the peak of perfection. Given the touch of sun and showers and a longer growing period, they are juicy and packed with flavor. Even so, the first fruits of summer are always welcome, as there's nothing better from the garden than a fresh tomato after a winter of dependency on those blah ones from the supermarket. About all *they* have going for them is color.

Some of us don't give a whoop about being the first to harvest anything, as we're going strictly for good quality vegetables for culinary use, and lots of them. Sometimes we reach the point of being sick and tired of more tomatoes, but we continue to harvest until frost do us part.

Whether you live in an area with a long gardening season, or one where plants can't be set out in the garden until the end of June, there are tomato varieties that are suitable for your climate. A good place to get advice is your local county agent's office. Also heed advice given by local gardeners. Many folks don't realize that there are umpteen varieties besides the highly advertised ones such as Big Boy, Early Girl, Beefsteak, etc. Some of the new hybrids are picture-perfect in appearance but they lack quality. The flesh is mealy, and they are firm enough to be hauled a thousand miles by ox cart without incurring a bruise. That may be well for the commercial grower, but the avid gardener seeks varieties that not only appeal to the eye but can only be described as downright delicious when prepared for the dining table. Most of the home garden varieties do not ship well, and folks shopping in supermarkets never have the pleasure of eating an honest-to-goodness flavor treat.

Trying varieties

I was born with an inquisitive streak, and I like to branch off from the well-known varieties and try some of the others. Living in Arkansas (Zone 8), where periods of high humidity and summer heat go hand in hand, I have learned by trial and error that not all varieties will grow here, even though tomatoes are generally known as a warm weather crop.

One of our favorite tomatoes is the **Thessaloniki**, originally from Greece. It is "indeterminate" (it needs staking) and mid-season bearing. It is a firm, full-flavored tomato about the size of a baseball. It has a deep red, meaty interior and is soooo good to slice and eat with toast for a snack. The plant has good foliage, and there's no trouble with cracking or sunburn. If I had to scale down to growing one

The Thessaloniki tomato, originally from Greece, is a heavy yielder with a deep red, great tasting interior.

Tomatoes come in many sizes. Park's Whopper and Sweet Million are two real winners in medium and small size tomatoes.

variety of tomato, I'd seriously consider making it this one.

For a large tomato, I am partial to **Supersteak** (indeterminate and mid-season). This one is not as smooth in appearance as Thessaloniki, but it has good flavor and a slice will cover a slice of bread and hang over the edges. Fruits generally weigh about two pounds and have good texture.

Quick Pick (indeterminate) is an early variety, as the name suggests. This is a medium size tomato with good flavor and will continue to bear until frost. Fruits are round but have an odd feature: they have a tiny point on the bottom. These tomatoes are just the right size for canning whole.

An oddity is **Evergreen** (indeterminate and mid-season). When ripe, these tomatoes show a slight tinge of yellow and are medium to large size. Evergreen has good flavor and texture and has a unique appearance in salads. In our garden, this one had a problem with wilt, leaving plants that were loaded with tomatoes but were goners.

We like to grow **Arkansas Traveler** (indeterminate and late-season). It is a hot weather plant and will continue bearing until frost. Flavor and texture

are good, and the tomatoes are about six to eight ounces in size. They are very good in salads and slightly less red than other tomatoes, thus providing variety in color.

Always leave room for a few small tomatoes. Generally speaking, these will need staking unless you are growing the patio varieties. Sorry, but I think the garden-grown ones have better flavor. One of our favorites and a heavy bearer is **Sweet Million**. It has a sweeter flavor than other cherry tomatoes and is a delight to pick and eat right from the vine while doing garden chores.

Growing tomatoes

All of our tomato plants are started in our small greenhouse, where we plant seeds in a heat-controlled seed starter, then transfer seedlings to styrofoam cups (with holes punched in the bottoms for drainage) or small plastic pots filled with a good quality potting medium.

When the danger of frost is past and the ground has begun to warm up, plants are about a foot high and ready to be *hardened off*—that is, given a

few hours of sunshine outside the greenhouse each day for several days in a spot protected from wind. We gradually increase the time of exposure until we know they are ready to move to their permanent place in the garden with no danger of *sunscald*. (Sunscald is over-exposure to the sun that causes leaves to bleach and severely damages plants.)

Tomatoes like a sunny spot in loose, moderately rich soil with a pH of 6.0-7.0. Every gardener who raises tomatoes seems to have a favorite method of planting. In our case, we have to take into consideration the fact that Mother Nature has a habit of turning off her water supply in mid-summer, leaving us to improvise if plants are to live through the dry season.

One preventive measure we use against drought is to plant the tomato plants deeper than we might in a cooler climate. We dig the holes deep enough to accommodate about a third of the plant, fill in plenty of well-rotted compost around the plants, and then water them well to eliminate any air pockets around the roots. Tomato plants will put out additional roots wherever the soil touches the main trunks, giving them access to moisture as well as providing good anchorage. Depending on the varieties, plants are spaced about 18-24 inches apart.

We also place a light organic mulch of leaves and pine needles around the plants at the time of planting. This prevents soil from splashing up on plants when heavy rains occur and also keeps the ground from crusting when it dries out. We add to the mulch as summer heat comes on to help retain moisture. In so doing we create a haven for earthworms—those diligent tillers of the soil.

Once our plants are in the ground and the earthworms take over, we forget about cultivation. However, a really tough dry season will bring out the water hose.

We set stout cages made from concrete reinforcing wire over our indeterminate varieties, which then grow

A real summer treat: stuffed tomatoes with slices of Evergreen tomato

up inside the cages. That makes for a lot less work than staking each plant. We drive in two short, stout stakes opposite one another against the wire inside each cage to assure that the cage will remain upright in strong winds.

Pests and diseases

Our main pest to combat is the **tomato hornworm**—that big, green, striped fellow with the horn on his tail. He has a voracious appetite and can consume quite a bit of foliage, as well as young tomatoes, in a few hours' time. Handpicking is the best and safest way to get rid of hornworms.

If **cutworms** are troublesome, a bit of 5% Sevin dust sprinkled on the base of the plant's trunk will solve the problem. After plants have matured and are out of the tender stage, cutworms should be no problem.

Tomato plant diseases—**wilts**, **mosaic**, etc—can best be dealt with by planting disease-resistant varieties. Also, if **nematodes** (tiny eel-like worms that live in the soil) are a menace, seek out tomato varieties that

show the letter "N" in the first part of their catalog description. For instance, Hybrid Beefmaster is VFN. "VFN" means "resistant to verticillium and fusarium wilts and nematodes."

Seldom is there any **bird damage** to our tomatoes, but I often hear complaints from friends about birds ruining their crops. Birds can be discouraged without resorting to violence. Just take some *dark* colored sewing thread and loosely tie pieces at random among the plants, being careful not to tie thread too tightly around the stems and thus interfere with the plants' circulatory systems. When birds fly into the threads, it startles them, and they will avoid the plants. (Maybe they think they have encountered a stout spider web.)

With all the variety we have in tomatoes—new ones as well as old standbys—no one should be bored with raising the same plants year after year. Give yourself a treat and explore. If you don't have much room, try some of the determinate varieties (which need only slight support) and patio varieties. Bush Beefstake, Celebrity, Pilgrim, Red Robin, Pixie Hybrid—the list goes on and on.

Reap your harvest and enjoy.

Some seed sources

Tomato Growers Supply Co.
P.O. Box 2237
Fort Myers, FL 33902

Geo. W. Park Seed Co., Inc.
Cokesbury Road
Greenwood, SC 29647-0001

W. Atlee Burpee & Co.
Warminster, PA 18974

J. W. Jung Seed Co.
335 S. High Street
Randolph, WI 53957-0001 Δ

> *When a just cause reaches its flood tide...whatever stands in the way must fall before its overwhelming power.*
> **Carrie Chapman Catt**
> **1859-1947**

My dog is old.
She limps.
Lying down and getting up
Come at great cost
And even her bark is gone.
(A stroke, the veterinarian suspects.)
It's hard to believe
She was once the guardian here
Whenever I was gone.
Now, she's just underfoot.
I keep her for no practical reason.
I hear her moan
And look down at my feet where she's sleeping.
Her legs twitch.
She's dreaming.
In a world only she can visit
She still runs like a dog.

John Silveira
Ojai, CA

A BHM Writer's Profile: Judith Monroe

Judith Monroe adopted Maine as her home state 40 years ago after emigrating from rural upstate New York. She raised three kids who, in turn, are raising their children—all in Maine. She has always loved dogs and has owned a succession of shelter foundlings. The one pictured here was a hound friend and a singer who needed just a little encouragement to sound off.

Her most recent acquisition is a Celtic harp which she found also sings on its own with a little encouragement—from the wind. Monroe is currently working on writing humorous prose and serious poetry.

A brick walk with little work and less money

By Robert L. Williams III

Because we often leave our house by the basement door, we have to cross 30 feet of often wet and muddy yard in order to get to the drive. What was needed, we decided, was a wide and rustic walk that could be built with very little work and practically no money.

We considered several options, but when we learned that used bricks were available to us at no cost, we decided immediately on the type of walk we would build. What we did can be done by virtually anyone with a little patience and energy.

Preparing the surface

The first step is preparing the surface of the soil. This means digging up and removing rocks, roots, and anything else that is in the way. This includes grass. What you want is a wide stretch of space that is nearly flat and ready to work. You may need to dig out enough soil so that you will have room for sand and bricks needed

Figure 1. Use a trowel to smooth the sand for the next bricks.

for the walk. If you don't use sand as a base, you may find that the bricks will sink in wet weather and in very heavy traffic.

Once rocks, roots, sand, and dirt are removed, locate some timbers (treated ones work well, but untreated timbers will last for a fairly long time and be replaced inexpensively, if you decide to leave the timbers in place) and line the walk area on both sides with these timbers. Then dump bucketfuls of sand between the timbers and rake the surface smooth.

If you prefer, you can put down a layer of black plastic before adding the sand. The plastic will help to prevent grass and weeds from coming up between the bricks. You can buy masonry sand, but this is expensive. You can use creek sand, as we did, and save money. The creek sand works beautifully once you discard pebbles larger than a marble.

Laying the bricks

Work in sections of about three feet at a time. Start with bricks stood on edge that are placed parallel to the house. Lay about a dozen of these bricks and then start a row of bricks perpendicular to the house. These bricks are started at the ends of the first bricks. You may choose to align these bricks exactly or you can, as we did, choose an irregular pattern.

One problem you may face is locating bricks that are free or very inexpensive. We found that a local community college offered courses in brick masonry. The students used a mortar made only of sand, lime, and water for their projects. Once the bricks had been used, they were not re-used and were free to anyone who wanted to haul them off. On weekends, we drove to the college and hauled 500 bricks per load until we had several thousand bricks on hand.

Figure 2. Lay a series of bricks, tap them down with the hammer, and level them. Notice the irregular exterior bricks that have already been mortared into place.

Our only cost was the expenses of operating a pick-up truck to haul the bricks.

We learned quickly that the mortar could be knocked loose with very little effort. We also learned of dozens of other places where bricks could be had for the asking. Some had to be cleaned of old-fashioned mortar, but we couldn't beat the price.

After positioning half a dozen bricks, as described above, use a level to check your work. If a brick is too low, lift it and put more sand under it. If it is too high, simply rake some of the sand away.

If your work satisfies you, keep placing bricks on edge until the first course is within eight inches of completion. Then, as you did in the beginning, turn the bricks until they are, again, parallel to the house. You may find that 20 bricks, plus the edge bricks will make a sufficiently wide walk. Sixty bricks, plus the edge bricks, will produce roughly three feet of linear surface.

Remember that you do not use any mortar of any sort between the bricks. You simply set in your edge bricks and then your interior bricks and proceed toward the end of the walk.

When you have completed the basic walk, you may wish to leave the landscaping timbers in place. Or you may remove them and leave only the edge bricks. Treated timbers can be costly, and in a typical walk, you may need as many as eight or ten timbers.

Earlier, I suggested that you use untreated timbers because you can move them as soon as one section is finished and remove them completely when the work is done.

One option is to go back after the interior bricks are laid and remove the edge bricks, a few at a time, and apply a bed of mortar where the bricks had been. Then "butter" the edge bricks and replace them. By doing so, you will have stationary bricks that will hold the interior bricks firmly in place.

When you come to the end of the walk, you can use a series of thin, flat rocks as the stepping-down area, or you can pour either concrete landing or a gently sloping terminus. Either way, you have rescued perfectly good bricks, helped reduce the loads of debris in the landfills, and in the bargain, you provided yourself with a delightful and useful walk that can also add beauty to your home. It is a bargain that is hard to beat. Δ

A BHM Writer's Profile: Jeff Fowler

Paul Jeffrey Fowler resides in Worthington, Massachusetts, in a passive-solar, solar-electric powered home with his family. He founded, developed, and later sold Fowler Electric, Inc., a successful business that supplies alternative energy components to power remote homes. Fowler wrote several successful how-to books and booklets on solar electricity while working at his former business. His most current book is The Evolution of an Independent Home; The Story of a Solar Electric Pioneer. Fowler has a B.S. in Biology from Tufts University and Masters Degree in Environmental Studies from Antioch New England Graduate School.

A BHM Writer's Profile: Bill Palmroth

Bill Palmroth pursued a newspaper career for 20 years, starting as a sports writer for the Grants Pass Daily Courier in 1958. In 1978 he started Media Specialist, an editorial and publicity service business. Loggers World Publications, in Chehalis, Washington, became one of his clients and he did field work for their logging magazines for five years before joining the company full-time in 1989. He then served as editor of the company's Log Trucker magazine for six years before moving to Belfair, Washington, in 1995 to become editor of the Belfair Herald. Over the years Bill has written articles for numerous outdoors and self-sufficiency magazines. As of 1999, he now operates his own store, Mr. Bill's Sportcards & Variety, in Belfair.

Lessons I learned while building my log home

By Dynah Geissal

When building a log home, the first order of business is getting your logs. Ideally you cut and deck all your logs in the beginning. We were unable to do that because we had so little time. We spent the weeks cutting, milling the logs to a uniform 6" width with our homemade Alaska Mill and transporting the logs that were manageable for the two of us.

On Saturday afternoons we had volunteer help so we needed to have enough logs ready to keep everyone busy. Twenty foot logs could be carried by six people using three steel bars. Thirty foot logs required eight people (the most we had available for carrying) and it would have been better to have had ten.

We milled the logs where they were cut so that they would be easier to carry. Many of our logs were ten feet and these we could carry to the site ourselves.

Selecting your logs

Your sill logs should be the strongest, straightest logs you have other than the ridgepole. Ideally they should be standing dead although ours were green. We cut half laps at the ends with a chainsaw and a chisel. To do that cut half the depth of each log and as wide as the log that is to lie on top of it. Either make a vertical cut and meet it with a horizontal cut or make multiple vertical cuts and hammer out the pieces and finesse with a chisel. It will look like this:

Be sure the sill logs lie firmly on the piers. If they don't, use wood shims (hardwood is best) until they do.

Besides the sill logs we have a sleeper which runs the length of the house and rests on the short end logs as well as on three wooden piers. We were advised that the 20 foot width of our house was too wide to use only the sill logs and that the sleeper down the

The beginning of the construction of Dynah's log home.

middle would greatly improve the strength of the house.

The short end sill logs do not run the entire width of the house because our house is on a slope. They go from the downhill pier to the center. A second log does the same. The third log lies directly on the uphill pier.

We were advised to put up three support pillars which would rest on the sleeper above the wood piers. These support the cross ties and ultimately the ridgepole. These pillars are 10" in diameter and 8' tall and were dead when we cut them.

Once again I wish we had time to study this for ourselves. I believe one support pillar would have been sufficient. Of course, the three add to the strength and stability and they do look

good, but they take up space and they divide the house, taking away from the open feeling we wanted.

If you do put up pillars they will have to be braced until they are attached to the cross ties. Support pillars are necessary only if you plan to have gales and, as I said, I really think three is overkill since we also have vertical poles in the gables which support the ridgepole.

Putting in the floor

Now you will need to decide whether to put on your floor or to wait until you have the roof on. We salvaged our flooring from a lumber mill. We bought pallets made of 2 x 6 tongue and groove boards which we had to dismantle. The pallets had been sitting out in the weather anyway so we weren't real concerned about them getting a little wet once they were nailed into place. Of course, when they were stacked we kept them covered so that they didn't warp. Another factor in our decision is that we only get 13" of precipitation for the entire year and most of that is from snow during the winter. So, in order to have a solid place to work inside, we opted to put in the floor.

We used the 2 x 6 tongue and groove boards for our joists also. We set them on edge 16" apart and secured them to the long sill logs and to the sleeper with joist hangers. Be careful with your measurements to avoid great frustration when you're flooring.

We chose the nicest boards for our floor, cut them to varying lengths of multiples of 16 and using finishing nails, nailed them to the joists. Two nails were used to secure the ends and the middle was toenailed in with a nailset used to countersink each nail.

Because our boards were used, there was some warpage and so the boards did not always fit together easily. When that happened we fit a third scrap board over the one to be nailed. Standing on the one we wanted to secure we smashed the third board with a sledge hammer. Usually that did the trick, but with an especially recalcitrant board we had to nail in one end and have a helper hold in the other end while it was hammered.

The house is divided by a step down which runs along the sleeper. The uphill side rests on top of the sleeper and in joist hangers on the sill log. Both sides rest in joist hangers on the

downhill side thus creating the step down. We started flooring at the stepdown reasoning that it would be easier to begin square when we didn't have to worry about the fit against a log. At the end we ripped boards to fit against the logs. We used relatively short boards because they were easier to custom fit.

Locating your doors

There are a number of things to consider when deciding where to put your doors. I believe every house should have two doors as a precaution against fire. They do take up quite a bit of space in a small house, but I think it's necessary anyway. So, where do you put your doors?

The short sides of our house face east and west. We were told to put the doors on those ends because you can't have your doors under the eves without building an additional roof. If you do, rain and snow will be pouring off your roof just outside the doorway. Made sense at the time. However, our prevailing winds are from the west and it is bad planning to have a door facing the prevailing winds. It is even unwise to have a door facing the opposite of the prevailing wind because it will always suck the wind inside. When our doors are open we have a virtual wind tunnel. In the winter we had to seal the door facing

west. Not good. So besides possible thoughts of convenience or aesthetics, consider the wind and never have two doors directly opposite each other.

Securing supplies

A word about supplies: prices vary tremendously. Be sure to shop around. At our "farm needs" store boxes of nails were 2/3 the cost of the same thing at the building supply store. We could get almost everything we needed there and the prices were always better.

We used 15" - 5/8 rebar and 10" spikes to anchor the logs. We used 7" spikes at first, but decided they were too small. In the beginning we used a brace and bit to drill the rebar holes and it was extremely difficult, but possible. Happily, a friend loaned us a generator and so then we were able to use an electric drill.

On the advice of more experienced people we put sill seal between the logs. When one log was anchored to the one below it we attached sill seal with a staple gun before placing the next log on top. The theory seemed good and my husband still thinks it was a good idea. I'm not happy with it myself. For one thing it's extremely expensive and for another it's plastic. It just doesn't seem to be in keeping with everything else involved in the construction of the house. The third and I believe most important aspect is that as the logs shrink there is space between them anyway and the sill seal inhibits filling these cracks with insulation. We have friends who are presently building a log house. They are cutting strips of fiberglass insulation and placing them between the logs. I think that will turn out to be a better alternative.

It is not necessary to have full length logs in most parts of the structure. The ones you do need to have full length are the sill logs and the logs directly above the windows and doors.

If you have the time you'll want to peel the inside and outside of your

The walls go up.

logs. We didn't so we did only the inside. It's easiest if the logs are off the ground so you don't have to bend over so much. Some drawknives are vastly superior to others - I like the old ones with thin blades. The new ones usually are much thicker and I don't like to use them. Always peel your logs when they are alive because, when dead, the cambium layer will adhere to the log.

Setting the logs in place

When you set the logs in place line up the logs as you look from inside the house. Outside they will not be uniform. If you don't do that it will be very difficult to hang shelves or whatever.

Even though you've milled the logs to a supposedly uniform size there are always going to be imperfections so keep your level handy and check after each log is placed. Shim when necessary. We had so many people working and were in such a hurry that levelling and plumbing didn't always happen when they should have. Brace the walls as they go up to keep them plumb. They will have a tendency to creep outwards. You'll need to decide how your walls are going to meet. What you choose will be somewhat determined by how much time you have. We had planned to use rabbit joints and indeed our first two logs (other than the sill logs) have them. We decided, however, that it was much too time consuming. We chose instead to use a half butt technique. In this method you alternate which logs butt up against the other. The short side is butted on one row and the long side on the next. You can make the long ends uniform or not, but it's best to leave them long until the house is finished. Then you can cut them all at once when you see how it looks. In any event, when you do cut them they need to be under the eaves. If they're sticking out they'll be exposed to the elements.

The log home before the roof went on.

When your logs are not full length join two shorter ones with a half lap as you did with the sill logs. The longer the "tongue" is the better—up to about three feet. Use your spikes to secure these joints. You will also want to spike every log every three feet or so and at each end. Your pins (rebar) go through or into 3 logs. They are staggered to give an equal distribution of strength. There should be one near the ends of the logs and every five feet or so. Mark where you put these with a pencil and also where you put your nails. That way you won't end up trying to drive one into another. Also, if you later want to cut into the wall to enlarge a window or some such, you'll know where the hardware is.

Planning your windows

When you have three tiers of logs up you'll have to plan for your windows if you haven't already. Windows are terribly expensive if you have to buy them new. Let people know you need them and check for demolition sites. Even rummage sales sometimes produce used windows. Glass stores sometimes have improperly sized thermopanes. The first time we sal-

vaged windows it seemed to take forever to get the first couple out, but we rapidly became proficient so stick with it.

After you have your windows you need to consider their placement. Books tell you to place your biggest windows facing south. In my case, however, south faces the road. My north side faces the meadow, which is my view of choice. Because we rarely have winds from the north we placed our biggest windows there. On the east end we only have one tiny window and that's really a mistake. We actually open the door on that wall in the mornings to let the sun warm up the house. Silly.

The other thing to consider is the height of the windows. Some windows you'll want to see out of when you're seated and so they will be placed differently than ones where you will most often be standing. In my living room area the windows are too high for when I'm seated. The one above the kitchen sink is so high I can hardly see at all. Part of the problem, I think, is that most of the people helping us were taller than I am. The rest

The log home completed

is just that I didn't have the time to get a feel for what I wanted.

In my case there is also the question of what part of the surroundings do I want to see—the mountains, the sky, the meadow or the yard? I find it frustrating to look out a window and see trees and sky, but not what the puppies are doing in the yard.

Another important consideration is the sun. In the north where I live I want the sun coming in all year. There is never too much and so I don't need to worry about letting it in in winter and keeping it out in summer. If you possibly can, experiment before you put in your windows. Put a chair in your unfinished house and see where a window should be. We managed to place two of ours well. Whether I'm sitting or standing I see the yard, the mountains and the sky.

We made our doors and window frames with our Alaskan mill. They are very attractive and fit the style of the house. We ripped 3 x 8 boards for the doors and 2 x 8s for the windows leaving the inside edge unripped for a natural affect. The door sill boards (also 3 x 8) are laid directly on the sill logs. If you are using green logs leave a 4" space above each door and window to allow for shrinkage. Only 2"

are needed if cured logs are used. Frame in the windows and doors, but leave the glass until the end to avoid breakage.

We installed used doors which saved us a great deal of time. They are good quality, but someday we'll make our own.

When you are ready to resume setting logs, use full length ones above doors and windows. When the windows are not all the same you may have to make the whole log the second one above the openings. These logs are called tie logs and are important for the stability of the walls. The top logs should also be full length. The ones on the long side are called plates and directly support the roof.

We were advised to use three cross ties, logs which are placed on the plates and across the width of the house. They rest on the support pillars. Two support the loft, otherwise, I believe, one would have been sufficient for a 20 x 30 cabin, but the three do look good. We left a 4" space between the support pillars and the cross ties to allow for settling. Into that space we drove wedges which theoretically could be gradually worked out. Rebar is driven through the ties and into the pillars.

As with the rest of the house, we are getting shrinkage, but minimal settling. This seems to be mainly due to the spikes we drove through the window and door frames into the logs. We finally had to cut them out and drive in 20 penny nails which stabilize the frames but yield to settling.

Locating a loft

If you intend to have a loft, now is the time to make your plans. We made a great mistake in having ours at the west end of the house. It is so dark in the mornings that I have to look up at the mountain tops to see if the sun is up. This, despite the fact that our one window is quite large. What a joy it would be to wake to a lightening sky instead.

Another consideration is where you will spend your evenings. Our living room area is directly below the loft. The heating stove is there and if it is warm enough to be comfortable sitting there, the loft is outrageously hot. This is greatly exacerbated by the fact that we did not build the loft floor all the way out to walls of the house so that hot air billows up from the stove directly into the sleeping area. A ceiling fan would remedy much of this, but the DC model is very expensive. The kitchen area is quite cold at night and we rarely keep the cookstove fire going after dinner. So sleeping conditions would be better there.

The final consideration is this—we have beautiful cathedral ceiling above the kitchen, but where we sit in the "living room" we look at the underside of the loft floor.

O.K., now for the actual building of the loft. We milled 3 x 12 joists with our Alaskan mill. The joists are notched where they lie over the two cross ties and the top log of the wall. They are spaced 18" apart. At the place where the stairs would be we made one joist about a foot shorter to allow for a landing. The most distinctive 3 x 12 finishes the front edge of the loft.

If we had it to do over we would make the loft the width of the house. We have a great lack of storage space and the area too low to be of other use could have served as storage.

For the loft flooring we used the same tongue and groove 2 x 6's that we had salvaged for the main floor.

Putting in the gables

Now is the time to determine the pitch of your roof. Talk to people who live in your area and research articles and books on the subject. Our roof is 10-12 on one side and 12-12 on the other. This means that for every 10" up you go 12" out. (See Figure 1.)

The reason they are not the same is that our step down is not in the center of the house. That means that the pillars are not in the center. In other words, one side of the house is wider than the other and so the roof angles cannot be the same.

There are many ways to build gables. The method we used was fast which was our primary concern as it was already Nov. 19 when we built them. I wanted them to be made of logs, but there was no time, and the weight of the logs at such a height seemed prohibitive without fashioning a way to lift them other than by human power. I would have been happy if we could have used boards, but there was no money to buy them and no time to mill them.

To my horror a friend brought up a load of pressboard that was left over from a construction project. I had been adamant that I would not use any plywood, particle board or anything similar in my house. But then it became apparent that the supplies were there and I could either use them or forget getting into the house before winter. Now, the outside is covered with the slabs which were milled from the house logs and the interior is finished with beautifully colored 1 by's which we milled. It looks great.

We built the gables from pressboard framed with more of the salvaged 2 x

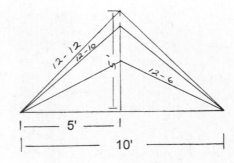

Figure 1

6's which were also attached as nailers. A support log 6" dia. extends from the top log of the wall almost to the peak of each gable allowing enough space on top to support the ridgepole. We built the gables on the loft. One was erected directly from there and we slid the other one across to the scaffolding waiting at the other end.

Lifting the gables into place was very exciting. It is very important to brace the gables until the roof is on. We used 2 x 4's for that.

Installing the ridge pole

Next comes the ridge pole. Let me tell you that getting that up even with

lots of bodies was quite a job. We had saved an especially fine, but even more importantly, a cured standing dead which was near the house. First we got it up on the top log and pushed it up to its pivot point. Then we had to get one end up the scaffolding and the other onto the loft. The end on the scaffolding went up onto the gable first. Then we slid the other end up the side of the gable which was no easy feat. It was wild and scary and almost dark, but finally it was up. Hurray!

Now you need to fill in the short logs that fit between the crossties because they will support the rafters. We used 5" poles for the rafters and spaced them 3 1/2" apart. They are spiked into the ridge pole at the top and the short logs and cross ties on the bottom.

When we had the rafters up we covered the entire roof area with blue plastic tarps. It was quite cold and snowy and even though we had a heat stove in the house it had become unpleasant to work. At that point we had to vent the heat stove through a window opening to avoid melting the tarp.

Next we installed the doors and windows and the cookstove which we

Dynah in her new log home.

also vented through a window. We installed insulation above the windows and doors where we had left space for shrinkage and settling. Someone had given us some cans of foam insulation which we sprayed in the corners and in the bigger gaps. While it did temporarily stop the wind it was actually a mistake to use it because it masks the openings if you aren't very thorough. You think it's closed off, but, in reality, it's only a thin covering between you and the outdoors—virtually useless, very expensive and ugly to boot. Don't waste your money on it. Later on we had to cut a lot of it away in order to chink properly—a real drag.

In order to maintain the integrity of the ridge pole we placed two 6" dia. logs on top of the two of the cross ties above the pillars. These were notched to fit around the ridgepole. We didn't put one on the third because it is under the loft. For structural support of the gables 4" diagonals were placed from the pillar to the gable top and from the same pillar to the next ridge pole support.

Our next step was to insulate the windows between the frames and windows themselves and to insulate the gables.

And then it was Nov. 24 and Thanksgiving. We brought in sawhorses and the beloved particle board and our family and friends piled upon it the most wonderful feast. The first of many in our new home. They had to bring their own chairs, eating utensils and candles. We managed to get most of the ice scraped from the floor and made a couple of benches from slabs and logs and had a very grateful day.

When we put in the floor we started in the middle at the stepdown. There was a space between the final boards and the bottom logs so at this time we custom ripped some more 2 x 6's to fit in those spaces. It was slow and tedious, but it stopped cold air flow which was great.

Building the spiral stairs

The weather was pretty bad at this point so instead of working on the roof we did indoor construction such as installing more structural support poles, planing and sanding the floors and beginning the spiral staircase which connects to the middle support pillar.

The spiral staircase has its pros and cons. It is very attractive and in a way is the focal point of the house. In reality, I guess, that's all I can say in favor of it. It really breaks up the house which is one thing we wanted to avoid. Our house is only 30' long and yet when one of us in the kitchen and one in the living room we can't see each other which makes conversation difficult. We're forever walking around the staircase to talk. Maybe even more importantly it takes up a lot of room. We had opted for one open room to give us the illusion of space, but then here is this big staircase right in the center of the house.

Another disadvantage is its unsafeness. Maybe if it had been built by a real professional it would be safer, but while the bottom steps have plenty of

The spiral staircase to the loft.

tread the top ones are sort of crowded together so that it's impossible to put a foot flat on the steps. In other words, we ran out of room. In addition, the railing is too low so that instead of using it we hold onto the cross tie and pillar when we go down.

I'll tell you how we built it in any case. Maybe you can correct our mistakes. The bannister or uprights that support the handrail are 3" poles. At the bottom they are spaced 12" apart which seems about right and toenailed into the floor. Each one is notched to hold a stair and the pillar is notched to hold the other end. The stairboards are 3 x 7's that we milled and 27" long. They are spaced for an 8" step. Our hand rail is about 28" above each stair and is made from peeled chokecherry whips.

Besides being toenailed the uprights are also glued to the floor. The stairs are spiked through the uprights and into the stairs and toenailed through the stair into the pillar. The top stair "floats" until the house settles. It is on top of the support pillar with a wedge between it and the pillar. There is a diagonal support from the pillar to the other end of the stair. That is because we cut off the upright to give us more space.

The landing is made of 2-2 x 6's. 2 x 8 boards form the 3 sides between the floor of the landing and the loft floor.

The weather remained poor so we put up more 3" poles, partly for support, mostly for aesthetics. We also installed cripples which are short 4" poles placed at an angle from the wall to the crossties. We worked, seemingly forever, planing and sanding both the main floor and the loft floor. Then we oiled the floors with soy oil. We used that because we could buy five gallons for $18.00—a real bargain. The floor looked very beautiful when we finished.

A friend gave us a DC light so we installed it in the kitchen and attached it to a car battery. We began spending more of our evenings in the house instead of the tipi. We would stay each evening until it got too cold to sit there.

When the weather finally improved we began again to work on the roof. We used salvaged 2 x 4's for purlins which we spaced two feet apart. On top of and perpendicular to the purlins we placed 2 x 6's on edge directly over the rafters. That allowed us space for R-19 insulation while letting the rafters show from inside. Over these "rafter extenders" we put more 2 x 4 purlins which serve as nailers for the metal roof. This was a lot of work and material whose only purpose was to have the rafters visible while still having space for the insulation.

Let me emphasize here how important it is to level and plumb continually. Some of our volunteers neglected to do that. The result is that every ceiling board has to be custom cut taking a tremendous amount of time. In addition, our roof is not square. So be sure to take the time. Eyeballing really isn't good enough.

Putting on the roof

Finally it was time to put on the roof. Along with insulation it was our main expense. We decided to buy new metal roofing and although we would have preferred green, we could not justify the added expense. Let me stress that metal roofing is the ONLY intelligent choice in the woods especially when we are miles from even a rural fire district. A roof of any other kind is simply not defensible in forest fire country.

When putting up the first sheet be absolutely certain that it is squared. Also, leave enough overhang for installation of the facia. Count the extra expense of roofing screws over nails as well worth it. Before installing the ridge cap attach screening to keep out insects.

We couldn't afford to insulate the floor so we just did the perimeter which helped some. It's a year later now and we still haven't done the entire floor. There's always something

Dynah in the kitchen of her new log home.

else that seems more important, like land payments.

We moved our solar panel and the two DC lights and the radio up from the tipi and our furniture from the shed and the house began to feel like home. We moved in on the winter solstice just in time for another holiday dinner with our family and friends.

We had salvaged some maple panels that measured 32" x 37" x 2 1/2 from a drugstore that was being remodelled. After much restoration we were able to use them as countertops. They are really beautiful now. They are supported by 3" poles. We used a hole saw to make holes in the walls of the appropriate size and inserted the poles. They are supported by diagonal poles.

Some friends salvaged a stainless steel double sink which set into one of the counters. Our water barrel sits on a platform nine feet above the floor and gravity feeds the cold water faucet. A metal cylinder sits on the woodstove and a hose connects it to the hot water faucet. The drain pipe goes under the house and into a gravel spillway.

For shelves we milled 2 x 12's and used pole supports that are inserted

into the walls in the same manner as the counters. These work well and look nice, but we used uncured wood and they began to sag as they dried. We shimmed them, but eventually we'll replace them.

We vented our heat stove through the floor so that the warm air would not be drawn from the house, thereby pulling in cold air from outside and we insulated around the stovepipe. Every day we stuffed more insulation into cracks.

We milled 1 by boards to cover the gables and the ceiling. As we milled them we kept them in order so that the grain and color have continuity. The boards for the gables are placed diagonally and the effect is very attractive. The ceiling boards run horizontally between the rafters. Milling all the boards is really time consuming and we still haven't finished, but we appreciate each board.

One of the last major tasks for our house was fabricating a tower for the wind generator, but that's another story. Δ

Ayoob on firearms

By Massad Ayoob

The Marlin Model 60 —
It's the classic backwoods home rifle

I recently bought a Marlin Model 60 .22 rifle. I needed it as an exemplar for a murder trial. An "exemplar" is an item identical to the one in evidence, which often cannot be accessed by defense experts.

The case involved a man who shot another man in his backwoods home. He claimed it was self defense. The prosecutor thought it was murder in the first degree. A single bullet had stopped the menacing giant who was moving toward the compactly-built 68-year-old householder. It caught him under the pectoral muscle, knifing through the liver and stopping in the spine. He died about an hour and a half later.

The Model 60 was designed to hold 17 cartridges. This one had been loaded with 12. The defense wanted to show that if murder had been intended, the defendant could have hosed a

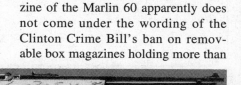

dozen bullets into the deceased instead of the one, or could have shot that man and his companion six times each. Hence, the exemplar rifle.

Most of my work involves firearms more potent than the Marlin .22, but working with this gun as we prepared for trial gave me an appreciation for it. When I tested it at the range, the first five shots (using Remington's lead bullet standard velocity round) grouped into half an inch at 50 feet. That's not the precision you'll need to win an NRA rifle match, but it's very good indeed for a mass-produced, low-priced semiautomatic rifle.

I suspect the accuracy comes from Marlin's patented Micro-Groove rifling, a 1953 innovation. The same feature has always made their Model 336 the most accurate of lever action .30/30 deer rifles. I have one that shoots just over one-inch groups at 100 yards. Instead of the standard rifling of five to seven deep grooves, Micro-Groove features many more grooves, cut more shallow.

I would never recommend a .22 for self defense unless the user was so physically challenged he or she could not handle a more powerful gun. That said, if I had to defend myself with a .22, I'd definitely want it to be a semiautomatic rifle containing lots of cartridges. (The integral tubular magazine of the Marlin 60 apparently does not come under the wording of the Clinton Crime Bill's ban on removable box magazines holding more than

ten cartridges, colloquially known as "clips.")

In performing the tests requested by the defense lawyers, I was able to pump a dozen Winchester high speed hollowpoints (the same load used in the shooting in question) into the middle chest area of a human silhouette 12 feet away in 2.5 seconds. The next test—one silhouette in the same place, another about eight feet to the side and another three feet further away— resulted in 12 shots fired in 3.67 seconds, leaving each target with four hits in the middle chest and two in the head.

Massad Ayoob

The rule of thumb is that with a short-trigger-stroke semiautomatic firearm, the average person can fire about five shots per second running at maximum speed. The thing with the recoil-free .22 rifle is that the running person can actually hit what they're shooting at, if they have a reasonably good idea of what they're doing, and are at reasonably close range.

Fortunately, the average purchaser won't need the rifle for this grim purpose, and will have a more potent firearm in the home should such a need arise. Where the Marlin shines is as a fun gun. The factory describes this rimfire as intended for small game hunting and "plinking," or informal target shooting. It should also do noble service for eradicating rural pests. A gun that puts every shot inside half an inch at 50 feet is all you need to permanently adjust the attitude of the freeloaders of the wild who believe your family garden is their salad bar, and it's accurate enough for barn rats and other disease-bearing vermin.

Between seven and eight million of these rifles have been made since the model was introduced in 1960. For the last decade, the factory has been producing about 200,000 of them a year. A lot have been sold through mass-merchandisers such as Wal-Mart. Many were produced for Sears under their J.C. Higgins private label (and, I suspect, their Ted Williams signature sporting goods series); for Montgomery Ward under their Western Field label; and for Western Auto stores as the Revelation brand. A great many were also marked Glenfield, Marlin's own economy grade in-house brand.

Current suggested retail is about $158, but it's almost universally discounted. Though I generally prefer to buy guns at gun shops (better point of purchase service, more knowledgeable advice, better follow-up service), none of the local gun shops had one in stock, so I had to go to a Wal-Mart. One store was retailing Marlin 60s for $123, but was out of stock; the other listed them for $97 and had one left. That one had gone back to the factory for reasons the clerk was unclear about, so I got it for $80. It worked fine. That's about the right price for a good used one. Use of cheap birch instead of traditional walnut for the stock, and other production economies that "take out the fancy and keep the performance" has kept the price reasonable.

Mine doesn't have a scope on it yet. If it shoots a half-inch cluster at 50 feet with the simple iron sights (post front, notch rear), Heaven knows what it'll do with a good glass on top. Any time you scope a .22, by the way, you'll be wise to avoid the narrow-tube models built expressly for that caliber gun. They tend to give a poor field of view and gather little light, and they don't stand up well to heavy use. A budget version of a high-power rifle scope with a full one-inch diameter tube is always a better choice. The optics are far superior, you'll shoot better with it, and it's much more likely to stand the abuse of farm use, particularly the constant vibration and

A BHM Writer's Profile: Allan and Marjorie Harrison

Marjorie and her husband, Allan, have been happily married almost 54 years and do almost everything together. They raised three boys and a girl and Marjorie put Allan through college. Today she is semi-retired but still works part time as a teller in a local bank and as Secretary/Treasurer of a recently formed nonprofit and tax exempt foundation located in Moreno Valley, California, called the Self Accountable Children's Society (SACS). It is designed to create self-reliant children at school and home, as depicted in her article published by BHM.

Allan, a captain in the Retired Reserves, began teaching elementary school in Moreno Valley Unified School District in 1959, where he innovated the "Harrison System" to instill self-reliance in children that Alice described in her article.

Later, Marjorie and Allan started and operated two different private elementary schools in Santa Ana and San Diego. Presently, Allan is President and Executive Director of the SACS Foundation.

Marjorie coauthored and self-published two book manuals with her husband in 1979 called "Discipline At School Made Easy" and "Discipline At Home Made Simple." With Allan's help she also wrote the article contained in this anthology.

jarring of riding along when you're on truck or tractor or snowmobile. (I've heard it said that the mark of the master rifleman is that he often pays more for his telescopic sight than for the rifle under it.)

At the age of four, I fired my first gunshots with an autoloading .22 rifle similar to this one (but no longer made), the old Stevens Model 87. I've found myself taking my new exemplar gun out to the range and shooting just for the heck of it. I haven't exactly rediscovered my childhood (though there's some speculation I might be entering my second one), but I've enjoyed shooting this inexpensive, lightweight, accurate little rifle.

Millions of these modest Marlins are everyday working tools in rural homes for pest eradication and the gathering of squirrels and rabbits for the larder.

If you know your livestock anatomy, such a rimfire rifle is all you need for humane slaughtering. A .22 bullet almost invariably stays inside the brain cavity of a steer or hog, but when placed in that brain, it kills as quickly and painlessly as a more powerful gun.

Marlin's Model 60 is a gun well suited for the lifestyle that *Backwoods Home* celebrates. It's plain, economical, unpretentious, and always seems to work. It does the job. It's fun. You can pass it on to your kids. It's the embodiment of backwoods living, rendered in birch stockwood and blued gunmetal. Δ

Think of it this way...

By John Silveira

Just how smart is that computer on your desk?

We were in deadline at the office. Things get hectic then. There are long days and even longer nights and a certain amount of tension permeates the office as we rush to prepare the magazine for publication. On top of that, the submissions were a foot-and-a-half deep on my desk and I wouldn't be able to get to them until after this issue went to print. But that didn't stop more from coming in everyday.

Outside, the sun was shining. It was teasing its way through the venetian blinds and I think it was calling my name. Behind me, O.E. MacDougal, the poker-playing friend of Dave Duffy, the publisher of this magazine, was taking his fishing reel apart. He'd arrived the night before and soon would be heading out to the lake.

When Dave walked in the door he looked at Mac. "When'd you get here?"

"Last night. Figured I'd stay here at the office."

"Good. Glad you could make it." He looked at the reel in Mac's hands. "Mac, I wish I had your job."

Mac smiled. "I lost $12,000 down in Reno last weekend."

"Is that a joke?"

Mac shook his head.

"Humph. Guess I'll keep my own job," Dave said and sat down as he flipped the switch to turn on his computer.

"You really lost $12,000?" I asked.

He nodded while he looked inside the disassembled reel.

"I can't believe you're sitting here getting ready to go fishing after losing $12,000. Of course, I can't even believe you play poker for a living."

He shrugged and continued to examine the reel. "I've lost big before. But I always make more than I lose by the end of the year. Besides, I get to go fishing whenever I want."

I shook my head. "There aren't enough fish for me to be able to live with a loss like that. I wouldn't be able to sleep at night."

Dave was staring at his computer. He watched it go through its exercises, one screenful of commands after another that have to be executed before he can use it. "These things take too long to boot up. I need a faster machine." He drummed his fingers on his desk. "Did you guys follow that chess match between the Russian and the computer?"

"Garry Kasparov and the IBM computer they call Deep Blue," Mac said.

"That's right. Did you think Kasparov was going to win as convincingly as he did?"

"Sure," Mac said.

Dave turned to say something but I interrupted, "How was that possible? How could a man beat such a sophisticated computer. I didn't think computers made mistakes."

Mac looked up from his reel.

"Do you guys play chess?"

We both nodded.

"Do you play well?"

"Silveira does."

"I'm just fair," I said. "I'm not really any good."

"In that case, I must be lousy," Dave laughed.

"You are," I said.

Mac smiled. "Well, most people think chess grandmasters play chess the same way they do, only better. But that's not how they play at all. Computers, however, *do* play like you do, only better."

"I'm not following you," I said.

"It would help if you understood the difference between the way you and grandmasters play. At your level of

John Silveira

sophistication, you look at a bunch of different moves and hope you'll see a way you can capture some pieces for nothing, and sometimes you even get lucky and find a way to pull off a sneaky checkmate your opponents have overlooked. I'm going to suppose you imagine that grandmasters play the same way, only better. But that's really not the way they play at all. They're too good to just leave pieces hanging out there to be captured for nothing and they don't carelessly fall prey to simple checkmates. Oh, there are some famous games where spectacular blunders have been made—grandmasters are still only human—but, in general, those things don't happen when they play each other."

"Then how do they play?" I asked.

"Instead of just grabbing pieces or instant checkmates, grandmasters look for strategic advantages, just like a good general does on a battlefield. A chessboard has its own terrain, like a battlefield. Getting your power concentrated in the center of the chessboard is like taking the high ground in a battle. Having freedom to move your pieces is like having good supply lines and mobility in battle. Secure lines of pawns can become incredible defensive positions. There are all kinds of analogies between war and chess, and, just like a good general in war, a good chess player will try to win all the tactical and strategic advantages he can before the big battle is fought.

"But most of the strategic advantages they fight for are so subtle that they're lost on the minds of average players. A grandmaster knows that if he wins these little struggles he can improve his position, even though the rewards won't be realized for 10, 20, or even 30 or more moves. And that's beyond what any player or even the best computers today can see."

"How many things could he possibly look for?" I asked.

"Well, it's been estimated that a grandmaster has about 100,000 rules of thumb stored in his mind."

"100,000?" I asked incredulously.

"Some are obvious like the three I've mentioned. There are a bunch of others like commanding open files, keeping pawn chains intact, centralizing knights. Any of these sound familiar?"

We both shook our heads.

"The ones I mentioned are the kinds of things you learn when you first decide to improve your game beyond the novice stage. But there are thousands of other things a grandmaster has to be aware of and that's what makes them great players."

"I don't know half of what you're talking about." I said.

"And I just look for moves," Dave added.

"And that's what both of you have in common with a computer because that's all a computer does. It has no feel for strategy. With its tremendous calculating powers, all it does is look for moves."

"But how can a computer play against a grandmaster if it plays the same way I do?" I asked.

"You can only look at a few moves at a time, but Deep Blue can calculate 80 to 120 million moves a second. That's more moves in a second than have been played in all the games between grandmasters since the game was first invented."

"Wow," I said.

A human can't look at more than a handful of the possibilities before him. But the computer, with it's incredible move-crunching abilities and lightning speed, can examine millions.

"How does it choose its moves out of all those possibilities?" Dave asked.

"The programmers put a software routine in that evaluates each sequence of moves the computer looks at; low values go to moves that are detrimental to the computer and high values go to moves that benefit it. From the millions of moves examined, the computer picks the move with the highest value."

"How many moves does a grandmaster look at?" I asked.

"Probably no more than either one of you do."

I was stunned. "But how can humans win when they look at so few combinations?"

"A grandmaster doesn't have to look at every combination. For one thing, he knows most are fruitless. For another, it's more profitable to focus on those strategic moves he knows are going to pay off further along in the game in situations than neither he nor the computer can see.

"Someone once defined a good chess player as one who knows what to do when there's something he's got to do, and a great chess player as someone who knows what to do when there's nothing to do. And that's the difference between Kasparov and the machine. The machine always knows what to do when things are obvious, but Kasparov goes beyond that; he knows what to do when there doesn't seem to be anything to do."

"Those little strategic goals," Dave said.

Mac nodded.

"How many moves deep can the computer see?" I asked.

"Within the time limits imposed on it by tournament play, probably no more than a dozen because at that point the number of possibilities exceeds what even the fastest computer can readily calculate."

"So," Dave said thoughtfully, "when a good chess player plays a computer, his best strategy is to play for those little strategic goals the computer isn't programmed to know exist, and to play for advantages further along in the game than the computer can see."

"That's exactly what they do."

"On the other hand," Dave said, "when the computer plays, its best strategy is to try on all the moves for size and see which one works."

"I like the way you put that because that's exactly what the computer does. It's the essential difference between men and computers."

"But the machine also has other advantages," Mac added. "It doesn't get tired, it doesn't make mistakes, it doesn't get upset, and it finds unusual lines of play that would never even occur to a human opponent."

"What do you mean by that last point?" I asked.

"A human can't look at more than a handful of the possibilities before him. There are just too many to consider. But the computer, with its incredible move-crunching abilities and lightning speed, can examine millions. It'll find unusual moves that are good that the grandmaster can't find because he doesn't know how to look for them."

"It'll find the 'needles in the haystack' that grandmasters wouldn't bother to look for," Dave said.

"That's right."

"How good will computers get?" I asked.

"Not only will computers in the future be able to look at even more moves and go deeper into the game, but with the help of good chess players they'll be able to build up a repertoire of good positions that will emulate the strategic rules of thumb the grandmasters use. One day, no human is going to be able to beat a good computer again."

"If a computer can beat a man at a game as complicated as chess," I asked, "is there any game we'll be able to beat them at?"

"Sure. Just change the rules. Instead of an 8 by 8 board, make it a 10 by 10 or 12 by 12 board and add some new pieces that have new kinds of moves. A game like that would suddenly overwhelm the computer—at least until the next generation of computers comes along—by making the number of possible moves it must examine go from the billions to the trillions."

"Why?" I asked.

"A huge increase in the number of possible moves isn't a big handicap to the human player because his play is based on strategy, and the quick formulation of strategies is always within the conceptual grasp of good players, even as the complexity increases.

"To the computer, however, if you increase the number of possible moves by a factor of 100, you increase its workload by a factor of 100."

"You're saying the brute force calculations would become less decisive, but the way we think, by generalizing strategies, would become advantageous."

"That's right."

"Why do you think Kasparov lost the first game?"

"I was surprised," Mac said. "I don't think any grandmaster's ever lost to a computer under tournament conditions before. Maybe a computer will be the world champion before we know it."

Chess and IQ

"Maybe computers will become as smart as we are," Dave said.

Mac gave Dave a funny look. "Actually, there's no correlation between the ability to play chess and intelligence."

Almost simultaneously Dave and I said, "I find that hard to believe."

"There was a Cuban player earlier in this century named Jose Capablanca. Some consider the him greatest player

What they found, to their own surprise, is that there is little, if any, correlation between chess ability and I.Q.

that ever lived. He didn't consider chess a game of intellectual prowess at all. He said it's an art. In fact, some of his contemporaries hated him because he said some of them were actually stupid."

"I don't see how you could be stupid and be good at chess," I said.

"In the 1950s, the Russians confirmed his assertion. Chess is a national obsession with them and they conducted extensive tests to identify potential chess prodigies. What they found, to their own surprise, is that there is little, if any, correlation between chess ability and I.Q. Some of the Soviet grandmasters were superb players, but otherwise of ordinary intelligence. However, they did discover that what makes a good chess player is the ability to manipulate objects in your head and to have good long term and short term memories."

"Then that's all the computers have going for them," Dave said.

"And speed."

"And speed," Dave added. "Otherwise, the computer is just an idiot."

Mac nodded. "The machines of science fiction that are conscious and more intelligent than man are just that—science fiction. Deep Blue can only play chess. Put some other kind of software on it, and it can only do that. A human mind can do a whole bunch of things—many of them pretty

well and quite a few others better than any computer.

"Before anyone makes a computer that can really compete with humans, something fundamental is going to have to change in the way we manufacture and program them. We're still a long way from making a computer that can duplicate, or even mimic, a human's brain. We can't even make one that duplicates a bee's brain."

"Why are the computer scientists wasting their time and energy on a computer that can just play chess?" I asked. "Why aren't they trying to solve some of the world's big problems?"

"Chess may seem like a waste of money and time, but it's not. By building a computer and devising programs required to play a world champion at chess, they're developing computer architectures, algorithms, and programming techniques that will be used to solve other problems once thought to be beyond the capabilities of humans and computers. Some will be as mundane as scheduling and routing airport traffic. Others will involve problems in economics, chemistry, medicine, and who knows what else."

"Well, why not go right after solutions to those problems?"

"Because those problems aren't as simple as chess. In chess, there are wins, losses, and draws. And even if your computer loses, its performance can be readily evaluated. If a computer can play a decent game of chess, maybe it'll be ready to tackle something tougher. But if it can't even play chess well, what chance does it have with more complex problems?"

"You know what I want?" Dave asked. "I want a machine just like Deep Blue on my desk."

"That power will actually be available to the consumer in the relatively near future."

"Really?" we asked.

"Sure. The chips Deep Blue used are all on the market now. One of the things this chess exercise did was show how the hardware and the software developed for it can work together. This kind of power will eventually be in the consumer's hands. It's just a matter of time."

"Well, I want one," Dave said and we all fell quiet for a few minutes. Dave and I started working while Mac reassembled his reel.

"Do you play chess anymore?" I suddenly asked Mac.

"No. I kind of lost interest in it."

"It's not like your game, poker," I said. "There's no chance in chess."

"That's not true," he said.

"You're joking."

Dave stopped working and turned around again. "There's chance in chess?"

"Do you remember the American who was world chess champion, Bobby Fischer?" Mac asked.

"Yes."

"When analyzing games, he often talked about winning chances. What do you think he meant?"

I shrugged.

"Well," Dave said, "it sounds like he meant that since there are billions of possibilities down the line, but no way to see which one's going to come about, that the chance lies in the decisions we make, even though, in theory, we should be able to see them all."

"That's right. In theory, chess is a game of perfect information, like tic-tac-toe."

"What's that mean?" I asked.

"A game of perfect information is one where you can see the result of every move and countermove, like tic-tac-toe. Even a school kid can see how every move in tic-tac-toe has a logical best countermove. In theory, chess is the same way, but…"

He hesitated there for a moment. I think he was expecting a response from us and suddenly Dave said, "But chess is so complicated that future moves get murky. Even a computer, whose forté is that it can look at hundreds of millions of combinations, can still only see so far. Beyond that horizon are unknown positions, and the advantages or disadvantages that are going to befall the players are unforeseeable. The choices we make to get to those futures are the chances we take."

Mac nodded. "It's almost a certainty that one day chess will be a game of perfect information, but only to a computer. It'll never be completely knowable to the human mind."

"Boy, that's a philosophical bone to chew on," Dave said.

"Do you see any downside to computers playing chess so well?" I asked.

"Sure. Just wait because someday, someone's going to cheat in a tournament with one."

"How?"

"Computers are getting so small that someday someone will conceal one on his body and use it to cheat in a chess tournament. It's conceivable that in some local tournaments, it's already been done. How would the tournament officials know?"

I shook my head. "How do you think of these things?" I asked.

He shrugged. "Active imagination?"

Computers and fishing

Dave was still thinking. "You know," he said to Mac, "I think I've learned a lot about computers today. If I had to sum it up, I'd say first that computers don't think like us—in fact, they don't think at all."

Mac nodded.

"Second, they're still nothing more than glorified adding machines. Third, our forté as humans is that we can take information and formulate generalizations and strategies from it instead of having to consider every possibility. Computers can't do that—yet."

Mac nodded again.

"And fourth, a computer doesn't even decide what to think about, or even how it's going to to think about it. We have to tell them how to do these things."

"I'd agree with everything you've said so far," Mac said, "but you're leaving out the most important thing."

Dave and I thought for a few seconds.

When we didn't say anything, Mac said, "They can't fish."

"What?" we asked.

"They can't fish."

I said, "Well, we could rig up some kind of net and one of those fish finders to a computer and they'd do a pretty good job of catching fish…"

"No, John, I'm saying a computer can't fish."

"But with the right electronic equipment attached to it…"

"You're not listening to me, John. You don't have to catch fish to go fishing."

"Oh, I see what you're saying. They can't…won't…" I groped for words.

"That's right, we enjoy life. A computer doesn't."

With that, he stood and gathered up his fishing equipment. "I'll probably be back for lunch. Maybe I can supply it."

He walked out the door. We could hear him get into his car and start warming up his engine.

Dave drummed his fingers on his desk. "You know, we speed up for deadline, we slow down in between."

I looked at him.

"How far behind are we?" he asked.

"Looks…bad," I said.

"Wanna just work like dogs, tonight?"

"Sure."

"Mac," he yelled as he jerked the door open.

Mac wasn't quite out of the driveway when he hit his brakes.

"Wait up," Dave yelled.

Dave grabbed his fishing gear out of his truck and I got mine from the trunk of my car.

"Hitch a computer up to a net and a fish finder," Dave mumbled to me as we jumped into Mac's van. "Where do you get those crazy ideas, John?"

I shrugged as Mac shifted the van into drive and we were off into the sunshine. Δ

Ducks contribute to a homestead in many ways

By Sylvia Gist

Free ducks! The ad on Tradio was irresistible. (Tradio is our local buy-sell-and-trade radio program.) I had always wanted to have ducks. It had never been a possibility before, but now that we had a place of our own out of town, we had the space and could think about raising them. In the beginning, I just thought they were cute. I learned they were far more.

When we picked them up, we found out they were Rouens, a "general-purpose" duck of fair size which resembles the mallard (only larger) and is sometimes called by that name. Within a few weeks, we chose two hens and one drake to keep over the winter. At that point, I was as yet unaware of the great asset they would become to our budding organic lifestyle and our effort toward self sufficiency.

From the start, their needs were minimal. Rouens will forage for themselves for a part of their feed if given the opportunity, so they do not require great amounts of commercial feed. For shelter, we provided them with a small building, perhaps 4' x 2' x 2' high, which they persistently ignored, sleeping in the open until the first measurable snowfall. At that point, they reluctantly moved inside. To go in the snow, they waddled out and quickly dropped to the ground, pulling their feet up in their feathers. They would flap their wings rapidly and attempt to skim the snow as they headed for their destination.

However, in spring, they thoroughly enjoyed sitting out in the rain. Only windy, blustery days would drive them to shelter. We constructed a makeshift shelter from straw bales to serve as an alcove in which to put their feeder (handmade by my husband from 2x4s). An old dishpan served as a waterer (and swimming pool). In very cold weather, we had to chip the ice and pour in hot water, which provided them very enjoyable swimming. This swimming hole was barely large enough to accommodate them in mating, so as the weather warmed, we provided larger water containers.

In spring, the hens laid eggs in the corner of the little "duck house," which had been abandoned with the warmer weather. This small shelter served the hens as they brooded for the required 28 days and continued to provide a home for the family as the ducklings grew. In just a few days, the little ones were out adventuring under the watchful eye of mama, seeking out the swimming hole, which, for them, happened to be a shallow black rubber feeder we had purchased at the farm store.

Liquid fertilizer

It was this swimming water (and any water they would subsequently be able to throw themselves into) which provided a major contribution to our ecosystem. Ducks "foul" the water, adding a lot of nitrogen, which, if the water is dumped, will go to waste. We were able to make use of this "liquid fertilizer" in the garden, which we were striving to grow organically. I transferred the water to five gallon pails (procured from a fast food restaurant), carried it to the garden, and distributed it by the quart to lettuce, leeks, and other nitrogen-loving plants. Carefully avoiding direct application to leaves, I poured it on the ground at the base of the plant. The result was big, beautiful heads of leaf lettuce, from which I trimmed the outer leaves. I then fed those leaves to the ducks. Since the two hens hatched out 27 ducklings, we had a plentiful supply of nitrogen-rich liquid fertilizer during the summer.

Delicious meat

Not only did this large flock provide a great deal of fertilizer, they went on to provide my family with a lot of delicious, tender meat. Although we slaughtered most of them between the ages of eight and ten weeks, we could have waited longer and

A BHM Writer's Profile: Mark & Lynn Klammer

Mark is by profession a computer technician and, by education, a geologist/chemist--but at heart he will always be a farmer. Lynn and their four children just try to keep up with him.

missed some of the pinfeather problems. For this reason, we ended up skinning many of them. Those which picked fairly clean, we froze for roast duckling. We cut up the skinned ducklings, separating the pieces, and packaged them to meet our needs. I saved all the livers for frying fresh—a real treat served with eggs and toast for breakfast.

There are plenty of recipes for roast duckling and various stuffings, but what does one do with skinned pieces? One recipe I borrowed became a favorite of ours. First dredging the pieces in seasoned flour or biscuit mix, I brown them in duck grease in a cast iron chicken fryer. Next I add chopped onion and some water. Then I turn the heat down, cover, and let them simmer until the meat is fairly tender. In the last 30 minutes, I put in small whole potatoes or chunks and allow everything to simmer until done, adding water as needed. Finally, I remove the meat and potatoes and make gravy.

The grease I use for browning is obtained from the drippings of a roast duckling. It also can be used as a substitute for butter on popcorn.

Eggs

Another source of food is the eggs. The Rouens are an all-purpose breed, which means that they are only average egg layers, as ducks go. My initial intent was to raise baby ducks, so I gathered the eggs only in the early spring when the nights were freezing and the eggs would be damaged. As soon as the weather improved (which happens in April here in western Montana), I left the eggs in the nests. Both hens laid in the same nest until one hen claimed it and began to set. As I watched the eggs pile up (and since neither hen seemed to be broody), I took out a few eggs, trying to keep the total between 12 and 15. These eggs I boiled, mashed, and fed to some new baby chicks we had at the time. The earlier eggs, however, I used for baking, allowing one duck egg for every two chicken eggs.

Down and feathers

Their contributions do not stop here. A by-product of slaughter was the down and feathers. Picking the ducks dry, we plucked the big feathers into one barrel. These feathers would go into the compost pile. We moved to another barrel to deposit the very small feathers and the down. To clean them for later use, I plunged them into a five-gallon bucket of warm water (adding soap if they were really dirty) and swished them a few minutes, transferring them by handfuls to a new bucket of clean water. I then used a pillowcase, turned wrong side out, as a strainer, pouring the water and feathers into it. (Don't put an excessive amount of feathers in one pillowcase, or they'll be so crowded they won't dry and fluff properly.) I squeezed out the excess water, put the wet ball of pillowcase and feathers in a mixing bowl, set it next to my sewing machine, and securely sewed the top shut. To extract more water, I used the spin cycle on my washer for a few minutes. Next, I threw it in the dryer on low for a while and then on "air dry" for a while. They come out soft and fresh-smelling. One just has to rip out the stitching and transfer the feathers to the desired destination.

Simple pleasure

A less tangible by-product of raising ducks is the pleasure I get from watching them. Excitement gripped me as I saw the tiny black and yellow heads peeking out from under the hen. A few days later we praised the hen as we admired her fluffy offspring—black and yellow like bumble bees—running energetically around in the pen, hopping gleefully into an opportune pan of water. A loud squawking from her would bring me running to the pen to see what trouble "Mother" couldn't fix by herself. A warning cry from the duck hen when a hawk flew over would send not only her ducklings to shelter, but also our young chickens and turkeys.

As the babies grew, they ate with the same zest with which they swam. In this energetic fashion, they learned that lettuce (the candy of the duck world) came from humans, and they would beg when I approached. As they grew, they were always optimistic—a delight to watch.

We provide our ducks with water, some feed, and minimal shelter, and they provide us with eggs, meat, feathers and down, fertilizer, and simple pleasure. They are economical, definitely giving more than they take ...all in all, a great addition to our farmstead. Δ

Concrete domes have some impressive advantages

By Lance Bisaccia

In the mountains above Ashland, Oregon, there's a place where you can pull your car off the road and look up and see three linked concrete domes whose sides merge into each other like 20-foot soap bubbles. Their appearance is a little strange and very pleasing. When I interviewed the owner/builder, Steve Wolf, I learned that they have a *lot* more going for them than their looks.

Steve was a builder for ten years, but he got sick of community design reviews and building regs that put inappropriate limitations on builders. He decided to design and build his own place. As he studied various construction technologies, he found himself increasingly impressed by the advantages of concrete domes—advantages that center around their structural integrity. A concrete dome transmits stresses through its structure,

which makes it very strong. This kind of structure can last for centuries, in case you'd like to make a house your great-grandchildren can enjoy.

There's a special feeling about being inside a dome, with its soaring spaces, unbroken by internal supports. Steve calls it "inspirational." He points out that a concrete dome is also

Fireproof: Not only will a fire *outside* the house normally be stopped by the concrete, but a fire *inside* the house probably won't spread to the forest (or in another setting, the neighborhood) around the dome.

Earthquake-proof, compared to conventional construction: It should handle a Richter 7.

Windproof: It has no vertical surfaces or overhangs for the wind to hammer and tear. About 70% of homeowners' insurance claims are wind-related.

Inside the air form

Steve showed me a photo of a nice-looking residential dome in hurricane country and said the owner just wasn't worried anymore.

Strong enough to berm or bury: You can berm up the side as high as you want, or even bury the entire height of it, and get your building out of the temperature extremes of the surface.

The construction techniques Steve used are fascinating. Some of them were also technically very demanding (the foam) and quite costly (leaving the air form in place). Later on in the article, we'll take a look at some alternatives that most of us would find more manageable and more affordable.

The dome is constructed in a pretty amazing way: the concrete is *shot* from a huge high-pressure hose onto the inner surface of an inflated air form that's as big as the finished dome. Does this mean that you're actually working *inside* a huge balloon? Yes it does.

Here are the steps:

Pour a concrete slab for your foundation, **and anchor to it (1) the air lock, and (2) the air form**, which is made of very strong reinforced vinyl. For Steve's house, the air form is being left permanently in place as a

The application of shotcrete is complete.

Framing for door opening. Blue air lock is visible in the background

vapor barrier. After a few years, sunlight would damage the vinyl, so it will be covered. (Part of Steve's domes will be finished with stucco and part will be bermed.) The edge of the slab is a "keyway foundation" from which sprouts the first course of vertical re-bar. Steve used a vibrator on this part to get all the air out of the concrete, for extra strength.

Inflate the air form with a powerful fan, which needs to keep running until the dome-sized grid of re-bar is complete. Vents maintain the correct pressure in the air form. Steve's air form was custom-sewn by a company called Monolithic Constructors in Italy, Texas.

Inside the air form, **place wooden forms to define doors and windows**. You'll create your grid of re-bar around these future openings.

Blow one inch of foam insulation over the entire inner surface of the air form (except your "framed openings"). Steve described this material as a "plural-component urethane foam," and he said that applying it was one of the most challenging parts of the project. The foam is very fussy, and it can't stand any moisture or tem-

peratures under 45°. It's sensitive to ultraviolet, so you don't use it on outside surfaces. It's not your ideal do-it-yourself technology: you'd probably want an experienced worker to apply it, which naturally increases the already considerable cost of the stuff. Fortunately, as I indicated earlier, its use is not essential to making a concrete dome, and we'll take a look at some alternatives later.

Once that first one-inch layer of foam sets up, **install *re-bar hangers*** all over the inner surface. Each of these ingenious hangers combines a staple that you drive into the foam, a flat surface that will be held in place by the *next* layer of foam, and a pair of six-inch wires that you'll twist to bind the re-bar into place. **Apply another two inches of foam**.

The foam has excellent insulation properties, and makes it possible to provide almost all needed heating for Steve's domes via solar gain. The domes' total floor area is 960 square feet, with eighteen-foot ceilings. In December of 1995, up there on the snowy mountainside, it cost him $14 to keep the domes at 60° for the month.

Create a grid of number-three re-bar on ten-inch centers, a grid that covers the entire inner surface of the dome (except the defined openings). Do the horizontals first, then the verticals. When the grid is complete, you can turn off the fan that's been keeping the air form and the foam in shape.

Install your electrical conduit and plumbing pipes, attaching them to the re-bar grid. They'll be inside the concrete.

Now it's time to **shoot the concrete onto the re-bar grid**. You use a special super-high-density type of concrete mix called *shotcrete*. Here is a typical recipe:

- one yard of sand
- seven sacks of concrete
- three ounces per yard of industrial soap (to create small air bubbles)
- Easy-Spread (Bentonite clay) to make the shotcrete flow better
- "cottony" polymer fiber to reduce hairline cracks and increase strength

You spray it on with a special electric shotcrete pump. A 185 cubic-foot/minute compressor adds air at the nozzle. Steve said this was the hardest part of the process. (Once again, an owner/builder might think twice about

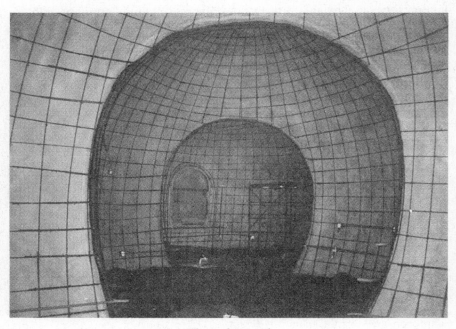

The re-bar grid

Rear view of the domes, covered by the air forms

trying to do this himself. We'll consider an alternative below.) You shoot on seven applications of a half-inch each, and at every coat, you trowel and scrape and smooth, using traditional concrete-finishing tools. When it's done and cured, you can finish the interior with plaster.

Inside the dome, you can use conventional stud framing to create interior rooms, a loft, etc.

Steve is planning to berm the back of his domes to a height of 12 feet. One of the virtues of the dome is that it's strong enough to permit this. Similar domes have been buried to a depth of 22 feet.

A different approach

After I spoke with Steve, I looked up a man named Miten Ahern, a contractor who has done concrete dome construction and is preparing to build them in a new and innovative way as part of his business. Miten was one of the first students at the dome-construction trainings offered by Monolithic Constructors (the company that created Steve Wolf's air form).

Miten's new and more affordable approach goes by the name of Eco-Straw Domes. In this technique, the re-bar grid is constructed *outside* the air form, and the shotcrete is applied to the *outside* of the form. This method became possible fairly recently, when a new and stronger fabric came into use for making the air forms. This stronger material can withstand a higher internal pressure, which makes the form more rigid, so it can withstand the high-velocity application of the shotcrete from the outside.

One of the important benefits of this new technique is that the air form can now be removed and re-used many times. What this means to the owner/ builder is that now you can *rent* the form instead of having to buy it. This brings a very substantial reduction in the cost of the house. Renting an air form costs about $1/square foot, plus about $1/square foot for shipping. You can rent both the air form and the inflation fan from Monolithic Constructors.

So: you do your slab and footing (a one-day pour). In this version, you install your electrical conduit and plumbing pipes (and hydronic tubes for heating) in the slab. Attach and inflate your rented air form, and erect your re-bar grid around and over the dome. Making the grid is likely to take two or three days. As with Steve's project, you'll place wooden forms to define your door and window openings and make the grid around them. You can climb on the lower parts of the grid to create the higher parts.

Once your grid is ready, you hire a shotcrete company (they're easy to find) to come in and apply the shotcrete to make a dome four inches thick. Miten says they'll do the job in

The view from the dome

one day. In fact, it's *important* for them to do it in one day, to create a dome that will cure as a unit for structural integrity and strength.

Can you apply the concrete by hand, to save the money for the shotcrete equipment and crew? No, you can't: this style of construction requires the high-velocity application of the shotcrete, in order to be strong.

So far, this method has resulted in a concrete shell that's very strong, but not so good for temperature control. You get your insulation by covering this shell with a layer of straw bales. You then cover the straw with a two-inch-thick outer shell of concrete, which is also reinforced with a re-bar grid, like the inner one. Miten says a "two-string straw bale" has an R-value of 40-45. By comparison, a conventional 3½" layer of fiberglass insulation has an R-value of 11 or 12. You

The living room in a finished dome

stack the bales and "pin" them together with re-bar spikes. On a 40-foot dome, the curves are gentle enough to be no problem to this process.

Straw must be kept dry so it won't rot. Concrete is not a good moisture barrier, so you spray or roll on a water barrier on the outside of the inner dome (about a day's work). Poly-butyl rubber is a likely candidate for this. When the outer shell is finished, you

treat that one as well. This waterproofing must be fail-safe, so the straw stays dry and continues to provide insulation. In addition, the straw space is vented, and the straw is "grooved" to accept perforated poly pipe. Any moisture that might find its way into the straw migrates to the perforated pipe by capillary action and is then conducted out of the straw space via the vents.

Miten says the cost of a dome like this is very competitive with conventional construction, but the building is far superior. He's planning a 40-foot dome for his own residence. That's big enough for a two- or three-bedroom home with two levels inside the inner shell.

With so much thermal mass in the concrete (to store and release heat), and so much insulation value in the straw, heating and cooling are no problem. Miten's dome will have a large glass area on the south with an overhang designed to *admit winter sun*, but *shade out summer sun*. He'll berm the north side. The air circulates very freely in a dome, so you don't get temperature stratification. And the concrete conducts heat, so if there is a hot spot (near a heat stove or sun space, for example), the heat is conducted away from it, and the inside temperature evens out.

Miten suggests that this type of construction also represents a livelihood opportunity, and he says that getting the training and certification from Monolithic Constructors is an excellent way to pursue it.

Speaking of Monolithic, their own dome office buildings provided dramatic proof of their virtues when they took a direct hit from a tornado. They suffered no damage, while the buildings around them were damaged or destroyed.

For more information about Eco Straw Domes, you can contact Miten Ahern at PO Box 608, Ashland, OR 97520, or send e-mail to miten @aol.com. Δ

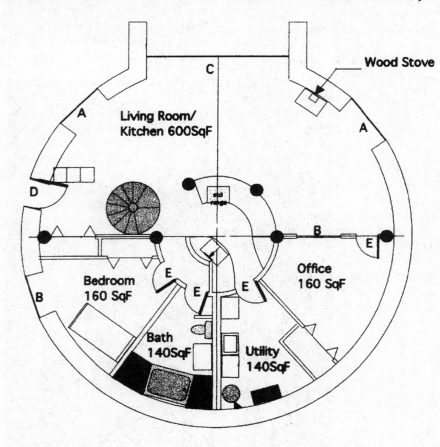

Floorplan for the downstairs rooms in a 40' residential dome

Cob construction is *literally* dirt cheap

By Marna Meagaen

Even as a backwoods woman, I never thought I'd be able to gather the skills to build a house of my own without some technical training, computations and measurements, massive power tools, and some expert advice. It was a delight to discover last summer while helping build Indigo Art Studio in Southern Oregon that I had learned practically everything I needed to know to create a house back when I was a little girl making mud pies in the backyard with my sisters.

Cob, meaning "small lump or mass" in older English, is an ancient earth building technique that is found—with many variations—all over the world. By mixing dirt with sand, water, and straw on old tarps, then moving and shaping it with many hands, it's possible to build houses, galleries, and outbuildings with the very land on which you stand. The walls feel rock-solid when the mix is dry. The sand makes it strong, the clay holds it together, and the straw helps it to breathe, as

A finished cob interior: the kitchen

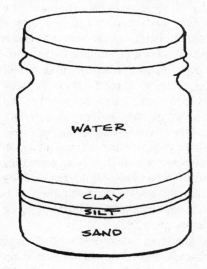

The jar test will tell you what your soil needs to make a good cob mix.

well as functioning as re-bar. It is remarkably resistant to water, although the foundation is usually brought to six inches above the ground, and the roof overhangs are usually large to minimize splash-back to the walls. Even without these protections, rain splash has only resulted in slight dents at the splashline in 400 year old cob houses in England.

A good mix:
Basic wall construction

Building with cob brings memories of childhood. You mix approximately equal parts of earth and sand on a tarp by pulling the edges of the tarp towards the center to roll the ingredients around. At the Indigo project, the recipe was ten shovels full of dirt to seven of sand. (See below for determining the recipe for *your* land.) Then you gradually add water from a garden hose and mix the concoction with your feet for five or ten minutes, until

the mixture is evenly moist and sticky. At that point, you add a handful of straw now and then (no more than a flake), continuing to roll the mix with the tarp and kneading it in with your feet. You end up with a big "cob pancake." The mixture's consistency is slightly more crumbly than modeling clay. It is added a chunk at a time onto the foundation (usually built of stone, although cement may also be used) and worked into the previous layer of the wall with thumbs, sticks, palms, and feet.

Testing your soil
to find the right recipe

The exact ratio of sand added to the dirt will vary depending on each site's inherent mix of clay, silt, and sand. To figure out the right recipe for your land, put a sample of your subsoil—one trowel full—in a one-quart jar. Fill the jar with water and shake it briskly, then set it aside. Sand will settle to the bottom, topped with silt and then clay.

For your cob mix, you want to have 50-80% sand. If that is what it turns out to be in your jar test, you probably don't need to add any sand to the cob mix—just use the soil and the straw. If you have to add a trowel full of sand to get the right percentage, then use one shovel of sand for every shovel of dirt. (In few cases will you need to add more clay.)

Run a few test batches of cob mix with that ratio of dirt to sand. Do other tests with more or less sand, and varying amounts of straw. Build some blocks, let them dry thoroughly, knock them over, hit them with a hammer, and use the mix that results in the strongest block.

Cob does not have to be built with topsoil. When levelling the site for the house, set the topsoil aside for your garden.

For the 240 square-foot structure at Indigo, we used 15 truckloads of sand in the bed of our 3/4 ton pickup. They cost $7 each from the local gravel yard. Ask for "concrete sand," a medium-faceted sand with varying grains.

The rounded sand found on beaches is not suitable for cob construction.

Make the walls 15 inches wide at the foundation for a one-story structure, 20 inches wide for two stories. As the walls rise, the inside wall should remain *plumb* (vertical), and the outside wall should angle inward slightly at the rate of two inches for every three feet. This slight incline increases the overall strength of the wall. We used a three-foot carpenter's level with a styrofoam angle taped to it to keep our walls straight and angled as needed.

Cob is different from stud frame construction: it doesn't require the constant checking to be sure that everything is level. While you want to be sure to check the walls as you go, the finish work you'll do with machete and plaster helps smooth over your "learning experiences." Because the walls are self supporting, leveling becomes much less crucial.

It is hard to describe the process of applying the cob. It is a cross between kneading a loaf of bread and sculpting a house out of clay. Some people have described it as "massaging" the cob. Basically, you are working with a

All the tools you need for cob construction

moist clay/straw slab and mixing it into the previous layer of cob by pushing firmly with your thumbs, by walking on it, or by pushing a stick into it with a slight twisting motion. Don't pound or slap the cob, because that would interfere with the setting up of its structure. Work it gently but firmly. Smooth and shape the walls as they rise.

It is best to add no more than a foot of fresh cob per day to your structure, as it cannot maintain its shape without drying some overnight. Too much cob (or too wet a mix) will cause it to "oog out," and you will need to hack it back into shape with a machete.

As the walls grow, the opportunities for sculpting expand, allowing hands to follow the guidance of heart and "error" as well as that of the mind. Cob is a wonderfully forgiving medium. I have seen one incredible cob sculpture of a panther, lying across the top of a window with its tail hanging down the side. It's quite a sight.

To "put cob walls to bed" at night, take a stick that is about an inch in diameter and poke holes two inches deep all over the top layer, four to six inches apart. These holes will help you work the next layer of fresh cob into the drier previous layer. Then

Supports for this scaffolding are built into the wall. When the project is finished, they'll simply be sawed off.

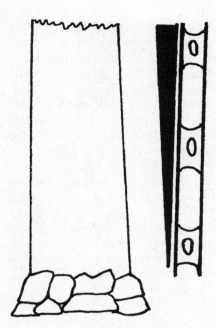

*Inner walls are kept plumb;
outer walls slant in a bit.
It's handy to have a carpenter's
level with a taped-on "slant gauge."*

cover the walls with several inches of straw and wet the straw lightly with a garden hose. If you expect rain overnight, cover the walls with a tarp.

You should have a design in mind before you build. Know where your door is, where you want your windows and shelves to be. These items are added in as you build, and you have some flexibility to shift windows, shelves and niches around as you go. In order to incorporate doors and windows into cob, drive bent, rusty nails into the sides of the wooden door- or window-frame that will be touching the cob. Position the frame using a level, and then cob up to the wood. The nails will grab the cob and hold tight for generations. This "porcupine" framing technique is detailed in the January/February 1996 issue of *Backwoods Home* (Issue No. 37). It is in the article by Harry G. Nemec, "Here's a cold storage house as good as our ancestors built."

When you install framed windows and doors using the porcupine method, you will need a longer slab of wood called a *lintel* sitting on top of the frame and extending beyond the frame in order to support the weight of the rest of the cob wall above the frame until the wall dries. For the Indigo project, we used cast-off 4x8s and railroad ties as lintels.

Windows that don't open can be incorporated by cobbing around a pane of glass—even a chipped or broken one. At the top, sculpt the cob into an arch—an extremely strong design —and the arch will easily support the weight of any cob above it.

As the walls rise, you can build the scaffolding for working on the higher levels of the wall right into the cob. When you're done, you can saw it off.

Plumbing and electric wiring can be run through PVC pipe through either the wall or the foundation. It's easier to cob around the PVC pipe low in a wall, rather than trying to build a sturdy, immobile rock foundation around a round piece of plastic. A small bush can be planted outside to cover the entryway of the wires or pipes to the house if you decide to plumb or wire through the wall.

Heating and cooling

As a building material, cob provides excellent thermal mass. The ten- to sixteen-inch-thick earth walls lend themselves easily to passive solar designs. Having a south-facing wall that is mostly glass windows with deciduous trees in front helps keep out summer sun and let in winter rays. In summer, the walls hold the night's coolness through the day's heat. Then they slowly radiate the stored heat of the day throughout the cool evening.

Another exciting possibility to try is a hybrid structure with a straw-bale north wall (making use of straw bales' insulative properties) and cob for the other walls. Cob and straw bale walls can be joined by driving wood stakes or branches into the straw bales and then building the cob up around and over those pieces of wood. One central Oregon cob house uses only half a cord of wood for its annual heating needs.

Cob is not a local phenomenon. Many traditional peoples have used earth architecture as their primary housing for as long into the past as memory holds.

Dirt cheap

Cob works well in situations where there are many willing and variously able bodies and few bucks. One of the first Oregon cob houses—one story with a loft and second-story study— cost only $500 for materials. Landfill and construction cast-offs can be scrounged and transformed into perfect cob house materials. At the Indigo project, a piece of wood from in front of the local laundromat became the lintel beam on top of the southern window wall. Rocks, broken or uneven pieces of glass, old teapots, broken plates, bottles, old 2x4's, rusty nails, and beautiful branches gifted from the forest floor can all become part of the structure.

Major costs can include paying for the levelling of the site (if done by rented machine or hired backhoe), purchasing and hauling sand and straw, water or electricity if pumping is required, and roofing materials.

It's best to buy the straw in season—after the spring cutting or fall harvest when availability is high and prices are low. Here in Oregon it costs $2.40 a bale in season, and more than $3 a bale out of season. The Indigo studio used about ten bales, and it was handy to have another bunch lying

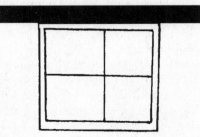

A lintel over a framed opening supports the weight of the wall above.

Nearing the top of the wall

around for makeshift scaffolding when the walls began to rise.

Applying plaster

One of the events that stands out in my mind as icing on the cake (almost literally) is combining and applying plaster to the inside and outside of the cob structure. My favorite plaster mix consists of one part clay, one part sifted dirt, one part well-aged horse manure, and some water. The horse manure is handy because the horses have pre-shredded the straw into just the right size for helping make the plaster bind. (There are many recipes for plaster. That will have to be a separate article.)

It's fun to find and gather different colored clays from various locations. Some of that heavy clay soil in your neighbor's yard could be a beautiful addition to your earthen house wall. You can also use lime to lighten the color of the plaster. If you do, be sure to *handle the lime carefully* (washing hands and tools right after application), as *it can be caustic to the skin.*

Now for the special fun. Mash the ingredients together, stand back from the wall, and apply by *throwing* the plaster at the wall. This allows for even coats. For those of more moder-

ate energies, a plaster trowel works just as well.

Cob does not need to be plastered in order to be preserved, but many people choose to plaster at least the inside of the structure to increase the light-reflectivity of the walls. Usually two or three coats are applied, in order to achieve a really smooth finish. Small pieces of tile, ceramic shards, or pieces of glass bottle can be inlaid in the final layer, and patterns or artwork can be etched into or raised from the surface of the plaster.

Tools

Shovels, a pickaxe, and a wheelbarrow help move soil to the mixing areas and onto the tarps. Old shower curtains, large pieces of plastic, and tarps are the mixing bowl for the dirt, sand, and straw that become cob. Hoses and a ready water supply are useful. Used shampoo bottles filled with water (to squirt water to wet down the top of the mix), pointed sticks that fit well to the hand (to massage in the new layer of cob), and more straw and tarps to cover the cob so that it stays moist are also handy. One tool that comes in handy is the modified three- or four-foot-long car-

penter's level I mentioned earlier. A machete is useful for hacking off bits of straw that stick out from dried walls. (This helps prepare the walls for plastering.) Various buckets, string, and a cement trowel are also put to work. These, along with willing hands and feet, are all that's needed to put up the walls of a cob house.

Of course your cob home will need a roof, the supporting beams of which can be incorporated into the cob walls. The roof can be anything from a simple standard shed or peaked roof to a recycled tire roof or living sod roof. The choice is yours. Cob itself is too heavy to use for a roofing material.

You might want to practice with cob before building a whole house. There are many smaller projects that are well suited to cob construction. Get your hands in the mud building a cob gazebo or garden bench or wall. These can be fun weekend projects with children, and will give you an idea of the beauty and pleasure of building with cob, as well as the amount of effort and materials you will need.

As Indigo Art Studio grew, we were mesmerized by the stunning beauty of the gently curving structure. The

A finished cob cottage

thought of returning to four square walls became unimaginable.

Both in terms of the medium—mud—and in the fact of working with other people, cob earthen construction is a lot like making mud pies. With few tools, little money, lots of friends, and free reign for creativity, the resurgence of cob construction makes an ancient building technique accessible for backwoods construction, dirt cheap.

For more information about cob, including a schedule of workshops, you can contact the folks that I learned from at Groundworks Earth House Building, PO Box 381, Murphy, OR 97533. They also have a handbook on cob coming out this summer. And you may want to visit my Web site about cob construction at http://www.tele-port.com/~sparking/cob/door.html.

An outline of the steps

Select site

Design house
Foundation, floor levels, door placement, and water/ electrical pipe locations are essential. Incorporate passive solar design.

Gather materials & tools
Materials: dirt, sand, straw, rocks for foundation, water, pipes for electrical/water, cement
Tools: wheelbarrow, tarps, shovels, water hose, hammer, rake, broom, sieve, etc.

Level site

Foundation
Create drainage (this can also be done after the building is complete)
Dig to solid ground, below frost level
Tamp under foundation
Plan under-floor cooler (optional)
Lay pipes for water & electricity
Lay water drainpipe at angle sloping out just above foundation, draining towards downhill side of home
Lay first layer of rock
Add mortar & pebbles

Continue adding rocks & mortar to 6" above ground level
Top foundation with pine tar or other water barrier (optional)

Door frame
Establish door threshold (must be flat) and seat for door frame
Set up and brace door frame with protruding nails to anchor in cob

The first two feet
Start laying cob
Experiment with mixes
Make walls curved & thicker for heavy support areas
Extra sand for heat retention, extra straw for insulation
Incorporate wood for
    Bench support logs or poles
        (inside & out)
    Lower ladder rungs
    Angled supports for counter
    Door for firewood (optional)
    Outside wood supports for wood shelter (optional)
Start cantilevers for cob benches (seat height usually 14")
Fire vents: incorporate into cob or foundation for fire to get fresh air

Windows
Start windows very low on north wall (or use a pipe with door & screen) to suck in cool north air in summer
Begin solar south window sills
Bury board support for shelves going from floor to ceiling

Stove/Fireplace
Incorporate stove and/or fireplace into wall; bury stovepipe in wall
Sculpt any relief art as you build (optional)

Two to four feet
Start windows
Bury shelf supports or create cantilevers for cob shelves, including under kitchen counter
Leave ledges to support counters
Create wall fridge above counter
Incorporate branches or other supports into cob for future expansion (all the way up)

Four feet and above
Incorporate wood into walls for:
    hanging artwork, branch for pot racks, closet racks, hat & coat hooks
    Lintels & arches over windows
Vent
Openable vent high on south wall
More niches for candles, etc.
    (outside near the door, too)
Ledges & support beam for loft support

Roof preparation
Supports for roof over door (if not done by roof overhang)
Bury deadmen for rafters
    (Deadmen are pieces of wood buried in the cob to which you can nail or wire other structural pieces)
Bury outer rafter supports
Bury rafters—plan for fascia & gutters & skylights (Use safety glass)
Insulation—lots of it
Holes for ventilation between rafters

Roof
Gutters
Stove pipe flashing & chimney

Floor
Level floor area
    (two different levels is appealing)
Create cold drop-off (one foot, no tamping, cover with small stones) for use for cool storage or wood (optional)
Tamp
Level guide nails
Sandy mix, chopped straw, two to three layers, dry in between applications
Score crack lines, fill with different colored mix
Varnish

Finishing
Plaster—porous paint or lime wash
Tiles above counters to protect walls (attach with plaster or white glue)
Lid with ventilation for floor cold spot

Landscaping

Hang door

Wood shelves, benches, counters, doors, lids, tiles. etc. Δ

Make quick and easy pasta

By Jennifer Stein Barker

One of the most simple, satisfying, quick and easy meals you can make is a meal of pasta with a salad. Whole-grain pastas have long had a bad reputation for being coarse and gummy; but this is no longer deserved, as pasta makers now search out higher quality grains and better techniques to formulate the products.

Look for whole wheat pastas made of 100% durum wheat, a hard wheat that is high in gluten. Our two favorite (and readily available in most health-food stores) pastas are Westbrae Organic Whole-wheat Ribbons and Vita-Spelt Shells. Products made of spelt grain are not only for the wheat-sensitive folks. They have a wonderful nutty flavor and great texture that everyone can appreciate.

General pasta cooking instructions

Bring a large kettle of water to a rolling boil before adding the pasta. Use at least one gallon of water for each pound of dried pasta you plan to cook. Some people like to add a little salt and/or olive oil to the cooking water to improve the flavor and keep the pasta from sticking together.

When you add the pasta, take a fork and give it a quick stir to separate the strands. This insures that it will cook evenly and not stick together. You don't need to stir it again; in fact, if you do, it will release more starch and cause your pasta to be gummy instead of firm.

Leave the pot uncovered. Bring rapidly back to the boil, then turn the heat down to maintain a gentle bubbling. Cook as long as indicated on the package; or, if you have no instructions, try 10 minutes as your starting point for whole-grain pastas. Adjust cooking time for doneness as you like it (usually between 10 and 15 minutes).

When pasta taste-tests done, drain immediately and thoroughly in a colander. If you want to pre-cook pasta for later use, try this trick: cook the pasta just under done, then drain and chill. When you are ready to serve, pour boiling water over the pasta, bring the pot quickly to a boil again, then drain. Voila! Dinner!

Confetti spaghetti

Use spaghetti, noodles, or shells for the pasta, just as long as it is whole grain. Choose hearty greens such as bok choy or savoy cabbage. Serves 4:

```
12 oz. dry pasta, cooked according to instructions
4 cloves garlic, minced or pressed
```

```
1 Tbsp. olive oil
1 cup grated yellow turnip
1 cup grated carrot
1 small hot pepper, finely sliced
2 cups shredded greens
2 Tbsp. tamari (or to taste)
```

Bring a large kettle of water to boil for the pasta.

In a deep saucepan over medium heat, warm the garlic, olive oil, grated turnip and grated carrot. Add 1/4 cup of water and 1 tablespoon of the tamari and cook, covered, for 10 minutes or until the vegetables are tender. (Start the pasta cooking in the boiling water during this time.) Add the hot pepper and the shredded cabbage, and more water if necessary, and cook another 5 minutes. Keep warm. When the pasta is done, drain it and return it to its kettle. Add the vegetables and the other tablespoon of tamari. Toss all together.

Serve hot, with grated Parmesan cheese.

Easy macaroni and cheese

This is a classic. My recipe gives the quick-and-easy version, as well as a more elegant baked casserole that will stand up for company. Our favorite pasta for this is Vita-Spelt Shells. Serves 4:

Sauce:

```
3 Tbsp. olive oil
3 cloves garlic, minced
1/2 cup fine whole wheat flour
3 cups milk, heated
1 Tbsp. prepared mustard
1 1/2 cups grated sharp cheddar cheese
1 tsp. tamari or Worcestershire sauce
3 Tbsp. sunflower seeds (opt.)
12 oz. pasta, shells or macaroni
optional additions: 2 branches broccoli
1/4 cup breadcrumbs
1 Tbsp. Parmesan cheese
1 tsp. basil
```

Warm the olive oil and garlic over lowest heat for five minutes to blend the flavors. Whisk in the flour and continue cooking over low for another minute. Then whisk in the hot milk.

Turn the heat to medium and cook, whisking constantly, until the sauce begins to thicken. Turn the heat back to lowest setting, and let cook, whisking frequently, for 10 minutes. Whisk in the mustard, cheddar, and tamari or Worcestershire sauce. Stir in the sunflower seeds.

While the sauce is cooking, you should be boiling the pasta. When the sauce is done and the pasta drained, you can just stir them together and serve immediately, or you can proceed with the more elegant version:

The elegant version:

Cut the broccoli branches into florets. Peel and dice the stems. Steam the broccoli just until it turns bright green. Stir it into the pasta and sauce, and turn the whole thing into an appropriately-sized casserole. Stir together the breadcrumbs, Parmesan, and basil, and spread openly over the top of the macaroni and cheese. Bake in a preheated 350 degree oven for 20-30 minutes, until bubbling and golden.

Either way, serve with a big green salad and your best smile.

Mama Gianna's easy vegie lasagna

This is a one-dish lasagna with nothing precooked. It makes a great sun-oven casserole, too. Make this lasagna in a two liter or larger casserole. If you do not have a covered casserole, you must use foil to cover the pan, because the noodles need the steam to cook. This is great with whole wheat lasagna noodles. Serves 3-4:

Sauce:
1-28 oz. can ground tomatoes
1/2 cup water
1 Tbsp. red wine
3 cloves garlic, minced
1 tsp. oregano
1/2 tsp. basil
1/4 tsp. fennel seed, crushed
1 Tbsp. tamari
Vegies:
1 medium carrot, grated
1 green pepper, diced
1/2 cup diced onion
Cheese:
1 cup ricotta
1/4 cup Parmesan
1 egg, beaten
freshly-grated black pepper to taste
Noodles:
8-10 lasagna noodles, enough to make 2 complete layers
Topping:
grated mozzarella for topping (optional)

Preheat the oven to 350 degrees, and get out a 2-liter or larger casserole.

In a medium bowl, mix together the sauce ingredients. In another medium bowl, toss together the prepared vegeta-bles. In a small bowl, stir together the ricotta, Parmesan, egg, and pepper.

Layer as follows in the casserole:
• 1/3 of the sauce
• a layer of uncooked noodles
• all the vegetables
• 1/3 of the sauce
• all of the ricotta mixture
• a layer of uncooked noodles
• 1/3 of the sauce

Cover the casserole with a lid or foil (this is necessary to keep the steam in with the noodles), and bake until the sauce has been bubbling vigorously for 1/2 hour. It should take about 1 1/2 hours total.

When the noodles are cooked, the lid can be removed and a layer of grated mozzarella may be added to the top of the lasagna. Bake 15-20 minutes more, uncovered, until the cheese bubbles and browns. In a sun oven, I merely kept this baking until it had bubbled vigorously for 1/2 hour (it took hours to bring it to the boil, but once things are boiling the cooking time is the same in a sun oven as in a conventional one). I removed the lid and added the layer of mozzarella to the top. It was delicious, but in order to be enough for four people we really needed the sourdough French bread, salad, and dessert we had with it. Δ

A BHM Writer's Profile: Mary Jo Bratton

Mary Jo Bratton and her family live in Lincoln, Nebraska. Their school project for 1991-92 was converting a barn into a house where they reside to this day. After being taught at home most of their lives, her children, Danny and Anna, are enrolled in college and are succeeding beyond their mother's wildest expectations.

Mary Jo writes for the local newspaper now. In hindsight, she wishes she's added two more tips (tips 11. And 12.) to her article on homeschooling: 11. Put away your television and skip most commercially successful movies if you want to raise creative, energetic, and mentally healthy children; and, 12. Cultivate a sense of humor. It is every bit as important as learning the times table.

White sage — the quintessential chaparral herb

By Christopher Nyerges

White sage (*Salvia apiana*) is a close relative of garden sage, and is one of the more common shrubs of the Southwest, growing throughout the mountains and chaparral areas and reaching to the desert. It grows from three to six feet tall, with its conspicuous whitish-gray leaves.

The plant is easy to recognize in the chaparral areas where it grows. Nothing else has quite that shade of whiteness. And if you're not certain by looking, you can crush one of the whitish-grey leaves in your hand and feel its stickiness and smell its pungent sagey aroma. Many who hike into sage areas may not know any other plants, but they know the white sage.

Some Indian tribes of the Southwest gathered, ground, and utilized the white sage seeds for a flour-like pinole which was used for bread products. The seeds resemble chia seeds, to which they are related. The tender tops of white sage were cooked and eaten by Indians who lived in Southern Nevada and throughout California's high desert. I have tried eating these tender tops, and they have a flavor and texture similar to cabbage, although the sage flavor is overpowering. If you want to eat these tops, I suggest you mix them with other vegetables or meats, or add them to soup.

The fresh or dried leaves infused in boiling water make a good-tasting tea. I've used it for years as my main dinner beverage. With just a bit of honey, it is very satisfying. Drinking sage tea is said to calm and strengthen the nerves. The tea has long been used as an aid to digestion after meals, and also has the reputation of relieving headaches. Sage tastes good and freshens the breath.

Because the fresh leaves can be applied directly as a poultice to stop bleeding and to soothe insect bites, it is a valuable herb to carry while hiking.

In her book, Indian Herbology of North America, Alma Hutchens writes, "The decoction (of sage) is used to cleanse old ulcers and wounds, and massaged into the scalp if troubled with dandruff, falling hair, or loss of hair if the papilla (root) is dormant and not destroyed." Fresh or dried leaves create a pleasant aroma when added to bath water.

I have routinely added dried and powdered white sage leaves into my various smoking mixes. Sometimes I use tobacco, sometimes not. But the white sage adds a pleasant menthol-like flavor.

Sage, regarded as a sacred herb among many Native Americans, is often used in ceremonies. Sometimes the fresh leaves are rubbed onto the body before entering the sweat lodge. Leaves are also sometimes sprinkled over the hot rocks inside a sweat lodge.

The fresh stems are also routinely bundled, allowed to dry, and then lit with a flame. This sage bundle—referred to as a *smudge*—will smolder like incense or a punk, but generally will not flame. It makes a pleasant incense, and the traditional smudging was intended to repel bugs in one's living quarters, such as a hogan or tipi. In fact, the leaves contain about 4% of camphor oil and eucalyptol, both of which have a history of use as insect repellents. Today, the idea of "smudging" has taken on a "New Age" meaning of "repelling evil spirits," somewhat akin to the use of incense during a high mass in the Catholic church.

Some folklore lends sage some mysterious overtones. One curiosity is the fact that wise men have long been called "sage." Another stems from the Latin and Spanish root words for sage being "salvia," meaning "to save."

The useful leaves of this evergreen shrub can be gathered year-round. However, the best leaves are those gathered from the stalks which haven't yet flowered, which is generally winter through mid-spring.

(Christopher Nyerges is the author of Guide to Wild Foods. For a free newsletter, which includes his schedule of wild foods outings, contact School of Self-Reliance, Box 41834, Eagle Rock, CA 90041.) Δ

Safe, delicious, and inexpensive home preserves

By Richard Blunt

Mankind has always been preoccupied with preserving his food, and long before recorded history he developed a variety of effective preservation methods. One of the earliest was the discovery that fruits and vegetables would keep longer if protected from moisture, air, and light. This protection was provided by coating fruits and vegetables with an impermeable substance such as clay or honey. Later, ashes or salt were used as coatings. This also removed moisture from the food and modified its appearance and flavor.

In areas where fire was still an uncontrolled mystery, or where salt was in short supply, simple drying was used to keep food from decomposing. As people learned to use fire, smoke and heat were used to cook as well as to preserve food. Smoke was also combined with other preserving methods, such as salting and brining, to produce various preserved meats and fish that still are popular today. Cured, smoked ham is a classic example of how this ancient technology has survived the test of time.

Another important discovery was that controlled fermentation could produce alcohol-based drinks from fruits, vegetables, and grains that would not spoil. Another type of fermentation was found to produce a potable acid-based liquid—vinegar. Both alcohol and vinegar could be used as food preservatives.

We think of freezing and freeze drying as types of preservation invented by modern man, but pre-Columbian Indians in the Peruvian Andes used Mother Nature's freezing mountain winds to freeze-dry potatoes and other vegetables long before anyone else figured out how to build a freezer.

Fruit, sugar, heat, and sterilization

Sugaring is another ancient technique that is still used to make fruits resistant to spoilage. Prepared fruit is cooked with sugar or honey and a small amount of acid, usually from citrus. This process removes most of the water from the fruit and replaces it with the sugar-acid solution.

In the 16th century, the Spanish began growing sugar cane in the West Indies on a large scale. Sugar became more common, and jams, jellies, and other sweet confections— once made only with honey, which was an expensive ingredient not affordable to most—became available to everyone. This marriage of fruit, sugar, and heat signaled the quiet, yet genuine, beginning of modern food preservation.

Unlocking the secret of preservation by sterilization was in its own way an invention as important as the discovery of fire, and it is the only preservation technique invented by

Richard Blunt

modern man. Sterilization was the method destined to be the basis for the bulk of all preserved food available on the planet today. Credit for this discovery in preserving goes to two Frenchmen, an English tinsmith, and an American.

In 1795, Napoleon Bonaparte was leading the French army to a series of stunning military victories in Italy. But his army suffered more losses from food poisoning and hunger than from enemy artillery. Spoiled food and starvation had been the scourges of armies since the dawn of time. So, in an attempt to solve this age-old problem, Napoleon offered a reward of 12,000 francs to anyone who could develop an effective method for preserving food and making it safe for consumption by the French military on the battlefield.

Fourteen years later Nicolas Appert, a little known French brewer employed as a confectioner, introduced a method of packing food into bottles, sealing the bottles with corks, then heat treating the filled bottles in boiling water. Appert held to the popular myth of the time that fermentation was the evil that caused all food to spoil. But he also believed that there was a realistic cure for this evil. He theorized that applying heat to a closed container would create a hermetic seal and remove all oxygen from the container, thus preventing "ferment" from becoming active. The system was not perfect, but it worked better than any other process known at the time.

Appert was awarded the prize. He quickly opened the world's first known canning factory and started processing preserved foods for the French military.

His theory was confirmed 50 years later by Louis Pasteur. Pasteur was researching the problem of young wine fermenting to vinegar during aging. He did not give credence

to the popular theory that fermentation resulted from spontaneous generation—life arising from nothing. He discovered that alcohol and vinegar fermentation were caused by the presence of plant-related micro-organisms that were everywhere—in the air, in water, and on all matter. More importantly he discovered there were some forms of these micro-organisms that did not need oxygen from the air to live and regenerate. This explained why wine could spoil in air-tight casks. Both types however, could be destroyed or rendered inactive using a modification of Appert's method.

The birth of mason jars

Peter Durand, an Englishman, and John Landis Mason, an American, further developed Appert's system of hermetic sealing. They both invented containers that were more reliable than the cork-sealed bottle. Durand invented containers made of steel, thinly coated with tin to prevent corrosion. Mason developed and patented a glass jar with a shoulder and a screw-top lid. These metal cans and mason jars have since become the standard for modern food preserving containers.

Until the end of World War II, home preserving was common in the United States, and families frequently traded their pickle, chutney, jam, and jelly recipes with each other. Large families often put up thousands of jars of preserved food to make it through the winter and to the next harvest season. But in the decades following the war, the old methods that reflected the culinary wisdom and creativity of our grandparents and great grandparents took a back seat to a succession of trends that included factory canning, prepackaged foods, and the disappearance of the small garden.

Then in the 1980s some of the old standards started to reappear. Home gardens were flourishing in more than half of the nations households. Road weary, plastic-choked produce was made unacceptable to the consumer by the increase in local farm stands and orchards which offered pick-your-own options. Many small farmers became truck vendors, driving through neighborhoods offering fresh fruits and vegetables picked only hours before being sold.

Home preserving also received new life during this resurgence of American culinary heritage. Seed catalogs began selling a wide selection of canning equipment. We are now in the last decade of the century and the upsurge in home preserving is not going away. This despite the fact that every supermarket, convenience store, many gift shops, and even drugstores offer a wide selection of jams, jellies, pickles, relishes, fruits, vegetables, and so on.

With all this variety within easy reach, and at generally good prices, it wouldn't seem practical to preserve foods at home. Especially when you consider the initial capital investment necessary to purchase pressure canners, boiling water-bath canners, jars, lids and other equipment necessary to ensure safe and effective canning. There is also an investment of time and physical energy. But home canning is coming back, anyway.

The reasons are many, but I think that superior quality and taste top the list. Preserves made with local fruits and vegetables that are processed shortly after being picked off of the bush or unearthed from the soil are far superior to those made with produce picked in some unknown part of the world and treated with unknown substances.

I am going to share with you a few favorite preserving recipes and techniques that were given to me by friends and family. All of these folks are experienced gardeners and view preserving as a creative way to extend the wonderful rewards of a successful growing season.

Follow these recipes using freshly picked produce that is being processed as close to harvest time as possible. The finished product will reward you with culinary delight that cannot be purchased in any store.

Home preservation basics

Let's get started with a review of some home preserving basics. This information will help to make your preserving effort successful and, above all, safe. Fruits and vegetables selected for preserving must be harvested while slightly underripe and free of all signs of decay and visible bumps and bruises. They must also be handled in a way that will eliminate contamination caused by enzymes, yeast, molds, and bacteria. Since these major food spoilers are omnipresent and can't be avoided, they must be destroyed before the preserving process is completed.

How do these food spoilers work? Enzymes are biochemicals contained in the cells of all plants and animals. They are essential for fruits and vegetables to ripen. If the action of enzymes is not stopped, their continued activity will cause food to rot.

Yeasts are plant-related micro-organisms that feed on sugars. This feeding starts fermenting the sugar to alcohol, which is fine for beer and wine, but does no justice to applesauce.

Molds are also plant-related micro-organisms that feed on the natural acid in food. Acidity in food acts to protect food against spoilage. Reduce the natural acid level in any food and decay will soon follow.

Of all the evils that can infect food, bacteria are by far the most dangerous. These seaweed-related micro-organisms are in the air, water, and soil. Most strains can survive temperature extremes that destroy other microbes. The most dangerous of the lot is the bacteria that causes botulism, *clostridium botulinum*. The poisonous toxin secreted by this microbe is so powerful that a teaspoon full is enough to kill hundreds of thousands of people. Botulinus bacteria will also live and reproduce in an oxygen-starved environment, so canned foods provide it with a perfect home. Foods infected with botulinus bacteria often show no signs of contamination.

The best safeguard against bacterial infection taking residence in your preserved food is faithfully maintaining high sanitation standards and following proven safe canning techniques. Taking short cuts will put the health of you and your family at peril.

How to keep the spoilers in check.

Heat is the only force that will stop enzyme activity. Precooking or blanching the food to be canned, then following the boiling-water bath or pressure processing methods will eliminate this problem. Some foods can be packed raw, then processed if proper heat treating procedures are followed. The best way to control yeasts, molds, and bacteria is to deny them a comfortable environment. Good sanitation procedures, consistently followed throughout the preserving process, are your best defense against these terrifying microbes.

Wash all fruits and vegetables with plenty of cold potable water before you begin processing. Wash all work surfaces and utensils with a 16 to 1 chlorine bleach sanitizing solution (1/4 cup of bleach to 4 cups of cold water) and allow them to air dry. The chlorine will dissipate into the air during the drying process without leaving a residue. Good sanitation and effective preserving techniques will eliminate all danger of bacterial infection in your canned foods.

There are two effective methods for processing all foods canned at home: the boiling water bath and pressure processing. The boiling water bath method is used when canning high acid foods, jams, jellies, and fruits doused in sugar syrups. Pressure processing is used to process all low acid foods and starchy foods like corn and potatoes and protein foods like meat and fish. All of the recipes included in this column were designed to use the boiling water bath

method. Pressure processing will be the subject of another column.

Essential equipment

Let's talk about the equipment you'll need to preserve food using the boiling water bath canning method. You probably have many of these items in your kitchen already.

• 8-qt stainless steel pot with lid for pre-cooking and blanching foods
• 21-qt. ceramic on steel deep water bath canner designed for processing quart jars. This 10-inch deep canner is necessary to provide the adequate top and bottom clearance for processing pint and quart jars. The jars must be elevated at least 1/2 inch to 1 inch from the bottom of the canner while providing at least 3 inches of space between the tops of the jars and the rim of the canner. This keeps the jars off the bottom of the canner so they don't break during processing, allows a two-inch water cover over the jars during processing, and gives at least one inch of clearance from the water cover to the top of the canner to keep water from splashing all over your stove during the boil.
• A good rack. The only problem with the rack that came with my deep water bath was the poor design of the jar rack. The jar cradles are almost too large to keep quart jars from touching the bottom of the canner and it's not at all usable with pint and half pint jars. Since I don't put up food in quart jars, I set the canner rack aside and purchased round cake racks. I support the cake racks on the inside of the canner with old mason jar screw bands without the sealing lids. This system works well and the 1/2-inch-thick screw bands give plenty of clearance on the bottom to ensure good water circulation during the boiling process.
• 1 case of 8-oz mason jelly jars with screw bands and lids.
• 1 case of pint-sized, wide-mouth mason canning jars with screw bands and lids.
• An accurate kitchen timer with alarm or warning bell.
• 1 pencil-shaped glass food thermometer.
• 1 ladle.
• 1 slotted stainless steel spoon for removing food after pre-cooking.
• 1 wide mouth funnel for filling the jars.
• 1 stainless steel colander for draining foods.
• 1 jar lifter for placing the jars in and removing them from boiling water
• plenty of clean dish towels
• Measuring cups in sizes up to 1 qt. (and including cup fractions)
• An assortment of measuring spoons, from 1/8 tsp. to 1 Tbsp.
• Jelly strainer with jelly bags for making jellies.

- 1 accurate food scale with at least a two-pound capacity.
- 2 narrow-blade heat-resistant spatulas.

Other Equipment:

If you don't own a food processor, a large wooden or plastic cutting board, and a professional set of kitchen knives, now is the time to treat yourself. These items are not essential but they will save you lots of time.

Let's get started

Canning, fermenting, drying, pickling, smoking, salt curing and deep freezing are all preserving arts that require the practitioner to follow a strict set of procedural rules to ensure success. The procedural rules for canning can be very difficult reading, especially if you are new to the craft. In an attempt to avoid a lot of general facts that are not required to successfully prepare the recipes included in this article, I have included enough information with each recipe to successfully prepare that recipe. If you are pleased with the results and want to learn more, I have included a list of suggested reading that covers most preserving methods in detail. But reading about food does not teach you as much as actually working with it.

Old World Apple Chutney

This is a recipe that my sister-in-law, Trudy, brought back from England. The apples she used in her recipe are fresh-picked Washington State Pippins but I've used Granny Smiths, Vermont Northern Spys, and Connecticut grown Romes with good results. Any firm, slightly underripe cooking apple will do as long as it is fresh picked. The flavor of this chutney will be even better if you buy whole ginger and cinnamon and grind them yourself.

Chutney is a high acid condiment and very safe for canning. Because of this, many books will suggest that the boiling water bath is not necessary. That may be so, but I process all of my canned foods by finishing them off with the boiling water bath method or pressure processing.

Ingredients

40 oz cider vinegar
1 1/2 lb brown sugar
1 1/2 tsp kosher salt
1 Tbsp ground ginger
2 tsp ground cinnamon
1 Tbsp pickling spice
6 whole cloves and 1 bay leaf tied in a spice bag
4 lbs fresh picked underripe apples
2 lbs Spanish onions
2 fresh garlic cloves, minced
1 lb golden raisins

Special equipment

8 qt stainless steel sauce pot
Boiling water bath canner
16 pint mason jars with screw bands and sealing lids.
Wide mouth funnel
Thin blade spatula
4-oz ladle or solid stainless steel kitchen spoon
A 9-inch pie plate for catching spills

Method

1. Combine the vinegar, brown sugar, kosher salt, ground ginger, ground cinnamon, pickling spice, and spice bag in an 8-qt. sauce pot. Mix and bring to a slow boil over medium to low heat for 30 minutes.

2. While the sugar syrup is cooking, peel, core and coarsely chop the apples. Peel and coarsely chop the onions, and mince the garlic clove. Uniformity is not necessary; this chutney is meant to be chunky.

3. Combine the apple, onion, and garlic in the cooked syrup and cook the mixture over low heat for 1 1/2 hours, stirring occasionally to prevent scorching.

Packing, processing and storage

1. While the chutney is cooking, carefully wash the jars, screw bands, and lids in hot soapy water and rinse with plenty of hot water. Fill the clean jars with boiling water and cover with a clean towel. Place the screw bands and lids in a bowl and cover them with boiling water. Let them stand this way until you are ready to fill them. Time this process so that the boiling water will not cool below 160° F or remain in the jars for more then 10 minutes.

2. Arrange all necessary utensils so that you will be able to fill, seal, and cap the jars efficiently.

3. Fill the canner to 1/2 of its capacity with water, place the racks on the bottom, and start heating it to a boil. Have an additional kettle of boiling water available to add more boiling water to the canner after the filled jars have been put into place.

4. Fill the jars with hot chutney to 1/2 inch from the top, using the wide mouth funnel to minimize spilling. Then set them, one at a time, on the pie plate. Remove any trapped air from the jars by running the narrow blade of the spatula down the sides of the jar. Carefully wipe the rim of the jar with a clean cloth that has been wet with boiling water to remove any traces of food. Set the sealing lid on the rim of the jar and screw on the band until it is firmly in place. Do not force or over-tighten the band. Put the jar in the canner. The 21-qt. canner will hold 8 pint jars and 12 half pint jars without crowding. As you are placing the jars in the canner, set them so they are not touching each other or the side of the canner.

5. Add enough boiling water to the canner to cover the jars with two inches of water. Do not compromise this step;

proper processing requires at least a two inch covering of rapidly boiling water. Less water may cause the whole procedure to fail. The yeasts, molds, and bacteria would love that.

6. Process the filled jars for 15 minutes in **rapidly** boiling water.

The further above sea level you are, the less heat required to boil water. From sea level up to about 1,000 ft above sea level, water boils at 212° F. At 5,000 ft water boils at only 203° F, and 194° F at 10,000 ft. Heat is essential to kill microbes in food. As you can see, getting the water hot enough for sterilization is more difficult at high altitudes.

To compensate for altitude add at least two minutes of processing time for every 1000 feet above sea level. This is a general rule that works well with high acid foods like jams, jellies, and fruits canned in sugar syrups.

7. When the processing is complete, turn off the heat. Using the jar lifter, carefully remove the jars from the canner and set them on a towel-covered flat surface to cool. It is important not to disturb the jar during the next 24 hours. During this period the jars will cool and the vacuum sealing will occur. With the modern mason jars the vacuum created during the cooling period will pull down the dome in the center of each lid to make the air tight seal. If the seal does not happen, just store the chutney in the refrigerator and eat it within a few days.

Storage

Food preserved in jars must be protected from light and excessive heat. A dark corner of the cellar where the temperature does not exceed 50° F is perfect. If cellar space is limited or non existent, wrap the jars in a sheet of newspaper, pack in a suitable size box, and store in a closet or cabinet that does not get direct sunlight.

The flavor of this chutney will continue to mellow and improve for 6 to 8 weeks—if you can wait that long.

Western blackberry jam

This recipe is a combination of two recipes I received from my sister-in-law Trudy, and John Silveira, the *Backwoods Home Magazine* senior editor. Last summer I sampled a blackberry jam John made from berries he picked across the road from the *BHM* office. Two years ago, while visiting Trudy, who now lives in southern Washington, I tasted a seedless blackberry jam she made with berries she picked in her back yard. (Blackberry bushes are so prevalent on the west coast that some folks consider them a nuisance.) Both of these blackberry delights had the most intense flavor of any berry jam I have ever tasted; so I asked them both to send me the recipes.

The recipes were so similar that I decided to combined them into one recipe with the option of making a seedless or a regular whole pulp jam by slightly modifying the procedure and the amount of berries. Once again, the success of

this recipe depends on the quality of the fruit. The berries must be picked when mature but under ripe, and processed no more then two hours after harvest. This is when blackberries contain a high amount of natural acid and pectin, both of which are necessary to ensure that the jam sets up properly.

Jell testing

This jam is made without commercial pectin, so you will need to test the cooked jam to determine when the jell stage has been reached. When this point is reached depends on the quality and age of the fruit. The more ripe the fruit is, the less natural pectin it will contain and it will have to cook for a longer period than slightly underripe fruit. If everything is as it should be, this berry mixture should reach jell stage in about 15 minutes. There are a few ways of testing jell stage; the following test is simple and works as well as more complicated methods.

With a clean dry spoon, scoop up a small amount of jell liquid and hold it above a saucer. Tilt the spoon so that the jell runs off the side of the bowl of the spoon. If it falls in two separate drops, it is not ready. If the two drops merge, and fall in one sheet, jell stage has been reached. If you have to test again use a clean dry spoon.

Ingredients

9 cups mature barely ripe blackberries (13 cups if making seedless jam)
4 cups sugar

Special equipment

8 qt stainless steel sauce pot
Boiling water bath canner

1 large medium to fine mesh sieve to strain seeds if
   desired
5 half pint mason jars with screw bands and lids
wide mouth funnel
4 oz ladle
9 inch pie plate for catching spills
large stainless steel bowl

Method

1. Sort and wash the berries, remove the stems and caps. Layer berries in a large stainless steel bowl with sugar, cover and allow to rest in the refrigerator for at least eight hours.

2. Transfer the berries to the sauce pan and bring to a simmer over medium heat and cook until the berries are soft, about 20 minutes.

3. If you are making seedless jam, strain the berry mixture through the fine sieve.

4. Continue cooking over medium heat until the jell stage is reached.

5. Ladle hot jam into prepared jars, as outlined in the previous recipe and process in the hot water bath canner for 10 minutes.

Storage

Store in the same way as the chutney.

Ruth's old fashioned zucchini pickles

As I set the summer squash plants in the soil, I could hear the little voice inside saying, once again, "What are you going to do with all of this squash?"

Usually, I dismiss this with something like, "This isn't as much as I planted last year."

Well, even though it is less, it is probably still too much. But this year I think I have a partial solution to the problem. The following recipe is a standard sweet pickle recipe that Trudy modified slightly so she could substitute green and yellow summer squash for cucumbers. I was skeptical about the concept until I tasted some that she sent to her father for his birthday. He wasn't thrilled about sharing them with anyone and, if you make a batch, you'll understand why.

For the best results, use only small, firm squash because they have more flavor and less water.

Ingredients

7 lbs zucchini or yellow summer squash
1 large sweet red pepper
4 large white onions
1/3 cup course sea salt or kosher salt
Ice water to cover
2 cups cider vinegar
3 1/2 cups sugar
1 tsp turmeric

1 1/2 tsp celery seed
2 Tbsp mustard seed

Special Equipment

Large stainless steel bowl
8 qt stainless steel sauce pot
8 pint mason jars with screw bands and lids
Large mouth funnel
Narrow blade spatula

Method

1. Wash the squash and pepper in plenty of cold water and drain. Slice the squash on the diagonal into 1/2 inch pieces. Cut the pepper in half, remove the seeds and slice it into pieces that are one inch long by 1/4 inch thick.

2. Peel the onions, cut them in half, and slice them lengthwise into 1/4 inch strips.

3. In a large stainless steel bowl mix the squash, pepper, and onions with the salt. Add just enough ice water to cover the vegetables. Let the vegetables stand for three hours, then drain.

4. In a sauce pan mix together the cider vinegar, sugar, turmeric, celery seed, and mustard seed. Bring this mixture to a boil over medium heat while stirring constantly. Remove it from the heat as soon as it starts to boil.

5. Combine the hot liquid with the drained vegetables in a large sauce pan and bring the mixture to a boil once again. Turn off the heat as soon as the boil starts.

6. With a slotted spoon fill the jars with the hot vegetables to 1/2 inch from the top. Divide the hot pickling brine evenly among the jars without exceeding the 1/2 inch head space. Follow the procedure outlined in the chutney recipe then process the jars in the hot water bath for 10 minutes.

7. Store the pickles in a cool dark spot for 3 to 4 weeks.

If you want to read more, find The New Putting Food By, by Ruth Hertzberg, Beatrice Vaughan, and Janet Greene from the Stephen Greene Press in Brattleboro, Vermont. The ISBN for the hardbound is 0-8289-0468-5 and for the paperback it's 0-8289-0469-3.

Home preserving, in all of its forms, is an ongoing chapter in the gastronomic story of America and it truly reflects the great bounty and many creative cooking styles that make American food worth writing about. Please drop me a line and share your favorite preserving recipe or method. I just purchased a 200 pound capacity commercial smoker and I need some good smoking recipes to share with the world. See you next time. Δ

When angry, count four; when very angry, swear.

Mark Twain
1835-1910

Plan your energy-independent home *before* you begin construction

By Paul Jeffrey Fowler

Over the years, as the owner of a successful solar electric business, I spoke with thousands of people about designing and installing a solar electric system. The majority of the customers who were building their homes contacted me after their homes were mostly completed, when many of their designs were irreversible. I always wished I could have helped these people with their choices before they had begun to build.

Obviously, I could have helped them to orient their houses for proper exposure to the sun and to plan for the installations of a solar electric array, system controls, and a battery room. In most cases, they had done fairly well on these aspects from reading solar electric books. I really wish I could have reached them early enough in their planning process so they could have built true alternative energy homes, not just houses with solar electricity installed on them.

In homebuilding, it is difficult to be creative, since a house is built with very standardized methods and materials. However, innovation is necessary in designing an alternative energy home, because it will use electricity much differently than a conventional "on-the-grid" home. In an alternative energy home, the goal should be to build a home such that the people using it will feel that they are enjoying a conventional level of comfort, though their source of electricity is an independent system.

A grid home in our area pays about 10¢ per kilowatt-hour for electricity, while a solar-electric-system owner pays an average of 30¢ per kilowatt-hour. Furthermore, the owner must invest up front in the equipment to produce 10 to 20 years of this

The author's home, with solar electric modules on the house and garage

30¢/kilowatt-hour electricity. My personal goal has been to use only one-third as much electricity as a conventional home of similar size and comfort by designing conservation into my home. In truth, solar electric homes almost never utilize a solar electric system to meet the typical energy demands of a conventional home. Solar electric homes are successful because of *conservation* of electricity.

Before you build your dream independent home, examine those loads that would be energy hogs if they were powered by electricity. These are normally heating, hot water, and cooking. You should try to power any heating load by another energy source. In the Northeast, even most grid homes choose to purchase less-expensive LP gas to power the kitchen stove and the hot water heater, and heat the house with wood, oil, or gas in preference to using electric heat.

Heating and cooking

Plan to buy a pilot-model propane stove. Standard propane stoves now come with an electric ignition feature

that creates some problems when it's used with an inverter's load demand function. (An inverter is the part of a solar electric system that transforms the direct current—DC—from the battery bank into the alternating current —AC—used in the home.)

Solar electric homes are successful because of conservation of electricity.

Solar hot water, wood-heated hot water, or a summer/winter hybrid of the two provide a renewable-energy hot water system. Conventional LP hot water heaters work well, but I prefer our more efficient Aquastar tankless model. Using LP is certainly not energy independence, since you are married to the gas company. However, it is more commonly used than wood for cooking or heating water. A home often uses only a 100-pound tank of propane per month, so those living far into the outback can transport the LP themselves.

Heating your solar electric home with a conventional oil or gas furnace is a problem: furnaces use a lot of electricity to run circulating pumps in hot-water systems or circulating fans in hot-air systems. Your alternative energy home should be designed to be heated by wood stoves, LP space heaters, passive solar energy, or any combination thereof, because these methods of heating require no electricity.

Solar heating

If you're planning to power your home with a solar electric system, you most likely have good solar exposure at your house site. I recommend incorporating some passive solar heating into your house design. This will require both south-facing windows and a heat sink (such as stone walls or concrete slab floors) that can absorb the heat of the winter sunlight. This will prevent the house from overheating during the day, while storing some heat for the night. Wood heat is a good partner for the passive solar heat.

...leafless branches in winter will reduce the solar energy by 35%

Many owners of independent homes find they are house-bound during the winter, because they can't leave their wood fires unattended for a weekend without the pipes freezing. Because you will not be using a furnace, you can plan for an LP space heater for backup heat.

Insulation

It is also possible to design a simple and affordable passive solar home that requires no furnace or backup LP heater. Our own 1800 square-foot, passive-solar, well-insulated home uses two cords of wood per year and will not drop below freezing in the

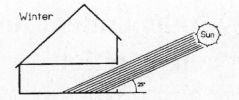

*Design your house
for passive solar heating.*

worst sub-zero weather while we are away. If you do plan to use passive solar heat, you will need to insulate your home more heavily than is standard for your area. In my town, homes are commonly insulated with six inches of fiberglass, but I used eight inches. You should also insulate the outside walls of the basement, or the perimeter of the floor slab, with two inches of foam insulation. One benefit of extra insulation is that it will lower the number of cords of wood you will have to cut each year for the rest of your life.

Cooling

In hotter climates, you will have to plan ways to keep your home cool without using standard electric air conditioning. Ceiling fans can be powered by super-efficient low-voltage DC motors that use a tenth of the electricity of AC fans. There are evaporative air conditioners or "swamp coolers" that use only a small amount of electricity for small pumps. The house site can be landscaped, and overhangs can be designed, to shade the house from the sun in the hot

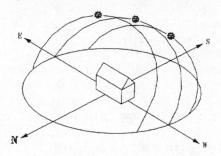

*In an unobstructed site, you get
maximum sun due south all year.*

months. Once again, the home must be well-insulated. Brave people can abandon a conventional home in favor of an earth-bermed, or underground, home that utilizes the earth to cool it in the summer and insulate it from the cold in the winter.

Water

An independent home needs its own water supply, and water-pumping can be a heavy electrical load to reckon with. A minority of folks can supply water using a spring on a hillside above the home that flows by gravity. Most people will have to drill a well. In dry areas of the country with deep aquifers, expensive deep wells require pump motors that are too large to be powered by an inverter in a solar electric system. In this case, you need to get a specialty jack pump powered by a low-voltage DC motor and an appropriately large storage tank. Look for help designing this system before you start building the house.

For homes with drilled or dug wells, there are choices for well pumps that work better with a solar electric system. If you can have a dug well close to the house, and the surface level of the water is less than 18 feet below the pump in the basement, you can utilize a centrifugal pump. The standard AC centrifugal pump (or its relative, a jet pump) is extremely inefficient. A better option is an efficient low-voltage DC pump that is powered from the battery bank. If you have a deeper well with a static water level that is lower than 18 feet, you can most likely use a 1/2 or 1/3 HP (horsepower) conventional deep-well pump. These pumps sit near the bottom of the well and push the water up, which is more efficient than pulling it up with a centrifugal pump. Deep-well pumps are normally 240VAC (240-volt alternating current), but they are also available in 120VAC, which is compatible with the 120VAC inverter in a solar electric system.

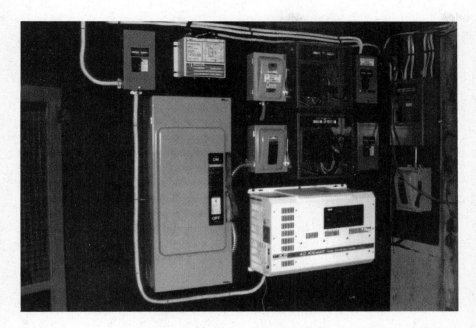

The inverter and controls, mounted on the basement side of the battery room wall

Getting enough sun

A solar electric home must have a daily minimum of six hours of solar exposure. Before you start building the house, you need to plot the daily path of the sun at your house site for the four seasons of the year. Shading trees must be removed. Even shading by leafless branches in the winter will reduce the solar energy by 35%. Most commonly, a solar house is oriented with one side facing due south (not magnetic south), with the ridge pole in an east-west line. The south wall can utilize extra windows for passive solar heating, and the roof can support the mounting structure for the solar electric modules.

Sometimes you can increase the total daily solar gain by shifting the orientation away from due south. For example, if there is a lack of solar exposure in the afternoon (maybe the sun passes over a ridge at 2 PM) and extra exposure earlier in the morning (an easterly valley), the orientation can be shifted 20° to the east to maximize your solar energy per day. Correspondingly, the house could be shifted to the west, if the ridge were to the east and the valley to the west.

Placement of modules, batteries, and controls

Solar electric modules may be installed on ground, wall, or roof-mounted structures. For a ground mount, you will need to plan for a ditch and a hole in the foundation wall for the underground cable from the module array to the battery bank. For a roof mount, you will need reinforced areas under the roof boards and between the rafters, where you will bolt the frame. You will also need a conduit, or interior wall space, to run the wires from the roof to the battery bank. If possible, the wires should be accessible after the house is finished to permit repairs and system upgrades. Solar electric module arrays send low-voltage DC electricity (usually at 12 or 24 volts) to the batteries. These wire runs should be kept as short as possible to reduce the need for thicker, more expensive cables.

The battery bank should not be inside the living area of the house. Lead-acid storage batteries smell when they are being charged hard, and they produce flammable hydrogen gas. Also, the batteries should not be installed in a cold environment, because the cold reduces their electrical storage capacity. A battery bank is ideally installed in its own ventilated room in a basement. Ventilation to the outdoors is necessary, so plan to leave an appropriate hole when you pour the foundation.

The system controls and the inverter should be as close to the batteries as possible without actually being in the battery room. Inverters typically draw 100-400 amps from the low-voltage battery bank, requiring large cables, preferably no more than five feet long. The controls will arc sparks when DC circuits are opened and closed, which could ignite the hydrogen gas produced by the batteries. Usually the inverter and controls are mounted in a four-by-eight-foot area on the basement side of the wall that separates the basement from the battery area.

If you plan to have a small solar electric system with 12V appliances and no inverter, you may want to locate the battery bank centrally to reduce the length of the circuits that will feed 12V electricity to the house, thus avoiding long runs that require thick, expensive cables.

A standard 15-20 cubic foot 120VAC refrigerator uses more electricity per day than your whole solar electric system could produce.

Most solar electric systems today utilize an inverter to change the low-voltage DC electricity from the battery bank to standard 120VAC electricity. Now that these inverters have become reliable and efficient, most people don't use DC appliances in their homes. Therefore, it is necessary to wire your home with the standard number of AC outlets, fixtures, switches, circuits, and circuit breakers. You may feel you do not need them now, but remember that it's easier to run wires before the walls are closed in.

Lighting

Lighting is a large load for your solar electric system. Furthermore, you will need more hours of electric lighting during the winter months when the days are short, which is also the time of year when we receive less solar energy to produce electricity. You can reduce your electrical consumption by choosing lighting fixtures that give you more light and supply that light where it can be best used. Avoid recessed fixtures that lose much of a bulb's light production to the black inside. Instead, seek out fixtures with globes or lenses that project the most light. Compact fluorescent bulbs are your most likely source of efficient and pleasing light. Unfortunately, these bulbs vary in size and shape. Try to select fixtures that can accommodate them. Some lights need to provide general lighting, while other lights need to be focused for detail work or reading. Choose your lights for where and how they will be used.

The best and most pleasing light for all activities is natural light. You can reduce the amount of electricity needed for lighting by matching window placement with areas that need light. For example, match your kitchen work areas to your kitchen windows so that electric lights are only needed at night. We rarely turn on a light in our home during daylight hours, because natural light does the job. Natural light is enhanced by white ceilings and walls to keep the light from being absorbed and lost.

Generators

Many solar electric homes use a generator to supplement their electrical needs in low-sun periods. If the generator is used often, it will need its own little shed or place in the garage, with an exhaust system to the out-

doors, hopefully out of noise range for the house and the neighbors. You will need to leave another hole in the foundation and a ditch for the underground line or conduit from the generator to the basement. If you have an LP powered unit, you will also have to plan for an underground LP gas line from the LP tank to the generator.

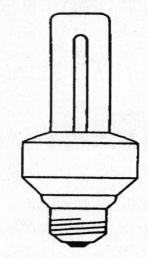

A compact fluorescent bulb

Cold storage

A standard 15-20 cubic-foot 120VAC refrigerator uses more electricity per day than your whole solar electric system could produce. Standard refrigerators are among America's most inefficient appliances and are not acceptable for an independent energy home. In sunny climates, you may choose a super-efficient low-voltage DC refrigerator. You will need to plan for an extra $1,000-1,500 investment in your solar electric array to power it. In climates like the Northeast, where I live, it is difficult to run even a super-efficient DC refrigerator, because it is a constant load even when the sun does not shine for several weeks straight. Most independent homes use an LP refrigerator that consumes about seven gallons of propane per month.

There are low-voltage DC freezers, but they consume about twice as much electricity as a DC refrigerator to

maintain the lower temperature and to cool the room-temperature foods that are added to them. LP freezers are small and extremely expensive. Most solar electric homes have no freezer. To compensate for this, I recommend planning a root cellar or cold storage room into your house design if you live in an area with cold winters.

The simplest cold storage room consists of a small room, well insulated from the basement and the warm ceiling of the house above, located in the north corner of the basement. In winter, the cold exterior walls of the foundation keep the room cool. Additionally, you may add one four-inch ventilation pipe that runs from just above ground, outside the basement, into the cold-storage room and down to its floor, and a second four-inch pipe from the ceiling of the cold-storage room, to the outside, and up the wall of the house six or eight feet. When the outside temperature is colder than the cold-storage room, cold outside air circulates into the space and warmer air rises out of the space.

A garden works well with the cold-storage room, because it supplies fresh vegetables in the summer, when the cold storage area is not cold, thus further reducing the need for a freezer and a large refrigerator.

To plan and design an independent home powered by solar electricity, you will need a lot more information than the few pages of this article. I hope I have started you thinking about the many facets of design that could help you plan and build an independent home—a home that uses far less power than your old "grid home," and at the same time provides you with a more comfortable existence, and a better and more sustainable life.

(Paul Jeffrey Fowler is the author of The Evolution of an Independent Home: The Story of a Solar Electric Pioneer, 1995, ISBN 0-9645111-7-7, distributed by Chelsea Green, available from *Backwoods Home Magazine*. He has written several successful how-to books on solar electricity.) Δ

July/Aug 1996
No. 40

Backwoods
Home magazi

practical ideas for self-reliant living

MAKING A LIVING ISSUE

13 Great Ways to Make Money While Living in the Country

Plus

Money-Saving Ideas
Natural Headache Relief
Perfect Wholegrain Bread
Graywater Disposal System
Proof of Psychic Powers?

$3.95 US • $5.50 CANADA

BULK RATE
U.S. POSTAGE
PAID
RIPON COMMUNITY
PRINTERS

DON CHILDERS

My view

Born of desperation

When I came to work this morning, John Silveira, *BHM's* senior editor who sleeps on a mattress on the office floor during deadline, was just waking as I walked in the door.

"What a nightmare I had," he said. "I thought I was back in DoD trying to get a job."

DoD is the Department of Defense. John and I worked for various DoD defense contractors for 15 and 10 years, respectively, prior to working for *BHM*. In fact, it took me two years and a constantly increasing wage offer to persuade him he should leave his high-paying and secure DoD job, which he hated, and come work for *BHM*, which I knew he would love.

"I dreamt I was at some defense contractors in southern California," he said. "I had quit the job three or four months before, I think, but I needed money to pay the mortgage so I was back there trying to get rehired. You were the only one I recognized; everybody else in the company had changed.

"You told me don't worry, that I'll get hired. At some point we went out to the roach coach to get something to eat, but you set the damn roach coach on fire and we had to run back in the building and hide.

"Then I was being interviewed by the boss, and he asked me why I quit. I told him I had gotten sick, that I was missing a day of work here and a couple of days there, then stopped coming in to work altogether a few months before because I was so sick. I told him I wasn't even sure I told the company that I had quit. He asked me what illness I had, but I couldn't tell him because what I had gotten sick of was the job. He asked me if I had any records from my doctor, but I hadn't been to any doctor. I could feel the job slipping away as he asked questions I couldn't answer. But I needed the crummy job to pay the damn mortgage. Man, was it depressing."

We had a good laugh. I knew the horror of such a dream first hand, and I had, in fact, lived it with minor modifications several times. In my 10 years working for defense contractors, I had quit many jobs, only to reapply to another company when the bills came due. Like John, I had hated going in for the interviews, hated going to work at the jobs, wished the day away so I could go home and do something I thought worthwhile, and lived for the weekends. I also grew to hate the growing metropolis that surrounded my home in southern California, and I grew weary of the rising crime, the increasingly congested roads, and the general din that reigns night and day in an overcrowded area.

Out of desperation, I eventually escaped to the backwoods and started a new life, not knowing just how I would make a living. This magazine was born out of the desperation I felt at the possibility I might have to return to jobs

Dave Duffy

that I hated. Luckily the magazine worked, and every issue Silveira and I work like dogs to make sure it keeps working so we won't ever have to go back to go-nowhere, miserable jobs in the city again.

There are many people out there today who are like John and I once were. They are good at what they do, but they can barely tolerate doing it. They need an outlet in the worse way imaginable. That's what this issue is about—an attempt to give you a few ideas of some of the possibilities of making a living. For most of you, the jobs depicted here will not be the jobs you will end up with, because in the end you have to create not only your own world in the country but your own job. You have to look at what you are good at, what makes you happy, what gives you the sense that you are spending your time well.

The compelling reasons that drove me to the country were job dissatisfaction and the citification of where I lived. But since arriving in the country and creating my own job, I have discovered many more benefits. Here are some of them:

My children visit me whenever they want on the job.
My children aren't exposed to drug pushers.
My children's mother is always at home with them.
I don't have to lock my house or car at night.
I look out the window and see wildlife.
I go fishing whenever I want.
All the neighbors know and depend on each other.
I look forward to going to work.
Silveira can sleep on the floor whenever he wants.

It's a great life. It takes a Silveira nightmare to wake me up and realize how lucky I am. But I quickly remind myself that I created my own luck. I took my life in my own hands.

If you feel a bit desperate about your job or where you live, you're welcome to use me as an example of what can be done. You don't have to start a magazine, but you should start something.

If you have some solid how-to knowledge to sell, writing and publishing a book is not that hard

By Skip Thomsen

Being able to earn your keep from your own home has a lot of benefits: no commuting, you set your own hours, you can involve your kids (to whom that participation can be a great learning experience), and there's just this wonderful feeling of autonomy that comes from being your own boss.

So have you ever considered writing for a living? If so, and if the thought of getting started was intimidating enough that you just put the whole idea aside, it's time to reconsider.

We are an information-hungry society. How-to books are hot sellers and are about the easiest kinds of publications to market on a small budget. Think about it: you're paging through your favorite magazine (the one that addresses your specific interests best) and you come across an ad for a book or booklet that promises to help you solve a problem that's been keeping you awake nights for some time. You'll go for it, right?

Getting started

I got started by accident. About 10 years ago, I was living on 108 acres of forest in northern Oregon. In the middle of this place, I built a 1600 square-foot house and a big shop. The house and shop had all sorts of electric tools, appliances, and gadgets, and I even had an office with a computer, photocopier, and two printers. All of this with no store-bought electricity. My place was about $10,000 away from the nearest power lines, and I really wanted to make my own power anyway, so I did.

Over the years, quite a few visitors voiced their surprise at how I could have all these electrical conveniences with "no electricity." (That's how most people perceive alternative power.) Several friends suggested that I write a manual on how to exactly duplicate my electrical system, since it had been working flawlessly for years.

Well, one day as I was sitting around wondering what I could do to earn a little extra cash, I remembered those suggestions, and I wrote up the initial draft of what was to become my first published writing effort.

If you have learned how to do some trade or even some specific facet of a certain skill...That, my friend, is marketable information.

The first printing was in 1989, and that little book has been selling ever since. It's now in its third printing, and it is just about time to get it ready for the fourth. This time, there will be some additional material included, covering new equipment that has recently become available. And I'm now working on my fourth book, and enjoying every minute of it.

Everybody's got a story

Almost everybody has got stories to tell, particularly you folks who have achieved some success at self-sufficiency. You've all mastered some tricks of the trade, ideas, and methods that you learned the hard way. You've all got helpful ideas to share with others.

Some people have a problem with "selling" ideas and thinking of this as "sharing." I consider myself fortunate to be able to buy, for a reasonable price, the information that somebody else has spent maybe years and lots of money learning. If you have learned how to do some trade or even some specific facet of a certain skill, you probably learned it over a period of time. Maybe you're like me, and you did it wrong the first several dozen times before you finally got it right, and when you finally did get it right, it worked better than you had ever hoped. That, my friend, is marketable information. You aren't the only one who has ever tried to achieve that goal, and you are in a position to offer the information on how to do it to everyone else facing the same challenge.

OK, now that we've got the philosophy out of the way, how do we become writers and publishers?

Writing the book

Your topics don't need to relate to what you're into right now, either. For example, if you are a serious homesteader living up in the piney woods, but you spent the last 20 years sailing the seas in your own blue-water boat, you no doubt have some ideas to share about sailing. There are few more dedicated audiences than the sailing folks, and they read every sailing magazine they can get their hands on. Same goes for doll-makers, bee-keepers, chefs, crafts-people, nurses, motorcycle mechanics—the list is endless.

Topics with small but excited audiences are the easiest to advertise to. I have a cousin who is making an exceptional living selling mail-order patterns for doll clothing.

The easiest topics are, of course, the ones with which you are intimately familiar. They're even easier if the topic is something you genuinely enjoy. Then you just write the how-to as if you were sitting there, talking with a friend. You know your subject, and the information just flows out.

Don't even try to create the perfect manuscript the first time out. Just pour out the ideas and thoughts. Hopefully, you're using a computer, because that makes it a whole lot easier. It can be done with a typewriter, or even by hand, but it's a lot more time-consuming that way.

Get the ideas down, and then spend the time to edit them into a logical progression. Don't worry too much about perfect grammar, either. Nobody's going to critique your work: they just want the information.

Should you be really worried about your writing ability, have a friend edit your manuscript for you. You can even have someone else do all the writing for you if you'll just dictate the information.

Once you're done with the last edit and you're satisfied with your writing, it's time to produce some marketable merchandise. The first step is printing the pages, and although a laser printer makes the best-looking page, you can get away with a letter-quality dot-matrix printer. What you're creating here are the "masters," the originals from which your actual production pages will be copied. Photocopying clear, sharp, letter-quality dot-matrix output makes it look almost as good as laser output, and certainly good enough for most how-to booklets. Just plain typed output works OK, too, but I must stress here that if you get even a little bit serious about writing, you need to get a computer. More on this later.

The "publishing" part — how it works

The detailed nuts and bolts of this business are beyond the scope of this article, but what I'll "share" with you here are the basics. Then if that builds a fire under you, check out the bibliography at the end of this article. Listed are the very best of the several hundred dollars' worth of books that

I've bought dealing with self-publishing and the marketing of your own writing.

The simplest way to get into self-publishing, and the way requiring the least money to get started, is to do booklets. Booklets can be printed inexpensively and bound with a low-cost saddle-stapler. Booklets are most easily produced in the standard 8½ x

The author at work in his home office

11" size of paper, or if you have a word processor that's capable of it, half that size (8½ x 11 folded in half). Booklets are great for single-topic publications, like how to grow bug-proof tomatoes, how to build a greenhouse for under $100, how to get the best firewood for free, how to troubleshoot computer problems, how to make your old truck run forever . . . this list is endless, too.

The book I did on my electrical system turned out to be over 80 pages (lots of drawings and diagrams), and since it was designed to be an instruction manual for a moderately-complicated project, it became a book rather than a booklet. I also wanted it to be a durable work-manual with a lay-flat binding. I did the first 1000 books by having the pages and covers printed by a regular print shop, and then I

bound the books using plastic "comb" (GBC) bindings. The machine that punches the pages and installs the bindings costs around $300.

When you start thinking in terms of bigger quantities, you should know that printing/bookbinding firms like to be paid up front. The cost per book goes down dramatically as the number of books printed goes up. The cost usually levels out a bit at about 3000 copies, so that's about a minimum practical order.

As an example of the quantity-discount thing, the next run of my power-system books was 3000, and the printer did the whole job, including collating the pages and binding the books, for less per book than it cost just to have the printing done on the first (1000-book) run.

The first run

If you're going to be doing booklets, you have several options. For just a few, like less than 100, the cheapest way is to have your nearest photocopy store make the pages for you, and then you can bind them with a stapler. A saddle-stapler is the best way to go here, because it is designed for that purpose. The booklet gets folded before stapling, and then it's simply opened again, and the fold is used to locate it on the stapler. The stapler then sets the staples right into the fold, and your product looks professional. Saddle staplers are also much heavier duty than common desk staplers, and they use heavier staples. They are available at most office supply stores, and if they don't have one in stock, they can order it for you. A desk stapler really is unsuitable for anything more than five or six sheets of paper. (See the Viking catalog in the bibliography.)

If your publication more closely resembles a book, and you want to use a comb binding, you can either purchase a binding machine or go to your copy shop and use theirs. Some copy shops will do the binding for you or let you do it yourself at a greatly reduced charge. They'll also have other methods of doing inexpensive binding.

For most booklets, regular copy paper is OK, depending on the quality of the paper and the printing process. The deciding factor is the transparency of the paper. Get a sample page with copy on both sides, and see how transparent it is. If you can see the printing on the back side coming through, the paper is too thin. *Always have the copy shop run a sample before printing a bunch of anything.* For a book, paper weight should be 50-pound stock. Anything thinner isn't durable enough and it just feels cheap. Covers should be heavier stock than the pages.

Explain what you're trying to accomplish and ask for suggestions. Often, copy places will have an oversupply of some paper that might suit your needs fine, and they'll sell it at an attractive price. Ask your copy shop about paper prices. If you find a good deal on paper, buy as much of it as you can afford. The prices rarely go down. Sometimes you can get a thicker paper that's less expensive than some of the thinner, more transparent

kind. And by all means, if you live where you have any choice, shop around. Prices vary a great deal from one place to another. Also ask about quantity prices. Some places offer price breaks at pretty low quantities.

Marketing your books

OK, now you are the proud owner of a box or two of your books. (You are now a publisher.) How will you market them? Classified ads in magazines addressing the book's field of interest are the most cost-effective on a limited budget.

Directly placing your product in stores that sell related supplies works, too. For example, a nursery or garden supply store would be a logical place for "How to grow bug-free tomatoes," or "How to build a greenhouse for under $100."

The easiest topics are, of course, the ones with which you are intimately familiar. They're even easier if the topic is something you genuinely enjoy. Then you just write the how-to as if you were sitting there, talking with a friend.

Many independent merchants will be happy to sell your books for you on consignment. The discount is usually 50%, so if the book sells for $4.95, you split that with the merchant. Consignment means that you place the books with the merchant, and he pays you for them as they are sold. Merchants are also more receptive to this idea if you can furnish some sort of display unit for your books, which can be as basic as a small cardboard box of the right size that will display the books standing up.

We've just scratched the surface of the possibilities in this article. If writing for a living sounds interesting to you, invest in some of the books listed below (or try your library). There is a lot to be learned in this business, but you don't need to learn it all at once. I recommend that you read completely through Dr. Lant's book, and then keep it around for reference. If the spark is there, this book will get the fire roaring.

About that computer

Let's get back to the computer thing for a moment. Excellent used machines are available in the $500-700 range, loaded with software, and often complete with a printer. (I recently sold one for $350.) Computer technology is advancing at such a rapid rate that what you buy new today is "obsolete" tomorrow. That makes it good for us folks who can get along just fine on yesterday's technology. I've written several books now on an ancient 386-DX/33 computer, which is considered totally obsolete. It does everything I need it to do, and then some. There are lots of complex businesses that depend on more antiquated computers than this one to do all of their accounting, word-processing, advertising, etc.

Don't let anybody sell you on the idea that you need the speed and capacity of a new machine. For word-processing, speed is immaterial. If you also want to get into the Internet, then you would do well do buy a faster machine, but even then a 486/66 or thereabouts will do nicely. And they're also dinosaurs and available cheap.

Bibliography

How To Make A Whole Lot More Than $1,000,000 Writing, Commissioning, Publishing And Selling "How-To" Information, by Dr. Jeffrey Lant. $39.95, ISBN: 0-940374-26-9. OK, that title really turned me off, too.

So did the price. But more than any other book I've read on the subject of writing and selling your work, this one is a bargain. Dr. Lant covers everything, with particular emphasis on the small-time writer of how-to material. With this information, you are set to go, and to take your new business to any heights you desire. This one is written in a casual, conversational style, and speaks to those of us who are entirely new at this game, as well as to those who are old hands at it. If you're only going to buy one book, this should be the one.

The Complete Guide to Self Publishing, by Tom & Marilyn Ross. $16.95, ISBN: 0-89879-354-8. This book is more for those who want to get right into real, full-size books. It's got a lot of info, and it's a lot less spendy than Dr. Lant's book, but this one is directed to a more commercial, "big-time" approach to publishing.

1001 Ways to Market Your Books, by John Kremer. $19.95, ISBN: 0-912411-42-2. This book is a gold mine of information on places and ways to market your books. It's a 500+ page, well-indexed resource that's a must for the serious writer.

Getting it Printed, by Mark Beach. $29.99, ISBN: 0-89134-510-8. This one is for when you're ready to produce your first serious, high-quality book. It covers everything you'll ever need to know about dealing with printers and getting the highest quality job for a reasonable price. Beach explains all the tricks of the trade, the processes used in every aspect of printing, and he takes the mystery out of "print-speak," the language used by those in the trade. It is important that you know this language if you're going to be dealing with printers. They all assume that you do, and if you don't, you're going to end up paying too much, getting something other than what you had in mind, or both.

Viking Office Products Catalog, 800-421-1222. This is a catalog, not a book, but it's a valuable resource. These folks are some of the best in the business, and they handle a very complete line of office supplies and tools (like saddle-staplers and binding machines). Their prices are the best around, they ship the same day, and the shipping is free on orders of over $25. If there's an error in any shipment (theirs or yours), they'll come pick up the wrong shipment and send another. It's a pleasure to deal with these folks. There is one catch: you need to be a business, so dream up a name for your new publishing business. You're going to need it pretty soon anyway, right? Call for a catalog. Δ

A BHM Writer's Profile: Darlene Campbell

One of Campbell's fondest memories is of her father's backyard rabbit hutches when she was a girl. There were always a few hutches of rabbits no matter where they lived, and she remembers how her mother often cared for the baby bunnies.

When she moved to Southeast Oklahoma in 1979 she and her husband, John, began raising rabbits commercially, but all her childhood memories hadn't prepared her for the losses they encountered in the beginning. Through trial and error she learned the right and the wrong ways to raise them. Later she wrote and sold her first book on rabbit management to TFH Publications, the world's largest publisher of pet books. Her next book was on raising parakeets.

Animals have always been a part of Campbell's life. On the farm she was able to surround herself with goats, calves, pigs, and poultry as well as rabbits.

When the rabbit venture folded she turned the building into a cattery and began raising registered Himalayan and Persian cats. She continued her writing about country life selling to such magazines as *Backwoods Home Magazine, Organic Gardening, I Love Cats,* and others.

In 1995 she began publishing "The Christian Homesteader," a newsletter geared toward homesteaders because she wanted to share her knowledge with others. The newsletter saw four successful years before it ceased publication due to other interests and lack of time.

Moving back to Arizona in 1998 Campbell is no longer farming but continues to write of her experiences so others may learn. She currently raises Yorkshire Terriers and makes turquoise jewelry in the historic town of Mayer.

Here are two country couples who diversified to make a living

By Dave Duffy

One of the best ways to determine how to make a living in the country is to go into the country and examine how people already there are making a living. What you'll find is that there are few ideal country jobs. In fact, there are few jobs period, and what jobs there are are lower paying than their city counterparts.

That's a daunting situation for a lot of people grown accustomed to a certain level of income. In many cases, people who are professionals or highly skilled in their field cannot find an opening related to the type of skill they have. They must do something totally new.

But as difficult a situation as that may appear to be, there is a bright side: the harder it is to find a job in the country, the less populated—and more desirable—the country becomes. If it were easy to find a good job in the country, the country would quickly fill up with people who would bring with them all the problems they sought to leave behind.

So if you want to make it financially in the country, you must be resourceful in how you pursue employment. And if you can't find a suitable job, you must create your own job, or diversify and perform several jobs needed in your area..

I took a look around my area in northern California to see how my neighbors made their living. I could have picked many of them to show as examples, but I picked just two couples. Both had given up good jobs to move from the city to the country years ago, and both had used their ingenuity to adapt to the sparser financial pickings of the country.

The key to their continuing success has been, in large part, their ability to diversify. Their example may give you an insight into the type of thinking often necessary to make a living in the county.

Paul and JoAnne Luckey

Paul and JoAnne Luckey owned a successful leather clothing consignment shop in Sausalito, located at the other end of the Golden Gate Bridge from San Francisco, California.

"We sold everything from hats to boots," Paul said. "I even went to Mexico and learned how to make cowboy boots." The Luckeys hired a U.C. Berkeley professor to teach tailoring for 6 months to 10 of the people who were consigning items to their

shop. "Seven of them went on to open their own businesses," Paul said.

By the mid 1970s, however, the Luckeys were "fed up with the drugs, alcohol, and crime in the city." They decided it was not a good place to raise their four children, and they began looking for "a simpler lifestyle ...cleaner and more healthy to raise the kids."

They chose northern California as their getaway. "It was during a severe drought in that part of California," Paul recalled. "I used to climb Mount Shasta and saw this incredible amount of water everywhere." In 1975 they bought a small Eagle Ranch near Montague, about 50 miles from Mount Shasta. And in 1980 they made the move, leaving behind a four-bedroom, three-bath home complete with jacuzzi, pool, and weight room, and moved the family into a two-bedroom trailer on the ranch.

Then the transition began. The Luckeys had money from the sale of their business and home, but they still needed to make a living. They needed

Paul Luckey with view of Eagle Ranch in background

Paul on his backhoe, making a living

a bigger house, too, to house a family that eventually expanded to seven children.

"I knew how to work hard in the country," Paul said. "I had worked in the coal mines of West Virginia when I was 10. At 13 I left home and worked on a dairy farm in Pennsylvania, and at 16 I went to Montana and worked in the copper mines and later on my grandfather's cattle ranch there."

Paul Luckey ended up becoming a jack of all trades, doing everything from cutting firewood for sale to operating a backhoe for hire. JoAnne became a teacher's aide and spare cook at nearby Bogus Elementary school, where she has now worked for 11 years.

They have done other things, too, as the opportunities presented themselves. In the early 1980s, during this country's energy crisis caused by soaring crude oil prices, legislation was passed that forced the utility companies to buy surplus electricity from private producers. So Paul, in 1982, started building his own hydroelectric power plant, taking advantage of natural springs on a hill above his ranch.

It took him, his sons, and his brother four years and 160 dump truck loads of sand and gravel to make the 300 yards of cement necessary to corral the creek and build a power plant, but he now has a 30-year lease selling electricity to the utility company.

The Luckeys have also raised cows on their ranch for income, but they sold the cows to pay off the ranch. They now grow and sell hay. Paul and his sons have also cut and sold firewood, cutting as many as 128 cords in a year.

Paul bought his own backhoe and bulldozer some years back, and now hires himself out (that's how I met him) to build new roads, dig septic systems, etc. He has also hired himself out to help build new houses, including his own, which is a 3600-square-foot home he built himself.

Because he has been self-employed most of his life, he would not qualify for social security if he were to retire today, so, since he won't turn 62 for another 10 years, he has taken a part-time job as janitor at local Bogus Elementary School to build up social security credits.

He also works for Excel Telecommunications, getting a commission on every local business he convinces to switch their long distance telephone service to Excel. *BHM* switched.

And in the past couple of years the Luckeys have managed to buy two rundown houses in town, fix them up, and rent them for extra income.

Paul admits he likes to work hard. "Work is very rewarding," he said. "You get immediate gratification at the end of each day."

The Luckeys are also religious. Paul, a Cherokee Indian, and JoAnne, an Apache, follow the Red Road. "All

JoAnne Luckey with Bogus School children

the national tribes follow the Red Road," Paul said. "You listen to the Great Spirit within you, and you'll find the answers to what you need to know. We've raised ourselves and our children not to depend on anyone else...to be independent, to be themselves, and to rely on God and themselves to make a living."

Paul and Margaret Boos

Paul and Margaret Boos live within a few miles of the Luckeys. They own Cold Creek Ranch, having moved there from Huntington Beach in southern California 22 years before.

Like the Luckeys, they had also given up their own company to move to the country. Paul, a clinical laboratory technologist, and Margaret, a nurse, owned and operated the Huntington Beach Clinical Lab, which provided services to doctors in the area.

It was the growing crime and congestion of Huntington Beach, along with increasing government regulations that consumed an increasing part of their workday, that prompted them to sell their 12-year-old business and leave their handsome, custom-built home. They and their two young chil-

dren moved into a tent while Paul built a cabin and dug his own well.

Only a few weeks after moving into their home-built cabin, they discovered 59-acre Cold Creek Ranch. "It was a small dilapidated place," Paul said. "It was made from an old cook shed, used when they built a dam on the Klamath River, and a chicken house. They put them together and made a house."

Paul had intended to go into the cattle business, but "the cattle business has been a bust." For a time he worked counting salmon for $5 an hour at a fish hatchery on the Klamath River. Eventually both he and Margaret fell back on their professions, working for Siskiyou General Hospital in Yreka.

Both have pursued side businesses while working in town. Paul saved and bought a Wood-Mizer sawmill, and he hires himself out to cut trees into lumber. That's how I met him. He also cuts firewood for sale, raises worms to sell fisherman who drive by his ranch, hires himself out on his backhoe, and raises registered Angus so he can sell the bulls and heifers. He also carves fish out of wood, and as a buyer of one of his pieces I can testify to their artistry.

Margaret Boos with her sheep

Margaret raises purebred registered cotswald sheep, and a few rambouillet, hampshire, and corriedale sheep, and she uses the wool to make hats, vests, felted balls, doll hair, yarn, and fleeces for Santa Claus beards. But it is the hats that make you go wow. They are fulled (as opposed to felted), beautiful, warm, and made from the natural color of the sheep she raises. She uses no dye or chemicals of any kind and, from the time she picks up the raw fleece, it takes her six to seven hours to make each hat.

Margaret crosses the wool to obtain the type of wool she wants. "I like the long fiber with luster and a small crimp," she said. "The wool never leaves the ranch. I care for them, they are sheared here, I wash the wool, card it, spin it into yarn, and knit it into a hat." She has made 150 hats, and you have to feel them to realize how luxurious a warm hat can be.

"I have a passion for wool," Margaret said. "And I like to do individual things. When I start I don't

Paul Boos with customer at Tulare Farm Show

Margaret's woolen hats

even know what I'm going to do to it. I don't want two people walking down the street and seeing the same thing on each other."

Margaret said she knits the hat to an oversized size, then washes it to shrink it to the desired size. She then shapes it on a form. Each of her hats bears a tag that says: "Homemade by Margaret Boos," and it has a photo of the sheep the wool came from.

About twice a year Paul and Margaret buy booth space at farm shows, such as the Tulare Farm Show in California. Margaret sells her hats and other wool items, and Paul sells "antique farm implements" that he has either found around the ranch or bought at auction or garage sales.

Margaret retired last year from her nursing job, and Paul will retire this year. They will use their side businesses now as their full-time occupations.

"There are hundreds of things you can make a living at," Paul said. "There are so many things you can take out of the country without hurt it, yet make a living. People don't take time to smell the roses."

By the way, if you'd like to take a look at some of Margaret's hats, she'll send you a little handout. Her address is Cold Creek Ranch, 16038 Ager-Beswick Rd., Montague, CA 96064. Telephone: (916) 459-3288.

I hope a look at the way Paul and JoAnne Luckey and Paul and Margaret Boos have made a living has given you a sense of the possibilities of making a living for yourself in the country. Remember, there is no magic bullet to making a living. You must fit

Margaret Boos demonstrating her wool hats at the Tulare Farm Show

A BHM Writer's Profile: Tom Kovach

Tom was born and raised in north central Minnesota and is now 54-years-old. He studied journalism at the University of Nevada-Reno and at Bemidji State University in Bemidji, Minnesota. He is divorced with two grown daughters and one grandson.

Tom served in the U.S. Army in Vietnam, Germany, and Korea. His hobbies include, hunting, fishing, hiking, walking, swimming, reading, biking, gardening, and travel. He has traveled all over the U.S., some of Europe, Asia, and Africa.

yourself into the country, ascertain what you can do, and adapt. Δ

A BHM Writer's Profile: Edith Helmich

Edith Helmich is a freelance writer working out of Tallahassee, Florida. She has been published in a variety of newspapers, magazines, and professional journals. She enjoys writing on a broad field of topics, using her life experiences as a base of knowledge.

Her background and experiences include teaching elementary and junior high school students and working as an educational consultant to colleges and universities in Illinois. Her graduate degree in Administration, and years of experience as an educational research scientist for the Illinois State Board of Education, provide a foundation for her articles.

A lifetime of fascination with fine foods and unique recipes provides an interest area that has expanded to provide a practical base for the culinary articles she writes. She has maintained a test kitchen for many years with a tasting panel that consists of her husband and three children, discriminating critics with healthy appetites.

The "night crawler condo" is a great way to make money

By Angela Jenkins

Raising worms to sell to fishermen is a time-tested way to increase your income, and this "night crawler condo" method will help you make such an operation more efficient and neater.

To build a crawler condo takes little more than a trip to the garden or farm supply store. Depending on the type of food store chain that's in your area, it may all be there in one stop.

To get started you need:

1. Styrofoam cooler with a lid (20-quart for the first one)
2. Peat moss
3. Clean soil such as potting soil for plants
4. Aged cow manure
5. Yellow cornmeal
6. Used coffee grounds
7. Rabbit food (alfalfa pellets)
8. Two dozen night crawlers (from a bait shop or your own back yard)
9. Water
10. Old towel or material that will hold moisture
11. Screen wire (2 pieces 4"x4")

First, the cooler must have ventilation holes cut into the sides about one inch from the bottom of each end of the cooler. Place the screen wire over the holes inside the cooler. The screen wire can be attached by using bent pieces of wire. The ventilation holes help to keep the contents sweet. Night crawlers will not thrive in soured soil.

Now the cooler is ready to be filled to within six inches of the top with a mixture of equal parts peat moss, potting soil, and cow manure. Add enough water to make the mixture damp but not wet.

Let this sit for a couple of hours to allow the water to soak through the peat moss and manure mixture, stir-ring the mixture occasionally to make sure the moisture is evenly distributed throughout the cooler. Then it's time to give the night crawlers their first look at their new home. Just drop them onto the top of the mix. Now take the soft cloth and thoroughly wet it with water. Wring it out and lay it over the top of the peat moss mix, making sure that the whole surface is covered (the night crawlers, too).

Twelve to twenty-four hours later, go back to the cooler and give those crawlers their first meal. While this might not sound inviting to people, crawlers love to eat this combination.

Mix together:
   1/2 cup of plain yellow cornmeal
   1/2 cup of rabbit food pellets
   1 cup of used coffee grounds

Sprinkle this mixture on top of the damp soil mixture and re-cover with the wet cloth. Additional used coffee grounds (about 1 cup) can be added about every ten days. Always keep the soil mixture damp, but not wet. The rate of moisture loss will depend on the air temperature and circulation around the cooler, so the dampness level should be checked at least once a week. If the soil feels dry, add water. The soil mixture in the cooler must never dry out completely. Night crawlers must have access to water to survive.

The upkeep of this crawler condo is quite simple. The night crawlers will come to the surface and eat the corn-meal and rabbit pellets. Check on them at least once a week to keep track of how much food they are eating. As they grow, they will require more food, but that's fine, because bigger night crawlers catch bigger fish.

As the food is depleted, simply add more by sprinkling the rabbit pellets, corn meal, and coffee grounds on top of the soil mixture and re-covering with the damp cloth. Always keep the cooler lid firmly in place after adding food or water. Placing a weight, such as a brick or a piece of firewood on top of the cooler is good insurance. Night crawlers are travelers, and they will crawl out if the lid is left ajar.

When the crawler condo is finished, place it in a cool, dry place such as a basement or garage. If the cooler is kept over the winter, a basement is a better choice in case there is exceptionally cold weather. In the cooler, the night crawlers cannot go deeper for protection from very cold temperatures as they can outside in the soil, so the protection of basement walls will hold them through the winter.

Night crawlers will grow to enormous size given this special gourmet treatment, and they are always available for a fishing trip with you when it's too hot to find them outside, or it's that first warm day in spring and the ground temperatures haven't warmed enough to bring them up near the surface.

This one-time setup will last three to four months. It's time to re-new the contents when the soil level has dropped to about half-way down the side of the cooler. At that time, just take out the night crawlers and put them in a separate container to hold them until you empty and replenish their home again. The peat moss and manure mixture being removed from the cooler will be an excellent addition to a flower bed or compost bin.

The worm castings in the peat moss mix are nutrient-rich food for plants.

When you replenish their condo with fresh bedding, you will find that the number of night crawlers has multiplied rapidly. Now is the time to set up other coolers with the extra worms, or better still, pull out those extra worms and sell them to the folks that didn't get their condos ready before winter.

Small grocery stores, bait and tackle shops, and service stations all sell night crawlers if they are situated around a lake or river area. Now even a few of the larger chain stores such as Wal-Mart and K-Mart are carrying night crawlers in the sporting goods section as a regular item. Night crawlers can best be packaged in styrofoam cups with lids. Fill the cup with dampened peat moss and add about a dozen worms per cup. Eight-to twelve-ounce cups will do the trick.

With the crawler condo setup, a supplier can easily raise thousands of night crawlers in a limited amount of space in a matters of weeks. Δ

When my pen is stilled
And my tongue is cold
And I can no longer
Hold you in my arms
My words will still be there
Read them
And though there will be other men
To hold you
I will still talk to you
From the poems I've left behind
And you will remember me
And when you've finally come
To join me
I will embrace you forever
And whisper poems of love
To you
For eternity

John Silveira
Ojai, CA

A BHM Writer's Profile: Michael Clayton

Michael Clayton was born in Jacksonville, Arkansas, and raised in Sherwood, Arkansas. He grew up with a backyard garden and started growing radishes and lettuce, and as the years went by he started helping to grow other plants including eggplants. Michael graduated from the University of Arkansas at Little Rock with a BA in Criminal Justice and in 1998 he completed a correspondence course in PC repair from the International Correspondence School. He is a member of the Council of Conservative Citizens and the American Nationalist Union for whom he was the Television Review for a short time in 1996 for their newspaper *The Nationalist Times*.

A BHM Staff Profile: Jean L'Heureux

Jean "Pop" L'Heureux is an Assistant Editor at *Backwoods Home Magazine*. His primary duties are maintaining the subscription database and inputting the "Letters to the Editor" for the magazine.

He has an extensive background in computers, operating them almost from their inception, and brings his knowledge to the magazine.

He vacationed in Gold Beach, Oregon, several years prior to the magazine's arrival there, and he loved it so much that he moved there, away from the hustle and bustle of a hectic city life. When *BHM* located to Gold Beach he postponed his retirement and joined the staff of the magazine.

Jean enjoys the salmon fishing available in the Gold Beach area, and he caught an 18 ½ pound salmon his first trip up the Rogue River.

Got some weekend residents in your area?
Then your home business is waiting to open

By Nanci Vineyard

Like so many of you who also read this magazine, I too once lived in the city and dreamt of getting back to the land. I pursued my dream for many years by lying on the couch, reading magazines, designing log homes in my mind, and wanting to kill the person using a leaf blower across the street. I put on pantyhose and mascara, drove on the freeway to a glass building, performed a well-paid but (to me) meaningless task, saved my money, and plotted my escape.

When I purchased a very secluded ten acres in the North Georgia Mountains, the pressure was eased somewhat, because at least I had a quiet place to escape to on the weekends. The first and most essential part of my dream had become reality.

After three years of land payments, I had enough equity in the land to swing a construction loan for a house. Despite hardly knowing the difference between a skill saw and an eyebrow pencil, I contracted the house myself. I weathered the alternate urges to commit murder or suicide, the house was finished, the mortgage secured, and I moved.

Although I loved hearing the rain on my tin roof, being able to have chickens and a huge organic garden, and no longer being constantly assaulted by blaring car alarms, I found that I had a new problem: how to make a living at the end of a dead-end dirt road. I had initially planned on meeting my financial commitments by commuting the two hours back to the city on a part time consulting basis, and this worked for about a year, until my main client went out of business. I did not want to spend huge amounts of time staying

overnight at friends' houses and rummaging up new clients. I desperately wanted to do something closer to home so that I would have the time to enjoy all the reasons I had moved here for.

With my back up against the proverbial first-of-the-month wall, I took a job at the only plant nursery in town, for an inadequate six bucks an hour. But the job barely kept the telephone and electricity turned on. I had to think of something, and fast.

One day while working at the nursery, I noticed a couple who came in and, unlike the locals, did not ask the price of plants. They just picked out whatever they wanted and handed me a VISA Gold card. They were "weekenders," people whose primary residence was in the city an hour and a half down the road, but who had a weekend getaway in the mountains. They started to include a particular

flowering shrub in their cartload of purchases one day, but put it back with the comment, "It requires so much watering, and we're only up here once or twice a month." Bingo! I had my idea, and in that instant my business was born. I named it "Weekenders' Angels" — corny but absolutely rememberable.

The underlying key to my success sounds so basic, yet it is so necessary: show up when you say you'll be there, do the work you promised to do, and charge as close as possible to the price you estimated.

It has been up and running for two years now, and I am happy to report that while it is not my ultimate, perfect, lifetime solution, it has proved to be a very workable idea for the present. I am paying my bills, providing a much-needed service to my community, meeting some nice folks, and having time to do the things I want to do at home.

The basic idea is quite simple: we perform whatever services out-of-town property owners want done and for whatever reason can't or don't want to do themselves. Our services run the gamut from landscaping, cabin cleaning, storm damage survey, carpentry projects such as adding closets or decks, plumbing and electrical repairs, house painting, and delivering firewood.

The execution of the idea has been like any new business—a couple of years of trial and sometimes error, learning, paying attention to what works and what doesn't, analyzing profits and losses, and making corrections. The underlying key to my success sounds so basic, yet it is so necessary: show up when you say you'll be there, do the work you promised to do,

and charge as close as possible to the price you estimated.

I have secured a trademark on my corny name, and have written a procedural manual which includes topics such as how to secure a client base, how to ascertain market rates for various services, how much start-up capital is needed and ways to get it, and how to deal with emergencies and cranky customers. It also includes examples of invoices, response letters, advertisements, accounting records, and what I hope are some beneficial as well as humorous anecdotes. I am marketing the manual, rights to use

the name, and my services as a consultant to others who find themselves living in a rural area which has a healthy component of non-resident property owners. While my particular situation involves mountain cabins two hours away from Atlanta, Georgia, the idea could just as easily work for anyone within driving distance of a ski resort area, lake, ocean, you name it, anywhere people have second/vacation homes or weekend getaways.

(Nanci Vineyard can be reached at (706) 276-4592 or Route 6, Box 533, Ellijay, GA 30540.) Δ

A BHM Writer's Profile: Dana Martin Batory

Though Mr. Batory studied for a B.A. in Geology at Ohio State University and is still an avid mineral collector he now operates a small, one-man, custom woodworking shop. He is the author of numerous how-to articles which have appeared in such magazines as *American Woodworker, Woodwork, Woodworker, Popular Woodworking,* etc. He has also written several articles on antique woodworking machinery which have been published in *Antique Week, Woodshop News,* etc. Besides having written Vintage Woodworking Machinery-An Illustrated Guide To Four Maunfacturers (1997), Dana supplies the section on antique woodworking machinery for Schroder's Antiques Price Guide which is Collector Books' number one best seller, and he has been on their Advisory Board since 1991. He is presently engaged in researching and writing other volumes in his planned series on American manufacturers of woodworking machinery. Volume Two will probably cover Whitney, Crescent, Parks, and Boice-Crane.

In order to raise needed funds to continue his research Dana is presently making selected items from his collection of vintage woodworking machinery catalogs and manuals available as photocopies. A 40+ page list (updated quarterly) is available for a $7.50 money order.

Dana is also interested in acquiring by loan, gift, or photocopy any and all documents, catalogs, manuals, photos, trade journals, personal reminiscences, etc. pertaining to woodworking machinery and/or their manufacturers, past and present, to continue his research. All assistance will be acknowledged in print. Loaned material will be treated with care and promptly returned. Dana Martin Batory, 402 E. Bucyrus St., Crestline, OH 44827.

Raising rabbits — for meat and making money, it's hard to beat this creature on the homestead

By Jayn Steidl Thibodeau

Rabbits. Everyone who has ever tried to raise a garden has cursed them at one time or another. Hunters stalk them in the cool autumn air, hoping to bag enough for a tasty stew. Moviegoers cry over Bambi's friend Thumper, or laugh as Bugs and Elmer Fudd battle in cartoonland. But domestic rabbits could add another dimension to this portrait of rabbits. Domestic rabbits (an entirely different species than the wild rabbit) not only have the capability of producing enough meat from a single pair to feed a family of four for a year, but also can be an economically viable commercial enterprise for your homestead.

Mike and I have raised rabbits for nearly 20 years, and believe me, we have made every mistake in the book —and a few not even listed. But overall, we have learned that rabbits are hardy, inexpensive to purchase and feed, and (providing a few simple rules are followed) not particularly labor-intensive, compared with other livestock.

Shelter

Housing will be the most expensive item in a beginning rabbitry, but used cages are available at reasonable prices in most locales, or it is a simple matter to build your own. Many rabbit raisers utilize an old shed to hang cages. Others simply put the cages under a tree in the great outdoors. We don't recommend the outdoor method because feed-to-weight conversion is better in a controlled environment. Close contact with wood also increases the incidences of an aggravating little critter called the ear mite. If you are using an old shed or a chicken house, be sure the ventilation is ade-

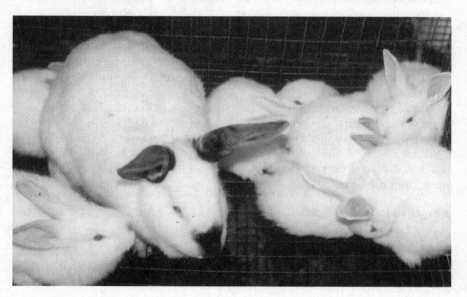
Here's a nice litter of California hybrids at three weeks.

quate and the roof doesn't leak. Walls and doorways should be secured to keep predators away. The neighbor's cat may look cute lolling about on top of a cage, but when a nervous mother stomps an entire litter to death, the humor in the situation is hard to find.

Having a source of water available is a must. You can utilize automatic waterers instead of using the old crock method, which often leaves the animals without water for extended periods of time. Automatic waterers are very simple to set up using either a pressure reducer or a gravity flow system. Several styles are available. The tube type is great for a warm climate and is really simple to repair. The PVC styles run into a bit more money to set up, but are great for cold weather areas. A heat tape can be run through the lines to prevent water freeze-up. These styles and others are available from dealers of rabbit supplies.

Much of the decision about what breeds to choose will depend on your market. Some people will find that a

pet market is what they are most comfortable supplying and will choose to raise a dwarf breed or one of the popular lop or Dutch belt breeds. There are commercial markets that buy pet rabbits for resale to pet stores. The main drawback to this particular operation is that demand is seasonal, peaking at Easter, but rabbits must be bred on a regular schedule year-round. Finding a market for a rabbit that weighs only two or three pounds is difficult, and many breeders resort to the snake food market for disposing of excess stock.

Show rabbits are another "iffy proposition." Out of a litter of five, there may be only one rabbit that is of show quality. What happens to the excess?

Some breeds, such as the Rex or the Satin, produce gorgeous pelts. If you tan hides well, you may be satisfied with these breeds and find a ready market for your wares at craft fairs.

But if you are interested in a really profitable rabbit, it is best to stick with a white-furred, pink-eyed meat breed such as a New Zealand or a California. These breeds have been bred for generations to be prolific and for mothering ability and rapid growth. Some other breeds, such as Flemish Giants, have been crossed on the New Zealands and Californias with great results for fryer growth rates, but when kept as does, they are usually too large and eat too much to be cost-efficient.

Colored stock occasionally surfaces in these white breeds, but commercial buyers discriminate in their pricing strategies against the coloreds, so don't save any for your own breeding stock, even if they are pretty.

Marketing

Commercial rabbit processors are located throughout this country, and rabbit is a popular export to Canada. Reports of widespread shortages of rabbit indicate that the market is in a stable cycle, and this is an ideal time to begin a rabbitry. To locate a processor near you, you could check with other rabbit raisers, or purchase a subscription to the magazine published by the American Rabbit Breeders Association (see below). There is a commercial section in the middle of the magazine which lists commercial prospects as well as current market reports.

Rabbit growers are an enterprising group of people, and the majority of rabbits raised in this country do not come from large rabbitries of 1,000 or more does, but rather from small back-yard growers of 10 or 12 does.

Those fortunate enough to live near a processing plant may deliver their own rabbits or have a driver with a designated route who will pick up the livestock at a pre-determined spot for delivery to the plant. Some groups of rabbit raisers have even formed informal co-ops with members arranging for large numbers of rabbits to be contracted by the processor and picked up. If you choose this method, be sure your members are reliable; if the con-

Freddy Rivera shows the proper way to hold a doe.

tracted number of rabbits is not available on the date specified, it will be difficult to deal with that company again.

Meat rabbits are also a popular item with home marketers. The meat, which is low in cholesterol and tastes somewhat like the white meat of a chicken, is in high demand from certain ethnic groups and is a popular barbecue choice. If you choose to sell your rabbits from home, be sure to sell them live and do any butchering only as a favor to your customer. Accepting money for butchering an animal brings you into USDA and health department jurisdiction, and the facilities required aren't cheap.

Choosing stock

When you pick out your stock, choose does and bucks less than one year of age. If a rabbit is being culled from a rabbitry because it is a bad mother or won't breed, you don't want to blow your hard-earned cash on it. If a doe hasn't bred by a year of age, she probably never will. Likewise, if someone offers you a couple of last year's Easter bunnies who have always lived together, avoid them like the plague. They probably won't breed.

Look for clean forelegs—rabbits clean their noses with their paws and dirty paws indicate illness—and clean anal areas. Hocks (the bottoms of the feet) should be free of sores; thin foot pads that can lead to sore hocks are a genetic trait you don't need passed on. The eyes should never be cloudy or filmy.

Teeth should be short. If an animal has teeth that don't quite meet properly, the result is malocclusion, or buck teeth, which curl around the mouth, making it impossible for the animal to eat. These teeth must be clipped regularly or the rabbit will starve. It is widely believed that this is more often caused by a recessive gene carried by the doe and the buck than by accident or injury, so don't introduce the trait to your rabbitry if you can possibly avoid it.

Check the ears for scaly brown scabs. This is a sign of the ear mite problem we mentioned earlier. If left untreated, it can cause nerve damage (wry neck) and the animal will have to be destroyed. If you do wind up with this problem, a dose of mineral oil or cooking oil will clear up the problem cheaply, or catalogs carry a variety of medications.

Run your hands over the body of the animal and feel for any hidden abscesses.

Prices

Rabbits are cheap in comparison to other livestock for the homestead. Prices vary according to the size and age of the rabbit selected. A good fryer-sized rabbit ($4^1/2$ to $6^1/4$ pounds) of about $2^1/2$ to 3 months should run less than $5, while an older doe of 6 months to a year may run as much as $25. If you opt for the higher-priced rabbit, ask to see the breeding records on the parents of that animal. They will give you an indication of how the animal will perform. The lower-priced fryer size won't come with records, as it is probably aimed at the meat market, but for the price, you may want to take a chance and just breed out any defects that appear in subsequent generations.

Some companies advertise the sale of certified or registered rabbits. These can be quite expensive and are certainly not necessary for someone who intends to produce a meat animal. Investigate such companies thoroughly before investing. Most are legitimate, but a few have had complaints.

Because rabbits are so cheap, you may be tempted to over-buy. As with any livestock, get your feet wet before diving in. Rabbits are a seven-day-a-week job, and you may find that they don't fit in with your lifestyle. Ten does and two bucks are an excellent number for a fledgling commercial enterprise. As you grow, you will want to save your own stock from your best animals. It is wise to keep at least one buck for every ten does, with replacements coming up at every stage of growth at all times.

Breeding

Every doe will need her own cage, plus a cage for her fryers after they are weaned. The does are ready to breed at about eight pounds or six months of age (later for the Giant breeds), and at that time you will take her to the buck's cage—*never the other way around*. Does are territorial and can hurt the buck if they feel threatened in their own territory. You will know that the doe is in season if the vulva is slightly swollen and purplish in color. She should breed within a few minutes. If she doesn't, remove her and try it another day.

The buck should breed her twice, and this will finish him for the day. (This is why two bucks are recommended for ten does.) Don't overwork your buck or you will lower the sperm count, resulting in smaller litters. Mark the date she was bred and which buck is the sire in a book or on a calendar.

Each doe will ideally produce seven or eight bunnies in 30 to 32 days, and you should have a nest box in the cage a few days before. Nest boxes can be made out of scrap lumber. They should be 9" wide by 18" long and 8" tall. We bought old wooden army surplus ammo boxes for about $2 each, and they have worked beautifully. The doe will put some of her fur into the filling material (pine shavings or fine hay) for the babies, which are called *kits*. The kits will be blind, deaf, and bald when they are born, but they grow quickly and will be out of the nest box in about 2½ weeks. You can breed the mother again at three weeks after delivery, although some commercial rabbitries do it sooner. The kits will be ready to wean at five weeks of age.

Some does will have more kits than they can raise, and other does may only have three or four. Neither is a desirable rabbit, but if you have a doe with too many, just remove a few from her box and give them to the doe who doesn't have enough. Most does will raise just about anyone's kit, no questions asked. Be careful when you stick your hand in the cage, though. Even though you selected calm, sweet-tempered does, maternal instinct is protective, and you may receive a nasty bite for your efforts to help. Wearing gloves might be a good precautionary measure.

Partial view of the rabbitry. There's a lot of manure under the cages, but the worms keep it from overwhelming us.

Feed

Feed is the most expensive item in a rabbitry, but costs can be cut by getting together with other raisers, contracting for larger amounts at one time, and negotiating for a lower cost. Lots of people try to mix their own feed, but nutritionally, a pre-mixed pellet is best for the rabbit. Most commercial feeds are non-medicated, containing about 17-18% protein, 17% fiber, and 2.5-3% fat, and the rabbits produce and grow well on these ratios. The most important things to remember about feeding are to find one brand and stick to it, and to remove any moldy feed.

Buying feed in bulk is cheaper, but storing feed for long periods may break down vitamins. Feed should be stored in a dry area, such as a plastic trash can, to prevent water damage. High humidity is also a problem, as the moisture causes the alfalfa meal in the pellets to swell and break apart, allowing mold to form. Moldy feed is a major culprit in rabbit enteritis.

Rabbits have very delicate digestive systems. Because they are so small, any slight diarrhea can kill in a matter of hours. Rabbits are like people when it comes to body condition. Some rabbits will get overly fat on just a little feed, while others are downright scrawny on full feed. A good rule of thumb is to keep your non-lactating does on about four to six ounces per day in the summertime, increasing slightly in the winter, while lactating does and fryers should have all they can eat.

Any change in feed should be introduced gradually. A little hay or alfalfa cubes are a helpful treat for your rabbit, but avoid such rich items as carrots, fresh grasses, or lettuce. Rabbits are best fed at night, because they pass soft feces that are re-ingested, much like a cow chewing a cud. Although they can do this at any time, it is usually a night-time activity and feeding in the evening seems to benefit the animal.

Summer heat is hard on a rabbit; they are more tolerant of colder weather. Older bucks have been known to go sterile in high temperatures, resulting in a lot of money spent on feed and no income from fryers. Keeping back some young replacement stock in January to be ready to breed in the summer months helps. We had one enterprising friend who moved her bucks into an air conditioned room, but she found that rabbit hair kept clogging up the cooling unit.

Cleaning the rabbitry can be a nightmare or a paying proposition, depending on your management. It still amazes me how many of those little round pellets a rabbit can produce, and when there are eight or nine fryers in the cage, the mountain just seems to grow and grow. Fortunately, rabbit manure is a commercial enterprise in itself. Gardeners love it, or it can be the basis for a commercial worm farm.

From our first year, local gardeners would show up at the rabbitry, shovel in hand, offering to clean the place for the manure. We tried this a couple of times, but found that it didn't really work out. The does were upset by strangers banging around in their house, and usually people weren't particularly careful about our equipment or the mess they left behind. A fellow rabbit raiser solved the problem by removing the manure to the back of the building and letting people load up feed sacks at a dollar or two a sack.

Being strapped for time with other livestock to care for, we decided to pursue a different route, and Mike's worm farm was born. The simple addition of a few thousand worms into the manure has kept the build-up under the cages to almost nothing and there is no problem with ammonia or odors. And as an added bonus, he has gardeners and fishermen lining up all spring and summer for the little critters. We still clean out, but only once a year for our own gardening purposes.

Rabbits can be a paying proposition with little more input than an hour or two a day for even a large rabbitry of 50 to 100 does. With proper management, a steady supply of fryers will not only pay the feed bill, but will also produce a regular income and even some excess meat for the freezer.

To appreciate the productivity of rabbits, consider this comparison: A 1,000 pound cow will produce one 500 pound calf per year. In contrast, one doe producing six litters of eight kits can produce 200 to 240 pounds of live weight in a year. So one hundred 10-pound does (that is, 1,000 pounds of rabbits) will produce 24,000 pounds of live weight per year, compared to the cow's 500 pounds.

A wide variety of marketing tactics can be employed with the enterprise, and even the waste products have a commercial value. The disposition of the rabbit is such that young children can help with the rabbit chores, and handling the rabbit requires no expensive equipment, like squeeze chutes or corrals. Literature is widely available, often at a nominal cost. And best of all, although the rabbit is very hardy, if a doe does die, the loss will not put you out of business, as she can be replaced for less than the price of a movie. Is it any wonder that the rabbit is the animal of choice for so many homesteaders across the country?

For more information

Mail-order catalogs carry a variety of rabbit-raising equipment and reading material. Listed below are some of the catalogs we have used or which have come highly recommended by fellow raisers. Prices vary with each catalog, so be sure to comparison shop.

Catalogs

Bass Equipment Company, P.O. Box 352, Monett, MO 65708. Midwest: (800) 798-0150. West Coast: (800) 369-7518. Fax: (417) 235-4312

Da-Mar's Equipment Company, 14468 Industrial Pkwy., South Beloit, IL 61080. (800) 95-BUNNY

Jeffers, P.O. Box 948, West Plains, MO 65775. (800) 533-3377. Fax: (417) 256-1550

K.D. Cage & Supply Co., 1820 S. CO 850 E., Newcastle, IN 47362. (800) 265-5113

Klubertanz Equipment Co., Inc., 1165 Highway 73, Edgerton, WI 53534. Orders: (800) 237-3899. Customer Service: (608) 884-9481

Morton Jones, P.O. Box 123, Ramona, CA 92065. (800) 443-5769

Safeguard Products, Inc., P.O. Box 8, New Holland, PA 17557. (800) 433-1819. Fax: (717) 355-2505

Reading material

The American Rabbit Breeders Association, Inc. Official Guidebook

Cash Markets for Rabbits, by Jack Messner

Domestic Rabbits, Voice of the American Rabbit Breeder's Association, Inc. Available to members of the ARBA. Membership is $15 per year for a single membership and includes a subscription to the magazine. Contact Glen Carr, Secretary, Box 426, Bloomington, IL 61702.

Domestic Rabbit Guide, an ARBA Publication

How to Start a Commercial Rabbitry, by Paul Mannell

Modern Commercial Rabbit Farming, by Jack Messner

Raising Rabbits the Modern Way, by Robert Bennet

Rabbit Production, by Peter R. Cheeke, Ph.D., Nephi M. Patton, D.V.M., Ph.D., Steven D. Lukefahr, Ph.D., and James I. McNitt, Ph.D.

All of these publications are listed in most of the catalogs we have mentioned here, with prices ranging from $2 to $26.95. Excellent information is also available from your local county extension agent or state university agricultural department, often free of charge. Δ

This family started a used bookstore for under $2,000

By Mary Kenyon

It only took 12 months of searching for a social work job for my husband, David, to consider the possibility of starting up a small business. His college degree and almost 10 years of experience working with clients proved to be of little value in his job search. After months of promising interviews, depressing rejections, and more wear to David's lone blue suit than in the 16 years since our wedding day, we were just about at the end of our rope.

It was typical of us to take 12 months to decide the direction our lives would take. In our 1979 wedding memory book, we promised each other to remain in our own little world, apart from society's rat race. Our dreams of owning acres of land, visiting Alaska, homeschooling our children, and running a small business were just that—dreams. Our oldest child was 12 years old before we finally tried homeschooling, and we've been enjoying home education for three years now. So, although the springboard to starting a small business was unemployment, the seeds of this venture were planted long ago.

Choosing a business

Why a used bookstore? The books and articles that advise potential entrepreneurs always suggest that you get involved with a business you can really love and that fills an obvious need. I'd been writing articles about what I knew and loved for years: articles about parenting, homeschooling, and saving money. Our bulging shelves of books attested to the fact that we were book lovers. And as homeschoolers and avid readers, we knew there was a need for a source of good quality used books. In our search for small busi-

ness opportunities, we also considered how our children could become involved, as part of their education. Pricing books, searching for books, and putting books onto a computer mailing list were duties we knew could be shared by our two older children.

Incidentally, an excellent reference book for those wishing to start a used bookstore is <u>Complete Guide to Starting a Used Book-Store</u>, 2nd edition, by Dale L. Gilbert, Upstart Publishing Co., 1986.

The initial investment

One of the most important factors in our choice of a business was the initial investment. The start-up costs had to be minimal. With no savings, no credit, and no rich investors up our sleeve, we had to consider borrowing a minimal amount from a generous relative. A business consultant we were working with was aghast at the $2000 amount we were starting with, but he didn't understand he was working with two expert penny-pinchers. He expected empty shelves and a hole-in-the-wall decor, but we surprised him with a starting stock of over 2000 books and a pleasant, clean atmosphere on opening day. Never mind that we bor-

rowed our children's prize doll house and colorful Noah's ark wall hanging to decorate the children's book area. Never mind that the beautiful pictures of children and adults reading that adorned our walls came from garage sales and helpful relatives. We strove for a comfortable atmosphere, and we succeeded.

Choosing the books

Our initial stock of books came from several sources. We advertised in a free weekly newspaper and by posting signs on a bulletin board at a local discount store. We were looking for good, clean used books, but at that time weren't aware of what would sell the best. Our gut feeling was that our homeschooling customers, whom we planned to reach through our mailing list, would be interested in educational books, classics, juvenile series books (such as the Nancy Drews and Happy Hollisters), and older adult fiction. We invested heavily in these, as well as collections of adult paperbacks and teen paperbacks. We bought private collections for as much as $100 and came away with boxes of books from garage sales that averaged 10¢ each. We visited thrift stores, but our sense of what would sell wasn't honed yet, and we came away with too many books that were just old, not valuable or collectible. We have read dozens of price guides and researched collectible books since then and have a much better idea of what a book is worth. The private collections netted some losers, too, in Book Club books from the 70s and 80s. All told, we spent approximately $700 of our money on books. I even sacrificed 200 of our own books for opening inventory, figuring that within a few years I could build up our collection again.

We continue to haunt thrift stores, garage sales, and library book sales for treasures, but now we know what we are looking for. Our customers bring in books, too, for cash or credit. In general, we give more in credit than in cash. We keep a running log on how much credit our customers have. Because we are a family store, and because we have targeted a specific customer base for our mailing list, we are constantly looking for certain books: newer adult non-fiction, older readers, pre-1960 juvenile series books, and cookbooks. We quickly found out we needed to beef up our selection of westerns, science fiction, and mysteries. The Book Club books and worn paperbacks were soon transferred to a 25¢ sale table.

Shelving

Shelving was another major expense. The few shelves we were finding at auctions just weren't going to be enough, and we wanted some kind of uniformity in the shelving of our store. My husband and two of my brothers-in-law spent several days building shelving and attaching it to the walls of the building we had rented. These homemade shelves would house all our adult books except the collector's books. We used various sizes and shapes of shelves in the children's area, including two shelves that came from our home. We were lucky to have run across a clearance sale on 72" white shelving at a local discount store which currently holds our best selection of juvenile books. Shelving took another $600 of our start-up money.

After purchasing a secondhand adding machine, receipt books, pricing stickers, and other office supplies, we were ready to roll.

Atmosphere

Our goal was to have a comfortable atmosphere for our customers to relax in and read. The building we rented isn't fancy, but it has a low rent, is close to a grocery store, and faces a small park and a bridge over a dam. The traffic over the bridge is a big plus, as we have many customers who come in because they saw our store as they drove over the bridge. The decor

of our store is attractive, yet simple. We bought a loveseat at an auction and set it up in the adult section with an end table full of interesting magazines next to it. The pictures on the wall follow the theme of reading. We expect to purchase additional pictures as we discover them at garage sales or auctions.

We designed the children's area to be family-friendly, with low-cost books on the bottom shelves for browsing and a few colorful toys for children to play with while their parents shop. We decorate the storefront window according to the season, and display a few interesting books in the window. During the summer months we set up our sale table out front, drawing customers who might not otherwise have stopped in.

Advertising

Advertising could be a major expense, but initially we didn't have the money to invest in advertising, so we made flyers on our computer and ran off hundreds of them at an office supply store for 2.6¢ each. We blitzed grocery store parking lots the week before we opened, and hung promotional posters in my sister's consignment store a block away from our bookstore. We sent out personal invitations to our grand opening to known readers in the area and packets of flyers and information to all the area schools to be put in the teachers' mailboxes. We offered Valu-cards to all

educators, including homeschoolers, which entitled them to 5% off all their purchases. We also sent out press releases to all the area newspapers. We have since had classified ads in the paper asking for books. We have found the best advertising to be by word of mouth from our satisfied customers. For our mailing list, we ran ads in several homeschooling magazines and newsletters offering our list of over 600 children's, adult's, and educational books for sale.

We opened up our store $70 in the red, not knowing what to expect for a day's sales. Thankfully, our first day netted over $100 in sales. Our mailing list is well received by the homeschoolers who have requested it, and several customers order over $50 worth of books at a time through the mail. Our diversification by selling through the mail to a target clientele will probably get us through the rough times we have at the store, like the weeks of over-90° weather in August when sales were down. The heat did not seem to affect the armchair shoppers in their air-conditioned homes.

My husband runs the store Monday through Saturday, while I manage the computer list at home, pricing books and updating our computer book list. When a particularly wonderful box of books is brought into the store, or when we discover a gem for 25¢ at a thrift store, I get chills up my spine. I love sifting though piles of books and discovering the treasures amidst the trash. Even our children have a new appreciation for good books.

Was it hard for my husband to change careers in mid-life? His answer: "Losing that job was the best thing that ever happened to me."

I don't know just how profitable our business will become, but I do know that we wouldn't mind doing this for the rest of our lives. And isn't that the way it should be?

(For a list of the Kenyon's more than 1,000 children's, adult's, and educational books, send three stamps to Once Upon a Time Family Books, P.O. Box 296, Manchester, IA 52057.) Δ

For headache, fever, or even rheumatism, relief is as near as the familiar willow plant

By Christopher Nyerges
Photo by Raul Castellano

Every now and then during one of my walks, someone will tell me that they have a headache. I peel off two slivers of bark from that ubiquitous plant of the streams, willow, and hand it to them. "Take two pieces of bark and call me in the morning," I tell them. Most people laugh when I say this, but some people don't get it, because they aren't familiar with willow or its history.

The inner bark of willow contains *salicin* and is **the original aspirin**. The bark of the younger shoots is strongest, and it is fairly easy to harvest. When steeped in water, willow tea is good for headaches, fevers, and even hay fever. Due to its strong **antiseptic** properties, the tea can also be used as a good mouthwash, or used externally on wounds. A willow wash is said to work wonders for **rheumatism** sufferers.

Willow plants are somewhat diverse in appearance. Some are small and bushy, and others are tall trees. Their **leaves** are nearly all **thin and lance-shaped**, and the plant is **always found along streams**. I have seen them at sea level and higher than 8,000 feet. They are found throughout North America. You might not know offhand how to identify a willow, but I can assure you that you have driven by one or hiked by one each time you were by a stream.

Willow plants are also a source of **food . . . sort of**. For example, the inner bark of willows has often been described as an emergency food, which is another way of saying that you'd probably never eat willow bark unless you were literally starving. As a practical matter, it is difficult to scrape out the inner part of the bark, and you generally end up eating all of the bark. Cooking renders it a bit more palatable. If dried and ground into flour and then cooked, it is even more palatable, though still in the realm of "emergency food." I have sampled this bark while backpacking with my brother and a friend. We rarely brought much food with us, preferring to catch fish and collect wild plants. We jokingly called our willow bark "wild spaghetti," which is a disservice to the reputation of spaghetti.

Euell Gibbons describes two species of Arctic willows (*Salix alexensis* and *S. pulchra*) whose tender young leaves can be eaten as a salad, or mixed into a salad. The flavor is said to be improved by cooking them first. Though I have never tried these species, I have nibbled on the wild willows of Southern California and would not include them in salads. They are a little bitter, but are improved by steaming or boiling.

In general, willow is a medicine tree, not a food source.

Willow is also one of the best sources of **craft material**. Whenever I collect willow, I go into the thickest patches, and I carefully cut only the branches I need with a sharp ratchet cutter. In all cases, when I return to those areas, I find the best and healthiest growths of new willow where I had done my careful pruning.

The author examines willow leaves.

I collect straight, dead pieces of willow branches for use in the primitive **bow-and-drill for fire-making**. Dried willow makes the best drill for fire-making. It is also an ideal wood to use for the baseplate in fire making—that's the flat piece of wood onto which the drill is spun.

Willows make interesting looking, lightweight **walking sticks**, and I have made many of these. Willow is a soft wood, so the walking sticks can easily be carved with faces or your name or anything that your abilities allow.

Long, straight willow stems are perhaps the single most useful plant in **basket weaving**. Willow is one of the most common traditional materials used in baskets, because it is light and easily worked, and it becomes flexible when soaked in water for about five minutes. Always scrape off the bark before using willow in your basketry projects.

I have seen **willow chairs and tables** at craft fairs, and there are craftsmen all over the U.S. who commonly use willow in these "backwoods" furnishings. They are very attractive. Though the Plains Indians used no chairs in their tipis, they did make a backrest out of willow. Using pencil-thick willow twigs, they lashed them horizontally onto two thicker vertical willow rods to create the backrest.

Because of willow's flexibility and common availability, I typically use willow whenever I make a **sweat lodge frame**. The sweat lodge frame is dome-shaped. Once the perimeter of the sweat lodge is drawn in the dirt, I dig holes into which I secure the willow poles. Then I bend them down and lash them together at the top to create the desired dome shape. The sweat lodge is covered with tarps, and very hot rocks are brought inside. Once everyone enters the lodge, it is closed up so that it is dark inside, and water is slowly poured onto the rocks, creating a high-temperature sauna or steam bath. This was and still is a tradition among Native American peo-

ples from North America through South America.

I have also used willow sticks for digging, and for the framework for a primitive **lean-to shelter**. It is a good plant to become familiar with, because it is so common and so versatile.

I have used long, dried willow stems as **pipes**, and—following in the tradition of Native Americans—I dry the bark of red willow and add it to my **smoking mixture**. I have sat outside my shelter made with a framework of willow, after sweating in my willow sweat lodge, and sat around the fire which was made with a willow drill, smoking some willow bark in my willow pipe. Willow is indeed a good friend.

(**Christopher Nyerges has been leading wild food outings since 1974. He is the author of Guide to Wild Foods and Testing Your Outdoor Survival Skills. A schedule of his outings appears in the *Talking Leaves Newsletter*, available from the School of Self-Reliance, Box 41834, Eagle Rock, CA 90041. The newsletter can also be viewed on-line at http://www.earthlink.net/~ nyerges/)** Δ

A BHM Writer's Profile: Albert H. Carlson

Albert H. Carlson was born February 13, 1959 in Chicago, Illinois, and grew up on Chicago's south side. In high school, he became interested in physics, computers, and electronics. The natural result was no clear idea as to a college major. His sister blindfolded him, gave him a pencil, and put a list of majors in front of him. He circled computer engineer, and that was that. His tuition was paid for by an Army ROTC four-year scholarship.

In college he married his high school sweetheart, Tina Anne Geeding. Tina was a Korean orphan adopted by a Chicago artist and his wife. They met as a result of a collision when Tina, who had a crush on Al, stepped in front of a very late Al in the school hallway. He never had a chance once she decided to keep him. In 1981 he graduated from the University of Illinois at Urbana with a bachelor in computer engineering. Two days later their first child, Ariana, was born; seven days later he was inducted into the US Army as a Second Lieutenant in Military Intelligence.

Following military service Al worked as an engineer and specialized in the design and production of integrated circuitry. His projects have included state-of-the-art designs in several markets, as well as project and engineering management.

Albert's family also increased during the intervening years, adding another daughter, Corine, and two sons, Robert and Alan. The youngest is now a teenager and the oldest is preparing to enter college as a physics major in the fall of 1999.

Al is now working on his Master's Degree in computer science, specializing in semantics and computational linguistics at the University of Idaho.

His interest in lightning began with a rush of lightning strikes around the Chicago area, where he still lives, in 1990. The lack of data available only served to make the subject more intriguing. He still studies the subject and closely follows advances in the field.

In addition to lightning, Al is involved in lapidary (rock and gem cutting, polishing, and setting), Sons of the American Revolution, Revolutionary Period Color Guards, fishing, fossil hunting, genealogy, and coin collecting. He is also beginning to develop land that he has purchased in Northern Idaho in preparation for retirement.

You can have a good career as a nurse practitioner no matter where you live

By Rodney L. Merrill

Diane Burlock is your run-of-the-mill modern day wonder woman. She's a wife and mother. She's working on a Master of Science degree in Community Health Administration and Wellness Promotion. And she's a full-time nurse practitioner. I didn't ask about her hobbies.

Burlock travels throughout the five regions of Northwest Territories and northern Alberta, Canada, providing primary health care services. Her story demonstrates how earning a living and getting an education are tightly interwoven; and how, today, you can do both, no matter how far into the backwoods you may live.

"If it were not for distance education," she says, "I might not be a nurse practitioner today. I'd be a Registered Nurse, but I probably wouldn't have finished the professional degree you need to become a practitioner. I certainly wouldn't be finishing my Master of Science degree."

What does a nurse practitioner do?

I asked Burlock to explain for *Backwoods Home* readers what the title "nurse practitioner" means. What does a person with this title do for a living?

"That depends," says Burlock. "Although all nurse practitioners are advanced nurses trained to be more independent in their assessment and treatment of patients, where you live can make a big difference in what you do."

She travels the far northern regions and northern Alberta, Canada, working at what Canadians call "nursing stations." These are clinics—much like a doctor's office—but they also have an emergency room, a chest and limb x-ray, blood analysis equipment for hemoglobin and white blood count, a formulary (pharmacy), and a two-bed hospital ward. Patients needing short-term observation or treatment (but not sick enough to warrant flying them out to a hospital) can stay overnight in this mini-hospital.

"Generally," she says, "where I work, nurse practitioners are the only on-site health officer. We obtain medical histories, perform physical examinations and general health assessments. From these, we diagnose health deficits and form a treatment plan."

These deficits often are common infections like a urinary tract infection, ear infection, or infected puncture wound, or the common communicable diseases like strep throat and pneumonia. But nurse practitioners also see and manage chronic conditions like asthma, high blood pressure, heart disease, and lung disease.

"There's the usual emergency room stuff, too," says Burlock, "the suturing of lacerations [stitching cuts and wounds] and removing embedded foreign objects like fish hooks and glass."

"In my situation," says Burlock, "I am often very isolated; and when elaborate testing is required, we have to fly the patient out to a larger facility. Consequently, we must rely more on our physical diagnosis and consultation-seeking skills than city practitioners who have ready access to sophisticated diagnostic equipment and tests." Based on the diagnosis, the nurse practitioner may prescribe medications and other treatments (such as physical therapy).

Nurse practitioners help prevent disease and promote health with screening, family planning services, prenatal monitoring, and care of pregnant women. The nursing station often sets aside morning hours for clinic and afternoon hours for health and wellness promotion.

Listening to Diane Burlock's story, I wondered, What about babies? If doctors and hospitals are so far away, do nurse practitioners deliver all the babies, too?

"We don't routinely deliver babies," says Burlock. She adds with a chuckle: "Though we do deliver a surprise package on occasion." What's *supposed* to happen and usually *does* happen, she says, is that the nurse practitioner assesses the risk involved in the pregnancy and schedules a "fly-out" to the nearest hospital two weeks to several weeks ahead. The exact timing depends on the risk assessment and the expected due date.

"In reality," Burlock says, "Women we've never seen before sometimes drag themselves into the nurse's station when they're already in labor. And even the best-monitored pregnancy can deliver early. So our *routine,* our protocol, is to schedule a fly-out, but we are capable and prepared to handle the occasional unanticipated delivery."

Whether or not they deliver the baby, rural nurse practitioners follow up with well baby checkups, childhood immunizations, growth monitoring, and general well child checkups. Later still, they monitor the adults these children grow into. They include considerable counseling and family health education as part of their health services.

Nurse practitioners also manage their patients' care by steering patients to related services and resources. When medical problems are beyond the scope of mid-level practice—even with outside consultation—the nurse practitioner refers patients to appropriate physicians and other specialists. They also arrange for patients requiring intensive care and long-term care to be transferred to appropriate tertiary facilities (like hospitals and skilled nursing homes).

Growth of the nurse practitioner field

The nurse practitioner movement began about 25 years ago as an advanced rural nursing specialty to provide primary health care services to under-served rural areas unable to attract primary care physicians. As nurse practitioners became more accepted, their practices began to spread to inner city clinics (also shunned by physicians). Nurse practitioners evolved as a service to the patients no one wanted.

In more recent times, the revolt against the growing price tag on health care has led government agencies and insurance programs to seek ways of transforming health care from a system dependent on acute care (high-tech hospitals and emergency rooms) to one more focused on primary care settings (offices, clinics, HMOs). The challenge is how to get medical care to more people and do it on a shrinking budget. As mid-level practitioners with mid-level salaries, willing to work where they are most needed, nurse practitioners have answered this need.

Today, nurse practitioners work in a variety of settings, both urban and rural, often as members of a health care team—in public health departments, rapid care clinics, group practice offices, corporate occupational health clinics, hospitals, and nursing homes—not as bedside nurses, but as mid-level primary care practitioners. Some set up their own private practices. Others join nurse practitioner group practices.

Their call for more independence from doctors, once automatically dismissed, is now being fostered through advanced training in clinical assessment and treatment skills and more liberal state licensing laws for nurse practitioners.

Licensing laws in many states still say that nurse practitioners must be "supervised" by a physician. Passage of these supervision laws was partly motivated by the sincere concern of lawmakers for protection of the public . . . but also by the suspicion that physicians would have revolted against the nurse practitioner movement without such a provision.

Diane Burlock

Rural nurse practitioners today are rendering the services once provided by physician general practitioners ("country doctors") before they were obliterated in the post-World War II rush to specialization, behemoth urban medical centers, and the abandonment of rural practice.

As Diane Burlock points out, "In remote areas, like the ones I visit—villages out in the Western Arctic with populations of 180, 300, 1800—it's a nurse practitioner or it's nobody. In

these situations, 'supervision' has a different meaning. A doctor might hold a clinic once or twice a month to see complicated patients, to look over your records, and discuss cases with you just to see how you're handling things. With our long, often severe, winter climate, sometimes 'supervision' amounts to consultation by phone or fax."

Can you make a decent living?

Burlock says a nurse practitioner in Canada gets "a base wage of about $54,000 Canadian, but there is extra pay for being on-call, for call-backs, for being in charge of a nursing station, which can bring the pay up to $75,000 to $85,000 Canadian per year." There are perks as well. Burlock says she is given a paid trip "out" at least once a year, a 50% rent subsidy, and additional hardship pay for working in such isolated areas.

It's harder to pin down nurse practitioner salaries in the United States. It depends who you listen to. The following figures were produced by the State of Washington and the U.S. Department of Health and Human Services. A nurse practitioner may start out anywhere from $30,000 to $40,000 per year. That works out to $14 to $20 per hour, depending on the salary and the exact number of hours worked per week. In the Pacific Northwest (where managed care is common) the average salary for nurse practitioners is $49,500 - $54,250 per year. The national average is $45,000 per year. Keep in mind that the average figure is diluted by a lot of entry-level salaries. Large salary increases come with each year of experience. Increases tend to level off at $60,000 - $70,000 per year. In certain specialties, though, advanced practice nurses can earn in excess of $100,000 per year.

That sounds like a lot . . . but imagine that you are a health care administrator with a primary care position open. A new doctor—with a dozen 25-year school loans at 8-10% compounded (non-tax-deductible) interest and a work life shortened by 11 to 15 years of post-secondary education and training—needs a six-figure income just to keep afloat. You can hire a nurse specialist to do the routine stuff (75-80% of the doctor's cases) for $50,000 - $75,000 a year. Those few nurse specialists who command $100,000 or more a year render the mid-level services of a physician specialist expecting to make $200,000 or more a year. Which would *you* hire?

And that is exactly what is happening. In both rural and urban settings, third-party payers are starting to balk at paying a doctor's fee for something that a less-costly mid-level practitioner can do. In HMOs, rural and inner city clinics, and other group practice settings, practices are being expanded by hiring nurse practitioners before hiring more physicians. As a result, mid-level practitioners are getting good salaries and greater respect. Career guidance experts are predicting persisting demand for nurse practitioners and other clinical specialty nurses; and this demand will allow them to continue getting $50,000 to $100,000 a year, depending on their specialty.

What is your status in the community?

"As the only on-site health officer, educator, counselor, referral agent, and public health officer," says Burlock, "your position is respected. The position is demanding and people know that. If you fulfill your duties to the best of your ability and act as a positive role model within the community, then you, as an individual, will be respected as well."

In talking with Diane Burlock and reading the notes she sent me, I get the impression that many rural patients and community leaders treat nurse practitioners with the kind of respect

once accorded to the general practice country doctor.

What are the training requirements?

Burlock says that the minimum requirement for nurse practitioner in Alberta or the Northwest Territories, Canada, is the R.N. license, the Bachelor of Nursing degree, and two or three years of rural nursing experience. New university graduates can take a fast-track intensive nurse practitioner course provided by the government and receive a subsidy *if* they pledge to serve two years' employment in the region which sponsors them through the course.

In the United States, the procedure for becoming a nurse practitioner is longer and usually requires more years of schooling. A nurse usually earns a B.S.N. (Bachelor of Science in Nursing) or B.N. (Bachelor of Nursing) and takes the Registered Nurse licensing examination. After three or more years of experience, s/he goes to graduate school for an M.S.N. (Master of Science in Nursing) or an M.N. (Master of Nursing) in a nurse practitioner specialty. This is the general idea. Specifics vary somewhat. Some people, for example, take their R.N. licensing exams before completing their Bachelor of Nursing degree. And requirements vary from one state to another.

Nurse practitioners may specialize in neonatal (premature birth) practice, pediatric and adolescent health, OB/GYN and women's health, geriatrics, family practice, psychiatric/mental health practice, and occupational health. Some advanced practice nurses may have different titles—such as Nurse-Midwife (labor and delivery) or Nurse Anesthetist (anesthesiology)—rather than nurse practitioner.

There are basically three routes to becoming a registered nurse today. Two-year colleges and vocational-technical schools offer an associate

degree in nursing which leads to "technical nursing" careers. Four year colleges usually offer the B.S.N. (Bachelor of Science in Nursing) or B.N. (Bachelor of Nursing) degree which leads to "professional careers" in nursing. Basically, "technical" nurse training focuses on direct patient care, whereas "professional" nurse training focuses more on the decision-making aspect of patient care and on managerial responsibility. Professional nurses tend to make more money and to have more opportunities for advancement into management or clinical specialty fields.

Another route to technical nursing careers is the hospital-based diploma program. I saved this one until last because there are advantages and disadvantages to this route. Hospital diploma programs exist because, during the nineteenth century, women were barred from most universities in the United States. Hospitals trained their own nurses by apprenticeship.

Rural areas are more desperate for nurses than metropolitan areas, and hospitals sometimes find it is easier to "grow their own" in a nurse training program than to recruit from the nearest university. Tuition is a lot more reasonable in hospital programs, too. Sometimes you can even get your training *free* in exchange for a promise to work in the area a certain period of time after graduation. The hospital-trained nurse gets a lot more direct patient contact and more practical, hands-on training than college programs can offer.

The main disadvantage to graduating from a hospital diploma program is that hospital-trained nurses tend to get pegged as hospital nurses. It may be harder to branch out into other fields with a hospital diploma than with a college degree in nursing. With hospitals downsizing, this could be a severe drawback. Still, don't despair if you are a hospital-trained nurse. It isn't hopeless. Read on.

Distance education opens new N.P. possibilities

The shortage of certain specialty nurses is stretching some rules and traditions. More colleges are offering "outreach" programs that allow hospital-trained nurses to demonstrate their knowledge for college credit. They then apply those credits toward their B.S.N. and complete their degrees-at-a-distance by satellite television courses, videotape, Internet courses by computer, and independent study.

That's what Diane Burlock did. She earned an R.N. through a hospital diploma program, then worked as a rural nurse for 12 years. When Burlock entered the Northwest Territories, she took a post-R.N. completion degree—the at-a-distance Bachelor of Nursing from Athabasca University—and became eligible to enter practice as a nurse practitioner.

Burlock is now making excellent progress toward a Master of Science (M.S.) degree through California College for Health Sciences. "If it were not for C.C.H.S. and its at-a-distance M.S. degree program," says Burlock, "I probably couldn't manage a Master's at all."

I asked Burlock what she saw as the benefits of studying at-a-distance as opposed to earning a degree by going to classes. "I can study when I have time," says Burlock, "and go at my pace, not according to some preset schedule. I can keep my job. The best part is, the California College of Health Sciences program allows me to schedule classes that are related to my current work assignments. They mesh. It's so much easier to learn new ideas when you can see the application in your daily work."

I asked her about the drawbacks to this approach. "For myself," Burlock says, "self-motivation can be difficult unless I work out a plan of action with definite steps. Many find that working on their own slows their progress, but I found that taking two courses at a time (rather than one) gave me the variety I needed to keep up the pace. I could not have gotten this far without the cooperation of my family. Many times, they have been a source of encouragement."

Diane Burlock is already a full-fledged nurse practitioner. She doesn't really *need* a Master of Science degree from California College for Health Sciences. So, I wondered, why is she working so hard to get it?

"There are many reasons," says Burlock. "Self-improvement, you know, to broaden my knowledge. But, also, because nurse practitioners—especially out away from it where I go—do a lot more than emergency and regular clinical care. I'm family life educator, health educator, counselor. (Luckily, nursing stations have recently started providing a professional social worker.) Anyway, you need many skills. The course content at C.C.H.S. directly supports my career and makes me a better nurse practitioner.

"Plus," she says, "the Master's degree gives me more opportunities. I can apply to the administrative relief positions. When I go to a one-nurse station, I can be left as Nurse-in-Charge. This means more responsibility; also a pay bonus. Luckily, I've found the content of my C.C.H.S. Master's-level courses directly helpful in these situations."

Except for her hospital-based R.N. credential, Diane Burlock has completed all of her education at-a-distance while living in a rural area, even while she has worked in remote and isolated outreach stations.

How remote is remote, you ask? "For six months of the year," says Burlock, "my principal means of transportation to work is snowshoe and snowmobile."

The primary care and specialty nursing shortage is worse in rural areas than in the city. Employers tend to be far less persnickety about your credentials coming from a big name school, or what study format you used to get them. If you've got the skills, you've got the job, and that's as it should be.

There once were many one-year non-degree nurse practitioner certification programs in the United States—for more experienced nurses—similar to the intensive program offered in Canada. There are only a few left today. In a bid for greater status, prestige, and independence, the nurse practitioner profession in the United States has pushed to increase higher educational requirements. Non-degree certification programs are fading and may disappear. Check with your state licensing agency to see if they provide alternate career pathways to experienced nurses.

In the end, you may get only as far as the B.S.N. by distance learning. You may have to leave town for your nurse practitioner Master's degree. But, as a rural nurse practitioner, the chances are extremely good that you'll be able to come back. Which means that men or women wanting to stay in the backwoods but desiring a good-paying, exciting, evolving—and admirable—career ought to look into becoming a nurse practitioner.

More information

National League for Nursing
Ten Columbus Circle
New York, NY 10019
1-800-669-1656
Internet: nlninform@nln.org

The NLN is the official accrediting agency for nursing programs in the United States, so they know if approved programs are near you. NLN also publishes many books on nursing, including an excellent introduction called Your Career in Nursing. Your library probably has it in the reference section.

P.S. Shortly after this article was written, Diane Burlock wrote me a note saying she had finished her M.S. degree. Congratulations, Diane. Δ

Consider small-scale hog production for delicious food and reliable income

By Rev. J.D. Hooker

Usually, when someone forms a mental image of a self-sufficient backwoods lifestyle, the idea of raising a few hogs forms part of the picture. Whether we're thinking about the hill folk of Appalachia, the mountain people of the West, or wherever, slabs of smoked bacon, home-cured hams, buckets of homegrown corn, and leftover slops seem to fit right into the picture.

Ever since the founding of Jamestown and Plymouth, the production of pork, both for good home eating and for marketing or trading purposes, has played a crucial role in the personal independence of many of America's rural people. Hogs possess an amazing ability to thrive under conditions where other livestock could not even survive, and they convert nearly any remotely edible waste into high quality meat. Without hogs, not very many southern folk, white or black, would have managed to survive the incredibly hard, lean years in the battered, beaten, and plundered South following our devastating Civil War. Prior to the enforced death-march of their "Long Walk" to the Oklahoma territory, part of the way in which the Cherokee peoples maintained their independence and increased their wealth was that every household raised at least a small swine herd for home butchering and for market.

Advantages of a small-scale operation

Some of you will have seen the ultra-modern factory-style swine production facilities that turn out several thousands of identical market hogs every year. The idea of attempting to compete with operations of such magnitude may seem impossible. However, you need to understand that the owners of these huge swine operations are virtually slaves to market factors and to their creditors. A single increase in feed costs, a drop in the market price, or a single otherwise-minor disease organism run amuck in their over-crowded pork factories can wipe out several years' worth of profits. The debt load carried by most such operations will often force the owners into bankruptcy after only one such incident, costing them the whole farm.

It's the small-scale pork producer, running between 100 and 500 hogs per year through the market, who might have an unfair advantage. Consider that selling about 110 hogs (no matter what the current price), for a 90%-plus profit will bring you about the same number of spendable dollars as selling 1000 hogs at the more usual 10% profit of the factory hog farm. Keeping a single good boar and five nice-quality sows, raising each litter to an optimum market weight of around 200 pounds per animal, and selling at the average market price will bring you an annual profit in the neighborhood of $13,500. Should the prices fluctuate upwards, you'd make even more income. And even if the market took a 50% nose dive, you'd still be able to realize about $6,750 that year (while a high percentage of factory-style pork producers would go bust). This might be an over-simplification, but you can see how the ultra-low-budget, small-time producer really is the one who has the edge.

Still, while it's potentially lucrative, even such small-scale swine raising isn't something that you'd want to jump into overnight. You'll need to do some homework and preparation before you begin.

Two types of hogs

The first step is to honestly appraise your own temperament and abilities, as well as the physical aspects of your country property. Then decide on the type of hog that you and your property are best fitted to produce. There are many breeds and varieties, and they fall into two major divisions.

First you have the "confinement" type of hogs, like the Duroc, Hampshire, and Yorkshire, that can do well in crowded conditions. They breed, bear, and fatten nicely while fenced and sheltered in a relatively small area. However, they require daily care, feeding, water, etc. These are possibly the ideal swine for the smaller farm or homestead, not requiring much acreage to bring in a reliable, steady income.

In the other major division are breeds like the Tamworth and Holstein (yes, there are Holstein hogs as well as Holstein cattle). These are capable of producing equally as well as the confinement breeds, while ranging loose in large fenced pastures or woodlots. These breeds require the absolute minimum of care, thriving and fattening quite well on grasses, acorns, roots, and such, which they can forage on their own. They require a much larger homestead acreage for successful production.

None of the confinement breeds do well when attempts are made to raise them under forage-type conditions. Forage-type hogs are equally unsuited for raising under confinement type systems. So this is something that you'll need to decide on before you set up your operation.

Strong and tight

Next you'll need to make a decision regarding what sort of facilities you'll need: shelter, fencing, farrowing huts, etc. This depends a lot on which type of hog you decide to raise. But keep in mind that *any structure, for any type of hog, has to be both strong and tight.* An adult hog is an immensely powerful animal, easily capable of breaking through poorly maintained fences or collapsing weak housing. And young pigs and shoats seem to delight in squirming out through the smallest break in any fencing or farrowing house. So whether you opt for wire field fencing or some type of wooden fence, and whatever sort of shelter seems right for your situation, make sure that your original installation is both strong and tight, and then make certain that it stays that way.

Feeding

It's in feeding the hogs where you'll find that the smaller producer has the edge over the factory farmer. It's the relatively high cost of commercial feed that forces these pork factories to work on such a high-volume, low-profit margin system. Sure, these high-dollar rations will normally bring their hogs to market weight much faster than less expensive feeds. But due to the feed costs involved, they usually need to produce *ten* market animals to match the profit realized by lower-volume breeders with a *single* marketable porker.

Many small-scale producers of forage-type hogs find that moving their herd three times a year works out the best for them. Their hogs spend the spring and early summer on mixed grass pasture; the late summer, fall, and sometimes early winter in the woodlot; and the largest share of the winter in the corn, bean, sorghum, or beet field that was planted for them, and left unharvested.

With our own Spot, Poland China, and Yorkshire confinement hogs, and our small operation, we've come up with a feed system that works great for us. We plant a mixture of corn, beans, and sorghum all together. The entire plants—cornstalks, beanstalks, and all—are harvested for feed. During the summer, we also feed a lot of fresh-mown hay or grass, saving the last cutting for winter hay. Also, every sort of garden waste, potato peels, damaged and spoilt tomatoes, wormy or bad apples, etc., is thrown to the hogs. We also feed them thoroughly cooked fish scraps and butchering wastes. To supplement the feed we produce ourselves, we've also found a bakery outlet store that will sell us a pickup load of stale bread, doughnuts, and other out-dated bakery products once a week or so, for next to nothing. This is a really worthwhile super-inexpensive addition for us, and they are happy to receive even a token

payment for this stuff, rather than paying to haul it to the dump.

Such mutually beneficial arrangements are well worth taking the time to find. Other small-scale breeders of confinement-type hogs have found restaurants, doughnut shops, produce wholesalers, supermarkets, farmer's markets, and other businesses whose owners have been happy to save their leftovers, damaged and imperfect produce, etc., for them in return for a token payment. Sometimes establishing such arrangements ends up being the determining factor in deciding the number of hogs your enterprise can support.

Buying your first hogs

As to the animals themselves, once you've determined whether you will be raising confinement- or forage-type swine, you'll need to settle on the particular breed (or breeds) you prefer. There are so many swine breeds (some common, others relatively rare) that this becomes mostly a matter of personal preference. Remember, though, that if there are other swine producers in your area, there will always be some demand for quality breeding stock, so it may be wise to stick with the breeds most popular in your area.

You'll need to select your own original breeding stock as carefully as possible. Check into the records of the producers you purchase your first stock from: litter size and survival rates, early weaning abilities, number of days to marketable weight, feed conversion rates, and related factors are all extremely important. Normally you'll pay quite a bit more for stock with a high production background, but it's well worth the extra cost.

Once our hog shelters, fencing, etc., were ready, and a steady and inexpensive feed supply assured, we were ready to buy our first hogs. Just-weaned shoats (young hogs)—one boar and four or five gilts (young female hogs)—is usually the best option. Starting out with these small, young animals allowed us to become thoroughly familiar with their care while they were still small and easily managed. We also found that by hand-raising our breeding stock like family pets, we ended up with calm, easily managed adult breeders. As we've continued our operation, all of the swine selected as eventual breeding stock has been handled in the same manner.

This is a method which I recommend highly in any sort of livestock raising endeavor. There will always be unexpected developments, whether it's a difficult birth or a thousand-pound boar on the loose. When these things happen, it's so much simpler and safer to deal with an affectionate beast, rather than an indifferent or belligerent one, that I think it would be foolhardy to use any other method.

Caring for your hogs

You'll need to use wire cutters (diagonal cutters seem to work best) to nip off the razor-sharp needle teeth of newborn piglets, to keep them from injuring their dam while suckling. Sometimes I have tried skipping this step with animals I think I might be keeping for breeders. This is because in our area, we frequently have trouble with feralized dogs attacking livestock. So far, though, I've had pretty poor results, as the mothers usually find those needle teeth too painful. The few successes that I have had, though, have proved that swine with tusks intact can hold off dog attacks.

It's necessary to castrate the young male shoats which you don't intend to keep or sell as breeders. This is a simple, relatively painless procedure, done while the animals are still small. I've found the best tool for this to be a finely-honed sheepsfoot pocket knife blade. I have read directions for attempting this procedure on your own, but I really wouldn't recommend attempting this by yourself on the first try. However, after watching someone

else, whether a veterinarian or an experienced hog farmer, cut a couple of shoats, you'll be able to do it yourself.

Hogs also have a few other needs. Chief among these is plenty of water. In fact, *fresh drinking water is the most important part of a pig's diet.*

They'll also need some way of keeping cool in the summer. Whether that would involve providing some sort of shade, a mud wallow or sprinkler, a creek or ditch flowing through your pasture or woodlot, or some electric fans in the barn, will depend upon your particular circumstances. Too much heat can kill a hog mighty quickly, so you'll need to come up with something.

Winter brings a different set of considerations. Adult hogs that aren't kept in seriously over-crowded conditions can stand an awful lot of severe cold, without any ill effects. *But, drafts can kill them off pretty quickly when they sleep.* Even forage-type hogs need someplace to curl up out of the wind when they sleep. You'll also find that any sort of hog shelter for winter use must either have a dirt floor, where the animals can scoop out a nice comfy nesting hole, or you'll need to furnish a plentiful supply of straw, sawdust, leaves, or other *dry* bedding, at all times.

While forage-type sows usually manage to care for their offspring just fine through weaning, you'll normally find that confinement breeds need a little extra care in this regard. That's because the adult sow can handle cold temperatures, but not heat, so she's constantly standing up, moving around, repositioning herself, and flopping back down in order to remain relatively cool and comfortable. However, *her offspring need to be kept warm all of the time*, and even a minor cooling off can kill them. There is also the constant danger of the sow crushing some of her offspring when she plops back down. There is a simple remedy: just hang an inexpensive heat lamp over one corner of the far-

rowing pen or hut. This supplies a steady source of warmth for the piglets. The small animals will tend to congregate under this heat lamp whenever they're not busy feeding off the sow, while their dam will avoid the discomfort of this added heat. That avoids the danger of her inadvertently crushing the infants.

Marketing

After a while, you'll learn to judge by eye just when your hogs reach the optimum market weight. After that, your only remaining difficulty is in loading the animals into an enclosed truck or trailer and hauling them to market. I've heard of a whole slew of methods for loading these generally reluctant creatures for hauling, and most of them seem to work well enough. But the only means of loading hogs into my truck that I've found satisfactory involves nothing more than a solid ramp with fenced sides and a good, hard-working dog.

If all of this sounds like a lot of hard work, remember that it's not some sort of easy get-rich-quick scheme, but just one method for independent-minded rural folks to provide themselves with a decent, steady, reliable income. It's not nearly as much hard work as all this might sound like, either, but it does require a steady daily routine of care and maintenance. So why not look into your own circumstances and see if this truly traditional slice of American independence can add to your own situation.

And remember the added bonus of providing your own succulent pork roasts, smoked hams, etc., practically *for free* as a side benefit of this profitable endeavor. That served as the final determining factor for us, when we first considered raising swine for profit. We feel as if this result alone, even apart from the income we've earned, has been well worth the effort. I strongly recommend small-scale pork production as one of the ideal backwoods enterprises. Δ

Felting is an ancient art that's still useful today

By Anita Evangelista

There's probably no simpler, more efficient method of turning wool into useful products than felting. Known from samples dating from as early as 6400 B.C., the process hasn't changed in the slightest since those primitive days.

At its best, a section of carefully handled felt can provide amazing warmth even when wet, and is remarkably durable, pliable, and strong. Felt is the ideal boot-liner during the cold of winter, an excellent wind-proof vest material, and is easy to cut and shape into slippers, mittens, handbags, hats, blankets, rugs, and horse saddle pads.

At its simplest, making felt requires nothing more than wool, soap, heat, and movement. Quality felt can be made at home, by hand, with a minimum of tools—most of which are commonly found wherever homesteaders reside. It's highly cost-effective (that is, cheap), and an excellent use of time (fun). Even small children can make usable felt swatches.

Felting is...

Felting takes place in wool nearly spontaneously. It can happen so quickly that most beginning woolworkers accidentally felt a certain quantity of wool in the process of washing it in preparation for spinning. The felted condition comes about in sheep's wool because of the unique "scales" present on individual fibers. When exposed to heat, moisture, and friction, the scales open, hook together, and bind tightly as the wool shrinks.

Some breeds of sheep produce wool that has excellent felting qualities, such as Romneys, Shetlands, Merinos, Karakuls, and Jacobs. While the wool

1. The completed stack of roughly 4"x4" pieces of carded wool.

of more common breeds, such as commercial Dorsets and Suffolks, isn't quite as easy to work with, it still felts sufficiently to make useable projects. Other types of animals, such as camels, llamas, and cashmere goats, produce hair and wool with some felting qualities. A few favorite spinning fibers, like dog or cat hair, angora rabbit, flax, or cotton, simply will *not*

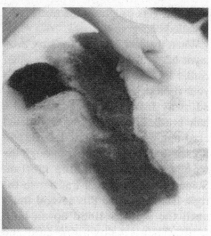

2. Laying out squares of carded wool to form the first layer.

felt—unless they are used in conjunction with a quantity of sheep's wool.

Equipment/preparations

It's possible to make exquisite felt with the most basic of supplies. That's one of the traits that undoubtedly endeared felt to earlier civilizations.

You'll need:

1. Wool. Two pounds of clean fleece will be more than enough to produce a thick square of felt. (I recently made a rectangle 16"x22"x$1/4$" thick, which weighed only seven ounces.) Any colors can be used, alone or in combination. The amount of wool needed to produce a specific amount of felt will vary with the final thickness of the intended piece, its size, and the type of wool used—something best determined by working experience with your fleeces.

2. Teasing comb, or hand cards, or drum carder. These tools are used to *card*, or fluff and lighten the wool, and to make it fairly uniform. If you

3. Pouring hot, soapy water over the first two layers.

only wish to work with a small amount of wool for a first experience of felting, you can successfully use dog "flicker" brushes—rectangular flat brushes with bent wire teeth. With a super-clean open fleece, which can be separated lightly by hand alone, carding might not be necessary. But for the first few feltings, carding makes the result more predictable and easier to bring to completion.

3. Soap and water. Homemade lye soaps make excellent felt, if you have any available. I've used "Dawn" dish detergent successfully, as well as a combination of "Dawn" and other dish detergents. Some folks use a plant

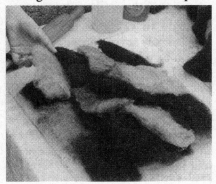

4. The third and fourth layers are laid over the first two layers. Notice the overlapping pattern.

mister or a laundry sprinkler to make handling the soap solution easier.

4. Washboard or dowel (broom handle, rolling pin, etc). These tools are used for the final agitation of the felt process, called *fulling*.

5. Towels, waterproof flat area, and hot water. A sturdy workplace (even a linoleum floor, or a table shielded with a plastic cover) is a boon—and you'll need quick access to hot-to-the-touch water and towels for sopping up excess liquid.

Preparing to felt

Preparation for felting means carding up a half to a full pound of wool, separating the carded fibers into flattened sections of about four inches square (make about a hundred of these), heating up a quart of water, adding a half-cup of soap to it, laying down a towel or two on your work area, and assembling the carded wool and water within easy reach.

How to card: Hold one of the hand cards or flicker brushes in your left hand, the handle in your palm and the rectangular brush surface lying against your wrist and forearm. This may feel awkward at first, but it will become very natural after a few uses. Now, using your right hand, place a small quantity of wool against the teeth of the brush, drawing the wool slightly so that it gets caught in the teeth. This is called *charging the card*.

When the card has a thin, fairly even layer of wool on it, pick up the other carder in your right hand. Hold this in your right palm with the brush extended away from you, as you would a hair brush. Now bring the right-hand card against the left-hand card, and lightly draw the right card through the wool in an easy combing motion. Some of the wool will transfer to the right-hand card. Do this several times until the wool is lined up on both cards. Then set down one card and gently remove the wool from the other card by rolling it from one end (it will

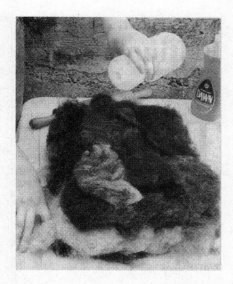

5. Pouring hot, soapy water over the final layer of squares

roll easier from one side than the other).

This small, fluffed piece of wool is your first carded piece. Continue to make these, allowing yourself plenty of time.

The process

There are a couple of things to keep in mind as you begin to work the wool: the overlapping nature of the scales on individual fibers, and the importance of working in the same direction (which will be clear in a

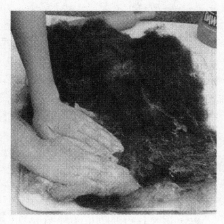

6. Pressing and gently rubbing the squares. Notice the soap bubbles beginning to rise around the fingers.

7. After a few minutes of rubbing, the wool has flattened and is beginning to stick together. Note the dirty, soapy runoff, which is a good reason for doing this project outdoors.

moment). Determine how large you would like this piece of felt to be: I would suggest somewhere around 20" by 20"—a random size that's easy to work with. Bear in mind that this sample will shrink a little (10 to 25%) in the felting, so you should make your work larger than you want the finished piece to be.

First, begin to lay down the roughly four-inch-square pieces of wool in

8. Fulling the new felt. The well-rubbed rectangle of felt is rolled onto the rolling pin and worked back and forth several times.

rows, starting at the lower-left-hand corner of your work area. Each piece should overlap the previous one by 1/4" to 1/2". When you reach the lower-right-hand corner of your predetermined-size piece, move up and begin a second row. Each square in the second row should overlap the first row, as well as the squares beside it. Continue making overlapping rows until you complete the size sample you wish. In our example, you should have covered an area roughly 20" by 20".

Now cover this first layer with a second layer that is placed in the opposite direction. That is, instead of moving left to right (west to east), place the squares from the furthest upper edge to the closest lower edge (north to south). Remember to overlap each square.

After finishing the second layer, take your hot soapy water and sprinkle liberally onto the felt-to-be. Now add a third layer in the same order as the first; and a fourth layer as you did the second. Wet again. If you have more wool squares, continue making layers,

alternating the direction of each layer. Sprinkle between every two layers.

When you've finished sprinkling the final top layer, you're ready to begin the actual felting. Carefully, using the palms of both hands held flat, begin to press and then rub the wool. There may be a tendency for some fibers to adhere to your hands at first, but the soap will eventually discourage that. Rub gently at first, in a circular pattern, always moving your hands in the same direction over a particular section of wool. This helps the minute wool scales to cling tenaciously. If you reverse rubbing directions, it will discourage that clinging action.

After a few minutes of pressing and rubbing, soapy water will work its way up through the wool and out the sides. Pause and use your towels as needed. If the fleece is clean, the water will be, too. Otherwise, it'll be a dirty gray shade. If the wool isn't thoroughly wet, add a few more sprinkles of hot soapy water.

Continue to rub with firm, regular strokes. Carefully turn the sample over after a few minutes, reversing sides now and then. Different wools take differing amounts of time to felt. About 20 to 30 minutes should be plenty of rubbing. The sample will become noticeably firmer and more compact as you work.

When a pinch of the topmost layer resists being pulled upward, the felting is done.

Now roll this still-damp square around the dowel or rolling pin. Then

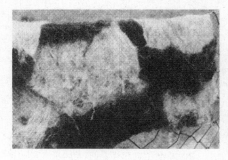

9. The completed piece of felt, still quite wet, hanging over a fence to dry in the shade.

10. A section of the felt has been cut out of the rectangle to line this slipper.

begin to roll the piece back and forth on a firm surface. This is the *fulling* process. Alternatively, you can gently fold your sample, exposing only a three- or four-inch area, and rub this on a washboard surface. Roll or rub for a few minutes. Unroll and turn the sample piece a quarter-turn, then re-roll on the dowel. Roll it (or rub it on the washboard). Do this from each side of the piece, so that it is worked in all directions. Fulling is now completed.

When you unroll this piece for the final time, you are looking at a section of completed felt. Rinse it in warm water, then in cool water to which you've added a dash of apple cider vinegar. Place it on a clean, dry towel to air dry, or you can pin it to a wooden frame to dry slightly stretched. You can also give this piece a "fleecy" surface by brushing it lightly in one direction after it has dried a little.

Finally...

The uses for felt are legion, particularly when you have a few sample-size pieces around. How about car seat covers? A baby blanket? Coat liners? Hats?

Some projects will require sewing the felt, of course, so here are a few thoughts on that: Felt can be loose or tight in structure, and that will affect its sewing characteristics. Commercial felt, for example, is very tight, and it will take hand- or machine-sewing, performing very much like leather. Home-made felt *can* be tight enough to sew that way, but if it's too loose, your sewing thread might pull out. If that's a problem, you can start by sewing a line of stitching parallel to the edge of the piece to make the felt more stable at the edge. You can sew pieces together so your thread goes inside the edge stitching. With or without the edge stitching, you might want to use an overhand stitch on pieces that are edge-butted or over-lapped. You might want to use heavy thread. Experiment with different batches of your own felt to see how they take sewing.

Pieces of compact felt can also be glued together. The glued areas won't be as soft as the rest, though, so don't use glue where that would matter (under the sole of your foot in a boot liner, for example).

Try felting different materials into your wool: mohair, plant fibers, or various designs of differently-colored wool on the outside layers. There is even a trend in textile arts to encompass exotic felted displays, which combine fancy textures, colors, and images.

For those with an artistic bent, this most-common of fibers around the shepherd's homestead can become an effective medium for personal expression. The November/December 1979 issue of *Fiber Arts* (50 College Avenue, Asheville, NC 28801, $4) is devoted to felt-making and includes many examples of felt-as-fine-art. And be sure to read about Margaret Boos' wonderful hats on another page in this issue of *Backwoods Home Magazine*.

From ancient times into the modern world, sheep and their products have offered more than they take. Felt is just one more part of this ongoing mutually-beneficial relationship. Δ

Simplify, save, grow food, and trade and you too can afford to work for yourself

By Dynah Geissal

Making a living in the woods is definitely not an easy task. It requires being constantly on the alert for possibilities. For me, though, there is no other option. I have chosen my way of life and cannot trade it for a job in town even if it would mean more financial security. I spend almost all my time here on my homestead, and still there is never enough time to get everything done.

Neighbors who commute to work leave in the dark and come home in the dark for a good part of the year. They are unable to do as much as they would like to do for themselves, because there is no time. Consequently, they need to buy most everything, and so they always need more money. Add to that the beating their vehicles take on our non-maintained mountain road. It is extremely stressful and frustrating for them, but it is a cycle that is hard to break out of.

To make ends meet without having a "real" job takes ingenuity and a basic attitude change. Leave behind the thinking that asks "what can I buy?" or "whom can I hire?" to solve a certain problem. Instead, make it a habit to brainstorm, experiment, and tinker, or just do the manual labor it takes to get the job done. If you work in town in order to hire someone to work with machinery at your home, who is having the better day? There can be an almost zen-like quality to work that is boring, tedious, and/or labor-intensive that can add more to the spirit than just the completion of the task.

Try to maintain the attitude that you can do whatever needs doing, and set about finding a method to do it. When you have to, ask a neighbor for help.

It's beneficial, of course, to have a partner, and in most cases to eliminate gender roles. Most successful homesteads consist of partners who share the work in most tasks and who each become proficient at whatever needs doing. It is absolutely vital in the case of sickness or injury of one person that the other knows how to run the farm.

Simplify and save

Saving money is about the same as making money, and the best way to do that is to simplify. How much do you really need? The answer is different for different people. Only you can answer this for yourself.

As an example, I think of our power situation. When we bought our land, we thought we would buy a generator to supply our power. A big enough generator could give us plenty of power, so that we would live pretty much as we did "on the grid." Money for such a generator was never available, though, and now we find that we are quite happy with lights and a radio supplied by sun and wind. In the beginning, we had only kerosene lamps, and that was OK for a while. As the nights got longer, however, the lamps seemed severely limiting, and our eyes were feeling the strain.

When we got our solar panel, we were able to have two lights, and that was wonderfully liberating. Our nights are so long in the late fall and early winter that we had hated having to huddle around our little lamps for five hours every evening. Now we have four lights, and we feel much richer. To us, light is extremely important for reading, cooking, and other evening projects, and in this case less was not better for us.

So don't be a martyr and give up things you really love. Just consider that some things maybe aren't so important or maybe are just habits that you could be happy without.

Raise extra and sell it

One way to bring in income without changing your life is simply to raise more than you need and sell it. For example, we need two pigs a year for meat, so we raise four and sell two. That gives us our pork for free. Everything you raise should pay for itself. That's a goal, of course, and it probably won't be achieved right away. Do more of what you already do and sell the surplus. Cut your ten cords of wood and then cut ten more to sell.

Some things work better than others, and there's no way to know which until you try. I can't raise enough chickens to fully supply the market (I raise 800 over the course of a year), yet selling rabbits is very difficult. I always seem to have a surplus. I think rabbits are way easier to raise and are very delicious, but there is a prejudice against eating "bunnies."

Where we live is open range, so getting fences up was very important to us. The range cattle were topping the tree seedlings, destroying the creek bank, and so severely overgrazing the meadow that exotics were taking over. It took six weeks to fence our lower 15 acres, but our only expenses were the nails and the fuel for the chainsaw. We built a jack leg fence, which is beautiful, functional, and cheap. Our nearest neighbor hired us to work on her fence when she saw ours. Every bit of work we can get up here is really appreciated, and helping Sarah was perfect.

Many ways to save

Now I'd like to talk about specifics. Let's start with your **vehicle**. It is vital to have one that can be used for just about everything, which generally means a pickup truck. Having more than one is a luxury we cannot afford. I can't imagine having to license, insure, and maintain a second vehicle. Remember that every dollar you spend is one more you have to earn. You must be able to be your own mechanic. Basically, that means you need an older vehicle. Ours is a '77 Dodge. It's very straightforward, and parts are cheap. (Example: $35 for an alternator.) When our transmission went out, we replaced it for $150. A clutch is $30. A breakdown is not fun, of

course, but with this kind of vehicle, it doesn't threaten our financial stability.

Next is **fuel**. If you live in the woods, you can probably get all the wood you need for heating, cooking, and hot water. You say propane is more convenient? I say, why pay someone else to provide your fuel? It would mean you would have to earn more money to pay someone when you could be working for yourself. Using wood becomes such a part of life that it doesn't seem at all inconvenient to me. It's just part of what I do, like brushing my teeth or feeding the livestock.

Grow your own food—at least as much as you can. We buy grains, beans, oil, and coffee. That's about it. Don't expect to achieve food self sufficiency in one year, but keep working toward it.

Become familiar with **herbs** and make your own medicines. Before I lived in the woods, I found it difficult to find the plants at just the right stage of development, but now I'm always watching and can pick at just the proper time.

Learn as much as you can about **wild foods** in your area. From April till October, I can find edible greens for a meal. In the summer there are mushrooms, and when we run out of onions, there are wild ones to dig. There are always trout in the creek. Add these free-for-the-taking goodies to what we grow, and we don't have to be dependent on the grocery store. We always have milk and eggs and rabbits in the pens plus all the fruits and veggies that we can and dry. In summer we pick strawberries, raspberries, currants, thimbleberries, gooseberries, serviceberries, and huckleberries—all growing wild right here. The surplus is preserved for winter use. In a few hours we can pick all the rose hips we need for a year's supply of vitamin C.

There are many **food items** you may not have thought **to make for your-**

self, but they're quite easy and save greatly on expense, including mayonnaise, ketchup, mustard, horseradish, salsa, hot sauce, seasoned salt, curry powder, and chili powder (although you will probably have to buy some of the ingredients). Being your own baker is a must.

When planning meals, rely on what you have. A recipe that contains one ingredient that you raised—a chicken, say—but requires you to buy a number of other ingredients is not what you're looking for (unless you can substitute with homegrown products).

Trade whenever you can. It helps everyone and feels good, too. Our neighbor Sarah loaned us her two 80-watt solar panels for the six months that she would be spending in Antarctica, where she works. We loaned our 50-watt panel to neighbors Dan and Marlene for the same period of time. They loaned us a DC water pump after they observed us siphoning water from a barrel in the truck up on the hill to our barrel in the house. Life up here is rough, and we love it or we wouldn't be here. Still, the feeling of community among our widely-spaced neighbors is very valuable to us. It's like family in many ways.

Right now we're just beginning to haul logs with our horses. We're hoping it will be another way to make money, but we've only been doing actual log pulling for four days, so we'll see how it goes. Everyone up here needs their blowdown cleaned up as well as house logs hauled, and if we can do it while being easy on the land, it may be just the niche we're looking for.

I hope I have given you some ideas about making a living in the woods or other rural areas. It's not easy, but the tradeoff is that you get to have your life instead of spending most of it working for someone else at a job you'd probably otherwise not choose to do. Δ

Ayoob on firearms

By Massad Ayoob

The price of machismo

In my last column in this space, I talked about the Marlin Model 60 .22 rifle, and about a man who had used one to defend his backwoods home. He stood charged with murder. I promised to tell you how it came out. Well, the good news is, we beat the murder charge. The bad news is, he was convicted of manslaughter. How such a thing could happen is far more important to a rural homeowner than what type of gun he or she might use to defend that home.

The defendant lived in rural Kansas. His home was a former chicken house that he had rebuilt with his own hands using scrap material. He was 69, and he lived there with his common-law wife (a retarded woman in her thirties) and her little girl that he considered his own.

On the night in question, one of his drinking buddies came by, along with another man, both pretty well in the bag. They sat down at the kitchen table and started drinking his beer. The old man joined them in a brew, though he wasn't under the influence. Soon an argument developed between the two visitors, which the homeowner tried to mediate with no effect. The drinking buddy went out of control, yelling and kicking a coffee table against a wall. The homeowner tried to calm the man down, and the guy grabbed him, ripping the buttons off his shirt. The wife tried to calm him down, and the man answered with an obscenity.

The homeowner was a small-statured guy, literally a "little old man." His assailant was in his early 40s, about six foot three, and strongly built. The old man knew he couldn't control this guy with his bare hands. He went into the bedroom for a gun. During this moment, the huge intruder—and intruder he was, because he had already been asked to leave—took a swing at the man's petite wife.

The old man emerged from the bedroom holding his Marlin .22 pointed at the floor, and ordered the raging giant to leave. It seemed as if he was going to comply. The man turned and went to the door...and suddenly, he was back in the tiny house, lunging at the old man, his eyes on the rifle and his hands reaching for it.

Fearing that the man would wipe out his family if he gained control of the rifle, the old man fired once. The big guy stopped in his tracks, stumbling back and sitting heavily on a coffee table. His drunk friend looked at the old man and asked, "Did you shoot him?"

"Hell, yes, I shot him," the homeowner replied, telling the man to get him to a hospital. The drunken companion did so, helping the wounded man out to his truck. There was no phone in the "home-made home" to call from, so in a short while, the old man drove to the nearest public place with a phone, a tavern/restaurant where the family had stopped to eat earlier and seen the two men who would later come to the house and set the stage for the tragedy. The pair had already returned there, he discovered, and the bartender had already called police and rescue, so he headed home.

The man he shot died later that night. The retarded wife made a statement to police to the effect that the man had been tearing up the house, so her husband shot him. To make a long

Massad Ayoob

story short, he was charged with manslaughter, and the charge was then upped to second degree murder. The prosecutor tried to jack it up again, to first degree murder, but the judge would not allow that.

All was going well in the trial—it was clear-cut self defense—until the defendant took the witness stand. The prosecutor had read him as an independent and stubborn man. He knew what buttons to push. He began an antagonistic cross examination that hit its climax with a question to the effect of, "If I came into your house and kicked a coffee table, would you shoot me, too?" And the frustrated, exasperated old man answered that if the prosecutor was going to do that in his house, he'd better be wearing a bulletproof vest.

That, as they say, was "all she wrote." After the "Guilty of Manslaughter" verdict, the jurors who were debriefed by the defense lawyers made it clear that once the defendant had threatened on the witness stand to shoot the prosecutor, there wasn't much else they could find in the way of a verdict.

There are lessons here for the sort of people who read *Backwoods Home Magazine*. If you weren't stubborn and independent, you wouldn't be reading *Backwoods Home*. Instead of planning for self-sufficient living (or experiencing it already), you'd be reading *Better Homes and Gardens* or *Architectural Digest*, and if you'd been in the same situation as this poor old guy, you might have been able to tell your butler, "Jeeves, throw this bounder out, and call one of my bodyguards if you need help."

Briefly, the learning points are these:

1) Have some form of communication available in your backwoods home. If the defendant could have called for police assistance on a CB or a ham radio or something as this situation developed, he would have been more clearly seen as the complainant instead of the perpetrator, and the sheriff's deputies might even have gotten there in time to prevent the shooting.

2) Never let a lawyer or anyone else provoke you to the point where you lose control. The old man had spent his adult life working with his hands. The lawyer who cross-examined him had spent his career working with his silver tongue. The old man was on the lawyer's turf now, playing the other man's game. Sentencing isn't complete yet, but I expect the old man will pay several months per word for the angry sentence he uttered when the prosecutor provoked him.

3) Don't invite out-of-control drunks into your house. Isn't that one of the things you left urban America to get away from in the first place? True, the old man didn't know how bad his friend was when he let him in, but he knew the man had a history of drinking and "losing it." He had told him it was OK to stop by when they met at the tavern. That was "the beginning of the end" for him.

The big thing that got the old man sent to prison—"hung by his tongue"—was his angry, threatening outburst on the witness stand. If ever you're being cross-examined, take it from a denizen of the courts: you're not talking to an advocate whose very job is to disbelieve your truth, you're talking to a dozen people on the jury who have basic, honest, human social values. Don't let a lawyer trick you into saying something that makes you look like you don't share those values, when in fact you do.

If you're interested in this case, I wrote it up for *American Handgunner* magazine as part of my regular feature there called "The Ayoob Files," a series of in-depth studies of shooting incidents. The back-order department of that magazine can be reached toll-free to order a copy at 1-800-537-3006. The case was *State of Kansas v. Willard Grooms*, and at this writing, Will Grooms is behind bars and will be there for some time; the woman he shared his life with has been institutionalized; and their little girl is in a foster home.

Who was it that said, "If we do not learn from history, we are doomed to repeat it"? Δ

A BHM Writer's Profile: Dorothy Ainsworth

Dorothy Ainsworth likes to write for *BHM* because the readers may be people just like her—possibly squeaking by on little more than minimum wage, but with a big desire for shelter, self-sufficiency, and the peace of mind that ultimately comes from being true to oneself.

As a waitress and single mom rearing 2 kids on her own, she fiercely wanted security without being beholden to anyone. At 40, with no previous building experience, she bought a piece of land with a farm loan, read stacks of how-to books, and started in. Her most powerful resource was drive. On a shoestring income she learned to use any cheap or free natural materials she could get her calloused hands on. "With logs, stones, straw, and mud, an energetic person with imagination and research, can create a home with his or her artistic signature in every touch."

Any discomforts of living on the barest necessities for a while were totally offset by indescribable feelings of fulfillment that came from everyday accomplishments.

Dorothy is now 54 and has 10 structures under her carpenter's belt: pump-house, water storage tank, root cellar, barn, shop, storage building, small guest cabin, piano studio, and 2 log homes (rebuilt main house that burned). The average cost was $15/sq. ft. and except for her land payment she's debt free. Tunnel vision paid off and the journey was so worth it.

Her future plans include writing a waitress book about her humorous experiences serving over 1 million people in 38 years. Also she hopes to find time to indulge in her life long hobby and first love—photography. Meanwhile she's in the process of editing the videotapes she took of building the original house.

You can make extra money as a stringer

By Robert L. Williams

Several years ago, I found that each month I needed a little—or a lot—of extra money. I was already working full-time and had erratic hours, so if I found part-time work, I had to do it all around the clock. Very few potential employers would even talk to me about hours early in the morning one day and late at night the next.

Then I picked up a newspaper and saw a byline with the notation under the writer's name, "Special to the Observer." This tiny message told me that the newspaper was buying a special article now and then from off the beaten track. Because we lived far out of town, we qualified for the off-the-beaten-track part of the work.

I called the state editor of the paper, told him what I'd like to do, and suggested a few stories. He agreed immediately to look at a story on one of my topics, so I did the interview, took a few photos, and wrote the story. I mailed it to the editor a day or so later, and almost immediately the story and a photo appeared in the paper.

That first article was about a karate expert who was also an accomplished cook, a seamster who made his own clothing, a gardener, a painter of excellent landscapes, and a college student. (More about this later.) The newspaper paid me $40 for what amounted to about five hours of work. I figured I could afford to work for $8 per hour, and I set about finding other stories.

Several stories in one day

What I quickly learned was that I could locate three or four stories in one area, and with one trip I could triple my income for the stringer work.

The author is shown with several issues of Foothills Magazine. *He did the cover photos for each issue, and the combined issues, with stories by him, resulted in a part-time income of about $4,500 over a period of four months. Total time invested was less than 40 hours.*

A stringer, by the way, is someone who is not employed full-time by a newspaper, but who writes on a semi-regular basis and has none of the perks offered by the paper.

By doing three or four stories on each trip, I could earn as much as $120 for about eight hours of work. I was now up from $8 to $15 per hour. Eventually I worked my way up to five to eight stories in a single morning. That is, I did the interviews and photos. Later I wrote the stories and prepared the photo captions.

Sell a story more than once

Then even greater dividends began to take shape. Remember the karate expert? He brought me copies of a magazine one day and asked if I thought his story merited space in one of the publications. I used the same photos (I always took more than I needed, just in case other opportunities arose), and I modified the story only slightly and sent it in.

I sold the story for $100 the first time, then for $150, and then for $350. I had now earned $640 for a total of about 12 hours of work. I was now earning more than $50 per hour.

In one issue of a newspaper special section, the type of publication referred to as "neighborhood journalism," I placed 11 articles at $80 each. That's $880 for about 20 hours of work. But it gets much better than this.

I did a story one morning and sold it to the paper. Then I sent it to a series of magazines. Understand that this was not a story of aliens kidnapping Elvis who had just captured a bigfoot at a reunion of James Dean, John Kennedy, and Jesse James. This was a rather commonplace photo and story.

I eventually sold the story for, in succession, $40, $45, $150, $150, $250, $300, $480, $850, $500, $175, and $550. And that was just the beginning. A total of almost $3000 for one basic story, at that point. I had invested no more than 15 hours in the entire photo layout, and I realized an income of about $196 per hour.

Once you have written the story, have it understood with the editor of the paper that you have the right to sell the story again and again, as long as you don't abuse the legal rights of either publication.

Then sell it to tabloids, regional magazines, and anyone else who will buy it. I sold my story about the 73¢ house 28 times, and always for a nice sum. When our own house was destroyed by a tornado and we built our new house with a chain saw and little else, I wrote the story of how we constructed the house for a fantastically low price. In the months that followed, I actually paid for the cost of the house by articles written about the house. The house is now valued at more than $200,000, but it didn't cost us anything close to that figure.

A word of warning: when you sell the story, ask the editor for permission to re-sell it. Then tell the new buyer where the story appeared earlier. Then ask him for re-print rights, and tell the third buyer where the story has appeared before. Keep on doing this and get it in writing, and you will likely stay out of difficulties.

Where do you find good stories?

The first question I am always asked when I speak to a group is, Where do I find good stories? My reply is, "Where can you go *without* finding good stories? They are all around us." I then offer a small wager that among the members of that club I can find a dozen publishable stories. After the speech, I talk with members and win my bet. I also find my next dozen articles.

The next question is, what makes a good story? My answer is, "Whatever reaches the heart, the brain, the funnybone, or the wallet." For example, touch your readers with a tender story of an 87-year-old woman who built her own house and chimneys, made her own furniture, painted the murals over the fireplaces, and did her own landscaping. I did such a story.

Or the story of a woman who lost both legs to cancer and then refused to accept welfare money, despite her poverty. She insisted that she could find work and support herself—and she did.

Show and tell the readers how they can make money (which is what this article is intended to do), save money (which is what many of my other articles in *Backwoods Home Magazine* do), amuse them with incredible but true stories that bring a smile and warm the heart, stimulate and challenge the reader intellectually, inform

The author's son Robert, age 19, is shown holding a copy of Foothills Magazine *which recently ran his square-split firewood story (after* Backwoods Home Magazine *had run it). Two paychecks are almost always better than one.*

him on matters that will help him now or later.

If you want to test the waters for a story, when you run across an interesting situation, tell a friend or family member about it. Share it with neighbors, students, etc. If they genuinely like the story, write it up and simply tell the story in print to readers.

Become a superior listener. When someone is telling you about his grandson who is playing the violin with a special orchestra, ask how old the grandchild is. You learn that he is only five years old, and you have a story.

As you drive, remain alert for something that catches your eye: a huge two-story house being moved, a blind person who takes photos, a 112-year-old preacher, a three-year-old professional photographer, a blacksmith still plying his trade. You might find a story in a survivor of a long-ago war, a woman who knew Thomas Edison personally, natural phenomena, people who fight back from devastating tragedies, a paralyzed person who types by using a straw held in his mouth, or a man whose hobby reaches around the world. All of the above are stories that I did within a few days of each other. The stories are everywhere.

Photo tips

One day I was driving to my regular job when I saw a superior photo opportunity and took the shot. The newspaper then began to buy what they called "wild photos" from me. These are photos without a story—or rather, the photo tells the entire story.

And of course photos will help you sell the stories you write.

If you can afford one of the throwaway cameras, you can take acceptable photos, but it's obvious that with a better camera you have a greater range of opportunities. My first suggestion is that if money is scarce, buy a cheap camera, then save all of your writing money until you can buy a better camera.

There are superior cameras on the market for under $500. You can buy an excellent used camera for much less, but have a camera instructor check out the camera for you before you invest too much in a used one. You can also rent cameras, but several rentals will go a long way toward the purchase price of a good camera.

When you take the photos, always ask first for permission, unless you are on the scene of a spectacle that will be covered by the media. Never, never trespass onto private property, and never shove a camera into a person's face without asking first.

When you shoot the photos, try to imagine the photo in print and cut out all unwanted elements. Don't have a tree growing out of a man's head, and don't snap the subject when he is picking his nose or scratching the south forty.

Don't invest in a darkroom. Use color print film and take the exposed rolls to Wal-Mart or other stores where there is a one-hour service. Go eat lunch while the film is being processed, and then pick it up and pay the $7 or so for the service. You can't develop and print your own photos at that price.

Write a good lead

When you write the story, work for an interesting lead, called a *hook*. This sentence is intended to capture the reader's attention instantly and keep it. Look at this lead, which was the hook in one of the first stories I ever wrote.

"On December 7, 1815, Marshal Michel Ney was executed by a firing squad composed of his own men. Death was instant, the result of eight wounds in the chest, three in the head, and one in the right arm. He was buried the following morning just outside Paris, and six months later he was teaching school in a small town in North Carolina." Will editors want to

Elizabeth Williams does a community calendar and a church news column for each issue of Foothills Magazine. *She never leaves the house to do the work, and she earns about $300 per month for the effort. If she goes out to do feature stories, she can make an additional $80 to $160 per month.*

read on? Several did, and this story, which I found in an old graveyard, earned me close to $800 for about six hours of work.

The story is perfectly true, with a bizarre twist, just like the story about the peaceful man who lived in a tiny town near my home years ago. He confessed on his deathbed that he was the infamous pirate Jean Lafitte, thought to have died long ago in Texas.

When you research the stories, ask more questions than you can possibly use. It's far better to cut out material than it is to try to stretch a few facts into a long narration. For example, in this story I cut the material about the Bigfoot that lived in our area for a while and was spotted by preachers, bankers, housewives, businessmen, and children.

You have probably noticed that many newspaper have Sunday supplements written by a small staff of writers. This is more of the Neighborhood Journalism movement. In our area the special Sunday section is called *Foothills Magazine*. I have written freelance articles for that publication since it started four years ago, and to date I have had at least one story in all but three issues. At times I have had

six or more articles, each at $80 or more per story. If your area newspaper has such a supplement, ask about writing for the paper. If it does not have one, ask if they are considering starting one.

All over this country there are newspapers that will buy occasional or frequent stories. All you have to do is make the proper contacts, sharpen your writing and photo skills, and locate the right stories.

Good luck, Tiger. The stories are out there. Go get them. If you don't, I will. Δ

Forage for wood lettuce and ground coral and you can spice up your outdoor eating

By Branley Allan Branson

Startling and spectacular moments in the woods do not always involve encounters with wild animals. Consider wood lettuce and ground corals. Unlike their name-sake counterparts of the garden and sea, both these life forms are rather strange and curious-looking fungi. They grow in long-established wood-lands throughout eastern North America, though there are many west-ern representatives, too. These fungi become particularly well-developed in mid-summer and continue to multiply through early fall.

Wood lettuce, or cauliflower mush-rooms, as they are also called, always startle campers when they encounter them. Only two species occur in all of North America, one in the east (the Latin sobriquet is *Sparassis crispa*) and one in the west (*S. radicata*). Many species also live in Central and South America, and in Europe and Asia, where they are staple food items. The eastern wood lettuce grows at the base of hardwood and pine trees, since it is a parasite on their roots, and appears in such places year after year. This fungus, often up to two feet across and half that in height, consists of myriad flattened, wavy, folded, curled, and crimped leaf-like parts arranged in a rosette. In color, the mushroom is strongly reminiscent of a collection of pale whitish-yellow egg noodles waiting for a cook. There is no root-like part, and in young spec-imens the leaf-like parts may be so tightly convoluted that the mushroom looks like a brain rather than like a head of lettuce or cauliflower. Most specimens weigh between one and five pounds, but exceptionally large ones may go as high as twenty pounds. The western species, which has a distinctive tapering rootlike part

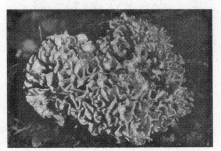

*Wood lettuce, or cauliflower mush-rooms (*Sparassis crispa*) are edible, weird-looking forest floor plants that startle first-time observers.*

buried in the ground, sometimes weighs as much as fifty pounds.

Wood lettuce bears little if any resemblance to any other mushroom in America, hence is easily identified. That is a lucky fact, for *Sparassis* is an edible species. A single specimen can feed a family of five or more, and the keeping qualities are exceptional. Under refrigeration, specimens may be retained for more than a week. *Sparassis* is a very fragrant and fla-vorful mushroom, but it must be cut into pieces, washed, and thoroughly cooked to remove toughness. I have found it best to parboil the pieces until they are tender, then gently sauté them in lightly salted butter until golden brown. However, large specimens may be parboiled then baked at 450° until golden-brown and tender. Wood lettuce is a perfect dish to accompany a pot roast or leg of lamb.

Wood lettuce is particularly abun-dant (in late July through early October) in the forests along the Blue Ridge Parkway in Virginia, and in most forests of North Carolina, Tennessee, and Kentucky. I have also found large specimens in southern Illinois and Indiana, and in the Finger Lakes region of New York.

Another delightful camping event occurs when one encounters coral fungi. These fantastic fungi occur throughout America, especially from mid-July through first frost. As the name implies, these often colorful fungi strongly resemble sea corals in shape. They consist of many upright branches that arise from a fleshy com-mon stalk. Colors range from whitish through tan, yellows, pinks, and greenish-to brilliant orange. Many of the small species grow directly on decaying logs, whereas the larger fleshy species grow on lignin-rich ground under trees. All of them are beautiful in their woodland settings, and many of them are favorites for the table. Since there are so many species of coral fungi in America, we shall only discuss a few representatives for introduction purposes.

One of these is the common crown coral (*Clavicorona pydixata*). This three-inch wide, four-to five-inch tall species is one of the few larger corals that grow directly on decaying wood. In the west, this fungus grows most commonly on aspens, willows, and cottonwoods, whereas in the eastern U.S. it is frequently found on dead oaks, maples, and sycamores.

The crown coral produces many branches from a common base, usual-ly in several tiers. The tips of the branches are enlarged into crown-like cups or fringes. Only one other wood-growing coral has these peculiar crowns, a grayish-brown western

*The crown-tipped coral (*Clavicorona pyxidata*) has many upright, brittle branches that end in crown-like tufts.*

species (*C. avellanea*) that grows on rotting conifer logs. The crown coral is whitish to pale yellow.

Like many other coral fungi, the crown coral is edible, but it tends to be stringy and tough, even after parboiling. However, because of its distinctive peppery taste, it makes an excellent addition to pot roasts and full-bodied soups. A hunting associate of mine uses it as an ingredient in venison stew.

One of the most common and widespread species in North America, the pinkish coral mushroom (*Ramaria formosa*) is a beautiful fungus that always elicits delight when found growing on the ground in the vicinity of conifer trees. It is a fairly large species, up to seven inches across and high, with multiple upright branches that are often grooved. The thick base is white close to the ground, colored like the branches above that, and tapers downward. The branches vary from light pink to pinkish-orange, salmon-orange, tan to reddish. The tips of the branches are yellow, regardless of overall coloration. When bruised or scratched, the flesh slowly turns brownish. The flesh never has a gelatinous consistency, but is always firm to rather tough. *This is not considered to be an edible fungus* because it has a tendency to produce cathartic effects when ingested.

There are many other species of *Ramaria* corals in North America, and most of them are very attractive. Some of them, such as the red coral mushroom (*R. araiospora*) are brilliantly

A beautiful woodland species, the jellied false coral (Tremellodendron pallidum*) has flattened, rubbery branches.*

red, resembling sea corals even more closely than the species we have already discussed. Other species, like the yellow coral mushroom (*R. rasilispora*) are brilliant yellow to saffron yellow. Some of these species dry very well and make interesting additions to dry arrangements in the camper.

Finally, several species of the jelly fungi often strongly resemble true coral fungi. Jelly fungi, as that name implies, are composed of gelatinous

bodies that may be soft and jelly-like or stiff and rubbery to the touch. Some species are brightly colored, oranges and yellows predominating, but the jellied false coral (*Tremellodendron pallidum*), which strongly resembles true coral fungi, is pure white to dirty white. The multiple upright branches are flattened and rubber-like, in sharp contrast with those of the true corals, which are brittle. Colonies are around six inches across and two to four inches in height, growing on the ground ln hardwood or mixed-wood forests.

Several of the jelly fungi are edible, and the jellied false coral is one of them. It is best used as an ingredient in soups and Chinese dishes.

Wooded areas surrounding campgrounds nearly always have interesting contributions to make to camping. Some of those contributions are curious, others are downright bizarre. Topping the list of the latter category are the species of wood lettuce and ground coral fungi. Δ

*The pinkish coral (*Ramaria formosa*), usually growing in the vicinity of conifers, causes sickness if ingested*

A working country moment

Rich Perrigo of Montague, California, uses a Wood-Mizer sawmill to cut a pine log into timber.

Perfect whole wheat breads
…some troubleshooting ideas

By Jennifer Stein Barker

Many people consider making bread to be a daunting task: they are afraid of fallen loaves, doughy centers, or bread that stubbornly refuses to rise at all. Others have perhaps been making bread for a while, but can't figure out why the loaves come out with an uneven texture or a hole in the middle.

A perfect wholegrain loaf is not an impossible dream. Bread making is both an art and a science. Flours and doughs react in normal and predictable ways, and learning the science of breadmaking will help you be at ease as you perfect the art of creating beautiful bread. Here are a few tips gleaned from years of experimentation that will demystify the yeast loaf. Following them is a troubleshooting section for those perplexing problems, and then some excellent recipes. Above all, remember these two things: yeast is alive, and the dough is your friend.

Proofing the yeast

A sure way to know if your yeast is really alive, and to nurture its growth, is to *proof* it. For proofing, use the amount of water, yeast, and honey called for in the recipe you're making. Measure out the water into a bowl. Test the water temperature with a thermometer or your hand. It should feel pleasantly warm to the touch, about 100°. Yeast likes to have the same friendly body temperature that you do in order to grow and multiply. The multiplication of the yeast produces carbon dioxide gas as a by-product, which makes the bread *rise* because the gas is trapped in the loaf. Sprinkle the yeast over the warm water and let it sit for a few minutes. Then stir gently to dissolve it completely, add the honey (to feed the yeast), and dissolve that. Let the cup sit in a warm place until the contents foam up, about 10 minutes. You have now given your yeast a good start in life.

Making dough

Gluten is what holds the dough together and traps the carbon dioxide in little pockets. Wheat is the grain with the most gluten, and *hard* wheats have more gluten than *soft* wheats (soft wheat is used to make pastry flour, because it does not have enough gluten to become "tough"). So look for flour marked "bread flour," which is made from high-gluten wheat. If you can't find whole wheat bread flour, or if your bread recipe has a high proportion of some low-gluten grain like rye, you may add what is called *gluten flour* (a highly refined product) in the proportion of one tablespoon per cup, to increase the gluten content. This refined gluten flour is not necessary to bake bread: it will simply make your bread rise higher.

Add the flour to your dough a cup at a time, beating well. When you have a soft dough, beat air into it until it forms strands between the spoon and the bowl (these are gluten strands). Continue adding flour a half-cup at a time until the dough forms into a ball and pulls away from the sides of the bowl. The dough is now ready for kneading.

Kneading

Sprinkle a layer of flour over your counter, and have your flour source handy in case you need more. Turn out the dough onto the floured surface. To knead, push the heels of your hands into the dough, then fold it over at the crease. Rotate the dough a quarter-turn, and repeat. Remember, the dough is your friend. Knead it vigorously and joyously, and it will respond. Do not beat, pummel, or otherwise torture your friend. When it is ready to be put to rise, after 5 to 15 minutes of kneading, it will fold over with a smooth and satiny stretch, and it will spring back with great life from any impression. Lay the dough in a clean, oiled bowl, turn it so the oiled surface is on the top, cover it with a cloth, and set it in a warm, draft-free place to rise.

The baking

The dough is ready to form into loaves when it has risen to double its original bulk. If you don't have time to deal with it right now, or if you want a loaf with a finer texture, letting it rise again may be advantageous.

Slap the risen dough vigorously with the flat of your hand. The air will hiss out and the dough will subside into the bottom of the bowl. Let it "rest" for a minute or two. If you're letting it rise again, just re-cover it and put it back in the warm place. To shape the loaves, turn the dough out onto a smooth surface. I just let the oil from the dough coat the surface, but if this doesn't work for you, you may have to get out the flour again, and flour the surface. Divide the dough into two (or more) parts, and work each into loaf shape: flatten the dough with your hands and work all of the air out of it. Roll, fold, pat, and otherwise shape it to fit your loaf pans. I find the baked loaves come free of the pans better if I oil them *lightly*.

Remember... the dough is your friend.

Cover the loaves and put them back into your warm place to rise the final time. They are ready to be baked when the dough has doubled in bulk (make note of the original bulk when you set it in the pans), and feels soft and giving when gently poked. Make sure your oven is preheated.

At the end of the specified baking time, check your loaves. The crust should be a lovely golden brown. Turn one out of the pan and tap it on the bottom. If it sounds hollow, it's done. If you hear a dull "thud," put it back in the pan and back in the oven for another 7 to 10 minutes. Cover the loaf with a loose foil cap if necessary to keep it from browning too much.

About salt

You can leave salt completely out of your bread if you wish. I find that in my sourdough breads, neither the flavor nor the rising suffers at all. In my sweet dough breads, however (such as oatmeal bread, recipe below), if I leave out all the salt, I get great big holes in the centers of my loaves. Now, I live at 5000' elevation. I tried leaving out the salt at 1000' elevation, and it worked just fine. You'll have to experiment for yourself and see how much salt you need for your tastes and your rising. If you're on a salt-free diet and don't like the holes in your bread, try letting the dough rise less.

Troubleshooting

Bread molds or sours quickly (in two days or less): You must keep your bread in the refrigerator if you have this problem, or use more of a preservative-type ingredient (salt or vinegar). Use 1/2 to 1 teaspoon salt per loaf (if you omit-

ted salt), or add 1 teaspoon mild vinegar (such as rice vinegar) per loaf to the wet ingredients.

Texture is uneven (air bubbles are bigger towards the top of the loaf, bread is denser at the bottom): You need to knead the dough longer. If the gluten is not fully developed, it will not adequately entrap the air bubbles and they will tend to rise towards the top of the loaf. Knead wholegrain doughs at least 7 to 10 minutes, until the dough is springy and smooth and does not stick to your hands or the board.

Big hole(s) in the center of the loaf: See "About salt" above. Also, try adjusting the ratio of sweetener in your loaf. If you already have salt in your dough, the problem could be too much sugar or honey.

Dough sticks to hands when kneading: First, try beating the dough well when you have only added a portion of the flour. This will develop the gluten before you ever have to get your hands in it. (People with wrist problems, take note: this can substitute for part or all of the kneading.) Then knead with cool hands and a firm stroke. Make it like a dance, and you will find the bread responding without sticking. If my dough sticks in the early part of the kneading, I rub my hands together to roll the sticky stuff off, and dip them in flour to begin again.

Flat-topped loaves: Your dough was allowed to rise too much before being baked. Try this test to see if the loaves are "just right" before you slide them into the oven: poke a loaf gently with a fingertip. The dough should be springy and lively, but a small depression will remain where you touched it. If a deep dimple forms, your dough is over-risen. You can still bake the loaves and they may not fall, but you may also choose to remove them from the pans and re-form the loaves. They will rise again just fine, and this will not hurt them at all. See also "Making dough" above (the discussion of pastry vs. bread flours). Your dough may not have enough gluten to trap the air inside.

Now let's move on to some bread recipes.

Basic whole wheat bread

This is a great all-purpose bread for beginners or anyone. This bread is wonderful for sandwiches, toasting, and goes equally well with sweet jams or savory spreads. Makes two loaves.

```
3 cups warm water
1 Tbsp. honey
1 Tbsp. dry yeast
1/4 cup oil
1/4 cup honey
1 tsp. salt
6 - 7 cups whole wheat flour
```

In a large bowl, proof the yeast with the warm water and the 1 Tbsp. honey. When the yeast has foamed up, measure in the oil, honey, salt, and enough of the flour to make a thick batter/thin dough. Beat vigorously until the dough forms long elastic strands. Add more flour, 1/2 cup at a time, until the dough is too stiff to stir.

Turn the dough out onto a floured board and knead for at least seven minutes, adding more flour as necessary, until it is smooth and springy. Place the dough in an oiled bowl, turn the oiled side up, cover and place in a warm spot. Let rise until doubled in bulk. Punch down, and let the dough rise a second time, if you have time.

Form the dough into two loaves and place in lightly oiled pans. Cover and let rise until double. Bake in a preheated 350° oven for 40 to 45 minutes, until the loaves test done.

Oatmeal bread

This bread has a lovely texture and a sweet flavor due to the oatmeal. If you want more tender oats, use hotter soaking water; for chewy oats, use cooler. Makes two loaves.

---

2 cups old-fashioned rolled oats
2 cups hot tap water (120 - 130°)
3/4 cup lukewarm water
1 Tbsp. dry yeast
1 tsp. honey
1/4 cup oil
2 Tbsp. honey
2 Tbsp. molasses
1 tsp. salt
2 Tbsp. gluten flour (optional)
about 5 cups whole wheat bread flour

In your bread bowl, stir together the oats and hot water. Let soak for 10 minutes.

In a two-cup measure, dissolve the yeast and the teaspoon of honey in the 3/4 cup warm water. Let sit for 10 minutes or until it foams up.

Add the oil, honey, molasses, and salt to the oat mixture. Stir in the proofed yeast. Mix the gluten flour with the first two cups of bread flour. Beat the flour well into the oat mixture until the dough begins to form strands. Add more bread flour 1/2 cup at a time until the dough becomes too stiff to stir.

Turn the dough out onto a floured board, and knead at least seven minutes, adding more flour as needed to prevent sticking. This dough will remain just a little sticky. Place dough in an oiled bowl, turn to oil all sides, cover, and let rise until double.

Turn dough out and form into two loaves. Place in two oiled 5x9" loaf pans and let rise until double. Preheat the oven to 350°, and bake the loaves until they are golden brown on top and sound hollow when tapped on the bottom (about 35 to 40 minutes).

Remove the loaves from the pans and cool on a wire rack. When thoroughly cooled, they may be stored in an airtight place or wrapped and frozen.

Sesame ring

This hearty sesame bread perfectly complements Mediterranean or Middle Eastern food. Makes one ring-shaped loaf.

---

1 Tbsp. yeast
1 1/4 cups lukewarm water
1 tsp. honey
1 egg
2 Tbsp. oil
1 tsp. dark sesame oil
1/2 tsp. salt
4 to 5 cups whole wheat bread flour
1 egg yolk
2 Tbsp. raw sesame seeds

Proof the yeast with the honey in the warm water. When the yeast foams, add the egg, oil, dark sesame oil, and salt. Beat in two cups of the whole wheat bread flour. Continue beating vigorously until the batter is smooth and elastic. Then add more flour 1/2 cup at a time until the dough is stiff enough to knead.

Turn the dough out onto a lightly floured board and knead until it is very elastic and smooth (about five to seven minutes), adding flour to the board as necessary to keep the dough from sticking. When the dough is smooth and lively, springing back vigorously from any impression, place it in an oiled bowl, turning once so the oiled surface is on top. Cover the bowl and set it in a warm place to rise until doubled in size, about an hour.

Punch down the dough and let it rest in the bowl for a minute, then knead a few times and form it into a smooth ball. Working your fingers through the center of the ball, pull and work the dough into a ring. Place the ring in an oiled pan (I like to use an oval casserole) which leaves room for the dough to expand. Cover the ring and let rise until doubled in size.

Preheat the oven to 375°. Brush the top of the ring gently with beaten egg yolk. Sprinkle the top of the ring with a layer of raw sesame seeds. Bake for about 50 minutes, or until the ring is golden-brown on top and sounds hollow when removed from the pan and tapped on the bottom. Δ

Think of it this way...

By John Silveira

Want proof of luck, ESP, and psychic powers?

We were riding down the Pacific Coast Highway—Mac, his girlfriend Carol, and I. Mac's the poker playing friend of Dave Duffy, the fellow who publishes this magazine. Mac and I have taken to palling around the last few years and on this particular afternoon, he and Carol had invited me to go along with them to a party her cousin was throwing in Malibu.

Mac drove with Carol beside him and me in the backseat. I was thinking about how he makes his living as a poker player.

I suddenly leaned forward and asked, "Do you believe in luck, Mac?"

"Do you mean as in good luck, bad luck, runs of luck, that some people are just plain lucky because they're blessed with it and others are doomed to be unlucky all their lives? Like it's some kind of metaphysical force?"

"Yeah."

"No."

"Really? The way you make your living, I would have thought you did."

He shook his head.

"I just thought all gamblers believed in luck," I said

"Quite a few do."

"How do you explain someone winning the lottery or a night when you get a good run of cards?" I asked.

"Well, in the first case, if you want to call someone who's just won the lottery lucky, you're using it as a descriptive word. It's like calling them rich. But if you're using it as a verb, as if some force called luck brought it about, no, I don't believe in that.

"As for the way I make my living, I don't win because I'm lucky. I win because I learned how to play the game well and I have the discipline to stick to the rules I've set out for myself. On a particular night, I may do a lot better or a lot worse than I ordinarily would, because of the random nature of the hands my opponents and I get. But that's just the way things happen."

"Do you believe in things like ESP?"

I saw him look at me in the rearview mirror. "No."

"You don't?"

"If it exists, no one's ever provided reliable evidence of it. Given all the people who say they have it or have witnessed it, I would have thought it would have been demonstrated to the satisfaction of science a long time ago."

"What about those guys like Uri Geller and others like him I've read about or seen on TV. How do you explain them?"

"Have you ever heard of a guy named James Randi?"

Looking in the rearview mirror, he could see the puzzled look on my face. "He bills himself as 'The Amazing Randi,'" he added

"The name's familiar."

"He's a magician. But he's best known for exposing psychics. Show him a feat that any of the psychics claim to perform by using supernatural powers, and he'll do the same stunt using nothing but the magic stuff he's learned over the years. Card tricks, mind reading, bending spoons, or whatever; he'll do them all, but he'll do them without claiming to use any psychic powers, only deception and sleight of hand."

"So what?"

"Well, if I know that a professional stage magician can do what these psychics do, why should I accept the explanation that psychic powers are involved, particularly when what

John Silveira

they're doing amounts to nothing more than parlor tricks?"

"But some of these psychics have convinced reputable scientists."

"Scientists are out of their league when they deal with these guys. Scientists are by and large honest, and they're not in the habit of dealing with people who are trying to fool them. They'd proclaim Randi a psychic if he told them he was one. I'm not impressed when some scientist proclaims one to be genuine. But let one of those guys get by a good magician and I might take notice."

I sat back and was looking out at the sea again. Carol looked back at me. Her window was open and her hair was floating on the breeze.

"Mac tells me you write," she said.

I nodded.

"He said you write poetry."

I was flattered to find out Mac talks about me.

She turned forward again and fished something out of the glove box. It was a notebook. She handed it to me over the seat.

"Tell me if these are any good."

I opened it and read the first poem. It was horrible. I read the second. It was worse. The third, fourth, and fifth were terrible, too. I was mortified. She wanted my opinion of them. I glanced up at her. She was watching me. How was I going to tell this beautiful woman, the girlfriend of a newfound best friend, that her poetry was atrocious. I read a few more.

I looked up again. She was still watching me. Looking into her eyes I knew if I wasn't brutally honest, she'd know I was lying.

I had to be honest. But my mouth opened and I lied, "They're pretty good. They're not quite what we put in the magazine…"

She screwed her face up. "Really? I think they stink. They're my cousin's girl friend's stuff. I can't believe you like them. When Jeff's girlfriend, Rita, heard you were coming, she insisted you read them before you got there."

She turned forward again. I must have looked mortified because Mac looked at me in the mirror again and started laughing. Carol looked at him, then back at me.

"You just said you like them because you thought they were mine, didn't you?"

I nodded.

She laughed. "You men are such cowards."

"Does the woman who wrote them want me to be honest with her?" I asked.

"Only if you think they rival Shakespeare's."

Mac laughed some more.

The rest of the trip was uneventful.

We arrived at a house in Malibu. It was one of those modern looking things that's all pastels and straight lines. We went in and Carol started introducing Mac and me around. She introduced us to her cousin, Jeff, then she introduced us to Jeff's girlfriend.

"Mac, this is my cousin's friend, Rita."

Rita was one of the most beautiful women I've ever seen. If there are desirable young virgins waiting on departed warriors in Valhalla, this is what they look like. She started to shake Mac's hand and stopped. "Oh, you're the poker player," she said and pulled her hand away like he was pond scum.

"And you must be the magazine editor," she said turning to me. Her face lit up and enveloped me. I was hers to do with as she pleased. My legs were like wilted celery stalks. No woman this beautiful had ever spoken to me before. She was going to ask me about her poems. I was going to lie. I'd hate myself in the morning. So what?

Her face changed. I no longer existed. I extended my hand but she didn't take it and just as suddenly as she'd appeared, she was gone. I was stung.

"Wrong guy," Carol said. "He couldn't make it. This is John, another card player."

Her face changed. I no longer existed. I extended my hand but she didn't take it and just as suddenly as she'd appeared, she was gone. I was stung.

"I told her that because you men are such cowards," Carol said.

"You should have let John handle that," Mac said.

"I would have told her anything she wanted to hear," I confessed.

"I know that," Carol said.

Mac watched Rita as she walked away from us, and Carol kicked him in the ankle.

"Hey, that hurt."

"Do you guys both need drool cups?" she asked and she took Mac's hand and they wandered around. Since I felt so out of place, I stuck close to them.

For hors d'oeuvres there were stuffed mushrooms I'd die for, marinated shrimp I'd kill for, and oysters on the half shell I couldn't get enough of. There were cases of wine I couldn't have afforded by the glass. I sensed there was so much money here a collection could have been taken up to buy Rhode Island and pave it over for tennis courts.

There were people talking the film business. I don't mean Fotomat but MGM and Universal. Others talked music. Everyone was dropping names the way baseball fans drop statistics.

We stopped to look out one of the bay windows and I found myself gazing on a view of the Pacific I couldn't afford. Suddenly, I was sure money could buy me happiness.

I looked around and Mac and Carol were gone. I felt awkward, like I was a fraud. I just hoped no one was going to ask me what I did for a living.

"Relax," a voice said. It was Carol. She was back. "These people are liars, just like you were in the car."

I laughed and wished I'd been honest with her when she'd shown me the poems.

"Mac's casing the place. He's trying to find out if there are any poker players here so he can wangle his way into their games." She rolled her eyes. "I think I'm going to get a nightgown made out of playing cards.

"Come on," she said and we walked into what I immediately realized was a large office. I still didn't know what her cousin did for a living. At least half the people at the party had congregated in this room. A man was sitting at a table and looked like he was doing card tricks. Carol and I got closer and heard him say:

"Everyone has ESP to some extent."

"That's what I think, Ron." The speaker was a woman named Helen.

"Here, let me show you," Ron said and he stopped shuffling the deck and spread the cards in what looked like a random fashion over the table.

We all moved closer to the table.

"I want you to point to…" He hesitated for effect. "…point to a red card. Make it a ten. Make it the ten of hearts."

She held her finger deliberately over the cards.

"Go ahead," he said.

She giggled and pointed to one.

"Don't touch it," Ron said.

"That one," she said. Her index finger hovered just millimeters over a card.

"Are you sure?"

She nodded.

He picked the card up and held it so only he could see it. When he looked back at her, his expression was non-committal.

"Pick another one," he said.

"Did I get the ten of hearts?" she asked.

"Just pick another one. Pick a black one this time." He thought a moment. "Make it a picture card. Make it the king of spades."

She hesitated. She was still thinking about the ten of hearts.

"Go ahead," he said.

"But I want to know if I got the ten of hearts."

"Point to the king of spades, first."

She let her hand hover again and slowly moved it in circles until she settled on a card in the middle of the table.

"This one?" Ron asked as he pointed to a card.

"The one next to it."

He moved his finger slightly. "This one?"

"Yes."

"Are you sure?"

She nodded.

He picked this card up and looked at it, too. He gazed at her again and she laughed.

"Let me see if I can pick one," he said. "Let's make it a small card. Let's make it the three of spades." His hand floated over the table until it settled on a card near him and he picked it up and looked at it for a moment, then looked at Helen again as he shuffled the three cards in his hands.

"Do you think I got mine, the three of spades?"

She thought a second and smiled. "How would I know?"

He threw the three of spades face up on the table. She looked surprised.

"Do you think you got yours, the ten of hearts and the king of spades?"

"I don't know," she laughed.

He threw the ten of hearts and the king of spades face up on the table.

"How did I do that?" She was incredulous.

"I told you, you have psychic powers. I can detect that they're not real strong right now, but with practice you could really start doing things with them."

She looked pleased with herself. "You know, I always could tell things, like when things were going to happen. And the night my grandmother died, I remember worrying about her and thinking of calling her and suddenly the phone rang and it was my mother. She told me my grandmother had just died. How could I have known that?"

"You just have to develop those powers," Ron said.

"Can we do it again?" she asked.

He was shuffling the deck again.

"Are you sure you want to?" he asked.

"Yes."

He spread the cards on the table again.

I suddenly realized Mac was with us now. I sidled up to him. "Did you see that?" I whispered.

He nodded.

"Do you know how he did it?"

He smiled and nodded again.

He turned and I followed him to a table that had more opened bottles of wine. He poured some for me, then some for himself. "I could ruin a perfectly good liver living here," he said.

Across the room, the rest of the guests huddled around the table where Ron was asking Helen to point to the ace of diamonds.

"How'd he do it?" I asked.

"The trick? Each time he finishes, he reshuffles the deck. As he shuffles, he'll glance at the bottom card. After he sees it, he can keep shuffling, but he makes sure the card he saw stays

on the bottom. When he spreads the cards on the table he knows where that bottom card is. Say the six of hearts is the card he saw. He asks her to point to the six of hearts."

"But she doesn't know where it is."

"That's right. But she'll point to some card. Whatever she points to, he'll pick it up and look at it, being careful not to let anyone else see it. Say the card she pointed to was the ten of spades, now he asks her to point to the ten of spades. She can't, of course, because it's in his hand, but she points to another card. He picks that card up and looks at it. Again he's careful to make sure no one else sees it. Say it's the queen of hearts. Now he says, 'I'll pick the queen of hearts, and he picks up the card that's on the bottom of the deck…"

"And that was the six of hearts that he asked for in the first place. So, now he has all three cards."

"That's right. He shuffles the three cards, just in case someone's noticed the order he had them in. Then, with a little drama, he shows the cards to everybody and we're all astounded."

"How do you know that trick?"

"It's older than I am."

We worked our way back to the table. Rita was at the table now and Ron was using her as the subject. She was certainly a lot prettier than Helen, and Helen stood by watching silently. I don't think Helen liked not being the center of attention anymore and she certainly didn't like not being the focus of Ron's attention.

"How do you do it?" Rita asked when he was done.

He shrugged. "We all have psychic powers to some degree. Most people don't know it, so their talents lie fallow. With practice, though, they become stronger. I can sense that each time you do it, you're powers are getting stronger."

"Are you sure this isn't just a trick?" Rita asked.

"It's no trick. Even if there were a way for me to pick my card, how does that explain the way you were picking your cards?"

She didn't have an answer for that.

"Let's do it again," she said.

I was itching to see what would happen when Mac exposed him. "Are you going to tell them how he does it?" I whispered.

"No. Everyone's having fun."

I watched Ron go on with the trick and suddenly I realized the reason I wanted Ron exposed was because I envied him and the way he was the center of attention. He'd already had Helen in his grasp, then threw her aside to focus on the vivacious, though vacuous, Rita.

When the trick was over, she said, "I'm not surprised. I've always known I've had psychic powers."

On the other side of the table, a fellow named Chuck, a technological type who later revealed himself to be a computer scientist, finally said, "I don't believe in ESP. That's just some kind of card trick."

"Then how's he do it?" Rita asked.

Chuck didn't answer but looked smugly doubtful just the same.

Rita was hanging on Ron, now. He wasn't interested in Helen anymore.

"It really is ESP, isn't it?" she asked Ron.

"What do you think?"

A woman on the other side of the table said, "My sister can tell what people are going to say before they open their mouths."

"Oh, come on," Chuck said. "This is just a parlor trick."

Others joined in the discussion and the room quickly broke into two camps: those who believed in psychic powers and those who didn't. Of the two dozen or so other guests, only about four said they didn't believe. Chuck was the most vehement of those four. Two of the other three, all men, merely said they were skeptical but wanted to remain open minded. Chuck's friend, Ira, halfheartedly supported Chuck but he really seemed to be a fence sitter, and if Chuck hadn't

been there, I'm sure he would have been in the other camp.

But the consensus seemed to be that if Chuck couldn't explain away all the psychic phenomena the others had seen, then he should concede their point. He wasn't willing to give in. But he wasn't articulate either, and his objections started to get more strident and he seemed to be making a fool of himself.

Mac left the room. I thought he'd gotten bored with the discussion. But just as suddenly, he reappeared at my side. He followed the discussion intently, and I wondered why he wasn't taking sides.

"Excuse me," he suddenly said. "I think I know a way that we can settle all this quite convincingly."

Only a few of the people seemed to notice he was talking, at first. But he went on and voices fell quiet as people paused to listen to him.

"I have a friend who can perform quite a spectacular feat and I think it would be a real eye-opener for everyone here."

"Who?" Rita asked.

"Well, since we're working with cards here, let me have the deck. He gathered up the cards before anyone could object.

"Someone…you, Helen…shuffle the cards a few more times and then remove a card from the deck."

She shuffled. "Now what?"

"Have Rita take a card from the deck. Any card, and show it to us all."

Rita took out one card and showed it around. It was the five of clubs.

"Are we all satisfied with the five of clubs?" Mac asked.

Several people nodded their approval, but no one seemed to know where this was going.

"I have a friend in Florida," Mac said. "She's half Gypsy and she has some uncanny powers that I've never been able to explain. But I think I can cast new light on the discussion here."

"What does she do?" Rita asked.

"She's a true psychic, the only real one I've ever seen. She can do things I

never believed possible until I witnessed her powers. She said they came to her after she had nearly drowned in a boating accident 10 years ago. Three other people died in the accident."

I was stunned. Could Mac really believe in psychic powers after what he'd said in the car?

"I want everyone to concentrate on the five of clubs," he said. "May I use your cousin's phone?" he asked Carol. "I want to call Madame Elinor in Florida. I'll use my credit card."

"Jeff's loaded, dial direct," she said.

Mac picked up the phone but used his calling card, anyway. Then he waited.

"Hello?" he said. "May I speak with Madame Elinor?"

He paused and seemed to stare intently into space. "Hello? Madame Elinor? This is O.E. MacDougal. Do you remember me?"

He looked down at the phone and asked Carol, "This is a speaker phone, isn't it?"

"Yes."

He stared at all the buttons on the phone. "How do you…"

Carol reached over and pushed the speaker button and Mac hung up.

"There. Can you hear us Madame Elinor?"

"Yes," the voice on the other end replied. It was a soft, smooth voice and sounded a little exotic.

"We're out here in California," he said, "and I'm with a group of people who are discussing the existence of ESP. I know you don't like to be bothered like this, but I was wondering if you could just give a short demonstration of your powers."

There was a pause on the other end. "If you know I don't like doing this, why did you call, Mr. MacDougal." Her voice was cold and accusatory.

"I want to apologize. I just thought perhaps you could help us."

"You already have me on the phone. So, go ahead." She sounded impatient.

"We've chosen a card out of a deck and I just wanted to show them…"

"Would you all please concentrate on it?" Madame Elinor interrupted.

All motion in the room seemed to have stopped. I was breathless. Where was this going? Mac had just told me...

"There is someone in the room who's mind is drifting," she said.

We all looked at each other accusingly, but I was sure it was me. We concentrated harder.

"I see a black card," Madame Elinor said.

There was another pause. It's a small card...but not a real small card...I think I see..."

I thought five of clubs as hard as I could.

"I see the five of clubs."

I was stunned. Rita started laughing. Even Ron looked surprised.

"Thank you," Mac said. "We won't be bothering you again."

"It's okay," Madame Elinor said. "I'm glad I could help you, Mr. MacDougal."

The phone went dead and Mac turned off the speaker.

"Wow, there it is," Rita said. She was jumping in place.

After everything Mac had told me, I wondered how this could have happened. I watched him for a sign, but he never even looked my way.

Those who believed in ESP were now triumphant. The three who had sided with Chuck now fell into the other camp. And even Chuck started to crumble. "Well, I want to be open minded," he said. "This might be the real thing. But most of the stuff you see I think is phony."

"What about what Ron was doing?" Rita asked.

Ron was silent now. He obviously wasn't about to let on he was just doing a card trick. Not now.

Strangely, Mac had backed out of the discussion and was just listening again. He seemed to be interested in how opinions had changed.

Chuck was obviously uncomfortable. He repeated that he still felt *most* demonstrations of ESP were phony.

"Oh, you scientific types are so anal," Rita said. "You just got living proof and you still want to deny it. Science can't explain everything," she said, and most of the people in the room agreed with her.

I was starting to have doubts about what Mac had told me in the car. I thought, I must have misunderstood him. He still didn't look at me.

Chuck fell silent.

"One other thing of interest," Mac said.

"What's that?" Rita asked.

"What you think you saw, didn't happen."

"What do you mean?"

"I mean, what you saw was not evidence of psychic phenomena."

"But you just..."

"There is no Madame Elinor. Earlier, while you folks were talking, I went to the phone in the hall and called my sister in Florida and told her what was going on. I told her that, when her phone rang again, she should pick it up and start saying 'Hearts, club, diamonds, spades.' I would say hello as soon as she called the right suit. After I asked to speak to Madame Elinor, she was to slowly start saying, 'Ace, two, three, four...,' etc. When I said hello again, she knew the face value. Then I put her on the speaker phone and...well, you know the rest."

"Why did you do that?" Rita asked and walked across the room to stand in front of him.

"Because so many people jump at the first romantic explanation for unexplained phenomena that is presented to them. If it's not ESP, it's flying saucers or visits from angels. I just wanted to show you that even after someone offers you proof of something unbelievable, you should be skeptical. Seeing is not always believing."

Then she kicked him in the same ankle Carol had and stormed from the room while he hopped about on one foot.

"It think she likes you," Carol said.

"I thought I was being helpful."

"People don't want you to help them. Do you think they play with you because they think they're better than you? About 30 minutes at the table and they know you're the best player but they think God, luck, or the poker fairies will help them beat you.

"You, of all people, should be grateful people are the way they are."

"I guess you're right.

"She kicks harder than you ."

"I'm sure that's all she does better than me," she said and kissed him.

The rest of the party didn't go well for Mac. Most who were there were aloof from him. Even Chuck was angry because he felt that even though Mac had basically agreed with him, he waited until he'd caved into popular opinion before saying anything. Chuck had wanted to be part of the "proof" that people are gullible.

On the way back to Ventura, Carol said, "Well, I'll tell you one thing, we won't be invited back to Jeff's for a while. Rita will make sure of that. But she won't last forever."

"Would he let something as beautiful as Rita go?"

"He tosses out women the way most men take out their trash."

"I just can't believe that backfired on me the way it did," Mac said. "I didn't anticipate them getting mad."

"They felt they'd been made fools of," she said.

"I still thought I was being helpful. I even had a lead on what could be a good game down in Hollywood. That's shot, now."

"There are other games."

"Well, you certainly made a fool out of me," I said.

"That wasn't my intention. It would just be nicer if people realized they should give some thought to things before accepting explanations, and even then to be skeptical."

"I just want to know when we're going back to your cousin's," I said.

"Why," Carol asked.

"I'm going to pick through his trash the day he throws Rita out." Δ

Money doesn't grow on trees, but you can grow it in your garden

By Robert L. Williams III

For many people, gardening is a splendid hobby that provides exercise, fresh air, and nutritious vegetables, berries, fruit, and melons. For many other people, gardening is a total mystery.

For nearly all people who are physically able, however, gardening can be not only pleasurable, but profitable. All that is necessary is to plant wisely, care for plants diligently, and eat or sell the harvest sensibly.

The first question is what to grow and how much of it. To a large extent, where you live determines what you can grow, but there are some universal favorites that find a place in a huge percentage of gardens.

If you plan to sell your produce, give careful thought to crops that are easy to grow and will show big profits. As an example, my tomato patch is usually a little larger than two modest rooms in a typical house, and the yield from this patch can be as high as 350 pounds a week. In the early season when tomatoes are scarce and sell in the stores for a dollar a pound or more, I can sell to markets for 50¢ a pound. When prices drop, I can sell for 25¢ a pound or less. This means that income from tomatoes could range from $70 to $175 a week. You can average $100 a week for three months, giving an income of $1,440 from tomatoes alone.

Other vegetables that produce high profits for a small amount of work are string beans, okra, squash, radishes, cu-

The author started gardening nine years ago, at the age of ten. Here he is with some of the produce from his first garden.

cumbers, strawberries, dewberries, and blackberries. Blackberries are ideal, because the berries can grow on their own. You rarely need to plant them, thin them, cultivate them, or spray them, once you have established a good patch. Typically, blackberries sell in the markets for $5 a gallon. From this amount, the grower receives $2.50 per gallon or slightly more. The growing season for blackberries is fairly short, but you can pick daily in the same patch. It is hard work, but you can pick up to 10 gallons in a day's time, if you have several good patches.

If you have enough space, consider growing corn, potatoes, sweet potatoes, pumpkins, watermelons, and cantaloupes. Once the vines or plants have matured, little care is needed until picking time. Watermelons bring $2.50 or more each in the early season and $1.50 when melons are plentiful.

If you have land that can be used for an orchard, you can earn considerable profits by growing apples, peaches, pears, plums, and cherries. From a healthy apple tree, you can pick about 10 bushels of apples, which will sell for $2.50 to $5 per bushel, or $25 to $50 from each tree. If you have 20 trees, your income can be $500 or much more per season. Peaches bring in $5 to $7 per bushel.

Grapes also grow well in many parts of the country. Scuppernong grapes and muscadines are extremely easy to grow and bring in great profits. The muscadines sell for one dollar for a large cup or small carton, and a dozen vines will produce gallons and gallons of grapes

Huge cabbages such as the ones shown above weighed 15 pounds each and sold for $2 to $3 apiece. They thrive on household vitamins.

and literally hundreds of dollars of income.

Cut your expenses

Growing vegetables and fruits is not all profit. In fact, if you do not manage it carefully, your garden may cost more than it earns. Seeds, plants, and fertilizers are expensive, and chemicals for pest control can be not only costly but harmful.

But there are ways to cut your expenses. You can save money by starting your own plants from seed, instead of buying starts. You can start seeds indoors or in a cold frame or greenhouse.

And, if you are not growing hybrid plants, you can save your own seeds. The seeds from one pumpkin, watermelon, cantaloupe, cucumber, squash, okra pod, tomato, turnip plant, or cabbage will be sufficient to plant a fairly large garden plot. You can save $40 to $50 by saving your own seeds.

You can save several hundred dollars if you buy root stock and graft your own apple trees. You can also

bud-graft peach trees. By reading a good book or magazine articles on the topic, you can do a variety of grafting work on all kinds of fruit trees.

If you have access to one or two good grape vines, when the vines are pruned, you can gather the clippings and then bury them in a shallow trench dug in loose soil. Leave four to six inches of the clippings above the surface and keep the soil moist and, preferably, covered with well-rotted sawdust or mulch. Not all of the cuttings will take root, but many will, and you can have as many grape vines as you wish with no cost at all.

You can also take a plastic bag and fill it with well-rotted compost. Be sure that the compost is moistened. Then take one end of a growing grape vine and push it all the way through the compost and the plastic bag. Tie a string at both ends of the plastic so it can't come open, so your compost won't spill out or dry. After several days, the vine will form roots, and you will have a "new" grape vine. Cut the vine below the plastic bag, remove the bag, and plant your new grape vine.

A third way to root a grape vine is to pull a section of vine to the ground and cover it with good moist soil. Leave the vine buried until roots form. Then cut the vine behind the roots and plant it out in your vineyard.

You can have tomatoes until frost by doing the following: as your adult plants start to fail, break suckers from the plants and push the end of each

A properly tended patch of green beans will produce several bushels of beans daily and hundreds of dollars annually.

"New" potatoes sell very well in early summer. This wheelbarrow holds about $35 worth of new potatoes.

sucker into good soil or compost, and within a week you will have new tomato plants a foot tall or higher.

To save money on fertilizer, save all table scraps and peelings and keep these in a compost bin until they decay. This compost makes superior fertilizer.

Save all your sawdust, bark, pine needles, small wood chips, leaves, and small twigs in a large pile. Turn the contents of the pile with a shovel every two weeks until everything is fully rotted. If you have a chipper, make your own mulch and clean up your land at the same time. Pile the mulch around plants and even between rows. By doing so, you prevent weeds to a large extent, and the mulch holds the moisture in the soil. At the end of the season, plow the mulch into the soil. (Don't plow in woody material unless it's fully composted, or it will retard next season's growth.) Producing your own mulch will save you money in at least two ways: you produce your own fertilizer and you save on the cost of watering your garden.

To market

Your next step is to market what you grow. Long before you are ready to harvest your crops, contact people who operate roadside produce stands. These people are often in need of all the produce they can get. Many produce sellers admit that they grow very little of what they sell. They also say that they have to drive long distances to buy the produce they need.

In preparing this article, I talked with produce vendors, and what I learned was surprising and pleasing. One roadside operator (who sells many thousands of dollars worth of produce each year) had this to say: "We don't even try to make a profit on produce we buy. We grow and sell fruit, and we are delighted to have gardeners bring their produce for us to sell for the gardener. We have found that many customers who stop to buy green beans and okra also buy our peaches and apples."

The largest roadside produce seller in our area does not grow his own vegetables and fruits. He said, "I drive 300 miles to pick up my produce. It would save me a great deal of time and money if I could buy it locally. I will buy all the green beans, okra, tomatoes, cabbage, and potatoes that local gardeners can produce. I am especially interested in fruits and vegetables that have a long shelf life."

He cited the following price schedule: $5 per bushel for Irish potatoes; $17 for a thirty-pound box of tomatoes; $10 per bushel for cucumbers; $12 for ³/4 bushel of squash; $10 for ¹/2 bushel of okra; $20 per bushel for string beans; $2 or more for watermelons; $8 for a 50-pound sack of cabbage; $4 a gallon for strawberries; $6 a gallon for blackberries; and $1.50 for pie pumpkins.

It is easy to see that green beans are very profitable. You can plant several hundred-foot rows and pick bushels of beans every day for weeks. As soon as your first beans bloom, plant more beans. Keep doing this all summer so that you will have fresh beans at all times.

One final thought: suppose you grow 20 bushels of Irish potatoes, 500 pounds of tomatoes, five bushels of

Watermelons produce well, and several plants will earn $100 or more.

cucumbers, ten bushels of squash, ten bushels of okra, 50 bushels of string beans, 300 cantaloupes, 200 watermelons, 150 pumpkins, 50 bushels of apples, 500 pounds of cabbage, 100 gallons of strawberries, and 50 gallons of blackberries. This may sound like a lot, but in reality, it is a small amount for an energetic gardener to produce. The total income for the products listed above will be more than $5,000.

That is not too bad for an activity that costs little, provides great exercise, brings immense pleasure, and also fills the table with delicious food. I started gardening seriously when I was in elementary school, and I learned that I could make a profit then. At age 19 I still garden, and profits today are even better. You too can make money from your garden, and the beauty of it is that the demand for fresh vegetables grows greater—as do profits—each year. Δ

Blessed is he who has found his work; let him ask no other blessedness.
—Thomas Carlyle, 1843

A country moment

Pat Ward of Fall Creek Ranch in southern Oregon took this photo of her ranch pond on a recent quiet evening.

(Note: If you have a country moment you'd like to share with our readers, please send it to us at Country Moment, *Backwoods Home Magazine*, P.O. Box 712, Gold Beach, OR 97444. Please include a self-addressed, stamped return envelope if you want the photo back.)

Where I live

By Annie Duffy

Working for a dad who works at home

I am homeschooled, and part of my homeschooling involves working for my Dad on this magazine. It has been a good learning experience for me. Not only have I learned how to work hard, but I have learned a lot about computers and writing.

Ever since Dad started *Backwoods Home Magazine*, I've worked for him in one way or another. Up to about two years ago, I labeled, stuffed, and stamped envelopes. I usually packaged our anthologies for mailing too. I always got to use the computer, usually playing games, but once the magazine grew a bit and we got a few more employees, I used the computer more often.

Since most jobs at this office have to do with the computer, I've learned many programs. Lately I have been teaching Linda, one of our employees, how to use Quark XPress, the desktop publisher program we use to make this magazine. She is typing in all of the zucchini recipes that readers have been sending in so we can publish them in a book later this year. I learned Quark XPress just by hanging around the office and asking my Dad and Lance, our associate editor, questions when I got stuck.

Another of my computer jobs is creating ads and editing photos using a program called Adobe Photoshop. Don Childers, our cover artist, has been teaching me that. Since he is a real artist, he can teach me things that only an artist would notice.

And, of course, I write this column, which helps me develop my writing skills. I also get credit for it with my English grade.

With the computers, I have access to the Internet. I can research stuff for my columns and for my schoolwork. I found some information about my goats, horse, and donkey too.

I also found some information about Veterinary Medicine, and since I hope to be a vet, I have been exploring these sections a lot. My goal is to have a business covering all aspects of animal care. Since I want to take full advantage of the preveterinary courses offered in highschool, I probably will not be homeschooled next year. Although I love to be at home, I think it will give me a good head start on my career.

My dad is buying a few acres close to my home where we will build our new office. We will also build a riding arena and a small barn. I hope to eventually locate my business there, too.

A fun part of working for my Dad has been traveling. My Dad and I have demonstrated *BHM* at many tradeshows in the western states, and a few in the east, to promote it. The shows are usually three days long, and I've had a chance to visit many places, such as Seattle, San Francisco, Portland, Los Angeles, Las Vegas, Salt Lake City, and Boston. I also get a lot of studying done in the car, by reading aloud to my Dad, who then quizzes me on what I just read. I usually read each section of my book three or four times, until I know it cold.

Since I am homeschooled and I work for my Dad, I also have a much

Annie Duffy

more flexible schedule, which allows me to take trips and do things that normally I wouldn't be able to do. Things like hiking, training my animals, and night fishing.

Just recently I was offered a job exercising horses for a neighboring couple. It's a job I really want, and thanks to my flexible hours, I'll be able to take it.

Since my Dad is a writer, and our senior editor, John Silveira, is a mathematician, I don't often have problems with my homework. John Silveira is like a walking encyclopedia so I can almost always get answers to the questions I have.

The advantages of homeschooling over public schooling are obvious for someone like me, since I live so far from town. The advantages of working for the magazine at home are even greater. I'm getting to learn all aspects of running a business, plus I still have the freedom to do things I love.

If you are offered a chance to work in your family business, take it. I hope you get the chance to learn as much as I do. Δ

Homesteading on the electronic frontier

By Martin Waterman

Cybrarian—a great Internet job

This column generates a great deal of e-mail and by far the number one concern among *BHM* readers is that of affordable Internet access. Although the competition among Internet providers in major metropolitan areas is fierce, resulting in a wide choice of providers and affordable pricing, rural dwellers have often been stuck with having to use expensive online services such as CompuServe and America Online, as well as often having to pay long distance toll charges.

Good news! Affordable Internet service for rural areas is arriving faster than anyone thought possible. This is for several reasons, the biggest of which is the entrance into the Internet service market by the larger telephone companies.

AT&T has announced that it will be giving inexpensive Internet access to its customers. The other phone companies are expected to follow to hold onto their respective market share in the competitive and expanding communication arena.

Another catalyst is the recent announcement by the Federal Communications Commission to open up the $100 billion local phone business to long distance companies as well as cable TV operators, the latter of which are already experimenting with providing high speed Internet access. The Internet is quickly becoming a vital component that will have to be offered by any company involved in telecommunications, lest their competitors have any advantage.

Cybrarians

The Internet is creating new jobs, and not just for the people providing the online services. A new position has been created that can be done from anywhere on the planet, provid-

ing you have access to the Internet. This is the position of being a cybrarian.

Cybrarians are one of the new jobs of the Information age, and not only are they in demand by businesses, but being a cybrarian itself can offer a great opportunity to be in business for yourself, particularly if you specialize in a particular kind of information that is needed.

Cybrarians are, of course, basically librarians but instead if being surrounded by books, they are nestled into a computer work station. There they are connected to the Internet and search the four corners of the globe to harvest information from thousands of universities, the World Wide Web, Internet News Groups, governments, businesses, professionals, and libraries such as the Library of Congress.

Consistent with the many facets of the Internet, there is more than one type of cybrarian. There is the traditional, institutional librarian who has made the leap to the Internet. The other type of cybrarian is more of a free-lance librarian, or, as an ode to the old west, a cybrarian for hire—a virtual information bounty hunter.

A third type of cybrarian that has evolved is the Corporate cybrarian. Many large businesses have always had corporate researchers to find market and other information. However, with the birth and unprecedented growth of the Information Highway, many businesses have found that the need for their own in-house or part time cybrarian if for no other reason than to monitor their competition. No matter the reason that information is needed, more and more organizations are finding they need someone to handle this task. This is usually because most managers, who need the information the most, do not have the time to surf and build an inventory of useful sites and find the information that they need.

The language barrier

The thought of marketing your wares around the world may seem intimidating, especially because of the different languages spoken. But the language barrier is not insurmountable, especially since English is the language of the Internet. There is also another factor at work that will help you do business around the world.

In the Orient and Latin America, many of the business people have very poor language skills when it comes to the English language. However, when it comes to written skills, most have excellent grammar. When dealing with a WWW site and e-mail, people in other countries are not intimidated and can take the time to compose a response. They may be very interested in using your services, as well as acquiring the rights to your product.

A real live cybrarian

I caught up with Lorna Peers, a real live cybrarian at the DISCscribe sit, which is located in Fredericton, New Brunswick, Canada (National borders, by the way, are irrelevant to the Internet). Lorna holds a masters degree in library and information science from the University of Western Ontario. She can be reached at http://www.disccribe.ca/disccribe.htm or e-mailed at lornap@disccribe.ca. If you visit her WWW home page you will see her photo and see that cybrarians are not chrome-plated info hunters from the future. Following is an interview I had with her:

BHM: What is your primary function as a cybrarian?

Lorna Peers: I locate information for clients or members of the company I work for using the Internet or commercial online databases. I think your term "information bounty hunter" is quite accurate. This includes individual requests from businesses and individuals, locating competitive information for use by companies, and background research and online promotion of clients who are on our Web server.

BHM: What percentage of your work do you find deals with online promotion?

Lorna Peers: I would estimate at least 50% and growing. I'm always finding new search engines and other places to promote our clients' Web sites. A lot of the time is spent locating the most appropriate category in a directory such as Yahoo.

BHM: How do you typically online promote a company?

Lorna Peers: At the design stage, I typically do some research to see what sites similar to the clients' may exist and where they are located in directories or indices. Once the client's site is ready, we write a brief press release or promo and post it in the appropriate newsgroups, mailing lists, search engines (i.e., Locos, etc.), subject directories, and What's New pages. Online promotion is very important to Web sites. Regardless of a site's value, it is of little use if it cannot be easily located.

BHM: What areas of the Internet do you find you use the most to find information for your clients?

Lorna Peers: I would have to say that I use the Web most often, primarily because of the Web design we do for clients. For more general requests, I use the Web (usually first, as it is the fastest growing portion of the Internet), gopher (less so, I often find the information out of date or reach dead ends), as well as newsgroups and mailing lists. On occasion, I may come across a Web site with a contact name and send a request by e-mail to see if he or she can supply more information. Other sources include library catalogs and periodical databases.

BHM: Is there such a thing as a common question you receive?

Lorna Peers: Not really. We've done some consulting for national organizations that want to get their offices on the Internet, so I'm often updating my list of Canadian ISPs (Internet Service Providers).

BHM: What is the biggest information request you have received?

Lorna Peers: One client wanted a fairly comprehensive list of Canadian companies that design and host Web pages, with contact and pricing information. Finding the companies wasn't difficult, but locating their list of services and pricing information, when available, took a while. Do you realize that some companies didn't have contact information on their pages? Not

very useful for the client who didn't have Web access.

BHM: Do you find that most of your customers are preoccupied with the status of their competitors' presence on the Internet?

Lorna Peers: No, not as much as they should be. Some businesses still see barriers to the Internet—e.g., cost of hardware, cost of access, learning curve—despite the fact that their competitor may already have a presence online. This spring we held two free seminars on using the Internet for local businesses. I think once they have the opportunity to see the capabilities for themselves, they may realize its potential.

BHM: What is the primary type of research you conduct and for what type of companies?

Lorna Peers: In terms of individual requests, many companies request a synopsis of "what's out there" that may be related to their type of business. In many cases these businesses don't yet have Internet access of their own, so the results may help justify the decision to purchase access. I would estimate that many of these companies are small businesses.

BHM: What does a cybrarian typically charge?

Lorna Peers: My rates range from $65 to $100 (Canadian) plus applicable taxes per hour for searching and formatting results. The rate depends on the volume of work and the urgency of the information.

BHM: Could you categorize for us the types of businesses that you find most often require the use of a cybrarian and for what purposes?

Lorna Peers: I've done a number of searches for government departments, where they required information for presentations, or for decision-making purposes, e.g., whether or not to proceed with a particular program. I've done research for insurance companies, telephone companies, manufacturing, public utilities, hotels, nonprofit organizations. The businesses, individuals, and organizations that have purchased our Web services range from the chambers of commerce to music groups. They like the fact that I can put together a list of links to other sites with related information, as well as promote their site.

BHM: What do you like or dislike about being a cybrarian as opposed to being a conventional librarian in a book-filled environment?

Lorna Peers: I like the fact that the Internet is constantly changing and evolving. It's all I can do to keep up on all the new sites, software, etc. Navigating the Internet can be a challenge, since there is no absolute list of its resources, but the tools and indices have improved significantly. I can't say I dislike anything. Who wouldn't love to surf the Net all day, and get paid? I'm also adjusting to being, for the most part, a telecommuter and working from home. I missed the daily interaction with co-workers at first, but there are lots of benefits. Also, since most of the communication and transfer of my results are done electronically, I rarely meet my clients face to face, and I for one would like to meet them now and then.

BHM: What is the strangest request you have ever received for information?

Lorna Peers: Well, we do have a site on UFOs. I put together a list of links to UFO pages on the Net. There's a ton of them. Another was for the availability of Internet access in St. Lucia, a Carribean island.

Opportunities

Many people now surfing the Internet as a hobby are becoming cybrarians. The field is wide open because it's still very young. If you're already surfing the Net, there may be a job there for you. Who knows, maybe one of your neighbors is putting in solar and he's reached a bottleneck because he needs information. Right there could be your very first customer. Δ

Pedestrian

She was awkwardly crumpled
Facedown in the street,
In the rain,
Her skirt up over her waist,
Her umbrella and purse
Separated from her
As if they didn't belong.
She stared unblinkingly at the wet asphalt
While the car that had surprised her in the crosswalk
Was stalled beside her in the roadway
Looking like a beast that had just stopped by to graze.
Far away, sirens wailed.
There was no way for them to know
There was no hurry.
I wanted to do something
To save her from the indignity
Of dying in the middle of the road,
Her ass in the air,
In the rain.
I wanted to close her eyes.
But our bus had come and I got on.
I watched from the window
As the bus pulled away.
A crowd had gathered
To stare at her.

John Silveira
Ojai, CA

A BHM Staff Profile: Mark S. Cogan

Mark Cogan is the layout and design editor of *Backwoods Home Magazine,* and as such is responsible for the "new look" the magazine has acquired during the past year (1999). He came to BHM from *Wind Tracks Magazine,* the nation's second largest windsurfing publication. Mark has worked as a design consultant and as a web developer for large corporations such as Harley Davidson Motorcycles, Neil Pryde Ltd, the world's largest producer of water sports products in the world, and 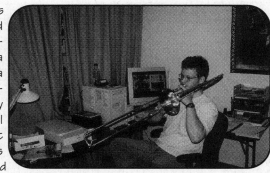 smaller outfits, like NetServe, Inc., Big Air Windsurfing, and several other lesser known companies.

Mark, 24, is also a part-time college student, majoring in Human Services and Sociology. He will leave the magazine in the fall of 2000 to become a full-time student. His hobbies include playing the trombone, singing Frank Sinatra tunes, and being a camp counselor during the summer.

Using trot lines, set lines, and jug fishing will increase your fish catch substantially

By Rev. J.D. Hooker

As I write this, it's past the middle of February, so spring's not that far off. Everyone is starting to look forward to the upcoming season change. Garden catalogs are all out by now, and ours are being researched regularly. Also, we've got a few poultry catalogs, and some new plans to go with them. And my wife and I intend to put up a small greenhouse pretty soon.

I'd have to say, though, that the one thing I'm most looking forward to is the ice-out—the day when, finally, all of the rivers and lakes around here are once again open water. Now, it's not a bad thing to sit out on a frozen lake, pulling fish out through holes chopped in the ice . . . especially if you have some good homemade Applejack to drink, and a pipe stuffed with good homegrown tobacco to keep you company. But that's just never been my idea of fishing.

Of course, my idea of fishing is a little different from a lot of other folks' anyway. If you're interested in providing a steady supply of delicious, high-protein, low-fat foodstuff for yourself, with the added bonus of producing a really high-quality supplemental feed supply for chickens, dogs, cats, and other homestead animals, then you might want to give some of my fishing methods a try.

Trotlines

Probably my very favorite fishing technique is using a trotline. Most folks will automatically associate this method with big-river catfish fishing, but the trotline is a highly effective means of taking large quantities of just about any sort of fish, from just about any water. By learning to be real adaptable in regards to baits,

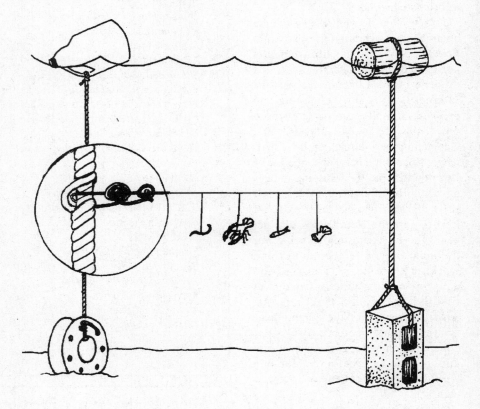

Trotline with a mid-depth set

depths, setting methods, etc., you can see how versatile the trotline can be. In addition to the various catfish and "rough" fish like carp and suckers, my trotlines regularly catch crappie, bluegill and other sunfish, largemouth and smallmouth bass, white and yellow perch, white and yellow bass, bullheads, drum, striped bass, sauger, gar, even walleye and northerns.

The method I use for setting out a trotline may differ a little from that used by most anglers, but I've found it to be the most effective and adaptable way to employ this technique. To start with you'll need an anchor, a float, and enough light rope to reach from the bottom to the water's surface, for each end of your trotline.

If you'll take a look back at my article on making canvas decoys in *Backwoods Home* Issue No. 35, you can see how to put together a simple kellick anchor. For trotline use, these will need to be quite a bit heavier than those used to anchor decoys, probably 15 pounds at the minimum. Other anchor options could include bricks (the kind with holes in them, for affixing the rope), cinder blocks, cement-filled coffee cans with U-shaped pieces of iron re-bar embedded in the cement, junk car rims, and plastic jugs filled with sand or gravel.

For floats you can consider things like empty plastic jugs (never glass), like bleach bottles, antifreeze jugs, milk jugs, and such; empty plastic buckets with tight-fitting plastic lids;

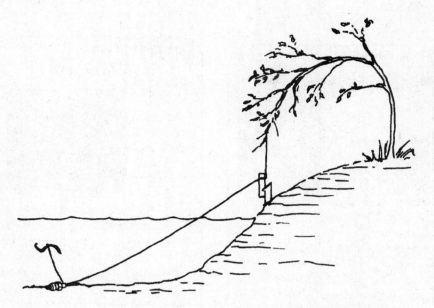

Set line using a sapling, an old spark plug sinker, and a trigger device

boards or sections of logs; two-foot or longer pieces of 4" PVC pipe, with end caps glued on; or just about anything else that will float. Should you have any concerns about punctures, any of the hollow floats can easily be filled with foam insulation. One can of insulating foam (sold at lumber yards and hardware stores) will fill quite a few such floats, and it is relatively inexpensive.

Usually quarter-inch nylon or poly rope is plenty strong enough for this sort of application. I prefer the braided ropes, but the regular twisted type works fine, too. You'll need some stout nylon cord (mason's line works fine), heavy braided fish line, and a large supply of hooks.

You'll also need to check your state's fishing regulations, as just about every state has rules regarding trotline length or number of hooks. In some states, in fact, trotlines are illegal.

Once you've determined the depth at which you'll be setting the trotline (see below), you'll want to attach the nylon cord to one of the ropes, as shown. From there, you'll attach two foot or three foot dropper lines, with baited hooks attached every two or three feet, until you've reached the desired length. Then attach the cord to the other rope, using the same method.

Effective bait

The depth at which you'll want to set your trotline, as well as the sort of bait you'll choose, will depend upon the water you're fishing and the species you're targeting. Nightcrawlers, corn kernels, pieces of fresh or tainted liver, marshmallows, chunks of Ivory soap, stink baits, or pieces of plug tobacco, fished a foot or so off the bottom, work great for catfish and other bottom feeders. Minnows, crayfish (or peeled crayfish tails), pork rind baits, nightcrawlers or redworms, and similar baits fished at depths from three to fifteen feet will attract many species of intermediate-depth feeders. And frogs (hooked through a thigh so they'll keep swimming), crickets and grasshoppers, salamanders, mice, crayfish, and other baits set right on the surface will bring in top-feeding bass and other surface feeders. If you want, you can set your trotline so that it angles up from the bottom to the surface to cover all three zones.

In most states, the fish and game regulations require that all trotlines be checked at least once every 24 hours. While that will meet the legal require-

ments, checking the set *at least twice* daily will normally produce much better results. I prefer to check trotlines just after sunup, and again right at dusk. It seems like fish left too long on the line are frequently chewed by turtles or other fish before I get to them.

Set lines

The trotline alone can bring in steady and reliable catches when properly located, baited, and maintained. But you can increase your yields by adding several *set lines*, or *limb lines* as they are sometimes called. Again, you'll need to check your state's rules, as the number of set lines you are allowed to use is usually specified. For example, here in Indiana, each person is permitted to use a maximum of 10 set lines. Other states have similar rules.

To rig a set line, affix a length of heavy fishline to a small sapling, overhanging limb, or something else of that nature, which is both fairly strong and relatively springy. Add a baited hook (and a sinker and/or bobber if you want), and toss it out into the water. A simple trigger device, like the one shown, will automatically set the hook and add a little to the effectiveness of this setup, but it isn't absolutely necessary. Used with a heavy line, and maybe a wire leader, the drop line is an effective method for taking snappers and other large turtles as well.

When I decide to use bobbers on some of my set lines, I usually just drill a small hole through a piece of stick, and run the line through this hole, threading an ordinary button onto the line at the desired distance to act as a bobber stop. This allows the bobber to slide down next to the bait, making it a little easier to toss out the line, and then slip back up for fishing.

Set lines are especially useful for folks who don't feel like going out in their boat every day to check on a trotline. They can just as readily be set up and maintained from shore as they can from the water.

Jug fishing

The third technique that I employ regularly is what's known as jug fishing. I attach a line with a baited hook to some sort of a float and set it adrift. Depending upon the location, I use lines between one and ten feet long.

Usually I set nine or ten such jug lines afloat, just before beginning to check on my trotlines and drop lines. Once I've finished checking these other fishing devices, I round up all of the jug lines. Every fish that has hit the bait solidly will still be "on the line," as these floats will play the fish at least as well as a professional angler with a high-dollar rod and reel setup.

Don't overdo it

When using any of these fishing methods, you do need to be realistic and responsible about what you're doing. Your goal is to bring in a large amount of succulent fresh fillets, but reducing the fish population too far is self-defeating. So just as soon as your take begins to slack off just a little bit, you'll need to move your whole setup to a different part of the lake or river, or maybe even to a different body of water altogether. That way you can return to your original location every year or two and start over.

For me, the real beauty of these fishing methods (except for the jug lines, which I only set out while already on the water) is that these trotlines and set lines are out there working 24 hours out of every day. I might be plowing, feeding hogs, eating breakfast, or playing checkers, but my simple setups are still fishing.

We use every bit of our catch. If you keep any animals that will eat fish, from hogs or chickens to hounds or barn cats, you might want to try feeding them what we call "scrap stew," so you can put all of your fish scraps to use. Just toss all of your fish heads,

entrails, fins, bones and such into a metal drum set over a fire. Add enough water to cover, and boil until all of the bones are soft enough to be eaten easily. Now, depending on what sort of animals you'll be feeding, add some sort of a thickening agent. For dogs and cats, cracked corn, soybeans (or other beans), stale bread, old cornmeal, weevilly flour, or things of that nature work fine. For livestock like hogs or chickens, chopped hay, freshly mowed grass, bad or cull potatoes or onions, sweet acorns, bad apples or other fruit, and similar waste produce can also be added. Spoiled or surplus milk or other dairy products can also be used up in this stew.

Let this stuff simmer, stirring it once in a while with a board or something, until it's thickened like oatmeal or mush. Then allow it to cool completely before feeding. All of this extra protein will put a really nice healthy shine on a dog or cat's coat, or fatten a pig very nicely, or put a really big boost into your chickens' egg output.

Before you start tossing your catch of carp and other "rough" fish into this kettle, however, you should try putting

them into your smokehouse for a while, even if you just use an old refrigerator with a can full of damp hardwood sawdust, or ground corncobs set on a hotplate. Smoking these fish is almost like working magic, as the fillets will turn from trash-fish into a true delicacy.

If you try any of these fishing techniques, you should see good results right from the start. As you gain experience using these methods in your local waters, these simple and inexpensive fishing methods will become really valuable "working assets." If you enjoy dining regularly on fresh fish, I promise you'll be impressed. Δ

You can make this effective gray water disposal system

By Steve Anderson

One of the things you need to worry about when you build your own home is waste water disposal. Even if you're starting with an outhouse, or installing a gas or composting toilet, you still need to safely carry off gray water waste from your kitchen and laundry. That muddy puddle (and the odor from it) at the end of a pipe run through the kitchen wall gets old fast. We solved the problem with a small, inexpensive, home-crafted tank and drainage system modeled on the big expensive ones.

It took us two tries to get it right ("us" being my son, my nephew, and me). Our first system functioned for about a year before failing. The first hint of trouble was a kitchen sink that seemed to take forever to drain. Finally it just stopped working during spring thaw, when the ground around the drainage system was saturated from snowmelt and heavy April rains.

Once the soil dried out enough for digging, we found a system totally clogged with matter that had the consistency of oatmeal. There were two major problems: We hadn't provided enough drainage—that much was obvious. But it wasn't until my son did a little research that the second problem became obvious. Modern septic tanks have an internal baffle system that keeps solids from getting from the tank into the drain pipe and leach fields. The purpose of the holding tank is to digest those solids before they reach the leach field.

Getting tanked up

We stuck with our basic design, though. The heart of our system is a blue plastic 55-gallon drum that we bought used for $10. To install the internal baffle, we cut off the top of the drum, about two inches below the rim. This allows plenty of surface area to re-attach the top with flat metal bracing. This bracing is available (pre-drilled for nuts and bolts) at the hardware store, or you can make your own.

We cut a four-inch hole in the top of the drum for the drain pipe from the house, then mounted a 15-gallon round plastic trash can (*with the bottom cut out*) on the inside of the lid, so the drain pipe from the house empties through it. This trash can acts as a baffle and keeps all *floating* vegetable matter away from the drain pipes that exit the drum. The stuff that *sinks* is kept *below* the drains, and everything is properly digested by bacterial action before making its way to the drain pipes. We mounted the trash can baffle to the top of the drum with three 90° zinc-plated corner braces. All the hardware is fastened with nuts and bolts after drilling holes through the plastic.

To finish the top, you need to cut another four-inch hole for a cleanout pipe. I used PVC cement to attach a plug at the top that I can unscrew to pump out the tank every few years. This way the system will work for a long time. We used four-inch PVC for this, once again mounting it with corner bracing. A four-inch PVC elbow was mounted to accept the drain pipe from the house.

You may be wondering why we designed this so we had to bury the drum standing up. Well, we learned from our first try: Yes, it required less digging to lay the drum on its side, but the weight of the earth collapsed the area of the drum above the drains.

Before putting the top of the drum back on, we cut two four-inch holes

The tank is in the ground with gravel laid underneath the drain pipes. Use plenty of gravel for proper drainage.

for the drain pipes 180° across from each other. These were cut just an inch or so below the seam joining the top and the side of the drum, so they are well above the bottom of the interior baffle. After the top was re-attached, and all the PVC installed, we applied generous amounts of 50-year silicone caulking wherever PVC goes through the tank. We didn't worry too much about a little leakage, because we dug our hole so we could get a generous foot or so of gravel underneath the tank, and four to six inches of space around it for the same treatment. Any leakage from the tank will simply drain through that, and leach back into the soil.

Laying the groundwork

As mentioned earlier, our first attempt at this project didn't provide enough drainage. We weren't going to make that mistake again. We dug two eight-foot-long trenches for perforated PVC drain pipe. We dug them deep enough to get eight inches of gravel underneath them. The whole system is deep enough so we don't have to worry about freeze-ups. The trenches are generous in width also, about 18 inches wide. The boys did the digging, and they were determined to get it right. They both thought doing it twice was enough, thank you very much.

If you're not sure about the drainage capacity of the soil, do a percolation test. Dig a one-foot-diameter hole two feet deep and fill it halfway with water. If there is still water in the hole an hour later, the soil is not suitable, and you need to pick a different spot. (You *could* construct a drainage bed with at least two feet of cracked stone underneath your drain pipes. I'd find another spot.)

We wanted good, clean gravel to use for the drain bed. The first time, we had used a sandy, stony mix that barely qualified as gravel. The problem was, we didn't need very much, and around here it's very hard to get as small a quantity as a couple yards of gravel delivered. But we found a solution, which I will describe. Without digressing too much, I'll admit that I'm a hardware store junky. A positive aspect to that is I probably know the inventory better than some of the sales help. I won't go into the negative aspects, except to say they usually involve spending too much money.

Tank with cleanout pipe mounted, hay in place, ready to be covered. Note generous amount of caulking around base of cleanout pipe.

But I had spied a pallet of about twelve bags of landscaping marble chips off to the side at one of the local stores (or "Dad's hangouts," as the kids call them). Since it was well past spring landscaping season, I was able to make a good deal on the whole batch and got out of it cheaper than if I had been able to find someone to deliver a yard of clean gravel. This went under the drain pipes, and six inches of hay went over them. The hay is to keep soil from filtering down and plugging the drains. We used what was left over of the old gravel to go around and under the tank. Then we covered the whole thing up. Later that fall, I went back and filled in the spots that had settled.

Venting

Septic tanks are designed to work with air and bacteria to digest solids into sludge. This greatly reduces the volume of the solids in the tank. A properly working system only needs to be pumped out every five years or so, depending on the number of people living in the house. You need to vent your system so the air outlet is above all the drains. My vent runs off the drain pipe under the sink (on the tank side of the trap), through the wall, and up the outside wall almost to my eaves.

The system described in this article has been in place for almost two years now and is working fine. There have been no back-ups or freeze-ups. To be perfectly honest, the kitchen sink does drain slowly when the ground is saturated in the spring. (By that I mean the sink is empty by the time I'm done wiping everything down after doing the dishes.)

A couple of rules

We also have a couple of hard and fast rules regarding the sink: Always make sure the drain basket is in the drain—always. I figure the more material I can keep out of the tank, the

Materials & costs	
Tank	.$10.00
4" PVC elbow	.3.99
Cleanout pipe & cap	.4.99
8 corner irons	.4.18
Caulking	.4.99
Two 8' perf. drain pipes . .	.11.90
Gravel	.12.00
Misc. hardware	.3.00
Total	.$55.05

longer it will be before I have to pump it out. Never let meat products (grease) into the sink. Coagulated bacon grease and other animal fat won't digest, so I try to keep it out of the system. Every now and then I dump in a half bottle of beer or so to keep the whole thing percolating.

If you're going to be successful at living independently, you've got to be willing to live by the old adage, "If at first you don't succeed, try, try again." Everything just isn't going to work the first time you try it. You don't become a jack of all trades overnight. Even doing this thing twice only cost us more labor and time. And you've got to learn from your mistakes.

Our second attempt is working fine, but if I had to do it again I would make it even better: I'd put in another drain pipe. I couldn't get the boys to dig that third trench. They swore two was enough, and so far they're right. And I'd look for stainless steel hardware—I'm not sure how long the zinc-plated stuff will last. You could also spend more and have each and every one of those holes through the tank waterproof, but all the fittings for that aren't cheap.

And there you have it: an inexpensive, safe, effective disposal system for gray water wastes for about $50, even if you have to go out and buy everything. I don't have more than $25 in mine. I had a lot of the stuff around before I started. It pays to be kind of a packrat. Δ

Backwoods Home magazine

Sept/Oct 1996
No 41

SPECIAL HARVEST ISSUE

practical ideas for self-reliant living

INCLUDING

using green tomatoes, tasty pickle recipes, harvesting greens in the snow, corn storage, pressing cider, homestead dehydrator, making your pectin, keeping apples, harvesting all year, cover cropping, sheet composting, using leafmold, storing onions, delicious meals from stored veggies

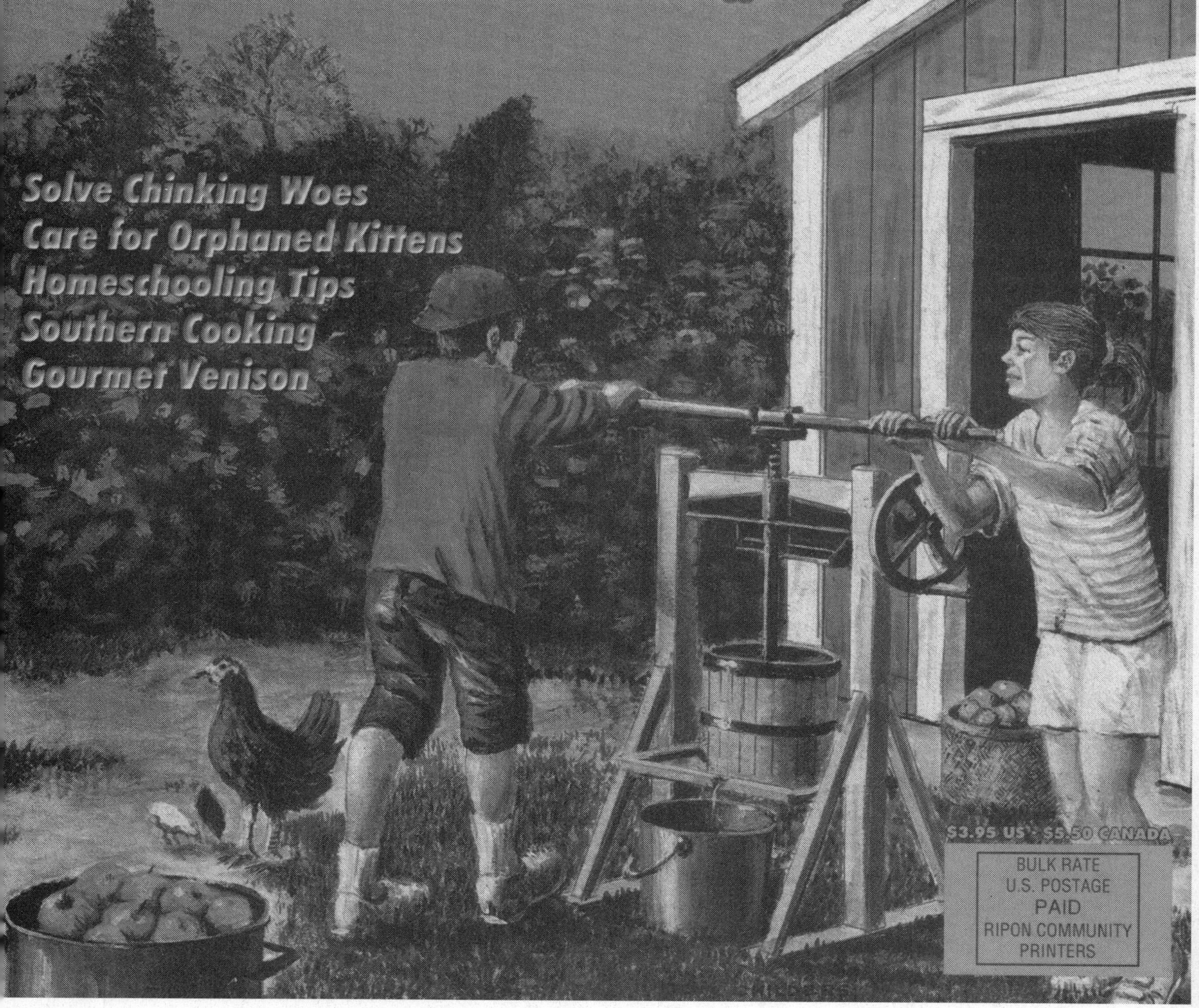

Solve Chinking Woes
Care for Orphaned Kittens
Homeschooling Tips
Southern Cooking
Gourmet Venison

$3.95 US · $5.50 CANADA

BULK RATE
U.S. POSTAGE
PAID
RIPON COMMUNITY
PRINTERS

My view

The "Leave Us Alone" coalition

Ever notice the way the news media and big government seem to work together, both at the national and local level?

At the national level it's fairly obvious: If President Clinton had been anything other than the big-government Democrat he is, the media would have deep fried him long ago over things like Whitewater, Travelgate, Filegate, Vince Foster, Paula Jones, Web Hubbel, Guy Tucker, the MacDougals, or any of his other friends who are either under indictment, on trial, or in jail. Imagine a Ronald Reagan surviving a portfolio like that?

But on the local level the collusion is much more subtle. I picked up my local newspaper this morning and read one of the main front-page headlines: *Property tax jump unlikely.* The slightly smaller subheadline read: *Assessor says values level off.* The prominently-displayed story was essentially a feel-good piece about the local tax assessor's office because he was not only not going to raise taxes, but he was going to lower some people's taxes a little. Wow, what a guy!

The same newspaper a week ago prominently featured a list of county services that would be cut unless voters passed two upcoming ballot tax levies. Ominously, libraries and fire services were at the top of the list. I couldn't help but link the two stories-you know, since they're giving us a break on property taxes, we should pass the two levies and save the libraries and fire stations.

But I'm probably just paranoid. After all I'm a right wing, knee jerk, mean-spirited conservative who could care less about libraries and fire stations, not to mention children, old people, and anything else big government taxing and spending is meant to help.

Buried inside today's newspaper is a story I consider important: *Taxpayers' bill passes in Senate*. The subheadline reads: *Legislation aimed at abuses of IRS.* The story is about legislation passed overwhelmingly by both houses of Congress to make it easier for taxpayers to sue the IRS for wrongful collection of taxes. The story termed the bill a "Taxpayer Bill of Rights" and listed all kinds of ways Americans could legally tell the IRS to take a hike. But I guess the newspaper didn't think that story very important, so it played it down by placing it inside the paper.

You know, I'm sick of the way the news media tries to feed me the news. They either ignore or play down stories I think are important, and they put on the front page news stories I often think are self serving to their big government allies in politics. From my local newspaper to national television news, they filter it through their own narrow big gov-emment-is-the-solution-to-everything prejudice. Did you know that more than 85% of the members of the news media admit to being liberals or Democrats? I suppose it's only natural for them to think big government is the solu-

Dave Duffy

tion to most problems. They probably can't begin to comprehend that someone like me just wants to be left alone, that I pay my property taxes grudgingly and think they should be abolished altogether, and that I think most tax levies are a waste of money, even the ones the lying (or stupid) news media claim are the only way to keep the libraries and fire stations from closing.

I am a member of that newest huge coalition that has emerged in America during the last few years-the "Leave Us Alone" coalition. We're made up of people with differing opinions, but what we share in common is we don't like big government with its tax and spend solutions, and we don't trust the news media which has become little more than the mouthpiece of big government.

And as many members of the "Leave Us Alone" coalition have done, I've begun not only resisting all attempts by big government to control my life, but I've begun turning off the news media and turning to alternative methods of getting news. For example, I have cancelled my subscription to my local newspaper and have stopped listening to most national television news.

Instead I rely on several good newsletters and radio shows, but in particular I rely on the relatively unfiltered versions of news found on TV's C-SPAN network and the comprehensive news CNN offers over the Internet on its World Wide Web page. Even though CNN still arranges news selectively on the Internet, it's easy to rearrange the news according to my own view of what's important, and it's easy to dig deep into a story, getting all the detail I want, even to the point of going right into a politician's email basket and telling him what I think.

The Internet, I think, is emerging as the greatest freedom tool of the twentieth century. No wonder big government is already making noises about controlling the Internet to save-get this-the children from pornography. What a laugh. Who they really want to save is—you guessed it—themselves. Δ

For large quantity food dehydration try this homemade gem from the past

By Rev. J.D. Hooker

The thing I like the most about *Backwoods Home* is that, unlike a lot of other magazines, the articles are written by folks who are actually doing the things they write about. Folks like Massad Ayoob, Don Fallick, and Dynah Geissal have already learned their stuff by trial and error, which can save the rest of us the time, troubles, and expenses of initial experimentation. It's good to fool around with new ideas, but we can use other folks' experience as proven starting points, and then adapt our own ideas and improvements into their concepts. As an example of building on someone else's experience, let me tell you how I ended up building the perfect large-quantity food dehydrator.

Since our garden, fruit trees, strawberry patches, etc., have always produced abundantly for us, we've worked at developing the skills to preserve this abundance from one harvest to the next. Canning and freezing only go so far, so for a couple of years we

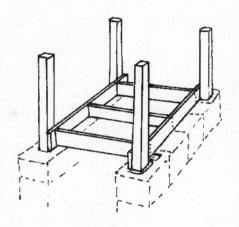

2. Install supports for trays.

fooled around with various types of dehydrators. The relatively inexpensive Ronco brand electric dehydrator we purchased at an area gun show works great for *small* quantities, and we find it very useful for that.

However, solar dehydrators turned out to be an entirely different story. I can tell you from experience that unless you're living somewhere like one of our southwestern deserts, where you can depend on plenty of hot, dry weather for lengthy periods, solar dryers (whether purchased or owner-built) just aren't dependable enough for real backwoods-type use. As a result, I fooled around with several other ideas, but none of them worked out to our satisfaction.

I might have given up on the idea entirely had it not been for the intervention of an elderly friend whose family has owned and operated an apple orchard for several generations. Not only did this gentleman show me more than I'd ever thought of knowing about apple varieties (best choices for eating, baking, sweet and hard cider, applejack, etc.), but he also showed me what was left of the big

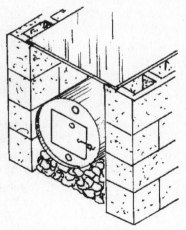

1. Dry-stack block to make three walls. Rest the barrel on a bed of stones. Set 4x4s in the corners and sheet steel on top.

wood-fired fruit dryers that his father and grandfather had used in the days before electric refrigeration, large commercial canneries, and such. While he explained how they were used, we looked them over. Remembering from his early youth, he also told me how his family, and other large commercial growers, would dry many tons of fruit every year. Demand always outran what they were able to supply.

Though the dryers on his property had pretty much fallen apart from years of decay and neglect, some simple measurements showed me that, when up and running, each one would have been easily capable of holding 30 bushels of produce. He assured me that regardless of the weather conditions, 24 hours was the maximum drying time, even for the juiciest fruit.

Although 30 bushels seemed much more than we'd ever need to dry in one shot, it was easy to see how such a simple wood-fueled dehydrator could be built in practically any size. There was a heat source at the bottom with interchangeable drying trays

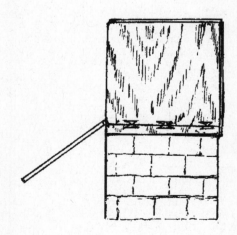

3. Cover three sides with plywood, hinged for access.

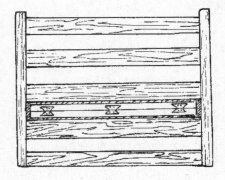

4. Leave openings in the fourth side for inserting and removing trays.

arranged over it, with eave vents and a sort of cupola vent on the roof (kind of like what you see on many older barns) to allow the rising warmed air to carry away the moisture from the drying fruit. I later learned that on cool nights, you can watch the vapor escape from these vents.

After tossing this idea around for a while, and fiddling with some figures to come up with a size more appropriate for our own use, I built a scaled-down version of those commercial dryers. Now, about 15 years later, it's still serving our family's needs perfectly. This simple design is so readily adaptable that you can include your own modifications to adapt it to your needs. So, while I'm going to detail the design that I used, remember that you can change practically any of the details and techniques to suit your own requirements and resources.

First of all, since I'd already located a reliable source for free, empty 55-gallon steel drums, I decided to build a simple barrel stove for the heat source. Laying the drum on the ground, I stacked extra-wide (16") foundation blocks around three sides of the drum, fashioning three un-mortared walls, two blocks taller than the drum. Next, I filled in the area between these block walls with ordinary field stones to the level of the top of the first row of blocks, so as to keep the stove up off the ground.

I dropped 4x4 timbers into the hollows of the corner blocks and fashioned a wooden framework to hold the drying trays. On three sides of the dehydrator, I used half-inch CDX plywood to close them off completely. However, each piece is hinged at the bottom, being held shut by hook-and-eye fasteners at the tops, to allow for easy access for cleaning after each use. On the fourth side, I left openings similar to those of a chest of drawers for inserting and removing the drying trays.

I built the trays from 1x3s and the lids from 1x2s. I used hardware cloth for the tray bottoms and metal window screen to cover the tops, which are fastened to the trays with hinges. I also used metal window screen to cover the eave and cupola vents to further prevent any possibility of insect damage. I used painted canvas for the roofing material (as covered in the May/June 1996 issue of *BHM*).

Note: Since this will be used for food processing and there is heat involved, you should not use pressure-treated lumber and avoid lead-based paint.

I used a hammer and cold chisel to cut an eight-inch-diameter hole in one end of the drum for fitting a stovepipe,

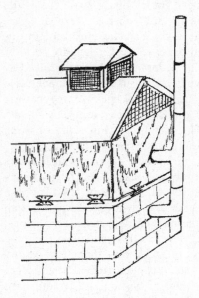

5. Install roof, vents, and stovepipe.

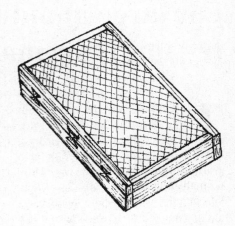

6. Hinge lids to trays.

and I cut a square access door in the opposite end. I used cheap hinges and sheet metal screws to reattach the square of metal removed from the door opening, along with a simple hook-and-eye to hold this door shut. This works just as well as the door provided with a purchased barrel stove kit; it just doesn't look quite so pretty. Adding a damper in the stove pipe, and being able to remove or reinsert either or both of the original barrel plugs, allows for heat control.

The most expensive part of this whole setup (and it didn't cost that much), was a piece of 1/8" steel cut to rest on the inside two inches of the top of the block wall. This creates a *much* more even distribution of heat, and the extra width of the block wall keeps the heat just far enough from the wooden outer walls.

In use, you'll need to rotate the trays every couple hours or so. Just remove the top tray, setting it aside for a moment, and raise each of the remaining trays one position. Then take the tray you'd removed from the top, and reinsert it in the lowest position. It's also necessary to keep a low fire going inside the stove during the entire drying process. During the day, we work in shifts, adding dry corn cobs and keeping the draft regulated as required. Then towards bedtime, we load the stove up with large, unsplit, only-partially-dried logs (remember, this is out-of-doors, not inside your living room, so a chimney fire isn't a major problem) and damper the stove almost all the way down. At least two or three times during the night, one of us will get up to go out and reshuffle the drying trays.

Usually we begin the drying process early in the morning. That way, by the time we're up and about the next morning, the dehydration process is normally completed.

Generally, we use dehydrated fruits and vegetables in one of two ways. There are plenty of other methods for using dried foods, but these two are our family favorites. The first method is simply to reconstitute the dried food by soaking it in water overnight, then using it in exactly the same manner as frozen food, in any recipe. This tastes a little better than using frozen fruit or vegetables, but otherwise you can't really tell the difference. The other method we like is to run the thoroughly dried food through our hand-cranked grain mill, producing pumpkin, potato, and other specialty flours, as well as apple, tomato, carrot, onion, and other "powders," which are terrific cooking aids.

Remember, you can vary the size, construction techniques, materials, and so forth to customize this design to fit your own circumstances. For example, you could build a really large masonry firebox, or use a smaller 30- or 15-gallon drum, or even an inverted washtub, for the heat source. You could substitute dowels, laths, or sticks for the trays, if you'll only be making jerky, drying fish, and such. Or you could make any number of other customizations. So whatever your food storage needs might be, a similar wood-fueled dehydrator could prove just as perfect for you as ours has for us. Who knows, you might even find that there's a market in your area for some of your delicious dried fruit. Δ

Cracking walnuts—"almost fun"

By Lydia Mayfield

Uncle Tol would never use any of the wonderful black walnuts that grew along the creek on his farm. He said a man would starve to death picking out the meats, and besides that, the bits of black hull that always got mixed up with the nut meats could poison him. That was before we got an old conventional washing machine and a commercial black walnut cracker. We already had an old hand corn sheller. Now getting the meats out of black walnuts is almost fun. Even Uncle Tol helps pick them up. This is the easy way to harvest black walnuts.

As soon as the walnut hulls are black and dry, hull them with a corn sheller. Sometimes it is best to run them through two times. Then fill the washing machine with cold water and wash them. Put in only a half bushel of nuts at a time, and wash them at least a half hour. The tumbling takes off all of the black hull. When you take them out, rinse them in cold, clean water and lay them out to dry. The water in the machine has to be changed frequently.

When the nuts are thoroughly dry comes the cracking. For this you can use any of the manufactured crackers on the market. All of these crackers crush the shell and allow the meats to fall out in large pieces, mostly quarters. There will always be a few meats left in the shell that have to be dug out with a pick, but for the most part the nut meats need only to be picked out from the shell, and there is no bitter hull left. It really makes picking out black walnuts almost fun. Δ

Keep your onions fresh... with panty hose!

By James Robertson

If you enjoy onions (like I do), then you probably enjoy eating fresh onions throughout the winter. The problem is keeping them fresh for long periods of time.

I have found that the best way to keep your onions is to put them in panty hose.

Panty hose?

Yep, you take a pair of panty hose and cut off the top part. Then put an onion all the way down into the end of the foot and tie a knot in the hose just above the onion. Put the next onion down on top of the knot and tie a knot just above that one, and so on. Hang the filled panty hose up somewhere cool and dry, and the onions will stay absolutely fresh.

What you're doing is keeping the onions from touching each other, thus eliminating the main cause of onions going bad.

You're also putting some extra miles on those old panty hose before they have to become part of a landfill somewhere. Δ

Pectin — You can rely on the grocer, or you can learn to make it yourself

By Rev. J.D. Hooker

It's difficult for most of us to realize that a lot of the things we take for granted today were unavailable not all that many years ago. Yet our ancestors seem to have managed just fine without them. As just one example, the vast majority of even the most independent-minded modern homesteaders would be pretty hard pressed to put by all those jars of delicious homemade jams, jellies, preserves, marmalades, and fruit butters, were it not for the ready availability of commercially produced powdered or liquid pectin, sold for home canning.

Yet my wife learned from her grandmother (more years ago than she'll admit) that such simple products didn't even exist until relatively recently. And no one ever noticed the lack of such a basic "necessity." Still, today, none of the women in her family ever bother with any of the various brands of "store boughten" pectin, relying instead on the following recipe, which has been verbally handed down through the female side of her family tree for longer than anyone can remember.

Place 10 pounds of stemmed and quartered (but unpeeled, and not cored) green apples into a large stock pot. Add water to cover, and bring to a full, rolling boil. Reduce the heat, cover the kettle, and simmer until the fruit is very soft (approximately 30 to 45 minutes). Using another pot to catch the liquid, strain the fruit through a jelly bag, allowing the fruit in the bag to continue to drain overnight. The next day, boil down this liquid (approximately three quarts to begin with), until only two cups of liquid remain. Store in tightly-closed canning jars. Use this home-produced pectin exactly as you would regular grocery store type liquid pectin, in any recipe.

You won't save a whole lot of money by producing and using your own pectin, since even the most expensive name brand fruit pectin is pretty cheap. But making your own pectin for home canning uses will let you have some fun, while providing a use for many of those apples that fall off your trees before ripening. It may also allow you to feel just a mite more independent, and most importantly, allow you to simply laugh off any future supermarket shortage on canning supplies. Δ

A few strings attached

By Marcia Brown

Grandma's pride and joy is three acres of flower gardens surrounding the family farmhouse. When a neighbor's game chickens began escaping from their pens and invading Grandma's carefully tended flower beds, she was frantic. These birds ate seeds and small bedding plants and even damaged shrubs.

Pleas to the marauders' owner brought effusive apologies but no fence mending.

One morning after Grandma discovered her seed beds destroyed once more, she wrote something with fierce strokes on several pieces of

paper. She then threaded yellow corn on long pieces of string, and to each end she tied one of the notes.

Shortly, several game chickens returned to her garden, eagerly gulping down the strings with corn and then running off with notes dangling from their beaks. That was the last we saw of invading game chickens.

"Grandma," I asked later, "did you write something rude about those birds?"

Her blue eyes twinkling, she replied, "Oh, I just invited their owner over for a few meals of exotic chicken—roasted, barbecued, and fried—and gave the dates!" Δ

Those leftover fall tomatoes are a delicious bounty that should be put aside for the future

By Alice B. Yeager
Photos by James O. Yeager

Some of us were brought up on stories of frugality and the merits thereof. You know, like the tale about the ant and the grasshopper. We were also introduced to bits of wisdom such as "Waste not, want not," "A penny saved is a penny earned," and so on. Not a bad way to go in this day of maxed-out credit cards, inflated prices, and other financial obstacles.

Gardeners are for the most part a thrifty lot. Maybe that's why we hang on to our old garden tools and try to get the most out of the plants we grow as long as there's hope for more yield. We appreciate vegetables fresh from our own gardens, and there's the fringe benefit of mental satisfaction in knowing we can grow our own produce. You might call it an independent-living kind of pride.

Among my seed selections each year are several varieties of tomatoes and peppers. (Perusing seed catalogs is a great winter pastime.) I compare prices and shipping costs, taking note of recommended growing zones. I am particularly interested in plants that "will do well under hot, humid conditions." This describes summers in Southwest Arkansas—Zone 8. It tells me that these plants are more likely to survive summer and produce a fall crop.

Later comes the spring work of soil preparation, transplanting, etc. After all of the effort put forth, I want to see healthy plants that produce as long as possible. Lack of water at the height of their production is one of the main reasons certain plants fail to survive to produce well in the fall. All that is needed is a little TLC to bring them through summer's dry spells. Plants need watering when drought conditions prevail, but the time spent watering can be reduced if a thick organic mulch is put down to help retain moisture in the soil. I like to use a mixture of leaves, pine needles, twigs, etc., as leaves alone tend to mat. These things add nutrients to the soil as they break down, and a good mulch also discourages weed growth. Earthworms will move in to till the soil and keep it pliable *if* they are not discouraged by the use of chemical fertilizers.

When the end of the gardening season is in sight, many of us think it downright sinful to let the bounty go to waste that is still being produced. Cool fall weather often brings out the best in plants that have endured summer's heat. Tomatoes take on a special zest. Bell peppers taste sweeter. The downside is that everyone has had their fill of tomatoes and peppers, and no one is enthusiastic about going out and gathering more. This is when a frugal conscience kicks into gear. Why not put more aside for the future? Home-canned vegetables are always in demand, for church suppers, gifts, and so on. Who knows what the next gardening season will be like? There may be an onslaught of Japanese beetles, too much rain—all kinds of negative things. Think about unpleasant winter days when it's nice to be able to avoid the supermarket. Surplus tomatoes, as well as other vegetables, can help stock a pantry with nutrition. (It's the ant and grasshopper story all over again.)

Plenty of jars of stewed tomatoes sitting in a pantry will not only be useful for soups, spaghetti sauce, Mexican dishes, etc., but they will cut down on the grocery bill. (See recipe below.) There's a world of difference between the taste of home-canned tomatoes and those that come from a metal can.

If frost threatens when vines are loaded with green tomatoes, the tomatoes nearest maturity may be laid on straw to ripen in a cool room (with no direct sunlight). These

Try stocking your pantry with some stewed tomatoes (red jars) and green tomato relish, or "fish pickles" (green jars).

fruits may not have the taste of the summer crop, but they'll be better than the ones at the supermarket. The small green tomatoes don't need to go to waste, either. Down South we turn green tomatoes into green tomato relish, that delectable mixture served at our catfish restaurants, as well as at home. We call them "fish pickles." (See recipe.)

Fried green tomatoes are now famous, thanks to the title of a recent movie. If you haven't actually tried this southern recipe, you are missing a real culinary treat that's not at all hard to make. This side dish probably originated as a product of necessity, but like so many others, it has become a favorite on our menu. Medium-size green tomatoes barely showing a tinge of red are best for frying. (See recipe.) Remember, don't knock it if you ain't tried it.

There are plenty of ways to turn late summer's produce into something delicious. Some of the best ideas come from books published by companies manufacturing canning supplies— Ball, Kerr, Mason, etc. Some books may be had for a small fee and others are free.

Be an ant—don't let that fall crop go to waste.

Don't let green tomatoes go to waste. Try making green tomato relish or fried green tomatoes.

Stewed tomatoes

> 1 gallon ripe tomatoes
> 2 cups onions, coarsely chopped
> 1 cup celery, coarsely chopped
> 1 cup sweet peppers, coarsely chopped
> 1 Tablespoon sugar
> 2 teaspoons salt

Wash all vegetables before using. Scald tomatoes in boiling water about one minute so that skins may be removed easily. Quarter tomatoes and then measure to be sure of correct amount. Mix all ingredients together in a stainless steel or porcelain pot. (Do not use aluminum.) Bring to a boil and simmer ten minutes. Stir occasionally to prevent sticking. Pour mixture into hot, sterilized jars and process in canner. Pints require 15 minutes and quarts 20 minutes at 10 pounds pressure.

Remove jars from canner, cover them with a light cloth, and let stand in draft-free place for several hours or until cool. Check to see that all lids are down or stay down when pressed. Jars with lids that have not sealed should be put in refrigerator and contents used within a few days.

Green tomato relish (Fish pickles)

> 2 gallons green tomatoes cut in bite-size chunks
> 1/2 gallon sweet peppers, coarsely chopped (use both green and red)
> 1/2 gallon white onions, coarsely chopped
> 10 Jalapeño peppers cut in rings (optional)
> 3/4 cup salt
> 8 cups sugar
> 1/2 gallon apple cider vinegar
> 1 Tablespoon crab boil OR pickling spices
> 1 teaspoon whole cloves

Put vegetables in a large stainless steel or porcelain container. (Do not use aluminum.) Sprinkle with the salt and let stand about three hours. Drain well. Do not rinse.

Dissolve sugar in vinegar and bring to a boil. Put spices in a clean cloth bag or large stainless steel tea ball and add to vinegar. Add drained vegetables and simmer until all are hot throughout and onions are clear. Remove spices. Pack mixture into hot, sterilized jars and seal. Cover hot jars with a light cloth and let stand in a draft-free place for several hours or until cool.

Fried green tomatoes

> 4 medium-size, firm tomatoes—
> green with just a tinge of red
> 1 large onion
> 1/2 stick oleo OR butter
> Salt and pepper

Thinly slice onion and fry in oleo until tender. Remove from pan and reserve to put over tomatoes. Slice tomatoes in 1/4-inch thick slices and fry in oleo about 1 1/2 minutes on each side. Sprinkle with salt and pepper while cooking. Remove from pan, place on serving dish, and cover with reserved onions.

Another version: Dip tomato slices in your favorite batter and fry. Batter may be enhanced with the addition of dried herbs such as sweet basil, thyme, etc. ∆

Apple-dapples — fun to make and even more fun to snack on

By Linda Gabris

One of my favorite memories of growing up was in autumn, when Grandmother's cozy kitchen was filled with the tangy aroma of apple. We'd sit at the table in front of the crackling wood stove with spools of string, threaded needles, and a bushel or two of washed, sorted apples ready for drying. While Grandpa cored and sliced, Grandmother and I strung apple rings into long, dangling chains ready to be hung from the ceiling behind the stove.

Today, I sit at my own kitchen table with my children, and we string fragrant apples in the same old manner as we did way back when I was a child. It's not only a fun family activity, but also a great way to use up your surplus apples. Dried apples, or "apple-dapples" as we still fondly call them, are one of my family's favorite snack time treats.

In my younger days, favored apples such as Macintosh, Spy, and Golden Delicious were stored in the root cellar for hand eating over the winter. Only bruised, overripe, or less sweet varieties, like crabapples, were strung and hung. Today, I dry whatever bountiful variety our trees offer, and I have found that even the tartest, sourest apple becomes a gem when dried.

After hours of singing, stringing, and hanging, the wall behind the kitchen stove is curtained in fragrant apples. The strings of apple rings will normally hang for about five to eight days, depending on the temperature of the room. But they can hang for an indefinite period with no harm done. The apples are ready when they are shriveled and leathery brown.

When the apples are dried, we cut them down and unstring the rings into gunny sacks to be stored in the attic for winter use. Apple-dapples are hard to resist, so you better hide a sack or two in the rafters for safe keeping as I do, or the kids will have them all eaten up before you know it.

On snappy winter evenings, we fetch the tin Chinese checker board out onto the kitchen table and herd our marbles into their corners. On such special occasions, I will bring down a heaping bowl of apple-dapples for nibbling while we take turns

jumping our marbles across the board. Those who can't keep their fingers out of the dapple dish will likely end up on the losing side of the board. A little dish of apple-dapples can also make homework time more pleasant.

At the first hint of a winter cold, I do as my Grandmother would have done: I quickly steep up a handful of dried apple rings and a few whole cloves in boiling water. Strained and sweetened with honey, it's a favorite medicine that never needs any coaxing. Sometimes I think that my kids can conjure up a cough or a sniffle at the mere thought of this pleasing drink. After a brittle day's worth of outdoor chores, dried apples steeped in boiled red wine and sweetened with lots of brown sugar are a sure cure for chilblains.

I use wonderful dried apples in desserts all winter long. They are great added to rice pudding and served with hot nutmeg milk. Another favorite is stewed dried apples served with buttered scones. Dried apples are as popular in my recipes as raisins or chocolate chips are in most kitchens. Although my family enjoys dried apples in many ways, I'm sure our very favorite way is apple-dapples right off the string. What a delightful, tart, chewy treat.

And when my kitchen is filled with the autumn aroma of drying apples, it fills my heart with beautiful memories. Δ

It's easy to build your own milking stanchion

By Janell Henschel

A few years ago, my husband and I purchased two F-1 heifers to add to our commercial beef herd. One of the calves was a Hereford-Jersey cross we named Rosey. She was very friendly from the start, and as her calving date drew near, it was obvious she was destined to become a family milk cow.

I began to purchase supplies in advance so l would be ready to milk my first cow. I bought udder wash, sponges, udder cream, a milk bucket, etc., etc. But where was I going to milk her? I didn't have a stanchion, and I couldn't locate a used one. Rosey's calf was due in a week and I was getting desperate. We had lumber left over from a project we had been working on, so I decided I would build my own. It turned out to be the easiest thing I've ever built.

Locate your stanchion in a well-lit area of your barn, especially if you don't have electricity. Using an existing space on a wall would be best: you will have one less post to buy, your cow won't be able to move away from you, and your stanchion will be sturdier.

Materials:

- 1 or 2 - 6" x 6" x 8' posts (2 if you don't have an existing post)
- 3 - 2" x 6" x 8' boards, cut in half to make 6 four-footers
- 4 - 2" x 6" x 6" blocks from scrap (or buy 2 - 8' boards and 1- 10' board and cut your blocks from it)
- A handful of nails (about 30)
- 4 feet of baling twine or light rope
- 1 brass snap
- 2 sacks of redi-mix concrete
- 1 tie ring with a heavy wood screw on the end

Set your posts two to three feet deep in concrete, four feet apart measuring from the outside edges. Make sure they are level and even. Refer to the diagram for measurements and order of construction. You will want your movable vertical board nearest to the wall or on the off side of the cow. Nail it with one nail only to the lower horizontal board, centering the nail. When you nail the outside horizontal boards over the vertical boards, nail at the ends only. If you nail through the vertical boards, your moveable board will not move freely. Tie a loop in your twine or light rope and place over the end of the moveable board. Tie the brass snap to the other end, adjust for the comfort of your cow, then snap to the tie ring that has been screwed into the post.

You should have some kind of non-porous floor for your cow to stand on. A cement pad, rubber mat, or even a piece of plywood will work. If you use plywood it must be kept dry or it will be very slick.

If, after building the stanchion, your cow still won't stand, there may be something bothering her. Check the udder for cuts, scrapes, bruises, flies, and fly bites. Use bag balm to help heal and prevent the flies from biting.

For a cranky cow that likes to kick, you can purchase cow hobbles or a stop-kick device from your local feed store or supply catalog.

If you can find a used portable milking machine at a reasonable cost, this may be your answer. After all is said and done and your cow still won't stand, your only other option is to sell her. There are plenty of good family milk cows available that would be a pleasure to own. Δ

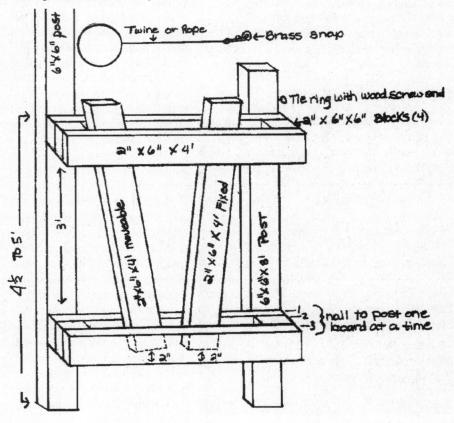

You can make delicious meals all winter with stored vegetables and dried spices

By Jennifer Stein Barker

Having a root cellar, attic, and pantry full of stored vegetables and dried herbs can make life pretty pleasant on the homestead in the winter. Instead of going to the grocery store, you just mentally run through the larder and ask yourself, "What have I got in storage?" before making up the menus.

Cooking frequently with the same ingredients doesn't have to lead to dull, repetitive meals, if you enjoy a well-stocked herb pantry and an international cooking repertoire. The vegetables you have in storage may be predetermined for the rest of the winter, but you can always change the meal's basic character by changing the carbohydrate: choose pasta, potatoes, bulgur, rice, or bread.

For added variety, change the flavors and seasonings to Oriental (ginger, garlic, and hot peppers), Italian (tomatoes, herbs, red wine, and garlic), or Russian/Yiddish (dill and yogurt).

My article in the May/June 1996 issue, "Quick-and-easy pasta recipes," contains some good recipes for using storage foods. Below, you'll find more ideas and recipes for a full meal using fruits and vegetables that can be found on well-stocked winter homesteads in most regions of the country.

Carrot-raisin salad

This salad is an American basic, and with good reason. The ingredients are very simple and always available. It stores well. And you can always take it with you, to potlucks, picnics, or parties. Serves four.

```
2 1/2 cups coarsely grated raw carrots
1/2 cup raisins
2 teaspoons fresh lemon juice
1/3 cup plain Lafayette yogurt
1 - 2 teaspoons maple syrup (to taste)
```

Toss the carrots lightly with the raisins and lemon juice. Blend the yogurt and syrup, and stir into the carrot mixture. Chill at least 30 minutes before serving.

Russian variation: leave out maple syrup and raisins. Add 1 Tablespoon finely chopped onion, 1/4 cup frozen peas, and 1/4 teaspoon dill weed.

Lima bean and sage chowder

A savory soup for fall and winter. Serves four.

```
1 3/4 cups small white lima beans
2 cups diced onion
1 Tablespoon olive oil
6 cups stock or water
1/4 teaspoon celery seed
2 bay leaves
1 Tablespoon tamari
3 medium carrots, halved and sliced
2 lbs. boiling potatoes, diced
1 daikon radish, quartered and sliced
2 teaspoons rubbed sage
2 Tablespoons tamari
1/4 cup water
4 Tablespoons fine whole wheat flour
```

Soak the dry lima beans overnight, or use the quick soak method: cover with plenty of water, bring the beans to a boil, and boil one minute. Remove from heat and let soak one hour. Discard soaking water, rinse beans, and proceed with recipe.

In a large stockpot, sauté the onion in the olive oil, covered, until beginning to brown around the edges. Add the

stock or water, celery seed, bay leaves, tamari, and soaked beans. Bring to a boil, adjust heat to simmer, and cook until the beans are just tender (about one hour).

Add the prepared carrots, potatoes, daikon, sage, and tamari. Cook about 20 minutes more, until the vegetables are tender. In a small cup, combine the water and flour to make a smooth paste. Remove some of the soup stock from the pot and mix with the paste, then return the mixture to the pot, stirring well to blend.

Cook another five minutes, or until the soup thickens. Serve immediately with a fresh salad or green garnish, and plenty of homemade bread.

Herbed potatoes

A quick and easy main or side dish to make from your root cellar vegetables and home-dried herbs. Serves six as a side dish.

```
3 pounds red or yellow potatoes
2 Tablespoons olive oil
2 cups diced onion
4 cloves garlic, minced
1/4 teaspoon celery seed
1/4 teaspoon dried marjoram
1/2 teaspoon dried savory
1/2 teaspoon oregano
1 small hot pepper
2 Tablespoons tamari
1 cup grated kohlrabi or carrot
1 cup meat or vegetable stock
```

Dice and steam the potatoes till tender. In a large, heavy skillet, cook the onions and garlic in the olive oil until they are tender and transparent. Add all the herbs, the kohlrabi or carrot, and the stock, and simmer gently until the liquid evaporates. Add the cooked potatoes, toss, and serve immediately or keep warm in a 200° oven for up to a half hour.

Apple pudding cake

This is a moist, sweet cake over a thick sauce full of apple chunks. Make sure you heat the sauce ingredients well. If you don't, the sauce will be too cold to bubble and thicken properly during the cooking time. Serves six.

```
4 cups finely diced apples (about 3 medium apples)
1 2/3 cups whole wheat pastry flour
2 1/2 teaspoons baking powder
1 teaspoon cinnamon
1 cup milk
2 1/2 Tablespoons oil
1/3 cup honey
```

Sauce # 1:

```
1 Tablespoon rum
1/2 cup honey
1 1/3 cups boiling water
1/2 teaspoon almond extract
2 Tablespoons fresh lemon juice
```

Sauce #2:

```
1 2/3 cups apple juice
1/2 teaspoon almond extract
2 Tablespoons fresh lemon juice
1 Tablespoon honey
```

Preheat the oven to 350°. Place the diced apple in the bottom of a two-liter casserole dish (do not use a smaller one). In a medium bowl, stir together the flour, baking powder, and cinnamon. In a measuring cup or small bowl, stir together the milk, oil, and honey until well blended. Add the liquid to the dry mixture, stir together well, and pour over the apples (don't worry about spreading it out evenly).

Now mix the sauce ingredients together (choose either Sauce #1 or #2) in a small saucepan, and bring to a boil. Pour the liquid over the batter and apples, but *do not stir*. It will sink down through the batter into the apples.

Bake for 45 to 50 minutes, until the cake is golden on top and the sauce has begun to bubble up around the sides. Serve hot, with the sauce spooned over the cake. Δ

CHILDERS/SILVEIRA

Ten off-beat metal cleaning tricks

By Sandy Lindsey

• You can clean and brighten tarnished metal gauges and switches on appliances by rubbing on a whitening toothpaste. And while you've got your mother-in law's toothbrush out, whitening toothpaste also works wonders on scratches on plexiglass.

• Clean chrome fittings and fixtures that are severely pitted with #00 Bronze Wool. If that doesn't do the job, dunk it in Penetrol for added effect, then give the job some old-fashioned elbow grease. The Bronze Wool/Penetrol combination will also work on stainless steel and aluminum. (*Do not* use Penetrol on metals that come in contact with food.)

• To remove tough build-ups on decorative stainless steel, rub on alcohol and kerosene. Use a 100% cotton rag. The kerosene will return it to a near-original shine. (*Do not* use kerosene on stainless steel items that come in contact with food.)

• Use metal polish and a standard bottle cork to clean particularly stubborn rust or metal discoloration spots. Dampen the flat edge of the cork first, so that it absorbs some of the metal polish, then apply more polish and rub away. Rub the cork over the spot. Its flat surface and naturally abrasive properties will do the rest .

• Kitchen metal surfaces sticky from a child's gooey hands? Pour vinegar or straight lemon juice onto a sponge and wipe down the goop. Let the vinegar or lemon juice sit for a few minutes to cut through the residue, then wash off with soap and water.

• When cooking gets your pots and pans so greasy and grimy that you think you're never going to get them clean again, place them in a heavy-duty garbage bag. Add one cup of ammonia and seal the bag tightly. Leave overnight. The following morning the grease and grime will hose off. (*Note: Be sure to avoid inhaling* the accumulated ammonia fumes as you open the bag. And *do not use this procedure on aluminum.*)

• You can easily restore aluminum yard furniture that is pitted and dull, by scrubbing until it's smooth again with a soapy Brillo pad. Rinse, then wax thoroughly with a car or boat wax to retard further damage.

• An easy way to wax the tubular railings of lawn furniture is to put an old sweat sock over your hand, dip it into the wax, and go to work. By curving your hand around the railing, you'll be able to cover more area, more completely, in less time.

• Clean bronze that has turned green with a clear teak oil. It will not only remove the tarnish easily, but tends to retard further tarnishing for months afterwards.

• To restore rusty outdoor metals such as iron and steel, spray with an instant galvanize, such as CRC Instant Galvanize. Δ

A BHM Artist's Profile: John C. Dean

John Dean is *BHM's* new Art Director, replacing the retiring Don Childers. Having pursued painting as a hobby while he raised three daughters, he began a career in jewelry design and manufacturing in 1980, and in 1990 included painting in his career. He is a well known artist in Brookings, Oregon, where he lives. Commercially his work has been put on post cards, maps, signs, logos, tote bags, front porch displays, murals, and, of course, framed and hung for customers. He is an excellent portrait painter and has painted the portraits of several *BHM* staff members. His art can be found at *BHM's* web site: www.backwoodshome.com.

John is also a musician and is the lead singer and guitarist for his band, Johnny Cardiac and the Cardiac Arrest, which performs around the Brookings area and for *BHM* functions. He has a Bachelor's Degree from UCSB in electrical engineering and a Master's Degree from Caltech.

Here are some simple tips on how to store apples for a long, long time

By Don Fallick

Almost any kind of apple will keep for three or four months, or even longer, if stored properly. It's cheap and easy to do. All you need is newspaper, a box or basket, and apples. A root cellar is optional, but not necessary.

The main causes of apple spoilage are time, bruises, and contact with a rotten spot on another apple.

Time

Time can be stretched by selecting long-keeping varieties of apples for storage. Tart and thick-skinned apples like Jonathans generally keep longer than sweet or thin-skinned ones like Delicious. Good keepers also have very firm flesh. The best keepers I have found are Spur Winter Bananas—from C&O Nursery, P.O. Box 116, Wenatchee, WA 98807.

They are yellow and tart at harvest, but get redder and sweeter, and actually taste better after a couple of months in storage.

Contact

Prevent contact between apples stored for the winter by wrapping them individually in sheets of newspaper. The easiest way to do this is to unfold a section of newspaper all the way and tear it into quarters. Then stack the quarters. Avoid sections printed with colored ink, which contains poisonous heavy metals.

Place an apple on top of the stack and fold the top sheet of paper up around the apple, wrapping it in paper. Give the corners a slight twist—just enough to make them stay wrapped. If you twist them too hard, the paper will tear. It's not necessary to exclude air. Just twist hard enough so the paper doesn't come unwrapped before the apples are boxed. The paper prevents contact between apples, so just one rotten apple won't spoil the whole bunch. With practice, you'll be able to wrap and store apples as fast as you can scan them for bruises and sort them.

Sorting

Always handle apples carefully, to avoid bruising them. Apples with even small bruises must never be stored with "keepers." Only perfect apples should be used for long-term storage. Even minor imperfections speed spoilage. While you're wrapping, check each apple for cut skin, soft spots, or bruises. Even bruised apples taste fine when they're fresh, so sort the best culls into a box to be eaten right away. If there are too many, make apple pie filling out of the excess. Use culls with extensive blemishes for cider. Or cut out any really gross parts and make applesauce.

My family owns two Victorio strainers. We blanch the apples to soften them, cut them in half, throw them in the hopper, and turn the crank. The Victorio separates the pulp from the skins, seeds, and stems, and produces fresh applesauce, ready for canning. With both strainers going, we can put up more than two bushels of apples an hour.

Canned pie filling, applesauce, and cider will keep for a year or more. Fresh cider that has started to turn sour can be made into hard cider, vinegar, or applejack (see Issue #35, Sept/Oct 1995). All three will keep indefinitely.

Storage

Boxed apples need to be kept in a cool, dark spot where they won't freeze. Freezing ruptures all of an apple's cells, turning it into one large bruise overnight. The usual solution is to store apples in a root cellar. But root cellars often have potatoes in them, and experts say that apples and potatoes should never be stored in the same room. This may seem incongruous, but there is a reason. As they age, potatoes release an otherwise harmless gas that makes apples spoil faster. If you can keep the gas away from your apples, they will keep just fine. Just don't store them right next to potatoes.

I keep wrapped apples in a cardboard box. It need not be airtight, just tight enough to impede air circulation. I've kept apples in an unheated basement, a pantry, an enclosed porch, an unheated attic, even in a root cellar, potatoes and all. Using these simple methods, I have kept ordinary apples until late February, and Winter Banana apples into March. ∆

Careful planning will make harvesting and preserving food a year-long process

By Dynah Geissal

What harvesting means to you will largely be determined by whether or not you have electricity. When I lived on my farm in the valley, I had power, and just about everything went into the freezer. Oh, I still canned fruits, pickles, tomato sauce, and such, but I had for the most part switched to freezing as my primary method of preservation. We butchered all the larger meat animals such as pigs, calves, and goats as soon as it was cold and/or whenever I had to start feeding hay. Only the breeders were overwintered.

Now, because I live on a mountain with no electricity, I have returned to canning. We also dry tomatoes, peppers, mushrooms, and berries on trays on the warming shelf of our cookstove. The lives of the smaller animals and some plants are extended to preserve "food on the hoof," so to speak. While we do maintain two freezers in town, the inconvenience of having our food over an hour away leads us to keep as much as we can here. I prefer to go out to the rabbit pen to butcher dinner, even though that may mean the litter is kept longer than optimal, rather than store them in the freezer.

Obtaining and preserving our food supply is as integral a part of our lives as maintaining our water system and our heat source.

Make a plan

Whatever method of preservation you choose, harvest planning is a year-round occupation. I suggest keeping a notebook or some such and writing in it what you expect to do during each month as you plan the harvest of your food. For exam-

ple: May 1—Buy weaner pigs; November 21—Expected butcher date for hogs. Of course, as time goes by, things change. These dates are not written in stone, but are merely a method of organizing an overall plan. For everything you plan to eat, write down dates of planting, breeding, butchering, preserving, or whatever. These tentative plans will help you to see your overall food design.

Year-round chickens

I start raising chicks in January so that I have live ones for most of the year. It's not easy without electricity, but it can be done. I heat bricks to keep them warm for the first couple of weeks, and their box is as near to the heat stove as it can safely be. The top of the box is covered with plastic so that they have light but also are kept warm. At night, I cover that with blankets and sleeping bags. If it's very cold, I get up during the night to replace the bricks with warm ones. When it's safe for them to move outside, they go into a refrigerator box inside the chicken house. Boy, do I miss my old brooder house. We hope to build our real barn this summer, and then we will have a more permanent setup for the chicks, as well as all the other animals.

I get new chicks every couple of months through September in order to have some for sale and some for eating. After September, I get a break from chicks. It isn't really practical to raise them in the fall. They don't grow well during the short, cold days, and they take way too long to reach butcher size. Slack times in the bird business means cleaning the chicken house and butchering and freezing the remaining cockerels.

Eggs from kerosene

During my first winter without electricity, I had just about decided that it made no sense to keep more than a few hens. The nights were so long and cold that I hardly got any eggs for three months. This year, however, I decided to try using a kerosene lamp. I hung a barn-style lantern from a hook attached to a crossbeam. It is out of reach of the chickens and provides plenty of light for our small shed. The amount of kerosene I used each night was determined by how much supplemental light I needed at that time to give a minimum of 14 hours. During the longest nights, I used a cup of kerosene. I wasn't sure at first if the use of kerosene would be cost-effective, but it turned out to be a great success. We had eggs all winter, and except for the molting period, we always had some to sell. We buy kerosene in bulk for about $1.75 a gallon, which is a real bargain for all the eggs we get.

Our temporary chicken house is sided with one-by's and has a metal roof. It's not tight and it's not insulated, so I think the hens did really well to maintain 80% production all winter. I feed whole grains, bone meal, kitchen scraps, and old produce from the health food store. I also try to break open the ice in their water every couple of hours during the day.

Year-round milk

Having a year-round goat's milk supply is important to me, although relying on the cheese I make when milk is abundant would be easier. Staggered breeding is the key. I keep records so that I know which does are most likely to breed early, and I get one of them bred as soon as possible. Then I breed one doe each month, saving my longest-producing doe for November breeding. Any doeling that

was kept from the previous spring is bred in December to give her plenty of time to attain good growth. In this way, I am never left with all dry does.

In addition, I usually have one older doe who produces prodigious quantities of milk and stays in good condition without being dried up at all. Nutrition is the key here. It is necessary to feed top quality alfalfa free choice, an adequate amount of goat chow, and a pasture block for any needed supplemental nutrition. Be sure to use a block suitable for goats.

It should contain no urea and is usually sold as a horse block or a "natural" cattle block. I think it does no harm to milk a grown doe all year under these conditions.

Many people breed a prolific milker only every other year. I like to have as many kids as possible for meat, for sale, and for replacement does, so I breed every year. Even so, some heavy milkers do not breed at all. It's the same as with nurse cows. Often the calves have to be removed before the cow will breed.

I've heard people say that they have such a hard time getting their heavy milkers to dry up at the proper time. If you have that "problem," just feed her up and keep milking. One of my does had no kids for three years and still gave a maximum of two gallons dur-

ing the spring and early summers and a minimum of one gallon during the winters. If your doe has kids on her, you need to milk her through the season. Don't wait until she weans them, because by then there will have already been a downturn in the cycle.

Be sure your breeding program is good so that you get the best-producing does you can. With staggered breeding and an occasional doe who milks year round, you'll never be without fresh milk.

Wild harvest

Part of my year-round harvest plan is to be aware of what grows wild where I live. I take advantage of the abundance in season and preserve some for other times. Fish, berries, and various greens can be foraged for dinner a good part of the year. I love to spend a couple of hours catching trout, then searching for edible mushrooms, greens, and wild onions to serve with it. I top this off by harvesting gooseberries to make a pie for dessert. That meal is appealing like no other to me. It is a harvest from the land and is there for the taking.

And speaking of wild things, don't forget herbs for tea and medicines. Yes, you have to learn what is what and what plant has what uses. Start small and learn five plants that are growing near you and are useful. Then build on that. I harvest and dry dozens of plants for medicinal use and have found them to be very effective. We use them especially for prevention, because we're rarely sick. If high blood pressure runs in your family, for example, there are many common herbs that can be made into a tea to drink every day so that maybe it won't happen to you. Besides that, you get the pleasure of picking something good for you and taking advantage of nature's bounty. I drink a tea of dandelion root, yarrow, and violet leaves. My husband drinks one of juniper berries, prince's pine, and Oregon grape root. These are only a few of the herbs that grow right on my land. Look around and see what grows where you live.

Produce preservation

In planning the produce you will grow, consider first how you will be storing your harvest. Look through your seed catalogs to determine which varieties are better for which methods of preservation. For those of us who are entirely reliant on what we grow for our food, it is imperative to choose wisely. If it isn't tasty or the texture isn't good, it doesn't matter how much you harvested: no one will want to eat it. Here's an example: I canned two kinds of beets. One was absolutely delicious with no dressing-up at all. The other lost its flavor, color, and texture, and no matter how I tried to make them more palatable, they were yucky.

Another quality to look for is extra vitamin content. Some varieties have a naturally higher nutritional content, and your seed catalog will note that in the description. When all your food is home-produced, I think it's worthwhile to take that into consideration. And of course, be meticulous in your method of preservation. Beginners will probably not be totally successful the first time canning, but do pay attention to what you're doing and produce the very best product you can. Winter can seem very long when your harvest is poorly preserved and it's all you have to eat for months at a time.

For those who are just beginning at self-sufficiency, don't spend too much time on fun, exotic things. Grow what will sustain you and will almost certainly be successful. Zucchini, for example, is fun to eat in the summer and is almost always successful, but it doesn't contain a lot of nutrition and is hardly worth preserving. Winter squash, however, is packed with vitamins and will keep relatively easily in a cool place.

In my climate, growing tropical plants is impossible, and while they are certainly more glamorous than root crops, it is more worthwhile for me to cultivate carrots, beets, parsnips, rutabagas, and so on, than to spend time on tomatoes or eggplants. I can always trade for these with people in the valley.

Growing a garden for self-sufficiency is somewhat different than growing a supplemental or recreational garden. Your quantities will be greater, and you will want uniformity and reliability. I use Garden City seeds from Hamilton, Montana, and in the catalog there are "market farming" tips for many vegetables. I find these to be very helpful for my garden.

Be sure to choose varieties that are suitable for your climate. Most seeds off the grocery store rack will not be, unless you live in an ideal climate. Choose varieties that are vigorous and give real food production. In my climate, earliness is vital.

Seed saving allows you to plant seeds that are successful for your micro-climate. If you choose to do that, be sure to buy open-pollinated seed. Growing food is difficult, especially in the north, so make it as easy on yourself as possible. There's nothing wrong with buying seeds, even hybrids, if you can afford to and if it makes producing food easier.

Keep your soil healthy with compost and biological controls. Your soil is your lifeline and must be treated as the living organism that it is. Nurture and pamper it, and you will be able to grow more bountiful crops than you ever thought possible.

I hope I have given you some ideas for your year-round harvest plans. Harvesting is more than canning or freezing. It is a year-long food design which incorporates every phase of production. Self-sufficiency is hard work, but it is such a thrill to be reliant on ourselves for our family's requirements. It puts us in touch with the earth to such an extent that it is a fulfillment in itself. Δ

A country moment

White pelicans on a serene mountain lake.

Make "recycled wine" from leftover fruit pulp

By Allyn Uptain

We're recycling-crazy around here. We recycle everything possible. Sometimes I hear the lunatic fringe of the environmental movement talking about our "doomed" planet. On other days I hear ultra-conservatives or libertarians talking about how the environmentalists are over the edge and we have enough raw materials to last until the end of time. It's hard to decipher the truth anymore, but we recycle anyway. It teaches discipline. It teaches us to make full use of what we have. I dislike the concept of waste and want to create as little waste as possible. It's also a good way to impress on my children that they should not be indiscriminate in their habits.

Now when I say "recycle," I do indeed mean saving bottles, cans, and paper, and taking some of that to the recycling center. Since the recycling center is about 15 miles from our place, stopping by the recycling center is just an accepted part of our trips to the city. But mainly we recycle by reusing. Everyone knows how to use a grocery bag as a garbage can liner. That's the best kind of recycling.

One of my favorite things to recycle is leftover fruit pulp from making jelly. When we make jelly, we always end up with a bunch of fruit peelings or the leftover pulp from squeezing the juice out of some fruit. What can you do with that stuff? Well, you could always feed it to the farm animals, but we prefer to make wine with it.

When jelly season hits, we usually have peaches, wild berries, and plums ready at about the same time, so each year we end up making a few batches of "jelly wine." It's different every year. One year we may have more peaches, the next year more berries.

But it is always good. This is also a good excuse for me to clean out any stored fruit we may have. Apples going bad? Throw them in the jelly wine. Same for oranges, grapes, or any fruit that looks like it's at or near the end of its storage life. Variety is definitely the spice of this wine.

Making wine is easy. Fill the largest sanitary container you have one-third full of fruit. If you don't have enough fruit, you can cheat by adding sugar. Add enough non-chlorinated water to fill the container to two-thirds full. Squash, stir, and mix until you think you have most of the juice out of the pulp. Add some good wine or champagne yeast. You can use bread yeast, but real wine yeast will make a much better product.

Cover the container so that nothing can get in, but excess gas can escape. A simple way to let the gas out is to attach one end of a plastic tube well above the liquid level and the other end in a glass of water. Watch it bubble for a couple of weeks.

As carefully as you can, pour off the juice and leave the pulp behind. Clean your container. Pour the juice back in, cover it, and let it stand for another two to four weeks, with your "gas lock" setup still in place.

Now syphon the wine into bottles, leaving all the sediment in the fermentation container. You can take the plastic tube, attach one end to a small bowl, sink it in the wine, and then syphon right into your recycled juice and wine bottles. Just make sure the bottles and lids have been sterilized with boiling water or chlorine. (Rinse extremely well or wait 24 hours if you used bleach water.) Now all you have to do is wait six months or more before drinking your wine.

While you wait, you can feel good about yourself for all of the stuff you recycled. The pulp left over from the wine-making process we usually give to the chickens, but if you are really into medicinal alcohol, it also makes a good brew for a distiller. You will have to add lots of sugar, but you won't need any more fruit or yeast. You can, however, add any kind of leftover grain you might have lying around, as well as old honey or syrup. Δ

Solve chinking woes with a mortar-sawdust mix

Robert L. Williams

In virtually any type of building there is always the problem of sealing cracks and crevices, and the most frequently used solution to the problem is to buy caulking or compound tubes and a gun with which to apply the sealer.

This solution works well with most smaller cracks, but if the opening is fairly large (wide enough for you to stick your fingers into the crack) caulk or sealing compound is not a practical manner of solving the difficulty. For one thing, the cost is prohibitive if there is much sealing to do. There are also locations where it is virtually impossible to use caulk from tubes. And if you use one of the foam sealers, you must then go back and cut away the excess that is left after the sealer expands.

Vinyl chinking

You can buy a vinyl chinking or sealer in five gallon cans (perhaps smaller). This sealer is excellent primarily because the vinyl basis for the compound allows for expansion or shrinkage in fluctuating temperatures, and the chinking never completely sets or hardens. Instead, it remains the consistency of hard rubber.

To use the vinyl chinking, you will need a wide-blade putty knife and a narrow-blade putty knife, a small trowel (of the flower garden variety), and a small container of water. When you open the containers you will find a compound that is the consistency of stiff and very smooth mortar. This substance will smell very much like bubble gum mixed with ammonia.

When you apply the compound to large openings, it is better if you can smooth it over the surface of wood that has been inserted into the cracks between logs or wide boards. If you

are chinking a log structure, and if the cracks are two inches wide, push lengths of 2-x-4 timbers into the opening and toe-nail the lumber in place. The outside edge of the filler lumber should come to within one-fourth inch of the horizontal surface of the logs or wide boards.

When you apply the chinking compound, use a putty knife and spread chinking one-fourth inch thick (no thicker) across the whole surface of the lumber. Feather the chinking upward and downward so that it is forced into the wood of the logs. When the basic work is finished (the application of the chinking) then use a clean putty knife dipped into water to smooth the compound. Work only in one direction, and leave the surface of the compound as smooth as finished concrete. In fact, it can be almost as smooth as wood.

Mortar-sawdust mix

The major problem with the vinyl chinking is expense. The chinking we used on one job cost $10 per gallon, or $50 for a five-gallon bucket. We found quickly that we would need 25 buckets of compound, which would have amounted to $1,250 for the job.

There is, however, one method that answers nearly all of the problems of sealing and chinking. This is the mortar-sawdust mixture. It is inexpensive, can be used wherever there is room for a narrow-bladed putty knife or trowel, can be done rapidly, cleans up easily, and requires no expertise except for basic manual skills.

Here's how to go about chinking or sealing with the sawdust compound. First of all, you need to mix a batch of mortar. If the job is very small, buy a bag of pre-mixed mortar and simply add water and mix by hand. Use a hoe or shovel for good results.

If the job is large, you may want to buy your own mortar mix and add the sand (the fine aggregate) and water. For our needs we have always used creek sand or roadside sand. It does not matter if there are small pebbles in the mix; in fact, the larger sand granules and small pebbles actually help the mix by serving as a course aggregate.

When you plan to do the chinking work, choose a time when the weather is good; that is, don't try to work in sub-freezing weather or during a rainy season. (You can, however, work in ultra-cold weather if you add a little antifreeze to the mortar. If you do not, the mortar will freeze while you work.)

Mix either in a wheelbarrow or a mortar box. If you don't have a mortar box (for larger jobs) you can knock one together by using plywood or wide boards with straight edges, but it is much easier to pay the money to buy an inexpensive mixing box or to

The walls when chinking began. Notice how large the spaces were.

use the wheelbarrow. The advantage of using the wheelbarrow is that you can move the entire mortar supply as you change work locations.

A basic mixture of mortar is a one-to-three ratio of mortar mix to sand. That is, use three shovelfuls of sand for each shovelful of mortar. The problem with mortar is that if you must have a wide joint, the mortar tends to crack. That's where the sawdust enters the picture.

The best type of sawdust we have found is chips from chain saw projects. We try to do the majority of sawing in the same general location so that our sawdust is in a single heap rather than all over the farm. When we rip logs for boards, we use a primary saw station, and the result is that we have wheelbarrow loads of sawdust available at all times.

If you have a workshop, sweep up the sawdust after each work session and store it in a bag or bucket. Do not worry if the sawdust or chips are green with sap, and the least of your worries is whether the sawdust is wet. In fact, you want to have it not only wet but saturated before you use it.

Here's why. When you are laying bricks or blocks, you should sprinkle the bricks with water before you install them into a course of work. If you do not, the dryness of the bricks will pull the moisture from the mortar and leave it too dry. The result will be severe cracking or crumbling.

The same is true of wood and mortar. You do not want to wet your logs or boards, unless you can sprinkle them lightly, so put the water-bearing sawdust into the mix and the problem is solved. The tiny wood chips cannot draw moisture from the mortar because it is already saturated. There will therefore be no appreciable amount of cracking, crumbling, or other deterioration of the mortar.

Another superior point is that the sawdust or wood chips (the tiny chips, that is, no large ones) will extend the amount of mortar needed, and you

actually save a considerable amount of money by using the sawdust.

Now to the proportions of sawdust to the mortar mixture: for every shovelful of mortar mix, add 1.5 times as much sawdust. So if you use six shovelfuls of mortar mix, use nine shovelfuls of sawdust, in addition to the sand.

If you cannot get a wheelbarrow close to the work site, use a mortar board to hold your sawdust-mortar mixture. To make a mortarboard, stand two 2-x-4 lengths (two feet long, each) on edge and then nail plywood or wide boards across the 2-x-4s. The final product should be at least two feet wide and two feet long so that you can have a large amount of mix on hand. You will use too much time and energy if you need to make trip after trip to get small amounts of mortar.

If you use the sawdust-mortar mix, you will not need to worry about the filler strips between cracks. All you need to do is load up a full-size trowel (brick masonry trowel as opposed to block masonry trowel) with mortar and push the mixture into the cracks so tightly that the mixture is forced upward and into the pores of the wood. Do not try to fill cracks loosely.

If you find that you are shoving mortar out the other side of the crack, there are two ways to handle the problem. The first way, if you have a helper, is not only simple and easy but also very efficient. One of you should work on the outside, and the other on the inside, and both of you should be at the same point in the wall. Each of you can scoop up a trowel-full of sawdust mortar and at the same time both of you should push the mortar mixture into the same crack. The pressure formed by the two masses of mortar meeting inside the crack will force more mortar into the pores of the wood, creating a better bond.

Remember that when you lay bricks, one of the purposes of jointing the mortar in each course is not just for decoration but to push mortar into the pores in the blocks or other masonry materials. The same principles apply to wood and mortar.

A second way, which works well if you must work alone, is to find short lengths of board (five to six feet long) and lightly nail the boards to the logs or wall boards so that the new board will cover cracks for several feet. The board will keep you from pushing mortar out the other side of the wall. When you have completed a stretch of work, leave the boards in place for a

The building when the chinking was completed.

few minutes until the mortar had has a chance to start to set. You must realize that setting up will not be complete for two to three days, so do not disturb the mortar-filled cracks for at least 48 hours.

Fill all the cracks that are covered on the other side by boards (you can use a sheet of plywood if you have one handy and get more coverage with less nailing time) and then move to the next work area and repeat the process. You can go back an hour to two hours later, unless the temperature is very hot, and use the back of a trowel to smooth the mortar. Dip the trowel in water and smooth as you would if you were finishing a small patch of cement or as if you were finishing the compounding of a joint.

For greater stability of the joints, you can go back to still-wet joints and push nails through the mortar at an acute angle until the point of the nail contacts wood. Drive the nail then until the head is even with the surface of the mortar. Use a punch to drive the nail until the head is covered.

Finally, when the mortar has set completely, if you see tiny strands of sawdust sticking out, use a sheet of sandpaper to brush the strands until they disappear. Your chinking job will then be completed, and at a price that is amazingly low and with a speed that is remarkable and gratifying. Δ

Sheet composting saves work

By John Fuchs

My work as a landscaper provides me with tons of grass clippings and leaves. I have utilized these materials to make compost piles. Last year, I decided to use some of these materials in a sheet composting experiment. The idea was to determine if I could save myself some of the back-breaking labor of building the compost pile, turning it, watering it, lugging it to the garden area, and then digging it into the soil to a depth of a foot or so.

In October, I spread a layer of leaves two inches thick over my garden area (primarily maple and sycamore leaves). The leaves had been partially shredded by my lawnmower. In order to hasten the decomposition of the leaves, I added a leaf activator that combined alfalfa, kelp, cocoa meal, and lots of microorganisms. I had used the activator the previous two falls in my compost piles with good success.

After spreading the activator on the leaves, I added lime and shoveled on an inch or so of dirt over the leaves. I then gave the area a good soaking. I did nothing else until late April, when I set out to plant some broccoli and lettuce.

I was pleasantly surprised to see that the decomposition of the leaves was largely complete. I estimated that 80 to 90% of the volume had decomposed. I passed the rototiller over the garden patch and incorporated the residue into the soil. Since the leaf breakdown was not 100% complete, I added a high-nitrogen fertilizer (28-3-3) that I use for lawns in the spring, as well as my usual 5-10-5. The extra nitrogen replaces the nitrogen that is "locked up" in the leaf decomposition process and released when the process is complete.

The results were excellent. Both my early crops (lettuce and broccoli) and my warm-weather crops (tomatoes, eggplants, peppers) produced heavily, and I saw no difference in yield from previous years when I had used traditionally composted material in the garden.

Undoubtedly, the years of adding traditionally composted matter had made my garden plot fertile, and, while I certainly would not discount the value of compost piles, sheet composting is a far less laborious way to incorporate organic matter into the soil. Δ

Based on years of personal experience, here are 10 good tips for homeschooling your children

By Mary Jo Bratton

Are you considering homeschooling your children, but don't know where to start? The following 10 tips will help answer some of your questions.

• Read, read, read.

But don't read too many "This is the way to teach your child" books. You'll end up confused and convinced that you can't do it. Instead, read a few "how-to" books and lots of books on world history, philosophy, religion, biology, psychology, literature, and other topics. If you don't know where to start, go to the library and look up all the children's books on the subject in which you're interested. The children's books will give you an overview, with easy-to-understand explanations that provide a base for more advanced learning.

• Relax: You're not having school-at-home; you're homeschooling.

Say the word "school" out loud. What's the scenario that comes to mind? Desks. Chalk dust. A U.S. flag in the corner. Teacher up front, lecturing to sleepy students. Lockers slamming. Bells ringing. Boring.

"School-at-home" is an image that needs to be ditched, in favor of "homeschooling." Rid yourself of the idea that having school means sitting at a desk in a stuffy room, taking notes for six hours a day while Mom lectures endlessly about history, biology, algebra, and French. When you homeschool, the emphasis is on "home." Sitting on the sofa while you do math problems, studying insect life under a dead log in the back yard, asking questions in the car on the way to the library, reading Western biographies instead of dry history textbooks, and writing papers about the novels of Agatha Christie or the Titanic or motorcycles, instead of

"What I Did Last Summer." It is also playing with your brothers and sisters at recess, and wearing what *you* like to wear, not what the group says is "in style."

• Tailor the program to fit your child's learning style.

What kinds of activities does your child enjoy most? Does she count with blocks, love fingerpaint and modeling clay, enjoy taking apart and putting together Legos or other building toys? Does he enjoy being read to or listening to cassette recordings of storybooks? Or is she happiest curled up with a good book and silence all around?

People learn in all three ways: **kinesthetic** (by touching and handling things), **auditory** (by listening), and **visual** (including reading). Of course, children learn through all their senses, unless they're physically disabled. However, since everyone tends to lean to one specific learning style, you can increase your child's learning enjoyment by adapting the curriculum to fit his style.

Materials good for **visual** learners are workbooks, flash cards, matching games, instruction books, and charts. Good materials for **auditory** learners are verbal explanations, cassette tapes and CDs (recorded books), educational songs and rhymes, and rhythm instruments (for music class). For **kinesthetic** learners, try nature walks, model kits, gardening, puzzles, and typing instead of writing (faster and less frustrating).

Using your child's learning style is especially helpful when you have to work through some of those sticky math problems. For a visual learner, try working out the problem on paper. An auditory learner may need only to have the problem read aloud. (My daughter asks for this help from time to time.) And a kinesthetic learner may need concrete objects (toothpicks, buttons) to stand in for the factors.

• Try lots of stuff.

How much would you pay for nine months at a private school? Probably $3500 and up. You don't need to spend that much to teach your children at home, but you shouldn't skimp, either. Education is *at least* as important as the amount you spent on Christmas last year, or on a trip to Disney World, or on a new Magnavox 31-inch television with a built-in VCR. If you set aside a specified amount for home school supplies at the beginning of the school year, you'll feel freer to buy that set of art prints or those German language tapes than if you have to dip into the family budget.

Caution: Don't buy anything you can't return. Ideally, you should have your hands on the book or program before you pay for it. Ask yourself: Is this simple to use? Will this appeal to my kids? Does it appeal to me? (If it isn't simple and/or appealing, you'll use it for two or three weeks and then stash it in the closet, where it will haunt you forever.)

• Write out your reasons for homeschooling and educational goals for each subject.

Why do you want to teach your own children? Do you want to ensure their religious training, academic achievement, individuality, continuance of family/ethnic traditions? Are you simply crazy? (You will be asked this plenty of times, believe me.) When the rubber hits the road, you'll need to have written-out reasons for taking on this more-than-full-time job, so you can read them often. That way, you'll remember why you chose to keep your kids home when everyone else was merrily pushing theirs onto the big yellow school bus.

Educational goals should focus on outcomes. What do you want your child to be able to do as a result of having been taught this material?

Here are some of my goals for my two children:

• **Language arts:** Be able to use the fundamental skills of communication —reading, writing, spelling, and grammar—in a way that will enable them to function in our society (letters, conversation, job applications, essays, etc.).

• **Social studies:** Understand and be able to explain the major world systems (government, religious beliefs, culture) and how they developed (world history).

• **Religion:** Have respect and appreciation for human values and for the beliefs of others.

• **Science:** Understand and be able to explain the physical world as represented through basic knowledge of the sciences.

My list of educational goals also includes mathematical skills, perseverance, intellectual curiosity, physical and mental health fitness, and more. Your list of goals should cover those areas which are important to you and your family.

• Sometimes it's not fun.

Nothing is fun all the time. Going to work isn't always fun. (Sometimes it's never fun, but that's another article.) Running a household isn't always my idea of a good time. And sometimes I'd rather dig in my garden than teach my kids.

Don't get me wrong. Life should be enjoyable and fulfilling. Unfortunately, sometimes you have to slog through the hard parts in order to make way for the good.

If you've done all you can to make grammar fun and the kids still gripe, explain that even though it's tough, an intelligent person must have a grasp of correct grammar. You can sweeten up the drudge with rewards along the way. For instance, I use index cards colorfully decorated with the words, "Coveted Candy Bar Card— Redeemable for one candy bar," to reward my kids for perfect papers. Or I give them something to look forward to, such as a "field trip" to an amusement park or campground after a particularly hard semester of schoolwork.

Face it, though. Some things are just not fun. They just have to be done. This is a lesson kids need to learn before they enter adulthood and have to write an annual report, cook dinner every evening, or stay up until 2 a.m. to meet a deadline.

• Give it a year.

One year of home education will not irrevocably harm your child, even if the only "schooling" you do is reading lots of books. (We're talking here about a literate family who gets out to the library now and then.) On the other hand, after a year, you should be able to tell if home education has been a success for you and your kids.

Be generous in your judgment of "success." Maybe your family has suffered a financial setback, death, illness, childbirth, or the like (in other words, normal life), and you've all had to pitch in to make it through tough times. In that case, "success" may mean a closer relationship between parents and children, and perhaps a talent discovered in carpentry, nursing, or clothing design. These family lessons are priceless and can only be taught at home, not in a public or private school setting.

• Do unit studies.

The beauty of a unit study is that the whole family can study a subject at the same time. You can take an armchair tour of a different European country every month, or follow the chronology of classical music throughout history. You may decide to take an in-depth look at Eastern religions for a semester. Or you can select a species of animal, research it, and then plan a field trip to its natural habitat. (See page 35: "A unit study on birds.")

In a unit study, each family member works to the limit of his ability. For an activity on a unit study covering the Revolutionary War, first graders may make a model of a hornbook with the alphabet and numbers printed on it. Ninth graders may reenact the signing of the Declaration of Independence.

You don't have to leave out the primary wage-earner when you do your unit study. Make posters charting the taxonomy of living things and hang them on the dining room walls. Plan an ethnically appropriate meal and have the kids cook and serve it. Watch a library video on Germany after dinner one evening.

Whatever you decide to do, set educational goals for your unit studies so specific skills are taught and assimilated. Give yourselves time to explore your chosen subject, and remember to keep it simple.

• Give life skills equal status with academic skills.

Driving a car. Planning and preparing a meal. Mowing the lawn. Reshingling the roof. Sewing kitchen curtains. Balancing the household budget. These are life skills and, while we may think they don't take a lot of brain power, life skills will most likely mean the difference between your child's future independence or her ineptness. It's extraordinary how much we worry about whether our children are learning biology, but then neglect to teach them the correct way to paint a room or a house, how to iron a shirt, how to cut or trim hair, or how to fix the toaster. Instead, we do these things ourselves or pay others to do them for us.

Make a list of life skills you'd like your kids to know before they leave your tender care. Teaching these skills not only helps the family now, but ensures that your kids will be able to take care of themselves later.

*And the **number one tip** for home educators:*

• Enjoy yourself.

Did you study the subjects you wanted to learn during your educational career? More important, do you *remember* any of it? My three years of French have withered away to one feeble chorus of "La plume de ma tante." I have even less memory of my Algebra II class (except that the teacher pronounced the word "function" in a very interesting way). Now I'm learning German and taking guitar lessons. And algebra is more understandable without all the distractions I had in tenth grade.

Who says school is for kids only? Now's your chance to listen to all of J.S. Bach's works for organ, investigate the ecology of your part of the country, or read up on hot air balloons. There's no limit to what you and your kids can learn when you have the freedom that home education brings. Δ

A unit study on birds

By Mary Jo Bratton

Here is a suggested unit study you can use in homeschooling your children. You can use this simple format in other unit studies you develop.

From a study of local birds, your children can learn many basic facts about a variety of subjects, such as animal life, geography, climate, aerodynamics, and the use of a compass.

Investigation

What birds live in our area? How do birds get ready for winter? Which birds stay here in winter and how do they survive? Which birds leave and where do they go? Are any of our local birds harmful to people or animals? Which ones are helpful? Why doesn't a bird fall off a limb when it sleeps? Questions such as these will help you write educational goals for your unit study and will help you think of learning activities that can be done, such as the ones listed below.

Activities

- Make a list of all the birds the children can name from memory. Look these birds up in a field guide. If some of the birds named are from other parts of the world, find their homes on a globe or world map. You may wish to check with your county extension service or state natural resources department to find the names of native birds. Don't rush your children through this step. Take lots of time to talk it over and discover what they already know.

- Find pictures of as many birds on the list as possible. The list and pictures can be used for teaching how to alphabetize, as well as for identification purposes. For very young students, you can teach colors, counting, and spelling with these names and pictures.

- Talk about what may be the cause for bird migrations. Check out children's books on the subject at the library. Point out flocks of birds and note the time of year and the direction they're flying. Watch for newspaper and magazine articles on bird migrations.

- Mark on a world map the destinations of various migratory birds. Study about flyways and note the amazing distances that some birds travel in their seasonal migrations.

- Invite a bird-watcher to visit your home and share his interest and information about birds. Or go to a local nature center for a bird-banding demonstration or a hike with a naturalist. People who love the outdoors usually love to share their knowledge with those who show an interest.

- Listen to tapes of bird calls. Imitate bird calls or try to describe them. This can be lots of fun, with the kids giving each bird call a different meaning. (Bedtime may become a little noisy at your house for a while, what with siblings sending messages via chirps and squawks.)

- Draw and color pictures of favorite birds. Ask, "Why is this bird your favorite?" "Because it's blue" is as good a reply as any.

- Keep a bird calendar. Record the last time certain birds are seen in the fall. In the spring, the same calendar can be used to record the return of migrating birds.

- When winter comes, set up bird feeders and research what seeds each type of local bird prefers. Study bird house design and build a few over the winter months. When spring comes, check your field guide to find out where certain species like to nest, and then mount the houses in similar places. You can continue your unit study throughout the year as you watch bird families choose dwellings, build nests, lay eggs, raise babies, and teach them to fly. Δ

Teach your kids math with the banking game

By Micki Warner

One of the tricks of successful education is the "exceptional teacher's" ability to make the process fun. When a parent takes over the teacher's job in the home, it is sometimes disastrous for both parent and student. The parent's intentions are good, but the part that gets lost is the fun.

The banking game described here can provide the fun and also accomplish the following teaching objectives:

• Improving basic math.

• Instilling organizational skills and neatness.

• Learning real banking methods.

• Encouraging saving money.

Along with these benefits, the program provides an opportunity for positive parent-child interaction during the educational process.

To get started, you need the following materials: several unused checkbooks, some deposit and withdrawal slips, a little "white-out" on an old bank statement, and two large piggy banks with enlarged holes for "ease of transaction."

At the ages of seven and ten, I introduced my children to the world of banking by opening the "Children's Bank and Trust Company," appointing myself Teller. Each child was given a stack of withdrawal slips, a new checkbook (with deposit slips), and a brand-new, simulated-leather checkbook cover. My only other contribution was a beginning balance of $5.

It was explained to the children that the *initial deposit* belonged to them, but thereafter, each *transaction,* whether a *deposit* (put-in) or *withdrawal* (take-out), must be accomplished according to the rules of the bank. They practiced writing checks

for different amounts and developed the skill of writing numbers in longhand. Addition and subtraction were used to complete the stubs, and instructions were given on how to deposit and withdraw money. Each time a child put money in the bank—or took some out—it was via a deposit or withdrawal slip. If they borrowed cash from other family members, we received a check, and the money was removed from the bank.

All transaction slips were kept inside the pig, and at the end of each month, there was an accounting. For this procedure, an old bank statement was used, by obliterating other transactions with white-out. We made photocopies of this blanked-out statement, and we used these sheets to tally up what the children had done. Following a real bank's format, we carefully filled out the statement with deposits and withdrawals. Cancelled checks and deposit slips were balanced and checked with the stubs in their checkbooks. The children rarely balanced, but we always had fun hunting for and solving mistakes.

Because we were a "small and newly opened bank," we had no interest (which might be excellent for older children). We also had no bank charges. The children thought this more than fair.

In the beginning, we had many "closed accounts" due to "insufficient funds," and after a few months we included a stiff fine for bouncing checks (one dollar). This dollar went to the salary of the Teller. The entire process was kept simple, and in a short time, the childen learned banking concepts, and their math skills were greatly improved. The children discovered the importance of neatness, since many mistakes were due to illegible numbers.

We kept up the game for many years. The children became "board members," and they enacted and repealed many by-laws for their bank. Some worked, some were enough to bring in the FBI. Their savings grew as it became an embarrassment to "bounce a check." When they began to demand interest, I turned them over to Alice, the teller at my *real* bank. ∆

Improve your poultry with selective breeding

By Jan Palmer

People don't usually think about poultry in terms of breeding—it's not taken seriously. People who wouldn't dream of inbreeding in other species take cockerels from the same hatchery (and probably the same genetic lines) to sire the next year's flock. Ducks and geese are not usually bred for specific traits, either.

Take a few minutes and think about what traits you want to preserve in your flock. Do you want the absolute largest bird? The one who is always out foraging for food, lays well, and is in good condition? The wild one that no predator can catch? The gander with such a good temperament that even the kids can be around him? The duck who lays exceptionally well? Do you want chickens for good laying ability and meat, but want to feed the meat birds differently from the start? Do you have rare breeds that you would like to preserve while selecting for your own selected traits? Each of these goals can take a different approach in selective breeding.

When selecting chicken breeders, look for cockerels that are at least six to eight months old (depending on breed) and pullets that have been laying for at least six weeks. Another option is using the older one- to two-year-old hens for breeders. This has a couple of advantages: if they've survived for over a year, they're disease-resistant and good layers (if they aren't, they should have been culled long ago). Therefore, they have proven themselves as carriers of traits that you want to have in the flock.

Keep the breeders as stress-free as possible, and have a way to separate them. Having three cockerels or roosters in with a dozen hens will leave you with a pretty ragged bunch of hens, and you won't know which male sired the chicks. Separating your breeders also prevents excessive inbreeding.

Other management factors: When you purchase your initial batch of chicks, you should make sure that they are vaccinated for Marek's disease. Keep the birds healthy. Make sure parasites are eliminated before setting to collect breeder eggs. Make sure the male is healthy and doesn't have too many hens to breed. A good rule of thumb is about a dozen hens per male. Give them room to move about. Make sure birds can comfortably reach into feeders.

Don't assume that layer rations are good for breeding: some have too little animal protein, vitamins, and minerals for embryos and vigorous hatching eggs. Look for a breeder ration (freshly mixed) or a game bird ration. If you can't find either, about six weeks before you plan to collect eggs for hatching, start supplementing your birds with a handful of dry cat food a few times a week, and add a vitamin/ mineral supplement to their water supply.

Poultry must receive 14 hours of light daily for best production. Use lights with timers. Gather eggs twice a day, and handle eggs gently: jarring the eggs decreases the chance of hatching. Wash your hands before collecting to minimize problems, and wash dirty eggs in water slightly warmer than the eggs.

Barred Plymouth Rock cock selected as a breeder. He is of good size and temperament and is an active forager.

If you are using a broody hen, make sure that she is reliable and won't abandon the eggs part way through incubation. Some people have had good luck with banty hens, Muscovy ducks, and some breeds of standard chickens. Orpingtons, Plymouth Rocks, Dominiques, and Sussex chickens all have members who are determined to be mothers. I had a Dominique hen a couple of years ago who had a few eggs in the bottom of a bucket. I picked her up and pulled the eggs out because I needed to use the bucket. As soon as I set it down, she was back in it, nestling down. That's determination.

However, don't rely on breed alone. Khaki Campbell ducks aren't supposed to be good setters, yet I had one who was downright vicious about protecting the eggs under her. She'd hatch any kind of eggs and would defend the nest with wing attacks, hissing, and well-placed attacks at the hand, foot, or dog nose near her nest. (She was of excellent temperament when she wasn't nesting.)

Of course, you may wish to use an incubator and set up a brooder in the corner of the barn, garage, or storage shed. Δ

Here are some cucumber pickles to make at home

By Olivia Miller

Preserving produce by "pickling" is one of the oldest and most delightful ways to save your summer harvst for your winter table. The word "pickle" applies to any food preserved in brine and/ or vinegar, with or without bacterial fermentation, and with or without the addition of spices and sugar.

Foods pickled with *vinegar* are usually cooked before the vinegar is added. Because the food is cooked, no fermentation is required. This method is usually restricted to fruits, though some vegetables can be preserved in this way.

Foods pickled with *salt* are usually covered with a brine solution of the proper strength to allow fermentation to set in. The rate of fermentation is determined by the strength of the brine: the weaker the brine, the more rapidly fermentation takes place; the more concentrated the brine, the slower the fermentation. One recipe from an old-timer said to make a brine strong enough to float an egg (one pint of salt to one gallon of water) for her recipe for cucumber pickles.

Quick-process pickles, also called *fresh-pack*, use a salt-and-vinegar method that has a brief brining period before the vinegar is added. Sometimes fresh-packed pickles are canned in a spicy vinegar solution without brining. Whole cucumber dills and sweet gherkins are prepared by this method.

Helpful tips

Here are some helpful tips for making cucumber pickles:

• Use *pure* salt (99% sodium chloride) with no non-caking material or iodine added, for fermented pickles. Usually called "granulated salt," "barrel salt," or "meat curing salt," it was once found at farm supply stores and speciality grocery stores, but now is available in most grocery stores in inexpensive 2^{1}/2 lb. bags labeled "canning and pickling

A display of cucumber pickles: icicles, bread-n-butters, sweet gherkins, cucumber relish, and crisp sweets.

salt." Regular non-iodized table salt can be used for quick-method pickles.

• **The lime used for pickling is calcium hydroxide** (*air slaked* or *builder's lime*). You'll find it beside the pickling salt in your grocery section with the canning jars and lids.

• **Ground spices can darken pickles and relishes.** Many recipes say to tie spices in a thin cloth bag and remove them before pickles are packed. Fresh spices give the best flavor. If dried herbs are used in substitution for fresh, use this ratio: 1 teaspoon dried = 1 tablespoon fresh. Spices and herbs lose their pungency in heat and humidity, so store them in airtight containers in a cool place.

Pickling spice, available at the grocery store, is made from ten to sixteen spices. Or you can make your own with the following recipe:

Pickling spice:

2 tablespoons mustard seed
1 tablespoon whole allspice
2 teaspoons coriander seeds
2 teaspoons cloves
1 teaspoon of ground ginger
1 teaspoon dried hot red pepper flakes
1 bay leaf, crumbled
a 2-inch cinnamon stick, crushed fine

In a bowl combine all the spices. Keep the mixture in a tightly sealed jar in a cool dark place for six months. Makes ^{1}/3 of a cup.

• **Dill is in season before cucumbers are ready for picking.** Gather the dill, do not wash it, break heads off the stem and place heads in mason jars. Put on a cap and screw band tightly and freeze immediately.

• **The vinegar used in pickling needs to be a 4 to 6% acetic acid, 40 to 60 grain strength.** Check labels. Cider vinegar has a good flavor and aroma. Clear distilled vinegar is used for onion and cauliflower, because cider vinegar discolors, but for cucumber pickles this is not a problem. White distilled vinegar has a sharp, pungent acetic acid taste.

Vinegar has been around a long time, pre-dating the Old Testament (which mentions Ruth dipping a bit of bread into vinegar). The name comes from *vin aigre*, which is French for "sour wine," and that is where it began. The bacteria *Acetobacter* sours the wine, dissipates the alcohol, and leaves a mixture of 4% acetic acid and water. Roman legions put wine vinegar into their drinking water to purify it. Vinegar was a by-product of wine makers and brewers until the 17th century, when the French separated vinegar making it into a separate industry. The English make malt vinegar from sour beer and ale. Americans make vinegar out of fermented apple juice.

• **Only fresh, firm, not-too-ripe cucumbers should be used for pickling.** Do not use waxed cucumbers, since the brine cannot penetrate wax. Cucumbers should be small or medium-sized. No more than 24 hours should elapse between picking cucumbers and placing them in brine. (If my harvest isn't adequate and I must buy more produce, I get the process set up before I go to the farmers' market to hunt for the right fruit, taking the farmer at his word that the cucumbers were harvested that morning.) Wash to remove dirt, blossom, and grit. Once in the brine, keep the cucumbers in a cool place; about 70° F is best. The fermentation process takes anywhere from a few days to several weeks, and is complete when bubbles stop coming up to the top of the container. Test for bubbles by tapping container on the side with your hand. Cut a cucumber: if it is the same color throughout and has no noticeable rings, fermentation is complete.

• **Hard water (that is, water with extra calcium salts) interferes with the brining process.** Purchase bottled water, or add ½ cup vinegar to a gallon of hard water.

• **For the brining process, use stone jars or crocks, unchipped enamelware, or glass containers.** Cover with a heavy plate or glass lid while brining. Use a filled jar of water to hold the cover down, so that vegetables are kept below the surface of brine. Pickles are soft and slippery if they're exposed above the brine or if the brine is too weak. Slippery stuff also results from storing in too warm a place, or cooking too long or a too-high temperature when cooking.

When heating pickling liquids, use glass, unchipped enamelware, stainless steel, or aluminum utensils. **Don't**

The right stuff for pickling: an unchipped crock, canning salt, vinegar, garlic, onion, sweet red peppers, fresh cucumbers, fresh dill, pickling spice, and jars and lids.

use copper, brass, galvanized, or iron utensils, as these metals will react with acids or salts and cause undesirable color changes in the pickles or form compounds which could be **poisonous.** Be attentive when timing the processing procedure. For fermented cucumbers and fresh-pack dills, start to count processing time as soon as the filled jars are placed in the boiling water. This keeps them from tasting cooked and loosing their crispness.

To sterilize jars and glasses for pickling: Wash the jars in hot suds and rinse them in scalding water. Put the jars in a kettle and cover them with hot water. Bring the water to a boil, cover, and boil the jars 15 minutes from the time that steam emerges from the kettle. Turn off the heat and let the jars stand in the hot water. Just before they are to be filled, invert the jars onto a dish towel to dry. The jars should be filled while they are still hot. Sterilize the jar lids for five minutes, or according to manufacturer's instructions.

Frightened? Don't be. Cucumber pickles are successfully produced in ordinary kitchens every year. I stick to the simple, quick methods for most of my canning, enjoying the special tastes that cannot be purchased at the grocery store. My one exception to the "quick and easy" is a favorite recipe for dills:

Fermented dill pickles

50 to 60 smooth small cucumbers
1 ounce whole mixed spices
dill
1 pound pure salt
1 gallon water
1 pint cider vinegar

*Author Olivia Miller takes bread-n-butter
pickles from the water bath, placing the hot
jars on a towel to let them cool before storing.*

Place a layer of dill in the bottom of a clean, four-gallon crock. Add 1/2 ounce whole mixed spices. Pack cucumbers to within three inches of top of crock. Then add another 1/2 ounce whole mixed spices and a layer of dill.

Make a cold brine of the salt, water, and vinegar. Pour brine over cucumbers. Cover with a china plate. Weight plate down to keep cucumbers below surface of brine. Cover top of crock with cloth.

Remove any scum that forms on surface of liquid.

Just as soon as bubbling ceases and active fermentation stops, place pickles in standard canning jars. Pour brine over pickles, screw on lids firmly tight, and immerse in a kettle of tap-temperature water. Bring to a boil and boil for 15 minutes. When jars are cooling, you can tell when each one vacuum-seals, because the lid will click down into a little indentation. Store in a cool, dry, dark place.

A variation of this fermented pickle is this mustard recipe:

Fermented mustard pickles

    50 to 60 smooth small cucumbers
    1 gallon vinegar
    1/2 pound (16 tablespoons) dry mustard
    1 cup salt

Wash cucumbers, pack into sterilized jars. Work the mustard into a paste using a little of the vinegar, then dissolve it in the rest of the vinegar. Pour cold solution over cucumbers to within a half inch of the jar top. Put on the cap, and screw the band firmly tight. When fermentation (bubbling) has stopped, process in boiling water bath 15 minutes. Makes three gallons. I prefer this method because the fermented

pickles are not moved into another container after the fermenting process.

There are many different kinds of pickles. Here are recipes for some of my favorites:

Fresh kosher style dill pickles

Kosher pickles are made in accordance with Jewish dietary laws. All ingredients are derived from vegetable matter only, and utensils used in the processing have not been in contact with meat products. I noticed the presence of garlic in all of my kosher cucumber pickle recipes. This is my favorite:

    30 to 36 cucumbers (3-4 inches long)
    3 cups vinegar
    3 cups water
    6 tablespoons salt
    fresh or dried dill
    1/2 to 1 clove garlic, sliced
    1/2 teaspoon mustard seed

Wash cucumbers. Make a brine of the vinegar, water, and salt. Bring to a boil. Place a generous layer of dill, garlic, and mustard seed in the bottom of six pint jars. Pack the cucumbers in the jars. Fill the jars to within a half inch of the top with the boiling brine. Put lids on jars, screw bands firmly tight. Process 20 minutes in boiling water bath. Pickles will shrivel after processing, but will plump up in the sealed jars, so don't panic and open the jars. Yields six pints.

Bread-n-butter pickles

Bread-n-butter pickles are a delicious condiment that adds sparkle to sandwich meats and blackeyed peas. My young children mound bread-n-butter pickles on top of lima beans, and even ask for a second helping.

    16 cups of cucumber, sliced 1/4 inch thick (4 pounds)
    6 cups of thinly sliced onions
    1/2 cup salt
    5 cups sugar
    5 cups cider vinegar
    1 1/2 teaspoons turmeric
    1 1/2 teaspoons celery seed
    1 1/2 teaspoons mustard seed

In a large (seven-quart) kettle, mix cucumbers, onions and salt. Cover with cold water and three trays of ice cubes. Let stand three hours. Drain, rinse well, and drain again. Set aside. In another large kettle, mix sugar and remaining ingredients. Over high heat, heat to boiling. Reduce heat and simmer uncovered 30 minutes, or until syrupy, stirring often. Get jars ready (wash and have hot), add cucumbers and onions to syrup over high heat, heat almost to boiling, stirring some, but don't boil. Ladle hot mixture into hot jars. Leave 1/2" head space. Wipe jar tops, put on rings and lids and process in boiling water 15 minutes. Cool. Makes six pints. For a Christmas variation, add two cups of sliced red sweet peppers.

Sweet gherkins

A *gherkin* is a variety of cucumber that bears small prickly fruit. The name also refers to the immature fruit of the common cucumber when pickled.

Use cucumbers no larger than two inches in length. Leave 1/4 inch or more of the stem on each. Wash and place in a crock. Add salt, using one cup of salt for each gallon of cucumbers. Pour boiling water over them and let them stand 24 to 36 hours. Remove the pickles from the brine and drop them into a solution of equal parts vinegar and water. Heat to the boiling point and remove pickles to sterilized jars. Add a teaspoon of mixed pickling spices to each quart, and also a fairly long strip of horseradish root. Add a cup of sugar per quart to the hot vinegar and water, and pour it over the pickles. Water bath 10 minutes.

Icicle pickles

"Icicle" pickle refers to the shape of the cucumber pieces, a lengthwise cut resulting in long slivers shaped like icicles. Cucumbers cut in this fashion can be dilled, sweetened, or fermented.

```
celery
pickling onions
1 quart cider vinegar
1/3 cup pickling salt
1 cup sugar
```

Cut large cucumbers into four to eight pieces lengthwise. Let stand in ice water eight hours or overnight. Pack into hot sterilized jars.

Fill the center of each jar with two pieces of celery and six pickling onions. Combine the vinegar, salt, and sugar. Heat to a boil. Fill jars and seal in water bath 10 minutes.

This is the basic recipe, and you make as much vinegar/sugar/salt solution as you need. I save unused portions in the refrigerator for the next day's pickles during canning season, or pour it over sliced cucumber, green bell pepper, and onion for a salad. The salad is best when chilled a few hours.

Start a collection of pickle recipes. Commercial canning jar companies produce recipe books with lots of tips. Δ

Enrich your soil with cover crops

By Inez Castor

Use it or lose it. That expression did not originally refer to soil, but it could have. Nature improves soil by growing plants on it continuously. In the wild, good soil is never without a cover of vegetation. Something will grow there, so it may as well be something you choose.

If you don't intend to grow a winter garden, plant food for the soil. Cover crops are grown only to be returned to the soil, to feed and protect the soil. They improve fertility, prevent erosion, and provide sanctuary for beneficial creatures while interrupting disease and weed cycles.

Cover cropping is a technique first practiced by the Chinese over 3000 years ago. Only in recent decades have American gardeners discovered its benefits. Planted immediately after the ground is cleared, cover crops act as "holding tanks," taking up nutrients and keeping them near the soil surface. They also add organic matter to the soil and protect earthworms.

A good cover crop, often called a *green manure*, should be easy to start, form a thick growth, and be easy to turn under in the spring. It will save you time and money, improve your soil, and increase your yields.

Not all manure comes from animals. Manure is anything that, through its decay, introduces organic matter and nutrients into the soil in compensation for those removed by crops, livestock, and the elements. Green manure is as much a fertilizer as barnyard manure.

Hairy vetch

Types of cover crops: legumes and grasses

Cover crops come in two main types: *legumes* and *grasses*. **Legumes** include peas, beans, clover, and vetch. These crops are great producers, not only of organic matter, but that all-important soil nutrient, *nitrogen*.

Legume cover crops are actually "nitrogen factories," but they need help from a kind of bacteria called *rhizobia*. These bacteria form white nodules on the legume roots, into which they bring soil-borne nitrogen. This nitrogen is absolutely useless to the plants until the bacteria eat it. The by-product of this process is the form of nitrogen that plants can use. This is called *nitrogen fixation.*

Legume seed must be *inoculated* with the necessary bacteria before planting. If your soil is in good condition, it probably already contains the necessary bacteria, but it's a good idea to inoculate the seeds anyway. The inoculants are inexpensive, easy to apply, completely organic, and will ensure that your legumes get all the nitrogen they can handle. Though there are several different types of inoculants, the type needed for the legume you choose will be available wherever you buy your seed. Inoculation is not a preventative, but a booster, like yeast. Seeds must be inoculated on the same day they're planted, or the bacteria will die.

Grasses are grain plants, including wheat, oats, barley, and rye. Although they don't produce nitrogen the way legumes do, grasses provide some nitrogen, as well as potassium, phosphorous, and trace elements as they break down. The main benefit of using grasses is that they create plenty of organic material that conditions the soil. They also make an especially efficient mulch.

All of the recommended green manures can be purchased in bulk much less expensively than the seed you buy in small packets. Seeds discussed in this article are available from these suppliers:

Territorial Seed Company
P.O. Box 157
Cottage Grove, OR 97424
541-942-9547

Bountiful Gardens Seeds
18001 Shafer Ranch Rd.
Willits, CA 95490
707-459-6410

Choosing

Choosing the proper winter cover crop depends on your soil and climate. I am familiar with the Northwest, so I'll use some of our sub-regions as examples.

In the coastal areas of northern California, Oregon, and Washington, where winter temperatures are moderate and the soil rarely freezes, fava beans, crimson clover, buckwheat, and annual rye work well.

In the Cascades and east of the mountains, where winters are colder, annual rye, winter wheat, and vetch are good choices. Vetch is the most cold-hardy of all green manures, and when mixed with a grain, such as rye, will give you the advantages of both the grains and legumes.

Be careful in your choice of cover crop. The easiest is always the best, and any crop that cannot be easily killed and turned under looks suspiciously like a weed. Annual grasses, such as rye, winter wheat, and barley work well, but perennial grasses can be hard to kill. And remember, where winters are mild (as on the coast), almost anything can become a perennial.

Annual rye grass is a good winter cover crop for both the mild-winter coastal areas west of the Cascades, and the colder areas to the east. It must be planted early in the colder areas so it can become well established before extreme weather sets in. In the coldest parts of eastern Washington and Oregon, rye should be planted by September 15.

In these coldest areas, rye will not make it through the winter, but the plant residue holds the soil and provides organic matter to be tilled under in the spring. In milder areas, rye can prevent heavy winter rains from eroding bare soil.

Bags labeled "Ryegrass" in your garden center are likely to be mixtures of annual and perennial rye. Look for labels that specify "Annual."

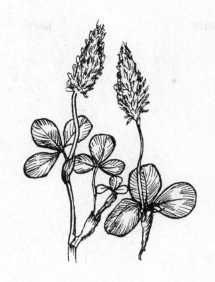

Crimson clover

Planting

While some experts maintain that soil preparation is unnecessary before sowing cover crops, a better, healthier stand can be obtained by prepping the soil just as you would for any other plants.

As soon after harvest as possible, remove all large plant residue, such as corn stalks. Till under small material and weeds, incorporating fertilizer or compost if the soil is depleted.

Broadcast the seed, and in the case of most of the legumes and grasses, just rake them in. If you want to use a rototiller, go over the soil quickly and shallowly, so that your seed isn't covered by more than an inch of soil.

In the case of clover, which wants a firm seedbed, press the seed in by tamping it down or using a light-weight roller. If you don't expect rain within 48 hours of planting, go ahead and water. A light mulch will keep the soil moist and improve germination.

Another option is to plant your cover crop between and among established vegetable crops during the last month of production. Simply broadcast a low-growing green manure among the vegetables to give it an early start. Once the vegetables are through producing, pull the residue and let the cover crop take over. This

is a good way to prevent post-harvest weeds from becoming established. Try planting clover among your corn stalks.

Timing is critical for green manures. It's important to let your crop get a good start before winter weather. Legumes should be planted six to eight weeks before the expected date of the first hard frost, and grasses should be in the ground four to six weeks before that date.

Varieties

Crimson clover is cold- and shade-tolerant, but it doesn't like acid soil. *Be very careful to get _crimson_ clover rather than one of the perennials, such as _red_ clover. These propagate through underground runners and can become a weed almost impossible to eradicate.* Crimson clover has beautiful, edible blossoms, but turn it under before it goes to seed. Seed production causes stems to become woody, taking longer to break down. This legume fixes nitrogen at a rate of one and a half pounds per 500 square feet. Plant four pounds per 500 square feet.

Fava beans: Banner is probably the best green manure fava. It is tolerant of cold to ten degrees and will survive temporarily water-logged soil. It can reach six feet, and provides an enormous amount of organic matter, as well as fixing nitrogen at a rate of one pound per 500 square feet. Sow it early in October, planting about five pounds of seed per 500 square feet. While the plants may be somewhat daunting in appearance, they are so brittle that they're easily tilled under. If you prefer, you can snap the stalks off and compost them separately, tilling in only the roots.

Vetch: While there are many vetches, wooly or hairy vetch is best, tolerating cold to zero degrees and growing well in poor soil. It fixes nitrogen at a whopping three and a half pounds per 500 square feet, and should be planted at a rate of five pounds per 500 feet. Vetch is shade-tolerant, and probably the best all-round green manure.

Buckwheat: This is a fast-growing grain, going from sprout to full bloom in about six weeks. In mild-winter areas, it usually winters over, taking a few frosts, but dying out if the ground freezes. It breaks up the soil well and grows to a height of three feet. It will grow on soil of low fertility, rapidly forming a dense cover. This cover crop accumulates phosphorus, which is released back into the soil when the crop is turned under. It has the best amino acid composition of all the grains, and attracts beneficial insects, including bees. If you raise bees, you'll find buckwheat honey is rich and dark. The brittle roots and foliage till in easily. Plant at a rate of three pounds per 500 square feet.

Annual rye: Annual rye is widely adaptable and very hardy. Sow it in late summer to produce both grain and organic matter. It will put on some early growth, then rest until spring. Rapid spring growth will produce seed heads for harvest in less than two months, so you want to work it up early. Plant at a rate of two pounds per 500 square feet.

Winter wheat: Hard winter wheat is cold-hardy and creates an abundance of organic matter. It is not drought-tolerant, but will survive acid soil. Plant in early fall for erosion control. Be sure to turn it under before seed heads form and stalks get woody. Plant at a rate of five pounds per 500 square feet.

Grains in general have several liabilities. They can be tough and slow to decompose if they become too mature. Winter wheat tills in easiest, but *be sure to work in all grains early*, or you'll be facing an unplanned prairie.

Green manure roots spread deeply through the earth opening up tight soil. When the roots die, they become food for microbes and earthworms,

Hard wheat

whose work continues the process of soil improvement. Over the years, a tight, compact soil can be turned rich and soft simply by having plants growing on it at all times.

Continue adding compost and manure, but as soon as a food crop is finished, plant a cover crop. Their wide diversity of growing habits gives you a choice to fit your needs.

Combine the types

In many cases, a blend of grains and legumes may be your best plan. Together they provide both nitrogen fixation and organic matter. Seeded together, the fast-growing grain protects the dawdling legume so it can make a good stand. You might try vetch with winter wheat in colder areas, or crimson clover and buckwheat in mild-winter areas.

Young, succulent legumes and grains provide more nutrients, while older, tougher plants provide more organic matter. Always allow at least two weeks for decomposition before planting other crops. Three weeks is better if you have the time. The decomposition process binds nitrogen, so it will not be available to nurture plants and seeds until decomposition is complete. The warmer the weather, the faster the residues break down.

Green manure plants can also provide you with food while they're enriching the soil. You can allow a small patch to go to seed, then thresh the grains for sprouting, or grind them into flour.

While fresh fava beans are routinely available in European markets, the only way to get them here is to grow them yourself. Shell them like peas and try them in a soup that includes onions, garlic, and carrots.

Crimson clover's beautiful blossoms are attractive and tasty in salads, and it makes a sweet, healthful tea. *But be sure you have crimson clover: **sweet clover is toxic.***

If we intend the soil to feed us, we must, in turn, feed it, and cover crops are a simple and economical way to nourish the soil. In spite of these beautiful days, winter is definitely on the way. Like you, your garden should be warmly covered before bad weather begins. Δ

Mice

Try to say something nice
About mice.

It's so hard to love them
When they rattle in the oven,
Just looking for food,
Yet souring our mood.

They scamper through the night,
Causing untold fright,
As they dash across the nose
Or shuffle over the toes
Of a sleeping canine,
Who reacts with a whine,
A howl, or a bark,
Shattering the dark.

Their style definitely encroaches
But they eat cockroaches.
Well, there's something nice
About mice.

**Diane M. Calabrese
Columbia, MO**

Here are some tasty ways to use those end-of-season green tomatoes

By Marjorie Burris

That gentle nip in the autumn air feels pleasant to your cheeks, but it also means that one more tomato season is about to come to an end. Although the *Old Farmer's Almanac* lists frost dates for most parts of the United States, it is quite candid and adds, "The possibility of frost occurring after the spring dates and before the fall dates is 50 percent." So at our house, when that time rolls around, we keep an ear to the radio for weather forecasts and an eye on the sky for cloud conditions. We want to protect those warm-weather-loving tomato vines as long as possible. We hate to give up those delicious vine-ripened tomatoes.

Tomato hay stacks

When we are convinced a light frost is imminent, we go into action. When we first transplant our tomatoes into the garden in the spring, we either stake them or set a cage over the plants. The method we use to lengthen the life of our vines in the fall involves the support of this stake or cage. First we pick all the small tomatoes that have no chance of ripening. Then we examine all the larger tomatoes and leave only those showing signs of having at least some blush of color. Next, we push old hay or straw up under and around and over each tomato plant, keeping the hay wrap loose and from three to four inches thick. Then we securely tie the wrap with twine around the tomato plant and its stake or cage. The stake or cage makes a good support for the "tomato hay stack." The tomato vines stay snug and warm under their cover, and the tomatoes will ripen without any more light. Later, when we pick the ripened tomatoes, we carefully part the hay without

pulling it loose, and pat it back into place until all the tomatoes are gone. Tomatoes protected in this manner ripen slowly until a very deep freeze hits, and best of all, they still have that wonderful vine-ripened taste.

The green ones

Now, about those other green tomatoes we picked before wrapping the vines. Once again, we sort the tomatoes, and we select the nicest large, full-grown ones to store.

We make sure the tomatoes are dry, then wrap them individually in newspaper. Some people don't like to use newsprint on food, even though most newspaper ink is now made from soy bean oil. If you don't like to use newsprint, inexpensive white paper napkins work just as well.

We store the wrapped tomatoes in shallow boxes or trays—no more than two deep—and set the trays in a place that does not freeze or get above about 65° F. Most green tomatoes will ripen in about four to six weeks if held at 55° to 65° with moderate humidity. To hasten ripening, I place a few unwrapped apples here and there among the tomatoes. And I check them periodically, so as to use the ripe tomatoes before they spoil.

One year, after a bumper crop of tomatoes, we sliced the last of our fresh, red tomatoes for Christmas dinner. Admittedly, tomatoes ripened this way aren't as tasty as vine-ripened tomatoes, but they sure are a lot better than those blobs they call tomatoes and sell in the grocery store in the winter time.

Green tomato relish

Because all produce, including green tomatoes, should be freshly picked (meaning not more than 24 hours old) before starting the pickling or canning process, I immediately start processing the rest of our green tomatoes. One way to use a large amount of green tomatoes is by making those good green tomato relishes. Most green tomato relish recipes tell you to chop the vegetables and let them set overnight in a salt solution. I can quickly chop the vegetables for relish and set them aside while I prepare more green tomatoes for other recipes. Here are our favorite green tomato relish recipes.

Piccalilli

1 quart chopped cabbage
1 quart chopped green tomatoes
2 sweet red peppers, chopped
2 sweet green peppers, chopped
2 large onions, chopped
1/4 cup salt
1 1/2 cups vinegar, 5% acidity
1 1/2 cups water
2 cups firmly packed brown sugar
1 teaspoon *each* dry mustard, turmeric, celery seed

Mix chopped vegetables with salt and let stand overnight. Next morning, line a colander with cheesecloth, pour vegetable mixture into colander, let drain, then bring edges of cheesecloth up over mixture and squeeze until all liquid possible is removed. Boil vinegar, water, sugar, and spices five minutes. Add vegetable mixture. Bring to a boil. Pour into sterilized jars to within a half inch of top. Put on cap. Process in boiling water bath five minutes. Yield: six pints.

Variation of Piccalilli: Use two quarts chopped green tomatoes instead of one quart cabbage and one quart green tomatoes. Also, two green sweet peppers can be substituted for the red peppers, but the relish won't be as pretty.

India relish

12 large green tomatoes
4 large sweet green peppers
4 large sweet red peppers
6 cucumbers (6 inches long)
2 large onions
6 Tablespoons salt
2 cups chopped cabbage
2 small hot peppers
2 1/2 cups sugar
3 cups vinegar, 5% acidity
1/2 teaspoon ground mace (or nutmeg)
1 teaspoon cinnamon
2 teaspoons ground ginger root
1 teaspoon turmeric
3 Tablespoons mustard seed
3 bay leaves

Remove seeds from peppers. Put peppers, tomatoes, cucumbers, and onions through food chopper, using coarse blade. Stir salt into vegetables. Let set overnight. Next morning, line a colander with cheesecloth, pour vegetable mixture into colander, let drain, then bring sides of cheesecloth up over mixture and squeeze until all liquid possible is removed. Chop cabbage very fine. Combine all the vegetables. Add sugar, vinegar, and spices. Mix well and heat to boiling. Boil three minutes. Pack into sterilized jars to within a half inch of top. Put on cap. Process in boiling water bath five minutes. Yield: eight pints.

Chow-chow

1 peck (12 1/2 pounds) green tomatoes
8 large onions
10 green bell peppers
3 Tablespoons pickling salt
6 hot peppers, seeded and chopped
1 quart vinegar, 5% acidity
1 Tablespoon ground cinnamon
1 Tablespoon ground allspice
1/4 teaspoon ground cloves
3 Tablespoons dry mustard
4 bay leaves
1 3/4 cups sugar
1/2 cup horseradish (optional)

Remove seeds from peppers and chop with the tomatoes and onions. Stir in salt and let stand overnight. Next morning, line a colander with cheesecloth, pour mixture into colander, and let drain. Bring edges of cloth up over mixture and squeeze to remove all liquid possible. Put in a large kettle. Tie the spices in a cheesecloth bag and add to the mixture along with the vinegar and sugar. Allow to boil slowly until tender, about 15 minutes. Add horseradish, return to boil. Remove spice bag. Pack into sterilized jars within a half inch of top. Put on cap. Process in boiling water bath five minutes. Yield: 10 or 11 pints.

Green tomato pickles

Next, I start making a few jars of green tomato pickles. Here are some good green tomato pickle recipes.

4 quarts thinly sliced green tomatoes
4 small onions, thinly sliced
4 green bell peppers, seeded, cut into strips
1/2 cup pickling salt
1 quart vinegar, 5% acidity
3/4 cup pickling salt
1 Tablespoon *each* black pepper, mustard seed, celery
    seed, cloves, allspice, and cinnamon

Sprinkle 1/2 cup salt over vegetables, let set overnight. Next morning, drain well but do not squeeze dry. In a large kettle, mix vinegar, 3/4 cup salt, and spices. Bring to boil. Add vegetables. Boil 20 minutes, pack into sterilized jars. Put on cap. Process in boiling water bath five minutes. Yields approximately eight pints.

Green tomato kosher dill pickles

Small, firm green tomatoes
Celery stalks
Sweet green peppers, cut into fourths
Garlic
1 quart vinegar, 5% acidity
2 quarts water
1 cup pickling salt
Dill

Pack tomatoes into sterilized quart jars. To each jar add one stalk celery, one green pepper, and a bud of garlic. Make a brine of the vinegar, water, and salt. Boil with the dill for five minutes. Pour hot brine over vegetables to within a half inch of top of the jar. Put on cap. Process in boiling water bath 15 minutes. This amount of liquid fills six quarts. These pickles will be ready for use in four to six weeks.

Green tomato sweet pickles

1 gallon green tomatoes (16 cups sliced)
1/4 cup pickling salt
1/2 Tablespoon powdered alum
3 cups vinegar, 5% acidity
1 cup water
4 cups sugar
1 Tablespoon mixed pickling spices
1/2 teaspoon ground cinnamon
1 Tablespoon celery seed
1/2 teaspoon ground allspice
1 Tablespoon mustard seed

Sprinkle salt over sliced tomatoes and allow to stand overnight. Next morning drain well, but do not squeeze dry. Mix alum with two quarts boiling water and pour over tomatoes. Let stand 20 minutes. Drain and cover with cold water, then drain well, rinsing alum away. Tie spices in a cheesecloth bag. Combine spices with vinegar and one cup of water. Add sugar and bring to a boil. Pour solution over tomatoes, let stand overnight. On the third morning bring the pickles and the solution to a boil. Remove spice bag. Pack into sterilized jars to within a half inch of top. Put on cap. Process in boiling water bath five minutes. Yield: eight pints.

Green tomato mincemeat

No season is complete without a little bit of green tomato mincemeat for pies.

3 quarts coarsely ground green tomatoes
3 quarts peeled, cored, coarsely ground apples
1 cup ground suet
1 pound seedless raisins
2 Tablespoons *each* grated orange and lemon rind
5 cups well-packed dark brown *or* raw sugar
3/4 cup vinegar
1/2 cup fresh lemon juice
1/2 cup water
1 Tablespoon ground cinnamon
1/4 teaspoon ground cloves
1/4 teaspoon ground allspice
2 teaspoons salt

Combine all ingredients in large kettle, bring to boiling, stirring frequently. Reduce heat and simmer until dark and thick, about two and a half hours, stirring occasionally. Use a pad under kettle to help prevent scorching. Pour boiling hot into pint jars to within a half inch of top. Process in a boiling water bath 25 minutes. Makes eight pints, enough for 8 eight-inch pies. Pressure processing is not needed for this recipe because of the very long cooking time.

Green tomato mincemeat #2

6 pounds green tomatoes
6 pounds apples, cored and peeled
6 pounds raisins
1 pound suet
1 1/2 Tablespoons salt
6 teaspoons ground cinnamon
3 teaspoons ground cloves
3 teaspoons ground nutmeg
1 1/2 cups lemon juice
3 pounds brown sugar

Grind apples, tomatoes, and suet. Put into large kettle with other ingredients. Cook until dark and thick, about two and a half hours, stirring occasionally. Watch closely to prevent scorching. Pour into sterilized jars to within a half inch of top. Put on cap. Process in hot water bath 25 minutes. Yields seven quarts.

Fried green tomatoes

Fried green tomatoes are ambrosia. Yes, they are fried in fat. Yes, they have a lot of calories. Forget all that. Upon occasion, some things are to be enjoyed without thinking of fat and calories. This is one of those occasions.

Slice large green tomatoes about 1/4-inch thick. Let stand in salt water (one Tablespoon salt to one quart water) four hours to overnight. Drain well. Pat dry. Dip each slice in flour. Fry in hot fat, turning once until golden brown. Serve hot. For extra flavor, add two Tablespoons bacon drippings to fat for frying. This is a good side dish or a good meat substitute with eggs for breakfast.

Variation: Dip each slice of tomato in beaten egg, then into cornmeal. Fry in hot lard.

Variation: Oven fry. Coat bottom of baking dish with cooking oil. Heat in oven. Layer coated tomato slices one thickness in dish. Bake 350° F. until golden brown and soft, about 25 minutes.

The brine-dill jar

This is by far our favorite. I like this recipe because I don't have to can these pickles unless I want to. Usually after a couple of weeks, there is nothing left to can, anyway, because my family eats them up so fast. This recipe is adaptated from the one given by the late Euell Gibbons, a nationally-known author and expert on wild foods. This is an imprecise recipe, and no two brine-dill jars are alike. You use what you have on hand or can forage. The only absolutely necessary things are onions, garlic, and dill, preferably fresh, but dried or frozen is all right.

Wash well and scald a gallon-size glass jar with a wide top. Pack a layer of dill in the bottom, add several cloves of garlic, then start layering vegetables into the jar, packing dill in between each layer. I put in several layers of small green tomatoes, about ping-pong ball size. Green cherry tomatoes are especially good. Use a layer of onions somewhere in the jar. If you don't have small boiling onions, slice larger onions. Peeled, sliced Jerusalem artichokes are good. Tender green or wax beans are good. (They are the only vegetables that must be cooked before adding to the jar. They have to be parboiled for about five minutes.) Cauliflower broken into small florets is great. Capers and a few red Tabasco peppers add a bit of dash. The white part of leeks and sweet peppers, either green or red, seeded and cut into strips, add interest.

But many times, I have used only the green tomatoes flavored with the dill, onions, and garlic.

Make a brine of 3/4 of a cup of pickling salt to 10 cups of boiled and cooled water. Add 1/4 cup cider vinegar of 5% acidity. Pour over vegetables in jar, insert a knife blade to remove air bubbles, then cover the top of the vegetables with more dill. Weigh down the top of the vegetables with something like a saucer weighted with a jar of water to keep everything below the brine, and let the jar cure at room temperature. Let the jar set about two weeks. Stand back when you open the jar: a stampeding family can be dangerous.

If you want to preserve these pickles, pack into hot, sterilized jars along with more dill. Strain the brine, bring to a boil, and pour over pickles. If you need more brine, use ½ cup pickling salt, four cups of 5% vinegar, and one gallon of water, and bring to a boil. Seal. Process in boiling water bath 15 minutes, starting to count the time when the hot jars are placed in the actively boiling water.

Finally, after we've stored and pickled and canned all the green tomatoes we can possibly use—and stand to look at—we are quite happy to dump the rest into the compost pile. We've found that the tomatoes compost best if we layer them in the compost pile not more than one tomato deep and separate each layer with some leaves, straw, and animal manure. Otherwise, they just sit and sog.

Ripe or green, tomatoes can be used in more ways than almost any other vegetable, which is one reason they have become the home gardener's favorite crop.

Making pickles: containers, salt, and vinegar

When making relishes and pickles or other acidic foods, use only glass, crockware, stainless steel, or graniteware containers. Acid foods react with aluminum ware, which should not be used to soak or cook those foods in.

Use only canning and pickling salt. Do not use table salt, either the plain or iodized type. Table salt contains fillers to keep it from caking, and those fillers react with pickling acids and spices, making the pickles dark, taste off-flavor, and sometimes spoil. Canning and pickling salt can be purchased at most grocery stores and is usually located beside the canning supplies or with the salt and spices. It can be purchased in two or five pound bags and will be clearly marked.

Vinegar used in pickling should be of 5% to 6% acidity. The strength of vinegar is usually shown on the label. If the vinegar is too weak, the pickles will spoil or become soft. Δ

Make grape juice the *easy* way

By Tanya Kelley

Squeezing and straining grapes for grape juice was not exactly my idea of fun. So when my neighbor showed me a faster, easier method, I was delighted. For anyone else tired of doing it the hard way, follow these steps for a delicious grape juice concentrate.

1. Wash and sterilize canning jars, lids, and rings. Fill water bath pan halfway with water to boil. At the same time, fill another pan with water to boil. This water will be added to the jars.
2. Wash grapes and remove stems and any damaged fruit.
3. Measure one cup of grapes and one cup of sugar for each quart jar.
4. Add sugar and grapes to jar. Don't bother mixing—it will mix when processing.
5. Fill the jar the rest of the way with boiling water. Leave $1/2$ inch headspace. Wipe jar top to clean. Screw on rings and lids fairly tight.

6. Place jars in water bath canner. Add boiling water to cover jars. Process 25 minutes.
7. Remove jars and place on rack or towel to cool. As you can see, the grapes may or may not float. Either way, the taste will be the same.
8. Serve in a pitcher with a strainer or drain juice off. Add $1/2$ to one jar of water to concentrate. (Taste to decide.) Δ

A country moment

Wesley Reynolds, age three, of Yreka, CA

(Note: If you have a country moment you'd like to share with our readers, please send it to us at Country Moment, *Backwoods Home Magazine*, P.O. Box 712, Gold Beach, OR 97444. Please include a self-addressed, stamped return envelope if you want the photo back.)

Where I live

By Annie Duffy

Walking the woods with friends and family

I love to explore the area around my home, and hiking and trail riding are two of the best ways. When you hike you can go across difficult terrain like steep mountainsides. When you ride a horse, you can explore a wider distance and travel through water with ease.

My dad and I went on a hike not so long ago on the mountain opposite the lake from our house. Before we left we went out on our porch and used binoculars to search for a spot where we would try to go. We aimed for a large clearing between a dead oak and dead pine tree. We brought my dog, Lucy, and planned to stay out only an hour or so.

On our way up the steep mountainside we were forced to go through large bunches of stickers that clung to our socks and pants. We got to the clearing we aimed for about an hour after we had started our hike, and spent about 10 minutes pulling stickers out of our socks and shoelaces.

Then we continued up the slope. In order to climb to the top, we had to cross over a bunch of rocks made up of an eroding lava flow that was hundreds of thousands of years old. Many of the rocks were about four feet across and we had to pick our way through them. Once we got by the rocks we were almost at the top, but then there was a cliff about 10 feet high made up of solid rock that we had to scale. We pushed the dog up first, because she didn't want to come back down if she couldn't make it. Dad went up first and gave me a hand.

The view from the top was spectacular, both of the lake and the opposite mountain above the lake. I was surprised how many more details of the mountain I could see from up there, such as the many ridges and ravines that were not visible from below.

We were higher than all of the birds except for the turkey vultures circling overhead. Even the golden eagles, bald eagles, and osprey were below us.

Behind us the view wasn't that exciting, except for a glimpse of Soda Mountain, where the cellular phone tower is.

Standing within five feet of the egde of the cliff we felt a cool wind, but taking a step back it was still and hot. Dad said the wind on the edge may have been from cooler air falling and lower warmer air rising along the mountain cliff.

Several bands of wild horses wander the mesa, but we didn't see any today. Many people think that the horses are actually mustangs, but none of them are pure. They are feral horses, which means they are decendants of domestic horses that have either escaped or have been turned loose. Some people capture and break them, but sometimes the horses can be dangerous. Ursula, my riding instructor, was on vacation when a feral stallion got in with her horses and killed her old mare, Balsam, while trying to mate with her.

We walked along the edge for about three-quarters of a mile before descending again near the office. Then we went to Gloria's store, which is the only store for about 30 miles, and had an ice cream.

Tomorrow, I'm going exploring in a different way—on horseback. Pat Ward of nearby Fall Creek Ranch has asked me to join a cattle roundup. It'll be my first cow chase and my first chance to show off my new horse Diego. I'll tell you about it next issue. Adios. Δ

VIEW FROM THE TOP—*Grassy area on opposite shore is Goose Meadow, and farther left (out of the picture) is my house.*

Keep fresh greens in your garden —
even in the snow — by using row cover

By Lance and Jennifer Barker

The idea of having fresh greens a month or two later than usual won't sound like a very big deal to folks who have long growing seasons. Many of us, however, live in places that have long, cold winters that start somewhere around Thanksgiving and continue for four or five months. Anything we can do to get something fresh, green, and home-grown during those months sounds mighty good to us. Here are some techniques that allow us to harvest fresh, hardy greens outside for a month or two after the snow and temperatures have fallen. Combined with root-cellaring and a few herbs on the window sill, that is as good as having a growing garden for half the winter.

Our objective is to grow hardy greens to full size before low temperatures and light levels stop their growth for the winter. Then we protect them from freezing and snow damage in place as long as possible, until either the ground freezes, or snow smashes the plants. (If you live in a more moderate climate where neither of these happens, you may be able to keep your garden green all winter.) In cold places, the amount of freeze protection you get depends on the temperature of the soil when the weather turns icy. What we are doing is modifying the microclimate around the plants by using the soil as warm mass for as long as possible, even if the air temperature outside plunges to zero.

We have drawn our inspiration from the farmers of France, who have long used cloches, row covers, and poly tunnels to extend the growing season. Our technique is synthesized from several different ones and adapted to

A boxed bed with a wood-and-wire frame keeps greens fresh well into snow season.

work best in our Zone 4 climate here at Morning Hill, where the temperature usually reaches zero by Thanksgiving.

We call our protection technique *bunkering*. This consists of wrapping and blanketing the beds with polyester row cover until we have provided many degrees of freeze protection. Combined with growing frost-tolerant hardy greens, it allows us to eat fresh green salads and stir-fries while the snow piles up and temperatures fall outside.

Build boxed beds

The foundation of the protected greens bunker is the boxed bed. Boxing a bed allows you to attach hoops for supporting row cover, provides a good seal for the row cover at the edges to keep warmth in, and separates your walking paths from your

growing areas. Unlike other boxed beds, however, *these should not be raised above ground level* any more than absolutely necessary. The objective here is to keep the soil from freezing for as long as possible into the fall, so ground level is best for these beds.

Our favorite method of building these is to terrace them into a gentle slope. This has the two added advantages of allowing for good air drainage (cold air flows downhill instead of settling on the garden) and letting us work from the downhill side for less bending. Our three-by-seven-foot beds are a good size both for reaching across and for covering with available widths of row cover. They are also more resistant to being smashed by snow than wider beds would be.

We make the sides of our beds with 2x4 or 2x6 lumber, with a wider board at the uphill side to hold the dirt back.

We don't have to use very wide boards, because we are not trying to make raised beds. The soil inside the bed should be level with or below the ground outside, because it will stay warmer if it is not raised. The purpose of boxing is to define the worked and improved soil area, and to give the row cover a surface to seal against to keep the cold air out.

Then we make hoops of 9-gauge wire and push the ends into the ground to hold the row cover up off the plants. A wooden frame may be used to hold the arch of the wire up, if you live in a heavy snow area. Row cover may be attached to the box at one side of the bed with a *batten*, a narrow strip of wood applied to the outside and screwed through the row cover to the box. It is then pulled snug over the hoops, and all free edges are held to the ground with small rocks or boards.

In the warmer days of late summer and early fall, one layer over the hoops is sufficient to guard against the surprise freeze, but as the freezing nights become more severe, more layers are added. The first additional layer goes underneath the hoops, supported directly by the leaves of the plants themselves (this is called *floating*). Then more layers are added on top of the hoops, as well as inside over the floating cover. Row cover, which lets some light through even multiple layers, is the best choice for keeping plants long-term. If plants are covered away from the light for too long, they will lose their chlorophyll and turn yellow, just like grass under a board. Ugh.

Opening and harvesting the beds

Obviously, there comes a point when the vegetables must be harvested because you need them or because conditions are becoming too severe for them outdoors. Once the ground freezes, plants are not able to take up water and will just wilt if temperatures thaw again. At first, we try to harvest on a day when we are having a warm spell and the row cover is not frozen to the ground. If we can do this without damaging the row cover, and the plants still look OK, we can just harvest what we need. Then we can re-close the bed, carefully pack snow back around it for insulation, and possibly store the remainder in place for another couple of weeks.

Another likely scenario, though, is that we will have to pry our way through the row cover even on a mild day. We sort through the greens and bag the best ones carefully for storage in our Sunfrost refrigerator (a 24-volt refrigerator which runs on our solar-electric system). Even greens which show freeze-damage may thaw in very good condition if they are put straight into the refrigerator where they will thaw slowly. Discard only wilted, broken, or rotten greens at first until you develop a feel for which ones will be OK when thawed.

If you have animals, the greens which are too smashed or freeze-damaged for use in the kitchen will make excellent supplements for their winter feed. Your favorite goat needs a taste of something green in the winter just as much as you do. Also, some of those vitamins will come back to you in your milk and eggs, so nothing is wasted.

Varieties to plant

Planting hardy, frost-tolerant varieties is the ultimate key to the successful growing of fall and winter greens. Plants that can tolerate frost can have some freeze-damage on parts of the plant and still be usable, while non-frost-tolerant plants will be flat on the ground the first frosty night.

Also, remember that as temperatures cool down, plants grow slower, so it is important to give your plants a good start before cold weather hits. We start ours in early August, because they will pretty much quit growing by the second week of October. It's not an easy time of year to get cool-weather plants started. Frequent misting of the young plants is our key to giving them the start they need.

Here are descriptions of some of our favorite varieties for fall planting:

Swiss chard: This perennial hardy favorite is also a good one for crop rotating, since it's not a brassica or a lettuce. It's in the same family as beets, and produces a flavorful green that is good in salads or steamed. It comes in a rainbow of colors and a variety of leaf types. This is a long-season plant, so be aware of its time needs when you plan your planting. We start chard much earlier than pak chois and lettuces.

Lettuce: A classic salad favorite. Some varieties are more hardy than others. These are a few of our favorite hardy ones: **Red Sails** and **Red Grenoble** are tender, flavorful, moderately curly leaf lettuces with rosy-blushed leaves. **Sierra** is a tough performer in the coldest weather, as its name implies. It is a Batavian semi-heading lettuce with smooth, hearty, red-tinged leaves, a great sandwich green. **Batavia Laura** and **Victoria** are hearty-flavored green Batavians. **Black-seeded Simpson** is the classic sweet, tender green leaf lettuce and stands chills well. **Tim Peters' Open-heart** is a heartier, darker green leaf variety. **Red Salad Bowl**'s burgundy-colored oak-leaf shape brightens and varies the textures for visual appeal. **Celtuce** is not exactly a lettuce, but it adds significant amounts of vitamins to your salad, and a different texture with its celery-like central ribs and soft leaves.

Cilantro: If you have read that cilantro must be planted after all danger of frost has passed, you might think it's a tender herb. Don't worry, it's super-hardy. We have let cilantro go to seed in the garden, and when the seeds were ready to come up in the spring, they germinated and grew, frost or no. In the fall, it's as hardy as anything in our garden. Cilantro is considered one of the basic food groups around our house, and we use it to flavor everything from Oriental salads to enchiladas. Two of us can eat a whole three-by-seven-foot bed of it. In fact, we haven't ever grown too much of it.

Mustards and pak chois: There are a zillion varieties of these, and we just grow a mixture of several that work well for us. Try **Tendergreen mustard** for a nice all-purpose green. If you have always thought mustards were too hot-flavored to taste good, just try growing them in cold weather to find out differently.

Since it's already garden season this year, don't wait till next year to try this out. If you've got more in your garden than you can eat (and what good gardener doesn't?), try this on any hardy greens, just to see how it works. Start small and get better at it every year. Try something different from what we have listed. We certainly haven't exhausted the possibilities for this technique.

Polyester row cover

Polyester row cover is a lightweight, spun-bonded plant protection fabric. It comes in several different weights and widths for different uses. Its uses include sun, wind, and temperature protection, as well as insect protection. We use it extensively in our garden, because we live in a place where it can and does frost all year round. We've had people say that our climate can't be as tough as where they live, because we have a garden and they can't. We just smile. Our secret is row cover.

Row cover is used by commercial growers to start tender plants in the early growing season, protecting them against a surprise chilly night. What we are doing with it in the application mentioned in this article is to moderate extreme cold for frost-tolerant plants. However, row cover is an extremely useful tool, and we have

found many places for it in our gardening.

We use it on almost everything in our garden. It floats over strawberry plants to keep frost off the blossoms and birds off the berries. (We remove it on sunny days so bees can do their pollinating duties.) It floats over potato plants to protect them from frost, because if the tops are frosted back, the plant puts its energy into regrowing them, and you get very small potatoes. Ours grow large and beautiful. We put it on hoops over tender green plants whose leaves we will eat, like lettuce and salad greens. And we use it to start hardy Oriental greens which can stand in the open later in the season.

If you want to try a small amount of row cover, just to see what it's like, you can buy the popular brand Reemay in smaller pieces at garden supply stores. Later, if you find this to be as handy as we do, you will want to buy large rolls of commercial quality row cover. The commercial type lasts longer and is much cheaper when bought by the bolt. Some people say commercial varieties are more abrasive to plant leaves than Reemay, but we haven't found that to be true.

But isn't polyester row cover a petroleum product? Yes it is. And using it is also creating solid waste. However, under some conditions, the choice is between using row cover and buying our food in the grocery store, because we couldn't grow much without the product. Grocery store food is grown by creating a huge amount of solid waste. Just because you don't see it doesn't mean it's not there. When you become familiar with commercial agricultural practices, using row cover will seem a small price to pay to have your own home-grown food available out of season.

We mitigate the amount of solid waste we create by having a "use hierarchy." New row cover gets used where an unbroken covering is important. As the covers develop a few small holes, we use them on hardier

stuff, and when they become tattered, we rotate them to use as underneath covers. Finally, they are only good for providing winter protection for things like strawberry plants and spinach, which seem to produce better in summer if they have been covered in winter. We can use several layers for this, so it doesn't matter if one is full of holes.

If you have cats, as we do, they may try to get on the soft, white covers. Keep them from damaging both your row cover and your plants by grinding black pepper over the covers. We don't know why, but this works.

Finally, we must consider irrigation. The manufacturers say that water will go through row cover, but in our dry climate that doesn't work efficiently. Perhaps rain will go through, but we don't get any in summer, so we can't say. Taking the covers off to water is cumbersome and adds wear and tear, so we provide drip irrigation under the covers. Foggers, mini-sprinklers, and drip all work more efficiently when row cover slows evaporation and increases humidity around the plants. Each type of plant gets the watering treatment it needs, and watering is as easy as turning a valve. We only have to take off the covers for weeding, inspection, and harvest.

Row cover sources

Zimmerman Irrigation
RD 3, Box 186
Mifflinburg, PA 17844-9534

Peaceful Valley Farm Supply
PO Box 2209
Grass Valley, CA 95945
916/272-4769 Δ

I don't like work—but I like what is in work—the chance to find yourself. Your own reality—for yourself, not for others—what no other man can ever know.

—Joseph Conrad
1857-1924

Traditional ways of keeping your corn crop and seed corn are still very effective

By Rev. J.D. Hooker

Corn . . . it's *the* traditional American crop. It doesn't matter whether the crop you'll be bringing in is intended for feeding your livestock through the winter, producing home baked cornbread and muffins, providing many quiet evenings' worth of popcorn, or any other homestead uses. This particular crop has been one of the mainstays of agriculture throughout all of our nation's history. In fact, until the 1990s, no other crop ever surpassed corn as America's number one cash crop. (And even then, corn was only surpassed by a bumper crop of an illegal drug.) When our forefathers (and foremothers) prayed, "Give us this day our daily bread," they were referring, almost without exception, to cornbread. Most of our early explorers and settlers never even tasted any other type of bread in their entire lifetimes.

Cornsilk was used as a tobacco extender or substitute; the cobs were

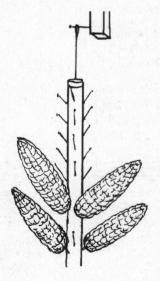

Corn-stick

used not only as pipe bowls, but as a heating fuel, for smoking meat (delicious), as easily replaceable file handles, jug stoppers, and many other simple but ingenious uses. The husks were stuffed into mattresses, braided into mats (and into sandal soles in the Southwest), fashioned into dolls and decoys, and used as livestock bedding. While the stalks were primarily used as cattle fodder and bedding, at times they were used as building materials. At one point during the Civil War, a train trestle was even built from nothing other than corn stalks, and it did hold up—for one train. Even the leaves were regularly employed as roof thatchings. While I would strongly recommend stopping short of the train trestle, there doesn't appear to be any reason for these "waste" products not to be used in similar ways today.

Of course, all the corn grown in early America was of open-pollinated varieties (with the exception of a very few hybrids developed among the Miami and Cherokee). Our frugal ancestors would never have been so foolish or extravagant as to keep purchasing fresh seed every year when they could so easily provide their own seed. No doubt these early Americans would be mightily impressed by much of our modern farming equipment, but I feel certain they would be appalled by most of our modern farming practices.

Maybe it's time that a whole lot of us—and especially us smaller-scale farmers and larger-scale gardeners—took a really hard look at the farming systems developed by our ingenious and independent-minded ancestors. Not only are most of their methods for producing this uniquely American crop well worthy of revival, but the simple processes they utilized for pre-

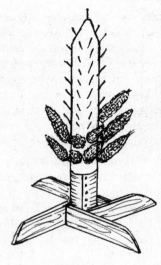

Corn-tree

serving their crop until their next harvest, and their seed-saving methods as well, can be just as valuable now as they were during the 1700s.

Saving seed

When it came to preserving their own seed stocks, not only our Old World ancestors, but the Indian farmers of that day (I've met very few "Native Americans" who don't refer to themselves as "Indians"), were mighty selective. Only the very best, earliest maturing, largest, most well-filled-out ears were kept for seed. Other desired traits were watched for as well, including color (usually based on personal preference), stalk and leaf size, tassel size (for pollination), etc.

Sometimes, the ears with the husks pulled back were fashioned into long, colorful braids and hung from the rafters to preserve seed for the next spring. While this was, and still is, quite colorful and decorative, it isn't really very practical. Not only would most of these braids eventually work loose and fall well before springtime,

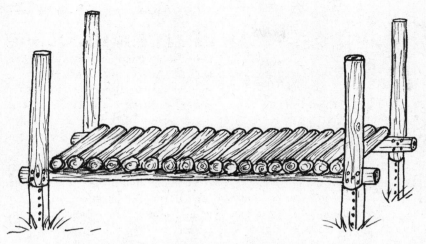

Corn crib posts and floor. For posts, use rot-resistant wood, such as catalpa, cedar, or redwood (4" minimum diameter). Post holes should be dug to below frost line. Fill holes with rocks or concrete.

but that method left the valuable seed supply vulnerable to rodents, squirrels, and other scavengers. The loss of even a single year's seed stock was not a minor problem, but a real life-and-death catastrophe in those early years. Therefore, safer storage systems were developed, or adapted from the practices of Indian neighbors.

Corn-stick and corn-tree

Two closely-related seed storage systems were almost universally adopted: the *corn-stick* and the *corn-tree*. Both methods work so well that they are still in use today among many people who grow open-pollinated seed varieties.

The corn-stick is just a long, peeled sapling pole, studded with finish-type nails. One husked ear is shoved onto each nail, and the "stick" is then hung from the rafters with a piece of heavy wire. Baling wire and coat hanger wire both work very well. Corn-sticks can vary considerably in length, as they need to be long enough to reach the overhead support, yet not so long that you can hit your head while walking under them. Of course, nails and wire were in pretty short supply among our ancestors, so the stick was generally bent like a shepherd's crook at the top end, with pegs substituted

for nails. That works just as well, should any of us ever be faced with a similar shortage.

Likewise, corn-trees work just as well now as they used to. Modern tools and materials make this a really easy project to put together. Many of the corn-trees that I've seen in use around here were fashioned from standard 4x4 lumber, chamfered to an octagonal shape. However, round posts seem almost as popular, and they're easier to fashion, and probably more traditional as well.

Four boards are nailed to the base of the post (as shown) to form the feet which will hold the corn-tree upright. The top of the post is then trimmed to a blunt point, and the post is studded with finishing nails for holding the ears. To prevent rodent damage, most of the corn-trees I've seen in use had the bottom 18" or so of the post wrapped with thin sheet metal, usually inexpensive aluminum roof flashing.

Corn-sticks seem preferable when storing your seed supply in a high-ceilinged structure, like a barn, while corn-trees seem better suited for use in lower-roofed buildings like storage sheds. One or the other (or maybe both) of these traditional seed corn storage appliances should work well for you.

How much seed?

Here is a tip you might be able to use when figuring your seed corn requirements. It's just a general guideline, but it usually proves to be mighty close to correct with most corn varieties. Generally, the seed saved from a plot of any given size is sufficient to re-plant an area equal to 75 times the size of the original plot. For example, if you were to save every ear from a 10' x 10' corn plot, you would have enough seed to put in a 75' x 100' area

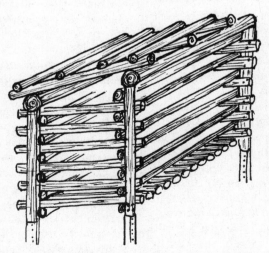

Framework for a simple corn crib. Wall poles are approximately 2" in diameter. Finish with waterproof roofing. Peel back husks before storing corn ears in crib.

*A roofed-over area between two corn cribs
makes a good parking, storage, or work area.*

the next season. Saving all of the ears from a one-acre field would allow for the planting of a 75-acre field the following spring.

The corn crib

If you are producing a sizable corn crop, whether for flour, corn meal, livestock feed, or whatever, you'll need a reliable method for storing this grain until it's used. Once again, our pioneering ancestors left us a pretty simple and reliable method for doing this. They adopted this storage method pretty much unchanged from their native neighbors.

You can see from the illustrations that a simple corn crib is easy to build. There are, however, a few things you'll need to keep in mind. First of all, if you were to build your corn crib any more than four feet wide, you'd lose most of your corn. Any wider, and you can't be certain of getting sufficient air circulation to wick away moisture from the innermost ears. If you space the support posts more than six feet apart, then the poles you'll be using for the sides of the crib will usually end up bowing outwards, allowing many ears to spill out. Also, if your area gets high winds, you won't want to build much over ten feet tall, and you'll want one of the narrow ends facing into the prevailing wind.

Before you begin, figure out how large a corn crib you'll require. This depends upon how much corn you use in a year's time; once you know that amount, the rest is simple. For each bushel of ear corn, you'll require 1.86 cubic feet of storage. For example, if you use five bushels of corn per day, which equals 1,825 bushels per year, you'd require 3,394$\frac{1}{2}$ cubic feet of space, which would equal a corn crib 4' wide, 10' tall, and 85' long. Of course, in most cases, building four corn cribs, each 22' long, would work out much better.

We use an awful lot of corn, some in cooking and baking, but most as stock feed. What we finally ended up with are two sets of 40' long corn cribs. Each 10' tall set has two cribs spaced 16' apart. We extended the roofs of these cribs, so that they cover the area in between them, providing some tremendously useful parking, storage, and working space.

Generally, you'll want to leave the poles used to fashion the sides of the corn crib unfastened at one of the narrow ends. As the corn goes down in the crib, easy access is always provided by simply pulling out some of the peeled saplings. And many folks install the floor so that it slopes towards the front of the crib, so it's almost self-emptying.

While it's traditional to install a thatched roof fashioned from corn

leaves, any sort of roof would work out just as well.

If you build the floor at least 18" above the ground, and encase the bottom 18" of each support post with light-gauge sheet metal, you'll have a rodent-proofed corn crib. And that leaves plenty of hunting space underneath for your cats to make some real inroads in any rodent population already on your property. (I strongly recommend good cats, from reliable, hard-hunting, barn cat stock, for rodent control. I *never* recommend poison.)

A variation

In building his own corn crib, a friend of mine has added some ideas that you might wish to consider. First off, he utilized used telephone poles as the support posts for his structure. Next, he added a barn-like loft over his two 40' corn cribs with a set of swinging barn doors at each end. Also, he replaced the poles normally used to fashion the sides of the cribs with welded wire fencing, as he felt he'd use up too much time collecting and peeling saplings. The floor of each crib is about 18" above the ground, and he closed it in with chicken wire, to keep out any animals, wild or domestic. Essentially what he's ended up with is a barn, complete with hayloft, built with corn crib sides. This design goes beyond the boundaries of a "simple" project, but it gives you an idea of how far you could go in building a corn crib, if your situation warrants such a major undertaking.

Anyway, there you have it: simple, time-tested methods for storing both seed corn and feed corn from one season to the next, without any of the muss and fuss of modern high-technology storage systems. Whatever your needs, building expertise, or available materials, I'm sure you'll find at least one of these valuable, functional, old-fashioned designs perfectly suited to your circumstances. Δ

Use plastic to get a head start on corn in the fall

By Mark and Lynn Klammer

As spring approaches each year, we can hardly wait for the feel of warm earth between our fingers. And so, while most avid gardeners let Mother Nature ready the soil for planting, we have devised a simple and inexpensive way to plant our garden outdoors just after the frost has left the ground. Our method, which uses sheets of clear plastic to warm the cold soil, suits plants that do not thrive indoors or transplant well. It allows us to get an early harvest from our favorite sweet corn, but it can also be adapted to coddle other plants, such as squash or sweet potatoes, that thrive under greenhouse-like conditions.

Begin in the fall by fashioning a seedbed consisting of foot-wide, six-to-ten-inch-high ridges of soil running in an east-west line. Space them as you want your corn rows spaced. (You *can* do this in the spring, but if your garden is poorly drained, you may find yourself in a bit of a mess.) As soon as the frost is out of the ground in the spring, spread a 10-by-25-foot roll of clear 4-mil plastic sheeting, available at any hardware store, over the planting area, laying it directly on the soil. Anchor the edges of the plastic with boards or stones or anything that will keep it from blowing away, including old croquet hoops or tent pegs.

After a few days (or longer, depending on the weather), when the earth under the plastic is warm to the touch, peel back the cover and plant the corn seeds halfway down the south face of each ridge. Then reposition the plastic, secure it, and begin a period of watchful

waiting. The ridges are important: they support the plastic until the seedlings grow, promote good drainage, and serve as heat reservoirs, gathering solar energy during the day and slowly releasing it inside the plastic at night. This technique, in almost any garden except one with a significant slope to the north, ensures that even when the temperature during a cold snap drops to a few degrees below freezing at night, the area under the plastic will not freeze. And despite some fluctuations, the temperature inside the "greenhouse" can be as much as 20° C warmer than the outside air.

As the seedlings grow, prop up the cover with wooden stakes, so that the leaves do not touch the plastic and the foliage is not scorched. Monitor the moisture level carefully, watering if necessary or airing out gently if it is too damp.

Around the time of the normal frost-free date, begin acclimating the young plants to the lower humidity and temperature of the outside environment by opening the ends of the plastic for a few hours on warm, still days. Repeat the procedure for increasingly longer periods of time for a week, after which you can remove the plastic completely and store it for use the next year.

A few days later, thin the corn to about six or eight inches. To support and protect the roots, take soil from the north side of the slope, pull it between the plants and fill in the trench on the south side.

The rest is easy. With some weeding, watering, and a little luck, you too can look forward to the sweetest—and earliest—corn around. Δ

Squash seeds are a delicious, nutritious snack

By Robert K. Henderson

Squash are a favorite homestead garden crop, offering abundant harvests for little effort. Yet many throw the delicious seeds on the compost pile, and that's a pity. Native Americans, whose talent for wholesome snacks gave us popcorn, tortilla chips, and beef jerky, valued the seeds of squash crops as much as the vegetable itself. In Mexico, "pepitas" remain an important staple to this day. Roasted squash seeds are a cheap, natural nibbler relished by kids and adults alike. Better still, they disappear like junk food while supplying fistfuls of nutrients: just one ounce of roasted pumpkin seeds contains five grams of protein and ten grams of dietary fiber, as well as significant quantities of calcium, phosphorous, and potassium.

Although pumpkins are the most prolific seed producers, all winter squash bear edible seeds. Even the hard, warty shells of over-ripe summer squash conceal a handful of small seeds that have a very delicate flavor when roasted. These are especially good in salads, on baked potatoes, and floating in soups. Roasted squash seeds also add character to granola, party mixes, and home-made ice cream. Dried, raw seeds may be oiled and sprinkled on cookies and quick breads before baking. With a little creativity, you can dream up

dozens of uses for roasted squash seeds. Once they become a part of your pantry, you'll wonder how you got along without pepitas.

To collect raw seeds, split the squash lengthwise. This makes it easier to reach the neat seed rows nestled in the interior pulp. Use your hands to strip the rows into a pan of water. Put your hand in the pan and clench handfuls of slippery seeds in your fist. They will shoot out from between your fingers like tiny bars of soap, removing residual pulp in the process. Pour the seeds into a colander and run water through the batch to drive the shreds of pulp to the bottom. Scoop the clean seeds onto the shiny side of a piece of aluminum foil and pat them into a single layer, so that each seed is exposed to the air.

Before they can be stored or roasted, squash seeds must be thoroughly dry. Incompletely dried seeds toast up tough outside and mushy inside, and will mold in storage. For certain success, leave the washed seeds out at room temperature for several days or pop them into a warm oven for an hour or so. Commercial food dryers do a fine job, too. Properly dried, raw squash seeds will keep almost indefinitely if sealed in an airtight container. Roasted seeds can be stored for several months, although the oil on their shells will eventually turn rancid. Freezing lengthens the shelf-life of roasted seeds considerably.

Because toasting time varies, you should roast different varieties separately. For example, Hubbard squash seeds brown about twice as fast as pumpkin seeds, so you don't want to toast the two together. As a general rule, glossy seeds such as those of the spaghetti squash roast up crisper. Seeds with a "flat finish," like those of jack-o'-lantern pumpkins, make for a chewier snack.

The following recipes can be whipped up in minutes, and are perfect for parties, trail food, or watching movies at home. They are also excellent nibblers to serve with fine home-brews or microbrews. All roasting times are based on pumpkin seeds. You may have to adjust them for other types.

Basic roasted seeds

| 1 cup squash seeds |
| 1 teaspoon oil |
| Dash of soy sauce |

Preheat oven to 300°. Place dry seeds in a mixing bowl and toss with oil. Add soy sauce and stir to coat each seed evenly. Spread seeds in a single layer on a foil-lined baking sheet and toast until crisp and golden brown, about 20-25 minutes. Be careful not to burn them. The soy sauce in this recipe adds a distinctive dimension to both the color and flavor of these nibblers.

Splitting the squash lengthwise makes it easier to remove the seeds.

Running water separates the seeds from the pulp.

Herbed seeds

1 cup squash seeds
1 teaspoon crushed dried oregano leaves
1 teaspoon crushed dried basil leaves
1/4 teaspoon sage
1/4 teaspoon thyme
1/4 teaspoon garlic salt
1/4 teaspoon black pepper
1 1/2 teaspoons melted butter

Preheat oven to 300°. Put all ingredients in a bowl, adding butter last, and mix thoroughly. Spread seeds immediately on a foil-lined baking sheet to prevent seasonings from settling to the bottom of the mixing bowl. Toast for 20-25 minutes or until crisp and golden. The butter in this recipe gives the seeds a delicate texture and flavor, and the black pepper lends just enough bite to keep things interesting.

Taco seeds

1 cup squash seeds
1 1/2 teaspoons oil
2 teaspoons taco seasoning

Preheat oven to 300°. Mix all ingredients thoroughly and proceed as for basic roasted seeds. For variety, substitute packaged pesto powder and melted butter, or instant spaghetti sauce and olive oil. Δ

Strip the seeds into a pan of water.

Spicy curry seeds

1 cup squash seeds
1 1/2 teaspoons olive oil
1 1/2 teaspoons curry
Dash of soy sauce
Pinch of cayenne

Preheat oven to 300°. Mix all ingredients thoroughly and proceed as for basic roasted seeds. Adjust cayenne to taste.

Mugwort — From aiding digestion to relieving fatigue, this flavorful plant has many good uses

By Christopher Nyerges

Of all the plants that are found in the chaparral of southern California, mugwort is perhaps the most steeped in lore and mythology. Mugwort (Artemisia douglasiana) is a multiple-use plant, having been used for food, medicine, fire-starting, and other things.

I have known people who ate the raw mugwort leaves in salad and added it to sandwiches, in much the same way that you'd add a pickle or a piece of lettuce. However, I have always found it too bitter for my taste to eat raw. But once simmered in water and cooked like spinach, its appeal is increased. Southern California Indians gathered the mugwort seeds and ground them into meal to make bread products. Still, the food value of mugwort is not its greatest asset.

Healing

As an infused tea, mugwort is said to improve the appetite, to be good for the digestion, and to relieve stomach pains and fevers. An infusion from the dried leaves is applied externally for inflammatory swellings. Bruises are reputed to heal quicker if bathed with a mugwort infusion. As a bath additive, it's used for tired legs and feet. Plus, in the bath water, mugwort gives the bathroom a pleasant aroma.

With some people, it is customary to rub the fresh mugwort leaves over exposed portions of their body before entering poison oak areas in order to prevent the rash. Some Indians used the fresh leaves externally as a cure for poison oak and wounds.

Before I immunized myself from poison oak, I used the freshly-crushed leaves of mugwort rubbed over newly-developing poison oak rash with good results. Aloe vera is the best treatment for poison oak that I have found, but you don't usually find aloe in the wild.

Mugwort gets its name from the English practice of putting a leaf of it in their mugs of beer to improve the flavor. ("Wort" is an Old English word meaning "herb.") This is still practiced in London pubs.

Vivid dreams

Sleeping on "pillows" of dried mugwort leaves is said to induce wild, vivid dreams and visions of the future. To test this, I placed several of the fresh leaves around my pillow. Those nights, I had very colorful dreams, though they were not what I would describe as "lucid," nor did I ever receive visions of the future. Nevertheless, some enterprising folks have begun to sell "dream pillows," which are small pillows stuffed with mugwort leaves.

Relief from fatigue

Folklore from various parts of the world says that a leaf of mugwort in the shoe will enable you to walk all day without leg fatigue. Nathaniel Schleimer of Pasadena, a student of acupressure, pointed out to me that there may be some factual basis for this "folklore." Schleimer told me that there is an acupuncture point on the bottom of the foot which is said to "regulate fatigue."

The mugwort leaves which have naturally dried on the plant are collected and used in a therapeutic technique called acupressure. These dried leaves, when rolled into small balls or into a cigar-shaped cylinder, are called *moxa*.

A Chinese species is said to be the best, but all species can be used in the following fashion, described by J.C. Cerney in his book <u>Acupressure — Acupuncture Without Needles</u>: "On the outside of the lower leg, below the level of the knee, is the head of the fibula. Just below and slightly in front of the head of the fibula is what the Japanese refer to as sanri or S 36. This is an important vitality-stimulating zone. It's a point where weary Oriental foot travellers applied a burning ball of moxa, and with energy restored, travelled on."

One of the most effective wilderness "punks" is made by gathering the leaves that have dried and browned on the stalk. Slide your hand along the lower stalk to gather the dried leaves and then roll them into a cigar. By lighting the end of this "cigar" and then wrapping the entire cigar in larger fresh mugwort leaves, you can effectively carry fire over long distances. This was the technique practiced by Southwestern Indian tribes for transporting fire from camp to camp. It can still come to the aid of today's campers where matches are scarce or unavailable.

I have tested dozens of tinders, using both natural and man-made materials, and mugwort has consistently proven to be one of the best natural tinders.

The pleasant aroma of the burning leaves, used as incense, helps bring the aroma of the mountains to the home. In the late 1970s, Timothy Hall would sometimes burn mugwort incense in his Trucker's Daily Bread Cafe, located in Highland Park (northeast Los Angeles), California.

Dried mugwort, mixed with other herbs, can also be smoked as a non-nicotine "tobacco."

Finding it

Mugwort grows along the shady banks of canyon bottoms and along riverbanks in foothill and coastal regions. You almost always find it near streams. Frequently it is found near poison oak.

The aromatic leaves are ovate to elliptic, and are often divided into three to five pinnate segments. The leaves near the top of the stalks become narrower, linear to lanceolate in shape, and generally are entire (not toothed). On the top side, the leaves are dark green and almost glabrous (hairless). On the underside, the leaves are covered with short, soft, white, wooly hairs, which is one of mugwort's dominant characteristics.

Twenty to thirty very small flowers are clustered together to make up 1/6-inch-high heads. These heads are tightly clustered along spikes or rod-like stalks, which in turn are arranged (alternately) along the main stalk. The flowers are followed by the seeds. The year-old dried stalks are usually found alongside the new young plants, and it is from these old stalks that you can usually collect the dried leaves to use for tinder or incense.

Some people believe that young mugwort leaves, which somewhat resemble a hand held out with fingers spread, are effective in warding off evil spirits. Mugwort is hung over doorways, windows, chimneys, and other openings on Halloween in the belief that it protects against the evil effects of witchcraft and the entrance of malevolent witches. Pregnant women and newborn babies were considered particularly vulnerable on Halloween. For this reason, a pregnant woman would wear dried mugwort around her neck in a small bag, and mugwort would be laid in or around young babies' cradles.

Mugwort's folklore and various uses make it an interesting and valuable plant to know.

(Christopher Nyerges is the author of <u>In the Footsteps of Our Ancestors: Guide to Wild Food</u> and other books. His schedule of outings is published in the *Talking Leaves Newsletter*, available from the School of Self-Reliance, Box 41834, Eagle Rock, CA 90041. The newsletter can be viewed on-line at http://home.earthlink.net/˜nyerges/.) Δ

A BHM moment

Dave and John celebrate the completion of another issue.

Ayoob on firearms

By Massad Ayoob

The backwoods hunter

"One does not hunt in order to kill," wrote Jose Ortega y Gasset in his classic Meditations on Hunting, "one kills in order to have hunted." Hunting is in many ways a metaphor of the backwoods lifestyle. One may have moved to the hinterlands to escape the blood lust of the cities, and find the killing of an inoffensive animal antithetical to their raison d'etre, while another might find the primal hunting, killing, and eating of a wild creature to be the very essence of "going back to nature."

The very argument is a part of the "live and let live" value system of the backwoods homesteader. Unless he's unclear on the concept, the vegetarian who wouldn't harm a fly won't dump on the hunter who kills his family's winter meat in the forest, and the hunter won't sneer at the vegetarian as a lightweight yuppie hiding out in woods he doesn't understand. Personally, I take a middle ground.

As a youngster, I lived to hunt: it was what you did every fall if you were a boy in rural northern New England. The male paradigm, male bonding, all of that. Late in my teens, when my only sibling died in my arms, I lost my taste for killing and stopped hunting for a long time.

I eat meat, venison being my favorite. Wild meat is the healthiest. Living in a nation of bloated hypertensives with fat-clogged arteries, I was struck in South Africa by the number of old Boers I met who were 80 and looked 60, or were 60 and looked 40, and had eaten the meat of the native antelope morning, noon, and night for all their lives. Little fat, no steroids...healthy food of the kind that made Homo Sapiens the dominant predator of the planet, whether the given specimen appreciates that heritage or not.

Being a meat eater, I'd be a hypocrite if I damned hunting. Buying your meat in a store is like paying the hit man to commit your murder for you: you have to accept moral responsibility for the death in question either way, and a middleman firing the bullet or slitting the throat does not exculpate you at all. Thus, while I will listen to anti-hunting arguments, I will listen to them only from those who wear cloth shoes and plastic belts and eat no meat whatsoever.

At the same time, if you are a hunter, the time should come when the animal is in your gun sights and you spare it if you don't absolutely need to kill it for food. You want to know in your heart that it was your finger pulling the trigger, not the trigger pulling the finger. The greatest understanding of the power to kill lies in the realization that you have the power not to. And—parents, proscelytizers of the backwoods faith to the urban refugees, and all the rest—hear me well on this: Never force someone to kill an animal if they don't truly want to have the experience!

That said, let's look to the mechanics. Take Hunter Safety classes from your local office of the state fish and wildlife department, or someone they've authorized to teach them. Learn navigation of the forest, and hostile environment survival skills, if you haven't already. Realize that hunting today is not time and cost efficient: hard labor at minimum wage

Massad Ayoob

will probably buy your family more food per hour spent than deer hunting. You do it for the sport and the venison, not for subsistence, unless you're desperate.

Use a good weapon and practice with it until you are skilled. Determine the distance at which you can place your bullet, your arrow, or your rifled shotgun slug into a six inch circle virtually every time, and do not shoot at an animal beyond that distance. This saves the animal needless suffering, and it saves you the grief and recrimination of crippling a beautiful animal or dooming it to an agonizing death. If you have dealt with Death, you know that "clean kill" is not an oxymoron, but rather, the responsibility of those who are for whatever reason involved with the legal and ethical ending of Life.

When it is over, you will one night sit down to a venison dinner that you brought home. The sensation will be rather like the satisfaction you feel eating vegetables you've sown into the earth, tended, and harvested. There will be a sense of accomplishment, of a primal circle having been completed, of independence and personal capability being confirmed.

Local gun dealers and conservation officers will give you the best advice on the types of guns and ammo or bows and arrows to use for the given quarry in the given topography, and they can steer you to local meat cutters who process game and can best advise you on how to dress, butcher, and cook the meat you harvest from the wild. The nearest village library in a rural area should be replete with books on hunting and tracking wild game and preparing it for the table. Read and absorb these books. If you're new to rural environs, let it be known that you'd like to find an old woodsman and trade his lore for yours, teaching him to surf the net while he teaches you to hunt in these parts. You'll be surprised how often such "skill barters" work, how often those who grew up in the wilds you coveted seek the accouterments of the high-tech advanced civilization you were wise enough to escape.

Give hunting a chance. It may add a new dimension to your backwoods home experience. At best, you'll know the exultance of eating meat you've hunted and harvested. At worst, if you come out against hunting, you'll have earned the right to an informed opinion, for someone who claims others shouldn't do what they themselves can't do are in the position of a eunuch preaching celibacy: their argument simply carries no credibility. Δ

A BHM moment

The old BHM office in the Siskiyou Mountains of Oregon.

Leaf mold is another way to build your soil

By John Fuchs

Leaves are an excellent way to add organic matter to the garden. However, using raw—or unprocessed—leaves has some drawbacks. Raw leaves are more acidic than composted leaves, and studies have shown that they take nutrients from the soil—particularly nitrogen—as they decompose. Because of this nitrogen depletion, adding raw leaves to your garden can reduce the yield of vegetable crops.

The solution to the problem is to compost the leaves and add the compost to the garden. The drawback to this approach is the time required to make the compost. In northern climates, it is even more difficult and time-consuming to make compost, because the leaves freeze solid, and the breakdown of the leaves is often incomplete come springtime.

A good compromise is to make and use *leaf mold*. Leaf mold is a halfway step in the process that turns raw leaves into composted matter. To make leaf mold, take raw leaves and shred them by running a lawnmower over the leaves. The shredding of the leaves greatly accelerates the breaking down process. I empty the mower bag into a plastic bag and add a handful of lime (to counter the acidity of the leaves) and a cupful of blood meal (to provide nitrogen). Then I dampen the leaves and shake the bag well.

Every few weeks, I open the bag and stir up the leaves. When the leaf mold freezes, I break it up as much as possible. Come springtime, the bags are full of friable black leaf mold which I spread right over the garden plot and till in. Studies have shown that leaf mold holds at least five times as much moisture as ordinary topsoil, so I always apply it to my flower beds instead of peat moss.

The advantages of leaf mold are many. It provides the tilth and moisture-holding capacity of compost and peat moss, but it's easier to make than compost and far cheaper than peat moss. While it doesn't provide as much nitrogen, phosphorous, and potassium as manure, it is rich in calcium and magnesium, which are essential for healthy vegetables. Best of all, the raw materials of leaf mold—leaves—are abundant in much of North America. Δ

Venison deserves gourmet treatment

By Edith Helmich

Whether you use a bow or a gun, bagging a deer is an adventure in the field, and a promise of succulent meals to follow. Too often, however, the venison is simply roasted or used in a few unimaginative recipes. Venison is a gourmet meat and should be the focal point of wonderful meals.

Good game recipes are hard to find. Cookbooks tend to feature meats that are available at the supermarket, and typically include only a few recipes for game. The recipes that follow were gathered from a variety of kitchens and culinary sources and modified over the years. They were chosen on the basis of taste, appearance, and ease of preparation. (Remember, you don't have to tell anyone that it took you so little time to prepare such delicious recipes.) Try them all, and you just may expand your reputation as a hunter to a chef specializing in game.

Dressing a deer in the field is fundamental knowledge among hunters, and will not be discussed here. Dressing the deer properly and promptly, of course, is very important to the flavor and quality of the venison.

Another well-known characteristic affecting the quality of the venison is the age of the animal. Some cooks believe that all game, particularly venison, should be marinated before cooking, but that is not necessarily so. The meat from a deer under one year of age (a fawn), or from one to two years of age (a yearling), is tender and mild-flavored

without any marinade. Certainly a mature deer's meat requires a good marinade to guarantee tenderness and minimize the wild or "gamey" flavor. Deer and elk meat are used interchangeably in most recipes for venison. Two of the recipes that follow call for a marinade, either to tenderize or to add flavor.

Venison steak St. Hubert

This recipe places the venison in marinade the night before serving, and requires a very short preparation time. The slightly sweet-sour sauce is wonderful on venison. Despite the gourmet title, it is an easy recipe to prepare. Serves four.

---

4 venison round steaks, 1/2- to 3/4-inch thick
  (about 2 pounds)

Marinade:

2 sliced carrots
2 sliced onions
1 chopped clove of garlic
2 cups of dry white wine
3/4 cup vinegar
1/4 cup water
1/8 teaspoon thyme
2 bay leaves
2 or 3 whole cloves
3 or 4 whole peppercorns
1/2 cup corn oil or olive oil

Place steaks in an enamel, glass, or earthenware dish. Pour the uncooked marinade over the meat, cover, and refrigerate for 24 hours.

Drain the marinade from the steaks into a saucepan, straining out the marinade vegetables. Bring the liquid to a boil and reduce by half.

Gently dry the steaks with a paper towel and sauté them in a small amount of hot fat until brown on both sides. Medium to medium-rare will provide maximum tenderness.

Place on a platter and cover with the following sauce:

Sauce Poivrade (1 cup):

2 Tablespoons flour
2 Tablespoons butter
2 crushed peppercorns
1 cup reduced marinade
3 Tablespoons red currant jelly

Brown flour in butter. Add peppercorns, reduced marinade, and currant jelly. Cook over medium heat, stirring until smooth.

Succulent venison stew

If you want to throw a bigger party, this recipe serves a crowd of eight to ten people. Again, the venison is placed in a marinade the night before, but this recipe requires a longer cooking time. This dish actually improves if made a day early and reheated before serving. A mature deer would work well with this dish.

3 to 4 pounds of fat-trimmed venison, cut into 2" cubes

Marinade:

2 thinly sliced onions
1 thinly sliced carrot
2 stalks celery, cut in large chunks
1 garlic clove, crushed
2 cups red wine
1/2 cup salad oil
1/4 teaspoon thyme
1 teaspoon salt
1/4 teaspoon thyme
2 bay leaves
10-12 black peppercorns
2 cloves

Place cubes of venison in a non-metal container, pour uncooked marinade over the meat, and refrigerate for a full 24 hours.

About two and a half hours before serving, drain and save marinade, discarding vegetables. Dry meat gently on paper towels. Continue with the following recipe for the stew.

Stew:

1/2 cup salad oil
1 cup diced salt pork
1 large onion, chopped
2 carrots, sliced
1 pound mushrooms, sliced
2 Tablespoons brown sugar, packed
3 Tablespoons flour
1 clove garlic, chopped or pressed
1/2 cup red wine
2 cups reserved marinade
Salt & pepper to taste

Sauté oil and salt pork until lightly browned. Add onion and carrots and cook until moderately browned. Sprinkle brown sugar over vegetables, stir well, and remove from pan.

In the same pan, sauté mushrooms until lightly cooked and remove from pan.

Still using the same pan and adding a little more oil (if necessary), brown stew meat. Sprinkle meat with flour and continue cooking until flour is also brown. Add wine and marinade (and additional water, if necessary) to cover meat. Cover pan and simmer on very low heat for one to one and a half hours. Add the reserved vegetables and cook for an additional 30 to 40 minutes.

Serve over rice and sprinkle with chopped parsley. A blend of wild and white rice is very good with this dish.

Roast leg of venison with lingonberry sauce

For a very large dinner, such as a special-occasion family gathering or holiday dinner, a traditional roasted leg of venison with lingonberry sauce is a delicious choice. Because this recipe uses no marinade, venison from a deer no older than a yearling is recommended. Serves 10 to 12.

1 six- to eight-pound leg of venison
1 teaspoon salt
1/2 teaspoon ground ginger
1/2 teaspoon ground pepper
1/2 cup beef stock
1/2 cup melted butter

Combine dry seasonings and rub into meat. Place roast on a rack in a roasting pan and cover with lid or foil. Roast in a 325° oven for approximately three hours, or until meat tests tender when pierced with a fork. Baste frequently with butter-and-water mixture while cooking.

Remove roast from pan to serving plate and cover with foil. Save pan drippings and liquid. While the roast sets its juices, make the sauce.

Lingonberry sauce:

1 eight-to-ten-ounce can of lingonberries with juice
Pan drippings (fat skimmed off)
    plus enough water to make 1 cup
6 - 7 Tablespoons of sugar
3 Tablespoons of cornstarch
    dissolved in 1/2 cup cold water
1 Tablespoon butter

Combine all ingredients in saucepan and bring to boil over medium heat, stirring constantly. Pour a small amount of sauce over the roast before carving, and serve the remaining sauce at the table.

Any one of these recipes will provide a memorable experience. Good hunting and good eating. Δ

Southern cooking that doesn't just whistle Dixie

By Richard Blunt

The southern region of the United States is almost as big as Western Europe, and despite the stereotype that non-Southerners have—that there is only one South—when someone says, "I am Southern," the South contains almost as many subcultures as Europe has countries. This cultural diversity shows especially in Southern cooking. A close look at the culinary practices in this region will reveal the influence of German, Dutch, Spanish, French, Scottish, Irish, Native American, Asian, English, and African cultures. The result has been the rise of three broad and distinctive Southern cuisines: Classic Southern, which is a blend of Anglo Saxon and African roots; Southwestern, with its Spanish influenced ranch style cooking; and Creole/Cajun, a mixture of French Canadian, Native American, and African cuisines.

English and African roots

Southern cooking—in fact, all "American" cooking—started nearly 400 years ago when a small group of weather-beaten, malnourished refugees landed on the eastern shores of North America. They'd left their homes, most of their relatives, and almost all their possessions in England and set sail for a new homeland where they sought religious freedom. In a very short time they established successful colonies at Plymouth in Massachusetts and at Jamestown in Virginia.

In spite of the dramatic climactic differences between the two colonies, the British women in both colonies set up their kitchens to accommodate the cooking style they had learned at home. But because winters in the Plymouth colony were cold and long, the settlers continued to rely mainly on the simple fortifying foods that were central to their Old World Puritan cooking style. Basic elements of this style survive today in New England Yankee cooking, e.g., when brine-cured meats and hearty leaf and root vegetables are combined to make boiled dinners.

Meanwhile, the milder climate experienced in the Virginia colony made life generally easier. And, though meals were also prepared along traditional lines, they were done so with a more relaxed attitude, meaning that in Jamestown the colonists made use of the more plentiful foods available there including a larger variety of vegetables and more herbs and spices. But even with this relaxed attitude toward traditional culinary practice, the food prepared in both was essentially the same.

Richard Blunt

There is a myth that early English cooking and, therefore, the cooking style the colonists brought with them, was plain, simple and unimaginative. The truth is that from the beginning of 17th century to the early part of the 18th century there was a Renaissance in English cooking. English cookbooks from that time show evidence that this was a cuisine rich with a variety of herbs and spices in which foods were crafted by techniques that contributed subtleties of flavor and texture.

At the center of all of this was the ancient art of open hearth cooking. This is the most dangerous and back breaking way of preparing food that I can think of, but it imparts a flavor and texture to food that is impossible to duplicate by any other cooking method. Cooking on an open hearth requires the use of very specialized tools and utensils. Adjustable spits used for roasting gave the cook complete control over the roasting process. An array of cranes and pulleys made it possible to move pots closer or farther from the heat. There were Dutch ovens, with long legs and tight-fitting deep-rimmed lids which were buried in the hot coals to allow the contents to cook while the coals slowly cooled, thus creating stews, soups, and other wonderful dishes that exuded flavors and aromas that are all but unknown today.

Using these and other special utensils like long legged chaffing dishes, iron forks and tongues, salamanders for browning, gridirons for frying and grilling, long handled waffle and wafer irons, and clay brick baking ovens all required a sense of timing and a mastery of this cooking technique that is nearly a lost art. By the time you read this column, I will be participating in a special workshop called

"Mastering The Art of Open Hearth Cooking." I will share that experience with you in a future column.

Southern cooking blossoms

More important to Southern cooking, however, was an event, scarcely noticed at the time, that took place at Jamestown. In 1619 a Dutch ship anchored off the coast and offered the colonists a handful of slaves transported from Western Africa. Thus began the slave trade in North America and for the next two centuries African slaves were put to work supporting all aspects of the South's agrarian economy. This included all of the food production responsibilities in many Southern kitchens.

Like their English sisters, the African women brought their native cooking techniques with them, and, once in the English kitchens, they demonstrated a natural flair for blending the ingredients they found there with other ingredients they were already familiar with, but which were new to the English palate. The resultant earthy foods, served in elegant style, have made Southern cooking legendary and it has survived political and social upheaval, wars, industrialization, and attempts by the commercial and fast food industry to bastardize it.

It was during the first half of the 19th century that Southern cooking really blossomed. All elements of the formula came

Thomas Jefferson

together and were supported by the South's rich economy. The tables of the upper and middle class households displayed some of the finest foods that could be found in this country.

Several critical events, however, would dramatically change the South and bring this era to an abrupt halt. When the War Between the States and the Emancipation Proclamation ended slavery, the legacy of African cooks running Southern kitchens came to an end. African cooks lost the Anglo Saxon influence and the Anglo Saxon households lost the creative ingenuity of the African cook. Poverty settled on the South, forcing most households to adopt simple diets of field peas, wild and cultivated greens, sweet potatoes, and a variety of dried corn products, supplemented by inexpensive pork products. A whole generation of Southern women left their kitchens and went into the work force, leaving little time for anything but essential cooking. Still, as meager as the food was, over the years even this food fare has been refined in Southern kitchens to the level of signature cuisine that any Southerner can be proud of.

Another factor in the nineteenth century that affected the cooking was the mass production of cast iron ranges that were sold at prices that most households could afford. This revolution in kitchen technology changed all American cooking because it signaled the end of open hearth cooking. But the inexpensive and convenient cast iron range could not produce the same results as spit roasting of meats before a hot fire and crusty breads like those baked in wood fired clay brick ovens.

Then the packaged food industry started to market off-the-shelf canned foods as an easy, but low quality alternative to the traditional labor-intensive methods of home preserving. The age of synthetic cheese, ham made with gluten, and imitation bacon had begun. American food was on its way to gastronomic disaster. It is a loss from which it has never fully recovered. Fortunately, in the South, tradition has never been considered an anecdote; and the legend of Classic Southern food has been kept alive throughout the region. And wherever Southerners have migrated, they have brought their cooking with them. On top of this, the culinary works of great 17th and 18th century authors have recently been revitalized to celebrate the past glories of traditional Southern cooking.

The first American epicure

The first great American epicure of note was from the South. He was Thomas Jefferson, to some, the greatest American President. He not only served as President, he was a governor of Virginia, Secretary of State under Washington, and an American minister to France. But his first loves were farming and overseeing all of the culinary operations at Monticello. He himself designed Monticello along with its kitchen, and he never lost an opportunity to play host. At times he entertained as many as 50 guests in his custom built dining room. But because of his fascination with French foods and wines, he was accused by other native Virginians of "rejecting his native victuals." It was an unfair accusation because Jefferson also relished such Southern delicacies as corn, dry cured Virginia ham, Jerusalem artichokes, scalloped tomatoes, peas, and rice. He grew 30 different varieties of peas at Monticello and risked becoming a criminal on death row because he smuggled seed rice from Italy into the United States for planting in his gardens—a capital offense at the time that was punishable by hanging. Every year Jefferson's April 13th birthday is celebrated with a lavish dinner party at his mansion. Of course classic Southern food is always a part of the menu.

To tell the story of Southern food would require an epic of several volumes. There are no boundaries where one can say Southern cooking starts and ends, and its ingredients are as varied as the mixture of different cultures that call the South home. There is no way I can do justice to it with the space I'm allowed in this column. But with what I do have, I will share with you some recipes that have been passed from my grandmother to my mother, and now they belong to me. There is nothing highfalutin (as my grandmother would say) about these foods. In fact, there is a certain grace in their simplicity and an elegance in the natural unmasked flavors that Southern fair offers all who appreciate good food.

Fried chicken

It would be blasphemy to discuss Southern food without giving some attention to fried chicken. The recipes and cooking methods for fried chicken are endless. Put a bunch of Southern cooks in the same room and they'll disagree on everything from the ingredients to the actual cooking

Beet, dandelion, collards

method. Some will insist that disjointed chicken, salt, pepper, flour, and fat are all that are necessary to make honest fried chicken. Others will make the same claim after adding to the formula various combinations of eggs, buttermilk, sweet milk, corn meal, bread crumbs, cracker crumbs, baking powder, and almost every variety of herb and spice known to man.

Some insist on frying in deep fat, others say shallow fat. They can't even agree on the type of fat. You'll hear lard, corn oil, and peanut oil each considered "best" by different cooks. So, if fried chicken is a must for you, I suggest that you consider you own taste and select the recipe and production method that you think comes closest to what you like.

Beware of recipes that tout themselves as "authentic Southern fried chicken" because there isn't any single such thing. But, if you want to try a chicken recipe that is as Southern as you can get, without going through the mind boggling variations of frying, my grandmother's Benne (pronounced *'ben ay*) Bake recipe is just the answer. Serve it hot for dinner with or without gravy, or chill it and plan a picnic.

Nanny B's Benne Bake

Ingredients

1 two pound frying chicken — cut into eight pieces
Undercoating
1 cup all purpose flour
1/2 tsp salt
1/2 tsp freshly ground black pepper
Middlecoating
3/4 cup Buttermilk
Overcoating
12 ounces ground pecans (ground with the coarse blade of a meat grinder or in a food processor)
2/3 cup white benne (sesame) seeds
1/2 tsp cayenne pepper (ground)
1/4 tsp nutmeg (fresh ground from whole seed if possible)
1/2 tsp salt

Method

1. Wash the chicken pieces in cold water and dry on paper towels.

2. Preheat the oven to 375 degrees F.

3. Combine undercoat ingredients in a brown paper bag and set aside.

4. Combine overcoat ingredients in a large bowl and mix.

5. Place middlecoating (buttermilk) in another large bowl.

6. Oil a roasting or baking pan that is large enough to hold all the chicken.

7. Place all of the chicken in the bag with the undercoating and shake until the chicken pieces are evenly coated with the flour mixture.

8. Remove the chicken pieces from the bag and shake off any excess flour.

9. Place the chicken pieces into the buttermilk and gently toss to coat each piece with milk.

10. Roll each piece of chicken in the overcoating until evenly coated and place on the oiled pan.

11. Bake on the middle shelf of the oven until the coating is a medium brown and the chicken is cooked through (about 40 minutes).

Note: This recipe produces a chicken that has a wonderful tasting and crispy coating that keeps the chicken moist and tender. If you are counting calories, this coating works with skinless chicken as well. It also works with center cut pork chops and firm fleshed fish such as catfish, eel, tuna, or swordfish.

Stewed Winter Sallet

Sallet (pronounce the "t") is an old English word for greens. Turnip greens, mustard greens, dandelion greens, Swiss chard, collards, beet greens, and spinach are some of the most popular greens that grow in profusion in the South. Today they are one of the mainstays of Southern cooking, but there was a time when greens were considered unattractive food at all but the poorest dinner tables. Over the years the ingenuity of those who did the cooking in poor households transformed this humble food into a distinctive cuisine by mixing and matching with other basic foods like corn, rice, beans, and inexpensive cuts of pork.

Cabbage, chard

Mustard, turnip

The following recipe, stewed winter sallet, has been served by my family at dinner on New Year's Day for as long as I can remember.

Ingredients

8 oz dry cured lean salt pork
2¹/₂ qts water
1 medium onion sliced
2 pounds fresh collards, kale, or cabbage (If you use kale, choose only young leaves. Kale becomes bitter as it matures.)
2 fresh hot chilli peppers cut in half, seeded and deveined.
Fresh ground black pepper to taste.
Kosher salt to taste

Method

1. Cut the salt pork into eight pieces and saute over medium heat in a heavy bottomed skillet until lightly browned. Combine the pork, water, and onion in a very large pot and bring the mixture to a slow boil. Reduce the heat, cover the pot, and allow the pork to cook for about a half hour at a very slow boil.

2. Wash the greens in plenty of cold water, cut away of any tough stems and cut the greens into 3/4 inch strips.

3. When the pork has simmered for a half hour, raise the heat to bring the broth to a medium boil; add the greens and chilli pepper and bring the mixture back to a boil. Reduce the heat to a slow simmer and cook the greens until they are tender. Cooking time will vary depending on the type of greens. Young kale takes only about twenty minutes.

Hardier greens like collards and cabbage will take up to an hour.

4. A few minutes before removing greens from the heat, taste the broth and adjust the seasoning with the salt and pepper.

Pepper Sherry

This is a table condiment used in the deep south to add extra zing to everything from soups to vegetables. I carry a small bottle with me when I go to food shows to help me through a day of tedious tasting. It will also enhance the taste of any cooked greens without masking the flavor. It takes only a few minutes to make and will last in the refrigerator forever. If you want to put some in a small bottle to bring to your favorite restaurant, it will live without refrigeration.

Ingredients

2 or 3 fresh hot chilli peppers. (I use habañero, Scotch bonnet, or jalapeno because they are both hot and flavorful.)
2 cups your favorite sherry

Method

1. Cut the peppers in half and remove the seeds. Dice the seeded peppers into medium chunks.

2. Scorch the peppers in a heavy bottomed skillet over medium heat being careful not to allow them to burn. Do not use any oil or other fat to lubricate the pan.

3. Combine the peppers with the sherry in a Mason jar or other suitable bottle, and refrigerate, covered, for 24 hours.

Kale, spinach

Before using this condiment, I suggest that you taste a little first, to see just how hot it is.

Hoppin John

This old Lowcountry rice and bean dish has a fascinating history that goes back to the late 1600s when Dr. Henry Woodward planted the first crop of Madagascar rice near Charleston, S.C. By the 1800s, Carolinians were using rice for currency and named their rice "Carolina Gold".

Slave cooks from West Africa slowly introduced this dish to South Carolina as they were allowed to introduce their cookery into planters' kitchens. Today Carolinians eat this dish on New Year's Day to bring good luck in the coming year. If you're interested in reading more about Hoppin' John history, buy a copy of The Carolina Rice Kitchen by Karen Hess. But first try this recipe to get a taste of a food that is as classic Southern as fried green tomatoes or baked yams.

Ingredients

6 oz lean salt pork cubed
1 medium onion diced medium
2 cloves minced garlic
1 cup long grain Texmati brown rice
2 1/2 cups water
1/2 tsp Kosher salt
1/2 tsp fresh ground black pepper
1 bay leaf (fresh if you can find it, but dried bay works well also)
1/4 tsp red pepper flakes or cayenne pepper
4 cups fresh or frozen black-eyed peas (I grow my own and freeze what I don't eat during the season. High quality frozen varieties are also available in most markets.)

Method

1. Place the salt pork in a heavy skillet (cast iron works best), and fry over a medium heat until lightly browned. Add the onions and garlic and saute until the onion is translucent.

2. Add rice and stir to coat grains with fat. Add the water, salt, black pepper, bay leaf, and red pepper; bring the water to a boil, reduce the heat to very low, cover the skillet and cook the rice on low heat for 10 minutes. Remove the cover and add the black-eyed peas. Do not stir.

3. Cover the skillet again and cook slowly for 30 minutes. Remove the skillet from the heat and let stand undisturbed for another 10 minutes. Remove the cover and gently fluff the rice with a fork to incorporate the black-eyed peas. Serve at once.

That's it for this issue, but remember, when they say, "The South will rise again," it's going to be because their cooks are taking over. Δ

Nov/Dec 1996
No 42

Backwoods Home magazine

practical ideas for self-reliant living

A DOZEN GREAT HOLIDAY CRAFT IDEAS

Plus

Holiday Breads
Shortwave Radio
CPR in the Backwoods
Growing Self-Reliant Kids
Finding Love on the Internet

HOLIDAY CRAFTS ISSUE

Corn Burning Stoves
Grow Your Holiday Turkey

$3.95 US • $5.50 CANADA

Keep the cooks happy with these easy-to-make kitchen helpers

By Rev. J.D. Hooker

After all of the decorations and gift giving, the brightest holiday memories seem to revolve around the dining table and the kitchen—turkeys, hams, geese and all of their trimmings, breads, pies, pastries, and all of the other mouth-watering delights.

Unless you happen to be one of the holiday cooks, however, you might not realize just how much real work goes into the preparation of one of these holiday feasts. Especially when you consider how New Year's comes right on the heels of Christmas, which comes right on the heels of Thanksgiving.

Sure, all of this preparation is generally considered as pretty pleasant work. But it's still work, enjoyable or not. So, for this special issue, it might be a reasonable idea to show you a few easy-to-make kitchen gadgets that can make some of these cooking tasks just a trifle easier.

Remember, this whole season, Thanksgiving right through New Year's, is really supposed to be a time of celebration, giving thanks to our Creator, sharing with friends and relatives, and expressing the joy and happiness in our lives.

So consider making up a few of these simple devices to distribute among the holiday cooks and bakers in your circle *before* the start of the season, so they can have the use of them as they prepare all of those wonderful holiday treats. I've found these small, unexpected early gifts to be greatly appreciated.

Oven hooks

The simplest of these kitchen helpers is an oven hook, a very handy

Trimmed from a forked branch

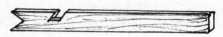

Cut from a wooden slat

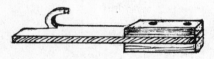

Made from metal stock

Pull out . . .

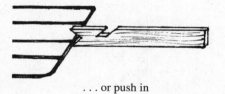

. . . or push in

Oven hooks

item for any baker. Whether fashioned from wood, iron, or aluminum, this easily made tool is a real finger saver.

One method of forming this oven hook involves nothing more than selecting a forked stick, with one limb of the fork being slender enough to slip between the wires of the oven rack. Cut this slender side of the fork off to leave about a 3/4" stub, and trim off the other side for a foot-long handle. Now, just notch the end of the stick so the tool can also be used to push the rack back in, and you're finished already.

A second way to make a wooden oven hook is to use about a foot-long hardwood slat that is thin enough to slip between the oven rack's wires. Just fashion a deep V-shaped notch in one end with a diagonal notch (as shown) about an inch further up the handle.

Iron, mild steel, or aluminum flat stock (1/2" wide by 1/8" thick works well) can also be handily fashioned into an oven hook. Just use a hacksaw to cut about a 1" slot in the end of an 8" - 14" piece of flat metal stock. Use pliers, a hammer, or some other tool to bend the metal on one side of the slot to a C shape. The addition of a riveted or bolted-on wooden handle, or even a tightly wrapped leather handle, makes for a fancier gift.

Wooden cooling trivets

Another handy kitchen helper is a set of quickly fashioned wooden cooling trivets. These can be built in various sizes to fit pie and cake pans, muffin tins, loaf pans, or whatever, but the basic structure of this simple device remains the same.

A pair of wooden slats (pieces of 1x2 furring strips work great for this) are laid down an appropriate width apart. Next, drill pilot holes and use wood screws to attach similar slats of a proper length atop these. These top slats need to be equally spaced, usually between 1/2" and 3/4" apart. Not only do these trivets allow for proper air circulation, for quicker cooling, they also prevent the bottoms of the

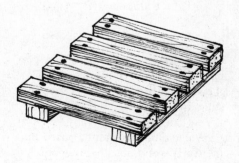

Wooden cooling trivet

hot pans from scorching the cook's counter or tabletop.

Cutting boards

Most holiday meal preparations include a lot of chopping, slicing, dicing, and mincing chores. A properly-fashioned cutting board can be a big help. "Properly-fashioned" mostly means selecting the right sort of wood. Woods in the oak, cedar, and pine groups should be avoided, as these will sometimes impart an unpleasant taste to the foods, while woods such as ash, birch, beech, maple, and hickory are generally preferred.

For best results, select a knot-free board between 3/4" and 11/4" thick, 10" or 12" wide, and between 18" and 20"

Cutting board

long. Use a band saw, jig saw, coping saw, or whatever to round off the corners and form a comfortable handle, then sand all of the edges nice and smooth.

You can just keep wiping coats of vegetable oil on the cutting board until the wood won't absorb any more, but I've found that it's much easier to just place the board in something like a

large sheet cake pan or even a metal roller pan for painting, then pour in a quart or so of vegetable cooking oil and place the whole thing in a low oven for a few hours.

After each session of use, the cutting board should be wiped clean and rinsed well. Then pour boiling water over all its surfaces before putting it away. Add a fresh coat of cooking oil occasionally to keep the cutting board looking nice.

Dough boxes

With all of the pie crusts, breads, rolls, biscuits, and other baked goods prepared for holiday dining, an old-fashioned wooden dough box is mighty handy for mixing up bread doughs, pie crusts, and other fairly stiff doughs. Usually cherished as a gift, many become family heirlooms.

Again, woods like ash, maple, birch, and beech are preferred, while those like pine and oak should be avoided. Standard 1" lumber (actually 3/4" or 7/8") is the best material to use. You can simply put the dough box together using screws, or you can get fancy and use dovetail or dowel pin joints if you prefer. An 8"x20"x6" deep dough box seems ideal for most bakers, but they can be made any size that suits individual needs.

Finish the dough box using vegetable oil, in the same manner as the cutting board. To clean the dough box after use, follow the same procedures

Dough box

as for the cutting board, but apply a fresh coat of cooking oil after each cleaning. This will go a long way towards preventing the dough from sticking.

In use, if the cooks will always remember to add all of the dry ingredients first, they'll love this mixing box.

Bread slicers

For many folks (like my family), home-baked breads are more than just a holiday delight. From the first cool evenings of autumn on, they usually become dietary staples. Anyone you know who bakes a lot of bread will appreciate a bread slicer just as much as my wife did when I built one for her.

Use any type of 1" lumber, or even 3/4" plywood, to fashion the base and the solid end. I used 3/4" dowels for the upright slicing guides, but you could use anywhere from 3/8" to 11/2" dowels, depending upon how thick you want the slices to be. Space the dowels so that the blade of your bread knife will slip easily between them.

Roasting spits

For more adventurous cooks, who also have an open fireplace in their home, a set of dingle spit roasters can make an ideal pre-holiday gift. While these roasting spits are exceedingly simple to make, they also happen to be my favorite method of cooking waterfowl. Try wild duck roasted this way, and you'll probably agree.

All that's needed to put together one of these simple cooking devices is a piece of stout cord, and a "whirl" of branches. Such "whirls," most commonly found on pine trees, are formed where several branches radiate out from the same spot on the trunk.

Trim the stem and the branches to proper lengths (branches about 1" for quail or Cornish hens, 2" to 4" for chickens, 6" to 8" for turkeys), and shave off all of the bark. Drill a hole in the end of the stem, so you can hang it. Allow the spit to season for at least a few weeks before putting it into use.

To roast meats or fowl, simply insert the spit through the meat and hang it by a cord in front of the fireplace,

Cheese presses

Kitchen wizards with a strong do-it-yourself bent will also enjoy this cheese press, which is just as easy to use as it is to make. Remove both ends from a coffee can, a large juice can, or

Cheese press

Roasting spit

above a pan or other container to catch the drippings. Just give the string a slight twist once in a while, to keep the meat rotating in front of the fire. When roasting wild duck or goose in this fashion, carefully keep ashes and such from falling into the dripping pan: you'll probably want to try these drippings as an ideal shortening for many sorts of baked goods.

a similar-sized metal container. Cut out a couple of plywood disks that fit loosely inside of the can. Drill several small holes through each disk, with a larger hole exactly in the center.

Use a piece of all-thread rod, with a regular nut and a large wing-nut to put it all together. In use, the curds are placed inside of the container, and the wing nut is tightened to apply pressure. Simple enough?

Like I said, these kitchen gadgets are easy to make. Some, like the oven hook, require no more than a few minutes to complete. None of them takes more than a couple of hours to build and finish. Most cooks would be very pleased with any (or all) of these handy kitchen helpers. So why not brighten someone's holiday season? Δ

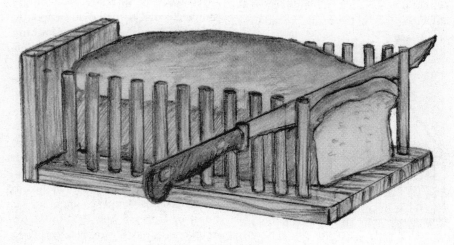

Bread slicer

Close encounters with the white deer

By Marjorie Burris

"Mom! Come quick!" Uncle David called in a loud whisper. "There's a *white deer* in the meadow!"

I took the griddle off the stove and hurried after Uncle David into the front yard. We could have pancakes any time—but a white deer was something very unusual. Uncle David pointed to the far side of the meadow just above the apple orchard. I could barely make out the deer in the early morning light, but it was white all right, and larger than the gray, long-eared mule deer we usually saw on the ranch.

"Where do you suppose it came from?" Uncle David whispered. "And isn't it beautiful?"

"Do you suppose it is a true albino?" I whispered back. "I wish we could see it up close."

We watched intently. The deer must have felt us, because it raised its head and sniffed the air, then bounced slowly away into the pine trees.

We were both excited. Uncle David looked "albino" up in the encyclopedia and found that true albino animals were white because they lacked normal pigment, and they had pink eyes and ears. He was eager to see if the deer was a true albino.

We hoped the deer would come back. That evening we got the binoculars and settled down quietly in the front yard to watch for the deer. We shivered with anticipation and kept our pact not to talk. But the deer did not come. We went to bed disappointed.

The next morning, Uncle David shook me awake early. "Let's go see if the deer will come back today," he said, and we hurried out to the front yard just as it was getting light. We hid behind the big juniper tree in the front yard. We didn't have to wait long; the deer came through the trees slowly, looked around cautiously, then walked into the orchard to eat some twigs off the trees.

We studied the deer through the binoculars, and were careful not to look at it too long at a time, so we wouldn't scare it off. We could see the pink of its eyes and ears clearly—and we saw something else, too. We saw bumps at the base of the deer's ears. He was growing antlers! We wondered if they would be white or pink.

After the deer left, Uncle David and I were so thrilled we could talk of

A BHM moment

*Inside the Backwoods Home Magazine bookstore
in Gold Beach, Oregon.*

nothing else all day long. Every morning we would look for the deer, and every morning it came back. And it started coming every evening, too.

A few days later Doug Vandergon, our forest ranger, drove up to the ranch to see us. He told us he had been seeing an albino deer on the other side of the mesa, and it must have changed grazing grounds and come our way. He also told us that the Goswicks, who had lived at the ranch in the 1940's, had seen a white deer a long time ago, but no one had seen one for about 25 years.

The deer became a regular diner in our meadow, coming both early morning and late evening. Grandpa, Uncle Duane, Uncle Don, and everybody who visited us watched for it. Over the summer, the horns on its head grew into a beautiful four-point rack. They were white with a pink tinge at the base.

When the apples ripened in the fall, we would leave a few on the ground for the deer. A little at a time, we would leave the apples closer to the house. The deer would eat the apples, then graze on grass closer to us. We were not so quiet as we had been when we first saw the deer, yet he did not seem to be afraid of us. He would

come up and eat in the grove across the road from the house, even when we were in the front yard. I wish I could say that he finally came up and ate out of our hands, but that isn't so.

The white deer came to our meadow regularly, both winter and summer, for about three years. We all thought he was very special.

The last time Grandpa and I saw the deer was one Christmas Eve. We were standing on the front porch, looking out toward the orchard. About three inches of snow had fallen during the day, and now, at dusk, the flakes had changed into large lazy fluffs as big as quarters. All the branches of the trees were weighted down with heavy, white snow. Our valley looked like a huge Christmas card. Suddenly, the white deer came walking through the gate at the end of the meadow. Following him, in single file, were six doe, their gray winter coats making a sharp contrast with the white deer and the snow.

Unhurried, unafraid, they started across the meadow. Halfway across, they all stopped and looked up our

way. The white deer held his antlers high, and the doe stood erect, as if in a pose. Grandpa and I hardly dared to breathe; we had never seen such a majestic sight. Then, still in single file, the deer slowly moved away into the forest above grandpa's workshop. It seemed they walked with a purpose.

Spellbound, we watched until the snowflakes covered the deer's tracks. finally, I turned to Grandpa and whispered, "Do you suppose they are on their way to pull a sleigh tonight?"

Grandpa put his arm around my shoulders and hugged me close. "Who knows?" he said, a twinkle in his eyes. "Who knows?" Δ

Here are five quick and easy craft projects

By Jan Cook

I've always found that crafts are more fun if they're quick and easy. Here are five that look a lot harder than they are.

Spruce up a kid's room

What you'll need:

Paint
Wooden furring strips
Wooden shelf (a few feet shorter than the length of the wall) and hardware to mount it
One roll of white picket fence border (a bit longer than the wall)
Hammer and nails
Two silk vines (as long as the shelf)

Measure and mark three feet down from the ceiling. Draw a line the length of the wall at these marks. Apply masking tape just below the line and paint the area from the line to the ceiling. Paint the furring strips and the shelf the same color.

Install the shelf along the line, centered on the wall (Fig. 1). Fill in the rest of the wall beyond the ends of the shelf, by nailing two furring strips to the studs, one along the line even with the shelving, the other about eight inches above it.

Figure 1

Align the bottom of the fencing starting at the left corner of the wall about six inches below the bottom furring strip. You'll need help for this. As one person stretches the fencing along the wall, the other person nails

Figure 2

the pickets to the furring strips, top and bottom. When you reach the shelf, the fencing will wrap out and around the front of the shelf, and you'll continue nailing (into the shelf now) along the lower line (Fig. 2). Having the pickets nailed into the furring strips (top and bottom) at the ends is important to provide stability, since only the bottoms of the pickets are nailed to the shelf. Weave the vines through the pickets and add furry friends (Fig. 3).

Figure 3

I did this in a kid's room to contain stuffed animals. For a kitchen or guest room, you may want to use a color with less contrast, such as pale yellow on a white wall, and put potted plants on the shelf in place of the animals. White felt or painted clouds add to the garden effect.

Christmas angels

Once you get all your supplies organized (a very difficult task for me),

this project takes about 15 minutes. I prefer the ivory lace, but I've made these in pale blue, pure white, and peach. A good source for inexpensive lace is your local thrift store. I bought a wedding dress recently that only had a small red stain (pasta sauce) on the bodice for only $7.50. I got several yards of usable satin and lace from the skirt for many dollars less than I could have bought it in a fabric store.

What you'll need:

White muslin, cut in a 12-inch circle
Batting
White lace
Three-inch, wire edged, gold ribbon or paper twist
Flexible gold trim
Glue gun

Place a wad of batting in the center of the muslin circle. Close the fabric around it and stitch through (or secure with yarn or a rubber band) to form the head. Wrap the lace trim around the neck to make the body. Cut a length (18-24 inches) of the flexible gold trim. Tie a knot in the center; this will form the hanging loop. Cut a 12-14 inch length of the ribbon or paper twist. Overlap the ends, and pinch in the center to make a bow (Fig. 4). Keeping the hanging loop and bow (these will form the wings) in

Figure 4

the center back, tie the ends of the flexible gold trim around the angel's neck and tie into a bow (Fig. 5) to secure the lace wrap. Shape the wire-edged ribbon into wings.

To make the halo, use the same flexible gold trim and wrap twice around a small bottle or bottle cap (approximately 1 to 1¹/₂ inches diameter). Apply hot glue to the trim to keep it in this shape, being careful not to get it on the form itself, or you won't be able to get it off. Place the halo on the angel's head and secure with hot glue

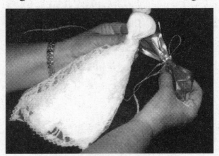

Figure 5

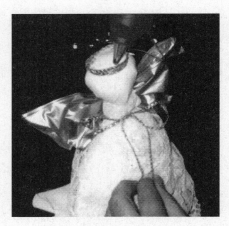

Figure 6

Figure 7

(Fig. 6). Figure 7 shows a basket of angels using iridescent twist ties for wings.

Painting with vegetables

You've heard of potato printing, where you carve a design in a potato, dip it in paint, and stamp it on paper or fabric. Well, this is much easier and a lot more fun. Finally, kids can make gifts for their parents that they'll actually use.

What you'll need:

Celery
Green pepper
Fabric paint: yellow, pink, lavender, white, etc.
Black paint or permanent laundry marker for outlines
Solid color place mats and/or T-shirt with shirt board
Rubber bands

If your place mats or shirt are new, wash and dry them first to remove any sizing.

Cut the celery in half and secure both pieces tightly with rubber bands. Slice off just the tips of both ends of the green pepper. These will form large and small flowers for the place mats.

Make sure you use fabric paint or add fabric medium if you use acrylic paints, to maintain flexibility. Acrylic paint used without fabric medium will be very stiff and uncomfortable.

Put dabs of paint on a paper plate to dip the vegetables in. Make sure all cut surfaces are thoroughly covered with the paint and blot excess on a paper towel. Press celery (or pepper) firmly on fabric (Fig. 8). Repeat as necessary to complete your design. Don't be afraid to mix colors. You can add glitter, too. Allow to dry. Figure 9 shows placemats painted with green pepper flowers.

Use black paint or permanent laundry marker to outline or emphasize flower petals (Fig.10). Draw or paint on some leaves if you like. I tried using real leaves on my test project,

Figure 8

Figure 9

Figure 10

but they don't work well. Veggies with hard edges turn out much better.

Always heat-set painted fabric by putting the items in a hot dryer for 10-15 minutes, or use a pressing cloth and press with a medium-hot iron. Avoid washing the project for 72 hours.

An easy bean-bag toss

I came up with this not-so-original idea for this game when I realized we hadn't planned any for my granddaughter's birthday party. I taped a couple of boxes together, cut a few holes, and whipped up some bean bags. The kids loved it and played with it for days afterward until it fell apart after getting rained on. For a longer-lasting toy, try making this out of plywood. Since this article deals with making things quickly and easily,

Figure 11

these directions are for the cardboard version.

What you'll need:

Two good-sized cardboard boxes
Duct tape
Paint
Knife
Old socks
Beans

Tape the boxes together to make a big target. Paint the outside. In Figure 11, Kevin and Ian are using the left-over turquoise from the kid's room project, but any color will do. Cut holes and paint around them in a contrasting color. I've used both faces and simple lines. Assign values if you like. The large holes are easier to score and should have a smaller value than the smaller holes.

Elissa holds a bean bag made with beans knotted into one of her stray socks (Fig. 12). Easy to make, and

Figure 12

easy to replace. But remember, if these bean bags get left out in the rain, they'll sprout!

Re-usable gift bag

I know, I know, all gift bags are re-usable, but the paper ones deteriorate quickly and are ridiculously expensive. What makes this cloth gift bag unique is its matching tag. This bag is 12x18, but you can make them in all sizes. Carry some in your purse when you go shopping, and you'll have your gift wrapped in less time than it takes the salesperson to ring it up.

What you'll need:

Fabric
Ribbon
Lightweight paper plate
Heat n' bond or similar bonding material
Sewing machine
Tissue paper

Cut a strip of fabric to the size you want. This one is 12x36. Match the short ends and sew the long sides together (right sides together) (Fig. 13). Turn the open edge over to form a hem and pin in place. In the center front of the hem, mark locations for two buttonholes about 1/2" to 1" apart. Make sure you only make them in the front of the hem area and not through both layers of fabric. The pull-tie ribbon will be run through here. Plastic paint can also be used in place of stitching around the buttonhole. Sew the hem in place. Insert the ribbon through one buttonhole, through the hem, and out the other buttonhole.

To make the tag, cut a square from a lightweight paper plate. Fold the paper in half to make a sharp crease before you bond it to the fabric, so it will open and close easily. Cut a square of heat n' bond the same size as the paper. Cut a piece of the fabric a little larger. With your iron, bond the pieces together as shown in Figure 14. Punch a hole in the corner of the folded edge and attach to the ribbon. Add the gift

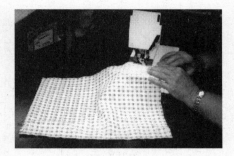

Figure 13

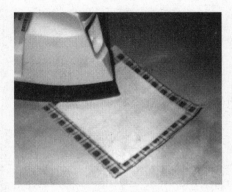

Figure 14

Figure 15

and the tissue paper, and you're done (Fig. 15). Δ

> *I shall tell you a great secret, my friend. Do not wait for the last judgment. It takes place every day.*
> Albert Camus
> 1913-1960

I heat my house by burning *corn*

By Judith W. Monroe

As I write this, it is fall in New England. If you burn wood, you are probably well along with the annual chores of chopping, splitting, and stacking. Back in the spring, you had your chimney cleaned of creosote buildup (or if you have no fear of heights, you climbed up on the roof to do the job yourself). Around that time, you might have walked the woodlot picking the right trees to drop for your next year's winter wood supply, and then the song of the chain saw was heard in the land. In the absence of a woodlot, you consulted the newspaper or a wood-burning neighbor to find seasoned firewood for sale at the best price. Any woodstove owner knows this routine well. It seems a fair exchange for the fire that warms your home during the coldest, darkest months of winter.

Or is it? Even you, who secretly believe your stove is the best woodburner of them all, have occasional misgivings. There was that October two years ago when an early sleet storm froze the uncovered woodpile into one great ice cube. How long was it before you could get to that wood? Or the cold night in February when the green logs bubbled and steamed inside the firebox, giving off the meager warmth of a lighted match. The farmer who delivered your wood swore that it had been drying at least two years. It seems he meant two months. And what about the worst scenario: that time when black ooze spilled down along the chimney, a warning of an impending fire. You've only had that kind of creosote buildup once, but it gave you chills no fire can warm.

With all your reservations, you have remained loyal to wood heat. After all, the other options do not stand up in comparison. Electric heat is incredibly expensive, and oil is not far behind. Natural gas would be nice, but it is not piped in to where you live, and bottled gas is more expensive than wood. A kerosene space heater that warms only its immediate area is not a consideration. You continue to stoke up the fire.

Still, thoughts rankle. There is the interminable nuisance of cleaning out the ashes. For every bucket that is carried outside, a fine dust remains in the air and on surfaces inside the house. Spiders build slovenly webs that capture this dust, giving certain corners in the living room an Addams Family look. Far more unsettling is the fact that any friend or relative who has emphysema, allergies, or asthma does not feel totally comfortable visiting in your home for any length of time.

Less vital, yet still annoying, are the problems of dry air and static electricity. No amount of boiling water on top of the stove brings the humidity up to a healthy 30-40%. Your skin is constantly dry. Some of your furniture shows signs of coming unglued. The dining room table wobbles dangerously. If you own a computer, you must remind yourself to touch the anti-static pad before you put your hands on the keyboard. To forget could mean wiping out the memory.

Heating with corn

For all of these grievances, big and small, there is apparently no ready answer. Until now. In the past ten years, there has been a revival of a heating method so obviously efficient that it is remarkable how few people know of it: using corn for fuel. A corn stove does not burn stalks or left-over cobs. It burns kernels, less than a handful at a time. No, the corn doesn't snap, crackle, or pop. (One of the things people ask is whether the corn pops as it burns.) Corn contains oil and ethanol, which burn cleaner than other fuels, and more cheaply, too. Once you learn how valuable this reasonably priced source of fuel is, you have to wonder why someone in the government has not caught on to the idea of using corn for more of America's energy needs. Given the current political climate in DC, maybe you don't wonder at all (but more about that later).

Corn stoves have been used in the South and Southwest since 1969, when the stove was invented by Carroll Buckner of Arden, NC. The most famous demonstration of the stove was in the Oval Office, installed during the administration of President Jimmy Carter. Even that, as grand a promotion as one could ask for, was evidently not enough to create a rush of orders nationally.

Here in New England where people are likely to mistrust ideas that come "from away," the corn stove might look to some like a southerner's gimmick to use up waste corn. Northerners might also think that any stove used in the South will not really do the job in their cold climate. They would be wrong about that.

In the last few years, corn stoves have been showing up for demonstration at county fairs all over New England. You might have seen one and passed on by, thinking it was just one more wood stove. The only difference, at first glance, is that the fire burning in the glass window is tiny compared to a wood fire. Small as it is, it is capable of producing 60,000 BTUs or more. A lot of heat.

Living with a corn stove

Pour a 50-pound bag of corn into the hopper, light the fire, and go about your business. Unlike the wood stove, after the initial lighting, you do not have to keep an eye on it, poke it, or refill it every hour or so. It burns for at least 24 hours. After filling the hopper of your corn stove, you can go away overnight in the winter without fear of the pipes freezing. To a person who is accustomed to burning wood, that is a luxury.

No more chopping or splitting. No more stacking. No messy ashes. There is no danger of fire, no smoke, no poisonous effluent released into the air, and a minimal amount

of dust settles inside the house. For every bag of corn you burn there is a small "clinker" left in the stove to poke out to the side of the fire box. Later, when it is cool, you crumble the clinker and add it to your compost or save it to sprinkle it on your lawn in the spring. The corn stove is safe to touch on its exterior surfaces. Only the door and its window would cause a burn if touched.

The corn stove does not have to use air from inside the house for combustion, although frequently it is hooked up to an available chimney. Instead, it can draw air for combustion from outside, thus alleviating the usual dryness that afflicts homes heated with wood.

There is no need to clean the chimney each year. In fact, you do not need a chimney. A corn stove can be situated free standing and without a hearth next to an outside wall. A dryer-like vent is all that is required.

Unless you have a woodlot, corn costs less to burn than all of the other fuels except for natural gas. A renewable resource, corn can be replaced in three months' time. Compare that to 30 years replacement time for trees, and 3000 years for oil, and you have one of America's largest and least expensive resources. Yet corn is actually stockpiled by our government, while it struggles endlessly with the politics and the cost of importing oil from other countries. The search for

more sources of coal, oil, and other fuels here in our own land is conducted at great expense to taxpayers, while corn and ethanol are, for the most part, ignored.

There may be other, more personal reasons why Americans have not yet begun to use corn for heat. New Englanders, for instance, are loyal to what warms their nest. They discuss wood stoves with the same fervor they ordinarily save for their cars and trucks. Models are important. Form and function are fascinating. Economy in terms of cords burned is as important as gas burned in miles per gallon. Although we New Englanders are not pioneers when it comes to trying newfangled gadgets, we reverted to wood burning quickly enough when oil prices skyrocketed a few years ago. Wood after all is a time-honored fuel.

Will corn catch on?

So when will we catch on to corn? Soon. At least 500 stoves have been purchased each year over the past three winters in Maine and another 700 in New Hampshire. Vermont is the slowest to acknowledge the advantages of corn heat. As the yarn goes, a Vermonter will not buy an item unless it is recommended by a Vermont native, preferably a neighbor or friend who already has one. That makes it a challenging market to break into.

Changing from one source of fuel to another can be expensive. Not everyone can afford to abandon a current source of fuel, even if corn is cheaper and cleaner. (I paid about $2000 for my corn stove. I've heard there will soon be a model available for half that.) Still, those who are tired of paying high fuel bills owe it to themselves to check on prices and do some figuring:

1. Research into actual heating costs in four north-

eastern U.S. cities found shelled corn fuel to have the lowest cost-per-unit of effective heat over nine other "traditional" heating fuels, from oil to wood pellets. (I got this information from the distributor who sold me my corn stove.)

2. It takes 2.2 bushels of corn to produce one million BTUs of heat, at an average cost of $8.79. Producing that much heat by burning wood costs, on average, $22.07. (You can use other oil-bearing grains, too.)

3. Heat from wood stoves can't be controlled as well, so there is some waste of heat. Corn stoves are designed to feed the burn unit automatically with the exact amount of fuel required to produce heat at a pre-set temperature. There's no waste. And corn stoves are much more efficient than wood stoves, so you get more heat from the fuel.

The downside

For those heating with wood, there are two advantages that corn cannot offer. One is radiant heat. I have heated with both wood and corn for years. Members of our family often stand near the woodstove for the comfort it offers (a habit so ingrained that they are apt to do it even in summer, when the fire is not burning). A corn stove, however, does not raditate that kind of immediate warmth. You can't cook on it, either. Although it can be every bit as attractive to look at as a wood stove, it is not hot to the touch, so the heat from within must be forced out by an electric blower.

The second advantage of wood heat is for emergency power outages. A corn stove needs electricity to operate the auger and to blow the heat into the room. When people purchase a corn stove, they often save their old wood stove as a standby for those occasions when the power fails and for the incredible sub-zero nights when extra heat is needed. Corn stove distributors also offer a 24-hour battery backup in

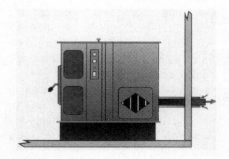

A corn stove doesn't need a chimney: it's vented through the wall.

case of outages, but that costs an extra $300 or more to install, and the battery, of course, has to be re-charged.

If you cherish silence in your home, the hum of the corn stove's motor may be a temporary annoyance. I live in rural Maine, and I had always heated with wood. The mechanical sounds of the corn stove, like the fan on my computer, seemed an intrusion at first. I had forgotten how quickly I became deaf to the sound of furnaces in other houses, as well as the refrigerator and the water heater in my own home.

In addition, like any other appliance or piece of equipment, corn stoves have little idiosyncrasies you learn to live with. You will need to experiment for a few weeks (or longer) to feel comfortable running the stove. Starting up the fire is not that much different from starting a wood stove. You can use paraffin blocks, twigs, or wood chips. Once started, the stove regulates itself. At first, you will need to watch for signs that the corn has actually caught and that the auger is dropping the right amount of corn into the fire box.

With wood, it is a given that there is some dirt and other residue attached to the bark. Corn, on the other hand, should not be dirty. If a piece of stalk, for instance, gets twisted and caught inside the auger, that slows down the fire and can cause the fire to go out. Sometimes there is a buildup of corn in the fire box, and then when more corn drops down, the fire is smoth-

ered. There are similar inconveniences with a wood fire, but on a different scale.

Use a good grade of corn

Buying corn from a farmer or a feed supply store means insisting on clean, dry fuel. Ask about the grade of corn for sale. The higher the quality of the corn, the hotter it will burn. Any grade corn can be burned, but the corn that supplies the most energy as animal feed also burns the hottest. Most suppliers are beginning to understand that there is a growing market for fuel corn. Those who do are glad to supply clean, high quality corn at a good price.

When thinking of storage for corn, think small. You can store two tons of corn in 50-pound bags in one corner of your garage (about six feet high, six feet wide, and two feet deep). That is the usual amount delivered at one time and is enough to heat your house for two or three months.

The corn stoves of today are much more efficient than the one invented in 1969. Even five years ago there were no thermostats for them. Today, thermostats are an option. Five years ago there were probably only two stove models available. There are at least six now. One early model, the one owned by the author, could be mistaken for a clothes dryer.

Occasionally, because our stove is attached to the chimney, on a day when we turn the corn stove down low, we notice the faint but sweet perfume of cooking corn in the air outside. This is in conspicuous contrast to the smoke billowing from a neighbor's chimney. Our corn stove, homely as it is, has won our allegiance hands down.

(Judith Monroe lives on a Maine mountain at the edge of a 600 acre wood. She buys her corn from a farmer in a nearby town and burns wood from her own land. She writes poetry and fiction, and is the author of two books about life on a Maine island where she lives in the summer.) Δ

Save time and money, and get that custom look, with hinges you make yourself

By Rev. J.D. Hooker

Many times rural folks get involved in a project that has to be finished right away but find themselves running short of time, money, material, or all three. So they end up with something that's sort of "temporarily" cobbled together. This temporary fix often remains in place until it breaks or falls apart, and needs to be totally redone.

A lot of these times, there really isn't any other alternative, and a little ingenuity and some baling wire can usually fix just about anything. At least temporarily. Believe me, there's a lot of truth to the old saying that "Without American ingenuity, and lots of baling wire, most of the world would starve." Other times, though, especially when it comes to things like simple hardware, it's really not difficult to come up with a reliable and permanent solution.

I realize that lots of simple things, like metal strap hinges, aren't very expensive. Almost everyone can come by the necessary cash to purchase a pair if they're really needed. For a lot

*Notch the door frame
and insert the hinge piece.*

of us, though, it's simply not worth the extra ten bucks in gasoline to run into town for a set of two dollar hinges. Other folks simply can't give up the time for that trip into town, without being forced to postpone completing the project completely. Still others find the clean, simple lines of some kinds of do-it-yourself hardware visually pleasing and its production satisfying.

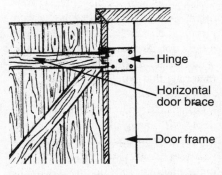

*Wooden hinge shown with door open.
The hinge is let into the door frame.*

Me? I'm one of those people who almost never seems to wind up having time and money both at once. I mean, it's always seemed pretty easy for me to end up with enough of one or the other, but all too rarely both at once. So I've gotten to be pretty good at putting things together while avoiding most of those extra trips to town.

From what I've seen, hinges are one thing where most folks will end up skimping by at first. I've seen a great many gates hung on a couple of loops of rope or wire; pieces of leather, or webbing straps, tacked on to swing chicken coop doors; lids that just sit on top, rather than hinging open; and so forth. I'm sure you have seen many of these and other such jury-rigged "get-bys."

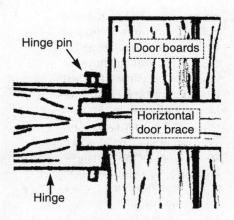

Closeup view of wooden hinge

However, like many other folks, I've found producing strong, not-bad-looking hinges, as needed, to be a pretty quick and easy undertaking. And these home-made hinges often add a nice custom-built look to a project.

Wooden hinges

My own first experience with making hinges involved building and hanging a Dutch door for an outbuilding. This solution turned out to be so sturdy, simple, and nice looking that with occasional modifications, I've adopted this method as my favorite way of hanging most doors.

Fashioning this type of hinge is simplicity itself, especially if you're putting together one of those simple and quaintly attractive cross-buck doors. Just allow the horizontal wood-

Bent metal hinge

en braces of the door to extend a couple of inches beyond the door's edge on the hinge side. Notch these cross braces as shown. Then cut mating notches in a similar piece of wood to form the other half of the hinge. Fit the hinge together and drill a hole with a diameter equal to half the thickness of the wood through both pieces (3/4" hole for 1 1/2" lumber, 3/8" hole for 3/4" lumber, etc.). Insert a slightly loose-fitting dowel for a trial fit.

Next, use a rasp to round off all the edges, and sort of smooth things up, until the hinge works freely. This usually requires the hinge to be assembled and disassembled through several trial runs, until everything is finally just right. Now you can sand everything smooth and apply your choice of finish. Once the finish has dried, hang your door and step back to admire your ingenious handiwork.

Gusset hinges

I've found gusset hinges to be handy for smaller items, like woodbox lids, cabinet doors, and chest or tool box lids. It's even easier to make.

Just cut a triangular gusset from metal, hardwood, or plywood, drill three holes, and attach with screws, as shown. That's it, you're done.

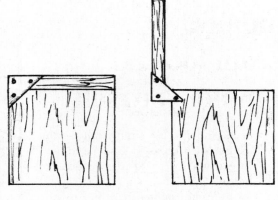

Gusset hinge

For lightweight items, gussets cut from galvanized flashing material will work fine. With heavier projects, or where plenty of strength is required, cut the gussets from 1/4" to 3/4" plywood, or even from plate steel. I have often used a torch to cut gussets from pieces of broken leaf springs, to use as hinges for larger tool boxes. I'm sure you can think of many other scrap materials that would work as well for your own needs.

Using this type of hinge, the lid (or door) will swing clear of the box (or cabinet) when opened, and will hold itself open as well. However, this hinge places a limit on how far the lid (or door) can travel. So this type of hinge is terrific for some applications, but not so great for others. It all depends on the requirements of each project.

Bent metal hinges

With many types of simple projects, like a lid for a rabbit hutch, good looks aren't that important, but reliability is. In these cases I've often found that very simple hinges fashioned from bent pieces of light metal (cut from tin cans, old license plates, or similar scrap), and any sort of wooden or metal rod to be ideal. Simply use tin snips to cut strips of the required size from whatever light-gauge metal you have available. Bend these strips over the rod you'll be using for the hinge pin. Then tack the

strips in place along the edges of the boards you'll be hinging together, as shown. Shove your hinge pin into place, and you're finished.

Kept painted, as protection from the elements, these simple scrap metal hinges will normally last for many years.

For the same kinds of uses, a row of fence staples can be driven into the edge of each board, with a dowel, long bolt, or other rod pushed into place as a hinge pin. This is another type of "instant hinge" for lighter-duty uses, where good looks aren't overly important. Should you wish to adapt either of these last two hinges for longer term outdoor use, tack a piece of scrap inner tube over the hinged area, to make a fairly watertight joint.

Temporary hinges

Finally, for applications that are intended for only short-term use, I've got a couple of temporary hinges you might find pretty handy. Both of these cobbled-together hinges were formerly used as hinges on salt box lids, where the corrosive action of the salt would waste away metal hinges. Ready-made hinges were pretty expensive in those times, so these cheap, easily-replaced hinges were popular.

Cotter pin hinge

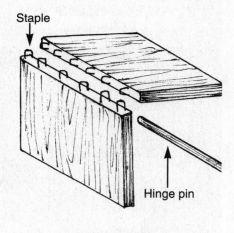

Staple hinge

Double staple hinge

For the first of these methods, just drive a fence staple into the edge of one piece of wood. Then drive a second staple through that first one into the other piece of wood to form a hinge. Eventually the staples will work loose, or they'll corrode if exposed to wet weather, salt, etc. But for short-term use, they're quick, simple, really inexpensive, and they work well enough.

The second method for fashioning temporary hinges is a variation of this method, but the staples are replaced by cotter pins. Just drill appropriately sized holes in the edges of the boards, link the cotter pins together, and drive them into place. If you place a tiny wooden wedge between the "legs" of each cotter pin before driving them in, they will hold better. Again, these are cheap, quick, and simple, but they're only suitable as temporary solutions.

So, whether you've decided to build a fancy wooden front door for your house, where a finely finished set of hardwood hinges would add that extra something, or you're tacking together a temporary home for a garter snake or other critter that one of your kids is bent on adopting, maybe you'll find one of these simple, home-made hinges to be just what you need. Why not *plan* on using one of these hinges on your next project. It's satisfying to realize that even the hardware resulted from your own skills and efforts. Δ

Listening to shortwave radio broadcasts from around the world is informative and fun

By Charles A. Sanders

The voice from the radio was clear, yet was speaking in an unknown language. Tuning in another frequency brought the staccato dits and dashes of a Morse code transmission. A little more tuning brought in an understandable yet noticeably foreign English broadcast.

If you can recall the first shortwave radio broadcast you ever heard, you may remember it as a crackling voice or melody, with the signal fading or growing in strength. The fact that these signals were coming from far around the world was amazing, to say the least.

One does not have to be a *ham*, or amateur radio operator, to enjoy tuning the airwaves. An amateur radio license is required only for transmitting on the air. As a listener, you are free to tune in to your heart's content. Long distance monitoring or "DXing" is not only an interesting pastime, it can be an efficient method of acquiring information not available elsewhere.

Unlike normal AM or FM radio broadcasts, shortwave radio depends upon the atmospheric layers surrounding the earth to "go the distance." These radio waves radiate from their transmission point, then actually "skip" off of the ionosphere, then back to earth to some point far distant from where they originate. The radio signal

may actually skip several times before it loses its strength. This characteristic is what enables you to glimpse life halfway around the world, via your radio.

A good, dependable radio receiver is a definite asset for monitoring these distant broadcasts. For the homesteader, or other remote location, or the casual listener, shortwave radio listen-

ing can be a very enjoyable and informative pastime. During normal times, dozens of entertaining broadcasts may be picked up on just about any evening. In emergencies or during events of international significance, these radios can help the listener monitor important events as they develop, often right where they are occurring in the world.

What's out there

There are identifiable shortwave broadcast stations in dozens and dozens of countries around the world. Some of the big "powerhouse" stations include broadcasters such as the Voice of America, the BBC World Service, Radio Canada International, Radio Australia, Radio Netherlands, Swiss Radio International, Deutsche Welle, Radio Moscow International, Radio Japan. Radio South Africa, The Voice of Free China, and many others. One thing you will learn about foreign broadcasts is that not everyone is exactly sympathetic to the United States.

Many religious broadcast networks use the shortwave frequencies. They broadcast their particular messages along with music, commentary, etc., all over the world, and seem to have a very large following. One of the largest and best of these broadcasters is HCJB in Quito, Ecuador. Others include WRNO, WCCR, WYFR Family Radio, and WHRI.

Other broadcasters direct their programming to "patriotic" groups and individuals. There are programs describing how to deal with the predicted economic collapse, how to buy gold and silver, acquiring various items for a survivalist's stores, and other subjects. Their news coverage and commentary convey a noticeably "conservative" stance. On the other hand, at least one broadcast station works to counter these with their own "liberal" broadcasts. Even the short-wave frequencies are not without some controversy and name-calling.

Scheduled broadcasts in English are made from almost every international station. Broadcast schedules can be obtained from most of the international stations, particularly the larger ones. Most of these broadcasters include their mailing addresses in their pro-gramming. Some stations even offer on-air language instruction as a part of their programming

As I mentioned, it is possible to lis-ten to events of international impor-tance as they develop, from where they develop. For example, back when Operation Desert Storm began, we had two television sets (tuned to two different networks) and our shortwave radio turned on. The shortwave was tuned to the British Broadcasting Company (BBC). After a while, we pretty well abandoned the network TV coverage in favor of the more com-plete shortwave coverage.

Universal Coordinated Time

One thing which you will quickly learn is that shortwave programming is set up on Universal Coordinated Time (UCT). UCT is the time at the *zero* or *reference meridian* on the globe. UCT was formerly referred to as "Greenwich Mean Time (GMT). GMT refers to the fact that the refer-ence meridian passes through Greenwich, England.

Time changes one hour with each change of 15 in longitude. EST, CST, MST, and PST are 5, 6, 7, and 8 hours "earlier" than the time at the reference meridian. They generally correspond to the 75th, 90th, 105th, and 120th meridians.

The table on this page is useful in computing listening times for short-wave radio broadcasts originating from countries around the world.

Buying your radio

Now that you've decided that you want to tune in the world, which radio do you want to buy?

A good quality portable radio can do double duty, serving as your AM-FM receiver to receive regular commercial radio broadcasts, as well as picking up shortwave broadcasts. The small portable set which I have does just that. I listen to shortwave broadcasts from around the world in the evening, and the radio wakes me up to the local stereo FM country station in the morn-ing. Select a radio that covers the por-tion of the radio spectrum in which you are interested. Fortunately, this is not as difficult as it sounds. Most portable DX radios on the market today include the standard AM-FM broadcast bands. Some may also offer some combination of bands to tune in aircraft, TV, weather, or police.

I recommend picking up a copy of the current Passport To World Band Radio, even prior to purchasing your radio. Not only will the book provide information on tuning in practically every international shortwave station in the world, it also contains informa-tion on most of the popular shortwave receivers available, all "star" rated by the editors. This book helped me to decide on the model which I pur-chased to replace my old radio. Another attractive feature of this guide is the hour-by-hour guide to what you can find across the bands.

Converting Universal Coordinated Time (UCT) to US times

EST	UCT	CST	MST	UCT	PST
1900	0000*	1800	1700	0000*	1600
2000	0100	1900	1800	0100	1700
2100	0200	2000	1900	0200	1800
2200	0300	2100	2000	0300	1900
2300	0400	2200	2100	0400	2000
0000*	0500	2300	2200	0500	2100
0100	0600	0000*	2300	0600	2200
0200	0700	0100	0000*	0700	2300
0300	0800	0200	0100	0800	0000*
0400	0900	0300	0200	0900	0100
0500	1000	0400	0300	1000	0200
0600	1100	0500	0400	1100	0300
0700	1200	0600	0500	1200	0400
0800	1300	0700	0600	1300	0500
0900	1400	0800	0700	1400	0600
1000	1500	0900	0800	1500	0700
1100	1600	1000	0900	1600	0800
1200	1700	1100	1000	1700	0900
1300	1800	1200	1100	1800	1000
1400	1900	1300	1200	1900	1100
1500	2000	1400	1300	2000	1200
1600	2100	1500	1400	2100	1300
1700	2200	1600	1500	2200	1400
1800	2300	1700	1600	2300	1500

* Or 2400. 2400 is associated with the date of the day that is ending, 0000 with the day just beginning.

Another book which you will find useful is the World Radio & TV Handbook. This guide offers information such as location maps, addresses of many broadcast stations, including standard AM-FM stations. As suggested by the title, it also provides information on television broadcasters throughout the world and satellite broadcasts.

Since most of us are not dripping with money, price will likely be an important factor in selecting your radio. However, quality enters into the equation, too. You do not need to sink a fortune into your new radio, but you will want to stay away from the really cheap ones.

For a world-band receiver, $50 to $75 is not going to buy much of a radio. You will be able to pick up most of the big power broadcasters, but anything beyond that will be more difficult and unpredictable. These less expensive radios lack the tuning sensitivity and frequency selectability that higher quality models have.

A decent portable world-band receiver can be purchased for between $175 and $400. With the higher prices, you might expect more and better features, and in most cases this is true. The Grundig YB-400 I have costs around $200 and is doing a very nice job. It has many features of larger and more expensive radios. As I occasionally travel in my work, its compact size permits me to take it along to use for entertainment, information, and wake-up duty.

One feature you should definitely look for in a radio is digital tuning. These sets are much more sensitive and accurate than the older analog or "slide rule" type tuners. It is simply much easier to tune in a station with one of these sets.

Sangean, Sony, Radio Shack, and Grundig are among the more popular manufacturers of compact receivers. They have models for just about any budget.

Drake, Kenwood, JRC, Yaesu, and others offer larger countertop radios with more features, but these will require a much greater investment. They are equipped with more sensitive tuning, more and better noise filters, and other features which make them attractive to the more serious listener. It is possible to tie up hundreds or even thousands of dollars on one of these sets.

For my money, I selected the Grundig Yachtboy 400. This radio offers standard AM radio, FM stereo, sideband capabilities to better monitor "ham" operators, and good coverage of all of the shortwave bands. It is portable, operable from either batteries or AC/DC, and has an external antenna jack as well as a good telescoping antenna. It includes an ear phone, a padded case, and an external portable reel-type long wire antenna.

External antennas

Speaking of antennas, you should note that in almost every case, shortwave reception will be substantially improved if you can attach an external antenna to your set. The familiar telescoping antennas which are standard equipment on most portable radios will do a very good job, but a simple external antenna can do a lot to improve your reception. The antenna doesn't need to be anything fancy. As long as you have an external antenna jack on your radio, any long length of light wire will serve as your shortwave signal grabber. Merely looping the wire along the baseboard in a room will work. So will running the wire out a window and out to a tree, bush, or post. An outside antenna will usually work a little better in improving reception, due to the fact that you are removing it from the network of electrical devices, wiring, plumbing, and metal structural members which can contribute to signal interference.

A simple way to convince yourself of the value of an external antenna is to tune in a fairly good shortwave station with the external antenna attached. Then unplug the external antenna, and you will probably hear the radio signal nearly or completely disappear.

There is one thing to remember about using an outside antenna, though. If it is suspended much above the ground, then **be sure to have a lightning arrestor hooked into the antenna** between the antenna and the radio. This simple device will help to prevent electrical disasters.

Regardless of the radio you decide to purchase, you will find a whole new world of music, news, and information waiting right at your fingertips. Those long winter evenings will become a lot more interesting as you sit with a hot cup, tuning the airwaves.

Suppliers

Listed below are a few suppliers of high-quality radios, accessories, guidebooks, and other items of interest to DXers. This is not a complete list by any means, but should get the new listener started.

Gilfer Shortwave
52 Park Avenue
Park Ridge, NJ 07656
Information: 201-391-7887
Orders: 800-GILFER-1
Fax: 201-391-7433

ACE Communications
10707 E. 106th St.
Fishers, IN 46038
800-445-7717 (24 hr.)

Electronic Equipment Bank
323 Mill St.
Vienna, VA 22130
Technical information:
 703-938-3350
Orders: 800-368-3270
Fax: 703-938-6911

Universal Radio
6830 Americana Pkwy.
Reynoldsburg, OH 43068-4113
Information: 614-866-4267
Orders: 800-431-3939
Fax: 614-866-2339 (24 hr.) Δ

These chocolate treats make great gifts and delicious holiday desserts

By Tanya Kelley

Just in case the world comes to an end, I plan on keeping plenty of chocolate on hand in my food storage. That is, if I can keep out of it. The trouble is, aside from just eating plain chocolate, there are too many delicious ways to use chocolate.

Although I have met *one* person who doesn't like chocolate, it's a pretty safe bet that holiday gifts of chocolate will be a hit. Fortunately they also meet my other requirements for gifts: inexpensive and quick to make. One size fits all, and no one will complain if you give everyone their own box of chocolates. No more struggling to find something for the person who has everything. And best of all, your recipient will need more again next year.

Here are a few of my favorites for gift giving as well as holiday entertaining. The cookies and candies below all keep well and ship well. Packaged in a box, they make a gift that few can resist.

Dark moons

These buttery cookies will melt in your mouth. Makes three dozen.

---

1 cup butter (not margarine)
1 cup confectioner's sugar
2 teaspoons vanilla
1 1/2 cup flour
1/2 teaspoon baking soda
1 cup of rolled oats
1 7-ounce chocolate bar, milk or dark chocolate

Cream butter and sugar until fluffy. Add vanilla and rolled oats. Sift flour and baking soda together and add to mix. Mix thoroughly. Shape dough in a two-inch roll and chill in

Chocolate cheesecake

Chocolate raspberry torte

refrigerator for one hour. Slice in 1/4" slices. Bake on an ungreased cookie sheet at 325° for 25 minutes, until the cookies are lightly browned. When the cookies are cool, melt the chocolate until it can be stirred smooth. Dip the side of each cookie in the chocolate, rotating it to make the crescent moon shape.

Milk chocolate truffles

Use either chocolate chips or chocolate bars for this rich candy. Dark chocolate can be substituted for the outer coating if desired. Makes 15 to 20 candies.

---

12 ounces milk chocolate (divide in half)
2 tablespoons butter
1/4 cup whipping cream
1 Tablespoon shortening
Sprinkles or finely chopped nuts

Melt half of chocolate and butter until it stirs smoothly. Stir in whipping cream. Refrigerate 30 minutes until stiff enough to form into balls. Freeze balls 30 minutes. Heat shortening, adding remaining chocolate until melted. Using a spoon, dip frozen balls in the melted coating until covered. Place on wax paper. Sprinkle tops with nuts or sprinkles before chocolate hardens. Chill in refrigerator for 10 minutes.

Turtles

Quick and easy. Makes 30 candies.

> 4 ounces shelled peanuts (preferably jumbo)
> 3-ounce milk chocolate bar
> 30 caramel candies

Preheat oven to 300°. Unwrap candies and place on buttered cookie sheet. Place in oven, bake for eight minutes, until caramels are soft but not runny. Push two peanuts in center and five around the outside of the caramel to make legs and head. Let cool. Melt chocolate. Spoon chocolate on top of caramels to make a "shell." Refrigerate for 30 minutes.

Chocolate caramel

Chewy and chocolatey. Makes 81 candies.

> 1 cup butter
> 2¼ cups brown sugar
> pinch of salt
> 1 cup light corn syrup
> 15 ounces sweetened condensed milk
> 1 teaspoon vanilla
> 1-2 ounces unsweetened chocolate
>   (depending on preference)

Butter a 9x9 pan. In a saucepan, melt butter. Stir in sugar, salt, and corn syrup. Slowly stir in the milk. Add chocolate. Cook over medium heat, stirring constantly, until candle thermometer reads 245°, when a small spoonful of the mixture dropped in a glass of cold water will form a firm ball. (Test with fresh water each time.) Cook for 12 to 15 min-

Truffles and chocolate caramels

Dark moons and turtles

utes. Remove from heat and stir in vanilla. Pour into square pan. When cool, cut into one-inch squares.

The desserts below are perfect for holiday get-togethers. The ingredients might look expensive, but when compared to store-bought confections, you save a bundle. (After all, you don't have the added expense of all the preservatives!)

Triple chocolate cheesecake

The crust is a little crunchy when cutting, but the rich taste will melt in your mouth. Serves eight.

Crust

> 1½ cups crushed Oreo cookies (about 10 cookies)
> ¼ cup butter
> ½ of a 1½-ounce chocolate bar

Melt butter and chocolate. Stir together until smooth. Mix well with cookie crumbs. Press the mixture on sides and bottom of a nine-inch cake or pie pan. Set aside.

Filling

> 2 eggs
> 8 ounces softened cream cheese
> ½ cup sugar
> ⅛ teaspoon salt
> 1 teaspoon vanilla
> 1½ cups sour cream
> 3 Tablespoons cocoa

Preheat oven to 375°. Beat all ingredients together until smooth. Pour into crust. Bake for 35 minutes. Chill before serving. If desired, drizzle top with melted chocolate or any remaining cookie crumbs. Top with whipped cream.

Raspberry chocolate torte

It only *looks* like you spent days making it! Serves 8 to 12.

Cake

```
1 devil's food cake mix
butter for cake
```

Filling

```
2 cups raspberries or pitted cherries (fresh or frozen)
2 cups sugar
1 cup water
3 cups whipping cream, whipped
1/2 cup confectioner's sugar
1/2 teaspoon vanilla
1   11/2-ounce milk chocolate bar, shaved into curls
    (use a potato peeler)
Maraschino cherries for garnish
```

Mix cake as directed on box, except replace the oil with the same amount of butter. Bake in a greased (not floured) nine-inch round pan according to directions. Let cool.

Mix sugar and water in a saucepan. Bring to a boil and add fruit. Boil for three minutes. If using raspberries, you might want to strain the syrup to remove any seeds.

Whip whipping cream on High until stiff. Add sifted confectioner's sugar and vanilla. Mix in.

Cut each cake layer into two layers (see * below), to make four layers. Place one layer, cut side up, on serving tray. Drizzle one-third of syrup mixture on layer. Spread one fourth of the whipped cream on top but not on sides. Place next layer of cake, cut side up, on first layer. Repeat topping with syrup and whipping cream with the next two layers. For remaining layer, place cut side down. Top with whipped cream, shaved chocolate, and cherries.

*A quick and neat way to cut a cake layer is to evenly space four toothpicks around the layer in the middle of the sides. Place a piece of sewing thread around the sides, resting on the toothpicks. Cross the ends of the thread and gently pull. The thread will cut evenly from the sides into the center, splitting the layer in two.

Tips for cooking with chocolate

Chocolate scorches easily, so heat on a very low heat in a thick-bottomed pan or in the oven at a low temperature.

If microwaving chocolate, stir every 15 seconds until melted. Do not overcook.

Do not let water get in the chocolate. The chocolate will harden into a lumpy mess.

To keep melted chocolate from cooling while working, place the container on a heating pad.

You can use any kind of chocolate bar for the treats above, but I prefer Hershey's or Nestle's.

Any of the recipes above can be made using white chocolate in place of the milk chocolate. Δ

A country moment

A serene Copco Lake in northern California.

Custom-crafted toiletries make very special gifts

By Joy Lamb

Aromas and scents wafting from the kitchen during the holidays fill us with nostalgia and hunger and a cozy comfort. Odors emanating from the bathroom usually do not.

Now, don't think of unpleasant odors. Think of luxury and relaxation and exotic places or even why you live in the country. Do you have a smell in mind? Would you like to package the scent and imagery as a gift? How do you wrap up comfort in gift paper with a pretty ribbon on top? One way is to give toilet articles that are personalized. You can make, rather easily and inexpensively, toiletries that convey both luxury and thoughtfulness. Obviously, this is not a panacea, but it is fun and fragrant to make and give aftershave, bath salts, bath oil, cleansing sachets, and essential oils.

Most of these gift products can be made up quickly. The ingredients can often be found already in your home or garden. If you need to purchase ingredients, look in grocery stores, drug stores, health food stores, liquor stores, and bath/aromatherapy shops. The ingredients are all easy to find. Packaging the toilet articles should be just as simple. Buy bottles and jars with interesting shapes and colors, or save food and drink bottles and jars, especially sauce bottles, olive and pickle jars, and vinegar, wine, and beer bottles. Any glass container that you think looks good will most likely work. The most appropriate-sized bottles hold six to ten ounces of liquid. A good jar size is one that holds one to three cups. Clean the container thoroughly and remove any labels. Right after the directions for making each toilet article, there is a discussion of the whats and whys of the ingredients and some packaging ideas. Keep in mind, these gifts should be fun to make and fun to receive.

The ingredients used in these toiletry recipes are basic. But before proceeding further, a caution is necessary.

Therefore, *WARNING: Do not take any of these products internally. Also, if a rash or any undesirable effect occurs, discontinue use immediately.*

We all know that making aftershave takes sophisticated chemistry and that it is full of unpronounceable secret compounds. Well, don't we? After all, we have read the ingredients list on the bottle. But guess what: Aftershave is basically alcohol. Adding astringents or moisturizers makes it...well...comfortable, but is hardly rocket science. Adding a scent makes it smell nice and lets you individualize it for the wearer. The ingredients can all be purchased readily and locally. High tech, chemistry lab equipment is not needed, so get out a glass measuring cup and a plastic stir stick or small spoon. This simple equipment and some very available ingredients plus a pretty bottle to hold the aftershave is all you need to make a delightful gift for a lucky man.

Each of the following recipes makes six to eight ounces of aftershave. The names are whimsical, and you can personalize them just as you can adapt the ingredients to fit the tastes of the wearer. The process for making aftershave is to measure and pour the ingredients into a glass container and mix them up. For instance, using a glass measuring cup, pour into it each ingredient from one of the recipes below. Stir the mixture and then pour it into a glass container for storage and cap or cork it. Then add a label.

Pirate Aftershave

The rum and citrus scents give it a reckless, Caribbean flair.

1/2 cup vodka
2 Tablespoons rum
3-4 drops oil of bergamot

Spicy Aftershave

The cinnamon scent is very manly.

1/2 cup 99% isopropyl alcohol
1/2 cup distilled water
3-4 drops oil of bergamot
5-6 drops oil of cinnamon

At Home Aftershave

Soothing for sensitive skin.

1/4 cup vodka
1/4 cup witch hazel
2 Tablespoons distilled water
1 teaspoon camphor spirit (USP grade)

Outdoorsman Aftershave

Moisturizing and gentle with a woodsy smell.

1/2 cup 99% isopropyl alcohol
1/4 cup witch hazel
2 Tablespoons glycerin
2 Tablespoons distilled water
2-3 drops oil of rosemary (or other essential oil)

After trying some of the above recipes, you will probably want to try some other combinations. Go for it.

About the ingredients

Alcohol: Two of the above recipes use vodka and two use isopropyl alcohol. They are interchangeable. Vodka has a nice feel to it but is more expensive. Most people have no problems using isopropyl, but it does make some people dizzy or sick to the stomach. Be sure to use the 99% isopropyl rather than plain rubbing alcohol, which is 70% and too watery. Vodka and rum are found in liquor stores, isopropyl is found in drug stores or cosmetic sections of grocery or variety stores. It is important to use distilled water because it is pure.

Oil of bergamot is an essential oil made from the rind of the fruit of a tree (citrus bergamia) and is often used in perfumes. The oils of cinnamon and of rosemary are also essential oils. There are lots and lots of essential oils sold in drug stores, health food stores, and bath or aromatherapy shops. Use the ones you like the best. Essential oils have pure and intense scents and are extracted from plant matter. You can make your own. There are directions later in this article.

Witch hazel is found in drug stores or cosmetic sections of grocery stores. It is an astringent, so it helps contract the skin's pores. It works nicely as an additive to aftershave because of this and because it freshens the skin and is a mild local anesthetic that soothes minor cuts.

Glycerin moisturizes and is a by-product from soap making. This sticky liquid is odorless and thick. It is used in many cosmetics. Buy it at drug stores.

Be sure to label the aftershave. Be imaginative in giving it a name. Then list the ingredients in the order of amount of each used, starting with the largest amount first, just like the purchased stuff. Put the date you made it on the label, too. You can purchase gummy labels to write on or labels that work on computer printers. Another idea is to design your own and tie it around the neck of the bottle.

For the bath

A bath duo that makes a wonderfully thoughtful gift for either a woman or a man is bath salts and body oil, because the recipient is encouraged to have a relaxing and indulgent time. Besides being easy, inexpensive, and quick to make, these products are *fun* to make. Experiment with color and scents, making them with the recipient in mind.

The easiest way to mix up bath salts is in a one-quart plastic zip-lock bag. Simply place the ingredients in the bag, expel much of the air, zip-lock the bag, and knead it. Knead by rolling and squeezing, much as you would bread dough. It will take a few minutes to completely distribute the contents and color. The bag can be used as the storage container, or you can pour the contents into a jar with a cap. If you don't wish to use a plastic bag, mix up the salts using a bowl and spoon. Be sure the storage container is airtight. The salts can get crusty or even solid if they take on moisture. Luckily, the salts will still dissolve in water.

Bath salts

2 cups Epsom salts
1/2 cup baking soda or cornstarch
scant 1/4 teaspoon essential oil
food coloring (optional)

Soaking in a warm or hot bath containing Epsom salts is very relaxing. It soothes tired muscles. Epsom salts (magnesium sulfate) can be bought in drug stores and beauty/health care sections of grocery stores. Both baking soda and cornstarch are, among other things, soothing to the skin. They are probably already in your kitchen. Otherwise buy them in the baking section of the grocery store.

Perfume may be used in place of an essential oil. Be creative when matching up the scents and colors. You can mix up one or more batches without the food coloring, then divide it up and make several colors. Layer these colors in a jar for a pleasing visual effect. Do not use more than one scent per package, as you don't know how they will interact. Be sure to label the salts with date and contents and use clever names that indicate the scent. To write directly on the plastic bag, try using a pen that is for labeling freezer packages. It is waterproof and smear-proof. Find it anyplace that sells canning and freezing materials. On the label, include instructions to add a big handful of the bath salts to the bath water as the tub is filling.

You might note that the bath water will be the color of the salts. Keep this in mind when making up the salts. Some people will prefer clear water, which means no added color in the salts. Oil of coconut might be an appropriate scent here. Others will find blue and green relaxing. Pine or lavender essential oils are very nice with these colors. Peppermint scent with red color is invigorating and invokes holiday memories of candy canes. Just hope the user sees the red bath water as funny, not scary.

To make a body oil to go with the bath salts, first find a glass bottle with a cap or cork that holds six to eight ounces of liquid. Recycled sauce bottles with those plastic inserts that allow you to squirt out small amounts work well. The process is simply to combine the oils and, if desired, add a fragrance. Cover the bottle tightly and shake well. That's it.

Body oil

> 1/4 cup each of three or four of the following oils: almond, apricot kernel, avocado, canola, coconut, corn, hazelnut, peach kernel, peanut, olive, safflower, sesame, sunflower, walnut, and wheat germ

A very nice combination for people who love the country is almond, sunflower, and walnut oils. Another winner is almond, avocado, peanut, and sesame oils. The oils used to make body oil are cooking oils and are found in grocery stores. A teaspoon of perfume or essential oil to match the bath salts is a nice touch, but this body oil can stand alone.

A fun and useful bath gift for adults or children is cleansing sachets. They are a use-once-and-toss-away sack that can be used for very dirty hands or to clean the entire body in the bath or shower. Personalize them with your own selection of herbs and essential oils. All the equipment needed is a kitchen grater, a measuring cup, and some small bowls for mixing.

Cleansing sachets

> 1 bar soap (plain)
> 1 1/2 cups oatmeal (regular, not "quick cooking")
> cheesecloth
> cotton string, colored yarn, or colored ribbon (colorfast)

To make these aromatic cleansing sachets, start by cutting the cheesecloth into squares, four inches on a side. If the weave is really loose, double the fabric. The above recipe makes about 45 sacks. Next, grate the bar of soap to make about 1 1/2 cups of flakes. Place soap flakes and oatmeal in a bowl and mix. Divide mixture into three small bowls so that you can add different herbs and scents to each bowl.

To each bowl add:

> 3 Tablespoons dried herbs (leaves rather than ground)
> 3-4 drops essential oil

After adding the herbs and essential oils, mix the contents of each bowl well. Each bowl will make about 15 sachets. Place one Tablespoon of mixture in the center of a cheesecloth square. Bring up the corners and twist. Secure tightly with string, yarn, or ribbon. Be creative, using different colors of yarn and ribbon for each scent.

Oatmeal is a cereal that is soothing and cleansing to the skin and can be bought in a grocery store. The herbs can be purchased, or use some you dried yourself. The same for essential oils: make them or buy them. The following are some suggestions for the herbs and oils to use in the cleansing sachets. They are listed along with fanciful names.

Paul Bunyan Washout: dried sage leaves and oil of rosemary
Sweetheart Clean: dried rosehips and oil of rose
Christmas Scrub: dried peppermint leaves and oil of peppermint
Relax in the Tub: contents of one bag of chamomile tea and oil of lavender

The above recipes use essential oils. They can be purchased in a variety of places. The biggest selection will be at bath shops, tourist shops, and aromatherapy shops. They are pricey at about $4-5 for 9-15 ml. This makes them the most expensive item that you need to make toiletries. However, you only need a few drops for each product.

There are two practical alternatives to buying essential oils. One is to use perfume that you already own in place of the oil. The other is to make your own essential oils using plant material from where you live. The following method is ancient and easy to do. It is called *effleurage* and uses sun heat to extract flower aroma. The only equipment you need is a small glass jar that will hold six to eight ounces of liquid, a measuring cup, and a tea strainer. When finished, you will need a tiny bottle with an airtight cap to store your essential oil.

Effleurage: making an essential oil

fragrant fresh flower petals (examples: gardenia, lavender, lilac, pink carnation, and rose)
light vegetable oil (examples: almond oil, very light olive oil, and sunflower oil)

Place flower petals in the small jar. Pour oil over petals to cover them. Place the jar in a sunny place and let stand for 24 hours. Of course, if your sunny place is outside, bring the jar in at night. Strain the oil into the measuring cup, pressing the petals with your fingers to get as much oil out as possible. Discard the used petals. Pour the oil from the measuring cup back into the jar. Place new, fresh flower petals in the jar, using as many as the oil can cover. Place in the sun for another 24 hours. Repeat this process for four or five days, or until you are satisfied with the scent. Each day you will have less and less oil, because it is impossible to get it all out of the petals. When finished, you will have a tiny amount of essential oil, which can be stabilized for storage by adding a few drops of castor oil, glycerin, or a pinch of orris root powder. Orris root powder is found in kitchen or spice shops.

Besides using essential oils in the toiletries described in this article, they can be used as-is. Simply put a drop on the skin and rub it in for an enchanting aroma. Another idea is to put some drops on dried flowers, leaves, or cones. Pine, cinnamon, and wintergreen are wonderful for the holidays. Δ

A BHM Writer's Profile: R.K. Henderson

Robert Henderson has studied rural history and traditional technologies in many countries. Following several unhealthy years as a public school teacher, he left the ranks of the salaried to become a writer. Today, he specializes in preparing tasty foods from unusual ingredients, and helping others to do the same.

Henderson's articles have appeared in *Backwoods Home* and other magazines. He also writes a colum on linguistics, a vestige of an academic past, for Suite 101.com. Henderson's guide to suburban wild edibles and his first full-length book will be published later this year by Chelsea Green.

In addition to food and cooking, Henderson enjoys and writes about amateur radio, social history, and traditional wooden boats. He currently lives with his wife in Canada.

A BHM Writer's Profile: Sally Denney

Sally Denney lives on a 23-acre farm in Warsaw, Indiana. She has been married to her busband, Randy, for 27 years and is the mother of four children and is the grandmother to Skyler James Boruff.

She enjoys living the country life where every day is different and knowledge is gained from the use of your own two hands.

Protect your land title before you buy

By Don Fallick

No one would buy a car without making sure he had valid title to it, yet many of us are content to spend much more money for land without the same assurance. There are three ways to protect yourself when buying land:

- **you can have the title history researched**
- **you can buy title insurance**
- **you can do a boundary survey**

In some states, one or more of these are required to purchase any land. The rules vary from state to state and according to whether the land is designated as "rural." All three ways make good sense.

A boundary survey

A boundary survey is conducted by a registered land surveyor. He measures the land itself, marking the corners of the parcel according to the "plat"—an official map registered with the county recorder. His corners should be accurate to within an inch or two, depending on the accuracy of the information he has to work with. A modern survey may not agree with one conducted a hundred years ago, or even thirty. Modern equipment is much more accurate. I have seen houses built right across property lines due to the inaccuracy of a century-old survey.

Surveyors work in pairs and charge by the hour, including travel time. In remote, mountainous terrain, it can take hours just to bring "control" to your land from a known position such as a section corner or survey monument. If you can find out who did the most recent nearby survey, you may save yourself a nice piece of change by hiring the same surveyor. If there's no control nearby, he will have to set his own work points from a distant monument, survey them, then work from there. He may need to do this anyway, if he can't see all the property corners from known monuments.

Surveyors keep records of their control points, and they can often re-use them. So it's smart to hire one who has control points on or near your land. If you can find the plats for your area, you'll know who surveyed it last. Surveys more than 20 years old may not be too useful. The markers may be impossible to find, or even missing, and the surveyors may have

retired or even died. But you'll have a better chance dealing with someone who has worked in your local area recently. What seems like a simple survey may turn out to be expensive. But not as expensive as neglecting to get it done.

Boundary disputes

I bought 17 acres of land in Colorado without either a survey or title insurance. My neighbor was a disputatious man who continually threatened to have our boundary surveyed, and warned me that I was going to lose a lot of land when he had it done. Finally, he hired a surveyor. It turned out that I lost about six feet of my driveway and a corner of my garden, while he lost nearly an acre of land, half his barn and five newly planted fruit trees. Since I had no desire to make him tear down his barn, we eventually agreed to trade. He kept his barn, I kept my driveway, and we stayed out of court.

It could have turned out a lot worse. One man I know recently found out that five square feet of his concrete driveway encroaches on his neighbor's land. The neighbor wants him to relocate his driveway, or buy the five square feet—for $5000. In another case I know of, a landowner actually started to build on the wrong lot. He eventually had to remove a full basement and restore the land—a very expensive mistake. But the money lost in a land dispute may by the least of your problems.

A horror story

In the Wasatch Mountains not far from where I live in Utah, there's a beautiful, two-story, log home on a hand-built, stone foundation.

The owner, a retired well-driller, just discovered he doesn't own the land it's sitting on—or any other land, for that matter. I've changed the names, as the case is still in litigation, but the story goes like this: John Doe and his three partners bought five parcels of remote land, intending to sell off the fifth parcel to pay for a community well and water system. When Doe met George Smith, the retired well-driller, he offered to trade him the fifth parcel in return for drilling the well and installing the water system. Smith drilled the well, then exchanged it and the system for a deed to the land, provided by Doe. Smith spent a year building his dream house and moved in.

Meanwhile, the Doe partnership broke up, and the land was sold to Piney Mountain Cooperative. They tried to evict Smith, and the matter landed in court. Doe's ex-partners testified that they knew nothing of his deal with Smith. The judge ruled that Doe had no legal right to convey title, so the sale and Smith's deed were invalid. Smith can try to collect from Doe for his work in drilling the well, but he will have to sue to do it. Piney Mountain is waiting to see if Smith gets enough money from Doe to pay for the land his house occupies. If so, they may sell it to him. Or they may not. Smith dares not spend any more time or money on his house or land until the case is settled. His position could not be more precarious.

Title insurance

Smith could have avoided some of his problems by securing title insurance when he contracted for the land, but that would only have paid his financial losses. It could not have compensated him for his labor of love in building his dream house. Nor would a land survey have helped, as the parcel boundaries are not in dispute. But a title search by a title company or real estate broker would have turned up the fact that Doe's partners'

names were on the title. Had Smith hired a broker or a real estate lawyer, either should have warned him that a deed without all their signatures might not be valid.

Brokers and lawyers

A broker is not the same as a real estate agent. Brokers must pass much more stringent tests than agents, but the biggest difference is in their function. An agent's business is to sell land; a broker's is to advise his client. Regardless of who hires him, an agent only gets a commission if a sale is made, so in a sense, an agent is always working for the seller, or at least for the sale. A broker charges a fee and gets paid for his knowledge, not his salesmanship. A real estate lawyer's job is to scrutinize contracts, including deeds, to make sure they are legal and say what you want them to say.

You shop for a broker, real estate lawyer, or surveyor the same way you shop for a doctor, accountant, or any other professional. Check the local Better Business Bureau to make sure there are no complaints, get names of satisfied customers, and ask them about their dealings. Make sure that your broker and surveyor are state certified or licensed, and that your lawyer is qualified in real-estate law. If in doubt, check with your state bar association.

Your broker should know and advise you about easements, rights-of-way, covenants, and restrictions on the land you are considering. A real estate agent may not know these things.

My friend Bruce spent his life's savings on 40 acres in a beautiful, remote area. His real estate agent assured him he could legally build his backwoods dream home there. The agent was right, too. A two-acre outcropping of rock in one corner of the parcel was legal for building, though not at all practical for it. The rest was protected wetlands, with a total building restriction.

Easements

A broker can tell you what easements apply to a parcel of land, but a surveyor can show you exactly where they are. It may make a difference. I surveyed one parcel for a client who was preparing to purchase it. There was a well on the land, owned by several local land owners in common. The deed specified a 100-foot square easement around the well head, but did not specify the orientation of the square. By orienting it properly, and including the orientation in the deed, the buyer greatly increased the available space in his front yard, which was the only level part of the parcel.

When you make your initial offer to purchase land, it's not a bad idea to make it contingent on the results of a pre-purchase survey. In one such survey, I found that a corner of the cabin being bought was not only off the lot, but it wasn't even in the same section.

But boundaries, buildings, and rights-of-way are not the only things a surveyor can look for. If you suspect problems with drainage, you may wish to include a contingency for a topographic survey. You will certainly need one if you intend to hook up to a sewer, or if you wish to build on a hillside. But you might also need one to put in a leach field for a septic system. The county building inspector can tell you the local requirements.

It can be quite difficult to judge relative elevations by eye. Yet even a difference of half a percent in grade can keep water from flowing properly. When I was young, I hand dug a 500-foot long, two-foot deep irrigation ditch, only to discover that it was sloped the wrong way. By the time I got the ditch deep enough to run water to the garden, it was way too deep to siphon water out of, and I had to build a water-lifting water wheel. But that's another story. Δ

The power to tax involves the power to destroy.

—John Marshall
1755-1835

Next year, grow your own holiday turkey

By Darlene Campbell

If you have difficulty finding the size or type of bird you want for your holiday table, consider raising your own next year. Turkeys are fun birds to raise—they seem to have more personality than other birds, even to the point of being somewhat affectionate, at least while you are carrying the feed bucket. A few turkeys will provide feasts all year long.

When we first started out with turkeys, we bought a trio of Broad Breasted Bronzes that were advertised in the classified section of the newspaper. These are the big guys that were originally bred from the wild turkey, so they still possess the wild turkey markings, only they're larger and meatier. You can select from several other varieties such as Bourbon Red, White Holland, Narragansett, Black, Slate, and even a few newer ones, but you may have to order them from a poultry supplier. Watch for ads in magazines like this one for poultry catalogs and then choose from there.

After breeding the Broad Breasted Bronze for several years, we went to the Broad Breasted White for two reasons:

1. We were living in the Arizona desert, and I thought the White would tolerate the heat better. Our Bronze tom got too heavy and died from the 110° heat when he was about two years old.

2. The White turkeys are smaller and better suited to a homestead. After all, who wants to put a dozen or so huge turkeys in the freezer? Small ones are perfect for company dinner all year long, and can be halved and frozen for family use.

Start with poults

It's always best to start with *poults* (young turkeys), rather than attempt breeding them yourself, because the tom is so large and cumbersome that he has difficulty mating. Most people don't realize that a 20-pound bird purchased in the store may have weighed as much as 40 pounds or more before it was dressed. Today most commercial turkey growers artificially inseminate their hens, but years ago the hen wore a muslin harness on her back to prevent injury during the mating process, and also to give the tom something to grasp. Without a harness, the hen suffers injury during mating. This can be lessened by clipping the tom's toenails and by using a young male that has not gained too much weight. At best, the hen will lose all the feathers on her back, and at worst she will have large lacerations that could become infected. One tom is sufficient for 12 to 15 hens.

Turkeys are seasonal breeders and will begin breeding in the spring when the tom starts his strutting. If the hen is allowed to roam free on the premises, she will choose a secluded spot to lay her eggs, one a day, and then begin sitting on them. If she is confined, provide her with a nest that is two feet square, with enough nesting material so that the eggs can pocket as they pile on one another.

You'll want to help hatch and raise them

Although provided with natural instincts to hatch and raise her young, the turkey hen is a poor mother, due to the size of her breast and excess weight. If she sets her own eggs, she is capable of breaking them, and when the poults begin to hatch, she may crush them with her weight. Some of the smaller breeds may be more efficient at raising poults.

At first, we removed the eggs from the hen and placed them under a setting hen. This is an excellent method, except that some hens will grow weary of waiting for turkey eggs to hatch. (It takes approximately four weeks for turkey eggs to hatch, compared to three weeks for chicken eggs.) Such a hen may leave the nest, thereby ruining your eggs. A duck's incubation time is more equal to that of a turkey, so a duck would be a good choice.

Another way to hatch turkey eggs is to place them in an incubator, turning them at intervals. This method has a very high rate of success. The temperature of the incubator should be increased each week, starting at 100.5° the first week and increasing one degree per week until the eggs hatch. Follow the directions supplied by the manufacturer of your incubator. Beware of power outages, as a power failure can cause you to lose all your incubating eggs.

Brooding turkey poults is much more difficult than brooding chickens. The poults must be taught to eat. We found the best method for teaching them to eat is to boil some eggs and remove and crumble the yolk. Drop the crumbled egg yolk from your fingers over the feeding dish. As the day-old poults see the yolk fall, they will peck at it and discover the feed in the dish. The egg yolk is also a good source of added protein. You may have to go through the teaching process for several days before the young birds learn to eat on their own. Turkeys are high-protein birds and require a game bird feed. Also give them access to grass and insects.

Keep them safe

Keep a light burning in a brooder box, the same as for baby chicks. If turkey poults become chilled, they are likely to pile on each other, smothering the ones on the bottom. Be sure to keep them warm with a light bulb or a thermostat-controlled brooder.

Also, be sure the place where you keep them is safely constructed. Don't make the mistake we made with our first hatch. I had constructed a temporary pen on the enclosed back porch of our house. The boards were not nailed in place, just leaning against the wall. One day when the poults were about three weeks old, I let a dog into the house, a good dog who never harmed the birds. I left her and the young birds indoors and drove to town to do some shopping. When I returned, the dog had moved one of the boards, probably to investigate the turkey poults, and the 1x12 boards fell on the young turkeys, killing them all. Because my pen was not safe, this could have happened with children around as well as the dog, so be sure to construct pens that are securely nailed.

After we lost our Bronze tom to the heat, we sold the hens (they were too old to be eaten) and began purchasing White turkey poults from a commercial hatchery. These birds, too, must be taught to eat, but we are always successful with them and dress them at six months of age.

I cut the carcasses in half through the breast with a meat saw and freeze them in two pieces. Each half is a meal for us, and I always keep two whole birds in the freezer for serving on the holidays.

Turkeys are delightful birds that bond to you. Perhaps it's because you must teach them to eat, just as nature intended the hen to do. But don't get *too* attached, or you might forego turkey dinner and decide on weenies for Thanksgiving. Δ

Here are 10 ways to beat corrosion in the garage

By Sandy Lindsey

1 To keep spare nails, screws, and other small parts from rusting, save empty jars of hand or face cream. Not only will the jar help keep the spare parts organized, but the greasy residue in the jar helps prevents rust.

2 To keep corrosion away from infrequently used tools, coat the tools with a thin layer of oil and wrap them in plastic wrap. Placing carpenter's chalk in a tool box will help absorb moisture and prevent corrosion, too.

3 Another popular anti-corrosion technique for tools is to store them in a wooden box with camphor and sawdust.

4 All new tools should be protected with the following anti-rust, anti-corrosion coating: $1/4$ cup lanolin and $1/4$ cup petroleum jelly. Heat until melted, stir until blended. While the mixture is still warm, paint it on your tools with a cheap paint brush. Allow to dry. You can reheat it in a microwave as needed.

5 For a quick cleanup of corroded tools and those with surface rust, dip a soap-filled steel wool pad lightly in kerosene and rub with some elbow grease on the offending areas of the tool. Then take a balled-up piece of aluminum foil and rub hard. Wipe off the residue with a paper towel and apply a fine coating of olive oil. **NOTE: Do not work with kerosene near an open flame.**

6 Cola and other carbonated sodas poured on a rusted screw or bolt will help loosen it.

7 To remove corrosion from car battery terminals, mix three parts baking soda to one part water, and apply the paste to the terminals to allow the alkaline baking soda to neutralize the corrosion. **NOTE: Always take precautions when working around battery acid.**

8 To prevent further corrosion to battery terminals, apply a thin coating of petroleum jelly or silicone dielectric grease.

9 To prevent a potentially dangerous moisture buildup in stored electronics (cameras, tape recorders, etc.), put some dry rice near them to absorb moisture. Heat the rice in a clean, dry frying pan until it browns. Place the brown rice in a cheesecloth bag to keep the grain from getting into the equipment and harming it. Check the bags frequently and replace as necessary when the rice becomes moist.

10 To keep spare batteries from becoming corroded, or old before their time, store them in a Zip-lock bag placed inside the refrigerator. Δ

Make this classic Shaker-style butcher block

By Dana Martin Batory

For a piece of furniture that is useful and at the same time will add a special touch to a rustic cottage, homestead, or log cabin, try your hand at building a Shaker-style butcher block.

This project is adapted from a block made at the Shaker community at Pleasant Hill, Kentucky, about 1850. The original can be seen at the Shaker Museum in Old Chatham, New York. Made from a sectioned three-foot-diameter sycamore tree, it is a testament to the Shakers' skill at seasoning lumber. Nearly 150 years later, the block shows no sign of checking (cracking).

Materials: one block, 21" in diameter and 13" tall; three legs, $2^{15}/_{16}$" in diameter and 24" long

Instructions:

Using a chainsaw (or a large one- or two-man crosscut saw) cut a 13" thick section from a sound tree trunk 21" across—sycamore or ash preferably, though other hardwoods will work. These dimensions are approximate, as the block can easi-

The finished butcher block

The rough-cut block (ash)

ly be made from larger or smaller wood. Mine came from a wind-damaged ash.

If it's from an old trunk, remove all badly weathered wood. Make the cuts as parallel as possible to save work later on. The bark can be peeled off and the exposed wood wire brushed, sand blasted, or sanded with a flexible flap-wheel. I prefer to leave the bark intact for a nice contrast. Even so, all loose bark, mud, stones, etc., must be removed with a stiff brush or a garden hose. I allowed my block to season under cover for over a year. But don't worry about checking, as it doesn't harm the block and only adds to its rustic charm.

Use a belt sander with increasingly finer grits to dress both surfaces as smooth and level as possible. Select the best side for the top.

Roughly determine the block's center. Using a compass, a trammel point, or simply a pencil tied to a string fastened to a nail driven into the block's center, draw the largest possible circle whose circumference falls within the block's bark ring. Lay out three 3" diameter holes at 120° intervals whose rims are about 1" in from the bark ring.

I prefer to make the holes with a drill press, but the throat on the average drill press is not deep enough. No elaborate jig is called for. I nailed together an auxiliary table that could be fastened to the drill press table with bolts and tee nuts. A temporary 80° drilling surface can also be made by simply tilting a plywood sheet on cement blocks, a bench top, etc., and securely blocking its bottom edge to prevent kick-out.

Place the block on the table. Rotate the block. Ideally the 3" drill bit should come within about $^1/_4$" of each hole's center mark. If the top and bottom are badly angled, then each hole must be custom-drilled to reach the 3" depth. This can be corrected later on. Run the drill press on

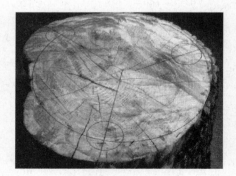

Layout lines on the block

*Drilling the block on
80° auxiliary table*

its slowest speed and back out the bit
frequently to clear the hole of chips.

After drilling the holes, sand off all
layout lines and varnish the bottom at
least twice. Try to keep the varnish
out of the sockets.

Prepare leg blanks about 28" long.
Any hardwood will work—oak, ash,
beech, etc. Turn to the dimensions
shown. The legs can be sanded and
varnished right on the lathe, but leave
at least three inches of the leg's top
bare. Glue will not adhere to varnished surfaces.

To determine the legs' correct
lengths, simply place a three-foot rule
against the hole's bottom and outside

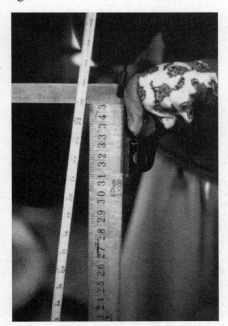

*Measuring for correct
height and leg length*

edge. Measure up from the ground
with another rule. The block should be
one or two inches below waist height,
so the point where your desired height
cuts the rule in the hole gives you the
correct leg length. It pays to check
each leg separately both for length and
fit. It's easier to correct any mistakes
at this stage than later on. Mark the
legs and their respective sockets to
avoid confusion.

Cut the legs to length. Apply glue to
the holes and push the legs into place
until they bottom out. Turn the block
upright so the weight of the block will

Turned leg (red oak)

act as a clamp. Wipe off excess glue
with a damp cloth. After the glue has
set, the leg bottoms can be sanded to
bring the top into alignment if needed.

Apply a salad bowl finish such as
Behlen's (or a non-toxic varnish) to
the block's top and sides, following
the instructions that come with the
product. Since you're treating end
grain, it will take at least three coats to
seal the top.

The block is heavy, about 150
pounds. I've found it best to move it
"litter fashion" by sliding a couple of
stout 2x4s underneath, running a strap
clamp or a rope around them and the
block, and putting someone else on
each end.

The beauty of the project is the fact
that the end result does not necessarily
depend on the quality of your tools
and machinery, but mostly on the
effort you wish to put into it.

The block can also be made totally
by hand. After the block is cut, it can
be smoothed using a jack plane or
block plane. The three holes can be

drilled with a brace and bit simply by
sighting the angle. Three straight tree
limbs can be cut to length and their
ends whittled down to fit the holes. Δ

Home Before Christmas

*For days before,
I thought of their surprised looks
If I crossed the country and appeared
    on their doorsteps.*

*And, for days afterward,
I thought of what it would be like
To arrive,
As if I were a late present,
When they thought Christmas was
    over.*

*By New Year's Eve I realized
I'd just spent another Christmas
Alone.*

**John Earl Silveira
Ojai, CA**

A Groaner

How far can a dog run into the
woods?

*Halfway, because then he's run-
ning out again.*

*The sole end for which mankind
are warranted, individually or col-
lectively, in interfering with the lib-
erty of action of any of their number
is self-protection.*

—John Stuart Mill
1806-1873

Seed art — it's fun to collect the seeds and to create these unusual pictures

By Alice B. Yeager
Photographs by James O. Yeager

Seed art is an old craft going back to long, long ago. Where the art of turning seeds into pictures first began is obscured by time, and I doubt that anyone of our day and age could solve the mystery.

However, I know where *I* came into contact with this fascinating craft. I attended a Junto Club meeting one evening when the program centered on crafts, and seed art was one of the crafts. Naturally, being an avid gardener and fascinated by plants, I was a prime candidate to get hooked on seed art.

You'll find seeds in lots of places

Creating seed pictures is a fun pastime. Anyone can participate, and it can be a year-round hobby. Collect seeds when the weather is good, then create pictures indoors when the weather takes a downturn. Seed hunting can be fun for the whole family. Select a nice day, see who can find the most varieties of seeds, and highlight the outing with a picnic. Watch how quickly young minds are alerted to different kinds of seeds.

Don't overlook the kitchen spice rack, as seeds are there, too. Saving seeds from your own plants is another way to start your collection. Involvement with seed pictures brings out artistic ability while teaching us about the plant world. And you can make unique and inexpensive gifts.

Remember to spread fresh seeds out on a tray indoors where they can dry thoroughly before being put in containers. Newly gathered seeds may mold if put away too soon.

Seed pictures are not confined to small frames. An example of this is the gigantic display on the outside of the Corn Palace in Mitchell, South Dakota. That large municipal auditorium is redecorated each year with huge amounts of grains and grasses depicting cowboys, buffaloes, Indians, etc. The theme varies annually. Those murals take a lot of effort and talent, and the end result is not only pleasure for human spectators . . . the bird population is most appreciative, too.

I have seen a few seed pictures of lesser dimensions in museums, but the artists' names are unavailable. I wonder who creat-

"The Prairie," 14" x 21¹/₂"
Flowers are cantaloupe seeds with an althea seed center. Larger flowers are dipper gourd seeds with acorn cap centers. The butterfly is morning glory and marigold seeds. Grasses are wheat and wild oats.

ed the lovely pictures and how they came by the art form.

Several years ago, when I was one of the judges of a craft show housed in a barn, I discovered someone's masterpiece of corn, sunflower seeds, and lima beans had been the target of hungry rats. Not much left to judge there.

I have learned from experience that destruction can also arrive in very small forms. Tiny seed-hungry bugs can create havoc. It's a good idea to spray seed pictures lightly with a non-oily insecticide every few months. Bugs love to discover a cache of unprotected seeds, so don't forget to protect your supply of seeds, too.

"Basket of Flowers," 8" x 9¹/₂"
Basket is made of grains of rice in alternating groups to form basket weave pattern. Flowers are made from seeds of mimosa, pepper, mustard, cantaloupe, and four o'clock.

*"Owls and Mushrooms," 5" x 9¹/²"
The tree is made of rice. The owls are
dipper gourd seeds. Each eye is a
pepper seed with a larkspur seed on
top. Each mushroom is a horizontal
cantaloupe seed over a vertical one.*

Materials

Egg cartons are useful storage containers. Names of seeds may be written on the lids, and the cartons stacked to save space. This is better than using odd-shaped bottles and jars. When my collection reached extensive proportions, I bought an organizer—a small metal cabinet with lots of drawers. Horizontal dividers in the drawers make it possible to keep many varieties of seeds separated.

Burlap is an excellent fabric to use as background for seed art. It is available in several colors and is usually reasonable in price. A yard of burlap

*Small flowers: Pepper
with mustard centers*

will make a number of pictures, depending on size. Buying half-yard pieces in several colors will provide variety. Not all colors will compliment all seeds. Light-colored seeds such as cucumber and pepper will not show up as well on a beige background as they would on a darker color. Mimosa and apple seeds won't stand out on brown. Light green is a good neutral color.

A lightweight board or a discarded piece of Masonite—something that won't bend—is recommended for a stiff backing. Cardboard is undesirable, as it will soon buckle. If you have a friend who has a woodworking shop, you're in luck, as there are usually scrap pieces of wood lying around that are free for the asking.

Here's how it's done

I suggest keeping your first picture simple in order to learn the basics. A 3x5" size picture is best for an initial attempt. Be sure that board is clean of all dust, and cut the burlap so that it is slightly larger than the board. Coat the board well with Elmer's Glue-All and place the burlap backing on it, smoothing out any wrinkles and keeping the fibers straight. Let it dry completely, then trim away the overlapping burlap along the edges of the board.

A vase of flowers is an easy subject. Use a piece of chalk or a pastel pencil to lightly outline the vase, keeping it centered and in proportion with your background. (Some folks like to draw a rough sketch on paper as a visual aid.) Seeds suitable for the vase itself include rice, mimosa, cantaloupe, and many others.

*Rose: Pepper with mustard center.
(Begin on outer edge and
work toward center.)*

Apply glue along the top edge of the vase. Touch the end of a toothpick to the glue and use the moistened tip to pick up a seed. Place the seed in the middle of the top line and work toward the left and right until the top line is completed. Repeat for the next line and so on until the vase area is covered, using glue as needed.

Select the highest center point for the flowers and taper downward toward the sides. This is the easiest way to keep the design balanced in appearance. There are lots of "flowers" to choose for your vase. Cucumber seeds make nice daisies. Four o'clock seeds give a cone effect to centers, such as those seen in black-eyed Susans. You can use pepper seeds to make perfect full-blown roses by laying an outer circle and lapping each inward circle until they meet in the middle. Finish with a mustard seed for the center. Four pepper seeds with

*Materials: Seeds, burlap on stiff backing, pastel pencil
or chalk for outlining forms, glue, toothpicks (touch
glue and pick up seeds), and imagination.*

*Owl: Dipper gourd with
pepper and larkspur eyes*

tips touching in the middle and a mustard seed for the center will make a four-petalled flower such as a bluet. These are good fillers for blank spaces. Another filler that gives an airy touch is fern made from a double row of dill seeds.

A dipper gourd seed resembles the shape of an owl sitting on a tree limb. To the wide end of the seed add two pepper seeds and a couple of larkspur seeds placed vertically on the pepper seeds, and you have a wide-eyed owl. Make a tree using rice grains and place a few owls on the limbs. Put some mushrooms on the ground simply by using a cantaloupe seed in a vertical position with another on top horizontally. Seeds are versatile. The same dipper gourd seeds may be petals for a large flower, with an inverted acorn cup as the center. Cantaloupe seeds make asters. You are limited only by your imagination.

Frame it

I consider it a downright waste of time and talent if I don't show off a seed picture masterpiece by giving it a proper frame. I don't use a fancy gilded design, as that type of frame detracts from the picture. A simple hardwood frame is best. I always put

*Small flowers: Grape
with millet centers*

A BHM Writer's Profile: Linda Wallin Smith

Linda Wallin Smith lives in Roundup, Montana, where with her husband she built her own earth bermed, rock and turf-covered roof log home using hand tools and horse power, while living in a tent year-round from 1980 to 1983. She also witched and drilled two water wells, and sews most of her family's clothes.

Linda has sold articles to BHM, Home Power Magazine, and Farm Journal, and is currently working with her husband on a non-fiction book series about some of the numerous miscarriages of the jurisprudence system.

my initials in the bottom right corner of my pictures. That's in case they get past the rats and bugs and end up in museums.

When special gift-giving days roll around, have some seed pictures handy. You'll be surprised how much people appreciate the extraordinary. You might consider entering some seed pictures in a fair or hobby show. Whatever you do, by all means display your creations in prominent spots in your home. They are great conversation pieces. Δ

A country moment

*The Backwoods Home Magazine bookstore
in Gold Beach, Oregon*

Make delicious, eye-catching holiday breads

By Richard Blunt

Beginning in early September and lasting through St. Patrick's Day, my mother's kitchen became the neighborhood's weekend community bakery. Our kitchen was not the largest in the housing project nor was it better equipped than many others. But on the weekends when my mother didn't have to work, women from our part of the housing project gathered in our kitchen to drink coffee and tea, munch on a variety of home-baked pastries, and discuss how to prepare each one. Before long the kitchen resembled a busy professional bakery, with women preforming various baking procedures while sharing with others some of the ethnic folklore associated with their bakery project for that day.

What follows is a composite of 15 years of listening, sampling, and sometimes helping during my Mom's weekend bakery seminars. Throughout this column I have scattered some of the homilies that were exchanged between my Mom and her local bakery group—things said by her generation and countless generations before hers, but which are rarely heard today. Things such as:

> ### A large hole in a loaf of bread is the sign of an open grave.

An old Hungarian saying claims bread is older than man. This isn't difficult to believe once you realize that the story of bread and bread baking reaches back over 15,000 years into the time when the 100 century reign of the last Ice Age was loosening its grip, and the earth's rock-hard frozen soil began to soften.

In the wake of the receding ice sheets and warming climate conditions, a wide variety of wild grasses and other edible plants began to flourish. The hunter-gatherers of this changing time found the seeds of the grasses to be a valuable food source. Using mortars and mills hollowed out of rock, they crushed the seeds of these grasses and mixed them with water to prepare crude porridge. Crushed nuts and roots were often added to the porridge to make tasty substitutes for the flesh of animals which were dangerous and hard to hunt on the partially frozen wastelands. The wonders of fire made it possible to cook the porridge, first over open fires, and later on hot stones to create the first breads.

These breads were totally flat and unleavened. Leavening wasn't possible anyway, because wild grass seeds were not really suitable to support any leavening action. Their hulls were hard and brittle and had to be parched to separate the germ and bran from the endosperm. This application of heat greatly reduced the effectiveness of the gluten-forming pro-

Richard Blunt

teins in the endosperm. A wheat plant with seeds that could be easily husked was necessary if the civilizing of man was to stay on course.

Just how this happened is not clear. One theory suggests that people in the ancient Palestinian city of Jericho, in 10,000 B.C., discovered that a small percentage of the wild wheat plants did not bear the characteristically brittle seeds. These seeds could be husked easily, without the use of heat. It seems as though, in a whimsical way, Nature had created a mutation. After a few accidental sowings by Mother Nature, and some innocent assistance by ancient farmers, a wheat perfect for bread making was born. It was now possible to make a gruel with a high percentage of raw wheat endosperm. The discovery of leavened bread would only be a matter of time.

In Egypt, around 4000 B.C., a small amount of bread dough, left unattended by an unwitting baker, became contaminated by wild yeast and, voila, the long journey to the age of Wonder Bread had begun. The Egyptians quickly made the connection between this activity in bread dough and the fermentation of beer, and by 300 B.C. yeast production was a specialized craft in Egypt. By the 12th century B.C., the Egyptians began to create baking techniques that were both creative and predictable.

> ### Set your bread to rise with the sun.

As time passed, baking techniques improved as the result of gradual improvements in the quality of wheat crops and milling practices which produced a finer flour. Each successive civilization left its mark, and Greek bread was better than that of the Egyptians, and Roman bread was far superior to that of the Greeks.

Agriculture shapes civilization

Agriculture colored the way civilization evolved. Generations of now-nameless men tilled the soil, put seeds in the ground, then watched the birth and death of the new plant that sprung from there. The following year, a new generation reappeared when the fruit of the harvested plant was returned to the soil. Why this should all happen was an ominous mystery to them. As a result, agriculture, and cereal plant domestication in particular, became interwoven with folklore, religion, and mythology, and bread became the supreme symbol of this wondrous relationship. The number of myths, fables, and mysteries relating to breads and cakes exceed all other food forms except salt.

Many early cultures believed that the existence of grain was the result of supernatural forces. The ancient symbolisms and superstitions attached to wheat and other grains by most civilizations center around a group of agrarian deities. The Egyptians believed that Osiris, a god that was cast into the Nile and returned to life, and the god Manerous were responsible for the sprouting of wheat.

The Greeks believed that bread was the gift of Demeter, goddess of the wheat field. Hestia, the Greek goddess of the hearth, who was known as Vesta to the Romans, along with Fornax, strictly a Roman goddess, bore myths that attached symbolisms of fertility and sexual fantasy to cultivation of grains and the act of bread making. Of course these myths start at the first sprouting of the grain and are carried through to the formation of the loaf in the oven.

Chinese emperors of the Chou dynasty were considered ancestors to the celestial deity, Prince Millet, and were regarded as trustees of the agricultural cycle.

Many of the ancient superstitions and myths associated with the cultivation and processing of

> *Put a slice of bread and a cup of coffee under the house and ghosts will stay away.*

grains were acted out in rites and rituals that were savage and sinister. In ancient Greece and in the Bible lands, people were burned alive to propitiate the sometimes terrifying agrarian gods and goddesses. Today there still exist remnants of bread folklore that are directly connected to the ancient rites of cannibalism.

To understand this connection, we must realize that the idea of ritualistic cannibalism comes not from the dearth of food, but from the belief that the strength and power of those devoured can be assimilated. In the bizarre ritual of sin-eating, once practiced in parts of Wales and England, bread was used as a totem object to divest a corpse of any virulent tendencies that might be directed against living relatives. The sin-eater, usually selected from the ranks of the poor, was positioned over the corpse just before burial with a small loaf of bread and a tankard of ale which he or she would consume while hovering over the casket. By doing so, the sin-eaters would take upon themselves the sins of the deceased. This wasn't all bad for the sin-eater as after the ceremony he or she was paid a fee for their services.

> *If wheat is cut in the light of the moon, the bread will be dark.*

Very few of the ancient rituals—which included everything from animal sacrifices to the burning of children alive—or the breads associated with these rituals, have survived to modern times. But some had their savage and sinister genesis removed and were adopted by the emerging Christian churches. Some were given a brighter "fun and games" image to make them suitable in public celebrations. Among them is England's Plough Monday, which is based on a pre-Christian fertility rite, but is now celebrated on January 6 when ploughs are blessed in front of the alter. Lassas Day, or "offering of the loaves," is an English festival celebrating the beginning of the harvest where the first wheat (called corn in England) is harvested and made into flour, baked into loaves, and offered in the church to God.

Some folklorists associate many of the foot stamping, hand clapping, and reeling folk dances of the British Isles, Ireland, and much of Northern Europe, to ancient Celtic sacrificial and fertility rites that were themselves associated with the sowing and reaping of grain.

The stories surrounding bread, harvests, and crops go on and on, and vary from culture to culture. They all extol the nutritional or the spiritual significance of bread. In the Bible, Jesus recognized bread as synonymous with nourishment. "Man shall not live by bread alone," he said. And in declaring, "I am the bread of life," he metaphorically associated bread with spiritual nourishment.

As we have seen, bread making is an ancient and universal craft that has afforded its practitioners much creative pleasure since neolithic times, while at the same time satisfying their nutritional and spiritual needs.

If you are a veteran home loafer, you already know that holidays are a golden time. They give you the opportunity to demonstrate your level of perfection in the art while providing you with many hours of creative pleasure.

If you are a newcomer to baking, you must realize that the fancy looking holiday and other festive breads that you see in markets and specialty bakeshops during the upcoming holiday season are not as difficult and complicated to prepare as their appearance may indicate.

To successfully prepare many of these breads all you need is a little time, a work surface, flour, water or other liquid, yeast, salt, and a means for baking the dough. Much of the long-winded technical stuff that you read in some cook books has its place, but bread making is not an exact art, and it is a surprisingly forgiving one. Many ingredients, including flour, salt, and liquid, can be eyeballed rather than measured precisely. I'm not suggesting that you completely ignore the measuring guidelines of a recipe, but scraping a knife across a cup or a measuring spoon to get an exact measure is not necessary.

The recipes I am sharing with you in this issue are all festive breads that were favorites in my Mom's neighborhood bakery. So relax, make a cup of coffee or tea, and invite a friend over to share in some old time baking fun.

One important thing to remember is that the fancy configurations I'm about to describe will not improve the taste, texture, or aroma of your loaf, but they will impress on your friends the fact that food is better when it's pleasing to the eye.

Braids, twists, ladders, etc.

Braiding and twisting adds a professional touch to yeast leavened breads. With a little practice it is possible to combine twists and a variety of braids into one loaf for a spectacular presentation.

Twisting is simple and requires only two 2" ropes of bread dough of equal length. To make the ropes, divide enough bread dough for one loaf into two pieces and form these pieces into ropes 2" thick. Now, loosely twist the ropes together and tuck the ends under the loaf.

The three rope braid is done using the same technique as braiding hair. Divide enough dough to make one loaf of bread into three equal pieces. Form three 2" thick ropes

Braiding bread dough

equal in length, and lay them on your work surface crossed in the middle. This will create a star with six legs, three on each side of the apex, kind of like a giant asterisk. Start on one side and braid the three legs as you would braid hair. Gently turn the loaf around and braid the other side in the same fashion. Pinch the ends together and tuck under the loaf.

Four and five rope braids may sound a little intimidating, but by using the simple formula that I outline here, you will be turning out complex looking braided breads without any headaches, anxiety, tears, or frustration.

Four rope braid

Divide enough dough to make one loaf of bread into four pieces. Form each of these pieces into ropes of equal length that are about 2" thick. Lay the ropes side by side on your work surface and pinch them together at one end.

Here is the formula: Starting from the rope on the left, number the ropes 1, 2, 3, and 4. It is important to remember before you start moving the ropes around that the numbers apply to the position that each rope is in, and not to each individual rope. Example: If you move a rope from the number one position to cross the rope in the number four position, that rope is now in number four position and the rope that was in the number four position is now in number three position. If this sounds strange, make a batch of your favorite white bread dough and practice using the steps outlined below. If you are not happy with the formation of your practice braid, you can knead it back into a ball and try it again. If you get tired of trying it, form the dough into standard loaves and bake them as usual. But don't try to use rope or string for practice because these multiple strand braids need the adherent qualities of bread dough to work properly.

Move each rope in the direction indicated in the box below:

Method:

1. Rope 1 over Rope 4 (to the right)
2. Rope 3 over Rope 1 (to the left)
3. Rope 4 over Rope 3 (between Rope 2 and Rope 3)
4. Rope 2 over Rope 4 (to the right)
5. Rope 1 over Rope 2 (between Rope 2 and Rope 3)

After you complete Steps 1 through 5 the first time, finish the braid using only steps 2 through 5 until all of the dough is braided, then pinch the ends and tuck them under the loaf.

Five strand braid

Method:

1. Rope 2 over Rope 3 (between Rope 3 and Rope 4)
2. Rope 5 over Rope 2 (between Rope 1 and Rope 2)
3. Rope 1 over Rope 3 (between Rope 3 and Rope 4)

Repeat the steps until all of the dough is used. Then pinch the ends and tuck them under the loaf.

Jacob's Ladder

I use this method more than the other braids because it is quick and easy. The braid forms vertically instead of horizontally and it adds a nice finishing touch to loaves baked in standard bread pans.

Method:

Divide enough dough to make one loaf of bread into two equal pieces. Form the pieces into ropes of equal length that are about two inches thick. Lay the ropes on your work surface so they intersect at their centers (see drawing). Take the opposite ends of the bottom rope and cross the ends over the center so the ends change places.

Do the same with the other two ropes. Continue alternating the folding of the ropes until all of the dough is used. Pinch the ends and fold under the loaf. Bake the loaf in a bread pan or free form style without a pan.

Now for the recipes.

Barmbrack

In my old neighborhood the Irish families called this bread Speckle Cake. The Irish moms would start making this bread at least two weeks before Halloween. They would store many of the loaves in my Mom's freezer to hide it from their own kids. If they didn't, there wouldn't be enough to pass out to all of us hungry trick-or-treaters who would start piling up at their doors as soon as the sun went down.

This recipe makes one medium loaf.

Ingredients:

¹/4 cup unsalted butter at room temperature
¹/4 cup whole milk
¹/2 cup water

Jacob's Ladder

¹/2 tsp sugar
1 pkg active dry yeast
1 egg (at room temperature) slightly beaten
3 cups all purpose flour (approximately)
¹/2 tsp Kosher salt
¹/2 tsp grated lemon peel
¹/2 cup dried currents
¹/4 cup chopped mixed candied fruit

Method:

1. Heat the butter, milk, and water in a small sauce pan to 115 degrees F, then combine with the sugar and yeast. Stir the mixture to dissolve the yeast. Set the mixture aside and let the yeast proof.

2. Add the beaten egg to the proofed yeast mixture.

3. Combine the yeast mixture with 1¹/2 cups of flour, the salt, and lemon peel and mix with a wooden spoon to combine.

4. Continue to stir in more of the remaining flour ¹/4 of a cup at a time, until the dough forms a shaggy mass and pulls away from the sides of the bowl. (This means you may need more or less than the three cups of flour.) Lift the dough from the bowl and place it on a floured work surface.

5. Knead the dough for about 10 minutes or until it becomes smooth and elastic. Place the dough in a greased bowl, cover and set aside until the dough has doubled in bulk.

6. Punch the dough down, remove it from the bowl and knead the fruit into the dough.

7. Shape the dough into a loaf and place it into a standard bread pan. Cover it and set it aside to rise a second time. When the dough is just above the edge of the pan it is ready for the oven.

8. Bake in a preheated 350 degree F oven for about 45 minutes or until the loaf sounds hollow when tapped on top. Remove the loaf from the oven and set on a rack to cool.

Challah

Challah (hal-la) was as popular in my neighborhood as bagels are in every metropolitan area in America today. Every bakery in the area had its own version. One of my mother's closest friends, Mrs. Sibley, lived in the apartment right below us. When she was expecting guests for dinner on Rosh Hashana or Yom Kippur, she would ask my Mom to help her make her loaves of Challah. She could make the dough from memory, but she had trouble forming the four strand braid or Jacob's ladder fold. When they were finished baking for the day, Mrs. Sibley would ask my mother to join her in the "act of Challah." They would both place a small piece of raw bread on a barbecue stick and burn it over the gas flame of our stove. This was a symbolic reenactment of a woman's creation.

The following is a recipe for three medium loaves.

Ingredients:

```
2 pkg active dry yeast
1 cup warm water (110 to 115 degrees F)
2 Tbsp sugar
1/3 cup light vegetable oil
2 eggs, lightly beaten
4 1/2 to 5 cups flour
1 tsp salt
1/2 cup dried currents
```

There is a glaze that goes with this.

Ingredients:

```
1 egg (beaten slightly)
2 Tbsp water
2 Tbsp poppy seeds
```

Method:

1. Combine the yeast, warm water, sugar, and vegetable oil in a bowl. Stir until the yeast is dissolved and set aside until the yeast shows sign of activity.

2. Add the egg to the proofed yeast mixture.

3. Combine the flour and salt. In a large mixing bowl combine 3 cups of the flour/salt mixture with the yeast mixture and mix with a wooden spoon to form a sticky paste, then add the currents. Continue to add flour a little at a time until the dough pulls away from the sides of the bowl.

4. Turn the dough onto a floured work surface and knead it until it is smooth and elastic, about 10 minutes.

5. Place the dough in a greased bowl, cover it with a clean cloth, and set it aside until it doubles in bulk.

6. Punch the dough down and knead on a floured work surface for 1 minute

7. Follow the instructions for shaping the dough into a Jacobs Ladder or 4 strand braid. When the loaves are formed place them on a well greased baking sheet.

8. Combine the remaining egg with the water and beat briskly with a fork until blended. Brush the egg glaze on the shaped loaf and sprinkle the loaf with poppy seeds.

9. Allow the loaves to proof, uncovered, until doubled in bulk, about 1 hour.

10. Place the loaves into a preheated 375 degree F oven and bake until the loaves are done, about 40 minutes. Remove the loaves from the baking sheet and transfer them to a wire rack to cool.

Italian Christmas Bread

This recipe was prepared by the Italian women in our neighborhood. It's called panettone (pahn-uh-toe-nay). Over the years I have prepared and/or tasted more versions of this classic bread than I can remember. The original recipe is

> *A cross cut on top of a loaf, lets the devil out.*

quite involved and takes at least two days to prepare. The following is a recipe that my long time friend Joe Troiano gave me. Joe was born and raised in the south side of Hartford, one of Connecticut's largest Italian neighborhoods, and teaches school there today. This free-form loaf is available year around in Hartford's Italian bakeries, especially at Christmas time.

Ingredients:

```
1/4 cup warm milk (110 to 115 degrees F)
1 pkg active dry yeast
1/2 tsp brown sugar
1/4 cup honey
4 Tbsp unsalted butter (melted)
2 eggs (at room temperature)
2 tsp crushed anise seed
2 to 3 cups flour
1/2 tsp kosher salt
1/4 cup chopped mixed candied fruit
1 Tbsp pine nuts
1/4 cup golden raisins
corn meal
```

Topping

```
1 Tbsp butter
```

Method:

1. Combine the warm milk, yeast, and brown sugar in a mixing bowl. Stir to dissolve the yeast and set it aside to proof.

2. Combine the honey, butter, eggs, and anise seeds in another bowl and beat with a wire whisk or fork until well blended, then add the yeast mixture.

3. Combine 1 1/2 cups of flour and the salt. Add the liquid ingredients to the flour and stir to make a soft sticky dough. Add the remaining flour 1/4 cup at a time, continue to stir until the dough pulls away from the sides of the bowl.

4. Place the dough on your floured work surface and knead for 10 minutes or until the dough is smooth. Continue to add flour, while kneading, if the dough shows signs of being sticky.

5. Place the dough in a clean bowl, cover it with a clean cloth and set aside.

6. Mix together the candied fruit, pine nuts, and raisins.

7. Shape the dough into a plump ball and pat down the top slightly to form an oval. Place half of the fruit mixture on top of the dough, fold the dough over and knead the fruit into the dough, then repeat with the rest of the mixture. Continue to knead the dough until the fruits are well distributed.

8. Place the dough in a well greased bowl, cover with a towel, and set aside to double in bulk, about one hour.

9. Remove the towel and punch the dough down. Place the dough on a floured work surface and shape the dough into a plump round ball. Place the loaf on a well greased baking sheet that has been lightly dusted with corn meal. Cover the loaf with a clean light cloth and allow the dough to rise for about 1 to 1½ hours or until double in bulk.

> **If all of the bread is eaten at the table the next day is sure to be fair .**

10. Preheat the oven to 375 degrees F.

11. Cut a ½ inch deep cross all the way across the top of the loaf with a razor. Place the loaf in the oven on the middle shelf. Five minutes after the loaf is in the oven drop the final tablespoon of butter on top of the loaf in the middle. Bake for about 40 minutes or until the loaf sounds hollow when tapped on the bottom. Allow loaf to cool completely before slicing.

Irish Soda Bread

This is a bread that was always available in my neighborhood. It was the perfect food for a hard working mom to prepare for her family and could be made in at least a dozen variations that I am aware of. This recipe was given to my Mom by Barbara Sullivan, a neighbor that lived on our floor. She had six children, and the original recipe produced 12 loaves. On St. Patrick's Day she would send a loaf of this bread to my Mom along with a mug of real Guiness Stout.

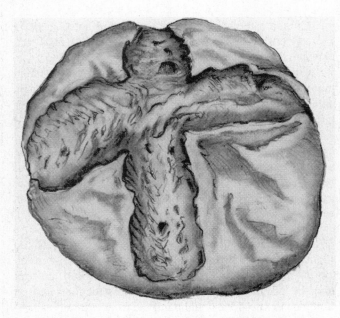

Irish Soda Bread with a cross baked into it

Ingredients:

> 2½ cups all purpose flour
> ½ cup sugar
> 1 tsp salt
> ½ tsp baking soda
> 1¼ tsp baking powder
> 1 Tbsp caraway seeds
> 4 Tbsp unsalted butter
> ½ cup dried currents
> 1¼ cup buttermilk
> 1 egg (slightly beaten)
> corn meal

There is no substitute for the buttermilk in this recipe. The acid in the buttermilk is critical to the leavening action of the dough. However, you can use powdered buttermilk if you can find it.

Ingredients for the topping:

> 1 Tbsp sugar
> 1 tsp water

Method:

1. Combine the flour, sugar, salt, baking soda, baking powder and caraway seeds in a mixing bowl. Cut in the butter until mixture looks like course meal. Slowly stir in the currents, buttermilk and egg. Mix all the ingredients thoroughly.

2. Scrape the mixture from the bowl onto your floured work surface. Control the stickiness by sprinkling flour on the work surface and rolling the dough in the flour. This dough is not to be kneaded.

3 Shape the dough into a plump ball and place it on a well greased baking sheet that has been lightly sprinkled with corn meal. Pat down the top slightly and with a razor blade cut a ½ inch deep cross on the top.

4. Place the loaf on the middle rack of an oven that has been preheated to 375 degrees F and bake it for about 45 minutes, or until it is browned and has opened dramatically along the cuts.

5. Just before the loaf is ready to be removed from the oven, mix the sugar and water for the topping. As soon as you remove the loaf, brush the bread with this mixture.

6. Remove the finished loaf from the oven and place it on a rack to cool.

There are many variations on the four breads I have just presented, so experiment and personalize these recipes until they're your own. Share with me any variation you create but, in particular, send me recipes for any festive breads you think I might enjoy.

Happy holidays. See you next issue. Δ

Where I live
By Annie Duffy

Chasing down cows at Jenny Creek

By Annie Duffy

A couple of months ago I went on Fall Creek Ranch's last cow chase of the season. Pat Ward, owner of the ranch, her daughter, Stevie Odom, a hired hand named Donnie, and I had to round up about 30 cows at Jenny Creek and move them to a different pasture.

I rode my new horse, Diego, a full blooded black bay Arabian gelding. He looks a lot like Pat's horse, a Peruvian Paso named Nevaro El Prim. We mounted up about 10 a.m.

The dirt road to Jenny Creek was fine until we got to the main hill down to the creek. It was slippery, dusty, and very steep. With every step, more dust flew into the air as the horses slipped. We talked calmly to our horses as if we were reassuring them, but we were really reassuring ourselves. After about 30 yards, our horses got used to the steepness and made it down the rest of the way fine.

In the winter, Jenny Creek is a raging river and impassable, whether by vehicle or horse. The only way to get to the other side is by an old foot bridge that sways back and forth. The first time my father took me on it I was six; I was scared at first, but then I found how exciting it was to rock the bridge back and forth as the creek roared past underneath. Now, however, the water was reasonably shallow and slower moving.

Once across Jenny Creek we followed the road around a bend and went about two miles over rocks, through low-hanging scrub oak trees, and thick bushes searching for the cows. The trail was on an incline that dropped off steeply to our right. Several fallen logs laid across the path, and we had to ride around them. I didn't see one log until we were right on it, and Diego surprised me by jumping it. Pat, riding just behind me, was surprised too. She said she'd never seen a trail horse fly before.

We finally found the cows at the farthest end of the pasture and saw that one cow was on the wrong side of the fence. Donnie got off his horse and took his wire cutters out of his saddle bag, thinking he would have to cut the fence to get the cow back into the pasture. As Donnie neared the fence, though, the cow panicked and jumped the fence with its front legs tucked under him just like a horse. We were all surprised, and Donnie was relieved he would not have to mend the fence.

Finally we started to move the cows. Included in the bunch were about eight calves and a bull. The bull, although huge, did not look very menacing, but I still kept my eye on him. The ride went fairly smoothly. One cow and her calf lagged behind and slowed the herd. The calf, looking only a few days old, was almost stepped on several times by Donnie's horse as he tried to hurry them up. A couple of cows tried to go back but were headed off by Pat, who reminded me that if a cow got by you it was okay to swear. Some cows went in the creek and had to be chased back.

We moved most of the cows to the new pasture, but a couple went through the wrong gate, and Pat and Donnie had to chase them down. Stevie and I remained near the pasture gate to block the road so they would go through the gate.

Once the cows were inside the pasture we closed up the gate and rested the horses. I was tired too. We drank from our canteens, and after about a half hour headed back. Ascending the hill from Jenny Creek was even more of a struggle than descending it, because now we were all tired.

But it had been a great day. I patted Diego on the neck, and I meant it when I said, "Good horse!" Δ

Pat Ward, left, Stevie Odom, and Annie Duffy prepare for the roundup.

This method lets you make quilts that are artistic and very personal

By Carole Perlick

My friend Gladney Weishaupt is a person with artistic flair. She has artistry and drama in her personality, and expressed these qualities for years, painting seascapes with her hands. After many years of enjoyment, she was forced to stop her painting due to lead poisoning acquired through the medium she used. When she was told that she couldn't paint again, she thought that she would go crazy. But as so often happens, when one door closes, another door opens.

During a visit, her niece asked Gladney if she could make a baby quilt to be given as a gift. This was a challenge to Gladney, and it sounded interesting. She took a soft white piece of cotton cloth, approximately 36 by 40 inches, and drew stick figures with an indelible black ink pen. She then filled in her drawings with bright colors, using acrylic tube paints. Following this process, each drawn figure was quilted around with black embroidery thread. Using quarter-inch batting as filler, the reverse side was finished with printed flannel to ensure warmth. The pieces were sewn together and strips of very fine ribbon were placed at intervals, through the three layers and back again, then knotted. The baby quilt was the hit of the baby shower!

Tasting success, Gladney expanded her vision and began making larger coverlets using designer sheets, embroidering various stitches and patterns that appealed to her.

It took her approximately two months to complete one of these coverlets, which were sold for over $500.

Outline quilting, not piece quilting, became a major source of expression for Gladney, and the following 15 years were spent making quilts for family and friends. Great nephew

Gladney and personalized quilts with her great niece and great nephew, Kady and Jason Lemke. (photo by Frank Tickle)

Jason, who is a normal rough-and-tumble kid, was given a Disney-designed quilt, much to the envy of his sister Kady. When Kady asked where her quilt was, Gladney felt that Kady should have a very personal quilt. It had to be different from her brother's.

Gladney took a piece of soft, white cloth 48 by 56 inches and began by drawing a house in the center of the material. On the house was a sign, "Kady's House." She then drew anything that was important to the child,

including Mom and Dad, brother, Sadie the dog, and finished it off with other figures that would appeal to a child that age. The quilt became a family project as everyone was allowed to draw whatever they wished on it. Gladney then took over and finished the painting and quilting as needed. The batting was one inch thick, and the backing was done with flannel and bordered with satin bias. Kady enjoys the feel of silk and satin, so this was important to Gladney. It took well over a month to complete this project.

The quilt was admired so much that Gladney went on to make one for her great-granddaughter Jessica and for other grandchildren of friends. At her family's urging, Gladney entered one of these special quilts called "Selena's House" in our local county fair under Children's Quilts and won second place. The judges wrote about her quilt, "Anyone would enjoy looking at this, but Selena most especially. There is great color, wonderful development of figures and the painting techniques work well."

My personal opinion is that these quilts are not only works of art but the story of a living family. There are a lot of "I Love You's" worked onto the quilt but there is also a lot of "I Love You" in the *making* of the quilt. Δ

Make your own nifty gift bags

By Darlene Polachic

Why pay big prices for Christmas gift bags when you can make your own for nothing, and use up all those scraps of wallpaper and gift wrap, and even the undamaged portions of last year's extra-nice wrapping paper that you didn't have the heart to part with?

Use the pattern given to create cute little 3" by 4" bags; double the measurements for larger bags; halve them for teeny-tiny bags that make great Christmas tree ornaments.

Materials

Paper for pattern
Ruler
Pencil
Scissors
Scraps of wallpaper, gift wrap, etc.
White glue
Hole punch
String, yarn, or decorative cord for handles (about 30 cm for small bags)

Instructions

1. Spread out paper. Press with a warm iron, if necessary, to remove creases.

2. Make a master pattern for the size of bag wanted and fold it as shown along all fold lines, beginning with top and bottom sections. Unfold and trace onto paper being made into a bag.

3. Cut out bag, and using the pattern as a guide, make the necessary folds, again beginning with top and bottom sections.

4. Lap section A over section B, with top cuff of B sliding snugly inside cuff of A. Run a bead of white glue all along underside of section A and press along the length of section B.

5. Fold side flaps at bottom in. Apply a bit of glue to get ready for next step.

6. Run a bead of glue around three sides of section X and press ends to glue to flaps.

7. Run a bead of glue around three sides of section Y and press to section X.

8. Punch holes where indicated through all thicknesses of paper.

9. Thread cord or yarn through holes and tie ends so knot is hidden inside a corner of the bag. Δ

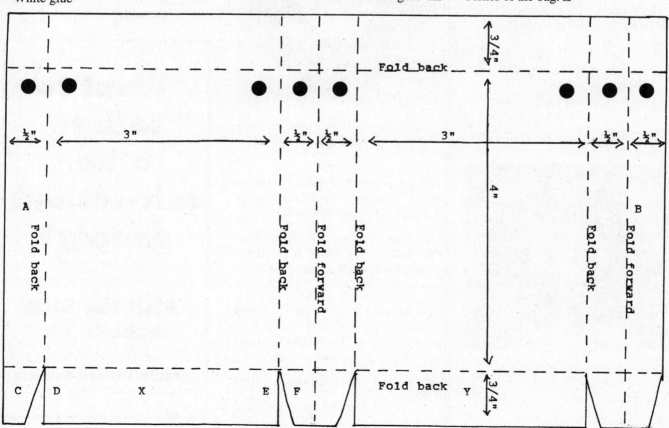

You can make these beautiful pinecone wreaths at home

By Darlene Polachic

Glue pinecones to form, beginning with an inside row.

Materials

14" wire wreath form
Newspaper
Black plastic garbage bag
Hot glue gun
Pine cones
12 to 15 clusters of artificial or dried
    berries with foliage
Dried baby's breath or seafoam
    statice
Spray shellac
Masking tape

When four rows of pinecones have been glued on, the wreath form will be pretty well covered.

Instructions

1   Crumple newspaper and stuff into back of wire form all around.

2   Cut black plastic garbage bag into three-inch-wide strips and wrap snugly around padded form using masking tape to secure ends.

3   Sort pinecones into three piles according to size. Beginning with the largest size, glue cones to inside circle of wreath, placing cones close enough so "petals" interlock a little.

Pinecone wreath with dried straw-flowers in place of berry clumps

Place a generous dollop of glue on base of cone and press to plastic, holding cone in place until glue is firm.

4   Add a second row of medium-sized cones, fitting as snugly as possible to each other and to the previous row.

5   Repeat for third row, then glue large cones around outside edge for a fourth row. The wreath form will be completely hidden.

6   Fill any holes with smallest-sized cones.

Completed wreath embellished with clumps of dried berries and baby's breath

7   Position clusters of dried berries on wreath as desired and glue in place. Glue a few sprigs of baby's breath to each clump and in any empty-looking spaces.

8   Spray the whole thing with spray shellac, particularly if natural dried berries are used. Let dry and hang. For a different look, substitute dried strawflowers for berries. Δ

Use these tips to avoid problems with your sewing machine

By Reuben O. Doyle

There never seems to be enough hours in the day to do all that we have to do. The last thing a sewer needs when she sits down at her sewing machine is to have everything go wrong. The needle breaks, thread jams in the bobbin area or keeps skipping stitches, or there are other frustrating problems that keep the project from being completed. These problems happen to the seasoned pro as well as the novice sewer, and while we would like to blame the sewing machine and perhaps "throw it out the window," there are measures the home sewer can take to correct most problems or even prevent them from happening in the first place. (I service sewing machines, so I know.)

The needle

The sewing machine needle is probably the number one cause of problems for sewers and crafters. This may sound silly, but the first thing to check when having stitching problems is whether the needle is in backwards. Oh, I know you're saying, "I've been sewing most of my life, and I know how to put the needle in the machine,"

but in about 25% of the sewing machine repair jobs I go out on, the only problem is that the needle was put in backwards. If your machine will not pick up the bottom thread or skips stitches badly, in most cases it's because your needle is in wrong.

Each sewing machine requires that the "flat" side of the needle be put in a specific way, facing the front, the back, etc., depending on your particular machine. Sewers in a hurry to get a project done may simply insert the needle, not pay attention to the position of the flat side, and immediately begin having problems. If by chance you have a sewing machine that takes a needle that doesn't have a flat side, you'll notice that each needle has a groove in it where the thread lies as it penetrates the fabric. Depending on whether your machine shuttle system faces to the front or left, the groove of the needle will also face front or left.

A needle that is dull, bent, or simply the wrong size or type can cause major sewing problems. Just because the needle "looks good" doesn't mean that it *is* good. A small "snag" on the tip of the needle can cause runs in the fabric, and a needle that is even slightly bent won't sew properly. A good

The author at work

rule of thumb would be to change the machine needle before each new project. And because some fabrics and fabric finishes can increase wear on the needle, you may even need to change the needle *during* the project if you notice stitching problems beginning to appear.

Always use the right size needle for the type of fabric you're sewing. I've seen sewers trying to sew denim with a fine lingerie type needle simply "because the needle was in the machine and still a good needle," and others trying to sew fine fabrics with needles that are much too large. A needle too fine for heavy fabric can bend or break when it hits the fabric, while too large a needle for the fabric can make puncture holes in the fabric and cause the thread to pull unevenly while stitching. Do yourself a huge favor and check the machine needle before you begin any new project.

The thread

The second thing to check is the thread itself. I have found that "cheap" thread is definitely *not* a bargain. The fibers of cheap thread split easily while you're sewing and can cause knotting or breakage of the thread, and can also cause a build-up of lint in the bobbin area and along the thread line

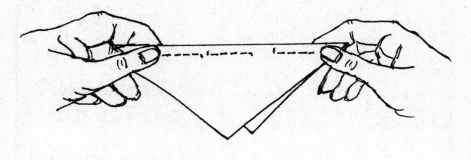

Testing thread tension

from the spool to the needle. If you hold a length of cheap thread up to the light, you can see the frayed edges and roughness of the thread. Stick to a good quality thread and you'll minimize the potential problems.

As you change projects and start sewing on different weight materials, you should test stitch on a piece of scrap material of the same weight before beginning the actual project, so you can adjust your upper tension to that particular material. As an example, if you're changing from a denim type material to a silky type material, you would definitely want to make sure the tension is correct and the stitching looks right before you start to sew on the garment.

To determine whether the upper tension is too tight or too loose for the fabric you're wanting to use, try the following test. Take a small scrap of the fabric, fold it, and stitch a line on the *bias* of the fabric (that is, diagonally across the weave), using different colors of thread in the bobbin and on top. Grasp the bias line of stitching between the thumb and index finger. Space the hands about three inches apart and pull with an even, quick force until one thread breaks. If the broken thread is the color of the thread in the needle, it means that the upper tension is too tight. If the broken thread is the color of the bobbin thread, the upper tension is too loose. If both threads break together and take more force to break, it means that the tensions are balanced.

Using different weights of thread on the spool and in the bobbin will cause ragged stitches, as well as other stitching problems. Never mix different sizes of thread in the bobbin and on the spool. (The exception is when you're doing sewing machine embroidery, where you might be using a heavier thread on the top to get a certain effect for the embroidery project).

You should also check to be sure the sewing machine is threaded properly. Each machine has a certain sequence for threading, and it only takes one

missed step in the sequence to cause your machine to skip stitches. If in doubt, take the top thread completely out and start all over again.

Many times it's the small things that cause a lot of frustration and loss of sewing time. Taking just a few minutes before starting a project to make sure everything is in order can avoid hours of "down time," not to mention frayed nerves and the possibility of an unnecessary trip to the repair shop.

(Reuben Doyle has written <u>Sewing Machine Repair For The Home Sewer</u> **($17.95 plus $2 P&H) and** <u>Serger Repair For The Home</u> <u>Sewer</u> **($17.95 plus $2 P&H). Write Reuben Doyle, 7267-F Mobile Hwy., Pensacola, FL 32526.)** Δ

A country moment

A little old house from the past.

A country moment

*BHM Publisher Dave Duffy and Paul Luckey shovel
out a frozen backhoe in the Oregon woods.*

Delicious holiday cakes don't have to be diet-busters

By Jennifer Stein Barker

Most people just sigh and forget about their diets during the holidays. That's because the main ingredients of most holiday treats are sugar, saturated fat, and eggs with just enough white flour to bind them together. The rationale for eating this stuff is that "it's only once a year." I'm telling you that you don't have to eat this way to feel like the holidays are special.

The principal ingredient of the recipes in this article is whole wheat flour. Its hearty goodness will satisfy your appetite more quickly than white flour and sugar, but you will feel you've eaten something special when you taste the vibrant spices and moist, soft texture of these cakes. They don't really need any dressing up, but for a festive occasion, try frozen yogurt, ice cream, or the honey cream cheese frosting recipe given here.

For a holiday buffet, arrange the pre-cut squares on a doily-lined plate. Don't pre-chill the frosting, but drizzle a little as a glaze over each square; then chill just to set before serving or wrapping up the plate for later use. These cakes go great in lunch boxes, too. Put these tender morsels in rigid snap-lid containers, and be sure to include a fork, as they are too delicate for finger food.

Gingerbread

A moist, gingery cake that is spiced just right. Use dark, or blackstrap molasses for best flavor. Makes an 8x8" cake.

```
1 2/3 cups whole wheat pastry flour
1 1/4 teaspoons baking soda
1 1/4 teaspoons ginger
1 teaspoon cinnamon
1/4 teaspoon ground cloves
1/3 cup oil
1/2 cup honey
1/4 cup dark molasses
1 egg
3/4 cup boiling water
```

Preheat the oven to 325 degrees and lightly oil an 8x8" square cake pan. Sift together the flour, soda, ginger, cinnamon, and cloves into a medium bowl. Spoon the mixture back into the sifter. Measure the oil, honey, and molasses into the bowl. Add the egg. Beat with a mixer until frothy. Sift the dry ingredients into the wet mixture in three parts, beating well after each addition. The batter will get very stiff with the third addition. Add the boiling water, and beat with a mixer or rotary beater for a full minute. The batter will be thin. Pour the batter into the prepared pan, and bake at 325 degrees for about 45 minutes, until the cake tests done.

Pineapple-coconut cake

Good when served warm for a treat. Makes a 9x9" cake.

```
2 cups whole wheat pastry flour
1 teaspoon baking powder
1 teaspoon soda
1 Tablespoon buttermilk powder
1/4 teaspoon nutmeg
1 egg
1/2 cup oil
2/3 cup honey
2/3 cup yogurt
1 cup crushed pineapple
1/2 cup unsweetened flaked coconut
1 Tablespoon lemon juice
```

Prepare a 9x9" cake pan by oiling it and lining with baker's paper. Preheat the oven to 350°. Sift together the flour, baking powder, soda, buttermilk powder, and nutmeg. In a large bowl, stir together the egg, oil, honey, yogurt, crushed pineapple, coconut, and lemon juice until thoroughly mixed.

Add the dry mixture to the wet mixture in three or four installments, beating with a spoon until well-mixed each time. Scrape the batter into the prepared pan. Bake 30 to 40 minutes, until the cake tests done. Let cool five minutes in pan, then remove from pan and cool on a wire rack. May be served warm or at room temperature.

Tahini spice cake

A simple spice cake, with a subtle nutty flavor. Makes an 8x8" cake.

```
1 3/4 cups whole wheat pastry flour
1 teaspoon baking powder
1/2 teaspoon soda
1/2 teaspoon cinnamon
1/4 teaspoon nutmeg
1/4 teaspoon cloves
1/4 cup cocoa powder
1 egg
1/4 cup oil
2/3 cup honey
1/4 cup tahini
1/2 cup yogurt
1/3 cup lukewarm water
```

Preheat the oven to 350 degrees. Prepare an 8x8" pan by oiling it lightly. Into a medium bowl, sift the flour, baking powder, soda, cinnamon, nutmeg, cloves, and cocoa powder. Set aside. In another medium bowl, put the egg, oil, honey, tahini, yogurt, and water. Beat until frothy and well-blended. Add the dry ingredients in four parts, beating well after each one until smooth. Scrape the batter into the pan, and bake at 350 degrees for 35 to 40 minutes, until the cake tests done. Remove from pan and cool on a rack.

Chocolate cake

A great classic chocolate cake: moist, heavy, almost gooey. A cake-and-ice cream cake. Makes an 8x8" cake.

```
1 cup whole wheat pastry flour
1/3 cup unsweetened cocoa powder
1/2 teaspoon baking powder
3/4 teaspoon baking soda
3 Tablespoons buttermilk powder
1/4 cup oil
1/2 cup honey
1 egg
1 teaspoon vanilla
3/4 cup boiling water
```

Preheat the oven to 325 degrees and prepare an 8x8" pan by oiling it lightly. Set your sifter on a plate. Measure the flour, cocoa powder, baking powder, soda, and buttermilk powder into it, and set aside. In a medium bowl, beat the oil, honey, egg, and vanilla together until frothy. Sift in the dry ingredients in three parts, beating each well until blended (be sure to use any bran left in the sifter and any flour that fell on the plate). If you are using a hand beater, you may have to finish this with a spoon. Add the boiling water, and beat for one minute. Batter will be thin. Pour the batter into the prepared pan, and bake at 325 degrees for 30 to 35 minutes, until the cake tests done. Cool in the pan, then cut into squares and remove with a spatula to a rack.

Honey cream cheese frosting

Use light or natural cream cheese. This is a soft frosting, almost more of a glaze.

```
5 ounces cream cheese, softened
3 - 4 Tablespoons honey
1 Tablespoon dark rum
  -or-
1/2 teaspoon vanilla
```

Beat the cream cheese and honey until they are well-blended and creamy. Beat in the rum or vanilla. Refrigerate at least an hour, or until somewhat firm, before frosting the cake. Δ

Ayoob on firearms

By Massad Ayoob

The best deal in home-defense guns

Backwoods home folks tend to be practical and economical. In that vein, they'll appreciate the best buy available today: traded-in police service handguns that glut the secondhand firearms market. There are two generations worth, and all are good buys.

Best of all are the "first generation" trade-ins. The majority of the nation's police have swapped their six-shot service revolvers for higher capacity, quickly-reloaded semiautomatics. Far from being worn out, many of these .38 Special and .357 Magnum revolvers were latest generation heavy duty weapons that were nearly new, such as the Smith & Wesson L-frame Model 686 or the Ruger GP-100. Virtually all got routine maintenance from factory-trained department armorers. I know that when my department traded in its .357s for Ruger 45 autos in 1993, a bunch of choice Ruger Security Six and GP-100 revolvers went out to be resold cheap to smart citizens. Some were bought back by our own officers as home defense guns.

Because there are so many of these trade-ins, hundreds of thousands of them, they're available dirt cheap...generally under $250 and often under $200 buys an excellent condition used revolver in the same condition as a new one that would sell for over $450.

The second generation of used guns are the high capacity 9mms purchased circa 1985 to 1995. They're being swapped by departments for identical pistols in .40 S&W caliber to give the officers more potent ammo. This is largely a tacit admission of the failure in the field of the 147-grain subsonic

9mm hollow point that the FBI popularized among police. Civilians, of course, can load a 9mm with much more effective high-speed 115-grain hollow points.

The Crime Bill of a couple of years ago banned new magazines of over 10-shot capacity. These guns, usually issued to officers with three magazines, are grandfathered and both guns and mags can be legally bought by civilians. However, the unavailability of new ones has forced up the price of the old ones to the extent that departments can trade even—old 9mms for new .40s—because the dealers expect to resell the old 9mms for so much to civilians. Thus, while still good buys, they're not nearly as economical as traded in late model service revolvers.

In the revolver, I'd recommend the .357 Magnum over the .38 Special. The .357 will take the more powerful round and mild 38 Special ammo for unexcelled versatility, but the .38 won't fire a Magnum cartridge. Adjustable sights let you zero in for out to 100 yards when you want to carry your gun afield to pot crop-stealing critters of various sizes. You wouldn't hunt a bear intentionally with a .357 Magnum, but if you have one and can't afford a .44 Magnum, the .357 always on your hip is better than no insurance at all against close encounters of the ursine kind.

Adjustable sight service revolvers include the Ruger GP-100 and Security Six, and any of several models of Smith & Wesson .357. You may also run across a few Colt Trooper and Lawman .357s. All are quality handguns you won't go wrong with.

I'd also recommend a stainless steel model, any of the Rugers or such

Massad Ayoob

S&Ws as the Models 66 and 686. Their slightly greater expense is offset by their easier maintenance for the all-weather outdoor person.

Frankly, you can get by with one of the rugged fixed sight guns that usually sell for less. I have an old Ruger Police Service Six that I bought for $100 in 1988. It shoots dead on for windage but high, so I just take a six o'clock aim on the target. With Federal Match .38 target wadcutters, it'll stay in the ten-ring of the regulation 50-foot NRA rapid fire target all day long. At six times that distance, a hundred yards, this old beater with much of its blue finish worn away in a policeman's holster put five out of five Pro-Load 125-grain .357 hollow points on a man-size target, from a standing two hand position on a tree-type rest. This is comforting capability if you're ever afield and run across some good ol' boy with a gun who thought "Deliverance" was a training film. Still, the gun would be even more versatile with the tough adjustable sights Ruger put on their more expensive Security Six and GP-100 models.

I no longer use a .357 revolver for deer hunting after shooting a petite doe twice in the chest with one and

COUNTRY MOMENT PHOTO: Wintering horses at Fall Creek Ranch in Oregon (Photo by Pat Ward)

watching her run an unacceptably long distance before collapsing. However, such credentialed handgun hunting experts as Robert Shimek and Dick Metcalf have had success with the .357 on whitetails. They recommend taking only standing shots, sideways into the rib cage, at reasonable distances. Fifty yards makes sense as a maximum distance limit for most people with an iron sighted .357, which will usually have a four inch barrel.

The traded-in police revolver makes excellent sense and gives the most "bang for your buck" in a home-defense handgun that also serves as a survival and forage tool in the great outdoors, and a source of recreation in target shooting. A top-quality brand in .357 Magnum caliber will give you the most versatility. It's simple to operate and easier than a semiautomatic to learn to manipulate safely. It's your most economical buy in a handgun today. Δ

For many people, these natural remedies can reduce high blood pressure

By Christopher Nyerges

People ask if there are any herbal remedies for high blood pressure. There is evidence that there are. So, as I set out to write this article, I spoke with several doctors and consulted my many books and files to come up with the latest medical findings.

Dr. Wayne Flicker from Sierra Madre sent me a thick wad of data from various sources, mostly medical journals. He pointed out that high blood pressure—referred to as *hypertension*—is a complex topic, and that whole books have been written on this subject. Dr. Flicker also pointed out that the causes are many and doctors simply don't always know what causes hypertension. The cause is ascertained in about 1 in 20 cases. Doctors refer to hypertension as "essential," which is medical jargon for "We don't know the cause."

However, I was able to come up with some concrete advice, some dietary and some herbal.

Lifestyle factors

Overweight: For starters, if you are overweight, lose some weight. This will probably mean that you increase your physical exercise, which in itself is a good way to reduce hypertension. If you simply can't get out to a gym, go for walks or exercise on a stationary bicycle.

Smoking: If you smoke, stop.

Alcohol: Excessive alcohol consumption may elevate the blood pressure. Hypertensives should limit alcohol consumption to less than one ounce of ethanol daily. That means less than eight ounces of wine, or less than 24 ounces of beer. Even better is to eliminate the drinking of alcohol.

Salt: In at least half of the cases of hypertension, the reduction of salt in the diet proved to be helpful. The elderly and Blacks are the most likely to benefit from restricted salt intake. Read the labels on foods, since you might be surprised to find out which foods are high in salt/sodium. A food is considered high in sodium if it contains over 250 mg. of sodium per serving, and this includes most cheeses, sausage, Danish pastry, many salad dressings, many olives, bouillon, etc. Read those labels.

Coffee: Drinking coffee is believed to be insignificant in hypertension. Thus, if you drink coffee, no change is warranted.

Though the above recommendations are considered some of the best ways to reduce high blood pressure, there has also been some attention given to the benefits of including calcium, magnesium, potassium, and fish oil in the diet.

The garlic and onion family

Garlic and onions have also been regarded as helping hypertension. In a variety of tests, garlic and onions (and members of that family) have been shown to reduce cholesterol, reduce high blood pressure, and reduce the incidence of flu. For example, Dr. Alan Tsai, Ph.D., of the Michigan School of Health, has tested rats and humans for the effects of garlic on cholesterol levels. He fed test groups high-cholesterol diets, with one group receiving garlic. Those who received garlic had cholesterol levels that rose about 4%, as opposed to those without garlic, whose cholesterol levels rose 23%. Dr. Tsai noted that the incidence of cardiovascular and other diseases is lower in countries whose populations consume large amounts of garlic, though he was reluctant to attribute this effect solely to garlic.

Studies reported in the *Indian Journal of Nutrition and Dietetics* concluded that both onions and garlic in the diet lowered blood cholesterol levels. Studies in Germany and in the U. S. have produced similar results.

Cholesterol builds up in fatty plaques on the artery walls, and so it is believed to be a major factor in the onset of heart disease. Anything that reduces high cholesterol levels helps to keep the heart healthy.

Dr. Truswell, at the Queen Elizabeth College of London University, conducted research by feeding human subjects high-fat meals with and without onions. He found that blood platelets stuck together faster after the high-fat/no-onion meal, whereas the effect was neutralized when onions were included. Platelets are a component of the blood that are an important aid in coagulation, but when they "malfunction," they can form clots in the arteries of the heart and brain, which can result in strokes and heart attacks. Dr. Truswell believes that by simply including onions in the diet, the chances of having a stroke or heart attack are reduced.

Though there are countless studies pertaining to the effects of garlic and onions on the human body, it may still be some time before doctors make conclusive statements, such as "Eating garlic will prevent high blood pressure." Again, this is due to the complexity of "high blood pressure," its various causes, and the fact that no two people are alike. Still, I eat garlic every day. For centuries, Russian folk healers and herbalists the world over have suggested that garlic be used to relieve a host of ailments, including high blood pressure.

We do know that garlic contains small amounts of selenium and germanium. Selenium is believed to prevent abnormal blood clotting, to normalize blood pressure, and to prevent infections. Germanium is being investigated for its reputed ability to retard or prevent the growth of some cancers. Garlic also contains a number of bio-

chemical compounds, such as allicin (considered to have antifungal and antibiotic properties), alliinase, allyls, allithiamine (which makes vitamin B1 more effective), and alliin (which makes proteins easier to digest). Allicin, left alone, turns into a substance that some researchers have called "ajoene," believed to be responsible for garlic's ability to inhibit blood clotting as effectively as aspirin.

Enough books and research papers have been written about garlic, onions, shallots, leeks, and the entire Allium genus to fill a small library. I will list a few of my references below, so you can pursue these on your own.

There are two other good sources of herbal information which I want to share.

Michael Moore

Herbalist Michael Moore has written several good books on medicinal plants. In his book Medicinal Plants of the Pacific West (Red Crane Books), he lists hawthorn (Craetaegus Douglasii and C. columbiana) as beneficial in cases of hypertension. He writes, "Hawthorn is a heart tonic—period. First of all, it is a mild coronary vasodilator, increasing the blood supply to the heart muscles and lessening the potential for spasms, angina, and shortness of breath in middle-aged or older individuals... I have seen it help the middle-aged mesomorph, with moderate essential hypertension, whose pulse and pressure are slow to return to normal after moderate exertion, and whose long, tiring days leave the pulse rapid in the evening. It will gradually help to lower the diastolic pressure and quiet the pulse... The benefits take weeks or even months to be felt, but are well maintained, not temporary."

In the "Preparation" section, he describes using the flowering tops or berries of hawthorn made into an infusion, and drunk three times a day.

In Medicinal Plants of the Mountain West (Museum of New Mexico

Press), he describes an herb found in China called Ligusticum wallichii, which is used clinically for lowering blood pressure. He only describes this herb in passing, since his main discussion is about a related Western U.S. herb named Osha (Ligusticum porteri). He says the Chinese relative is nearly identical to Osha.

Indian herbalogy of North America

Over the years, I have found useful information in Indian Herbalogy of North America by Alma Hutchens.

Among her references to high blood pressure, she includes black cohosh (Cimicifuga racemosa). The root is made into a tincture which is used alone or mixed with other herbs to treat high blood pressure.

She also states that in Russian folk medicine, "They have found that corn oil is prophylactic for high blood pressure." Though she provides no more details, I presume that these benefits are derived by consuming the corn oil with salads or other foods.

Hutchens includes onions on her list of herbs which are used for high blood pressure, citing as her source the Atlas Lekarstvennych Rastenia USSR (Atlas of Medical Plants of the USSR).

See a doctor

Anyone suffering from high blood pressure should seek competent medical advice. The dietary and herbal information provided above is to be considered general information, but due to the chemical and biological differences between human bodies, there is no way that this general information can substitute for talking face to face with a doctor who can interview you and consider your particular situation.

((Christopher Nyerges is the author of In the Footsteps of Our Ancestors: Guide to Wild Food and other books. His schedule of outings is published in the *Talking Leaves Newsletter,* available from the School of Self-Reliance, Box 41834, Eagle Rock, CA 90041. The newsletter can be viewed on-line at http://home.earthlink.net/ nyerges/.) ∆

With papier mache, you can make treasures from trash

By Sally Denney

In the late 1700s, a pioneer woman named Sarah Miller needed a tray for her home. The general store was a day's ride away, so a quick trip into town to buy one was out of the question. She had far too many chores to do before she could allow herself so many hours away from her homestead, but she still needed that tray. What did Sarah do? She used the art of papier mache to supply her with her emergency needs.

Women settlers used papier mache techniques to supply their families with containers, wall decorations, lamp bases, and other household requirements. The lightweight items were easily made, strong, and conveniently transported.

Today in the United States, papier mache is making a comeback, due to recycling efforts. The art form allows you to make new and useful products from articles you would normally throw away.

The process is great family fun, it is economical and environmentally practical, and children can easily learn to master the method. I learned the process and techniques during a high school art class. I liked the flexibility of the wet paper and the durability of the final dried product. While in high school, I filled my bedroom walls with papier mache art. My favorite piece was a pretend stoplight I made using toilet tissue holders and shoe boxes.

Today, as a source of added income, I rent space in two craft malls. My craft booths are now filled with a variety of papier mache products: holiday decorations, birdhouses, fake fruit, puppets, jewelry, jewelry boxes, sewing boxes, and canisters.

The items cost me very little to make. The only purchased supplies I use are paint, masking tape, and all-porous glue. I have also had good luck using a homemade flour paste as the binding material. (Recipe follows.)

Finished birdhouse ornament

The papers I most often use are newspaper and brown craft paper (in the form of used lunch sacks). I have also used wrapping, construction, tissue, and typing papers. It is best to *tear* the paper into usable strips, because the torn edges stick better and the product will have a smoother, stronger finish. When dry, the ragged seams are also more easily sandpapered.

The bases for my articles are objects I find around the house (or scavenge from friends): boxes from bar soap, butter, tissue, and cereal are some of my favorite containers to make into birdhouses, jewelry and sewing boxes, baskets, and canisters. Round oatmeal or salt boxes can be turned into band boxes, or trunk-style lids for a more masculine jewelry box.

The tools needed are common household supplies such as scissors, a utility or razor blade knife, a pencil, masking tape (used to strengthen base seams), paint brushes, and a bowl or ice cream bucket for mixing and dipping the newspaper strips into the glue.

Before starting any project, it is a good idea to cover the work space with several layers of newspaper, so that cleanup will be easier. I also take my telephone off the hook or turn the

Here are the steps

ringer off before my hands are immersed in the glue. I learned this after having to wipe glue from the telephone receiver one more time than I wanted.

Always allow the papier mache to dry completely after each coat of paper and glue. By doing this, you will greatly reduce the amount of overall drying time for each finished product. Papier mache usually air dries within 24 to 48 hours.

Like Sarah Miller, whenever I need a new decorative item, toy, tray, or bowl on my homestead, I study the form of the object I want and then start searching for a base I can form my papier mache around. Soon I have an article very similar to the one I first desired, only better because I've painted the item to match my home's decor.

One fun Christmas decoration I have made and sold in my crafting business is a birdhouse made from a five-ounce bar soap box. Here are my directions so that you can make them for your tree, too.

Birdhouse Christmas ornament

Materials

Five-ounce bar soap box
Cereal box
Newspaper
Brown lunch sack
Flour paste, or white all-purpose glue (Elmer's or equivalent brand), or wallpaper paste
Ruler
Scissors
A nickel
Pencil
Utility knife
Masking tape
Decorations: Spanish moss, rose hips or red beads, arborvitae or pine sprig
A used wooden match stick (for a perch)
Paints: antique ivory acrylic, gold Testers model enamel
Paint brushes

Instructions

Step 1: Remove opening flaps from soap box. Mark the centers of the wide sides of the bar soap box (front and back) at the top where the tabs were removed.

Step 2: Make marks two inches from the bottom on the edges of those sides. Draw a line from the left-edge two-inch mark to the top-center mark. Draw another line from the right-edge two-inch mark to the top-center mark. Do this on both sides of box. This is the pitch for your birdhouse roof. Along the narrow sides of the box, draw a line from the front two-inch mark to the back two-inch mark.

Step 3: Cut along the lines, creating the roof pitch. Also cut along the narrow sides front to back on the two-inch line.

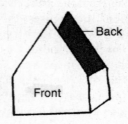

The box should look like this at the end of Step 3.

Step 4: From the cereal box, cut a roof piece 8¼" x 2". Fold in half, printed side facing out. You should have at least a half inch overhang on each side of the box. Eaves will be less than ½".

Step 5: Secure roof to soap box with masking tape.

Step 6: Cover the house with a layer of paste or glue-coated paper sack which has been precut (or torn) to the dimensions of the birdhouse sides, bottom, and roof. Allow these to dry.

Step 7: Decide which side is the front of the birdhouse. In the center of the front, trace around the nickel with a pencil. Cut this section out with the utility knife. This is the birdhouse opening. Centered ¼" below this, use your utility knife to make a small X

pattern of slits for inserting the wooden match for a perch. Glue perch in place. Paint birdhouse with antique ivory and roof with gold metallic paint. Paint perch to match either the roof or the birdhouse. Once paint is dry, seal with a coat of all-purpose glue or varnish. Air dry.

Step 8: Place a small piece of arborvitae or pine sprig at the top of the peak. Glue this in place. (I use a glue gun, but all-purpose glue will work, too.) Glue beads or rose hips to the greenery. If you wish, use white paint on top of the gold metallic at roof peak and roof edges to give the effect of snow.

Step 9: Insert some Spanish moss inside birdhouse. Glue a piece of gold string or red ribbon to the roof of the house so you can hang the ornament on the Christmas tree.

Flour paste recipe

1 cup flour
1 cup sugar
1 Tablespoon powdered alum
3 cups water
30 drops of clove oil or wintergreen or liquid Lysol (to prevent mildew)
1 quart boiling water

Place first four ingredients in a double boiler. Blend until mixed to the consistency of a smooth paste. Gradually add the quart of boiling water. Cook until mixture is clear and the consistency of a thin to medium white sauce. Remove from stove and add the mildew preventative. The paste will last for several months. Pour extra paste into jars.

For more information

Creative Papier Mache by Betty Lorrimar
Papier Mache by Robin Capon
Papier Mache Style by Alex MacCormick
The Step by Step Art of Papier Mache by Cheryl Owen △

Here's how to make a musical bamboo flute

By Robert E. Kramer

Materials

1 propane or butane torch or
   campfire to heat up metal rod.
1 steel rod at least 1/2" diameter
1 oven mitt or heavy cloth
1 fine-tooth saw such as a hacksaw
1 grease pencil or magic marker
1 sheet fine grit sandpaper
1 old 1/4" drill bit
1 pair of vise grip pliers
1 old bamboo fishing pole
1 measuring tape
Linseed oil and rag

Instructions

Cut out a piece of bamboo, at least 18" to 20" long with a diameter between 3/4" and 1", from the bottom of an old fishing pole. Be sure to cut it so as to leave one end blocked by the fibrous material that is between the sections. (See Figure 1.)

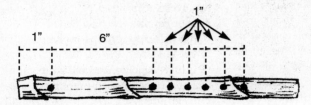

Figure 1

Measure and mark a spot 1" from the blocked end of the bamboo. Then measure a distance of 6" from your first mark and then make five more marks at 1" intervals. You should, when finished, have a total of seven marks. (See Figure 2.)

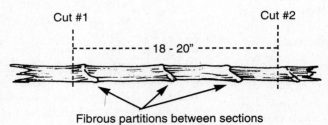

Figure 2

Your next step is to use the 1/2" steel rod to burn out the unneeded fibrous material. To do this, heat one end of the steel rod until red hot. ***CAUTION*** — BE SURE TO USE THE OVEN MITT OR A HEAVY CLOTH TO HOLD THE UNHEATED END OF THE ROD, AS IT WILL GET VERY HOT. When the rod is hot, insert it into the open end of the bamboo and apply moderate force to burn through the fibrous partitions. *Be sure to leave the last (end) section of fibrous material intact.* (See Figure 3.)

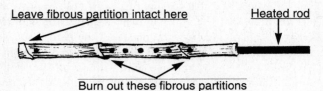

Figure 3

Next you need to heat the 1/4" drill bit until it is red hot. Use the vise grips to pick it up and burn out the holes at the places that you measured. Do not drill out the holes in the bamboo, as this may cause the bamboo to crack. (See Figure 4.)

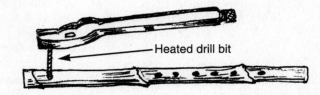

Figure 4

Take a piece of fine-grit sandpaper about 3"x3" and roll it up. Use the rolled-up sandpaper to remove the black charcoaled bamboo from around the holes that you have burned. You can also use the sandpaper to widen the blow hole. This will make it easier to get a sound, but be sure not to make the hole too large. (See Figure 5.)

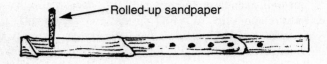

Figure 5

Rub a coat of linseed oil on the finished flute. Cover the last six holes with the first three fingers of each hand. Blow across the blow hole as you would on a soda pop bottle. Keep trying until you get a constant note. Now you can remove a finger to get a different sound. Experiment and practice. Have fun. Δ

Homesteading on the electronic frontier

By Martin Waterman

Looking for love in cyberspace

I have always said that the Internet is more a social phenomenon than it is a technological revolution. It continues to enhance and change people's lives by bringing people with common interests closer together as well as making the task of finding information and products much easier. The Internet has also been credited with providing a medium which has resulted in many new relationships from simple friendships to marriage.

Recently, there has been much written and published about Internet romance as online romances flourish and become more commonplace. Meeting someone online has completely different dynamics than meeting someone in person, with the former becoming increasingly easier to do than using the traditional methods.

A hundred years ago, or so, many rural-based men often ordered a mail-order bride. Today, finding that special person, for both genders, continues to be a difficult proposition especially if you are far from major urban centers and population areas. However, the Internet is responsible for making the entire world a much tighter-knit global community and is causing relationships to spring up all over the planet which was not one of the anticipated benefits of the Internet.

There are probably two principal reasons that explain why Internet romances are occurring at such a great frequency.

As human beings we are very diverse creatures. Normally, we tend to date and marry people from our immediate environment such as our neighborhood, workplace, church, etc. If that special person for you is one in a million or even just one in a thousand, it is unlikely that you may meet them in your immediate area. By using singles groups on the Internet and on the WWW, you can expose yourself to potentially hundreds of thousands (or more) of members of the opposite sex which gets the laws of averages working in your favor to find that special person.

Another reason the Internet is such a potent match-maker is that it is still a somewhat blind medium. In the real world, when you meet someone, you are prejudiced by many factors such as what an ideal mate should look like and a number of other factors based on your past experiences, morals, values, even the television shows you watch. The Internet forces you to get to know a person first without arbitrarily dismissing them because they are too tall, too short or perhaps bear too close resemblance to some man or woman in your past for which you may have not had a good experience. In other words, you are less likely to throw away a person who might be the ideal mate on a decision that judges them primarily on physical appearances and other aspects which alone could do little to guarantee the success, intensity or longevity of any union. Furthermore, in getting to know them on the Internet, the bonding process has already started. Since you don't have to worry about your appearance or mannerisms in front of the computer, you can feel free to be yourself. How many times, in the real world, have you wanted to approach someone only to be too shy or fear rejection and then be left to wonder "what if" for the rest of your life.

Cyberspace is a fertile environment for communicating and establishing friendships which as we all know often lead to something else.

How and how-not to find a Cybermate

More and more and more people are getting their own WWW sites and posting their photos on the Internet. This is one way but not the best way to start to let potential mates find you on the Internet. However, if you do have your own Universal Resource Locator (URL), this can be used once you have a rapport with someone or used in conjunction with an ad in the USENet news groups and the WWW.

Of course, people are always meeting because of common interests, because they participate in mailing lists or meet in chat groups. However, if you really want to use the full power of the Internet in your favor, you have two potent options; singles news groups and single sites on the WWW.

Singles news groups

There are dozens and dozens of news groups that cater to singles on the Internet. However, most of them are unmoderated and are frequented by those who are marketing 900 numbers or some other products or services. But many are still a great place to advertise because of the high volume of people who read the ads.

The different groups represent different attitudes. Two of the most popular are alt.personals and alt.personal.ads. There are also other more specific groups such as alt.personals.tall and regional groups such as chi.personals (Chicago area).

Single sites on the WWW

Single sites on the WWW represent some of the best and easiest ways to find a mate. If you do a WWW search using the words or the word "Cupid", or go to http://www.cupidnet.com you will find links to the most important single sites on the World Wide Web. Although you can find the modern equivalent of mail-order brides from Russia, South America and the South Pacific, the two biggest and most popular groups are American Singles and WebPersonals. While the majority of ads are from North America, both have people from around the world placing ads, and of course anyone on the planet with WWW access can answer your ad as well.

Placing an ad on American Singles or Web Personals is quick and painless. You simply fill out a form and specify such things as if you are looking for a Pen Pal, Just a Friend and Maybe More, A Committed Relationship possibly leading to Marriage, Marriage as well as other options. Some of the sites allow you to search a data-base using key words. For instance, under activities or hobbies you can immediately find all those who list sailing or boating.

Another popular WWW singles site is WebPersonals. These sites are very potent and many internet matches have been made many of which lead to marriage. Many of the sites have a collection of "happy endings" available.

Writing an ad

Writing an ad is not difficult. The first consideration is to be honest. If you are not, it will eventually catch up with you. The second thing is to take some time to consider two very important things; what you have to offer and what you want. This is important and studying other people's ads may spark some ideas.

One of the most common mistakes is when people go overboard on the "wants". For instance, if you say you are looking for a person who is blonde, with blue eyes, a preferred height and other qualities, the more you say, the more potential respondents you eliminate thus reducing your chances of finding that special someone. Furthermore, many women find it objectionable when men list physical requirements so that even if she does measure up, she may never respond.

Unlike a newspaper ad, the Internet allows you more words to work with. Good things to mention are your dreams, ambitions, hobbies and personality traits. Simple things such as whether you like to cook, like pets or have a sense of humor are important as they can be the initial spark to get a reply or start a conversation that leads to something special.

If you are particularly nervous about writing your ad, there are two very simple solutions. First, have someone else, a friend perhaps who is objective, write the ad for you. Second, and probably best, read the Internet ads and see which ones have phrases or qualities you feel describe yourself. Borrow these to help you build your own ad.

Another very important piece of advice is that it is far better to place an ad than to reply to one. A good ad may bring in hundreds of replies. Therefore, if you reply, you may be just one of the crowd. If you place the ad, you get to pick and choose.

Getting someone to answer your ad is usually not the difficult part. Checking your e-mail can become a very exciting proposition as you never know when there may be a response. Once you are communicating with people the challenge becomes finding out how compatible they are with you. The trick is to have fun, be yourself, and do not be in too much of a rush.

Many of the sites offer you the chance to use anonymity so that no one need know who or where you are until such time as you wish to make that information available. This is comforting for many people since the Internet is but a reflection of the real world meaning that there is some pretty strange characters out there.

If you are a man and really serious about finding a companion, an excellent book on the subject is A Man's Guide to Advertising for a Woman by Sebastian Phillips (Loompanics: ISBN 1-55950-146-4). It can be ordered by calling 1-800-380-2230 and is an inexpensive investment for $16.95 when you consider the book has so much useful information that may help you find that mate for life. It is my understanding that the publisher is considering a similar book for women but published the book for men first since men have the most difficulty writing ads that can solicit the large volume of replies that women's ads seem to do almost automatically. Of course, the challenge for women is to qualify and sort through all the replies to make sure they are getting what they are seeking.

One of the great things about the WWW single sites is the fact that they also have information on placing and replying to ads. Using this information and a site that suits your style, you can quickly place an effective ad and be meeting potential mates in the comfort of your own home or wherever you have your computer. With e-mail, you can carefully consider your replies (unlike a personal encounter) and correspondence and unlike snail mail, the interchange can speed to quite a fervent pace if the chemistry is there.

Of great importance is that you can find someone who shares the same love of the backwoods as well as your other values and beliefs. Of course, you will also be introduced to all kinds of new philosophies as you meet other people. Internet dating will also give you the benefit of having a social circle similar to that of a large metropolitan area without all the drawbacks that led you to embrace the backwoods home lifestyle in the first place. Δ

In the classroom and at home, this system will help you grow self-reliant kids

By Marjorie (Sultzbaugh) Harrison

My husband Allan started teaching sixth grade at the Moreno Valley, California, Unified School District in September of 1959, without even slightly knowing how. Fortunately for him, teachers were needed so badly that the district hired just about anybody. They grabbed Allan fresh from military service and shoved him into a classroom without any training in teaching methods. (He had a BA degree.) Although it didn't seem so at the time, this also proved very fortunate for the many pupils, parents, and teachers he later taught.

Since he'd not been trained in methods of instruction, Allan had to devise his own. This required an examination of his colleagues' techniques. The more he scrutinized contemporary teaching methods, the more dissatisfied he became. It was obvious that pupils were being taught to need management forever, rather than become self-reliant and self-responsible.

The classroom management methods taught to teachers in college, approved by school administrators, and advocated by teachers' unions (the controllers of education) made students rely on an authority for almost everything. Pupils were offered little opportunity to think for themselves. Even a drink of water or a trip to the bathroom must be approved first. When the teacher couldn't force the student to do his will, he had to try to rely on the parent for coercion. This seemed a terrible way to teach in America. (Of course, in Nazi Germany or Communist Russia, the rulers would have been delighted.)

Self-responsibility

Allan decided authoritarian methods were not for him; he would quit teaching first. But how could self-reliance and self-responsibility be taught? Allan realized that they can't. It is something one learns by being self-accountable and relying upon participatory laws for self-rule. In other words, the rule of law must prevail, rather than the rule of authority. It was that simple.

To accomplish this required a "scorekeeper" to get kids involved— something similar to our adult money. Academic test scores would be ideal. He could call them Scholar Dollars, or Points. The Points could accumulate in Student Bank Accounts, recorded in a notebook with a sheet for each student. His best pupil would be allowed to earn the position of Banker for the

month, and the next best could become his Personal Secretary to record grade scores. Each would be paid a monthly wage in Points for the chore. Thus the program would be run by the kids. The students would learn self-responsibility, and Allan's teaching workload and stress would be reduced.

Making the Points valuable was easy: all he had to do was ask himself what his pupils would buy in exchange for Points. At an auction held once a month, Allan sold the following to the highest bidder:

1. The right to move a desk next to a friend
2. King or Queen for a half day (advises teacher on the fun subjects taught)
3. Teaching contracts (with a miniature lesson plan, a set time for instructing the whole class, and a test given when finished)
4. Bulletin boards
5. Extra credit projects
6. White elephant items brought from home and no longer needed
7. Six seats in the teacher's car going to the beach, mountains, or desert once a month for a two-hour educational outing
8. Classroom "companies" which help the teacher and are motivational to kids, since the operator collects the fees charged (*e.g.* the Bathroom Company, the Water Works, the Pencil Company, the Finance Company, the Service Company, the Clean Up Company, and many more as needed)
9. First, second, or third in line at dismissal or lunch.

Self-discipline

Now that Allan's pupils were self-motivated, they needed to become self-disciplined. This required Classroom Laws to take *him* out of the management business and put the students into self-management and self-

punishment. With Allan's guidance, pupils devised a Constitution (for inalienable rights) and voted proper Laws (with fines for infractions) into existence. These were all set forth in a loose-leaf notebook for all to read at any time.

The only thing remaining for a good self-accountability learning program was a simple system of justice. Since Allan remained the only person in the classroom who was completely neutral, he automatically became the "Judge and Jury" for deciding damage amounts, collecting fines, or hearing evidence of guilt.

Student teachers

To reduce his classroom workload to a minimum, and to offer leadership opportunities to students, Allan devised an earned Tutorship or Student Teacher position for the top pupils in each major subject. This worked fantastically well. Perhaps an example can explain why.

Of the 30 pupils, five of the top students in math, English, social studies, etc., became Student Teachers, and they selected five pupils each from the remaining 25. After Allan taught an important concept, he turned the five groups loose for reinforcement instruction. He paid each Student Teacher a bonus of 10% of what each of their pupils earned at test time. Thus the whole class moved rapidly along together, without any horseplay.

Eventually his class size was raised to 66 pupils in a "pilot project," supposedly to test the productivity of self-accountability learning. Actually, his administrators believed and hoped this would torpedo the program for good, since they had agreed to his request that the other sixth grade teachers in his district would send him the students that *they* didn't want.

The administrators got a rude surprise. With an average IQ of 94, Allan's pupils *doubled* their overall achievement averages in six months. Moreover, all his pupils so drastically

improved their previous *attitudes* that most of the teachers wanted their former students to return. Instead, Allan secretly taught teachers at home to implement self-accountability methods in the classroom, much to the teachers' delight and the dismay of administrators.

The reason for administrative dismay is this: all of the controllers of education know that self-reliant and self-responsible pupils will eventually destroy the educational empire and eliminate the need for much management.

Allan maintains that there is no magic in self-accountability learning. Any teacher can achieve better results teaching 180 self-managed pupils than an instructor can achieve attempting to manage 30 dependent students. The reason for this lies in the Tutorship technique. For instance, suppose a teacher had 180 fifth grade pupils with 30 Student Teachers who had five self-reliant and self-responsible pupils each. The adult teacher could easily teach 30 top pupils who knew they would be expected to impart that information to their peers and then be paid for their efforts on a productivity basis.

Proof of this can be found in the early newspapers of the 1800s. Joseph Lancaster, a Quaker schoolmaster in New York and Pennsylvania, taught 1,000 elementary school pupils all by himself and at the same time. Furthermore, he started over 100 private schools that did the same thing. His accomplishment lay in his ability to get self-responsible pupils to help self-responsible pupils, as any good self-accountability teacher should do.

A program for the home

After the great success of the pilot project, one of Allan's parents asked him, "Why haven't you designed a program for the household? It's just as badly needed at home." So Allan helped him set up a self-accountability learning program for his home.

John and Mary Jones's family consisted of four children, ages 12, 10, 8, and 4. Allan asked John to purchase a hand-held calculator, two notebooks with loose sheets in each (one for the Bank Book and one for the Law Book), and some tokens to be used for keeping score, such as foreign money, play money, poker chips, or even credit slips John and Mary designed. Then the parents selected a household Banker whose position would rotate monthly among the capable persons in the home.

Next, Allan suggested that everyone regularly hold a Family Council meeting once a week or once a month. At the meeting, John and Mary were asked to decide how much of a vote each child would exercise, depending upon their capabilities. Tom, age 12, was permitted 3/4 of a vote; Steve, age 10, was allowed 1/2 of a vote; Alice, age 8, was given 1/4 of a vote; while little David, age 4, was not considered capable of voting yet. Nevertheless, David could express opinions and desires which would help him earn a portion of a vote in the future. The parents possessed a full vote each, which reserved a majority control of the household to them. The children's fractional vote could increase at the discretion of the parents, as capabilities were demonstrated.

A monthly budget

Allan asked the Family Council to devise a monthly budget. The Council decided on $2,400. This meant that 24,000 Points (real money times 10) would be available for a self-accountability program. Since the family is made up of six people, each person's "fair share" contribution should be either $400 in cash or 4,000 Points earned around the house doing chores, or any combination of the two.

John and Mary agreed to contribute $400 cash each, so each received 4,000 Points they could use to pay their children for their own personal needs at home, such as shining their

shoes, etc. Tom, age 12, said he wanted to contribute $100 cash from his paper route, so he received 1,000 Points for personal use. He was required to work at household tasks for the remaining 3,000 Points. Steve, age 10, thought he could contribute $25 cash and got 250 Points for personal use. He was expected to work for 3,750 Points. Alice and David had to work for their 4,000 Points each. Henceforth, any household work Mom or Dad cared to contribute free would be greatly appreciated by the other working members of the family.

Naturally, Allan said, the parents also had to contribute the other $1,475 in cash, but what they received in return would be truly wonderful.

First of all, the Jones family would be welded together in a family partnership. Kids even as young as David would now know why some things could not be purchased and where the money must go. All things could be discussed and solutions discovered with the whole family behind decisions. This generated a great feeling of strength that "management" households cannot match. Moreover, the family would draw closer together as self-control, self-reliance, and self-responsibility were exercised, and as the family learned to work together and make decisions together.

Allan next advised the Council to make a list of household tasks and then assign Points to be earned for each (without exceeding the total available). The children were then allowed to select enough tasks to fulfill their Point requirement of 4,000 (or less). Thus the kids would learn self-responsibility while the parents' work and stress were reduced.

Household laws

After this, the Council was required to devise a Constitution and then make a list of household Laws with infraction fees which were placed in the Family Law Book. A system of justice was implemented. Mom and

Dad rotated monthly as "Judge and Jury" to hear lawsuits, try criminals, set penalties, and award damages.

Spending Points

Finally the Council discussed ways that Points could be spent. The following were approved for the month (with many more added later):

1. TV and telephone time carried a set price unless two or more wanted the same time; then it was auctioned.
2. Overnight sleeping rights at friends' were popular.
3. Rental of vehicles such as bikes was spirited (cars come later).
4. Real money allowances for each child could be bought at a 20-to-1 rate ($20 for 400 points, $10 for 200 points, etc.).
5. The household "companies" were normally auctioned because they were popular and earned points for the operator (Baker, Mechanic, Cook, etc.).
6. The parents agreed to take each child to some special place he or she desired for a specified number of points. Also, special meals, attire, etc., would be permitted if a set number of points were paid.
7. Tickets to games, special events, etc. carried a set price.
8. Toys and games wanted by the children would be available for a set price or auctioned.

Basic necessities, such as ordinary food, water, etc., were not sold. How motivational an item was for the child determined whether it would be sold (unless it was clearly harmful; if it was, the Council denied the item). Thus the Council managed the household, rather than just the parents. This effectively eliminated most parental stress and guilt.

(Anyone needing further assistance or do-it-yourself manuals can write to the author at 21863 Brill Rd., Moreno Valley, CA 92553. Please enclose a SASE for a reply.) Δ

Grow winter salad greens on your windowsill

By Sally Denney

Greens for your winter salads can be as close as your windowsill. When the price for iceberg lettuce doubled at the grocery store, and I had leftover summer garden seed stored in my freezer in a resealable freezer bag, I decided to try growing lettuce in containers on my windowsills.

I had extra seeds from each of the four varieties of lettuce. My leaf lettuce types were Black Seeded Simpson Oak Leaf (heat tolerant) and Salad Bowl. These mature in 40 to 50 days. Butterhead varieties on hand were Buttercrunch and Bibb, which mature in 60 to 75 days. Romaine matures in 75 to 85 days. Head lettuce, Iceberg, matures in 85 to 95 days. I wanted lettuce as quickly as possible, so I considered Romaine and Iceberg impractical for speedy indoor use. I settled on Black Seeded Simpson, with Buttercrunch for my experimental crop. My impatience prompted me to use the Buttercrunch leaves like the leaf types, although the plants did eventually form heads.

If you have no saved seed, check your local seed suppliers. They will often have seed left over from the growing season. If you choose to buy seed through mail order, be sure to explain that you want the seed sent immediately, or they may wait until your regular growing season begins.

Cool but sunny

Having grown lettuce outside for over 20 years, I know lettuce to be a shallow-rooted plant which loves cool but sunny growing conditions. To adapt my house to these growing requirements, I used a window in a room with a southern exposure and a consistent room temperature of 65°. I also used a sunny east-facing enclosed porch window in the morning, switching the pots in the afternoon to a sunny west-facing window. These pots grew equally as well as the southern-exposed pots, but required more of my time and energy seven days a week, switching them from one place to another.

Knowing I needed to use the most sunlight available for lush plant growth, I removed the window screens and kept the windows clean. I also made a tinfoil backdrop to reflect as much light as possible back to my plants. I also used mirrors in the places where I could prop them up without their being accidentally bumped and broken.

The plants grew almost directly against the window glass. Since lettuce is cold-tolerant, the plants thrived under these cool conditions on some extremely cold nights. (We have no storm windows, but the windows are double-paned.)

Keep an eye out for any curling of leaves and for signs of minute spider webs, which are signs of spider mite infestation. To keep spider mites at bay, prevent the plants from drying out. Spider mites love to attack plants suffering under arid conditions. I ran a humidifier near the plants during the day. If the plants still appeared to be dusty or dry, I occasionally spritzed the foliage with temperate water. If I had suspicions of insect invasion, I took the plants to my kitchen sink and used the vegetable sprayer for a quick shower. This usually took care of any pests.

During short winter days, or if cloudy days were numerous, I found it helpful to supply the plants with supplemental artificial light for at least 16 hours per day to help keep them growing vigorously.

Creating planters

The containers I chose to use were inexpensive. Since growing indoor salads was a spur-of-the-moment decision, I used plastic bowls as growing containers. Whipped topping and margarine tubs work well. They were four inches deep and fit comfortably on my windowsills.

I did not make any holes in them for drainage. To keep the lettuce roots from becoming waterlogged, I filled the bowls in layers, using a few small stones first, then vermiculite, and topping it with a thicker layer of seedling starter potting medium. Do not use the heavy black potting soil sold for re-potting houseplants: it is too heavy for potted lettuce. Their roots need a light, loose soil to thrive. Use a mix with a good portion of peat moss that is relatively light to carry when bagged.

Another alternative to this would be pure decomposed compost.

When watering, keep the plants moist but not soggy. To fertilize the plants, I used fish emulsion (one-half capful to one and half quarts of water) each time I watered them.

Planting

A dozen plants were sufficient for four to eight people (the number depended on how many of the older self-supporting children showed up at mealtime), but I also have a couple of non-salad eaters in my family. Plant two or three seeds per six-inch pot, or about three to four inches apart in a larger container. Barely cover the seeds, no deeper than their size. After watering the seed, I covered the pots with plastic to prevent them from drying out and placed them on top of my refrigerator to speed sprouting. This took two to four days at 75°. Germination was spotty at temperatures above 80°, so it is a good idea to place a thermometer near the pots, so you will know what conditions they have while they are sprouting. Refrigerated saved lettuce seed tends to emerge more quickly for me than seed stored at room temperature.

As soon as the seeds develop, move them to a sunny windowsill, where it should be much cooler. With vigilant care, the lettuce will be ready to use in six to seven weeks. To have a steady supply of fresh lettuce, start a new batch of plants every two to three weeks. Plants grown inside with temperatures averaging around 65 to 70 degrees take longer to bolt, which allows you more time to use them. I began harvesting my lettuce when the leaves were of useable size. Plants which ooze milky liquid when broken or cut are past their prime and are usually bitter tasting.

The only thing I am planning to do differently this year is to start the pots earlier, so I will already have a supply of lettuce maturing when the price of lettuce doubles at the grocery store. A

good time for me to start these pots will be in the fall when I thin my outdoor-grown seedling crops. I will re-pot the plants I would normally discard and be a few weeks ahead of schedule for my first indoor winter harvest.

For added flavor for your winter salads, you may also want to try growing chives, parsley, and sweet basil in windowsill pots.

Dressing for loose leaf lettuce

> 2 strips bacon
> Pan drippings from bacon
> 1 Tablespoon flour
> 1 cup water
> 1 Tablespoon sugar
> 1 Tablespoon vinegar
> Dash of salt (optional)
> 2 Tablespoons sour cream
> 2 hard-boiled eggs, diced

Cut up bacon in one-inch bites and pan fry. Use part of pan drippings to make pan gravy with the flour. When brown, stir in water. Let boil and then add sugar, salt, vinegar, and sour cream. Fold in boiled and diced eggs. Just before serving, add the lettuce.

Mail order seed suppliers

R.H. Shumway's, P.O. Box 1, Graniteville, SC 29829; Thompson & Morgan Inc., P.O. Box 1308, Jackson, NJ 08527-0308; Gurney's Seed & Nursery Co., 110 Capital Street, Yankton, SD 57079; Park Seed Co., Cokesbury Road, Greenwood, SC 29647-0001. Δ

> *Fear of serious injury cannot alone justify suppression of free speech and assembly. Men feared witches and burned women. It is the function of speech to free men from the bondage of irrational fears.*
> — Louis D. Brandeis
> 1856-1941

Other titles available from
Backwoods Home Magazine

❀ *Best of the First Two Years of Backwoods Home Magazine*

❀ *Backwoods Home Magazine: The Third Year*

❀ *A Backwoods Home Anthology—The Fourth Year*

❀ *A Backwoods Home Anthology—The Fifth Year*

❀ *A Backwoods Home Anthology—The Sixth Year*

❀ *A Backwoods Home Anthology—The Seventh Year*

❀ *A Backwoods Home Anthology—The Eighth Year*

❀ *A Backwoods Home Anthology—The Ninth Year*

❀ *A Backwoods Home Anthology—The Tenth Year*

❀ *A Backwoods Home Anthology—The Eleventh Year*

❀ *A Backwoods Home Anthology—The Twelfth Year*

❀ *A Backwoods Home Anthology—The Thirteenth Year*

❀ *Emergency Preparedness and Survival Guide*

❀ *Backwoods Home Cooking*

❀ *Can America Be Saved From Stupid People*

❀ *Chickens—a beginner's handbook*

❀ *Starting Over—Chronicles of a Self-Reliant Woman*